Front Door
to the Past

Front Door to the Past

How an exploration of the history and ownership of a single Victorian London house and its surroundings leads back to the 16th century, uncovering a most surprising web of people and other places and events linked by their connection to the land.

Jennifer Brown

Jennifer Brown

First published in 2016 by
Jennifer Brown
352 Cromwell Tower
Barbican
London EC2Y 8NB

ISBN 978-0-9955599-0-5

British Library Cataloguing in Publication Data
A catalogue record for this book is available from the British Library

Typeset by Makar Publishing Production, Edinburgh
Printed in Great Britain by CPI Antony Rowe

Contents

Part Three – The Lethieullier era 1721–1798

Part Four – Closing the circle 1799–1952

Appendices

List of illustrations

Text and illustrations permissions

Permission has been granted to reproduce the Ordnance Survey maps by Bruce Castle Museum (Haringey Culture, Libraries & Learning). Photographs of the Candler and Pycock family by Patricia Turner and Jane Fawls. Photographs and documents of the Pitman family by Sylvia Fuller, Cynthia Pitman and Lindsay Clubb. Images of Charles Dorman, Laurence Charles Dorman and Francis Thomas Dorman by Charles Dorman. Deeds and extracts from the Middlesex Deeds Register by the City of London, London Metropolitan Archives.

Preface

There is little more banal than a most ordinary, almost nondescript area of North London touching Stamford Hill at one extreme and Seven Sisters Road at another, within it Vartry Road, one of its calmer Victorian streets. Not part of the urban village life of Stoke Newington, nor the busy High Street flavours of Tottenham, Finsbury Park and Wood Green, nor the urban chic atmosphere that parts of Islington purport to have, nor the leafy suburbanism of Crouch End and Muswell Hill, yet the local area touches on and reflects all of them.

Vartry Road and the area in many ways embody all that makes London a great city. The Hasidic Jews of Stamford Hill, with their sombre clothes and purposeful look, the mix of Greek, Cypriot and Turkish migrants now firmly established, the smattering of Afro-Caribbean and South Asian Londoners in numerous forms, the more recently arrived Polish and other Eastern Europeans and the whole range of other working-class, arty, professional and media types all seem to combine relatively easily with each other.

But within every street and local area lie stories of people, buildings, places and events. In Vartry Road, there is a unique house that stands out a little from its neighbours and which opens a door to a body of social history and interconnected relationships linked by the land on which it sits. As every picture tells a story, every house tells a great number of them.

This is a history of a house, its occupants and those connected with its local area. The research began purely as a short investigation but developed and evolved much further, with the obsession growing and leading into countless unforeseen places. Therefore, the book deals with the land on which the house sits and the pockets of land surrounding it, in effect a triangular area in its immediate environs, and the people who owned or were even remotely or unknowingly associated with it. The people and story cover a period from the late 1500s to 2014, a key event during that period being 1897, when the land ceased to be space but a home.

This book offers snapshots of various events, people and their lives and there undoubtedly are many other related stories that might otherwise have been included. While every care has been taken to cite historical document references, should there be inaccuracies, apologies are offered for this and for any references to documents and sources that have not been fully acknowledged. The research and writing have been a huge challenge but, it is believed, a productive one. Research has been a pleasure, even though it has occupied as much as fifteen years of my life in this and the writing. Naturally, there is never a true conclusion and so the author would value and welcome other contributions to the story. Every day more information comes online and the story will probably be an ongoing one, even if not mine. Any such contributions can be made via *http://www.jenniferbrown.org.uk/contact.htm.*

The project could not have been completed without the help and information provided to me by many people, one way or another connected to the families discussed in the text. My thanks are to Jane Fawls, Hugh Barton Candler, Sylvia Fuller, *née* Pitman, Cynthia Pitman, Lindsay Clubb, Charles S. Dorman, Primrose Reynolds and Aryeh Wolfin. Grateful thanks go also to Valerie Crosby, Deborah Hedgecock and Clare Stephens at Haringey Local History Library and Archives, Bruce Castle Museum, for all their help. My special gratitude is to Robert McKay for driving me all over the country to look at memorials and for his editorial guidance. I am immensely indebted to everyone who has helped me on this project.

Part One

The House, its occupants and their stories

1

A very fine house

Jenny Brown and Robert McKay bought the house on 11th May 1984 from Mike Phillip Halsey and Steve Barnes, the former of whom is a weaver of repute. Halsey is the author of a number of books on the subject, including *Foundations of Weaving, Double Cloth, Spindle Weaving and Introducing Tapestry Weaving,* some of which were written while he lived at number 54. On 3rd April 1975 Halsey and Barnes had bought the house for £19,000. Besides living in the house they also used it as a school for weaving. By 1984, it was in a moderately run-down condition, though structurally sound and was purchased for £55,000.

The house was constructed on a triangular site with, on the front, red bricks and pebbledash with imitation beams to the top two floors, similar to the houses and tenements in the rest of the street. At the back, again, there is a mixture of red brick on the ground floor and stucco to the first floor level. The houses to either side at the back have traditional yellow brick of lesser quality.

From 1984, a process of renovation and restoration began, not to any monumental extent, but enough to return it to a comfortable family home and to pay respect to the ideas, work and materials that had gone into its original design and construction. A number of key alterations were made, mainly with a view to retaining the original character of the house, most of which was intact.

An imposing dark oak front door leads into a large triangular hall, over twelve feet wide, which has a grey and white speckled terrazzo floor with dark pink and black striped border. This had been badly stained with ink from a printing machine which had been placed there but it cleaned up perfectly well. Keen to retain that which linked most directly to the earliest days of the house, some of the original anaglyptic wallpaper which was loose was taken away, repaired and replaced by paper conservationists recommended by the Victoria and Albert Museum. The coat cupboard underneath the stairs then had the original green paint and wood effect paint finish in dark brown. On the first floor there had been a partition on either side of the banister rail and a door to separate the top floor from the rest of the house. Fortunately, when it was removed, the damage was barely visible. This partition may have been constructed by the previous occupants, Halsey and Barnes or more likely, the family that preceded them, the Locketts. The top floor flat may have been occupied by Mrs. Eileen Lockett's mother and father.

The late 20th century and beyond were acknowledged by the removal of a quite narrow servants' entrance door and the corridor directly to the rear of the house that had prevented servants and trades-people coming through the main hallway and for the delivery of coal to a coal store off the corridor.

When the back study was being redecorated, a piece of wood from an old slatted blind above the smaller window was found, with the name of *Candler* (of whom more later) written on the back. When the house was being rewired, the electrician discovered an old screwdriver and a silver mustard spoon underneath the floorboards. Another room uncovered various layers of wallpaper that, over the decades, had been put up. A chard of a blue and white plate and a lead lion toy were found in the garden. Some original pieces of a cast iron table, similar to the three-legged ones used in Victorian pubs were also found in the garden. These little artefacts were all that was left from the eras of previous occupants.

On Friday 12th December 1986, when some woodworm was discovered and the wood was to be replaced, an old rolled up newspaper was found, stuffed behind the door frame of the old coal store, next to the kitchen. The *"Croydon Advertiser"* from Saturday 12th December 1896 had many references to the suffragettes and topical items including an advertisement for a gallon of whiskey for fifteen shillings. It was a joyous coincidence that it was found on the exact same date, ninety years later. It also proved that the house was being worked on at that time.

The quality of the materials themselves gave the clue that this was more than just an ordinary house, relative to others in the vicinity. The tongue and groove pine floors are superbly constructed. The weighty doors are made from a combination of pine with pitch pine panels. All the fireplaces in the house still exist and are in fine condition. Some had originally had brass canopies but only one of these was found in the garden in a very poor state. The living room fireplace was restored using another old cast-iron insert from the same period. The original dark oak surround has classical style carving. The dining room has a beautiful cast-iron fireplace with oval mirror and the bedrooms upstairs have white marble surrounds with tiled inserts. The banister rails are made from mahogany, the spindles are barley twist and the newel posts are also in mahogany and very substantial. The hall was so grand and elegant that it was the key selling feature when seen in 1984.

The original conservatory was demolished and rebuilt to a different design but the existing windows and frames were re-used in the revised structure, partly to retain the 19th century, yet remarkably modern window furniture that had been originally fitted. A snow guard on the roof prevented the snow from falling onto the roof of the conservatory.

The garden had grown wild and much of the rubble and broken tiles of the roof of the house that had been replaced earlier were strewn all around. It was put in order and thereafter carefully tended, but the terrace area was merely tidied up, with all the clutter removed. Later, the area was remodelled, introducing plant areas, tiling and a wooden deck, making the area more useable in the warmer months. Small sections of the original oak fence remain at the front of the house, indicating that it was of good and sturdy quality.

The house was again sold to new custodians on June 3, 2014.

The residents of 54 Vartry Road

The Lockett Family era

In 1984, while renovations were taking place, Leslie Lockett, a previous owner, introduced himself and came to the house to discuss it. By this time, his family lived just around the corner in Manchester Road, so had moved within the area to a smaller flat on the ground floor and their daughter lived upstairs. He was worried that we were going to discard the fireplace in the living room but we reassured him that this was not going to happen. He explained that his wife, Eileen, was responsible for the removal of the original Victorian dresser in the dining area as interior decoration styles changed and the doors had been covered in hardboard, as was the tendency at the time, to make them look more modern.

Eileen Lockett too and her daughters spoke about the history of the house and its inhabitants. From their own supposed first-hand experience, members of the family were convinced that for a time the house was haunted. Eileen believed that she had heard strange noises when alone in the house. They claimed that a former servant of the house, Hannah Cohen, notable, allegedly, for her withered arm, was seen by them and/or their house guests, her presence apparently having the effect of turning rooms cold. They also reported that, as a result, they invited spiritualists to the house to cleanse it of bad spirits. The procedure appears to have worked, as Hannah has not been seen, certainly since 1984. Nor is there any evidence that a Hannah Cohen lived in the house as Electoral Registers did not record all women until the Equal Franchise Act 1928 and she may have lived there before that time. Whatever, the period between 1984 and 2014 at 54 was a very happy one and Hannah appeared to be at peace.

Leslie and Eileen Lockett lived in the house between the years 1941 and 1975. They found out about the *Woodberry Lodge Estate*, within which the house sat, from Eileen's sister, who had just been married and had come to live there with her husband, having had a recommendation, which will have been necessary for these homes at that time. She, in turn, recommended her parents, Annie and Frederick Donovan, her sister Eileen and brother-in-law, to Stanley Rolls, who was the *Woodberry Lodge Estate Company* estate agent. According to Eileen, no-one who rented a property on the estate could wear a uniform, even that of a postman or bus driver. In fact, in 1941, when Eileen and Leslie, who was a uniformed policeman, first applied to live in 54 Vartry Road, they were told that they could not have it. Leslie was quick to point out to the managing agent that he was being promoted on the following Monday to plain-clothes CID, so they managed to satisfy the criterion. The house, having been converted into two flats, had been rented out before the War to a succession of people. However, Eileen said that before they rented it, they had been told that it was unoccupied for a period and at the start of the War was used for fire-watching, as it had a third floor and a view stretching as far as Alexandra Palace. When Leslie was away fighting in the War from 1943 to 1946, the house was shared by Eileen and her parents. The rent for each of the two flats in 54 Vartry Rd, one for her parents and her own, was £1.2s.6d, by 1945.

After the War, Eileen and Leslie continued to live there with her parents and two daughters Anne and Doreen. Eileen recalled that when she moved in, it had a beautiful old floral toilet which, clearly, she enjoyed. By all accounts, there were great parties at the house over the years. Eventually the whole property was sold to the Locketts in 1951 and was then first registered with the Land Registry.

The standard of building and maintenance was good on the estate, as many of the electricians, carpenters and plumbers who had worked on the houses continued to live in the area. Eileen had been told by them that George Candler had brought wood from all over the world to use in various parts of what became her house and that he had been most particular about the quality of work in it. According to her, in her time, original bells were still in the kitchen and in each of the rooms there were devices beside the fireplaces to summon the servants. The one in the living room still worked, she recalled.

Behind the house, on the other side of the wall at the end of the garden at 54 and 56 Amhurst Park, there were a number of older houses, which had in their time been elegant but had become dilapidated. The local children used to play in their large gardens during the War as there even was a gate at the end of the garden to gain entrance and the Locketts used to grow vegetables in them. The house was not then overlooked, as the present Samuel Lewis Trust flats had not been built to replace the crumbling ruins. More recently, as there were many developments in the 1950s and 1960s, some of the older houses on Amhurst Park have been demolished, with few remaining on the north side of the road. Remaining today is a fig tree but there had been other fruit trees in the garden. Eileen recalled that in the front garden there had been a beautiful large pot which she took with her to her new flat and retained. Bomb damage occurred during the War in the Tiverton and Seven Sisters Road area, when many were killed. Apparently the front door of 54 was blown in but unharmed by the blast and many buildings in Vartry Road were damaged.

The Deeds of 54 Vartry Road show the people involved when the house was sold in 1951. It was first registered with H.M. Land Registry on 17th May 1951 prior to it being sold on 22nd August of that year by *Woodberry Lodge Estate Company,* whose registered office was at 23 Essex Street, Strand, London WC2, to Leslie Albert Lockett, a police officer. L. C. Dorman was named as the director of the company. The greater part of the money (£1,200) was paid to that company and a small part (£300) was paid to H. W. C. Davies, of the *Woodberry Development Company*, whose registered office was at 115 Vartry Road. Laurence Charles Dorman was the grandson of another Charles Dorman, more of whom later. Eileen Lockett had suggested that Mr. Davies was the owner of the Company and the transaction would appear to confirm it. At one time, a

Henry and Emily Davies, qualified to vote through occupation and husband's occupation, lived at 37 Franklin Street and it may be that they were related to H.W.C. Davies.

Some of the other buildings surrounding the house were still owned by the *Woodberry Lodge Estate* in 1951 and were referred to in the Charge Certificate from the Land Registry as "*unsold portions.*" There was a restrictive covenant which stated that written permission was required for any part of the land or building to be used for the "*purpose of any trade business, manufacture or occupation of any description or in any other manner than as a single dwelling house..... provided that the user of the property for the purpose of a medical practitioner or dentist shall not be deemed to be a breach of this stipulation.*"

Eileen Lockett knew about many of the houses and the tenants, some of whom she recommended for placement to the *Woodberry Lodge Estate Company*. Some of her family owned *Woodberry Lodge* flats and houses and several still lived in the area in 2004 but have since moved out of London. When the houses were put up for sale, around the time that Mr. and Mrs. Lockett bought theirs in 1951, their prices apparently did not reflect their true market value. There was a set price for tenements, small houses and larger ones. Eileen suggested that Mr. Davies, who bought the Estate, did not know much about the area, of its history or of a previous agent, George Candler.

Other occupants of the house

Table A explains entitlement to vote in 1918 and 1928. Table B lists the occupants of 54 Vartry Road, from 1901 to 1939, compiled from the Electoral Registers at Bruce Castle Museum, Lordship Lane, Tottenham, London, census records and other sources. Women could not vote in parliamentary elections before 1918. The qualifications for voting changed with the Representation of the People Act 1918 when business men and women, graduates, women aged 30 and over and the wives of local government electors were eligible to vote. In 1928, all women over the age of 21 were entitled to vote, with the passing of the Equal Franchise Act.

Key early names are those of George and Constance Mackenzie Candler. The Electoral Registers placed George Candler in the occupation section and not the ownership section, when that was a criterion for voting. Constance became qualified to register after 1918 through her husband's occupation. The residents named in the Electoral Register from October 1930 to 1934 had no known connection to the Candler family. These five individuals were probably tenants. They did not seem to be related or married and they may have all been in employment.

Anne Brackley and Lilian Brackley, evidenced from jury service records in different years, may have been one and the same. Listed in the Census of 1911, there were only four people named David Victor Williams and they were from Glamorgan. There was only one person by the name of David Robert Woolf recorded in Hackney, at 126 Geldeston Road, Upper Clapton. He was an assessor and collector of government taxes and land evaluation offices. He

Table A. Entitlement to vote 1918-1928.

1918-28 Men & Women	After 1928 Men	After 1928 Women
R Residents qualification	**R** residents qualification	**Rw** residents qualification
BP Business premises qualification	**B** business premises qualification	**Bw** business premises qualification
O occupation qualification	**O** occupation qualification	**Ow** occupation qualification
HO qualification through husband	**D** qualification through wife's occupation	**Dw** qualification through husband's occupation

Table B. Occupants of 54 Vartry Road 1901-1939. The two columns with PE are for Parliamentary elections and LE for local elections.

Date	Occupants	PE	LE	Notes /sources of information
1901	George Candler Emma Wilson Ada S. Milton			Census 1901 Emma Wilson (housekeeper) Ada S. Milton (domestic)
1905	George Herbert Candler	O		Listed as occupier in Rate books
1911	George Herbert Candler Constance Mackenzie Candler Harriet Jane Brawn	O		Census of 1911. Women were not listed on electoral registers. Harriet Jane Brawn (domestic)
1915	George Herbert Candler	O		
1918	George Herbert Candler Constance Mackenzie Candler	R HO	O HO	R for resident's qualification. O by occupation. Constance qualified to vote because of husband
1923 1926 1928	George Herbert Candler Constance Mackenzie Candler	R HO	O HO	Electoral register. Women appeared on the electoral register because of husband's occupation
1929 May 1930 Oct	George Herbert Candler Constance Mackenzie Candler Ada Elizabeth Butler	R R Rw	O O	Register was produced on 1st May before George died. Constance left house between June 1929 and October 1930.
1930 Oct 1931 Oct	Christopher Bevan Anne Brackle David Grenig Lewis David Victor Williams David Robert Wolff	R Rw R R R	Ow	
1931 Oct 1934 Oct	Christopher Bevan Anne/Lillian Brackley (J) David Victor Williams David Robert Wolff	R Rw R R	Ow	J for Juror
1934 Oct 1939 Oct	Annie Sherman Hyman Solomon Sherman Abraham Stiller J Pearl Stiller	Rw R R Rw	Dw O O Dw	J for juror. These residents left the house some time during the war.

was fifty three, single and born in Manchester, living with his widowed sister. That placed him in the right area so would make him potentially a tenant, although by the time he was living in Vartry Road, he would have been about seventy-two years of age.

The tenants listed at the house in October 1935 and into 1936 had names that suggest that they may have been Jewish. However, Abraham Stiller had been a juror, which would indicate that he was well-established in the country. There were no electoral registers produced during the War years to support or challenge the view of Eileen Lockett that it was empty, although her information had the benefit of closeness to the time and events.

The *Birth, Marriage and Death Index* on *www.ancestry.com* reveals that a Pearl Rubenstein married Abraham Stiller in Hackney in the third quarter of 1932 (*Ib 1248*). A Hyman Solomon Sherman married Anne Stiller in Stepney, also in the third quarter of 1932 (*1c 684*). Anne was the brother of Abraham Stiller. The couples were related, therefore, by family and by marriage. Hyman Solomon Sherman was born in 1906 (Apr/May/June) and his birth was officially registered (*1c 359*) as the Parish of St. George in the East. His wife, Annie Stiller was born in 1912 (Jan/Feb/Mar) and her birth was also registered (*1c 564*) as the Parish of St. George in the East. As it was after 1912, her mother's maiden name was included and given as Skiop. Abraham Stiller was born in 1910 (Jul/Aug/Sept) and birth registered (*1c 263*) in the Parish of St. George in the East. The birth of another person by the same name was registered in 1896 (Oct/Nov/Dec) (*1c 368*). The latter was, possibly, another son born to the same family but who died. Pearl Rubenstein was born in 1910 (Jan/Feb/Mar) and her birth registered (*1c 209*), in Whitechapel.

3

Neighbourhood development

Taken from the *Ordnance Survey Maps, Middlesex Sheet XII. 7&11, from 1864 and 1894/6,* of which two sections of are reproduced overleaf, the *Old Ordnance Survey Maps, Stamford Hill, London Sheet 21 (The Godfrey Edition),* for the years 1868, 1894-96 and 1913 provide useful information on the area. They show the development of the land from fields to housing. The earliest of these maps delineates a number of plots, notably 922-936, that are relevant, covering some of the area around which Candler and/or Dorman later owned or managed houses. James Giblett of *Woodberry Lodge,* a cattle dealer and local landowner, was described in the notes attached to the Godfrey edition map of 1868 as a *"fox-hunting looking man, never without a riding whip".*

St. Ann's Church was built some time around 1861, mostly funded by the wealthy builder, Fowler Newsam. The 1861 Census places him as the occupier of house and land opposite Hanger Lane. In the Old Ordnance Survey maps of 1868 and 1894-96 of Stamford Hill *(The Godfrey Edition),* *"The Newsams"* was the name shown on the map on the land next to a large house called *Fowler Newsam Lodge,* opposite the junction of the newly named St. Ann's Road and the High Road. This was recorded in *"Hall's Notes on Tottenham".* Hanger Lane became St. Ann's Road in 1869, renamed for rating and electoral purposes and because it had a poor reputation in the 1860s, due to a number of violent deaths there. In 1619, there was a Hangers Green and Chisley Lane, which became Hangers Lane. In older documents, maps and books Hanger Lane is sometimes written as Hangers while in more recent times as Hanger's Lane. Its name is thought to refer to the fact that there had been a gallows at Stamford Hill. The word *"hanger",* in this context, means a wood on the side of a steep hill, meadow or enclosure by a wood. *"Great Hanger"* is referred to in the *History of the County of Middlesex, Volume 5,* as early as 1455 at the time of the dissolution of the monasteries. The population of Tottenham increased dramatically around this time.

The largest houses on Hanger Lane in what is now the St. Ann's Road area of South Tottenham were *Woodbury (Woodberry) Lodge, Albion Lodge, Barnfield House, Coleraine House, Markfield House and Gothic House,* set in their own grounds with surrounding land. On the Ordnance Survey map of 1894-96, *Gothic House* had been extended to become the *"Tee To Tum Club"* but by 1915 it had been demolished. There appeared to be some sort of sports field behind the building, which was separated from St. Ignatius College, then under construction, by the Great Eastern Railway Enfield Branch. Howard, Frinton and Thorpe Roads were built on the site between 1894 and 1915.

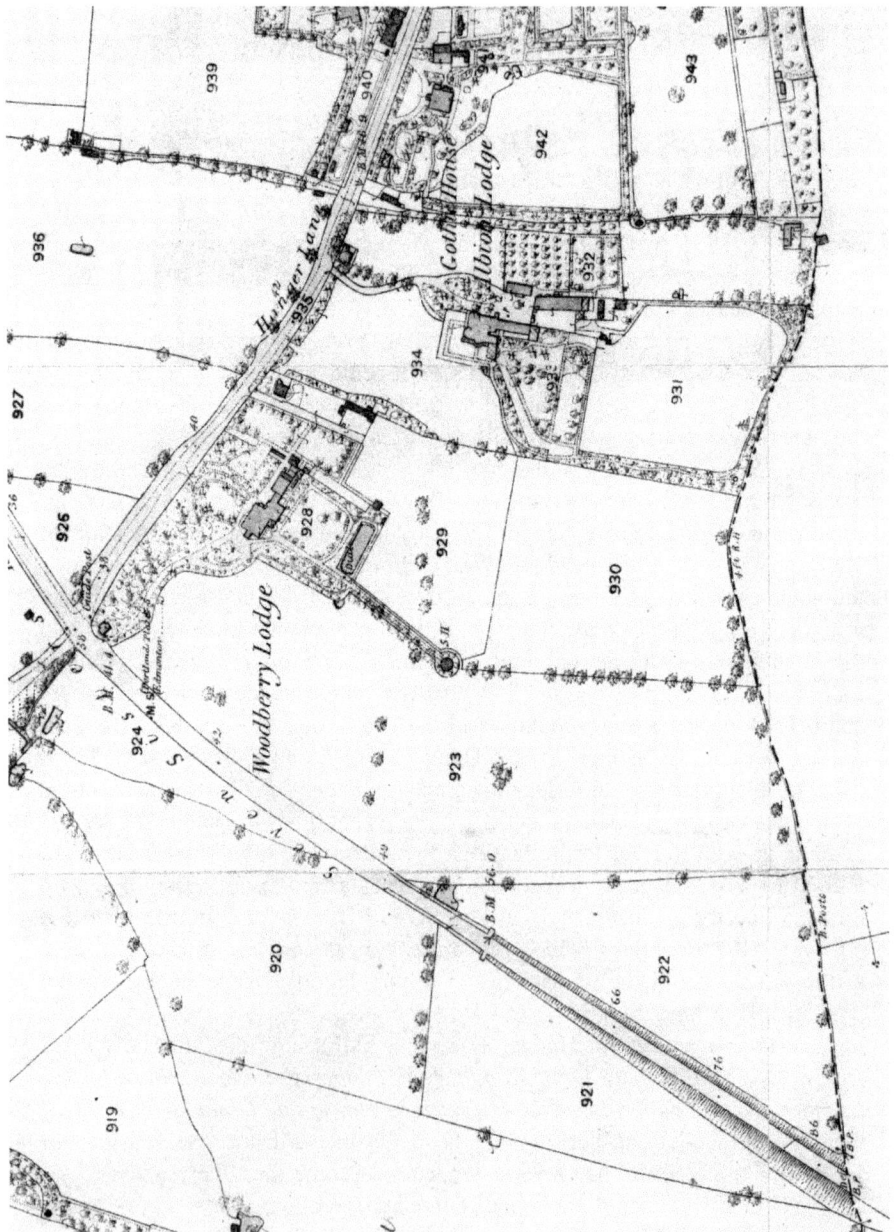

3.1 1864 OS map, Middx sheet XII. 7 & 11, detail.

3.2 1894–6 OS map, Middx. sheet XII. 7 & 11, detail.

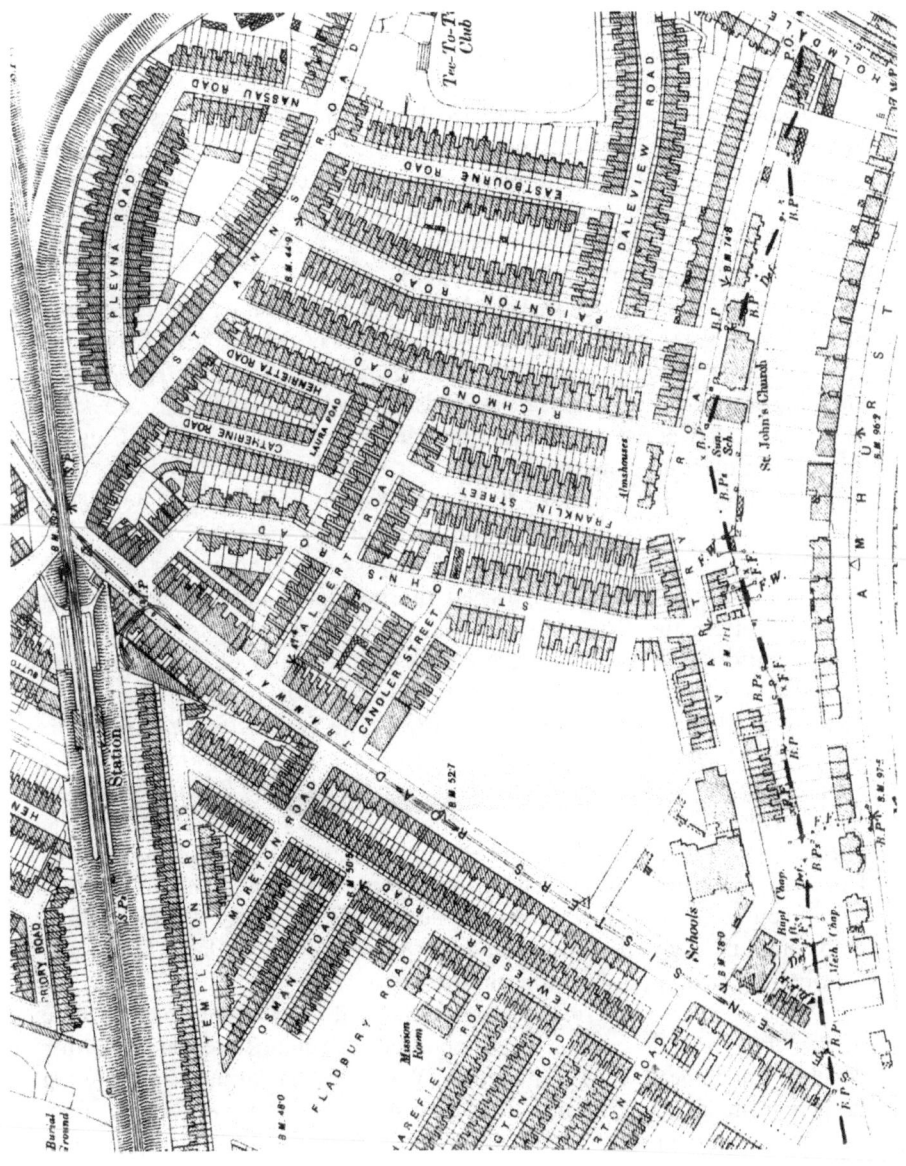

The roads, railways, tramways and other affordable transport opened up the area to development in the nineteenth century. The Great Eastern Railway's Cambridge Line was linked after 1868 with the Midland Railways Gospel Oak Station by the Tottenham and Hampstead Junction Railway. From 1st May 1871, trains began to call at South Tottenham Station. In 1872 the Great Eastern Railway Line to Enfield opened with stations at Stoke Newington and at Stamford Hill. Amhurst Park, which was begun in 1864, reached Stamford Hill in 1873. Its purpose then was to link Clapton with Seven Sisters Road. The new tramway opened in the late 1870s and ran down Seven Sisters Road. For the first twenty years, the trams were pulled by horses and then became electric powered, along with railways, around 23rd September 1909. The railways signalled the beginning of the end of the Woodberry Lodge Estate and the other more grand houses on St. Ann's Road as the area was divided up by railway lines and stations and redeveloped.

A typed copy, transcribed from a hand-written account by a local resident in the 1860s, listed some of the people involved in the narrative *(Pamphlet box 872: St Anns and Its Environs in the Sixties by a One Time Pupil in his Seventies at Bruce Castle Museum)*. It also indicated the different names for St. Ann's Road over the years, including Hanger, Hangers, Chitchelly, Chisley, Wood and Coleraine Lanes.

According to the account, there were, south of Hanger Lane *"three buildings all invisible from the road. The entrance to the first was near the Cottage. The second lay far back in a park like expanse the third was Dan's."* It was said that Dan owned the meadows and the cattle-sheds towards Tottenham. Dan also, according to the author, had all the land from Stamford Hill as far as Abney Park. Dan's employer was Mr. Giblet *(sometimes spelt with one "t")*. He was the substantial cattle dealer, referred to above, who: *"lived in the big house far behind the high split oak fence which divided a very lofty, very dense, very magnificent thicket of yellow buried holly and oaks from Hangers Lane. His Estate was called Woodberry Down but locally knew no name but 'Dan's'."* According to the deeds at this time, it may have been Giblett, James Kingsford or Charles Dorman, or a combination of them, who owned the land. The description would appear to be of the houses on the *Woodberry Lodge Estate*, hidden by bushes and trees. Giblett, in the late 1860s, lived in the large house and Dan Pelling in another building on the estate.

The account also describes that when the Railway was constructed, some of the clay from the cutting was deposited at South Tottenham. Another development of the time was that Hornsey Wood became Finsbury Park. During the period, on Saturdays, the new Road (Seven Sisters) will have been busy from early morning to mid-afternoon with flocks of sheep and herds of cattle being driven from Tottenham Hale Station to Holloway, where there were holding pens for the market. The road was lifeless during the week. There were very few houses in the area and much of the land may have been used for grazing cattle. According to the commentator, the land, as far as the eye could see, down to Abney Park cemetery, belonged to Giblett.

In the same account is an anecdote of a man by the name of John Robbins who was collected every day by another called Pickard, in the latter's omnibus and delivered to the Bank by 10.00 a.m. Robbins then left the Bank at 5.30 p.m. at Threadneedle Street and Pickard drove him back through Dalston and Stoke Newington, where Robbins was deposited 150 yards from his gate at Stamford Hill, opposite the end of Hanger Lane. Pickard continued his journey north to Palmer's Green. John Robbins was the-son-in law of Fowler Newsam.

One of the people referred to was Dan Pelling. In the 1861 Census, in the Parish of Tottenham High Cross, Daniel Pelling, a shepherd and Sarah, his wife, a dairy maid, were recorded at Hanger Lane, at Shepherd's Cottage, beside Woodbury Lodge. In 1871, Daniel Pelling, head farm bailiff and his wife were registered at the Farm next to Woodberry Lodge, at St. Ann's Road. Daniel Pelling, senior was born in 1829 at Barnet in Hertfordshire and Sarah was originally from Stevenage. Their son, also called Daniel, was according to the census, living with his father, born in 1857 at the same address in Tottenham. Another son was Bob. By 1881 Dan was living at 1 Tron Villas, West Green Road and was registered as a cattle drover. This might indicate that the land had been cleared for development between 1871 and 1881 as they had been living on the farm. The elder Pelling's gravestone is in Tottenham Cemetery, where he is buried with Sarah; he died around 1905.

London Metropolitan Archives retain a Memorial of a Deed registered 30th May *1876* and dated 4th May (*MDR/1876/14/150*) and (*ACC/0489/024*), in the Deeds of Vartry Lodge (formerly Albion Lodge, Tottenham), which is part of the Holmes Family Collection. George Holmes of Crescent, Norfolk Road, Shacklewell, Middlesex, purchased from John Jackson, Esq. and others, *"All that piece or parcel of ground situate lying and being in Hanger Lane"* known as Gallow Hill or Gally Hill; the sum of £6,400 (£3,993. 15s. 9d + £2,406. 5s.8d) was paid. It included Vartry Lodge, formerly known as Albion Lodge, once lived in by John Watson. The indenture included a plan with areas outlined in red, blue, yellow and brown. The main section (1) was outlined in red (7 acres 26 perches); the section (4) outlined in blue (23 perches) referred to an earlier indenture from 1817 (*B9 539*) and was between land marked as owned by John Giblett; the yellow section (2) (1 acre 2 roods 18 perches) was next to a road belonging to the Great Eastern Railway Company and beyond land owned by Mrs. Townsend; the brown section (3) was shown next to Hanger Lane. On the south was land belonging to the Tyssen Amhurst Estate. On each of the indentures is a memorandum to confirm that Charles Cleverley Paine acquired a lease on the land in 1881/1882. Another Deed, dated 24th December, 1877 and registered on 15th January 1878 (*MDR/1878/2/683*) and (*ACC/0489/026*) was an exchange by way of mutual conveyance of land at Stamford Hill in the County of Middlesex. Mary Holmes of Avalon House, Norfolk Road, Hackney, Middlesex, a widow, exchanged land which she had inherited from her deceased husband, together with Charles A.D. Tyssen and others, trustees of the Tyssen Amherst settled estates. In the margin, on a plan marked A, outlined in green, a long parcel of land on what is now part of Vartry Road was to be exchanged for two parcels of land, marked B, outlined in red and orange, on the new road, next to the railway line. The plan confirmed that new roads with all the necessary services were to be created by Mary Holmes. These were to be named later as Holmdale Terrace and Vartry Road.

4

The Woodberry Lodge Estate

It was in 1866 that a valuable freehold property known as the *"Woodberry Lodge Estate"*, situated at Hanger Lane and Seven Sisters Road, near to Stamford Hill and Green Lanes, in the Parish of Tottenham, five miles from the Metropolis, including a spacious family residence and valuable building land, containing some forty-one acres, was to be sold by auction. The land was intersected by the Tottenham and Hampstead Junction Railway and was advertised as close to an intended railway station and the new branch of the Great Eastern Railway. The sale was to take place on Wednesday 17th October 1866 at Tokenhouse Yard, by Messrs. Norton, Trist & Co. Particulars were also available from Kingsford and Dorman, solicitors and from the auction house. A copy of the brochure and accompanying plan of the Woodberry Lodge Estate (*PS 089, 1866*) is held at Bruce Castle Museum. Figure 4.1 is a purely indicative drawing.

Below are details of the six lots representing acres (A), roods (R), perches (P):

Table indicating lots and their descriptions on Woodberry Lodge Estate

Lot No. on plan	Description	A. R. P	Notes
Lot 1 pink	1.House, offices and garden	2 1 26	Mansion, stables, lawn, yard, grapery & fishpond
	2.Stabling, etc.	0 2 26	Cottage, kitchen garden & orchard
	3. Plantation	0 0 25	Let on lease for a term of 86 years from 1st January, 1817, at a rent of £1 12s. per annum and the purchaser will be entitled to such rent
	4. Meadow	7 0 11	
	5. Ditto	12 3 26	
	6. Ditto	4 3 31	
	Total	28 0 25	Possession (with the exception of the plantation No. 3 on plan) was to be given on completion
Lot 2 blue	Freehold building land	0 3 4	Plot suitable for erection of semi-detached villas
Lot 3 yellow	Freehold building land	1 3 5	Plot suitable for erection of semi-detached villas
Lot 4 Brown	Freehold building land	0 3 20	Plot suitable for erection of semi-detached villas
Lot 5 Green	Two enclosures of free-hold building land	8 3 6	*"The cattle layers and sheds upon this lot will be removed by vendor prior to the completion of purchase"*
Lot 6 Purple	An enclosure of freehold building land	0 0 16	

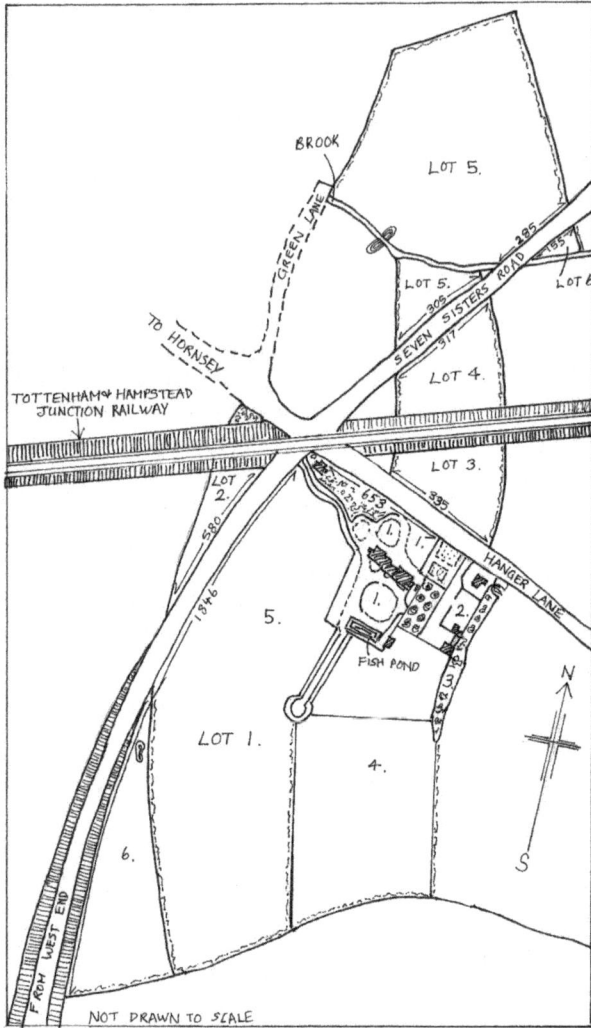

4.1 Woodberry Lodge Estate plan, 1866.

Lot 1 was described as a family residence approached from Seven Sisters Road by a lodge at its entrance and a carriage-drive. Accommodation on the upper floor of the mansion consisted of three bed chambers, two dressing rooms, a boudoir, day and night nurseries and two lavatories. On the ground floor was an entrance hall, dining room, elegant drawing room measuring 34ft by 18ft, opening on to a veranda with steps to a conservatory, breakfast-room, billiard-room, with steps to garden bathroom, lobby, lavatory, butler's pantry and two servants' sleeping quarters. The basement had a kitchen, back-kitchen, dairy, larder, knife-house, coal and wine cellars, a lavatory and other rooms. The estate had a detached double coach-house and a four-stall stable, harness-room and carriage-yard. It also had a cow-house, piggery, shed, poultry-yard, fowl-house, brew-house and farm buildings. It provided *"delightful pleasure grounds laid out in lawns, flower beds and shrubbery walks, with avenue of fruit trees leading to a fish pond and rustic summer-house, greenhouse, productive kitchen garden, melon ground and forcing pits, surrounded by ornamental paddocks containing together twenty-eight acres and twenty-five perches"*. The property was available for the erection of detached and semi-detached villas *"without interfering with the enjoyment of the residence"*. It was a working farm, which suggests that a farmer or cattleman occupied it at that time. Other descriptions of the same indicate that there were five or eight bedrooms in the property; there may have been an error in transcription. The area in Lot 1, which included No. 6 on the plan (4 acres, 3 roods and 31 perches) was not part of Oatfield and Snaresmead. It will be discussed later in the book.

Woodberry Lodge was again identified on 9th March 1872, in an advertisement in *The Times,* as being close to Stamford Hill, Green Lanes and Finsbury New Park. The Woodberry Lodge Estate, included a:

> ...very valuable and important freehold property within five miles of the Metropolis, close to Stamford Hill Station and the Tottenham and Hampstead Railway and the intended Tottenham and Edmonton branch of the Great Eastern Railway which will have its terminus at Liverpool Street Station. The estate consists of a capital family residence with pleasure gardens and offices and nearly forty acres of meadow land, possessing a very important frontage of several thousand feet in St. Ann's Road and Seven Sisters Road. The whole immediately available for the erection of detached and semi-detached villas, so much in request in this delightful neighbourhood.

The exceedingly valuable freehold estate was for sale by auction, particulars to be had from Messrs. Kingsford & Dorman, solicitors, of 23 Essex Street, Strand, the owners and the auctioneers. This sale offered the opportunity for highly profitable building speculation.

Then on 27th May 1876, an advertisement in Saturday's edition of *The Times*, gave a description of a house at Stamford Hill, Middlesex, which was to be sold by order of the trustees. As will be discussed in later chapters, around this time one of the owners, William Jones, was involved in a bankruptcy case. The Estate agents were Debenham, Tewson and Farmer and the sale was to be on 15th June. The spacious family residence came with freehold and vacant possession, had stabling, coach house and paddock amounting to three and a half acres. The house had *"commanding extensive views"* and was only ten minutes walk from Stamford Hill Station on the Great Eastern Railway and South Tottenham Station on Midland Railway. The *"charming freehold,"* *Woodberry Lodge*, St. Ann's Road, Stamford Hill, was approached by a long carriage drive from a Lodge entrance. The house had *eight* bedrooms, two dressing rooms, drawing room, dining room, morning room, billiard room, conservatory and office, stabling for four horses, coach house, poultry house and piggeries. The grounds were described as beautifully shrubbed and clothed with well-grown timber: "*There are pleasant shrubbery walks, a walled kitchen garden, a mushroom house and paddock.*" The complete residential house and land had a considerable frontage to St. Ann's Road, although the advertisement was qualified by the suggestion that it was "*unusually well placed for sub-division for building.*" Other parts of the estate must have already been sold off separately.

A *Times* reference, in April 1882, to freehold building land described some 63 plots on the *Woodberry Lodge Estate*, Seven Sisters Road, Laurie Road and Vartry Road. The area was described as:

> ...one of the most improving and popular positions in the northern suburbs with unequalled facilities of access being within a few minutes walk of three railway stations. There is a new church on the estate and a new station is in the course of being erected adjoining the property in Seven Sisters Road. The plots fronting the main road are particularly suitable for shops and the plots for villas are all of excellent depth. No charge made for the construction of roads and sewers will be made to purchasers.

The address given was the firm of Charles Dorman at Essex Street, Strand. The indentures supplied the evidence of the transactions although the documents did not explain clearly who owned the freehold and leasehold of the land. *The Times* then carried an advertisement in June 1882 for a portion of the *Woodberry Lodge Estate* on Seven Sisters Road, situated close to Stamford Hill and the railways:

> ...comprising of valuable freehold and leasehold shops and numerous dwelling houses for investment or occupation. Also several eligible plots of building land, having extensive frontage to good roads, the whole of the estimated value of upwards of £2500 per annum in 40 lots.

Woodberry Lodge, the original house from which the Estate and company took their names, must have been demolished between 1876, when it was still a residence, and 1882, when the land was being sold for development.

5

From fields to homes, people and places

Vartry is the name of a river in County Wicklow, in Ireland. It runs by the scenic village of Ashford, home to the famous Mount Usher Gardens. Dating from 1860, Mount Usher Gardens combine a famous collection of over 4,000 species of plants, gathered from all corners of the world. The gardens cover 20 acres along the banks of the Vartry River. Perhaps the Dorman family, with Charles' interest in orchids had a connection to that part of Ireland.

As early as 1878, Vartry Road was referred to for the first time in the notes in the Tottenham planning books when a builder named Lee submitted a proposal for a Stamford Hill Estate. Vartry Road existed in 1881, evidenced by the census of that year, when there was a list of streets shown at the beginning of that document. These included Albert Road, Candler Street, Paignton Road, Franklin Street, Charles Street, Catherine Street, Daleview Road, Holmdale Road, Eastbourne Road and Vartry Road. A map from 1883, held at Hackney Archives, shows the layout of Vartry Road, although it was not quite the same as the one existing today. It started at Holmdale Road, beside the railway and then took a right diversion at Paignton Road and started again across from Daleview Road. Cranwich Road linked across Amhurst Park with a space between two houses almost opposite where Berkeley Road is now. Berkeley Road was formerly Lawrie Road. The houses in Manchester, Heysham and Berkeley Roads were built after 1896.

Deeds for 1-6 Florence Villas, Vartry Road relate to the first six houses next to Stamford Hill School at the Seven Sisters end of the street. Mr. E. Homer lived at 1a Florence Villas in 1884. In 1891, he properties were bought by James Davis from J. Kingsford, L. Cockburn, mortgagees, and Charles Dorman. Townsend Road, which is referenced in some of the plans, later became St. John's Road. George Candler filled in the gaps, so to speak, in the street with his new tenements and houses in the 1890s.

The new Stamford Hill Lower and Middle School at the end of Vartry Road was constructed after 1882. An indenture (*MDR/1882/11/899*) bearing the date 21st March, was registered on 4th April 1882. The parties were Charles Dorman, a gentleman, the vendor, of the one part and the Tottenham School Board, the purchaser, of the other part. The parcel of land at Tottenham, Middlesex, had been recently part of a portion of the Woodberry Lodge Estate, bounded on the north east of a road intending to be called Lawrie Road and south east of a road intended to be called Vartry Road. The remaining side of the site on Seven Sisters Road was the property of the vendor.

J. T. Adams (builder) submitted plans for Stamford Hill School on behalf of the School Board Office, Tottenham, on 31st January 1883 but it was not built until 1891. The site was described as *"the corner of Woodberry Lodge Estate and Seven Sisters Road"* and the architects were Edward Ellis and Son.

A further indenture (*MDR/1926/22/704*) relating to the school, was registered on 15th June 1926. The document shows:

> Francis Thomas Dorman of 23 Essex Street Strand in County of London, gentleman and Laurence Charles Dorman also of 23 Essex Street Strand, vendors of the one part and trustees under the will of Charles Dorman the probate of which will was registered in Middlesex 1902 (B12 No. 565) and the Urban District Council of Tottenham in the County of Middlesex, purchasers of the other part, a piece of land 112ft × 256ft next to Stamford Hill School, at the corner of Vartry Road and Seven Sisters Road together with all mines and minerals lying and being within the undersaid land.

The trustees of Charles Dorman sold to Tottenham Urban District Council the parcel of land between Seven Sisters Road and Stamford Hill School for the playground.

In 1981, *The Weekly Herald*, a local newspaper, published an article recording a fire at the school. As the firemen were leaving, the fire started again and the top floor rooms were extensively damaged. Walking past the school on Vartry Road, it is possible to see that the second section of the building has been remodelled and the upper section of the school damaged in the fire, was never rebuilt. Four stations were involved in putting out the fire and arson was suspected. A local fireman, Paul Wood, who had attended the school, recalled the story on via a social media web site.

Mr. J. Owens is recorded in various Planning and Rate Books and he lived at 27 Paignton Road when he built 51-59 Vartry Road in 1881. He later moved to No. 59 Vartry Road. Mrs. S. Owen was living there in 1908.

Planning applications 1890-1899

The archivist at Bruce Castle Museum, writing in 1985, had suggested that a George Herbert Candler was one of the builders responsible for much of the housing development in the Seven Sisters/St. Ann's Roads area of South Tottenham in the 1890s.

The information in the table, *Planning Applications 1890-1899*, at the end of the chapter, is collated from the Tottenham Urban District Council Registers of deposited plans in the *Surveyors Report Books for New Streets and Buildings*, indexed by depositor and places *(1/TLA/B/4/Volumes 3-5)*, for the years 1890-1901 and held at Bruce Castle Museum Archives. The table outlines George Candler's involvement, along with that of other individuals, in the development of the South Tottenham area, as it relates to the surrounding streets. When Candler made his building applications, some were for houses and others for tenements and extras such as bay windows. John Farmer's plans for dog kennels at the rear of No. 25 Vartry Road were not approved due to issues of drainage.

In May, 1890, George Herbert Candler was given approval for 24 houses in Charles Street (later Richmond Road) and 20 in Townsend Road (later St. John's Road). In 1891, 21 were approved in Townsend Road. Later in the same year, a further 19 houses were approved in Townsend Road. In October 1894, 4 in Richmond Road (previously Charles Street), 4 in Franklin Street and 25 in Vartry Road were approved. Candler applied for building approval of the plans for 54 Vartry Road in July 1896 and for the conservatory in December of the same year. The conservatory was obviously an after-thought and was built, at the earliest, in 1897. In 1896, plans were approved for 23 houses in Manchester Road. A soup kitchen was approved for St. John's School in January 1897. In 1898, 15 houses were approved in Laurie Road (sometimes Lawrie Road and later Berkeley Road). In 1899, 31 houses were approved in Heysham Road and another at 25. Planning permission was given subject to the provision of adequate drains, sewage and manholes.

The exact locations of the houses or tenements were not defined but one might assume that two tenements counted as one unit; there were also single houses. In Vartry Road, up to 1899, planning permission was given for a total of 46 units. Numbers 61-75 corresponded with 4 units, 87-111 with 10 units and 113-139 with 7 units on the north side of Vartry Road. On the south side of Vartry Road, corresponding with numbers 26-52 (7 units) and 56-78 Vartry Road (8 units), were numbers 90-124 (10 units), adding up to 25 units. The house at 54 Vartry Road was proposed as a unit on its own. A further 8 units with 16 tenements, numbered, 152-182 are named Devonshire Terrace, near the Baptist church at the end of the street. They are in a similar style and bear the dates of construction as 1901 and 1903. If Candler's, they might add a further 8 units to the total proposed by him to 54. The Table of Rates for 1900 below shows the units in Vartry Road that he was managing to total 53. This is explained thus because one of the units, 78 Vartry Road, was then owned by W. Blackwell.

In 1890, Mrs. Jewell's amended plans for 16 workshops at Vartry Road and Lawrie Road were approved. In the same year, she had applied for planning permission for 20 houses in Vartry Road, two of which were not approved. At that time they were numbered differently and are now numbered 82-88 and 126-150. One of these houses is now 130 Vartry Road. It is a double-fronted house with a space at the side, so that if Berkeley Road (Laurie Road) had continued across Vartry Road, there would have been a gap for a road. As late as 1894-96, on the Old Ordnance Survey maps of Stamford Hill *(The Godfrey Edition)*, there was still a space on Amhurst Park for two houses. By 1915 the Ordnance Survey map showed that two houses had been built on this space. Oddly, the last address that Candler used when he applied for planning permission for 25 houses in Heysham Road was 150 Vartry Rd, which was then owned by Mrs. Jewell. The back garden of Number 56 Amhurst Park backed on to 54 Vartry Road and the tenements numbered 56-70. This was a large house named *Suffolk Lodge*, with a side access to the back garden and stables at the rear. In 1894-6, Henry C. Smith lived at that address.

Candler made his first building applications from 37 Albert Road and later from 12 Albert Road, where he was living with his second wife, when approval was given for 54 Vartry Road. By the time of the last applications in 1899, he was listed as the occupier and owner of 54 and 115 Vartry Road. He was still living at 54 Vartry Road in 1923, the year in which the last *Tottenham Street Directory* was compiled. Construction of the other houses in Vartry Road must have commenced after the planning applications in October 1894. Candler's wife died 3rd October, 1899, shortly after the last application listed. There may have been no urgency to complete the house in his period of mourning as he was probably living on his own at number 115.

It is probable that Candler was also responsible for the building of at least two tenements in Candler Street (*20/22*) which are of a similar style to those in the area.

There were a number of brickworks and a tile works in the Tottenham area, one north of Hanger Lane, west of Seven Sisters Road and the railway lines and another further south in the vicinity of Eade Road, still there in 1894. These may have been the source for bricks to build the houses, though the red bricks came from outside London. Most of the brickworks were built over as the area became redeveloped. By 1913, a blouse factory, a confection-ery factory called *Maynards*, that made *Wine Gums* and a lace-paper works had taken their place. Some of these factories on Eade Road now contain carpet warehouses, Cole & Son, wallpaper manufacturers (infamous much more recently for supplying expensive wallpaper for the official residence of the Lord Chancellor) and offices. In 1928, Haringey Greyhound Stadium, just north of the New River, opened but it was demolished in the 1990s, to be replaced by Sainsbury's and a shopping precinct.

Rate Books 1900 and 1913

Table 5.1 is a summary of who are recorded as the owners of the houses and tenements in *Woodberry Lodge Estate* in the various streets, as compiled in the Tottenham Parish Rate Book of St. Ann's Ward, 19th April, 1900 and the last column for the half year to September 1913. The Poor Rate Books were an *"Assessment for the relief of the poor of the Parish of Tottenham"*. The numbers of the houses are in bold to differentiate them from the tenements.

In 1900, Mrs. Jewell owned 12 houses at 126-150 Vartry Road. Those at Heysham Road were not completed until October 1900 and were owned by Kingsford, Dorman & Co. and *"owned"* by Candler in 1913. Charles Dorman owned a house and farrier shop at 5 and 6 Woodberry Mews, accessed from St. John's Road, as well as the victualling house called the *Woodberry Tavern* at 618 Seven Sisters Road. At some point after the death of Charles Dorman, in 1901, his executors relinquished their *"ownership"* of the houses and tene-ments, as did Kingsford, Dorman & Co. and George H. Candler appeared in the *"owner"* category in 1913, at which time he was managing hundreds of purpose-built tenements and houses.

Table 5.1 Tottenham Parish Rate Book, St. Ann's Ward, April, 1900 & September 1913.

April 1900	April 1900	April 1900	September 1913
George Candler	**Charles Dorman**	**Kingsford, Dorman & Co**	**George Candler**
Vartry Rd 26-52, **54**, 56-70, **72, 74, 76, 90, 92,** 94-124, 61-75, **87,** 89-99, **101-111,** 113-139			Vartry Rd 30-52, **54**, 56-70, **72, 74, 76, 78, 90, 92,** 94-124, 61-75, **87,** 89-99, **101-111,** 113-139
	Richmond Rd **26-62,** 79-125		Richmond Rd **32-62,** 79-125
		Berkeley Rd **1-29**	Berkeley Rd **1-29**
			Heysham Rd 1-47, **49,** 51-57, 2-68
		Manchester Rd 2-48, 1-41	Manchester Rd 2-48, 1-41
St John's Rd 33, 33a-37, 37a, 49a-55	St John's Rd **2**, 22, 22a-52, 52a, **54, 56, 58,** 7,11, 39, 39a-47, 55a-73, 73a	Land and sheds at corner of St John's Rd and Candler St	St John's Rd 22, 22a-52, 52a, **54, 56, 58,** 33, 33a-73, 73a
		Franklin St 1, 38	Franklin St 39-53
		Candler St **5, 17**	
		Albert Rd **29-38, 12-28**	
	Seven Sisters Rd **610, 616, 644, 652, 656** house & shops, **618** Tavern	Seven Sisters Rd **483, 485**	Seven Sisters Rd **612** tenement and ground floor **614** house and shop

The *Poor Rate Books* for St. Ann's Ward show that Candler was listed as the *"owner"* of 54 and 115 in April 1900 and 1913. However, rate books for the years 1905 and 1910 introduce contradiction. In 1905, 115, and 113 Vartry Road were said to be owned and occupied by Candler and the latter, the upstairs tenement, was recorded as being empty. In 1905, Candler was listed as the owner of 26-52, 56-76, 92-124, 61-75 and 87-139 Vartry Road. In 1905, the house at 54 Vartry Road was shown to be owned by the executors of Dorman and not by Candler. The house had the highest gross estimated rental value in the street, of £50 a year, even more than St. John's Vicarage, valued at £45. Tenements varied in rental value from £15 to £19 a year. Smaller houses, such as 87, were valued at £24 a year. Again, in 1910, in the Rate Books, the owners of the house at 54 Vartry Road were shown to be the executors of Dorman. Candler was still the *"owner"* of 115. The estimated rental values for the houses and tenements had not increased so inflation was not a critical factor. Between 1910 and 1913, Candler acquired ownership of 54, if the information in these books is to be believed. By 1913, the tenements at 26 and 28 Vartry Road were owned by other people. Candler is unlikely to have owned 54 and 115 in 1929, when he died, because they did not form part of his assets in his will. They may have been partly owned by a Company, in which he had shares or he was simply a leaseholder or tenant. The definition of owner is not specified in the Rate Books.

George Herbert Candler and Charles Dorman were involved in some form of business relationship because George submitted the plans to build the houses on land whose freehold was owned at that time by Charles Dorman and he may have been acting as an estate agent for Kingsford, Dorman & Co. When George Candler made the building applications for many of the houses, he was living at either 12 or 37 Albert Road and these houses, as noted from the rate books, were owned in 1895 by Kingsford, Dorman & Co. Unfortunately the deeds and documentation, marking the exact area of land involved and legal documents were destroyed at their premises at 23 Essex Street. Kingsford, Dorman & Co. still existed in 1913 but many of the properties previously owned by them in 1900 were then owned or, more likely, managed by George Candler. George Herbert Candler certainly chose the biggest house in the street, after the Vicarage, for his own home, which suggests that he had standing and held a position of some responsibility. As Constance left the house shortly after the death of her husband, it might be assumed that they were living there as long as he was house agent.

According to the Middlesex Deeds Registry, in many of the Memorials, after 1901, addressed in detail later, Francis Thomas Dorman and Charles Herbert Dorman are cited in connection with transferring land, as both Charles Dorman and James Kingsford were by then dead. Annie Candler, George Candler's sister-in-law, bought property and land in South Tottenham at St. Johns Road and Heysham Road in 1914, after her husband died. Charles Herbert Dorman himself died in 1915 and the sales may have been initiated because of death duties or probate. Laurence Charles Dorman, the son of Francis Dorman, was admitted to the Solicitors' Roll in 1927. He is referred to in the Memorials in the 1920s and 1930s when many of the other uncles and aunts had died or had given up being trustees of Charles Dorman's will.

George Candler, Charles Dorman and Kingsford, Dorman & Co. are recorded in the rate book of 1900 as owning many of the houses. What is unclear is whether George owned leases on the houses and was a leaseholder rather than a freeholder. The will of a Stephanie Henrietta Pedder, who died in 1912, indicated that she left a considerable estate amounting to £22,054 and 16 shillings to James Henry Kingsford and Charles Herbert Dorman and, in consequence of her will, the freeholds of many properties reverted to their respective families. The *Woodberry Lodge Estate Company* owned some of the properties when they were sold and registered for the first time after 1951.

The *Woodberry Lodge Estate* may have had gates when it was first built and apparently no two houses were identical. The facades vary, especially on the gables and there are different floor plans and types of access to the gardens outside. Some of the older residents in Richmond Road, one of whom died at the age of 97, recalled that she had seen the road being built; her husband had a connection with the *Woodberry Lodge Estate Company*.

From the *Rate Books* it is apparent that the tenants worked in a variety of jobs, since public transport had been much improved and people did not necessarily work locally. The Books showed that it was normal for some properties to be sublet and there are still some sitting tenants in the flats. One of them, living at St. John's Road, has been able to display the original varnished wallpaper on the wall in the hall. Mrs. Lockett had an old rate book belonging to a Mr. Hosking, a late friend of hers, who lived in the upper flat at 51 Franklin Street, in the street opposite 54 Vartry Road.

One Rate Book shows that George Candler owned or managed 51 Franklin Street during the period 1908 to 1912 and the rent was 9s.6d. per week, commencing on 27th January, 1908. At the top of the rate book is the heading *Woodberry Lodge Estate*. Candler was still registered as the owner of this house in 1913, the last year when rate book records were available. The statement accompanying the agreed terms of tenancy declared the following:

> A week's notice to quit from the Landlord, or a Week's, Notice by the tenant, or the payment of one week's rent by the tenant shall terminate the tenancy. The keys, in all cases, to be delivered to the Landlord, or his Agent, before 12 o'clock, on the day on which the notice expires.
>
> The tenant to deposit with the landlord at the commencement of the tenancy the sum of twenty shillings, which sum will be returned to the tenant at the end of the tenancy, provided no wilful damage has been done to the premises and leaving the fittings belonging to the landlord, such as keys, locks, door furniture, range fittings, windows, copper lid, dustbin, etc., intact, the floors clean and premises free from rubbish. The Landlord to have the right to apply the whole or any portion of the deposit towards making good any loss or damage done to the fittings or premises during the tenancy, and should the deposit be insufficient to satisfy such damage or loss, the tenant to be liable for the difference.
>
> No fowls, Rabbits, Pigeons, Goats or Dogs are to be kept.
>
> Tenants must not interfere in any way with the paintwork or alter any part of the woodwork of the premises and no electric bells, extra locks or other fittings are to be affixed without the approval of the Landlord.
>
> The portable dustbins are provided for dust only. All vegetable matter should be burnt, so as not to become a nuisance.
>
> The tenants of the houses and ground floor flats are respectively asked to keep the forecourts and front gardens in a neat and orderly manner, also to abstain from placing window boxes on the sills, as continual watering rots the woodwork of the windows.
>
> The register tops of kitchen ranges should be kept clear of soot, and the chimneys frequently swept to avoid catching fire.

Tenants are asked not to drive nails in the walls or woodwork of the property but to use the brass picture suspenders secured by small pins.

No payment of rent will be recognised unless entered in this book and signed for by the agent or the person authorised by him to receive it.

G.H. Candler, 115, Vartry Road, South Tottenham.

This was an extensive list of requirements and rules to be followed and tells of a way of life not entirely dissimilar to today but perhaps more strict in relation to animals and fowl.

In 1945, Sydney Hosking still lived with his sister, Gladys Freeguard at 51 Franklin Street. This house was demolished in the 1960s, along with others in the street, allegedly because they were poorly maintained and in a dilapidated state. The decision to demolish and rebuild might be questionable, as so many other houses in the area were built around the same time and still survive today.

In 1918, Ada Jane Darkins, of 115 Vartry Road, was registered to vote, by virtue of occupation. There are three rooms in the downstairs tenement so it is conceivable that one of those rooms was for collecting rent and the occupants may have lived in the other rooms. George Candler was obviously using 115 Vartry Road as a rent collection office in 1929, as it was referred to in his will. In 1928-29, Amy Young lived there and was eligible to vote by virtue of occupation. In 1937, it was the office of the *Woodberry Lodge Estate Company*. Mrs. Lockett recalled that a Mr. Rolls lived there in 1941 and he continued to collect rents for years. In 1945, at the end of the Second World War, no one was listed as living at that address.

Local People

Evidence from a wedding certificate offers information on a family that once lived at 116 Vartry Road. On July 6th 1901, Arthur John Webley, a nurse, aged 23, married Ellen Martha Beament, a spinster, aged 28, at St. John's Church; William West was the officiating minister. The two gave addresses at 137 and 116 Vartry Road, living directly opposite each other, in the upstairs maisonettes. Ellen's father, Edward William Beament, whose occupation had been that of a commercial traveller, was deceased and electoral registers showed that Rebecca Beament lived at 116. The census of 1901 shows that Rebecca was the head of the family and lived there with her two daughters and her son, whose names were Ellen, Florence and Charles. She was 61 years of age and her place of birth was the Parish of St. Clement Danes in London. The sisters, Ellen (27) and Florence (25), were machinists and dressmakers and Charles (18) was a printer; Florence was a witness to the wedding. The census shows that 137 was owned and lived in by William Warren (33), his wife Alice (31) and son Stanley (5). Perhaps Arthur, who gave his address as 137 Vartry Road, was in fact a friend staying with William or a lodger at the time of the marriage. He did not appear after this date as a lodger in the electoral registers. By 1906 Rebecca Beament had disappeared from the electoral registers and by 1928 Cicely Louise Rowsell lived at 137 Vartry Road.

The 1901 Census also shows that a Harold A Barnett lived at 56 Vartry Road with his wife Emma and daughters Gladys and Doris. He was an architect and surveyor but there is no evidence that he was responsible for the development of the houses in the area. It may only be a coincidence that he lived next door to George Candler, the builder and Estate manager.

Some of the houses at the railway end are architecturally different from those built by George Herbert Candler and date from an earlier period. They are much taller than the remainder of the houses in the road and were, at the time, in what became Hackney rather than in Haringey. They were the subject of separate building applications from those of Candler and his peers. Indeed, one of the earliest references to residential housing in Vartry Road was for seven houses and shops at the corner of Vartry Road and Holmdale Road, beside the railway, approved on 3rd June 1882, and built by the Paine Brothers of 109 High Street, Stoke Newington. In 1882, the brothers were also listed as living at 37 Vartry Road, although sometimes their addresses are conflicting. These houses were all built around the same time, as evidenced by the fact that they are of a similar style. In an entry in the *The Edinburgh Gazette* of October 1891, John William Paine and Charles Frederick Paine (trading as Paine Brothers) of 1A Holmdale Road, Hackney and residing at 29 Vartry Road, Stamford Hill, Middlesex, builders, were recorded in bankruptcy proceedings. According to the census return of 1871, John William Paine was a carpenter, his mother Mary an ironmonger and his sister Clarinda, an assistant ironmonger. The brothers were nephews of Charles Cleverley Paine, who also trained as a carpenter and was responsible for building many houses in various parts of Hackney, in partnership with George Bignall Jordain, son of John Jordain, a retired timber merchant. In 1871, Paine married Ann, daughter of John and Elizabeth Nowell Jordain and after the death of both George and John Jordain in 1875, Paine and his wife inherited a share of the estate held in trust by his widowed mother-in-law. In 1881, Elizabeth N. Jordain had acquired leases for numbers 1-11 Vartry Road, 9-19 Daleview Road and 3,4,5,6,7,8 and 9 Holmdale Road, from Thomas Lee, a builder, of 7 Holmdale Road when Lee was declared bankrupt (*Assignment of lease M 3138 Hackney Archives*). *Kelly's Directory* of 1908/9 shows that the builder, Charles Frederick Paine was living at 29 Vartry Road. In the 1911 Census, Charles Frederick Paine (52), a builder's manager and his wife, Kate Agnes Paine (41), were recorded at 29 Vartry Road with their children, Alex William (15), Muriel Cleverley (9) and Norah Kate (2). Electoral Registers showed the couple still there in 1929.

13 Vartry Road

The census of 1891 recorded James Loveday, aged 49, a commissioning agent, living at 13 Vartry Road with his wife Florence and daughter Hannah, a music teacher. The census of 1901 recorded Samuel William Clifford living there; he was a warehouseman and hairdresser. In 1911, Samuel William Clifford (42), his wife Amy (39), son Sidney (14) daughters Doris (8) and Marjorie (3) were still there. Samuel W. Clifford had become a salesman and manager of a "*hair department*". He appeared in the Electoral Register in 1914.

Local resident, John, from the terrace in question, discovered photographs, left behind at 13 Vartry Road after the previous occupants left. The house had been empty for some time and had fallen into disrepair. The photographs included images of weddings and posed family groups taken in London, Manchester, Melbourne, Buenos Aires, Chicago and New York. Notes on the back of some of the photographs were written in Hebrew and others in Russian. The people in the photographs were dressed in all their finery. One, taken around 1930, in Melbourne, Australia, as dated by fashion style, was a woman's graduation photograph.

A large card, dated 1915, on which there is a collage of photographs, was addressed to I. Hirshowitz, Esq., at 31 Faraday Avenue, Cheetham, Manchester and sent from Lewis Mendelssohn, 26 Sackville Street, Bangor, North Wales, commemorated the life and death of Lewis' wife, Beatrice. He described her as his "great *lernd* wife". Research confirmed that Lewis Mendelssohn, formerly Chalcovitz, of Sackville Street, applied to become a naturalised English citizen on 4th October 1911 (*The London Gazette* dated 3rd November). At the time of the census of that year Lewis and his wife Beatrice, both 36 years old and born in Russia, were living at 26 Sackville Street, Glamorgan in Wales.

Another signed photograph taken by a photographer in Chicago, dated 19th September 1930, was of a boy named Sidney D. Hirsh, then aged 3. Research confirms that Sidney Hirsch, at the age of 77, died on 11th March 2005, residing prior to his death at Wilmette, Illinois, Cook County (*Announcement in Chicago Tribune dated 14th March 2005*). He was survived by his wife Jean (*née Michael*) to whom he had been married for 44 years and daughters Danielle, Elise and Susan. Susan Greenberg, his daughter, opined that her grandfather was born in Russia, moved to Manchester as a baby and went to America when he was 18 years of age. I. Hirschowitz was Sidney's grandfather and a rabbi. Sidney's father was Meyer Hirsh (Hirshowitz). It was common for surnames to be changed.

Meyer Hirsch, his wife, Ethel, and Sidney were recorded in the American census of 1930 with other members of his wife's family, whose surname was Levy. The records show that Meyer (33) was born in England and spoke English; his mother and father were both born in Poland; Ethel (30) spoke Yiddish. The census further indicates that the couple married when he was 25 and she 22. Sidney was two to three years old at the time. The document adds that in 1912 Ethel and other members of her family had arrived in America from Poland and Meyer Hirsch came in 1913 from England. By 1930, as recorded in the census, Meyer was a naturalised citizen. The date of their marriage was 3rd December 1922 (*Cook County Marriage Index*/ www.ancestry.com); Meyer's birth year, as deduced from the census, was 1897. Meyer stated that he was a salesman in a department store. According to the census of 1940, Meyer then 43, again indicated England as his birth place, with Ethel, 40, born in Poland

and Sidney, 12, born in Illinois. They were then living at 98 Lawrence Avenue, Cook, Illinois (One of the photographs found at Vartry Road had 3rd December 1922 written on the back, suggesting that this was indeed Meyer's and Ethel's wedding). Meyer, Ethel and Sidney were still living with his wife's family in 1940 and Meyer died on 18th October 1985, aged 90.

An Israel Hirshowitz, a rabbi, is recorded on passenger lists as travelling from Hamburg to Grimsby in 1902, 1905 and again in 1909. It was noted in 1909 that he was then 46 and married. Israel Hirshowitz died on 8th June 1939, aged 76, at Salford Royal Hospital. He was living before his death at 26 Kelvin Grove, Cheetham, in Manchester. Administration of his will was executed by Esther Rose Hirshowitz, his widow and Annie Israel, a married woman. Esther Rose was living at 51 Huxley Avenue, Cheetham in Manchester when she died on 12th December 1941. Her death at 74 years of age was registered at Southport. Her estate was administered by Annie Israel, the wife of Lewis Harris Israel, in 1943.

Israel Hirshowitz had three daughters. Annie Hirshowitz married Lewis Harris Israel, in Prestwick, Lancashire in 1923. Lewis H. Israel, aged 59, died on 6th June 1951 at Hackney Hospital. He had lived 32 Knightland Road, London E5, Upper Clapton and the will was administered in Manchester by Annie Israel, widow. The marriage of Sarah Hirshowitz to Joseph Wolfin was registered in the first quarter of 1928 at Manchester north. Their daughter, Shoshana was born in April 1929 at Marylebone and their son, Bertram, was born in the first quarter of 1934, in Hackney. In 1933, the family was living at 40 St. Kilda's Road and in 1938 at 18 Wilderton Road, Hackney (*Electoral Registers*). Bertram, now known as Aryeh and living in Israel, remembered that at the age of five when the War started they were evacuated to South Wales but returned to London. Joseph was in the silk-trimmings and textile business. In 1939, Joseph and his elder brothers, Harry and Nathan were recorded in the London telephone directories at home and at business premises at 66 Goswell Road, EC1, 1 Charterhouse Buildings, EC1 and at 27 Stoke Newington Road, N16 respectively.

Joseph and Sarah (Sara) were living at 11 Holy Park, London when Sarah died on 11th March, 1958. Her estate was administered by her husband, a company director. Sarah's death, aged 55 was registered in 1958 at Hendon. Minnie Hirshowitz married Abram Abramovitch in Hackney in the first quarter of 1936. In the census of 1911, Abram Abramovitch, aged 16 and born in Romania in 1895, an errand boy in a clothing warehouse, was listed with his mother, Clara, brothers, Bernard, Morris, Harry and Saul and sister, Kate, at 7 Kent Street, Cheetham, Manchester. Their mother had at that stage been married for 17 years. The three youngest children were born in Manchester, suggesting that the family moved there around 1903. Their father was not in the house on the night of the census but he may have been away on business or out of the country. Minnie and Abram may have known each other as children, as both lived at Cheetham. Abram, of 13 Vartry Road, London N15, died, aged 57, on 16 February 1952. Probate was granted on 26 March 1953 to Maurice Thei, an accountant. In May 1953, in *The London Gazette*, Minnie appeared in a list of aliens who received Certificates of Naturalisation. She was described as a knitwear manufacturer of 13 Vartry Road and her place of birth was shown as Lithuania. In 1957, she travelled as a tourist passenger on the *Queen Mary* to New York and visited her brother, Meyer and his family at 7625 East End Avenue, Chicago 49, Illinois and returned home in September. Her date of birth is shown on the passenger list as 5th March 1900. Again her address was 13 Vartry Road and her occupation manufacturer.

Deeds show that 13 Vartry Road was originally leased on 2nd January 1880 for sixty years by Charles Cleverley Paine to James Edward Bramley. On 27th October 1952, Minnie, then a widow, had taken a lease from the Prudential Assurance Company for sixty years on 13 Vartry Road. Electoral registers and telephone records show that Minnie was living there from 1954 until 1977. Minnie Abramovitch died on 21st March 1979 and was buried on 23rd March at the Adath Yisroel Cemetery, Enfield. Shoshana Wolfin, her niece, was her executor and it was she who cleared the house; Maurice Thei was Minnie's accountant and Minnie left a sizable estate (*Probate London 7th September 1979*). Shoshana, in her eighties and with limited eyesight, identified from the photographs her father and mother. She also recalled that Abram Abramovitch had been ill for some time before he died. Shoshana confirmed that there were knitting machines on the ground floor of the house at 13 Vartry Road, which were used to make cardigans and jumpers; Minnie lived in rooms above and took in lodgers. Many others were listed in the Electoral Registers during Minnie's years at that address. Other family photographs from the later part of her life show Minnie and her sister, Sarah, dressed in various patterned jackets, possibly produced by the former. They show that Minnie very much resembled her mother, Esther Rose Hirshowitz. The photographs, sent by family members from around the world to Rabbi Israel Hirshowitz and his wife, had ended up with Minnie Abramovitch. Minnie and Annie did not have children.

Other houses

The five houses from 16 to 24 Vartry Road originally belonged to Lady Amherst, who was one of the largest landowners in Stamford Hill and who donated the land for St. John's Church; they were marked on the Ordnance Survey map of 1894-6. These double-fronted houses, each with a small back extension, are different in style again from others in the street and were for estate managers or professional people. In 1889, *The Times* carried an advertisement for these same houses, to be let, at auction, at an annual rent of £154 by Edmund W. Richardson, an agent. Alf and Lily Clark lived at 22 Vartry Road from 1937, when they were tenants of a Dr. Bragg, who had previously lived there. In 1990, Alf and Lily moved out to sheltered accommodation but continued to own the house. Lily died in 1995 and Alf in 2002. This information came from a relative, whose cousin saw the deeds of the house, which showed that the house and grounds originally were part of the Amherst Estate.

The deeds of 22 Vartry Road show that a succession of members of the Amherst family owned the freehold for some considerable time. The house was sold by Lord William Cecil and Lord John Pakenham Joicey, members of the Amherst family, for £850 in 1927 (*MDR/1927/48/842*) to Asher Amstell, a commercial traveller of 76b Amhurst Park, Stamford Hill. Then, on 11th January 1932 (*MDR/1932/2/372*), Dr. Tom Bragg bought the house. He moved from 337 Victoria Park Road in Hackney. The house was sold for £1500 to the Clarks, who were sitting tenants, on 11th September 1963. The owners by that time were Mrs. G. J. Bragg and William Russell Newman. Dr. Tom Bragg died in September 1942. The house changed hands again in 2008.

In 1900, according to Poor Rate Books for St. Ann's Ward in Tottenham, 2-16 Vartry Road were owned by J. Conning. The shops in the Terrace, 2-14 Vartry Road, beside the railway, listed in 1908/9 from Kelly's Stamford Hill and Tottenham Street Directory were:

Table of occupants 2-14 Vartry Road (1908/9).

Number	Trade	Name of occupant
2	Grocer	Mr. Arthur Smith
4	Post Office	Mrs. Warner
6	Confectioners	Mrs. Harwood
8	Shirt and collar dresser	Mr. Applegath
10	Dairy Farmer	Mr. A. K. Hislop
12	Draper	Mr. William Westwood
14	Greengrocer	Mr. Daniel Griffin

Before washing machines, it is understandable as to why there was a need for Mr. Applegath's shirt and collar dresser shop, as many of the people who lived in Vartry Road would have had white-collar jobs in the City. The railway and station were important means by which many of the residents in the area went to work in the City as bank managers, solicitors, clerks and the like. Indeed, some early photographs of the street show men wearing top hats. Stamford Hill station is close by and took them quickly to the City. By 1911, Frederick William Applegath was listed at 57 and 59 Oldhill Street, which was an up-and-coming area, nearer to Stoke Newington. Mr. Hislop kept his cows at Upper Clapton Dairy Farm and his shop later became occupied by United Dairies, perhaps the result of a takeover.

In the Post Office Directory of 1937 the following people were listed as owners or traders at the Terrace at the end of Vartry Road.

Table of occupants 2-14 Vartry Road (1937).

Number	Trade	Name of occupant
2	Grocer	Thresher & Co
4	Stationer, Post Office money orders, Telephone Call Office & Savings Bank	William Ernest Grantham
6	Confectioner	James Rippengale
8	Boot Repairer	Albert Ernest Wilkinson
10	Dairy	United Dairies London Ltd.

Number	Trade	Name of occupant
12	Kosher Butcher	Sol Grodsky
14	Greengrocer	Horace & Jesse Perry/Perez
14a	Motor Engineers	"Sussex Garage"
14b	Motor Car Hire	Herbert Langridge

Those listed in 1936/7 in the Electoral Register, at No. 8 Vartry Road were Albert Ernest J. Wilkinson, Gwendoline Rose Alice Wilkinson, Rose Alice Wilkinson and Ann Boyce. The "*Coach House*" had listed, at 14a, an Anthony Terence Rampoller Burgess and Florence Bertha Burgess and at 14b, Rose and William Patrick Vaughn. They must have moved around this time as in 1937, Herbert Langridge, a motor car hire business, was listed along with the Sussex Woodware and woodware manufacturers at 14b. The building was divided into the upper and lower part. In 1942 Reginald Edward Dunkley was registered as a motor engineer at 16 Manor Road, N16. It was for the first time, in 1949, that 14a & 14b Vartry Garages, motor engineers, were named and John Dunkley's father, Reginald, arrived to the site. The upper part of 14b was occupied by Maurice Viner, a glove manufacturer. Many of these buildings were used by clothes and wedding dress manufacturers before demolition.

Gwendoline (Gwen) Bland, *née* Wilkinson, lived at the terrace of shops at 8 Vartry Road until March of 2003, when, according to John Denton, a neighbour and friend, she died at the age of 93, She was born in 1910. Her family lived in an upstairs flat at those premises, operating the commercial premises below. Her brother was a carpet fitter and the same or another brother played an instrument, having been taught by her husband. Gwen had a great affection for her father, Albert. Unfortunately her son, who had moved to Norfolk to live, died of a brain haemorrhage at a relatively young age. John said that Albert made and repaired shoes and people used to come some distance to have him do their work.

Gwen lived most of her life in Vartry Road, except for a few years after she was married, when her father became ill and she came back home to look after him. Gwen went to Stamford Hill School and was married at St. John's Church in Vartry Road. She spoke of many Quaker and Jewish people living in the area. She also talked about a music academy in 51 Vartry Road at the corner of Paignton Road, which she attended. In 1937, a Miss D. Henshaw was registered in the Post Office Directory as a teacher of music, living there. There was a physician and surgeon called Simon Gardner at 37 Vartry Road. Earlier in 1908/9, Albert Tooley and his wife lived at 101 Vartry Road and were listed in the Post Office Directory as teachers of the pianoforte.

Bert Ambrose

Gwen recalled stories about the people who lived at No. 22 Amhurst Park, because the top floor of her house overlooked the large house on the corner with Holmdale Road, next to the railway line. She recalled, as a young girl, watching garden parties with bands playing music and trees draped with fairy lights. During the 1920s and 1930s, she said that the family of a famous bandleader called Bert Ambrose (1896-1971) lived in the house. *Ambrose* was the name of his band and it regularly played on the radio in the 1930s.

In 1911 the following people lived at Amhurst Park: 22 Robert Gunn McKay, 24 Miss Goodman, 26 Herbert Mitchell, 32 William Owen, 40 Henry W. Lee and 78 Joseph Lockley. William Owen may have been related to one of the builders who developed houses in Vartry Road. The large houses in Amhurst Park had a variety of different uses and by 1937, Number 46 was a nursing home.

In 1915, Woolf A. Rutkowski lived at No. 22. The Ambrose family must have moved to the area after 1918 when no one was living at that address. In 1921 Louis or Lewis Ambrose was listed in the Post Office Directory at 22 Amhurst Park. The Electoral Registers show that in 1923 Lewis and Rebecca Ambrose lived at the address, as did Ethel and Godfrey Joseph and there was a Bert Ambrose living in the same house in that year. One might assume that he was the musician. Lewis Ambrose, likely to have been his father, was a wool merchant who had previously lived in another part of North London. Ambrose was known by many nicknames, such as *"Ammy"*, Bert (sometimes Bird) short for Bertram and it is said that his formal name was in fact Baroukh, a Hebrew name. On his death he was listed both as Benjamin and Baruch.

In 1927, Bert Ambrose was elected musical director of the Mayfair Hotel where he started to assemble what, over the next 20 years, was to become the finest dance band in the UK. He was extremely successful, made a fortune and gambled a great deal. He stayed at the Savoy Hotel, married a singer and played for the princes who later became kings. Another of his claims to fame was that he made Decca's first ever recording, on February 7, 1929. He played at the Embassy Club, which he partly owned and he also lived and played in Biarritz, Cannes and Paris. In 1934 a Bert Ambrose lived at 34 Hereford House, North Row, Park Lane, W.1.

Bert had started playing a violin at a very early age. At fifteen he went to America with his aunt, where he continued his studies. His first professional job was as a violinist at the Palais Royal and he became a conductor of a band in New York at the age of twenty. A magazine, *Memory Lane,* suggested that he had returned to England in 1922 because his mother was ill. This fits in with the only record in the Electoral Register of a Bert Ambrose that year at 22 Amhurst Park.

From 1937 to 1940, Vera Lynn sang with his orchestra and later Bert Ambrose discovered the singer, Kathy Kirby, when she was only 16 and singing at the Ilford Palais, at a point in the 1960s when his career was declining. She had great success with the song "Secret Love". He managed her career and there was talk of a relationship. She was said to be so devastated by his death that her career ended and she became a recluse and died in 2011. Apparently the only family member at his funeral was a cousin who was not known by any of the musicians who attended. He was married to at least one person and there my have been two children; a Patricia Ambrose, whose mother's name was Tyler, was born in Spring 1934. There was also another child called Monica. A blue plaque commemorating his achievements adorns an exterior wall at the Mayfair Hotel, London.

In 1931, David and Hetty Javerbaum had replaced the Josephs at 22 Amhurst Park. By 1935/6 two other families, one, Jack, Sarah and Sylvia Figoff, the other, Anne, Louis Frankel and Alice Hillman had replaced the Javerbaums as neighbours of the Ambroses. In 1936/7, Louis and Rebecca Ambrose had moved or died, as Esther and Morris Woolf lived in their house.

In 1939, for the first time, a block of flats now called Cambridge Court was listed as an address, having been built on the site of those houses some time between 1937 and 1939. The architecture is clearly 1930s in style with curved windows and wrought ironwork.

Alfred Hitchcock

Someone of great fame who had connections with the area was Alfred Hitchcock, who was born in Leytonstone in 1899 and around 1910 went to the Jesuit College beside St. Ignatius Church on the corner of St. Ann's Road and Stamford Hill. He did not live in the area but he moved as a child to Salmon Lane in the East End of London, where his father owned a greengrocer's business. His parents wanted him to have a strict Catholic upbringing so he was dispatched to St. Ignatius College every day by train, from Limehouse, arriving promptly for Mass before school at 8.45 a.m. He will have arrived at Stamford Hill Railway Station, on the Great Eastern Railway Line, situated at the end of Vartry Road. In fact, Hitchcock had a strange fascination with travel and as a child frequently travelled for pleasure all over London on trains, trams and buses.

The small college of some 250 students and the school symbol on the boys' hats was "*SI*" and the students were often teased about their "*silly idiot*" hats, as they walked down to the River Lea to eat lunch. The school had been constructed in 1894 and when Hitchcock attended in 1910, the church was still under construction. It has been said that the tower scene from "*Vertigo*" was inspired by the towers of St. Ignatius College. A priest who taught at the school remarked that there were always many pigeons flying around the top floors of the church and college buildings, which may have influenced "*The Birds*". The front part of the college, which was similar in style to the façade of the church, has since been demolished but the back of it is still there. In an interview that Hitchcock gave in 1973 to the "*Ignatian*", the magazine of the college, he said he had not forgotten his days at Stamford Hill. He described the method of corporal punishment used at St. Ignatius as "*highly dramatic*" and that one of the ways in which he learned to create suspense in a film was from his experience as a schoolboy waiting to receive the ferula. Sir Alfred Hitchcock died in 1980; his college has since moved to Enfield.

The Coach House, 14a/b and Terrace, 2-14 Vartry Road

Some of the earliest buildings in the area at that time were in the Borough of Hackney and Haringey or partly in both. In fact, some houses in the Haringey part of street must have had gardens in Hackney. A large building at the end of Vartry Road, originally a coach house and stables, is marked on the 1894 Godfrey map. Planning books at Bruce Castle Museum archives show that approval to a builder called Goodman was given on 6th January 1882 for two stables and a coach house. Presumably the house in which he lived was built just before that time. Later in July, other stables and a shed were added. It was later recorded in 1908 with different units and uses. The hay lofts and living quarters were upstairs with a high ridged loft ceiling. The building was not of any great architectural value but interesting historically because it had changed use over time with evolving transport modes.

On the back of the Ordnance Survey map for Stamford Hill of 1894-96 (*The Godfrey Edition*), Mrs. Goodman is recorded at Cambridge House (24 Amhurst Park) and Alfred Probyn at Gloucester House (26 Amhurst Park). Their rear gardens went all the way back to Vartry Road. Information on access to Cambridge House and Gloucester House from Vartry Road was recorded in the Rates Book of 1900. The coach house, stables and rooms over the stables were at the end of the back garden of 24 and 26 Amhurst Park and were shared by both houses. They were owned by Mrs. Goodman, who paid rates for them to St. Ann's Ward in Haringey as they were in a different borough to that of her house. Cambridge House was then occupied by Benjamin Goodman and Gloucester House was occupied by Robert Prevost. Goodman, the builder, may have been from the same family but he may have died earlier. At the time of the 1911 Census, Miss Goodman was still living at 24 Amhurst Park but by 1913 it was occupied by William Alfred Watts. In 1915, houses at 24-30, Amhurst Park, had gardens extending to Vartry Road.

By August 2004, the old Coach House building, prior to demolition, was in a sorry state upstairs, with water damage and floorboards partially lifted. On the first floor, in a room at the front of the building, there was one original cast iron fireplace, without surround, probably taken by the people who removed some of the floorboards for salvage. This may be where the stable boys and footmen lived. There were other smaller rooms but they may have been added later. The main spaces were large, with some of the large wooden rafters still visible between roof panels. Downstairs, there were three spaces, one where the garage used to be and two smaller rooms. There was only one brick fireplace in one of the spaces. The chimneys had already been removed by this time as there was no evidence of them on the outside. A few of the wooden supports still were visible and they were, according to the asbestos removal people, covered for fire prevention purposes with asbestos. This was taken away prior to demolition in October 2004 to build new houses.

There was an old sign on the front of "*Vartry Garages Motor Engineers*", illustrated with motorcars and an old petrol pump situated at the corner of the building. Previously, there had been another advertisement attached to the front but it had gone. The metal plaque on the side wall of the coach house which had on it the following inscription, "*Parish of St. John at Hackney, 1898, J.W. Whiter, J. Schofield, Church Wardens has now gone*". The boundary between Hackney and Haringey near the coach house was moved in 1989 and the whole of Vartry Road is now in Haringey.

John Dunkley operated a mechanic's workshop from the building, repairing cars. He explained how he had come to the area to work in the garage with his father as a child over fifty years previously. His father, originally from Stoke Newington, operated the garage, despite having lost his hand in an explosion, when he was twenty-three years of age. It was never a hindrance, though, to his success. John had completed his apprenticeship with another firm in Southgate and then returned to work with his father. His father had looked after a 1937 Wolseley 9 Hornet belonging to a Mrs. Milton, a woman of modest means, for many years. It was sometimes seen parked outside the building. John also had an old Rover, in beautiful condition, which he kept in the garage for some 19 years.

John recalled that when he first came to the area, the land to the side and back of the garage, where he used to play, was a bomb site. This was at 26 Amhurst Park, hit by anti-aircraft shells on 18th September 1940. 42 Amhurst Park, behind St. John's Church and the vicarage and 66 and 68 were destroyed by high explosives on 23rd September 1940, as documented by Jennifer Golden in her book, *Hackney at War*. There are photographs at Hackney Archives Department of some of the damaged houses.

John's father died in 1966 and his mother shortly after and John took over the garage. His four children have been successful in their endeavours and his second daughter, Georgina Dunkley, is a well-known and successful potter once based at the Chocolate Factory, Stoke Newington, N16. She makes striking, tall, twisted, clay, lamp bases, some up to six feet high.

John Dunkley remembered a story about the day he was tending to the garden behind St. John's Church. It was quite dark at the time and he put the shovel against the wall for a rest. Moments later there was light and the whole length of the wall had collapsed, fortunately for him, in the other direction. He recalled also that previously another mechanic repaired cars on the adjacent site where other new houses are now situated. According to John, the trees on the street in front of it blocked this man's way and it was said that he went out in the dead of night and chopped them all down. Everyone knew that it was he who had done it but the matter was laid to rest.

John moved to Suffolk to live and work in the early 2000s and sold the site in October 2003. He did a fine job repairing old and classic cars and in fact some of his customers continued to go to Suffolk to have their cars repaired, such was his service and their loyalty.

The Aged Pilgrim's Friend Society's Home, 1883 – No. 81 Vartry Road

One of the largest, grandest and oldest buildings in the street is directly opposite 54 Vartry Road. The *Aged Pilgrim's Friend Society's Home* was created and endowed by Sarah Ward, its building work having commenced and been completed in 1883. A great plaque of Portland Stone on the front of the building commemorates the benefactor. Miss Ward originally had the intention of leaving money in her will to build the almshouses but then decided personally to supervise the buying of the land and the project. This was a considerable feat as she was in her eighties at the time and in poor health. Her father had been associated with a Home in South London but she chose to build one at Stamford Hill because she lived, at the time, at Sydney Place, Stamford Hill and was able to oversee the work. An indenture (*MDR/1882/34/124*) bearing the date 12th October 1882 and registered the same day was made between Charles Dorman of No. 23 Essex Street, Strand, a gentleman, of the one part and Sarah Ward of Sydney Place, Stamford Hill, a spinster, of the other part. It was for all that parcel of land in the Parish of Tottenham High Cross in the County of Middlesex near Stamford Hill, measuring approximately 77 ft. by 143 ft., for messuages and tenements. The plan shows Paignton Road, Charles Street, Franklin Street and Vartry Road. St. John's Church was directly behind the site.

A year later, Sarah Ward of Sydney Place, Stamford Hill, of the one part, transferred this land with ten messuages and tenements, now No. 81 Vartry Road, to the trustees of the Aged Pilgrims' Friend Society, including William Heathfield of No. 44 Lincoln's Inn Fields, Thomas Marshall and many others, of the other part. The indenture (*MDR/1883/34/910*) dated 8th November was registered on 14th November 1883. Miss Ward, lived for a further three years until January 29th, 1885. The architect was William Henry Sainsbury Gilbert and no expense was spared. The building is faced with Portland stone and red bricks from outside the area and the back has the more traditional yellow brick of London. When it was built, it overlooked the iron church and fields. Each pensioner received a pension of ten guineas a year from the endowment and each resident had two rooms, so often sisters shared, with a warden to look after them. It was linked to the Woodberry Down Baptist Church, which recommended pensioners to the Society.

Notes kept by the Society make it clear that Tottenham had pockets of poverty as the area developed and "*there was a problem of crime in the locality and the Home Committee wrote to the police in 1892 requesting more police in the area*". The home was surrounded by railings and locked at nights. The Society sold the home in the 1980s to a developer and its apartments are now privately rented.

St. John the Divine, Stamford Hill, Vartry Road, 1886

St. John the Divine, "*St. John's*", was an "*Iron church*" originally in Franklin Street, opened on 24th February 1880, by the Bishop of Bedford. Its planning and construction had been organised by Mr. Walter Letts, son of the Vicar of St. Ann's, the Reverend J. D. Letts and it had been funded mainly by Fowler Newsam. St. John's, at its inception, was a "*Chapel of Ease*" and the "*gift of the Living*" was vested in the vicar of St. Ann's. The church at that time could not fulfil all the duties of a normal church.

It 1885, a site was given for a new church of St. John's at Hackney, Vartry Road, and the foundation stone was laid by Princess Christian of Schleswig-Holstein on 6th March, 1886. A separate parish was formed and the Reverend Reginald Letts, the second son of the vicar of St. Ann's, became the first vicar. S.W. Grant was the architect of the church, which seated 650 people. The total cost was £5,600 and the church was consecrated in July 1886. A parsonage was added in 1887 and completed in 1889, the latter being the only building which survives today, now converted into flats. The vicar of St. Ann's had wanted a church for the poor, of whom there were many in the area. The greater part of the building work had been contributed to by St. Ann's Parish and the final debt was cleared as a result of a bazaar in 1889, attended by Princess Christian. The land for the church and vicarage was donated by Lord Amherst and the Bishop of London's funds contributed to the building, which straddled the boundaries of Haringey and Hackney. Bishop William Walsham How, who worked and lived in East London, had a house at Upper Clapton where his associates were always welcomed. He was rector of other City of London Churches and the prime mover in raising large amounts of money for the East London Church Fund, being primarily interested in the spiritual uplifting of the members of his east London Diocese. He accepted the position of Bishop of Wakefield in 1888.

An indenture (*MDR/1892/12/309*) dated 28th April was registered on 29th April 1892. The parties were Charles Dorman of No. 23 Essex Street, Strand, of the one part, to Trustees of the Bishop of London's Fund, of the other part. The parcel of land, 60 ft. wide, south of Vartry Road, approximately 92 ft. deep, was in the boroughs of Tottenham and Hackney. The plan was marked in pink to show the Tottenham part and yellow for Hackney. St. John's Church was marked on one side and the land to the left of the site belonged to Charles Dorman, what is now Nos. 26-58 Vartry Road. Most of the site was in Hackney. The land was for the new St John's Hall and School, completed by 1894. The purchaser had permission to use the sewer.

In 1896, Candler submitted an application to build a soup kitchen in St. John's Hall and School. The plans were approved on 21st January 1897. Following the Provision of School Meals Act 1906, according to the minutes of an education meeting, on the 22nd January in 1908, it was decided to give break- fast to 450-500 children from three local primary schools, in St. John's Hall, next to the church, which had been refurbished. It was then the only building in the area which was equipped to serve food to the children from the schools. Breakfast was of currant buns and cocoa. Reginald Letts lived at St John's Vicarage in 1900.

On Friday, May 28th 1937, *The Weekly Herald* reported an incident relat- ing to St. John's Church headlined "*Shot vicar succumbs*". The story goes that the Reverend Charles Sykes was called to the church hall to investigate some trouble. Alfred Kirby (26), former churchwarden and scout leader, shot at Reverend Sykes and other members of the church and then killed himself. Walter Longhurst, an official from the church who lived at 11 Berkeley Road said how he was shot at by a man in the church hall at about ten that Wednesday morning, when he was laying out some scones. Someone yelled to him "*Don't move*" and then shot at him three times as he walked towards the stage. He dashed for the door just as the Reverend Sykes was about to enter the church hall. He told him not to go in because the man was armed and just as the vicar entered, he was shot in the face by the gunman, who was hiding behind some curtains on the stage. When the police arrived, they found the vicar in a serious condition and the mystery gunman dead, on a platform above the stage, with a gun beside him. Reverend Sykes was taken to hospital and died the following Sunday from his wounds. The verdict at his inquest was *"wilful murder"*. The vicar did not know who had shot him. The family of Alfred Kirby said at the inquest that he had been close to a nervous breakdown on a number of occasions and he had been suffering from ill-health but would not tell his family what was wrong. His father had given him a gun some time before, when he said that he wanted to go rabbit-hunting. After being asked by his father to get a license for it or get rid of it, Kirby must have taken it to the church for safe-keeping. The verdict from the coroner was that he shot himself while the state of his mind was unbalanced. The family had lived in Richmond Road until the previous year and Kirby had been an enthusiastic participant in the Scouts and in church organisation, working every evening in the church or the church hall, until he moved. The relationship between the Reverend Sykes and Alfred Kirby had been a good one, according to church members. No other reasons were given for the incident.

During the Second World War, St. John's had also suffered bomb damage to its roof, which was repaired, but the church lost its local support in 1950s. The final straw came in 1966 when the heating broke down and the church authorities took the unusual step of consecrating a wooden hut, built inside the church, as a way of trying to keep the worshippers warm, when funds could not be found to repair the fabric of the building. Finally, the late 1970s, after the demolition of the church, Jubb Powell House was built on the site.

Few records for St. John the Divine, Vartry Road, Stamford Hill exist at the London Metropolitan Archives, because of the chaotic nature of the decline in the building. However, some beautifully decorated and printed invitations and programmes for concerts from the 1890s did survive. The concerts were organised to raise funds for the church to administer food for the poor in the soup kitchens as well as funding the refurbishment. Other documents referred to the sequence of events relating to the transfer of the parish. In September 1975 the Parish of St. John's, Vartry Road was united with St. Bartholomew, Stamford Hill and St. John's old church was declared redundant and demolished. It confirmed that St. John's Worship Centre and mission church, in what used to be the Vicarage, was in the Parish of St. Bartholomew, Stamford Hill. In 1980 it was transferred to the Parish of Holy Trinity, High Cross, Tottenham.

By 1984, there were only twelve members of the congregation and the Worship Centre on Vartry Road was finally closed down and sold to developers for private apartments. A bid by the Servite nuns to buy the vicarage was rejected; they run the sheltered accommodation in Jubb Powell House, standing on the site of the original church next door. Reverend Brian Smith was the curate when the church closed and he confirmed that all the papers had gone to Holy Trinity. He also provided some useful articles from newspapers explaining what had happened. He was disappointed that the church had closed due to a lack of funding and a decision by the church hierarchy to refuse to help churches in less well-off areas coping with many pastoral problems.

Woodberry Down Baptist Church, 1882 (No. 190 Vartry Road)

Records exist of a meeting among local Baptists who made the decision to build a satellite church linked to Hackney Downs Baptist Church. The deed, dated 21st March 1882, showing transfer, was registered on 24th April 1882 (*MDR/1882/13/927*), between Charles Dorman of the one part and the Reverend Vincent Tymms of 224 Evering Road, Clapton and others identified as James Theodore Griffin, William Richard Rickett, William Payne, Thomas Ogden, William Phillips, William Foster, Cox and Cleeve Hooper, trustees, of the other part, from the Baptist Church. The land in question was referred to as part of :

> …all that triangular piece of meadow land situated in the Parish of Tottenham High Cross in the County of Middlesex containing in the whole by estimation 4a 3r 31p be the same more or less bounded on the west by the Seven Sisters Road on the north east by the land of one John Giblett and on the south east by land now or late of ____Wilson Esq.

A drawing of the site showed the rectangular parcel of land was 80 feet by 120 feet. William Page, W.T. Ogden, Vincent Tymms and J. Austin Meen, elders in the Baptist Church, were responsible in 1873 for buying the land on which the church was built, although no documents confirm this date. John Allen and Sons, of 24 Helburn Park Road, submitted plans to the Council on 11th June 1882 for the new Woodberry Down Baptist Church at the corner of Vartry Road and Seven Sisters Road. The architects were Paull and Bonella. The foundation stone was laid in 1882 by the Reverend T. Vincent Tymms, who was Head of the Baptist organisation in London. It certainly was one of the earliest buildings on what used to be farmland in the area. The church used to have a steeple, which was struck by lightning and badly damaged in the 1970s and it was not replaced.

Table of Planning applications 1890-1899 for Woodberry Lodge Estate.

No. of Plan	Name	Address	Date of plan notice	Nos. of houses or alterations proposed	Locality	Remarks from engineer and surveyor's office
1618	G H Candler	37 Albert Rd	13 Mar 1890	12 11 20	Charles St NE side Charles St SW side Townsend Rd	Disapproved 15 April 1890.
1618	G H Candler	37 Albert Rd	13 March	As above	As above	Approved 6 May 1890
1618	G H Candler	12 Albert Rd	13 Mar 1890	1	Charles St	Approved 2 Dec 1890
1618	G H Candler	37 Albert Rd	21 Feb 1891	21	Townsend Rd in lieu of 20 disapproved 29/4/1890	Amended plans approved

No. of Plan	Name	Address	Date of plan notice	Nos. of houses or alterations proposed	Locality	Remarks from engineer and surveyor's office
1646	Mrs Jewell	86 Amhurst Park	14 July 1890	20	Vartry Rd	Approved with the exception of 17&18. These have not sufficient space at rear. The Board will not undertake nor be responsible for the drainage of cellars
1651	Mrs Jewell	86 Amhurst Park	29July 1890	14 workshops	Vartry Rd & Lawrie Rd	Amended plans approved
1663	Mrs Jewell	86 Amhurst Park	12July 1890	2 workshops	Laurie Rd	Amended plans approved
1750	G H Candler	12 Albert Rd	26 Jul 1891	16	Townsend Rd	Approved 19 Sep 1891
1858	G H Candler	12 Albert Rd	9 Sep1892	3 7 14	Townsend Rd Vartry Rd Vartry Rd	Approved 13 Sep1892
2003	G H Candler	12 Albert Rd, South Tottenham	30 Aug 1894	2 storey bay windows	Vartry Rd	Approved 26 Sep 1894 (one corner of Charles St (Richmond Rd) and one next to Mr. Owen's house (59 Vartry Rd)
2008	A. Porter	702 Tottenham High Rd	10 Oct 1893/4	Mission Room	St John's Mission Room, Stamford Hill	Approved
2142	G H Candler	12 Albert Rd	11Oct 1894	4 4 25	Richmond Rd Franklin St Vartry Rd	Approved subject to SW drain not passing through sewer manhole 30 Oct 1894
2200	John Farmer	25 Vartry Rd	13Feb 1895	Dog kennels	Rear of 25 Vartry Rd	Disapproved on account of drainage
2317	G H Candler	12 Albert Rd	9 Dec 1896	Soup Kitchen	St. John's School Vartry Rd	Approved 21 Jan 1897
2352	G H Candler	12 Albert Rd	21Feb 1896	22	Manchester Rd	Approved subject to separate surface drain to each house 3 March 1896
2411	G H Candler	12 Albert Rd	18Jan 1896	1	Manchester Rd	Approved 1896
2412	G H Candler	12 Albert Rd	18 June 1896	1	Vartry Rd (54)	Approved 1896 (Page 116)
2412	G H Candler	12 Albert Rd	7 Dec 1896	Conservatory	Rear of 54 Vartry Rd	Amended plan approved Dec. 1896 (Page 135)
2999	G H Candler	12 Albert Rd	20 Dec 1898	15	1-29 inclusive Laurie Rd	Approved
3087	G H Candler	115 Vartry Rd	11 May 1899	31	Heysham Rd	Approved 29 May1899
4049	G H Candler	150 Vartry Rd	23 Aug 1899	1	25 Heysham Rd	Approved 29 May 1899

6

Early days of the Candler family

Documents in the possession of the Candler family, gathered in 1883 by a researcher, recorded information about the family. The notes showed Richard Candelar, in the sixteenth century, originally coming from Walsingham in Norfolk.

John Candler, who died, aged seventy, on 24th July 1782 and his wife Ann, who died on 10th July 1776, aged sixty, were buried in the churchyard at Benacre, in Suffolk. A number of entries in the *19th Century British Library Newspapers* database after 1816 record Stephen Candler of Benacre as one of the members of South Cove Association *"for prosecuting horse stealers and other persons guilty of a felony."* Stephen and Mary Candler were also buried in the churchyard of St. Michael, Benacre, which is close to Covehithe. Stephen Candler, a tenant farmer, died, aged eighty-two, on 6th February 1842 and his wife Mary on 26th July 1843. On 11th August 1843, a matter of weeks after her death, there was an advertisement in the local newspaper that said that the entire household effects of the late Mary Candler, including her furniture, beds and Suffolk hemp sheets, were to be sold by auction at Wrentham. They had a son named George, who died in 1824 at the age of twenty-one. Census information suggests that Samuel Candler, born at Covehithe, may have been an elder brother of this George Candler, as his date of birth was around 1795. Stephen was the father of Samuel Candler and George Herbert Candler and Samuel Horace Candler, born at Alresford, in Essex, were Samuel Candler's sons.

Samuel Candler married Elizabeth Fennell on 10th October 1817 at Covehithe in Suffolk; he would have been around twenty-two at that time. The couple moved from Suffolk to Alresford to live in one of the grandest houses in that area. It is possible that Samuel inherited land or money from his wife's family and it may have been that the family farm was run by his father and elder brother, Stephen.

At the time of the 1841 Census, Stephen and Elizabeth Candler *née* Newson, aged forty-five and forty respectively, were living at South Cove. He was a farmer and their three children were Frederick, aged fifteen, George aged fourteen and Edgar aged seven. Frederick William Newson Candler was born on 1st September 1824 and George Alfred Stephen Candler was born on 21st August 1826. The children were born at South Cove. By 1851, Stephen was a widower, running a farm of one hundred and ninety acres and employing more than seven men. His birthplace was given as Covehithe, which was the same as his brother Samuel. All his children were still at home.

In 1853, an advertisement was published in the local newspaper for the sale of a farm at South Cove, situated inland from Covehithe. The tenant farmer, Stephen Candler, was to show prospective buyers around the farm. He may have taken it over after his mother died in 1843; he still had another one in the area. The advertisement declared that it had one hundred and thirty-four acres of land, a house, barns, a cottage and the best partridge shooting in the area. Stephen Candler's obituary confirmed that he died on 19th February 1879, aged eighty-five, which made his date of birth 1794 and older than Samuel. The fact that the Candlers were tenant farmers with more than one farm suggested that they were relatively wealthy.

At the time of the census of 1881, Stephen's son, George Candler, was fifty-four and head of house at South Cove, still farming one hundred and ninety acres, employing eight men and one boy. He was unmarried and had an unmarried housekeeper. On 12th June 1883, an Ipswich newspaper published the obituary of George Alfred Stephen Candler, a farmer, of South Cove in Suffolk, aged fifty-six. Memorials show that he was buried in the churchyard of St. Laurence, South Cove, in Suffolk, with his father. The will declared that he was late of South Cove, near Wrentham in Suffolk and confirmed that he had died on 6th June 1883. It was proved by his brother Frederick William Newson Candler of Southwold, a retired farmer and Edgar Robert Samuel Candler, of Bungay, in the said county, a commercial traveller and hotel keeper, his brother and executor. His effects amounted to £2,420. Edgar Candler was recorded in the census of 1881 as a commercial traveller with his large family and a young wife at Regent Road, Great Yarmouth, in Norfolk. His first wife may have died, as there was a twelve years difference in age between him and his wife Sophia, aged thirty. His wife and eldest son, by his first wife, were listed as drapers. His elder daughters were scholars. Edgar obviously had started a business as hotel-keeper at Bungay by the time his brother died. The George Candler in question was a cousin of George Herbert Candler, who had had several cousins at Great Yarmouth.

The earliest document confirming that Samuel Candler, the father of George and Samuel, was living at Alresford Lodge was a tithe document, dated 1839. He was listed as the owner/living in Alresford Lodge and Lime Kiln Farm. Today, the house is situated next to a quarry. A burial was recorded for Elizabeth Candler, aged fifty-two, on 16th April 1841, at St. Peter's, Alresford. An entry in the *Ipswich Journal* on Saturday 17th April 1841 confirmed that she was the wife of Samuel Candler:

> ...9th inst, after a long and protracted illness, which she had endured with much Christian patience, deeply lamented and deservedly respected by her family and friends, Elizabeth, wife of Samuel Candler of Alresford Lodge, Essex, aged fifty-two years.

In the 1841 Census, Samuel Candler, a widowed farmer, aged forty-eight, was recorded at Alresford. He was living with two servants named Will Bowls, aged twenty and Henry Rand, aged fourteen. Less than six months after Elizabeth had died, church records at St. Peter's, Alresford show that on 4th October, 1841, Samuel Candler married Sarah Whittaker Wade, a spinster and a farmer's daughter. A birth was registered for Sarah Whittaker Wade, daughter of Thomas and Susanne Wade, on 10th September 1809, at Alresford. In relation to the marriage, Samuel's father was shown as Stephen Candler. Witnesses were Philip Kingsley and Thomas Wade. The marriage was registered at Tendring in Essex Oct/Nov/Dec 1841 (*Vol XII 491*). According to the 1841 Census, there were other members of the Wade family living in the Alresford area.

As Elizabeth, his first wife, died in April, Samuel did not wait long before he married again. Sarah Elizabeth, daughter of Samuel and Sarah Whittaker Candler, of Alresford Lodge, was born on 13th April 1842, and was baptised on 12th July, that year. She was born prematurely and may not have been a healthy baby as on 30th May 1843, there was a record of a burial for Sarah Elizabeth Candler, aged thirteen months, of Alresford Lodge. No further births were recorded for Samuel and Sarah Candler but on 25th November 1846, a burial was recorded at St. Peter's, Alresford, for Sarah Whittaker Candler, aged thirty-eight. Samuel Candler was widowed for a second time.

Six months later, on 10th June 1847, another marriage between Samuel Candler, a widower, and Mary Ann Cross, a spinster, born at Holbrook, was recorded in the Parish Church of Frating and was registered at Tendring in Essex. Samuel would have been around fifty-four by this time and Mary Ann almost forty. Her father was John Cross, a farmer and she was living at the time of the marriage at Frating, in Essex. Among the guests at the service were William and Hester Caldecott, who lived at Frating Lodge, near Colchester, Anna Cook, Henry, Suzanna and John Cross. Within two years, on 20th June 1849, their first son, Samuel Horace Candler was born; his father referred to his son as Horace. Samuel Horace's birth was registered at Tendring, in Essex, in September 1849 (*XII Page 257*). His birth date is recorded on his gravestone, as is the fact that he had lived at Alresford Lodge.

7

The Candler brothers

Documents at Essex Record Office at Chelmsford show that around 1850 the elder Samuel Candler was involved in a lengthy legal dispute. A letter forming part of the documents was addressed to Samuel Candler at Alresford Lodge. He was one of the named executors of the will of Arthur May, of Weeley, in Essex, when it was proved that year. There were debts owed to the deceased by various people and the executors called in the debts so that the estate could be paid to the beneficiaries as directed in Arthur May's will. Samuel Tillet, another executor, who lived at Hill House, Lexden, was eventually forced to sell the contents of his house, presumably to pay back money owed to the estate; Candler and Tillett were on opposite sides in the dispute. These events were happening around the time when Samuel Horace and George Herbert Candler were born.

The 1851 Census confirms that the Candler family was living at Alresford Lodge:

Table of occupants in 1851 at Alresford Lodge.

Name	Age	Relation/Occupation	Birthplace
Samuel Candler	56	Head/Farmer 240 acres employing 7 men and 2 boys	Covehithe Suffolk
Mary Ann Candler	41	Wife	Holbrook Suffolk
Samuel H Candler	1	Son	Alresford Essex
George H Candler	6 mths	Son	Alresford Essex
Anna Marie Mann	34	Niece	Sotterly Suffolk

Mary Ann was born in 1809, at Holbrook, in Suffolk, which is some distance away from both Alresford, in Essex and Covehithe, in Suffolk. Samuel Candler was fifteen years older than his wife. In the census of 1841, Samuel Candler's age had been stated as forty-eight but he was born some time between 1793 and 1795.

In 1861, the family was living at Lodge Farm but it was farming only 190 acres.

Table of occupants in 1861 at Lodge Farm.

Name	Age	Relation/Occupation	Birthplace
Samuel Candler	66	Head/Farmer 190 acres employing 5 men and 2 boys	Covehithe Suffolk
Mary Ann Candler	51	Wife	Holbrook Suffolk
George H Candler	10	Son	Alresford Essex
Anna Marie Mann	44	Niece	Sotterly Suffolk

There were also two servants living at the farm.

The 1871 Census still showed the residence as Lodge Farm.

Table of occupants 1871 at Lodge Farm.

Name	Age	Relation/Occupation	Birthplace
Samuel Candler	76	Head/Farmer 200 acres employing 5 men and 2 boys	Covehithe Suffolk
Mary Ann Candler	61	Wife	Holbrook Suffolk
George H Candler	20	Son	Alresford Essex
Anna Marie Mann	54	Niece/housekeeper	Sotterly Suffolk

There was a slight increase in the number of acres farmed; up from 190 to 200. Anna Marie Mann was the unmarried daughter of Samuel Candler's sister, Mary, still living with her relations and helping with the running of the household.

Samuel's sister, Mary Candler married John Mann on 25th November 1806, at Covehithe in Suffolk. By the time of the census of 1851, Mary and John had already died. Their son, Charles Mann, aged forty-three, was head of house, living with his sisters Caroline, Ellen F. and Emmeline Mann, aged thirty-six, twenty-five and twenty-one respectively. He was running a farm of three hundred and thirty-five acres employing eleven agricultural labourers and four boys. Charles was born on 19th April 1807 and Caroline was baptised on 19th July 1813, both at Covehithe. Anna Marie was born on 29th April 1816 and Ellen Julia born on 20th October 1824 at Sotterly. Emmeline was also born there on 4th August 1828.

When Samuel wrote his will in 1864, he was residing at Alresford Lodge. He appointed his wife, Mary Ann Candler, William Cross of Frating, a farmer, and Henry Pearl Cross of Henley Hall, Suffolk, also a farmer, possibly her brothers, as executrix and executors. It would appear from the will that, at that time, Samuel had copyhold lands, which he instructed his trustees or their survivors to sell by auction or private contract with *"full power to fix with a reserved bidding"*. He wanted all his real and personal estate to be converted into money and £2,000 to be converted into government securities in England, by way of a trust. The interest and dividends were to be paid to his wife for the maintenance and education of his two children. His sons would eventually receive equal shares as tenants in common. The trust made allowances for a sum, not exceeding a third of their share, to be made available *"during their minority for their advancement in the world"*. If they died before achieving the age of twenty-one and their mother survived, the trust was to be for her sole use. A further £1,000 was to be divided at the discretion of his wife or trustees and given in equal shares to his nephews and nieces unspecified. His niece, Anna Maria Mann, was the only extended member of his family to be named in the will and was to receive £19. A codicil was added on 3rd June 1871 replacing the two members of the Cross family with his sons Horace and Herbert Candler, who were then over twenty-one. Samuel lived for a further six years after writing the will.

The family gave up the farm after 3rd June 1871 and before March, 1877 as by the latter year they were living at West Bergholt. It may be that his elder son, Samuel Horace Candler, having decided to take up a career as a solicitor after his law degree, did not want to return to the farm. George Herbert Candler, likewise, may not have wanted to take over the farm from his father. Alternatively and/or additionally, it may be that they were forced to give up the farm for financial reasons or were unable to renew their lease.

The date of death of Samuel Candler, aged eighty-four, was recorded on his grave in the churchyard of St. Peter's, Alresford and in his will as 2nd March 1877. It was proved by his wife Mary Ann and his two sons, Samuel Horace Candler and George Herbert Candler, to whom admon was granted, on 23rd April 1877. His effects were under £3,000 and in the will was written "*no leaseholds*". A note was added, when the will was proved, to say that their names were in fact Samuel Horace Candler and George Herbert Candler and not Horace and Herbert, as written in the will.

By the time of the census of 1881, George Herbert Candler, then aged thirty, was living at Colchester Road, West Bergholt, Essex with his wife and widowed mother. George's stated profession was that of farmer (out of business). His mother, Mary Ann Candler, declared herself a farmer's wife and independent and she was the head of house. Mary Louisa Candler was described as a farmer's wife. They had only one servant. George's cousin, Anna Maria Mann, had left their home and was back living with her brother, Charles Mann, aged seventy-three, at 7 Holton Road, Holton, in Suffolk, at the time of the census of 1881; Charles was no longer a farmer. Anna Maria was then sixty-four years of age and described as a farmer's daughter. Their niece, Emmeline Cass, was staying with them.

Samuel Horace Candler

The elder son of Samuel and Mary Ann Candler, Samuel Horace, known as Horace, was recorded at Trinity Hall Cambridge, as an undergraduate at the time of the 1871 Census. The following information was given by the Alumni Office at Cambridge:

> ***Candler, Samuel Horace*** Adm. Pens. (age 19) at Trinity Hall (Cambridge) June 4, 1868. Son of S. Esquires., of Arlesford, Colchester. Matric. Michs.1868; B.A. and LL.B. 1872; M.A. 1897.

The family has a photograph of Horace when he received his M.A. in 1897. Presumably in memory of family and childhood days, Samuel Horace Candler called his London house *Alresford* and George may have applied the style of architecture prevalent in that part of Essex to the houses that he built in this area of South Tottenham. It is easy to understand why Alresford Lodge made such a lasting impression on Samuel H. Candler. The house is set in a wonderful location overlooking the River Colne and Wivenhoe with splendid gardens and view, near the ford; there are said to be Roman ruins in the Garden. The front of the house was built in Tudor times and has different brickwork from that of the side. According to the owners, in 2004, the side was damaged in an earthquake in the 1700s and rebuilt with different bricks, very similar to those at the house in Vartry Road. They and their successors have since made other alterations. The other families associated with the house in the 1870s were the Bartons and the Higginbothams who were owners of large sections of land in the area. The owners in question retained a number documents relating to the history of the house. The earliest known documents (*D/DGd E38*), relating to *Alsford* (Alresford) Lodge, date from the period 1698-1715 and are held at Essex Record Office. They give details of the condition of the house and a valuation. Other papers include the will of Sir John Lawson, whose will was proved, on 25th September 1665. He may have been a previous owner. John Lawson was knighted by Charles II in 1660 and died from wounds received at the Battle of Lowestoft, in 1665, while Vice-Admiral of the Fleet.

In 1896, Samuel Horace Candler acted on behalf of the village school in Alresford, when it was extended by public subscription. He may, in fact, have been one of the trustees. He stayed at Alresford Grange, a grand house which still exists, during this time, so he still maintained links with the area. He drew up the conveyance using his firm, Kingsford, Dorman & Co. of 23 Essex Street, Strand.

Samuel Horace left Alresford as a boy to go to boarding school and then to university. By the time of his marriage to Annie French, on 18th September 1877, at St. Clement Danes, Westminster, in the Strand (*Vol. 216 Pg.125*) he was settled in London. He gave his address as 23 Essex Street, Strand. Annie was born at Edgware, Middlesex in 1850. She was twenty-seven and Samuel was twenty-eight years of age; she was registered as a spinster and he as a solicitor. The two witnesses were her father, William French, a gentleman and her sister, Helen French. The marriage produced no children.

Legal documents (*C16/933/F43*) at *The National Archives* show evidence of a legal action, French v. Sims, dating from 1874, involving Samuel Horace Candler and his wife. The plaintiffs to the action were Jane Sophia French, Annie French represented by William Henry Lee, "*her next friend*" and Helen French; William Henry Lee was a clerk at Kingsford, Dorman & Kingsford. Horace Candler joined the suit in 1877, after he married Annie French as did Helen French in 1882, when she married Walter Herbert Cook, together with, at the same time, John Cook, Walter's father. The defendants were Eliza Sims, wife of the testator and William French, executrix and executor of the will of Thomas Sims.

The action concerned the will of Thomas Sims and it was not settled for a number of years. Sims had stated in his will that his wife Elizabeth was to receive any rents from his freehold, leasehold and copyhold land and that after annuities were paid, the residue of his estate was to be divided half between George Thomas Sims and the other half among the three children of his cousin, William French. Thomas Sims was living at St. John's Wood, in London, when he died on 23rd April 1874. His will was proved by his widow, Eliza Sims and William French, draper on 4th May that year. His effects were under £9,000.

The Chancery pleading said:

> The plaintiffs are desirous of having the personal estate of the said testator administered and the trusts of his said will and codicil carried into execution and the property subject thereto ascertained and secured for the benefit of themselves and all other the persons interested therein under the decree of this honourable court.. The said testator was at the time of his death seized and possessed of real and leasehold estate of considerable value and was possessed of personal estate also of considerable value and more than sufficient for the payment of all the legacies... under the said will and codicil.

The action was filed on 4th May 1874 by Messrs. Kingsford, Dorman & Co., solicitors for the plaintiffs. A sworn affidavit, made by William French, to say that the three plaintiffs were his daughters, was included with the documents.

Samuel Horace Candler joined Kingsford, Dorman & Co. in 1877, the year that he married, having been admitted to the Roll in 1876. but it was not until 1881 that he was listed as one of the partners at Kingsford, Dorman, Kingsford, Candler and Moore. It was not just coincidence that he was practising there while the above action was taking place. It is likely that he met Annie French at their offices and would have known a great deal about her personal circumstances and potential inheritance.

In the census of 1871, William French, aged fifty-seven, linen draper, was recorded as being at the High Street in Edgeware in Middlesex along with his wife, Anne aged fifty-six. Their children were Jane Sophia, thirty-four, Annie, twenty-one and Helen, eighteen, all then unmarried. His wife, Anne died between the years 1871-1881.

At the time of the census on April 3, 1881, Samuel and Annie, the latter described as a housewife, were living at 21 Josephine Avenue, Tulse Hill, in Lambeth. Her father, William French (67), born at Stanmore in Middlesex, then a retired draper and her sister, Jane S. French (44), were visiting. The two other guests were John Pycock Candler and Alice Mary Candler aged seven and five respectively. These were the children of George Herbert and Mary Louisa Candler and possibly they were visiting their uncle and aunt, as the Easter holidays and the census happened in April. However, it was confirmed by John Pycock Candler's daughter, Patricia Turner, that one or both of the children, at some point, went to live with their aunt and uncle.

In the 1891 Census, Samuel's mother, Mary Ann Candler, was recorded at 16 Trinity Road, Lambeth along with a cook and housemaid. She was eighty-two and living on her own means. This was the house where her son and daughter-in-law lived but they were not registered in London at the time of the census. Mary Ann died in October, 1898, at the age of ninety. Her death was registered in Lambeth, South London and she was shown to have been living with her son, Samuel, and his wife Annie, before her death. Mary Ann Candler was buried with her husband Samuel in the grave at Alresford on 4th November 1898.

On 25th August 1892, William French died at 6 Torrington Park Villas, in Finchley and left most of his estate, worth £6,000, to his son-in-law, Samuel Horace Candler and daughter Jane Sophia French.

On the night of the 1901 Census, Samuel and Annie Candler were staying at the Victoria and Albert Hotel in Torquay, a grand establishment. In the same year, after Charles Dorman died, Samuel Horace Candler became the eldest partner in the firm and died in 1903 at the age of fifty-four.

Information and photographs of Samuel Horace Candler, George Herbert Candler and the latter's son and daughter, John Pycock Candler and Alice Mary Candler were in the care of Patricia Turner, George's grand-daughter, who died in 2008. Patricia intimated that possibly there were difficulties involving George Candler and the Dormans. However, Annie Candler bought property in South Tottenham with the Dormans in the 1920s so it seems unlikely that this would have happened if there had been bad feelings, or the issue may have been confined to only one part of the family.

On 17th March 1903, Samuel Horace Candler was buried next to his parents in the graveyard of St. Peter's Church, Alresford. Below is a summary of his will:

> **Candler**, Samuel Horace of "Alresford" 16 Trinity Road, Tulse Hill, Surrey and of 23 Essex Street, the Strand, Middlesex, died 12 March, 1903 at "Alresford". Probate London 16 April to Annie Candler, widow. Effects £19,177 11s. 4d. (Probate year 1903)

When Jane French died on 13th June 1905, she left her estate to her widowed sister Annie and to Francis Thomas Dorman. Jane was living, at the time of her death at "*Abbotsford*" Torrington Park, North Finchley, the same address as Annie occupied at the time of the census of 1911. This is a summary of her will:

> **Candler**, Annie, wife of "Abbotsford", Torrington Park, North Finchley, Middlesex widow died 1 September 1933. Probate London 30 September to Lawrence (sic.) Charles Dorman solicitor, John Pycock Candler, bachelor of medicine and Edith Nellie Constant Cox (wife of Edward Scrivener Cox). Effects £41,332 13s 5d. Resworn £41,298 15s. 9d. (Probate year 1933)

Annie was cremated at Golder's Green and her ashes interred with her husband in the churchyard at St. Peter's, Alresford on Wednesday 6th September 1933, by Reverend Pelham Thompson, the vicar of Christchurch, North Finchley. She died at the age of eighty-three. Annie made provision in her will, in the sum of £200 for the rector and churchwarden at Alresford, to ensure that the graveyard was kept in good order. The church itself is now a ruin, having been destroyed in a fire in 1971 but the Candler graves, made from granite and engraved are in extremely good condition. She also left £200 to her servant Ada Aylott. John Pycock Candler inherited his aunt Annie Candler's house, this having been recorded in the Memorials of the deeds in the 1930s at the London Metropolitan Archives. A trust was set up by Annie Candler for the recipients of her estate. Edith Nellie Constant Cox, cited in the will, was the niece of Annie Candler and the daughter of Helen Cook, *née* French.

George Herbert Candler

Records show that George Herbert Candler was born on 11th September 1850 and he was baptised on 10th October that year at St. Peter's, Alresford, in Essex. His father's place of abode was Alresford Lodge and his occupation was given as yeoman. The birth was registered in Braintree, Essex (*XII Page 26*), in December of that year. His father also referred to his son as Herbert.

George Candler married Mary Louisa Pycock on 9th January 1873, in the parish church at Newton-on-Rawcliffe, in the county of York. She was living with her family in the vicarage at Newton and George gave Alresford Lodge as his address. The marriage was registered in the Pickering district of Yorkshire. Her father, Joseph Pycock officiated as the minister of that parish. Her brother William Joseph Pycock and Samuel Horace Candler, the groom's brother, were witnesses at the wedding. As a gift, George Herbert and Mary Louisa had been given a bible by Reverend James Hopkins Swainson, the rector at Alresford. Its front page recorded the same date of marriage and, later, the births of their two children. Swainson was living at the rectory, at Alresford, at the time of the 1851 Census.

Mary Louisa became pregnant within months of the marriage. John Pycock Candler was born 7th October 1873 and Alice Mary Candler on 26th July 1875. Baptismal records at Alresford show that John Pycock Candler was baptised on 26th October 1873, and Alice May Candler on 12th September 1875.

By 1886, George and his wife Mary Louisa were living in London. He is recorded in the electoral rolls in the Tottenham area at 37 Albert Road in 1886, 1887, 1888, and 1889. Perhaps coincidentally, Edmund Wood, a builder developer, gave 37 Albert Road as his address in 1882. George was registered to vote in 1890, 1893, 1896 and 1898 at 37 Albert Rd. In the census of 1891 George Herbert and Mary Louisa Candler were listed, aged forty and forty-five respectively, along with Sarah Scrivener, a servant. The census confirmed his place of birth as Alresford and his wife's as Morley in Yorkshire, where she was baptised on 6th August 1845.

George made building applications from this address and the original houses in the street no longer exist. In 1895 and 1900, however, they were owned by Kingsford, Dorman and Co., George's brother's law firm.

Mary Louisa Candler died, possibly of cancer, on 28th July 1893, aged forty-seven. Her death was registered at Edmonton in London. George Herbert and Mary Louisa were living in rented accommodation at 12 and 37 Albert Road in South Tottenham, London, when she died. The latter address was recorded at South Metropolitan Cemetery, Norwood, where she was buried on 2nd August 1893; John Pycock, her brother officiated at her funeral. The *Ipswich Journal*, on 5th August 1893, announced the death at Stamford Hill of Mary Louisa Candler. She was described as the wife of George Herbert Candler and the eldest daughter of the late Reverend Joseph Pycock, formerly rector of

Newbourn, Suffolk. She was the third member of her family to die young, with only one brother and one sister left alive in 1893. On 17ᵗʰ October 1894, probate was granted to her estate agent husband George Herbert Candler. Her effects amounted to some £53, approximately.

George H. Candler took a second wife, May Annie Rose Parfitt. He married a year after the death of his first wife. A copy of the marriage certificate gave the date as 20ᵗʰ November 1894. They were married at All Saints Church, Finchley Road, in St. John's Wood, in the Parish of Marylebone. Unfortunately, her age was given as "*full*", which means over twenty-one and not specified. The witnesses were named as James Wallis Butcher, and Annie Eleanor Harman. The latter may have been May's sister. May Annie Rose was living, at the time of the wedding, at 49 Townshend Road, London NW8, which is close to All Saints Church. Townshend Road runs parallel to Avenue Road, which leads on to Regent's Park. It was and still is an expensive area in which to reside. George Candler gave his address as 12 Albert Road, South Tottenham. May offered evidence of no occupation and George's occupation was stated as "*estate agent*". Her father's name was Ponsonby May Parfitt, already deceased and described as a "*gentleman*". James Wallis Butcher, according to the Census of 1891, worked for the Metropolitan Police and his wife was a music teacher; three of his children were clerks. In 1888, he was a chief inspector in the criminal investigations department at Scotland Yard.

The 1891 Census confirmed that Ellen Parfitt was the head of household at 49 Townshend Road. She was a widow, living on her own means and aged fifty-seven, making her year of birth around 1834. Also living with her were May, aged twenty-five, born in 1866 at Deal in Kent and Florence, aged twenty-one and born around 1870. Ponsonby May Parfitt must have died between 1869 when Florence was born and 1881. As the family lived at Chatham in Kent, it is possible that the father's occupation was connected to the Navy or shipping.

On the night of the 1881 Census, May Parfitt, aged seventeen, was staying with her sister, Ellen Harman, a "*mantle maker*", aged twenty-nine and her family at 3 Stephen's Cottages, Camberwell, in Surrey. Ellen's husband was George Harman, a builder, born, as was his wife, at Chatham in Kent. On that night, besides George and Ellen's four children, three of whom were born in Camberwell, were also Florence Parfitt, her younger sister and Ellen, their widowed mother, then aged forty-five. George Harman may have worked for George Candler, developing the houses and flats in South Tottenham.

George Candler and May were married for only five years, as she died in 1899. Her death, aged thirty-six, was registered in Edmonton (*3a 213*). She must have owned property or other assets in her own right, as in her administration it was shown thus:

> **Candler**, May Annie Rose of 115 Vartry Road, South Tottenham, Middlesex (wife of George Herbert Candler), died 3 October 1899. Administration London 15 January to the said George Herbert Candler, estate agent. Effects £1544. 2s. 7d. (Probate year 1900)

By 1901, George was still a widower. At the time of the census he described himself as a house agent working on his own account and as head of the house. He was managing properties in the *Woodberry Lodge Estate* and, possibly, taking in rent. Also living in the house then were Emma C. Wilson, a twenty-seven year old married domestic housekeeper who had been born in Toronto, Canada and Ada S. Milton, a twenty year old single domestic servant, who had been born in Rickmonsworth, Hertfordshire.

George moved on. In the autumn of 1903 he married Constance Mackenzie Pitman, recorded in Hackney (*1b 940*). She was then thirty-nine years of age and George was fifty-two. The couple married on 13th November 1903 at St. Olave's Church, at Manor House, London, in the Parish of Stoke Newington. George was shown as a widower and estate agent, living at 115 Vartry Road but not registered at 54 Vartry Road, although the 1901 Census placed him there. Constance was a spinster of 2 Woodberry Grove, Finsbury Park and her father was Nathaniel Gerrard Pitman, a gentleman. The witnesses at the wedding were Frank G. Pitman, her brother, and F.K. Pitman, most likely her sister, Florence Kate Pitman.

Hugh Barton Candler, George's great-grandson, after consultation with his aunt, Patricia Turner, George's grand-daughter, identified a photograph of a man whom he believed, due to perceived family likeness, to be George Herbert Candler. There was certainly a family resemblance to photographs known to be of John Pycock Candler and Alice Mary Candler, George's children. It is an original "*Chromotype*" photograph produced in the studio of G.C. Crawford Barnes, Colchester who "*guarantees this photograph to be*

7.1 Left, John Pycock (provided by George Candler's great granddaughter Jane Fawls) and right, taken in the same studio, George Herbert Candler.

absolutely permanent". As the words "*Chromotype patent*" are printed on the back of the original photograph this indicates that the photograph will have been taken between c.1878 to c.1884. The quality and thickness of the paper further confirms the period. Candler would have been around 28-35 at that time which is reasonably consistent with the image in the photograph. At that time he was living in West Bergholt, Essex not far from Colchester. This would place Candler close to where he was living at the time in question.

8

The Pitman antecedents

Captain Colin William and Helen Jane Lindsay

James Mackenzie married Jane Martin on 15th May 1813 at St. Giles, Camberwell, in London. Helen Jane was their eldest child; Martin Mackenzie was baptised at 2nd April 1819 at St. Mary, Lambeth, in London and a third child named William Thomas Peter Mackenzie was born on 13th October 1826 and baptised at St. Leonard, Shoreditch, on 3rd December that year. The Mackenzie family moved around quite considerably so her father may have been in the Navy, as Helen married at Teignmouth, Devon.

Photographs in the possession of the family identify Captain Colin Lindsay and Ellen Lindsay. He is dressed in naval uniform holding a sword. It was taken at the studio of George A. Dean, in Douglas, Isle of Man. Dean had a studio there from 1847 until he went to live in New York in 1877. A photograph of "*Ellen*" Lindsay was produced at the studio of Abel Lewis, Douglas. Lewis was known to have a studio at Douglas from 1862 to 1885, when he moved from the Isle of Man. Her dress suggests that it was taken around 1865-1875 and she was wearing black mourning beads.

Lindsay Clubb, a descendent of Charlotte Emma Pitman, suggested that Colin Lindsay was, in fact, Colin William Lindsay. He had a copy of a marriage certificate showing that on 27th October 1846 Helen Jane Mackenzie married Colin William Lindsay, by licence, at East Teignmouth, a seaside town in the district of Newton Abbot, in Devon. The certificate showed Colin William Lindsay to be a bachelor and a Royal Navy lieutenant and she a spinster. Her father's name was James Mackenzie and his father was William Lindsay, both gentlemen. Witnesses to the wedding were Eliza Lindsay, Margaret Davy, Mary Rose Bradley, Muriel Spencer, Leah and Margaret Spratt. The minister was also named Bradley. Lindsay Clubb was of the opinion that as Muriel Spencer was a witness and this confirmed that it was the family in focus, as he believed that Helen Jane Mackenzie's grandmother was Sarah Spencer. Colin Lindsay was living, before his marriage, at Marylebone and Helen Jane at East Teignmouth.

Eliza Lindsay may have been Colin's sister. A birth was recorded for Eliza Lindsay, daughter of William and Charlotte, at St. Marylebone, on 31st May 1811. William Lindsay had married Charlotte Neaves Raine on 14th February 1804 at the Old Church of St. Pancras, close to Marylebone. Leah and Margaret Spratt were both baptised at East Teignmouth on 22nd June 1828 and so obviously were local girls. Possibly, Mary Rose Bradley was related to the minister.

A scrapbook, of some eighty pages, was passed down through the Clubb family. Its title page has the following dedication to Charlotte Unwin, the mother of Constance Mackenzie Pitman:

Charlotte Unwin from her affectionate friend Elizabeth W. Long
November 24th 1847...

Charlotte Unwin would have been about seventeen when she started the scrapbook. The first page contains an embroidered picture of a posy of flowers entitled the gift of friendship. Another page explains that friends were invited to contribute to the book. Most entries date from the years 1848-1849. Emma Crowther, Elizabeth and Mary Ann Long, George Carter and Henry Hilliard contribute on a number of occasions. Henry Hilliard, from Glasgow, contributes with a poem by Robert Southey (Robert Harvey Hilliard was one of the executors of Elizabeth Unwin's will so Henry may have been a relative). On 14th June 1857, Charlotte copied a poem by William Cowper, a religious poet and hymn writer (Cowper eventually died in an asylum in 1800 but he lived with a couple named Morley and Mary Unwin and married Mary Unwin after her husband died).

Some pages in the scrapbook include small floral collages and landscapes, printed pictures of fashionable women in dresses of the period, poems, some attributed to various people and many copied, and postcards from the Great exhibition of 1850 showing Russian, French and Austrian stands with images of sculpture. Some of the men who contributed may have been friends or suitors from the time before she met Nathaniel. There is also an original watercolour of a little cottage by a lake, signed by Colin William Lindsay, with a poem on the same page, which was dated 23rd September, 1848, added by George Carter. In addition, there are some competent unsigned pencil sketches, one of Loch Lomond, possibly by Lindsay.

Colin William Lindsay may have met Charlotte Unwin only after his marriage, in 1846. His wife, Helen was at least twelve years older than Charlotte and possibly her cousin and Helen's marriage to a Royal Navy officer probably seemed most romantic. The stories that Colin Lindsay must have told Charlotte as a teenager about his travels to far-off places are likely to have been enthralling.

The Lindsays were certainly staying in London at the time of the 1851 Census. Lindsay was on half-pay from 1848 so he may have taken a trip with his wife to visit relations or to what may have been his family's birthplace in Scotland and then have given Charlotte the sketches on his return.

The scrapbook offers an interesting insight to the intellectual abilities and interests of this educated young woman.

O'Bryne's *A Naval Biographical Dictionary* 1849 contains a record of the early career of Lieutenant Colin William Lindsay. He passed his naval examinations in 1827, when he was sixteen. He then obtained a commission on 10th January 1837 and was appointed on 8th February, 1837 to *The Russell*, under the leadership of Captain William Henry Dillon, serving in the Mediterranean and in Lisbon. On 8th April 1839, he transferred to *The Curacao* under Captain

Jenkin Jones, helping with the fitting for the South American Station. When he returned home at the end of 1842 he was paid off. On 23rd February 1844 he joined *The America* under the Honourable Captain John Gordon, attached to the forces in the Pacific. Lindsay was said to have left this ship on his arrival back in England in 1846. By 1848, according to O'Bryne, he was on half-pay.

The Times gave an account of an incident that took place while Lindsay was Lieutenant on *The America*. The first entry was dated Monday, 24th August 1846, when there was an announcement of Lindsay's promotion to First Lieutenant on the ship *"America"*. The previous First Lieutenant, Agassiz was unable to fulfil his duties, due to illness. He had been taken to Haslar Hospital after the ship had arrived at Portsmouth to be refitted. The freight from *The America* had been landed at the Royal Clarence Yard and then housed in the South West Railways Company Carriages before the cargo was conveyed to London on a special train at three in the morning. The *"treasure"*, perhaps gold and/or money, arrived at the bullion offices of the Bank of England by six that evening.

A reference to Colin William Lindsay was dated Thursday 27th August 1846 in the form of an account of proceedings at the Court Martial of the Honourable Captain John Gordon of *The America* that took place at Portsmouth. Gordon was answering a charge that on 26th April, 1846 he sailed from Valparaiso in Chile for England, in disobedience of orders from Sir George Francis Seymour, in breach of the 22nd Article of War. The First Lieutenant, Agassiz, gave evidence, despite his ill-health; Lindsay was also called to give evidence in his capacity as Second Lieutenant on *The America*.

The Court Martial hinged on the interpretation of orders between the Honourable Captain Gordon and his superior officer, Rear-Admiral Sir George Francis Seymour. The Captain decided to take his ship across the Atlantic, understanding that if he had not taken that decision he would have to have had to wait three months, in Chile, to receive further orders. It was this decision that caused him to be before the tribunal to be court-martialled. Gordon had taken the *"treasure,"* described above, belonging to merchants at Valparaiso, in Chile, valued at around two million dollars and transported it to England. The merchants also gave evidence and explained that it was their opinion, in January 1846, that the cargo should be transported as quickly as possible, for safe-keeping. Despite the safe arrival of the cargo in England, the Rear-Admiral questioned Captain Gordon's decision as he thought that there was a risk that by not waiting for further support from other naval vessels, for the first part of the journey from Valparaiso, the fifty-gun frigate had not been sufficiently well protected. The Rear-Admiral believed that there was a risk that England was potentially on a war-footing with America.

It was a high profile case, as one of the captain's brothers was the Earl of Aberdeen and another of his brothers, the Honourable W. Gordon, was lately an M.P.; both attended the hearing. Second Lieutenant Colin Lindsay, who had a slight speech impediment, was called upon at very short notice to give evidence in the trial and he protested that he was not prepared. The report of the hearing intimated that Lindsay was withholding information but that his interrogator was patronising and aggressive in his manner, *"putting words in his mouth*", as the witness took so long to answer questions. Second Lieutenant Lindsay was reprimanded for his "*confused testimony*" as he did not seem to know the capabilities of other naval vessels in the area. Other accounts of the proceedings reported that Lindsay had been badly treated at the Court Martial. The Honourable Captain Gordon was not court-martialled and received a reprimand for taking the decision he had done. It was noted by the court that Gordon had not taken any pecuniary advantage, given the value and risk involved in transporting the cargo.

In the *Caledonian Mercury* of 21st September 1846, another report explained that following the Court Martial, *The America* went to Plymouth, where it was refitted, under the direction of First Lieutenant C. W. Lindsay. The Honourable Captain Gordon later complimented Lindsay by stating that he had completed the job "*in the most perfect style*". First-Lieutenant Agassiz was then invalided out of the Navy at Portsmouth and the ship was to go to the Mediterranean after refitting. Maybe as a result of his reprimand, Acting First-Lieutenant Colin William Lindsay was then replaced by someone who was eight years older and possibly more experienced than he. If O'Bryne's account is to be believed, it seems that Lindsay did not rejoin *The America* after refitting and stayed back, marrying a month later at East Teignmouth, in Devon.

At the time of the census of 1851, then aged thirty-nine, London-born Colin Lindsay was living at 17 Gloster Street in the Regent's Park area in the Borough of St. Pancras. The street was just off Queen's Square in Bloomsbury; it does not exist today. His occupation was shown as "*Lieutenant in the Royal Navy on half-pay*". The age of his wife, Sheffield-born Helen Jane, was, recorded as twenty-eight, making her year of birth 1823.

On Saturday 26th March 1853, the *Hampshire Telegraph (Portsmouth) and Sussex Chronicle* recorded that Lieutenant Colin William Lindsay had been appointed to command the East End Lane Coastguard Station, near Sheerness. In the *Caledonian Mercury (Edinburgh) edition* of 31st May 1859, it was noted that Lieutenant C. W. Lindsay had been removed as inspecting Lieutenant from East End Lane Station to Douglas Division.

At the time of the census of 1861, Colin William Lindsay, then aged fifty and Helen Jane, his wife, apparently aged forty-four, were listed at 74 Love Lane, Onchan, on the Isle of Man. His occupation was given as "*coast guard inspecting Lieutenant, Isle of Man division*". In 1863, Lindsay was shown in the Post Office Directory to be living at 2 Auckland Terrace, Douglas. There was a further reference in that year to Lieutenant Colin Lindsay, as the inspecting lieutenant, when he visited a coastguard station at South Quay on the Isle of Man. In the naval and military news section of the *Daily News*, on Saturday 15th April 1865, it was noted that Lieutenant Colin William Lindsay has been placed on the retired list, with the rank of Commander.

Colin William Lindsay died at Auckland Terrace on Christmas Day 1865 and was buried at Braddan Churchyard, Douglas on 29th December. This was reported on Saturday 30th December. He was fifty-six and may have been ill before his retirement in April that year. This confirmed his year of birth as 1809. He left a will, proved in 1866, which bequeathed everything to his wife.

By the time of the census of 1871, Helen Jane Lindsay, a widow, was at 9 Beislane Street, aged forty-eight, living on a widow's pension, comfortably off, with a servant. Letters in the *Manx Recollections, Memorials of Eleanor Elliot,1894,* by Katherine A. Forrest, make reference to Mrs. Lindsay, widow of a naval officer. Mrs. Elliot wrote that Mrs. Lindsay had offered to read out the letters that her husband had received from the Pitcairn islanders and invited her friends to her home one evening. Everyone invited was delighted at the prospect of the reading. She referred to her husband as Captain Lindsay, which may have been the title he used after his retirement from the Coastguard service. Mrs. Lindsay said that her husband had visited the Pitcairn Islands on more than one occasion during the early part of his career and he had talked of how enchanting were the people of the island and of their prowess at swimming and climbing; even the older women. When her husband left the islands, the women hugged and kissed him, asking him to return and some of the islanders considered Lindsay to be their friend. His travels were obviously an exciting topic of conversation. A letter, dated 1843, is reproduced in the *Manx Recollections*, written to Lieutenant Colin Lindsay by Frederick Young, a direct descendent of Edward Young, one of the mutineers from *The Bounty;* Edward was the nephew of Sir George Young. In the letter, he explained that some inhabitants of the island had died from Influenza and that Mr. Fletcher Christian was a magistrate on the island. Many of the mutineers on *The Bounty* were from the Isle of Man and stories about their descendents were of much interest to the inhabitants there. Another letter from the same writer, dated 1849, confirmed that Captain Lindsay had recently married, as he tells him that his sister had decided to name her daughter after Captain Lindsay's bride. Of course, communication between these places will have taken a long time. Given that Colin Lindsay was recorded at various places in the Southern Hemisphere, in the Pitcairn Islands and in South America, it is likely that he knew his wife-to-be for some time before he married, as there was not much time for courtship between August and October 1846.

When Colin Lindsay visited the Pitcairn Islands, he was either on *The Curaceo* or *The America* as both ships visited that part of the world. It would appear that Colin William Lindsay was no ordinary naval officer. He was also an accomplished artist. His detailed watercolours, long before photography was available to the masses, show an incredibly talented artist recording places, events and native people in Spain, South America, California, Hawaii, and the Sandwich Islands going about their everyday lives; an album of his watercolours was sold at Christie's in 1990s. Mrs. Lindsay had said that her husband had visited the Pitcairn Islands, in the South Pacific, so he may have recorded some of the inhabitants there.

Helen Jane Lindsay, was recorded in the census of 1881, aged fifty-nine. She was living at 51 Athol Street, Onchan, on the Isle of Man. She had a native islander, Elcanor Cain, as a boarder, the latter living on income from rents of houses and dividends. In 1891, the census showed that Helen Jane was lodging at 11 Belmont Terrace, Douglas, Isle of Man, then aged seventy and living on her own means.

Over the years in five census returns from 1851 to 1891, Helen Jane Lindsay's stated year of birth varied from 1818 to 1823. A baptism was recorded for Helen Jane Mackenzie, daughter of James and Jane Mackenzie, at St. Peter's Cathedral, Sheffield, on 6th October 1817. This tallies with her age in the census of 1861 and her place of birth but it indicates the extent of the other discrepancies.

Helen Jane Lindsay, at eighty years of age, was buried with her husband in *grave 3101*, at Braddan Cemetery on the outskirts of Douglas, on 13th November 1896, suggesting that she was born around 1817. Also commemorated on the same gravestone was Captain Martin Mackenzie, brother-in-law of Commander Lindsay, the former having died, aged twenty-five. Helen Jane Lindsay left everything she had to her spinster cousin, Mary Ann Jenkins, who lived at *"The Grove"* Greater Stanmore, London. It might be assumed that all of Helen's immediate family members were by then dead.

9

The Pitman family

The matriarch, Elizabeth Unwin and her family

Nathaniel Pitman's mother-in-law, Elizabeth Unwin was listed in the census as blind. Thirty years earlier, on the night of the 1851 Census, on 30th March, her family was recorded as living at 198 Upper Thames Street, in the Parish of St. Michael, Queen Hithe; Elizabeth was described as an annuitant. She was even then a widow, aged fifty-seven, having been born in Sheffield, in Yorkshire. Two daughters were living with her; Sarah, aged twenty-nine, born in Yorkshire and Charlotte, aged twenty, born in London and her son, Joseph, aged twenty-two, his birthplace having been listed as Stepney, in Middlesex. His occupation was that of an iron merchant's clerk. The family moved from Sheffield to London some time between 1822, the year in which Sarah was born and 1829, Joseph's birth year. The baptisms of Joseph and Charlotte Unwin were registered at St. Dunstan, Stepney on 17th April 1831, as the son and daughter of Joseph and Elizabeth Unwin.

The third wife of George Candler, Constance Mackenzie Pitman's middle name was the maiden name of her maternal grandmother; she never met her maternal grandfather, as he died on 16th June 1849. Records show that Joseph Unwin married Elizabeth Mackenzie on 1st October 1817 at St. Peter's Cathedral, Sheffield, in Yorkshire. Elizabeth Mackenzie was born on 19th November 1793 but she was baptized on 5th May 1796 at St. Peter's Cathedral on the same day as her three brothers, William born in December 1788, James in December 1790 and Thomas in January 1796. Their parents were Peter and Sarah. According to their descendant, Lindsay Clubb, Peter Mackenzie married twice. His first wife was Sarah Spencer, whom he married in Nottingham on 1st January 1788 and the second was Betty Bell, whom he married on 22nd January 1800.

Listed in the same household, both in 1841 and 1851, was George Mackenzie (or *McKenzie*), in 1851 aged forty-five, making make his year of birth around 1806; he was born in Derbyshire. A George Windleborough Mackenzie, whose parents were George and Mary, was baptised on 28th April 1807 at All Saints, Derby. Other documents in archives in the Court Rolls of the Manor of Thundridge in Hertfordshire link, the Mackenzie and the Windleborough families. George Windleborough Mackenzie may have been a cousin or lodger. Like Joseph Unwin, Elizabeth's son, Windleborough Mackenzie's occupation was shown to be that of an iron merchant's clerk, though McKenzie was a good deal older than Joseph Unwin; they, possibly also with Elizabeth's husband until 1849, may have worked at the same company.

The will of the elder Joseph Unwin, Elizabeth's late husband, described as a commercial clerk of Thames Street in London, was proved on 27th September 1849. He left everything to Elizabeth and George Mackenzie was a witness to the will. It is possible that George Mackenzie worked with the father as well as his son, Joseph.

In the census of 1861, George *Mackenzie*, was still listed with Elizabeth Unwin, her son Joseph and daughter, Sarah *"Spencer"* Unwin, at 198 Upper Thames Street. This was the only time that Sarah had entered another Christian name. The fact that her middle name was Spencer would appear to confirm a family connection, as her grandmother's maiden name was Spencer. By then, Charlotte had married and had left home. George Mackenzie's relationship to the head of house was now described as *"lodger"* and his occupation had changed to that of commercial clerk; Joseph Unwin's occupation had changed to that of a commercial traveller.

The Gerrard and Pitman family names are listed in an old document in the possession of the Pitman family, recalling dates and times of birth, so it will have been written by a close family member. The names of the Pitman children were Nathaniel John, born and baptised in 1810 at St. Nicholas, Wesleyan-Methodist Church in Colchester, who died 1812, William Henry, born on 20th September 1814, Louisa Ann, born on 29th August 1816 and baptised at an independent church at Hereford, Nathaniel Gerrard, born in 1822, Rebecca Ann, born in 1826, who died 1827. There is a record of a baptism for Nathaniel Gerrard Pitman, son of Isaac Pitman and Elizabeth Gerrard, on 21st February 1822 at the Wesleyan Church of St. Michael, Hereford; he was born on the same day.

Nathaniel's mother, Elizabeth (Eliza) Gerrard was born on 22nd June 1786 to John and Anne Gerrard. Isaac Pitman married Elizabeth Gerrard on 22nd October 1809 at Wyke Regis in Dorset. The family document shows the Gerrard births to be in Dorset and these are confirmed in records at Old Meeting Hill Street, Presbyterian Church in Poole, in Dorset.

Charlotte Unwin married Nathaniel Gerrard Pitman on 13th May 1852 at St. James, Tollington in Middlesex. The minister who officiated at the wedding was W. B Mackenzie, possibly a relation. Joseph Unwin, her brother, was present at the occasion, along with Anne Crowther and Anne *Goodhaugh*. Isaac Pitman was shown to be Nathaniel's father. Charlotte was twenty-one and nine years younger than her husband. She gave her place of residence in the Parish of St. Michael, Queen Hithe. He stated his address as Holloway, so they may have married close to where Nathaniel lived. At that time, Nathaniel was working in a silk manufacturing business at 12 King Street, Cheapside, in the City of London, not far from Upper Thames Street and he may have been living with his brother before the marriage. Nathaniel and his brother William may have worshipped at St. James' Church and met Charlotte there, where William Bell Mackenzie preached. According to the census of 1861, William B. Mackenzie, aged fifty-five, was born in Sheffield in Yorkshire and was described as the incumbent of St. James', Holloway. He was living at 10 Canonbury Park North, in Islington with his wife, Maria and family. By 1871 Maria C. Mackenzie was a widow.

Family photographs exist of Nathaniel Gerrard Pitman and Isaac Pitman, taken by Henry Lock, whose studio was at 248 Shoreditch, London. There is also one of Joseph Unwin, probably the son, taken at Pumphrey Photo of 21 Paradise St. and 101 New St., Birmingham and at 3 Market Square, Wolverhampton. Alfred Pumphrey was quite a famous photographer, from a Quaker background, who had studios in both places, certainly at the time he married in 1863. Joseph Unwin had a fresh complexion, bushy beard, dark hair and was prematurely bald and looked then about thirty-five. The clothes he wore were typical of the period 1860-1870 with a high-necked waistcoat, collar and bow-tie. Joseph, being an iron merchants' clerk in 1851 and a commercial traveller in 1861, may have had photographs taken while travelling in the area, Wolverhampton being a city closely connected to the lock industry and metal trades.

A family photograph probably of Elizabeth Unwin, Nathaniel's mother-in-law, was taken at 10 Barnsbury Park, Barnsbury, in Islington. This was at the photographic studio of T. C. Turner, a famous Victorian photographer, who worked at this address from 1870 to 1900. Turner also had a studio at 17 Upper Street and previously at 3 Cheapside, between Newgate Street and Paternoster Road, close to where Nathaniel worked. The studio at Barnsbury was quite close to Park Street, where it is known that the Pitman family were living after 1860.

Below is a table with the names of the children of Nathaniel Gerrard Pitman and his wife Charlotte with dates of birth, baptisms, addresses and Nathaniel's stated occupations. It also gives an idea of the movements of the family between the years 1855 to 1870.

Table of details of children recorded at various addresses.

Date of Baptism	Christian Name	Address	Occupation of father	Church
10 June 1855 Born 20 May 1855	Charlotte Emma	4 Finsbury Place South	Warehouseman	St.Giles, without Cripplegate
15 March 1857 Born 9 Dec. 1856	Frank Gerrard	4 Finsbury Place South	Warehouseman	St.Giles, without Cripplegate
18 July 1858 Born 22 June 1858	Elizabeth Helen	Shepperton Cottages	Warehouseman	St.Mary, Islington
11 November 1860 Born 29 May 1860	Annie	Park Street	Warehouseman	St.Mary, Islington
3 July 1861 Born 6 June 1861	Joseph Unwin	Park Street	Warehouseman	St.Mary, Islington
22 February 1863 Born 14 Nov. 1862	Florence Kate	Stonefield Street	Silk Manufacturer	St.Mary, Islington
20 November 1867 Born 19 Oct. 1864	Constance Mackenzie	5 Highbury Park South	Silk Manufacturer	St.Mary, Islington
20 November 1867 Born 24 Nov. 1866	George Ernest	5 Highbury Park South	Silk Manufacturer	St.Mary, Islington
23 October 1870 Born 25 Nov. 1869	Colin Lindsay	73 Hungerford Road	Silk Manufacturer	St.Mary, Islington

The *Post Office Directory* of 1856 confirms that Nathaniel Gerrard Pitman was registered at 4 Finsbury Square South. A birth was registered for Elsie Mary Pitman in Islington, Middlesex during the third quarter of 1875 (*1b 335*).

The family was living at 18 Park Street at the time of the census of 1861, though in March 1870, Charlotte Pitman wrote a letter, still in the possession of the family, to her son, Frank, which gave her address as 5 Highbury New Park South. He must have been away at boarding school and she mentioned that when he returned on Saturday they were to look at an address that contained the words "*St. John's, Highgate Hill*". There are two addresses at the bottom of Highgate Hill; St. John's Way and St. John's Villas. Perhaps she was thinking of moving there at around that time. When their son, Colin Lindsay Pitman was baptised in October that year, they were living at 73 Hungerford Road, Lower Holloway, in the Parish of St. Luke's, so the family moved house between March and October.

Elizabeth Unwin was shown to be living at Manor Road (now Manor Gardens) and Hungerford Road was the Pitman family's address at the time of the census of 1871 but Annie and Joseph had died and Frank was back at home. Along with the family, there was an Irish cook from Kerry and a widowed nurse from Plymouth. Perhaps Charlotte was not well and needed support to look after her younger children. Nathaniel was then employing between fifty and seventy people, so his business had almost doubled in size between 1871 and 1881. As the family increased in number, they will have needed to move to larger accommodation. Charlotte's death was recorded, in the third quarter of 1875 (*1b 222*), at Islington. She died on 1st September 1875, at the age of forty-four, from Pyaemia (blood poisoning caused by the spread of pus-forming bacteria in the bloodstream from a source of infection), following the birth of Elsie, her youngest daughter. Nathaniel was present at her death at 12 Manor Road, Upper Holloway, Islington. Her obituary was recorded in *The Standard*, dated 4th September 1875 and gave Nathaniel's address as Well Street, Cripplegate. The family appears to have moved in with her mother; they were certainly living together by 1875. In the Post Office Directory of 1878, Nathaniel Gerrard Pitman was listed as residing at 12 Manor Road. By 1881, Elizabeth was blind, so their living arrangements may have been dictated by this disability. The circumstances of Charlotte's death may also explain why Elsie was not baptised at this difficult time.

The death of Joseph Unwin, Charlotte's brother, aged 49, was recorded at St. Pancras, in London. His will was proved on 7th March 1878 by Elizabeth Unwin of 12 Manor Road, Upper Holloway, mother and sole executor. It states that Joseph was formerly of 198 Upper Thames Street in the City of London but lately of 12 Mansfield Road, Kentish Town, not that far from where his mother and brother-in-law lived. The will confirms that he had died on 9th October 1877. His personal estate amounted to £800.

Elizabeth Unwin died on 2nd September 1882 at 2 Woodberry Grove. Hers was a double probate. The first will, with a codicil, was proved on 29th September. It was proved by two of the executors, Robert Harvey Hilliard, M.D., of Aylesbury in the County of Buckingham and Charlotte Emma (in the codicil written Charlotte Pitman), of 2 Woodberry Grove, a spinster and the grand-daughter of Elizabeth Unwin. Her estate was valued at around £1,776. Charlotte was the eldest child of Nathaniel Gerrard Pitman and obviously someone whom her grandmother trusted to be able to execute her wishes.

The will was written on 18th July 1878 in the year following the death of her son Joseph. Robert Harvey Hilliard, the surgeon, was living at 8 Belgrave Terrace Holloway (by 1882 he had moved to 7 Church Street, Aylesbury) and Frank Gerrard Pitman, her grandson, were named as executors and trustees. Elizabeth Unwin left specific instructions for them to purchase annually from the government commissioners an annuity of £65 for her "*dear and afflicted daughter Sarah Spencer Unwin now an inmate at Dr. Millers at Bethnal Green, Cambridge Heath*". Sarah's mental condition may have been the reason why she disappeared from census records in 1871, 1881 and 1901. Elizabeth Unwin requested that this annuity be paid for clothing, board, lodgings, maintenance and for the "*personal and peculiar benefit*" of her daughter. The executors were to receive a sum of money in consideration for their trouble. As a condition of the will, she also asked that the trustees visit the institution to observe first-hand her daughter's state and condition and promote her comfort and welfare. All the residue of her estate was to go to Robert Harvey Hilliard and Frank Gerrard Pitman and their heirs, executors or administrators. When her daughter died, her funeral was to be conducted in a decent and respectable manner. Any residue left after the death of Sarah Spencer Unwin was to go to the child or children of her late daughter, Charlotte, to be shared equally, when they attained the age of 21. A new trustee was to be appointed in case of the death of her nominated trustees with the consent of the eldest child, to ensure that there were not less than two of them. Nathaniel Gerrard Pitman was one of the witnesses to the will. A codicil, dated 11th September 1878, gave £50 to her "*nephew*" Robert Harvey Hilliard and £10 to Charlotte and Helen Pitman, her grand-daughters as well as what she had already given to them. She then appointed her eldest grand-daughter Charlotte, then over 21, to be an executor with Hilliard and Frank Gerrard Pitman. The will was proved, with a codicil, by the oath of Robert Harvey Hilliard and by Charlotte, named in the codicil therein "*Admon was granted. Power reserved of making the like grant to Frank Gerrard Pitman, the grandson the other executor named in the will*". The will was proved a second time on 13th November by Frank Gerrard Pitman, gentleman, grandson of the deceased and other executor.

Robert Hilliard was described as the nephew of Elizabeth Unwin, though in fact he was more distantly related by marriage. His father was Harvey Hilliard who, in Glasgow, married Jane Wilson on 29th September 1835. Harvey Hilliard was born on 16th May 1810 at Cathedral St. Peter's, in Sheffield. His parents were Robert and Mary, who was, possibly, Mary Mackenzie, the sister of Elizabeth Unwin, *née* Mackenzie, as the latter's birth was also registered there. George Hilliard, named in Charlotte Unwin's scrapbook, may have been a relative of Robert Harvey Hilliard. A document at the *TNA* suggests that, in 1854, Harvey Hilliard patented a machine for sharpening cutlery, perhaps another link to Sheffield and the manufacturing of cutlery.

Dr. Robert Harvey Hilliard was staying in the Old Steine Albion Hotel in Brighton at the time of the census of 1881. He was recorded as being married and he gave his birthplace as Lanark in Scotland. However, his wife, Elizabeth Isabella Hilliard, was listed as being head of house, aged 31, her birthplace being London and now living at Fairmead House, Holloway Road, along with her four children, Emilie Pearson and her widowed sister-in-law. They had also a governess, a page, a nursemaid and a cook. Emilie was also born in Lanark, Scotland. Robert Harvey Hilliard was born in Dundee, studied in Glasgow and died at the age of 52 on 8th July 1891 at 51 Eversfield Place, St. Leonards-on-sea, Sussex. His will confirms that he had been lately living at 7 Church Street, Aylesbury. His son Harvey followed in his father's footsteps and was studying medicine at the time of the census of 1891. He trained at Charing Cross Hospital. Emily Rosalie Hilliard had married Mandell Pearson in Edinburgh on 27th June 1871.

Nathaniel Gerrard Pitman and his Family

An Isaac Pitman, recorded in a document at The National Archives, was born in the Parish of Milbourn Port, which is not, in fact, on the coast. He served in the Hereford and Somerset Militia from 1803 to 1824, when he was discharged at the age of forty. Some of the Pitman children were born in Hereford and the Gerrard family were known to have been from Dorset. The document *WO 97/1106/38*, an official release paper dated 19th December 1823, indicates that Isaac was Nathaniel's father. Isaac Pitman had enlisted in the 2nd Somerset Militia on 1st April 1803 until 4th March 1815 as a trumpeter or drummer; the regiment was known to have been fighting in the Napoleonic Wars from 1804 to 1815. Six months later he enlisted again on 19th December 1815 for unlimited service, when he was in Dublin, this time into the Hereford Militia as a trumpeter or drummer; his commanding officer was Sir George Cornewall. Isaac held this position for seven years and was promoted to the rank of corporal, for one year and ninety days, before his discharge on 24th March 1824 as a result of his chronic rheumatism but it was recorded that he was a good soldier. The document served to sign off that he had been paid all that was due to him. In order that no one else could impersonate him and request any further money, a description was given of Isaac Pitman. He was five feet six inches in height, had dark hair, grey eyes and fair complexion and before enlistment, had been a shoemaker. When he was discharged, he had served twenty years and sixty-nine days.

Isaac Pitman is seen in the census of 1851; he and his wife Eliza were living at Church Street, John Place, at Gillingham, in Kent. Both were aged sixty-four and Eliza's birthplace was stated to be Poole in Dorset; his occupation was given as a retired straw hat dealer. In 1861, they were living in Wellington Street at Milton in Gravesend in Kent. His wife, then aged seventy-four, was said to be a fund holder; her death was recorded at Poplar in the last quarter of 1868. By 1871, Isaac was living at 138 "*W Lane*", possibly West Kennington Lane, in the Parish of St. Peter's, Lambeth with his son William

Henry Pitman, aged fifty-six, whose birthplace was in Ireland. By then, Isaac was a widower and William was single. Isaac was described as an annuitant and William's occupation was as an Inland Revenue Officer. Isaac died aged eighty-nine, in Lambeth (*1D 385*) in the second quarter of 1875.

According to the census of 1881, William Henry Pitman, then aged sixty-six and unmarried, was recorded living at 120 Caledonian Road, as a pensioner of the Inland Revenue. He stated that he was born at Hereford but this entry conflicts with the census of 1871, completed by his father, which said that he was born in Ireland. If it is the case that William Henry Pitman was born on 20th September 1814, it will have been while Isaac was serving in Ireland with the Somerset Militia. His wife Eliza was also living there, the assumption being that wives were stationed with their husbands. The family moved from Colchester in 1810, went to Ireland in 1814 and then to Hereford in 1816. Their daughter, Louisa Ann Pitman, was born in Hereford on 29th August 1816. Eliza was in Hereford in 1822 when Nathaniel was born. Rebecca was born on 19th September 1826, after Isaac had left the Militia but she died in the following year. Eliza had returned to Hereford before her husband left the Militia.

At The National Archives, a document (*CUST 116/28/63*) dated 1837, confirms that William Henry Pitman had entered into the Customs Service as an excise man. In the census of 1891, William Henry Pitman was recorded as a lodger, aged seventy-six, a retired C. S. in the Inland Revenue, born in Ireland and living at 34 Colebrooke Road, a prestigious address in Islington. William was living at 199 Liverpool Road, Islington, Middlesex when he died on 7th December 1896, aged eighty-two. Probate was granted to his brother, Nathaniel Gerrard Pitman, a trimmings manufacturer. He left £5,253, 1s. 6d., quite a large sum of money for a retired government official.

Family papers and photographs offer insight into the Pitman family and business. In an article published in *The Furniture Gazette* on 25th November 1876, it was explained that Messrs. Pitman and Holliday's business of manufacturing fringes, tassels and upholstery trimmings had originally been set up in 1835 at 12 King Street, Cheapside by Mr. James Walmsley. Nathaniel Gerrard Pitman had worked for the business for some thirty years and eventually became a senior partner. Mr. J. Holiday managed the manufacturing department and worked for the business for some twenty years. Pitman and Holliday had premises at 3, 4 and 5 Well Street, Falcon Square. The elaborate and complicated construction of some of the fittings was explained in great detail and the article was most complimentary about their working practices, compared to those of other companies. Trimmings were for the home as well as for the export market. According to the article, the light in the premises was good, to assist in colour differentiation when making up the goods, the premises large, workrooms comfortable and sanitary conditions good. The businesses maintained a library of some three hundred and fifty books paid for by the workers out of a small weekly subscription and Mr. Holliday undertook a bible class for those who wanted it. The article opined "*We are convinced that the more employers make their workpeople's happiness their own, the more pleasurable and the more profitable will the results on both sides be found*".

Sylvia Fuller, *née* Pitman, Frank Gerrard Pitman's grand-daughter, when she was aged eighty-two, said that she believed that some of their silk trimmings were used on seats and curtains in theatres in the West End of London. Some time after 1876, Holliday was no longer with the company, which was then listed as Pitman, Son & Co., at 5 Well Street.

This article suggests that Nathaniel was not from a wealthy family, as he had worked his way up within the company. However, a reason why he worked for that particular company may have been that James Walmsley was his brother-in-law. His sister Louisa Ann Pitman had married James Walmsley in the third quarter of 1838 at Hereford (*Vol. 26 Pg. 175*). According to family records, Louisa Ann was born on 29th August 1816 so she was 21 when she married and James was older than she. Nathaniel must have joined James Walmsley's company at the age of 24.

In 1861, the Walmsley family was living at 17 Highbury Grove Villas, near to where Nathaniel was living, suggesting that the families maintained a close relationship. James' place of birth was Staffordshire and his then stated occupation was that of a silk and worsted manufacturer. At the time of the census there were some seven children still alive; Louisa, born in 1844, Emily Ann, born in 1847 at Cheapside in London; Mary Ann, born in 1850; Ellen, born in 1852; William H.; born in 1853; Fanny, born in 1855 and Horace, born in 1858. They had a son named James Pitman Walmsley who died, aged two, in 1845 in London.

A document in the *Bednall Collection Part 2 (BC2) No. 854*, dated 20th May 1864, confirms that James Walmsley's addresses were by then 13 Aberdeen Park and 14 Cheapside in London and his occupation was that of a fringe manufacturer. The document concerned the dissolution of the partnership, operating in the name of M. Walmsley & Co., of James, John, Hezekiah and Thomas Walmsley; John, Hezekiah and Thomas Walmsley were all silk manufacturers from Leek, Staffordshire. James was to receive £1,500 for giving up all the rights in that firm to the other three parties. The arrangement was to advance £500 each to the other three parties and leave the £1,500 in the business and James Walmsley was to receive the sum of £4 a month, in interest, for the term of the loan. The four parties were or may have been brothers.

By the time of the census of 1871, James Walmsley's age was given as 61 and Louisa's as 49 (this is probably inaccurate) and he described himself as an annuitant. Their son, William H. Walmsley, aged 18, whose occupation was in oil refining, was living with them at 41 Craven Hill Gardens in the Parish of St. John, an address close to Bayswater and Hyde Park and an affluent part of London. William's place of birth was given as Barnsbury. Also in the house were Horace (13), Louisa Ann (25) and Ellen (19), the elder girls being unmarried. In a company directory of 1871, *Pitman, Walcot & Holiday* were shown as patent Tuscan fringe upholsterers and trimming manufacturers at 4 and 5 Well Street, Falcon Square, so it would seem that Nathaniel had already taken a share of the company before the death of his brother-in-law. James Walmsley died in Kensington on 2nd November 1872, aged sixty-two (*Morning Post*).

In the census of 1881, Louisa Ann Walmsley was shown to be living at 8 Mount Ararat Villas, Richmond. Her son, William Henry, aged twenty-eight and unmarried, was then described as a traveller and Louisa Ann as an annuitant. Her son, Horace, an unmarried merchant sailor, was staying in a boarding house at Plymouth at the time. When Louisa Ann Walmsley, still a widow, died at 46 Durley Road, Stamford Hill in Hackney on 4th October 1894, her age was given as seventy-eight. Her effects were valued at £2,582. The executors of her will were her brother, Nathaniel Gerrard Pitman and her nephew Clarence George Beardsworth. An announcement by her executors in the *London Gazette* in late October called on creditors to make contact before December.

An entry in the *London Gazette* of 23rd October 1900, gave notice that the partnership of Nathaniel G. Pitman, Robert Harker, Samuel Dobbs, Edward Adamson Thompson and Frank G. Pitman, under the name of Pitman, Son & Co, carrying on the business as Trimmings Manufacturers, at Paternoster Buildings, in the City of London, had been dissolved on 1st September 1900. All debts owing were to be received and paid by R. Harker, Edward Adamson Thornton and F. G. Pitman, who were to continue the business in the same style. Nathaniel was then nearly eighty years of age and was handing over his share to his eldest son.

Cynthia Pitman had been told by her late husband that Pitman, Son & Co., run first by Nathaniel and then his son, Frank Gerrard Pitman, lost everything in a fire, as the Company was not insured. There was, in fact, a devastating fire in London on Friday 19th November 1897, reported in *The Times*, on Monday, 22nd November. Pitman's premises at 5 Well Street were only one of a large number affected, as the fire seems to have covered an area of some seventeen streets of factories and warehouses, six or seven stories high, backing on to one another and packed with combustible products. Beardsworth and Cryer, another trimmings manufacturer, was operating at 17, Well Street. They were next door to 15 Well Street, an ostrich feather dealer, where it was later discovered that the fire started due to a gas explosion. It spread along the streets and everything was destroyed. Even the roof of the Church of St. Giles, Cripplegate caught fire but its interior was saved, although water damaged. The streets described in the article no longer exist as most of the buildings must have been demolished and a new street layout established. Fifty-six buildings were lost, sixteen burnt out and a further twenty-four damaged.

A relief fund was set up to help compensate the four thousand workers thrown out of work, most of whom were women. In the fire, they lost their sewing machines and clothes, valued at £10,000. The annual rateable value of the properties involved exceeded £32,000 and amounted to one sixth of the total in the Parish of St. Giles without Cripplegate. The insurance valuation for all the companies' losses did not exceed £1,000,000 but many of the firms were not insured.

Phoenix-like, the Pitman business continued to operate. They must have moved to their new premises at Paternoster Buildings after the fire but by 1904 Pitman, Son & Company, upholsterer manufacturer, was recorded in the Post Office Directory at 2-5, St. George's Row, York Road/City Road. A company card, still in existence, confirms that Pitman, Son & Co. operated at the Georges Works, London Wall, telephone number 1468.

9.1 Pitman, Son & Company business card.

On the night of the 1881 Census, at 2 Woodberry Grove, in the Parish of St. Mary, Stoke Newington, there were in the Pitman household:

Table of occupants in 1881 at 2 Woodbury Grove.

Name	Relation	Age	Occupation or profession	Birthplace
Nathaniel G. Pitman	Head widower	59	Silk and Worsted Trimming Manufacturer employing 60 men and 40 women.	Hereford
Charlotte E. Pitman	Daughter	25		Middlesex City of London
Frank G. Pitman	Son	24	Warehouseman (trimmings)	Middlesex City of London
Helen E. Pitman	Daughter	22		Middlesex Islington
Florence K. Pitman	Daughter	18		Middlesex Islington
Constance M. Pitman	Daughter	16	Scholar	Middlesex Islington
Elsie M. Pitman	Daughter	5		Middlesex Islington
Elizabeth Unwin	Mother-in-law	87		Yorkshire Sheffield

Elizabeth Unwin was a widow. George Ernest Pitman and Colin Lindsay Pitman were not recorded at Woodberry Grove as both were boarders at Bedford County School, Kempston.

There were two servants, one called Laura Grange (17) from Holt in Norfolk, who was a housemaid and a Mary Duddenham (21), from Snoring in Norfolk, a cook. It was a large household and Nathaniel appears to be a successful businessman, employing several people. The house still exists today although it is now converted into flats.

In the 1891 Census, Sarah Spencer Unwin was listed as an inmate at Bethnal Green Lunatic Asylum, in the Parish of St. John's. She is shown to have been born in 1820/22. The death of Sarah S. Unwin, aged ninety, was registered at Bethnal Green, in the first quarter of 1911. She lived to a remarkable age despite her mental state and her living conditions. Two of the trustees taking care of her welfare had died, namely Charlotte Cryer, *née* Pitman in 1889 and Robert Harvey Hilliard. The only other executor was Frank Gerrard Pitman, so another trustee must have taken their place.

On the same night at 2 Woodberry Grove, there were in the household:

Table of occupants in 1891 at 2 Woodbury Grove.

Name	Relation	Age	Occupation or profession
Nathaniel G. Pitman	Head, widower	69	Manufacturer in silk & wool
Frank G. Pitman	Son	34	
George E. Pitman	Son	24	
Colin L. Pitman	Son	21	Mercantile seaman marine
Florence K. Pitman	Daughter	27	
Constance. M. Pitman	Daughter	26	
Elsie M. Pitman	Daughter	15	
Kate Talbot	General servant and domestic	22	City of London

George Ernest Pitman and Colin Lindsay Pitman had returned to the family home but probably Colin was on leave, as he had joined the Merchant Navy.

Kate Talbot worked for the family before Frank Gerrard Pitman married her on 28th March 1896 at West Ham. He was twelve years her senior. They were married in the presence of Alfred Abbott, Nathaniel Gerrard Pitman, the groom's father and George Ernest Pitman, the groom's brother. Her father was Thomas Talbot, a florist.

Twenty years earlier, Thomas Talbot had been listed as a milk carrier, living then at 1 Rifle Street, in Bromley-by-Bow but he went on to make a career move. Ten years later, Thomas and Elizabeth Talbot were living at Elizabeth Cottages, Essex Street, Westham, at Forest Gate, close to Westham Cemetery in Essex. His occupation was then stated to be a gardener and his birthplace as Brentford in Middlesex. Kate was listed as a scholar and her grandfather, who was visiting them, was named as Edmund Birch, a widower, aged seventy-eight, born at Ibstone in Buckinghamshire. Kate was one of five children and the census indicated that she was born in the City of London. There was a baptism recorded for Kate Talbot on 10th May 1868 at St. Bride, Fleet Street. It is known that Nathaniel was interested in gardening and there are letters full of information on that subject.

A memorial card, in the possession of the Pitman family, connects Thomas Talbot with a William Talbot. Probably Kate's uncle, William died in 1910, in his seventy-first year and was interred in Sonning churchyard. At the time of the census of 1881, William's occupation was stated as a gardener, as was Kate's father's. Thomas was born around 1831 and William in 1840 at Harefield. William Talbot of "*The Elms*", Sonning Eye, Oxfordshire, died on 19th January 1910 leaving his estate, valued at £1,700 to Sarah Elizabeth Talbot, a widow and William Fitch.

At the time of the census of 1901, Frank Gerrard Pitman was living at 59 Stanwick Mansions in Fulham, in the borough of Baron's Court, along with his wife Kate and their two sons, George Gerrard Pitman and Frank Talbot Pitman. George Gerrard Pitman had been given the name of Gerrard from his maternal great-grandmother, Ann Gerrard and subsequent generations continued with this tradition. George was born at 59 Stanwick Mansions, Fulham on 10th February 1899 and Frank on 11th July 1900.

In 1901, the only people shown to be at 2 Woodberry Grove, at the time of the census, were Constance and Florence Pitman, still unmarried, with one servant. However, on 10th October 1905 Nathaniel wrote from 2 Woodberry Grove to his daughter-in-law Kate, letting her know that his gardener was tending certain plants but Nathaniel had no room for them and could not have them there as they could not be kept outside in the winter as they could not stand frost. He asked if she could spare room for them in the warmest part of her conservatory if he sent them over in the next two weeks. He suggested that she may have a customer for the largest and she could keep the others if she would like to. He hoped that she was better and that the boys were well. He signed the letter "*yours affectionately*" so it seems they got on well. In passing, he said to tell Frank, his son, that he had sent some small plants to a friend of Fred Garston, his cousin and Nathaniel had suggested to Fred that he would send the remaining specimens to his friend, if he wanted them, at a price of 50 shillings, as he did not want them himself. He had three larger plants but they were worth 15 to 20 shillings each. Nathaniel was clearly a pragmatic man who was not wasteful with his money.

Nathaniel Gerrard Pitman died eight months later on 11th June 1906, at the age of eighty-five. An account of his will in a newspaper gave information on the recipients of his estate, amounting to £18,745. It implied that he was still part of Pitman, Sons and Co., at York *Street* (author's italics) E.C., in London. Obviously he had not lost everything in the fire. The testator bequeathed the following amounts to his family:

Table of beneficiaries of Nathaniel Gerrard Pitman.

Amount	Relation	Name
£1,360	Daughter	Elizabeth Helen Beardsworth
£1,660	Daughter	Florence Kate Pitman
£1,600	Daughter	Elsie Mary Reed
£1,600	Daughter	Constance Mackenzie Candler
£1,250 in trust	Son	George Ernest Pitman
£1,000 in trust	Daughter-in-law	Annie Pitman (wife of Colin Pitman)

Furthermore: *"He left a debt due to Messrs. Beardsworth and Cryer as to one half to his daughter and one half in trust for the children of his deceased daughter, Mrs Cryer, and as regards a debt due to Messrs. Pitman, Sons & Co to be directed that £1,644 part thereof may remain as a loan forming part of his residuary estate and he left the balance to his son Frank Gerrard Pitman and subject to some other bequests left the residue of his estate to his four daughters, Mrs Elizabeth Helen Beardsworth, Mrs Elsie Mary Reed, Mrs Constance Mackenzie Candler and Florence Kate Pitman. The executors of his will are Frank Gerrard Pitman, of the "Homestead," Church Lane, Barnes, trimming manufacturer, son of the deceased, Mr George Herbert Candler, estate agent of "Lisnabrin," Stamford Hill and Mr Charles George Reed, of 73 Palace Gardens, Muswell Hill, North."*

(It might be assumed that "Lisnabrin" was the name Candler gave to 54 Vartry Road as this name was used, albeit found only once, in the above document. "Lisnabrin" is the name of Croker family residence at Lisnabrin House, Curraglass, Co. Cork, in Ireland.)

Nathaniel Gerrard Pitman, his children and their families

Nathaniel left £1,250 in trust for his son, George Ernest Pitman. He was around thirty-nine when his father died and may have been living at home with him and never married. Nathaniel also left £1,000 in trust for Annie, wife of his son Colin. Colin Lindsay Pitman had married Elizabeth Anne Morris (Annie) in Glamorgan in 1893 (*11a 1135*). A death was recorded in the last quarter of 1894 for a Charlotte Emma Pitman, a baby who died at birth in Swansea. It is likely that she was Colin Lindsay Pitman's first daughter, named after her aunt who had died four years earlier. In the census of 1901, Colin, an assurance agent aged 31, born in London, along with Elizabeth, 29, born in Glamorgan, Swansea and their daughter Constance, aged 2 were all recorded residing in Monmouth. This suggests that he had given up his career as a mercantile seaman, perhaps having earlier made the decision to travel the world and not to work with his father and brothers in the manufacturing business. It might have been family life that changed his mind about his chosen career after his daughter, Constance was born in 1899. In 1911, Constance Jane Pitman, aged 12, was recorded at Glamorgan at the home of her grandmother, Margaret Morris, from Glamorgan, Swansea, whose occupation was that of a housekeeper.

The two sisters, Helen E. and Charlotte Emma Pitman, had married into the business of Beardsworth and Cryer, trimmings manufacturers, run by Nathaniel Pitman's two sons-in-law, John Cryer and Clarence Beardsworth. Attentive to the interests of his sons, daughters and grandchildren, in his will, Nathaniel had stated that he had a debt owed to him by Beardsworth and Cryer but he instructed that the monies due were to be paid back, half to his daughter Elizabeth Beardsworth, then a widow and the other to the children of his deceased daughter, Charlotte Cryer. These debts may have related to the fire of 1897 as Beardsworth and Cryer also lost their stock and possibly were not insured. Nathaniel may have lent John Cryer and Clarence

Beardsworth money to start up again. There was also a debt due by Pitman Son & Co. to remain as a loan of £1,644 forming part of his residuary estate and the balance to be left to his son, Frank Gerrard Pitman, who was one of the partners running Pitman, Son & Co.

Nathaniel's will made reference to his daughter not as Helen E., as listed in some of the census returns but as Elizabeth Beardsworth, named after her grandmothers, both with the Christian name of Elizabeth. Elizabeth Helen Pitman had married Clarence George Beardsworth at St. Mary's, Stoke Newington, on 10th October 1883; the Reverend C. White, brother-in-law of the groom, officiated. Beardsworth described himself as a widower and manufacturer, aged forty and she was a spinster, aged twenty-five. They both gave their address as Woodberry Grove. His father was named as George Beardsworth, a clerk in Holy Orders. Nathaniel Gerrard Pitman and Annie Charlotte Beardsworth were witnesses, Annie being Clarence's sister. On the date of the census of 1881, Annie Beardsworth, a spinster, had been with her sister, Marion, aged twenty-seven and brother-in-law, Reverend George C. White, at Southampton, Hampshire.

Charles George Beardsworth had married Welsh-born Ashfield Ann Ponting on 28th June 1876, at St. Peter's, Notting Hill, in Kensington (*1a 158*). He had been living in the Parish of St. Matthew, Bayswater. His father was a vicar from Selling in Kent, where Charles was born and hers was Henry Ponting, a farmer. They were married in the presence of Mildred Beardsworth, the groom's sister. George Coupland Beardsworth was born on 19th November 1877 and baptised on 5th February 1878, when the family was living at 66 Foulden Road. Constance Margaret Beardsworth was baptised on 29th December 1879. George's mother Charlotte, *née* Neame, died at Selling in Kent in 1897.

At the time of the census of 1881, Clarence Beardsworth, aged thirty-seven, was still residing at 66 Foulden Road in Stoke Newington, along with Ashfield and children, George and Constance, aged three and one, who were born in Stoke Newington. His occupation in 1881 was described as that of an agent of silk goods. Ashfield died between 1881 and 1883 and his manufacturing business was established during the same period. Elizabeth Pitman became the step-mother of two very young children, perhaps having looked after the children at her father's home at Woodberry Grove, prior to the marriage.

The marriage of Charlotte Emma Pitman to John Cryer had taken place on 19th July, 1884 at the Church of St. John the Evangelist, Brownswood Park, close to Finsbury Park (*The Times*). The marriage certificate noted that John was the second son of the late Henry Cryer, Esq., a farmer of Heyes Hall, Fillongley in Warwickshire. The groom was a bachelor, aged thirty-two and the bride a spinster, aged twenty-nine. His occupation was given as that of a manufacturer. Before the marriage, John had been living at 33 Portland Road. Their daughter, Margaret was born in 1886. John Lindsay Pitman Cryer, named, in part, after Colin William Lindsay, was baptised on 15th May 1887, at St. Paul's Hornsey, Finsbury Park, when his parents were living at 33 Portland Road. Eric was also baptised at St. Paul's on 29th March 1889. Charlotte may have died shortly after the birth of her last child, as did her mother, her death having occurred in the second quarter of 1889 at Edmonton, in London (*3a 131*). She was thirty-three years old when she died.

At the time of the census of 1881, John Cryer, described as a silk agent, was boarding with a clergyman's widow at 112 Markhouse Road, Walthamstow. By the time of his marriage in 1884 he was in the manufacturing business.

On the night of the census of 1891, the Beardsmore family was living at "*Chelwood House*" Oakleigh Park, at Friern Barnet, in the Parish of All Saints in the Borough of Enfield. Clarence, Elizabeth and one of the children, Constance Beardsworth, then aged eleven, were shown on that evening to be with John Cryer and his three children, Margaret, John Lindsay and Eric, aged five, four and three respectively, as guests or living in the house. It might have been that, as the younger children's mother, Charlotte Emma Cryer, had died just two years before, there was a practical, short or long-term arrangement to reside with the Beardsworth family. The eldest son of George Beardsworth, also called George, was not shown to be at home, so may have been away at school. Mary Mackenzie, aged eighty-five, described as the widowed "*aunt*" of Clarence, the head of house and born in the Parish of St. Luke's, London, was also staying at their house. It is more likely that Mary was Elizabeth's great-aunt, as she was a Mackenzie and may have been the same Mary Mackenzie, a widow, then aged seventy-five, who was living with her friend and lady's companion of the same age at 47 Penn Road Villas in Lower Holloway, ten years earlier. The Beardsworth household was all being looked after by a cook/domestic servant, a housemaid and a nurse; a total of eleven people in all.

In 1901, the Beardsworth family was living in the Parish of St. John's, Whetstone, in Finchley. Clarence recorded his occupation as a manufacturer of children's blouses and dresses and was then fifty-seven; Elizabeth was forty-two; Constance, of whom the family retains a photograph, was twenty-one and George was twenty-three; Margaret was classified as a scholar. The Cryer family had moved to "*Forest side*" Epping, Upland, in Essex and John Cryer was described as a manufacturer of shirts, collars and belts, etc. Beardsworth and Cryer had both moved away from the manufacturing of trimmings and were in the business of making clothes and accessories. The death of Clarence Beardsworth, aged sixty-two, was recorded at Barnet (*3A 188*) in 1905. He died before his father-in-law, unexpectedly, without making a will.

At the time of the census of 1911, Elizabeth Beardsworth, then a widow, aged fifty-two, was living at 35 John Street, Shoreham, in Sussex. Her nephew, Eric Cryer, aged twenty-two, born in Finsbury and a warehouseman for a clothing manufacturer, was staying with her. His father, John Cryer, then fifty-nine and a widower, employer and clothing manufacturer, was listed at another address along with his daughter, Margaret, aged twenty-five, born at Hornsey, Middlesex. John Cryer was obviously still in the manufacturing business and may have still been in partnership with his sister-in-law, Elizabeth Beardsworth. John's son, Eric Cryer joined up to fight in the First World War and died of wounds received in battle on 15th November 1918, just a few days after the armistice was signed.

Frank Gerrard Pitman was living at *"The Homestead"* Church Lane, Barnes, when his father died. On 7th April 1900, *The Times* reported that a Charles Talbot Rotherham, perhaps a relation of Frank Pitman's wife, was declared bankrupt, while living at this same address. On 25th April, an announcement was made in the paper about the circumstances of his bankruptcy and Rotherham had explained that he was not a financial agent but a secretary of public companies who had become overstretched financially when he proposed to buy *"The Ship Restaurant"* at Charing Cross. He was declared bankrupt owing around £5,000. Frank may have been the next occupant of the house after April 1900 but his family was still living at Stanwick Mansions at the time of the census in 1901. Some time after March 1901, Frank Gerrard Pitman moved into *"The Homestead"*. Written on the backs of family photos of Frank Gerrard Pitman's wife and two children, are words to indicate that the scene was set in the garden of their house there. Cynthia Pitman revealed a letter addressed to Mrs. Pitman at *"The Homestead"*, dated 6th May 1908. It said:

The Homestead, Barnes

My Dear Kate,

I enclose Bank Notes for ninety pounds as a gift to you and with which I wish you so purchase the furniture and effects at the above address as I desire that all of it shall become your property and under your absolute control and further make a free gift of all my furniture and effects which are at the above address for your own use and benefit absolutely.

It was signed *Florence Kate Pitman* and was addressed to her sister-in-law, Kate. Florence Pitman must have cleared some of the contents of 2 Woodberry Grove to *The Homestead*, after her father died in 1906, when he may have been living there with her brother. The letter might be evidence that Frank was in financial difficulties in May 1908 and Florence Pitman was obviously giving her brother financial support under difficult circumstances. The letter had the name and address of Florence Ellen Hewson, 33 Nassau Road, Barnes, written at the bottom and she may have owned the furniture and the property.

On 27th November 1908, Frank Gerrard Pitman, trading as part of Pitman Son & Co., called in the Official Receivers and was declared bankrupt. It would appear that either through crippling debts, changing fashion in drapes and furniture or other factors, the business had to be wound up.

A notification in the *London Gazette* of September on 30th September 1909 suggested that Frank was still using *"The Homestead"* Church Road, Barnes, as his address when bankruptcy proceedings were under way at the High Court of Justice in relation to his business. The Barnes address, arguably not a lucky one, was still being given in the *London Gazette* on 1st February 1910, when the bankruptcy proceedings were still continuing. However, on 15th September 1909, Sir Ralph Denham Rayment Moor, the first High Commissioner for

Southern Nigeria, was living at "*The Homestead*" when he took his own life, his will having been proved at that address.

Sylvia Fuller/Pitman, the grand-daughter of Frank Gerrard Pitman, suggested that he and his family went to Indiana in the United States and stayed for four years; her father, Frank Talbot Pitman had told her about their trip. He had said that her grandfather had bought over one hundred acres of land there. The family was listed as passengers on a ship named *St. Paul*, which sailed from Southampton on 22ⁿᵈ March and arrived on 30ᵗʰ March 1911 at Ellis Island, New York. Frank declared his occupation to be that of a "*grocer*" and the name of his nearest relative or friend was Mrs. Bulbeck, Moor Villa, Sandown, on the Isle of Wight. In the census of 1911, Maria Bulbeck was registered on the Isle of Wight. Her house was shown in the 1921 Electoral Register to be on York Road. The ship's manifest recorded that they were going to stay with friends, a Mr. *Torno* at Elm Hill, Milton, Indiana. The table below shows the Pitman names, ages and comments from officials on arrival at Ellis Island.

Table describing Pitman family on arrival at Ellis Island in 1911.

Name	Age	Colour of eyes	Disability	Colour of hair	Height	Where born
Frank Gerrard	54	Blue	Scar on left eyebrow	Grey	5ft 7in.	London
Kate	44	Brown	None	Dark	5ft 3in.	London
George Gerrard	11	Brown	Brown spot on right eye	Dark	Slight	London
Frank Talbot	10	Blue	Limp right leg	Dark	Slight	London

Presumably, the attempt at farming must have failed as the Pitman family returned from America and eventually settled in Winchester. Sylvia remembered that her father worked for a while in an office at Jury Street, Winchester but he decided that it was not for him. According to her recollections, he joined up before the end of the war in 1918. She believed that Frank and the family spent some time on their return, on the Isle of Wight, possibly with his sister, Florence. She also remembered the address of her grandfather's shop in Winchester as 137 Upper High Street, which her father, Frank Talbot Pitman, had said was a tea shop. She believed that it was her grandmother, Kate who had the business acumen. However, Frank Gerrard Pitman was made a Freeman of the City of London on 28ᵗʰ February 1924.

It can be seen from the 1911 Census, at the Grosvenor Estate, at Kayleigh, in Essex that George E. Pitman, Constance's brother, who was 44 and single, was boarding with Mary Cole, a widow and charwoman. Mary Cole was born in the Parish of St. Luke's, London. George E. Pitman described himself as a retired warehouseman from a furnishing and drapery business and gave his place of birth as Barnsbury. When the family business collapsed in 1908, George would have also lost his source of income and have become prematurely retired. Meanwhile, his brother-in-law, Charles George Reed was living at "*Sturley*" in Woodcote Park in Surrey. He was aged thirty-five and described himself as an estate agent and employer, born in Brighton. His wife was Elsie

Mary Reed, aged thirty-five, born in London. The couple had been married for twelve years. Florence Kate Pitman, then forty-eight, Elsie's sister, was staying with Charles and Elsie Reed at the time of the 1911 Census. Florence may have been closer to her youngest sister than she was to Constance.

Frank G. Pitman died on 29th April 1930, aged 74 and his death was registered in Winchester. According to Cynthia Pitman, having been told the story by her father-in-law, George Gerrard Pitman, Frank's wife Kate had died of cancer on 13th January 1926, aged 57, at Winchester. Her death certificate, in the possession of the family, showed her husband's occupation as a retired grocer. Frank spent the last few years of his life living in a council house in Winchester, where he had gone by 1926. Cynthia remembered two addresses in Winchester, one at Mildmay Street and the other at Clifton Road. Their sons Frank Talbot Pitman and George Gerrard Pitman had nursed first their mother and then their father and lost both to cancer. George continued to live in the family home after his father's death.

The will of Florence Kate Pitman, a spinster, of "*Fernleigh*", Lake, in the Isle of Wight, was written on 13th November 1937 and identified all the members of the Pitman family that she knew to be alive at that time. (Sylvia Fuller, *née* Pitman, the daughter of Frank Talbot Pitman, recalled that, when she was a small child, her family went to visit Florence on the Isle of Wight.) Her burial was recorded at Sandown Cemetery (*Plot E69*) on 9th January 1939, aged 74. Florence appointed Charles George Reed, of Malvern House, 68 Holywell Hill, St. Albans, her brother-in-law, a retired Captain in His Majesty's Army and County Secretary to the National Farmer's Union, Hertfordshire Branch, as executor and trustee of the will. Among her beneficiaries, she had named her two nephews and their wives; George Gerrard Pitman was married to Eva, living at 12 Mildmay Street, Stanmore, Winchester and Frank Talbot Pitman was married to Betty, *née* Rebecca Casson, who was living at Restholme, White Hart Lane, Porchester, near Southampton. Florence wanted all her jewellery, linen and personal belongings to be divided equally and distributed to their wives. She left £100 to her nephew, George Gerrard Pitman and a lesser amount to her other nephew, Frank Talbot Pitman. Among others, she identified her niece, Margaret Clubb, of "*Chelwood*" Connaught Avenue, Frinton-on-Sea, the wife of Herbert W. Clubb, as a minor beneficiary. Florence's brother, George Ernest Pitman of 43 Middle Street, Southsea, Southampton was given £5. Next was her brother Colin Lindsay Pitman, living at 25 Livingstone Road, Hove, in Sussex. Everything else went to Florence's sister, Elsie Mary Reed.

Florence Kate Pitman was not listed in the electoral registers on the Isle of Wight in 1921, so had moved there after that date. Later, she was recorded at various addresses in the Parish of Sandown and Shanklin, Isle of Wight. In 1929, Florence was living at "*Cottage on the Cliff*", Cliff Road, in a long and large two storied Victorian house at the top of a high cliff, overlooking the sea and pier and the town of Sandown; it has since been converted into five flats. In 1933, the following people were listed at 6 Cliff Road, the same address as above: Marie Adelaide Marsh, Alice Helen Marsh, Florence

Kate Pitman, Mabel Drusilla Shopto, Florence Mackenzie Pitman and Barrie Pulcher. Florence Kate Pitman, it might be presumed, was renting rooms from Mary Adelaide Marsh, the owner. The baptism of Florence Mackenzie Pitman, daughter of Charles and Frances, of 49a St. John's Road, N15, was recorded on 2nd July 1893 at St. John's, Vartry Road, Stamford Hill; Charles who, like Isaac Pitman, was born in Somerset, was then an omnibus driver. In 1901 he was a Stamford Hill coffee house keeper and by 1911 was running an off-licence in Bermondsey. In 1938, Florence Kate Pitman had moved to *"Fernleigh"*, on The Fairway, a street of detached houses built around 1933. She was living there with Fanny Brown, the owner, Sarah Jane Cave and Alice Helen Marsh the last of whom had been living in her previous house. Although on the Isle of Wight, she was only a short journey away, by ferry, from Portsmouth, Porchester and Southsea, where other members of the Pitman family lived.

On 25th November 1940, George Ernest Pitman died intestate; he would have been around 73 years of age. The letters of administration, dated 11th March 1941, where he was described as a bachelor, without parent, were granted to his *"lawful sister of the whole blood and one of the persons entitled to a share of the estate"* She was named as Elsie Mary Reed, wife of Charles George Reed, who was living at 68 Holywell Hill, St. Albans. Her brother left around £1,000 and Elsie was the youngest of the Pitman siblings. George's address was 43 Middle Street, Portsmouth, although he died at 85 White Hart Lane, Porchester, in Hampshire. White Hart Lane was the home of George's nephew, Frank Talbot Pitman.

Frank's daughter, Sylvia, recalled the circumstances of George's death. Apparently, during the aerial bombardment of Portsmouth, in the Second World War, the house in which George Ernest Pitman was living was hit by enemy fire and for eight hours he was trapped under rubble. Sylvia had a newspaper cutting from the Evening News, Monday, 18th November 1940, which gave an account of the incident on the previous Saturday evening. It reported her uncle George Pitman, by name, aged seventy-four and although the article stated that his grand-daughter died in the bombing of the house, Sylvia and other sources confirmed that George was a bachelor and this was not the case. She thought that he was probably a boarder in the house. The newspaper report did not give the address to confirm if it was in fact 43 Middle Street where the bomb struck. Rescuers said that George's life was saved by a fallen beam but others in the rubble were less fortunate and four people died of their injuries. George was dug out alive and taken to hospital, where he was thought to have responded reasonably well to treatment. He left hospital and went to stay with Betty, the children and their grandmother at White Hart Lane, as his home had been demolished. Unfortunately, George never really fully recovered from his injuries and died of pneumonia a week after the incident, explaining why he never made a will; he was buried at St. Mary, Portchester. Sylvia was only thirteen when George Pitman died; she did not know why her great-grandfather, Nathaniel had left money in trust for George as she believed him to be capable of looking after himself. She remembered that George Ernest Pitman used to call her Sybil instead of Sylvia.

Sylvia Fuller, *née* Pitman also recalled that she spent some of her childhood holidays at Middle Street, Winchester with her uncle George Gerrard Pitman, who lived there with his family. She liked going there and remembered that there was a sword and a barometer hanging in the hallway and was of the impression that the sword was connected to the Mackenzie side of the family. Alternatively, it might be that the sword was passed down from Isaac Pitman to his son Nathaniel Gerrard, then to the latter's son, Frank Gerrard Pitman and then his eldest son, George Gerrard Pitman. The furniture, she remembered, was large in scale and probably came from the previous homes of Frank Gerrard Pitman, her grandfather. Frank lived with his son George and his wife Eva after Kate Pitman died in 1926. Sylvia remembered beautiful china and Chinese vases in that house. There was a rosewood desk, which she believed her father, Frank Talbot Pitman, had bought for his mother Kate. There was also a large tapestry signed by all the girls in the Pitman family. Some of these items were in the front room of the house, which she should not have entered. She remembered that the curtains were especially heavy with olive green tassels, with sunflowers in yellow and gold protruding from the surface. They may have been made by workers in the Pitman factory. Very few items of family heirlooms, furniture, personal papers and old photographs survived when houses were cleared after family members died, to offer further clues to the family history and the various relationships. Sylvia was also told by her relations that the Pitman's were extremely religious and were not allowed to do any work on a Sunday; they even had their own pew at church. A keen motor-cyclist, according to Sylvia her father, Frank Talbot Pitman, occasionally took his mother in his side-car on a trip to visit relatives. Of the various family photographs in which Frank Talbot Pitman appears, one is of a handsome young man taken after he joined the Navy in 1920, when he was twenty-one years old.

Frank Talbot Pitman died on 14th October 1941, on war service. Sylvia revealed a newspaper cutting of the incident that caused her father's death. He was a leading telegrapher on board *HMS Fleur de Lys*, west of Gibraltar, when the ship was torpedoed by a German U-Boat (206) and it went down; there were only three survivors. Letters of Administration were granted to his widow Rebecca Pitman (Betty), on 18th December 1942. His address at his death was given as 85 White Hart Lane, Portchester, in Hampshire. Frank was something of a writer and poet, keeping a diary for ten years, though the only reference in his diary to Sylvia was to record her date of birth on 1st October 1927. Sylvia's brother, also named Frank Talbot Pitman, was born on 9th December, 1933, when the family was living at 5 Roger's Terrace, Portchester; he had a daughter names Helen. Sylvia also remembered that the family was stationed at Gibraltar for four years, when she was a child.

Charles George Reed was living at Malvern House, 68 Holywell Hill, St. Albans, when he died on 4th February 1947. His will was proved by his widow, Elsie Mary Reed on 22nd May in that year. Elsie was his sole beneficiary and received over £8,500. There was a memorial service for him at St. Alban's Cathedral on 7th February 1947, indicating that he may have been a leading member of the community.

9.2 Frank Talbot Pitman in 1920, aged 21.

Sylvia Fuller, *née* Pitman, met her "*uncle*" Colin (in fact her great uncle), on a number of occasions when she was a child. After the War ended, in 1946 Sylvia went to live in Canada, as she had married a Canadian serviceman named Carl, the son of a farmer. It was shortly after the birth of her daughter, Sonia, that Colin wrote to her there from his address at 43 Cross Street, Sandown, on the Isle of Wight, where he had moved after 1937. Sylvia kept the letter, dated 2nd February 1948, which had been sent by air mail to arrive in the space of a week, instead of a month by ship. In it, Colin refers to rationing, thanking her for sending him and "*Aunt Doll*" (perhaps his second wife) a cake and explaining that they seldom saw bacon, eggs, butter and suchlike since the War and was very envious about the produce on their farm. The Electoral Register shows that Colin Lindsay Pitman was not living on the Isle of Wight in 1938 but he was at 43 Cross Street in 1947, so he moved there between 1937 and 1938. Colin Lindsay Pitman died intestate, aged 80 and was buried on 29th December 1949 at Sandown Cemetery (*plot E95*) on the Isle of Wight. Sylvia lived in Canada for fifty-five years and after her husband died in 1995 she returned to live in England with her grand-daughter, Catherine.

Eva Maud Pitman of 12 Mildmay Street in Winchester, died in hospital on 19th September, 1957 and in her will left her estate to her husband, George Gerrard Pitman, a clock repairer. Alan was their only son and, according to Cynthia Pitman, his widow, her father-in-law had a withered leg. George, apparently, had been dropped by his nanny as a child and had suffered permanent damage. George Gerrard Pitman married again in 1960, much to the chagrin of many in the family. His son Alan married Cynthia Padwick around the same time but George's new wife did not go to their wedding.

The youngest sister of Constance Candler, Elsie Mary Reed, died on 4th August 1956, aged 80 at Malvern House, 68 Holywell Hill, St. Albans, where she had lived with her husband. Her estate was administered by Barclays Bank Ltd. of 54 Lombard Street in the City of London; she made the will on 20th July 1955. Among her legacies, one was to her "*niece*" Betty Keyzor, of Gosport, which is relatively close to Porchester where Betty had lived with her first husband. The latter was the widow of Frank Talbot Pitman and she had married again. Frank and Betty had two children named Sylvia, born 1929 and Frank and subsequently Betty had a child to her second husband, Jack Keyzor. Sylvia met Elsie Mary Reed and thought that she was a generous, lovely woman. Connie and Dorothy Pitman, living in Manselton, Swansea, who were linked to the family, were also recipients of legacies of £50. They may have been the children of Colin Pitman by his first wife, who died in late 1949. Most of Elsie's real and personal estate was divided into seventeen parts, and bequeathed in different-sized segments to relatives and friends, namely, Margaret Clubb of the Cottage, Partridge Green, in Sussex, Eric and David Clubb of 8a Salisbury Road, Hove (Eric and David were the sons of Herbert and Margaret) and George and Alan Pitman (George was her nephew and Alan his son), both of 12 Mildmay Street, Stanmore, Winchester.

10

The Mackenzie Pitman and Candler period at Vartry Road

Charles George Reed, a commercial traveller, was the husband of Nathaniel's youngest daughter Elsie Mary Pitman. Both twenty-three years of age, the couple had married on 11th February 1899 at the Church of St. John the Divine in the Parish of Tottenham, the marriage having been registered in Edmonton (*3a 420*); Charles may have been working for Elsie's father. Elsie's brother, George, was a witness, as were Harriet Reed, the groom's sister or mother and Constance Margaret Beardsworth. George Herbert Candler, Nathaniel's son-in-law, was living at 54 Vartry Road in 1906. Charles' address was recorded as 54 St. John's Road, a house rented out by George Herbert Candler and the church in question was in Vartry Road. As George Candler must have known Charles Reed as a tenant, it may be that Constance met her future husband through her brother-in-law to be. In 1906, the only unmarried daughter left at home at 2 Woodberry Grove was Florence and she must have left the house soon after her father's death. Presumably the furniture and personal effects of Nathaniel were divided up among the brothers and sisters, including Constance, when Florence left the very large house at 2 Woodberry Grove.

In 1910 George Candler was included on the jury lists, still as an estate agent. He inherited two houses and money after the death of his second wife in 1899, when he was already involved with the *Woodberry Lodge Estate*. Constance then inherited funds from her father in 1906, which George may have invested in mortgages on tenements and houses on the *Woodberry Lodge Estate,* as evidenced by the Rate Book for 1908 in which Candler's name was given as the landlord of a property in Franklin Street.

By the time of the census of 1911, George was sixty and he described himself as a house agent living at 54 Vartry Road, South Tottenham but was not shown to be an employer. Constance was aged forty-six and gave her place of birth as Highbury. According to the records, they had completed seven years of marriage and had a general servant/domestic named Harriet Jane Brawn, who was single, aged 40 and born at Plymouth in Devon.

George Herbert Candler was noted in *The Times* on 18th August 1925 in relation to a house for sale. A freehold house with four and a half acres, orchard and paddock at the price of £1,500 or to rent at £70 per annum at Barton near Ampthill in Bedfordshire, was to be let or sold; it could be sold without the orchard at a lower price. The house had five bedrooms, two sitting rooms, bathroom, kitchen and two sculleries and was fully repaired and decorated throughout. The correspondence address shown was Candler's office at

115 Vartry Road, his name was specified and no agents were to apply. While it is not clear whether or not George owned the property himself or he was selling it for someone else, if he had been the owner of the house, this might account for a large part of the money he left in his will.

The British Telecom Archives confirm that George Candler was registered in 1929 as an estate agent at 115 Vartry Road, N.15 and his telephone number was Tottenham 3022. He did not have a telephone at No. 54, which may be due to the fact that one of the covenants attached to the house was that it was not to be used for commercial purposes. Stanley C. Rolls was listed in the telephone directory as an estate agent at 115 Vartry Road in 1930, 1939, 1943, 1950 and finally in 1952. He took over from George Candler, collecting rents and managing the flats and houses for the company.

George Candler died at the age of seventy-eight and his death was registered in Edmonton (*3a 560*) London. *The Times* reported his death on Friday 24th May 1929 and his burial on Monday 27th May. The funeral service was at St. John's Church, Vartry Road at 10 o'clock followed by interment at 11.45 a.m. at West Norwood Cemetery, normally a burial place of the wealthy, indicating that when the plot was bought, George was relatively well off. His first wife, Mary Louisa was buried in a double plot, to be joined when George "*passed over...in 1929*" A map of the plots in Norwood cemetery identifies their burial place, three rows from Doulton's path, near the back of the cemetery. The simple headstone confirms also that Mary Louisa Candler had died on 28th July 1893, with both their names engraved in the stone and inlaid with metal, in contrast with the more elaborate ones surrounding theirs; the cross on top has long since fallen off and it and the middle section of the headstone may have been added later. The inscription read "*Even so father for so it seemeth good in thy sight*". As at 1930, the cemetery records show that John Pycock Candler and Constance Candler were responsible for the grave for, as Mary Louisa Candler was John Pycock Candler's mother and Constance Candler was his step-mother, it seems appropriate that George should have been buried with his first wife and the mother of his two children. This is a summary of George Candler's will:

> **Candler**, George Herbert of 54 and 115 Vartry Road, died 24 May 1929 at 54 Vartry Road. Probate, London, 10 July to Constance Mackenzie Candler, widow and John Pycock Candler, doctor of medicine. Effects £2550 8s.11d. (Probate year 1929)

That was the gross value of the effects but the net value was under half that at £1146 19s. 11d. Comparative statistics show that £2500, in 1929, would be worth about £125,000, gross in 2014. In his will, George appointed his wife Constance, his son John Pycock Candler, M.D. of "*Ashleigh*", Brighton Road, Coulsdon, Surrey and his daughter, Alice Mary Candler as executors and trustees. All his personal property went to Constance but he requested that any part of his personal estate consisting of shares in commercial companies was not to be sold but on her death was to be left to his son and daughter in equal amounts. Constance had no legal obligation to comply with his wishes and his intention was not to favour his son and daughter. He requested that his wife ask his old friend Dr. Vaughan Price to arrange the sale of his Rigby gun, with the case, cartridge belt, cartridges and other accessories including the old wildfowl guns in the homemade case in his bedroom. His two freehold houses at 21 and 22 Casselden Road, Harlesdon, Middlesex and all other real estate which he possessed at his death was to be sold and converted to money as and when his trustees saw fit. They were to remain unsold in the year following his death and any income from rent was to be used to pay the interest on the existing mortgage on No. 21, Casselden Road. When they were sold, any balance of money was to be invested in trust funds to pay an income to his wife during her life and then to his son and daughter. Mindful of his occupation, he asked that his real estate was to be kept in a reasonable state of repair and insured against loss or damage by fire. The will was dated 12th November 1927 and witnessed by Stanley Charles Rolls of 47 St. John's Road, South Tottenham, an estate agent's clerk and John William Hemmings of 46 Heysham Road, South Tottenham, a decorator.

Stanley Charles Rolls and his wife Dorothy Venner Rolls lived at 47 St. John's Road from 1926 until 1934, as recorded in electoral registers for Stamford Hill Ward; after that year they moved. Rolls was listed in the telephone directory at 37 The Meadway, Bush Hill Park, Enfield (Laburnum 3865). Stanley was born in Stoke Newington on 9th September 1895 and lived with his family at 35 Maury Road. In 1914, aged 18, he joined up to fight in the First World War and returned to live with his family in Stoke Newington in 1918. He married Dorothy Venner Webb in Hackney, in the third quarter of that year. A local resident confirmed that Stanley C. Rolls went to live in Brighton where he may have had an office as an estate agent. Apparently, Mr. Rolls was last seen locally in the mid-1980s by Mrs. Lockett's sister, before she died, checking to see how the area had changed. Mr. and Mrs. Lockett were both of the intriguing opinion that Stanley Rolls had *"more than the role of an administrator or manager of the Estate"*. Death records show that Stanley ended his days living at Cockermouth, Cumberland, in the north of England where he died in 1983 aged 88. His widow Dorothy died there in 1993, aged 97.

Houses that Candler owned at his death were 21 and 22 Casselden Road, Middlesex, London. The former was one of the houses which he and his second wife, May Annie Rose, had bought from Henry Brazell in late 1897. Below are summaries of the deeds relating to Casselden Road held at City of London, London Metropolitan Archives:

Memorial of a deed registered 9th April 1897 (MDR/1897/13/566)
Dated 9th April, 1897. Endorsed on a deed dated 3rd day of February 1897 made between Henry Brazell of No. 23 Casselden Road, Harlesden in the County of Middlesex, builder of the one part and George Herbert Candler of 12 Albert Road, South Tottenham, Middlesex, Agent of the other part, registered 4th February 1897 (B4 No. 911). Parties within named George Herbert Candler of

the one part and the within named Henry Brazell of the other part. Description of lands affected. All the hereditaments and premises comprised in the within written indentures. Witness to execution of deed by the said George Herbert Candler. James Allward of James Allward, 10 Gray's Inn Square EC.

This indenture relates to the property at No. 22 Casselden Road. as George H. Candler stood as surety for that property.

Memorial of a deed registered 9th April 1897 (MDR/1897/13/654)
Dated 9th April, 1897. Parties: May Annie Rose Candler, wife of George Candler of 12 Albert Road, South Tottenham in the County of Middlesex (herein after called the mortgagor) of the 1st part the said George Herbert Candler hereinafter called the surety of the 2nd part and Ellen Mary Southgate of Hazelwood, Upper Norwood in the County of Surrey, spinster and Charles Francis Southgate of 7 Kings' Bench Walk, Temple in the City of London, Gentleman (hereinafter called the mortgagees of the 3rd part).

Description of lands affected. All that plot of land in Casselden Road, Willesden, Middlesex, which constituted part of Lot 30 of the land described in the lithographed plan published with the particulars and conditions of Mr. F S Priest's Sale by auction at the Willesden Junction Hotel, Station Road Harlesden on the 4th May 1891. Together with the _____ messuage and premises erected therein and now known as or intended to be known as No. 22 Casselden Road aforesaid. Witness to execution of Deed by May Annie Rose Candler and George Herbert Candler, Evelyn H. Pollock, solicitor, 7 Kings Bench Walk, Temple EC.

The solicitors dealing with the documents were T. Southgate & Sons and May Annie Rose Candler's signature was scrawled and very poor.

Memorial of a deed registered 21st June 1898 (MDR/1898/24/260)
Dated 21st June, 1898. Parties: May Annie Rose Candler of 12 Albert Rd (crossed out then replaced with) 54 Vartry Road, South Tottenham in the County of Middlesex, the wife of George Herbert Candler of the same place, Estate Agent, of the one part and William Richard Garwood of 47 Cazenove Road, Stamford Hill in the County of Middlesex, gentleman of the other part. Description of lands affected. By recital of a deed dated 16th April 1895, registered the 18th day of April 1895 (B11 No.627). All that plot of land in Casselden Road, Middlesex, which con-stituted Lot 29 of the lands delineated in the lithographed plan published with the particulars and conditions of Mr. J. S. Priests' sale by auction at the Willesden Junction Hotel Station Road, Harlesden in the County of Middlesex, on the fourth day of May one thousand eight hundred and ninety one was conveyed to the said May Annie Rose Candler.

In operative part: All the land hereditaments and premises comprised in the herein before recited Indenture of conveyance together with the messuage or tenement and dwelling house erected thereon and known as No. 21 Casselden Road aforesaid.

When May Annie Rose Candler died in 1899, her estate passed to her husband, George and he kept the two freehold messuages at 21 and 22 Casselden Road. Electoral Registers for these properties in the 1930s showed that no family members lived in the houses so they continued to be rented out up to his death.

Candler certainly owned shares in commercial entities and he may have had an equitable interest in the *Woodberry Lodge Estate Company*. His personal estate, including the shares he held was to go to his wife. Houses that, according to the Rate Books in Tottenham, he may appear to have owned in 1913, may in fact have been held by a company or George may have sold some of the tenements to other people after this date.

Dr. Vaughan Price (*spelt in various documents as Prisce, Price and Pryce*), was to sell his guns. (*John Rigby was an Irish gun manufacturer of some repute and early ones are worth quite substantial sums today*.) The commentary on the back of the Old Ordnance Survey map of Stamford Hill for 1913/1915 *(The Godfrey Edition)*, reveals that a Harold Vaughan Pryce F.R.C.S.Eng., M.A., M.B., B.C. Cantab., physician and surgeon, lived at 104 Bethune Road. Born in Worcester, in 1873, he studied at St. John's College, Cambridge and was the same age as George's son, John Pycock Candler who was a contemporary; the two may even have known each other there. Harold worked as a surgeon and anaesthetist at many hospitals, including St. Bartholomew's, in the City of London, the German Hospital, Dalston, Tottenham and Great Ormond Street (*Alumni Cantabrigienses*). In 1913, Harold was working at the Invalid Asylum and Stoke Newington Home Hospital for Women at 187 Stoke Newington High Street, which, in 1916, was renamed the Stoke Newington Home Hospital for Women. It is now *The Yum Yum Restaurant*. The building next door (189) was a charitable dispensary. The hospital provided nursing and medical care for servants and shop workers, who through illness were unable to continue work but were not ill enough for hospital. Patients of "*good moral conduct*", were expected to look after each other and clean the wards. In a Street Directory in 1921, Dr. Pryce was listed as working there.

At the time of the 1881 Census, the Pryce family was living at "*Henley Lodge*", Amhurst Park Road. According to the census of 1891, Robert Vaughan Pryce, M.A., LL.B., D.D., was a Professor of Theology at New College, Finchley Road, Hampstead, London. By the time of the census of 1911, Harold's father, the Reverend Robert Vaughan Pryce, then aged 76, was an independent minister of the Stamford Hill Congregational Church, living at 68 Bethune Road. His then wife, Kate, was aged 35. Her husband died in 1917, aged 83 and he was buried in Abney Park Cemetery. It would appear from his obituary that he was a highly respected member of the church and college; the former does not exist today as it has been replaced by the Stamford Hill Library. The wall at the end of Vartry Road, next to the railway line and the 1930s apartment block, is built from large carved stones that may have come from the demolished church at Stamford Hill. In 1930, Dr. Vaughan Pryce was still living at 104, Bethune Road with his wife Violet, along with Frank Stiles and Nellie Williams, who may have been employees. Harold Vaughan Pryce died suddenly at Welshpool in Wales in December 1946. His widow, Marion Frances Violet died in 1978, aged 103. She was the daughter of Reverend Walrond Clarke of Devon.

George's grand-daughter Patricia, who would have been about eight at the time of his death, hinted that there may have been no love lost between George's third wife and other members of the Candler family. After his death, Constance did not go to live with her sister-in-law, Annie Candler or John Pycock or Alice Candler, George's son and daughter, who were all alive then.

11

Constance Mackenzie Candler (after 1929)

After George

Constance was no longer living at 54 Vartry Road, nor was her servant, Ada Elizabeth Butler, by 15th October 1930, when an Electoral Register was compiled and the house was rented to a number of successive tenants. Whatever the reason, her move, so quickly after the death of her husband, appears dramatic, though it may have just been that the house was too big for one person or too expensive to run. Alternatively, if George did not own the house before his death, because he was merely working as a house/estate agent for the Dorman family, Constance may have lost her right to live there. She had a degree of financial security though, having received funds from her husband's will and her entitlement to a share in any money made from selling shares or property.

Constance Mackenzie Candler may have gone to live with other members of the Pitman family. In 1929, Frank was seventy-three, Elizabeth seventy, Florence sixty-six, George sixty-two, Colin, fifty-nine and Elsie, fifty-four. Florence was a spinster when Constance married in 1903 and probably knew her sister best as they lived at home with her father before her marriage.

A document in the possession of Hugh Barton Candler, the great-grandson of George Herbert Candler gives evidence of Constance's whereabouts and movements. The name of Mrs. Logan was recorded in the estate accounts, prepared by Kingsford, Dorman & Co. for Alice Mary Candler, daughter of George Herbert Candler, who died on 2nd May 1943. Included in the list of her personal property and estate is the item "*interest expectant on the death of Constance Mackenzie Logan under the will of George Herbert Candler*". As Alice died in May 1943, clearly Constance Mackenzie Logan was still alive when the papers were prepared after Alice's death.

The National Records of Scotland, Edinburgh reveal that a Constance M. Candler married Adam Logan on 18th February 1937 (*644/8 379*), at Blythswood, in Glasgow. Her marriage certificate gives her address as 4 Trebovir Road, at Earls Court, London SW5 and her name is shown to be Constance Mackenzie Pitman or Candler. A commercial directory from 1937, at the local archives at Kensington, shows that 4-6 Trebovir Road was the address of a private hotel called the *Kerrisdale*, situated on the south side of the road but it would seem that the address was a temporary one. Constance's father was recorded on the marriage certificate as Nathaniel Gerrard Pitman, a silk mercer and her mother as Charlotte Emma Pitman *née* Unwin, both of whom were deceased by this time. The marriage was confirmed by declaration before the Sheriff substitute of Lanarkshire at 136 Buckanan Street, in

Blythswood, in Glasgow in the presence of George Reid Logan of Cloncaird Farm and John Lees Logan of Mossend Farm. Adam Logan was also living at Mossend Farm at the time of his marriage and George Reid Logan and John Lees Logan may have been his sons. Given that Constance's maternal grandmother was a Mackenzie, born in Sheffield but probably hailing from Scotland, the couple may have met while she was visiting relatives. There may have been a holiday romance.

This declaration proves beyond doubt that Constance had married again but the marriage certificate gives rise to a few observations. Adam Logan was described as aged sixty-one and divorced and Constance as a widow. On the document, Constance had recorded her age as sixty-five when she was in fact seventy-three years of age, having been born in late 1864, so she had married a man twelve years her junior. However, she appears to have remained married to Adam Logan until his death.

Adam Logan

Adam Logan, at the age of five, was recorded in the 1881 Census for Scotland. He was the son of George Reid Logan, a farmer who lived at Cloncaird Farm, Dalrymple, near Ayr. George's father had also been called Adam and his eldest brother had gone into the grocery business. On 3rd June 1874, George Logan married Janet Murdock, the youngest daughter of James Murdock, said by some to be a first-class farmer and an intelligent man and Marion Galbraith. Adam Logan was the eldest son, born at Cloncaird on 23rd September 1875. The family had three other children, James, born 14th July 1877, Marion born 21st July 1879 and Susan, born 21st November 1881. It is known that Janet's mother, Marion Murdock, died at Cloncaird Farm on 30th May 1886, aged seventy-nine. It is likely that Adam, as the eldest son, would have inherited the Cloncaird farm on the death of his father.

Adam Logan married Janet Lees, also known as Jessie, on 29th December 1904, at Lagg Farm, Fisherton by Ayr, in the district of Maybole in the County of Ayr. Fisherton is an area down the coast from Burns Cottage, south of Ayr. There had been a proclamation of Banns, according to the Forms of the Church of Scotland and the marriage was registered on 31st December 1904. Adam was a described as a bachelor and farmer and Janet as a spinster and a teacher of modern languages. He was twenty-nine and living at Martnaham Farm, Dalrymple and she was twenty-six. Martnaham Loch is near the farm and is mid-way between Coylton and Dalrymple, where other members of the Logan family lived. Jessie was living at Dunoon, which is just across the Firth of Clyde, at Glasgow. Jessie may have been working there or perhaps her father, Robert Lees farmed there. Her father was still alive although her mother, Agnes Lees, *née* Drennan, was deceased. Adam's parents, George Reid Logan and Janet Murdock, were both alive and probably still living at Cloncaird Farm. William Murdock, who officiated at the wedding, was the minister at Fisherton and was the uncle of the groom. The witnesses were James Logan and Lilias Lees, obviously relatives of the bride and groom.

Adam and Janet Logan had three children over the next few years. George Reid Logan was born at Dalrymple in 1908, Adam was born in 1913 and John Lees Logan in 1920; these last two births were registered at Dalrymple. It was probably George Reid Logan who died aged seventy-seven, at Ayr, in 1985.

Janet (Jessie) Logan died on 18th May 1925, aged forty-six at Challiners Road, East Ayr and her usual residence was recorded as Cloncaird Farm, by Ayr. A post-mortem was performed and it was said that she died from shock resulting from an operation which she had undergone some nine months before for the removal of a carcinoma. Her husband was present at her death, registered on 21st May 1925 and both her parents were by then deceased.

A year later, on 3rd June 1926, the widowed Adam Logan married Rebecca Norman Murray, a spinster of 5 Westercraigs, Glasgow, at the Grand Hotel, Glasgow, after Banns were read according to the Forms of the Established Church of Scotland. The marriage was registered on 7th June 1926 and the officiating minister was Dr. F. Liddle of Blackfriars Parish Church, in Whitehall Street in Glasgow, also known as Dennistoun Blackfriars Church. Adam Logan was aged fifty and she was forty-seven, making her year of birth around 1879. Her late father, James Murray, had been a merchant sailor and her mother's Christian name was Matilda. G. Logan, of Cloncaird, Carrick Road, Ayr, probably Adam's father, was a witness, along with James M. Reid of 14 or 16, Derby Crescent, Glasgow. The fact that the name of Reid was also the middle name of other members of the Logan family suggests that James was related in some way to Adam Logan. This was the second time that Adam Logan had married someone who lived outside his own area so he may have met his future wife while visiting relatives in Glasgow. This marriage lasted nine years and the couple divorced in 1935, as seen by a record of the divorce being stamped and signed in the margin of their marriage certificate.

Having then married Constance, Adam Logan, aged sixty-six, died in a nursing home at 29 Racecourse Road, Ayr, on 5th March 1942 (*578/1 156*). The address was apparently on "*a very nice street*". His death certificate recorded his profession as retired farmer normally living at Mossend Farm, near Ayr, where he had lived with his second son, Adam, Junior. Today Racehouse Road is the site of a council-run residential home which may be the one in which Adam lived before his death. Written on the death certificate was the following information: "*Adam Logan was a widower three times over; his first wife was Jessie Lees, the second Rebecca Murray and the third was Constance Mackenzie or Candler*". George R. Logan, his son, of Cloncaird Farm, provided the information for the death certificate. As he was the eldest son of Adam Logan, he took over Cloncaird Farm from his father. Adam Logan was buried in the Cemetery at Ayr, as was Jessie.

If Adam was described as divorced, when he married Constance in 1937, the declaration on the death certificate that his father had been widowed three times, implied that all his wives were then dead. In fact, Rebecca Norman Murray, also known as Logan, died in 1961, aged eighty-two in the Cathcart District of Glasgow. After the divorce, Rebecca had returned to the area where she knew and grew up.

Adam Logan left a will (*SC/46/69*), written on 10th January 1940 and witnessed at the offices of John W. & G Lockhart, solicitors in Ayr. He wrote:

> I, Adam Logan, residing at Mossend Farm, by Ayr, hereby assign, dispose and bequeath to my son Adam Logan, Junior, residing with me at Mossend aforesaid, as his absolute beneficial property, the whole means and estate, heritable and moveable, real and personal, of what nature whatsoever and wherever situated, which may belong to me at the time of my death and I appoint the said Adam Logan, Junior to be my sole executor and universal legatory.

An inventory (*SC/6/44/134*) was presented for registration on 28th December 1942, showing that Adam Logan had poultry and poultry houses on the farm as well as crop implements valued at approximately £229. His household furniture had been valued by a licensed valuator at £46 and small sums were due from the Kilmarnock Equitable Co-operative Society Ltd. The movable or personal estate and effects, outlined in the inventory, did not amount to much and he appeared to have amounts owed to his creditors. Mossend Farm was to go to his son Adam, Junior. Presumably Adam, Senior had already passed over Cloncaird to his eldest son George Reid Logan in 1939. This seems likely, given that Logans or their descendents were still living at Cloncaird Farm until 2006. It would seem that Adam Logan was ensuring that his third wife, probably estranged, was to receive nothing from his will. "*Blood is thicker than water*" as the saying goes.

The electoral registers at the British Library had placed Adam Logan but not Constance at Mossend Farm in October 1937. Electoral registers show that George Logan was still living at Cloncaird Farm in 1948 as was Mary Logan, possibly a wife. There was an Adam Logan recorded at "*Bergerwal*", Drongan, Ayr, Coylton, married to Jeanne Logan and an Adam Logan recorded in 1948 at 50 Burnton Cottages. Jeanette Logan was the owner of Cloncaird Farm in 2006.

A succession of G.R. Logans lived in this area, each generation appearing to have had a G.R. Logan. Some were known by the name of George and others by Reid. One of the living G. R. Logans was kind enough to add more information about the family. He confirmed that both Cloncaird and Mossend Farm no longer belonged to the Logan family and had been sold and Cloncaird redeveloped. The present George Reid Logan, who lives at Coulton, had spoken about Constance to his uncle, John Lees Logan, who now lives in a nursing home. He was, at the time eighty-seven and blind but would have been seventeen when Adam married Constance in 1937. He had a recollection that Constance was from London. A significant reason for remembering her was that apparently Constance had put him out of the house following a disagreement and John then enlisted and went off to fight in the Second World War. This might explain why John Lees Logan was not included in his father's will. The father may have been annoyed with his son for leaving the farm and going off to war. John Lees Logan would only have known his stepmother for a short time so it is entirely understandable that his memories of her were limited. The fact that his middle name was Lees confirms that he was the youngest son of Adam's first wife Jessie Logan, *née* Lees. His red-haired mother was, by John Lees Logan's account, an educated woman and a teacher of German. John was only five when his mother died in 1925 so his memories of her would have been limited. His elder brothers, George Reid Logan and Adam Logan would have been seventeen and twelve at the time of her death.

Constance Mackenzie Logan's later years

Constance Candler had inherited the houses at 21 and 22 Casselden Road, Willesden, which George Candler had inherited in 1899 from his second wife, May Annie Rose Candler. However, the first time that 21 Casselden Road was registered at the Land Registry was by Kingsford, Dorman & Co. of 23 Essex Street Strand, solicitors, acting for the estate of the deceased, George Herbert Candler, on 26 May 1952. Both properties at Casselden Road were shown by the Land Registry to be in the same ownership until 1952. Constance was still alive in 1952 and her solicitors were Kingsford, Dorman & Co., so it may have been she who instigated the sale of the two houses.

Copies of the wills of Charles George Reed, Florence Kate Pitman and Elsie Mary Reed and the contributions of two surviving members of the Pitman families who allowed access to family documents in their possession, fill in critical gaps in the family history.

In her will, made in 1937 and proved in February 1939, Florence Kate Pitman bequeathed £5 to her sister Constance Mackenzie Logan, of "*Moss End Farm*" by Ayr, the wife of Adam Logan. This address confirms that Constance had been living for a time at Mossend and not Cloncaird Farm, when she was in Scotland.

The youngest sister of Constance Candler, Elsie Mary Reed, died on 4th August 1956, having made her will on 20th July 1955. One of the first legacies, of £200, was to her sister Constance Mackenzie Logan then of Salisbury Lodge, Queen's Road, Worthing, in Sussex.

Upon the death of Constance Mackenzie Logan, she was described as a widow of 55 Shakespeare Road, Worthing and formerly of Worthing Lodge, Stoke Abbott Road, Worthing, who died on 25th July 1958 at the Seaward Nursing Home, 10 St. Michael's Road, Worthing. The net value of her estate amounted to £488 when it was granted in August that year to Margaret Clubb (wife of Herbert Clubb), her sole executrix, who was then living at "*Chelwood*" in Henfield in Sussex. Constance had been born in the last quarter of 1864, making her a remarkable ninety-four years of age when she died. Her will had been written on 17th October 1938, when she was residing at Worthing Lodge and she declared herself to be the wife of Adam Logan and the widow of George Herbert Candler. All the stocks, share and securities to which she was entitled under George's will were to go in equal shares, as tenants-in-common to her stepson and stepdaughter, John Pycock and Alice Mary Candler, if they were living. Their children were to receive their share if the parents had died before Constance. Finally, all her property and effects, both real and personal, were to go to her niece Margaret Clubb and in the event of Margaret prede-ceasing her, to her godson, Lindsay Clubb, the only child named in the will. The solicitors dealing with Constance's affairs were Kingsford, Dorman & Co. and the witnesses were Winifred and Frank Page, the latter a retired Police Detective Inspector and Feray D'Esmar, fellow residents at Worthing Lodge. She left Adam Logan nothing, which suggests that by later 1938 the marriage might have broken down. By the time of her death, John Pycock and Alice Mary Candler were both dead.

It is possible that Constance was on holiday in Worthing or had left the marital home and her husband in Scotland, when she wrote the will. She had married in February, 1937 and by October of 1938 she was not recorded in the electoral register in Scotland. The electoral registers in Worthing confirm that she was living at Stoke Abbott Road in 1938/9. In 1939/40 the three witnesses to the will, named above, were still registered there but not Constance. In the 1939 Register, Constance M. Logan, a widow, is recorded at 24 Tisbury Road, Hove, Sussex, a guesthouse. Her birthdate was given as 19 October 1874 but the actual year was probably incorrect. She appears again, however, in elec-toral registers at Worthing in the year 1950/51, at "*Rudham*", Rowlands Road, Heene Ward, in the same area. Rowlands Road is a few streets back from the seafront, parallel to the sea and close to her next address. During the years 1952 to 1956 she was recorded in every year at 16 Queen's Road in Heene Ward, a house identified as "*Salisbury Lodge*" as was referred to in her sister's will. It is a large detached Victorian house about fifty yards from the sea, on a road running at right angles to the sea front. In 1956/7, she was recorded at 55 Shakespeare Road, in Clifton Ward. This small Victorian terraced house, in a quiet street, had five people registered as living there and was some distance from the sea front. The houses not dissimilar in style, coincidentally, to the houses and tenements in Vartry Road and Constance must have had a room in the house. The last entry for her in the Electoral Registers in 1957/8 was back at 16 Queen's Road, then in Clifton Ward, where there were twelve residents. This was not the address shown in her will, that being 55 Shakespeare Road but she might have moved there again between October and July, before she died in the nursing home. Indeed, the houses may have been boarding houses or small hotels in those days. Constance was living independently well into her nineties and must have managed her finances carefully. As she was living in rooms, all her belongings must have fitted into suitcases and there was probably none of her furniture from Vartry Road left by that stage, as she had moved to Scotland and then back to Worthing. She ended her days alone and without immediate family, as she was the last Pitman of her generation to die.

Constance Mackenzie Logan was buried in a now unmarked grave at Durrington Cemetery at Worthing (*Section: 20, Row 8, Grave: 48*, on 30th July 1958). On one side of her plot is Elizabeth Stephenson, buried in June 1958, aged eighty three and on the other side is Anne Elizabeth Cripps, buried on 31st July 1958, aged eighty-nine.

Constance Mackenzie Logan's beneficiaries

The major benefactor of the estate of Constance Mackenzie Logan was her niece, Margaret Clubb, the daughter of her sister, Charlotte Emma Pitman and John Cryer. Electoral Registers at Frinton-on-sea, in the Harwich area, show that in the years 1929-1930 Herbert Wentworth Clubb and his wife, Margaret, were living with John Cryer and Ethel Mary Burton at "*Chelwood*" Connaught Avenue. Again in 1930-1931 and 1931-1932, the same three members of the family were recorded without Ethel. John Cryer died in 1936, aged eighty-four and his death was registered at Tendring, in Essex. His daughter, Margaret Cryer and Herbert Wentworth Clubb had three children, Eric Wentworth Clubb, Oswald Lindsay Clubb and David Selwyn Clubb. Constance's godson, Lindsay Clubb, who was named in her will, was also known as Lin, apparently disliking the name Oswald. Lindsay Clubb was killed in action at Pihen-Les-Guines in 1942. In *The Times* there were two entries for him; one was "*In Memoriam*", on 12th March 1943, placed by his family and inscribed:

> In proud and loving memory of Sergeant Pilot Oswald Lindsay Clubb R.A.F.A.R. (Fighter Command), on this his 21st birthday, Friday 12th March. He made his last flight April 27th, 1942 and was killed in action over Northern France.

He was only twenty when he died. A letter to *The Times* from his father, H. Wentworth Clubb, headed "*An Airman's Grave*", dated Wednesday, 13th June 1945 explained that his son, Oswald Lindsay Clubb, of 111 Squadron, died over Northern France while engaged in defending heavily attacked bombers. Herbert had received a letter from a French official to say that the grave at Pihen, near Calais, was well looked after. The Germans had given his son a "*solemn funeral*", which apparently they had not done before, with a military band and guard of honour with a "*magnificent wreath in admiration of the courage shown in combat*". The father was obviously exceptionally proud of his son's achievements and comforted by the fact that the enemy would honour the British war dead.

Herbert Wentworth Clubb died in 1962 and left his estate to his wife Margaret and his sons. Margaret Clubb died in the second quarter of 1968, aged eighty-one and her death was registered in the New Forest area. Their son, Eric Wentworth Clubb died in 1983 and his brother, David Selwyn Clubb, in 1995. The Clubb/Pitman line follows through Eric and his wife Muriel and their sons, Colin David Berryhill Clubb, Lindsay Wentworth Clubb and Julian Clive Mackenzie Clubb, who are still alive today. Presumably the latter's name was an acknowledgement of the Mackenzie Logan and Pitman/Unwin ancestry.

Lindsay Clubb, the great-grandson of Charlotte Emma Cryer, *née* Pitman, has engaged in extensive family research. He suggests that the "*aunty*" in many of the photographs taken with his grandmother, Margaret Clubb and her sons, was in fact, Elizabeth Beardsworth.

There was clearly a close relationship between the Cryer and Beardsworth families, going back to the time when the families were living together after

11.1 Margaret Clubb, two sons and "aunty" in 1929.

Charlotte Emma Cryer died. Elizabeth, in effect, brought up the Cryer children with her own stepchildren and indeed Eric was with his aunt Elizabeth on the night of the census of 1901. Figure 11.1, a photograph taken in 1929, shows a white-haired, elegant lady, wearing spectacles and dressed in clothes of that period, standing in the back garden of their home at Frinton-on-sea with her niece, Margaret Clubb and her children. Alternatively, given that Constance left her estate to her godson, Lindsay Oswald Clubb, it may be that the lady in the photograph is Constance and not her sister Elizabeth Beardsworth. Lindsay recalled that, as a child, he was taken by his parents, Eric and Muriel, to visit some old ladies on the south coast. Margaret and Herbert Clubb were living at "*Chelwood*", Connaught Avenue, Frinton-on-sea in 1937, so it might be possible that Constance went to stay with her niece after George Herbert Candler died in 1929. Margaret Clubb named many of the homes she lived in "*Chelwood*" because, when she was a child she had stayed with her aunt and uncle, Elizabeth and Clarence Beardsworth, at *Chelwood* in Friern Barnet and it had obviously made a great impression on her.

Lindsay's parents, Eric and Muriel married in Hove in December, 1950. His grandparents moved to *The Cottage*, Partridge Green, where they were living in 1955. Elizabeth Helen Beardsworth was living in Flat 4, 15 Palmeir Square, Hove, when she died on 26th February 1953, aged ninety-five. Probate was granted on 4th May to Charlotte Alatha Rosalie Adams, a widow and her effects amounted to £145. When Constance died in 1958, Lindsay's grandmother, Margaret Clubb was living at "*Chelwood*" Henfield, in Sussex. Hove, Worthing and Henfield being not far from one another, it would be charming to think that Constance and Elizabeth, despite their longevity, kept in touch with their niece, Margaret Clubb.

12

The Pycock and Candler families
and their descendants

Earlier Pycocks

Joseph Pycock's grandfather, also Joseph Pycock, was born at Adlingfleet on 12th October 1736. He married twice; his first wife Margaret was the mother of Mary, born on 28th July 1765. Margaret died on 2nd July 1770 and Joseph then married Mary Mell on 4th March 1773. John Pycock was born on 28th August 1774. A number of documents from this period relating to the family are held at East Riding of Yorkshire Archives and Records Service. The first (*DDCL/2264*), is dated May 1782 and is a lease and release relating to land at Ousefleet. Joseph Pycock, a gentleman of Adlingfleet, in the same area and Sir Clifton Wintringham of Dover Street in Middlesex together were the parties to the agreement. The property consisted of a messuage and farm, over one hundred and sixty acres in size and another thirty-six acres of arable land, with a total rental income of £120 a year; the value of the transaction was £5,000. One of the witnesses to the agreement was John Kilvington of Gray's Inn. Another six acres were leased for £500 in June that year by Joseph Pycock and Edward Wilkinson, a farmer of Ousefleet. The Pycock family was quite wealthy and was involved in several land deals with people from all parts of the country.

Joseph Pycock was buried on 22nd October 1789 at Adlingfleet. Documents (*DDCL/2265*) include a will for Joseph Pycock, written on 17th October 1789. Among his executors were John Mell, Pycock's father-in-law and the beneficiaries were his daughter Mary and his son John. Among the documents is an abstract of title deeds of Mary Pycock, the mother, to premises at Ousefleet for the years 1782-1789. The document describes land at Adlingfleet. Another lease (*DDCL/2267*), for one year, was dated 22nd March 1831 and one of the associated parties was Mary Pycock, a spinster, of Ousefleet who died on 23rd June 1839.

The Pycocks in the mid-late 1800s

At the time of the census of 1871, Mary Louisa Pycock, then aged 25, was unmarried and living with her sister Sarah Lavinia Pycock, aged 23, her brother John Pycock, aged 22 and another brother, William Pycock, aged 20. The head of house was their father Joseph, who was at that time the rector of Newbourn, in Suffolk. Joseph Pycock was born on 31st March 1811 to John and Mary Pycock at Adlingfleet, north of Scunthorpe, then in Yorkshire and now in Humberside.

Joseph may have met his wife Sarah when he was minister at Morley cum Churwell not far from Armley. Sarah, aged sixty, baptised at Armley, in the conurbation of Leeds in Yorkshire on 4th September 1810, was the daughter of Phillip and Mary Abbey. Of the children, Sarah Lavinia Pycock's baptism was recorded on 28th April 1847 at Morley in Yorkshire. She attended Prospect House, a ladies' seminary at Malton, Yorkersgate, North Yorkshire

Entries in the British Library newspaper collection offer insight into the movements over the years of Joseph Pycock and his family. An entry from 1849 is a reference to a published letter, giving his address as Morley near Leeds, that the Reverend Joseph Pycock wrote to Hull Town Council. On 4th April 1857, the *Hull Packet and East Riding Times* published an article entitled "*Testimonial to a clergyman*". It was a glowing account of the party to mark his departure, after sixteen years as minister at St. Peter's Church, Morley cum Churwell, when Joseph was presented with a timepiece, amid much cheering. Another entry, dated 27th June 1857, explained that Reverend Joseph Pycock had been appointed to a new position at Helperthorpe in Yorkshire, a small village, where the parish duties were probably much easier. Some time between 1857 and 1871, Reverend Pycock moved to the Parish of Newbourn near Ipswich.

On 1st November 1871 the *Ipswich Journal* published an obituary for the youngest son of Reverend Joseph Pycock, Henry Abbey Pycock, aged eighteen, who had died at Newbourn Rectory. Another obituary was for William Joseph Pycock, of Jesus College Cambridge, described as the second son of Reverend Joseph Pycock, former rector of Newbourn in Suffolk. William died on 21st March 1877, aged twenty-six, at Newton-on-Rawcliffe near Pickering in Yorkshire. His will explained that he was a medical student and that his father was his next-of-kin; he bequeathed under £1,000. It is possible that George Herbert Candler met Mary Louisa Pycock while both were visiting their brothers studying at Cambridge.

The Reverend Joseph Pycock died on 3rd June 1880, aged sixty-nine and his obituary noted that he was, prior to his death, vicar of Newton-on-Rawcliffe in Yorkshire. His will was proved by his son and surviving executor, Reverend John Pycock and his effects had a value of under £9,000. His widow, Sarah would have lost the right to live at the vicarage at Newton after her husband died and indeed she was living at 104 North Marina Road, Scarborough, when she died on 2nd March 1886. Her will was proved at York, by her son, Reverend John Pycock, late rector of All Saints, Huntingdon, the sole executor; the value of her effects amounted to £9,653.

Reverend John Pycock

On 4th December 1874, John Pycock graduated with an M.A. from St. Catherine's College, Oxford and followed his father into the Church. By the time of the 1881 Census, aged 32, he was still unmarried and was the Rector of All Saints, Huntingdon, living with two servants in the High Street, in the census district of Huntingdon St. John. It was not until 1885 that, according to *The Times*, he was appointed Vicar of All Saints, Huntington and surrogate for the Diocese of Ely. All Saints and St. John's were the same church after 1668 and later became known only as All Saints; Oliver Cromwell was the most noted resident of Huntingdon and attended school next to the church. In 1892, Pycock gained another ecclesiastical appointment as the Rector of Hatley, St. George's, in the County of Cambridge. During the third quarter of 1893, he married Mary Minshaw in Kensington, in London (*1a 219*). By the time of the census of 1911, John Pycock was aged sixty-two and living with his wife of seventeen years at Clifton Rectory, Biggleswade. Mary had been born at New Cross in Kent and she was forty-five years of age in 1911. John Pycock eventually rose to the position of Canon in the Church of England.

John Pycock died in 1938 at the age of eighty-nine and left his estate to his widow, Mary Minshaw Pycock. His obituary in *The Times* recorded that he had died peacefully on Wednesday 20th April 1938, on the eve of Easter, at Oak Tree House, Brockenhurst. He was described as a priest, formally the rector of All Saints, Huntington, Hatley and Clifton, Bedfordshire. His funeral was to Lyndhurst Cemetery.

Mary Minshaw Pycock died at the family home on 23rd October 1944 at the age of 80 and in her will she left half of her £30,000 estate, a sizable sum, to her nephew's son, Horace John Pycock Candler; the other half went to her solicitor. Probate was settled in January 1945.

John Pycock's sister, Sarah Lavinia Pycock, was living in a retreat at York when she died on 24th June 1912 at the age of sixty-six. She never married and the letters of administration were granted to her brother for the value of her estate, £1,927 9s. 8d.

Alice Mary Candler

Alice Mary Candler was born in Tendring, Essex (*4a 299*) and her date of birth was shown on the front of a family bible as 26th July 1875. She was the daughter of George Candler and she did not marry. According to George's grand-daughter, Patricia, she had been told that "*George did not want, or feel able to cope with his children so his brother Samuel and his wife Annie took John Pycock Candler in and brought him up as their son, having no children of their own*". In fact, John spent much of his early life at boarding school and of course, at university, separated from his family. George may not have had an especially close relationship with his son and Alice may also have been brought up by her uncle and aunt. On the night of the census of 1891, John Pycock Candler and Alice Mary Candler, aged respectively seventeen and fifteen, were staying with their uncle John Pycock at 84 High Street, Huntingdon.

John Pycock Candler had already left home to study at Cambridge in 1892. Samuel and Annie Candler are likely to have been considerably better off than George as the elder brother was a partner in a significant firm of solicitors. George was beginning his new career building houses in South Tottenham at this time and perhaps unwilling or unable to provide suitable accommodation for his children. According to Patricia Turner, when his wife was dying of cancer, George was being comforted by a lady who may well have been his next wife.

Alice Mary Candler's niece, explained that "*Auntie Tots*", as she knew her, was educated and at some stage during her life she went to Germany to study music. A photograph was provided by Patricia, taken by *E. Beiber, Königl Bayer & Herzogl Sachs, Hof-Photograph, Hamburg, Newer Jungfernsteig 20 or Berlin W, Leipzigerstrasse 128*, probably during her period studying music in Germany. This might have been an adventurous challenge for a single woman in those days and she might have been any age between twenty and thirty. Alice's travels might explain her absence from the census of 1911. Other elegant photographs of her are in the family's possession, taken when she must have been around thirty. In Alice's early life, her education and activities may have been supported financially by George Herbert Candler. She appears to have been a patriotic, caring individual who become involved in the war effort.

The National Archives retains a medal card for Alice Mary Candler, as she was part of the Voluntary Aid detachment during the war years 1914-1918. Patricia reported that Alice contracted an illness which left her an invalid for the rest of her life. After the War, she lived and was looked after by a lady who owned a house in Hounslow at 36 Bulstrode Road. Only at the end of her life was she in a nursing home, hence her final address shown in her will.

Alice had written her will, revoking all other wills, on 22nd May 1929, just a week before the death of her father. When her administration and will was proved in 1943, it explained that her executors were her brother, John Pycock Candler and Francis Thomas Dorman (named as Frank in her will) who died during her lifetime. There was no reference to her stepmother. She left one hundred pounds each to Mary and Evelyn Cross and some loan stock and a diamond ring to Elizabeth Beryl Cross, who may have been members of the family who looked after her before she went into the residential home. Besides leaving a small sum of money to her niece and nephew, Patricia and Horace Pycock Candler, she also left money to Mrs. Edith Cox, who was the niece of her aunt Annie Candler and to some other female friends. The bulk of her personal estate was left to her brother but as he had already died it then went to Patricia Anne Candler "*the lawful niece of the whole blood and one of the persons entitled to share in the undisposed estate of the said deceased*".

Alice Mary Candler died at the age of 68 in 1943, less than six months after her brother John and her death was registered at Staines (*3a 45*). Her estate was left to be administered in the hands of Kingsford Dorman and Patricia remembered visiting their office to collect her aunt's possessions from Laurie Dorman (Laurence Dorman). Below is a summary of her will:

Candler, Alice Mary of Gloucester House Resident Nursing Home 149-151 Uxbridge Rd, Hampton Hill, Middlesex, spinster, died 2 May 1943. Administration (with will) Llandudno, 7 June to Patricia Anne Candler, spinster. Effects £2,649 2s.4d. (Probate year 1943.)

12.1 Alice Mary Candler and John Pycock Candler.

John Pycock Candler

John Pycock Candler was born on 7th October 1873 in Tendring, Essex. When he reached the age of twenty-one, on 6th October 1894, an application was made on his behalf by his father, George Herbert Candler, to claim part of an inheritance belonging to his great grandmother. The action, pursued through the High Court of Justice, on 1st December 1896, was between John Pycock Candler and the defendants, who were members of the Ingham family, Carrall, Garner-Smith, Hutton, Wood-Hughes, William Hall, Reverend John Pycock and Sarah Lavinia Pycock. The Reverend John Pycock was the uncle of John Pycock Candler and Sarah Lavinia Pycock was his spinster aunt. William Hall was the sole surviving trustee of the will of a Matthew Bateson who had died in 1822. Bateson had left his estate to his four daughters Ann, Mary, Nanny and Sarah. Ann died a spinster on 26th January 1846 and after this her share of the estate was divided among her surviving sisters, all of whom had married. Their father had left them, as tenants in common, considerable real estate which included land near Leeds. In 1855 a court order declared that the descendents of the surviving daughters were entitled to a conveyance of the share of their father's estate and to all rents and profits. However great was the exact extent of the wealth of Matthew Bateson, his brother, Joseph was a miller and Matthew had interests in cotton mills.

Mary Bateson, one of the daughters, had married Philip Abbey in 1805. She died on 2nd March 1873 and her share of the estate went to thirty-nine people. She had a daughter named Sarah, born in 1811, who married Joseph Pycock, a minister. Mary Louisa Candler, *née* Pycock, was the grand-daughter of Mary Abbey and one of the beneficiaries. She became the wife of George Herbert Candler and her son John Pycock Candler, although he was not born at the time of Mary Abbey's death, was deemed to be "*en ventre sa mère*". George Candler and Mary Louisa Pycock had married around 9th January 1873, two months before her grandmother's death on 2nd March. Mary Louisa Candler was already pregnant when Mrs. Abbey died and was entitled to her fortieth share of the "*Abbey third*" inheritance, as there were relatives of the three sisters left alive. An action was taken by the trustees against all defendants in June 1893, before the death of Mary Louisa on 28th July 1893, who died intestate. John Pycock Candler was added to the action in December 1894, after his mother's death.

George Herbert Candler transferred his first wife's share to his son in an indenture dated 23rd November 1896, by which time he had married May Annie Rose Parfitt. George transferred to his son a share in the latter's own right as heir in law to his birth mother and a share was apportioned from his mother, since dead. Altogether three shares were allocated to John Pycock Candler and three to the Reverend John Pycock. George Herbert Candler was clearly looking after the interests of his only son who had not as yet finished his studies at Cambridge. Whatever was the amount of his mother's share of the inheritance, George and Mary Louisa Candler were in receipt of it for the whole of their married life as Mary Abbey had died in 1873. If the Candler family had suffered financial hardship, having had to give up Alresford Lodge, to move to West Bergholt, this inheritance would have been a crucial one for them. It may also explain why Samuel Horace Candler, John's uncle, took a great interest in his nephew's inheritance.

The claim by John Pycock Candler was to recover 1/40th share of the net rents from the date of death of Mary Abbey in March 1873 as he was, technically, alive at the time, having been conceived. One of his other demands was for a 1/40th share from that moment forward. Another was a demand for the other beneficiaries to repay to him any excesses from any sales made during the period 1873 until the date of the case so that he would be on an equal footing, together with damages, by way of compensation. He asked that a receiver be appointed for rents and profits and that the only trustee surviving should be prevented from any further action until his case had been adjudicated. All costs were to be paid by everyone who had part of the third share of the estate of Mary Abbey.

A letter from a solicitor in Leeds in September 1896, prior to the writ of December 1896, showed the progress in building their case against the Bateson Trustees in pursuit of John Pycock Candler's own share. He requested more proof that John Pycock was conclusively born on 7th October 1873 and not 26th October 1873 as recorded in his baptism at Alresford. These three weeks were considered crucial to the case and his uncle, Samuel Horace Candler made an affidavit on his behalf to verify his date of birth. His mother had also made an affidavit to confirm to the authorities in Cambridge that it was 7th October but her declaration has since been lost. His demand for compensation from the previous twenty odd years from the proceeds of sales of the extensive residual estate of Matthew Bateson and the Railway companies would have to be addressed on another occasion. He continued by explaining that the Ingham family had now bought out most of the Pycock descendents shares and the six owned by Huttons. The solicitor seemed to think that the Pycock and Hutton families would not oppose his right to his own share. In April 1897, a letter from the solicitors explained that Ingham, one of the other shareholders, had made a request to buy up the Pycock/Candler shares. The solicitor thought his action inappropriate at that time with the result of the case pending. His solicitor also suggested that the shares would be a sound and improving investment as he said that he knew that some of the land in question was at the time being rented out at £320 per acre. The land in question was located inside the boundary of Leeds, Wortley and Beeston and around Gildersome, Churwell and Morley. It included an early eighteenth century large residence called Turton Hall. The solicitor also advised that, in his opinion, each share was worth around £550. Unfortunately, the final outcome of the case was not reported so the case may have been settled out of court.

In the statement of claim in the High Court of Justice, John Pycock's sister, Sarah Lavinia Pycock was described as being of unsound mind and unable to make a decision on her own. John Pycock's uncle also aligned himself with the other beneficiaries and trustees against the action of his nephew John to prevent him having 1/40th share of the inheritance.

John Pycock Candler, it appears, was a car enthusiast of the day and excelled at cricket. Quite short, he had been a handsome young man and looked exceedingly elegant into old age. Jane Fawls, his niece, thought that there might have been a Candler ancestor from the Mediterranean. His daughter, Patricia, believed that he played for the Marylebone Cricket Club, the MCC, though it is more likely that he played for Cambridge University at the Oval, at Lords and elsewhere in 1894 and 1895. An analysis of his performance in these matches, in the *History of Cambridge University Cricket* by W.J. Ford, from 1820-1902, acknowledged that John Pycock Candler was good at bowling but, according to the librarian at Lords, was a "*tail end*" batsman.

The Times carried a handful of items about John Pycock Candler in his capacity as doctor. The first was reported on 1st February 1901, after he was awarded Master of Arts on 31st January 1901 and qualified as a Bachelor of Medicine and Surgery from Corpus Christie College, Cambridge. The second was much more dramatic, involving a fatal accident reported on 7th January 1902 from Westminster Coroner's Court. The death was announced of Herbert Arthur Towse, one of two Bridge Masters of the City of London. He had "*accidentally*" fallen from the top of an omnibus in the West End, late on Friday afternoon and was knocked unconscious. He was taken to Charing Cross Hospital by ambulance where he died later that evening. Witnesses to the accident said that he had joined the bus at Chancery Lane, going westward and outside Coutts Bank on the Strand he had decided to make a call into the bank. However, as he was going down the stairs he had fallen over the handrail onto the roadway. The bus was going at a slow walking pace at the time but the staircase was slippery. John Pycock Candler was the house surgeon at Charing Cross Hospital, who performed the post-mortem on Towse, who died from injuries he received. His skull was fractured in a number of places. Having been otherwise healthy at the time of death, a verdict of accidental death was recorded.

John Pycock Candler was married to Margaret Ann Kerr in a civil ceremony in Chelmsford in late 1906 (*4a 1011*). However, there is evidence of a wedding in St. Matthew's United Free Church of Scotland, in Glasgow on 5th April 1907. From the wedding certificate it is clear that Margaret Ann Kerr's father was deceased by 1907 and his death, at the age of 57, had been recorded in 1905. She came from Ardrossan in Scotland, where her father had owned the Ardeen Iron Foundry. John Pycock Candler was living at that time in Kingsbridge, Marlborough Road, South Woodford, Essex and his job then was as an Assistant Pathologist in the London County Asylum.

At the time of the census of 1911, John Pycock Candler was living at 9, The Terrace Woodford Green, Essex. He was 37 and his wife, Margaret was 26.

Cambridge University Library offers information on John Pycock Candler, from John and J.A. Venn's, *Alumni Cantabrigienses from the earliest times to 1900 (Cambridge University Press: 1922-54 10 Volumes*).

> **Candler John Pycock:** Adm. Pens. at CORPUS CHRISTI Oct. 1, 1890 of Essex. Son of George Herbert, deceased, born Oct.7, 1873 at Alresford. School, Merchant Taylors' Matric. Michs. 1892; Scholar, 1893; B.A. 1895; M.B., B.C. and M.A. 1901; M.D. 1908. At Charing Cross Hospital. D.P.H., R.C.P.S. (London) 1903. Resident Medical Officer to the borough Sanatorium and Medical Officer for Health, Brighton. Pathologist to the West London Hospital. Assistant Pathologist to County Asylums. Medical Officer to the Ministry of Health, Whitehall. Of "Sunnylands", Smitham Bottom Lane, Purley, Surrey, 1939. Author, medical. (Merchant Taylors' School. Reg.; Medical Directory, 1939.)

When George Candler died in 1929, John Pycock Candler was living at "*Ashleigh*", Brighton Road, Coulsdon, Surrey. British Telecom Archives show that in 1939 a Dr. J. P. Candler was listed in the phone book (*Uplands 5912*) at 52 Smitham Bottom Lane, Purley, where his daughter, Patricia, said she enjoyed living; he may have moved after his father died. Patricia also had a vague memory that her father went to Scotland at some point. She believed that it had something to do with a settlement, perhaps set up with Constance Mackenzie Candler after George's death.

John Pycock Candler died, aged 69, on 4th December 1942 at St. Mark's Hospital, City Road, London EC1. His address was given as Church Cottage, Brampton, in the County of Huntingdon, but formerly of "*Sunnylands*" 52 Smitham Bottom Lane. The estate was administered by Margaret Candler, the widow and her son, Horace John Pycock Candler, a solicitor, both resident at Church Cottage. The explanation for the father's move from Purley became apparent from Patricia. He had already retired as a doctor when the Second World War started but the Ministry of Defence asked him to return to work. He went either to Addenbrooke Hospital in Cambridge or to a large house at Hinchingbrooke, to help turn it into a military hospital and he was living at Brampton during this time. His will shows that he left over £6,300 gross to his widow, Margaret, Horace John Pycock Candler, his son and in trust for his daughter, who was not then twenty-one. The net value of the deceased estate was around £2,150. John Pycock Candler had written his will on 22nd May 1939 and added a codicil on 26th July 1940, the same day that his wife, Margaret drafted her will. The will was comprehensive and referred to his aunts, Mary Minshaw Pycock, wife of Canon John Pycock and the late Annie Candler. The executors of John Pycock Candler's will were his wife Margaret Ann, son Horace John Pycock Candler and Cecil Montague Jacomb Ellis of 17 Albemarle Street, who died in London in February 1942. Candler left to his wife *"one half of the original share in the residuary estate of my said aunt* [Annie Candler] *by her said will settled on me and my children"* and the other to his aunt, Mary Minshaw Pycock if Mary did not predecease him. It also said that *"if I survive my Aunt Mary Minshaw Pycock, my Estate will be considerably increased on her death"*. His aunt was at this stage a widow. There was no reference in his will to his stepmother, Constance. It may be that he had severed all links with her, financial and social, since his father's death. Hugh Barton Candler discovered a reference to Constance Mackenzie Logan in papers left to him by his father, Horace John Pycock Candler. These included correspondence with Kingsford, Dorman & Co. and in particular Laurence Dorman, one of the beneficiaries of Annie Candler's estate. Hugh also confirmed that there was no love lost as between both John Pycock Candler and his sister Alice and at least one of their stepmothers.

St. Mary Magdalene's Church in Brampton, in its adjacent cemetery, is the burial place of John Pycock Candler. A small headstone carries his name with Alice Mary Candler, his sister, who died 2nd May, in 1943 buried in the same grave. They died within six months of each other and were obviously very close and John Pycock's widow clearly thought that the brother and sister should be reunited in death. Brampton is a village that Samuel Pepys visited and where he stayed many times. Some of his family lived there and his uncle managed the estate in Hinchingbrooke, which is only a mile from the village.

Margaret Candler lived for a further seven years and her death was recorded in Surrey in 1950. This is a summary of her will:

> **Candler, Margaret Ann**, of Sunnylands, 52 Smitham Bottom Lane, Purley, Surrey, widow died 25 February 1950 at 15 Smitham Bottom Lane, Surrey. Probate London 29 April to Horace John Pycock Candler, solicitor. Effects £10,265 9s. 4d. (Probate year 1950)

Her will was drafted on 26th July 1940 at the premises of Ellis Peirs and Company of 17 Albemarle Street, in London. Cecil Montague Jacomb Ellis, a solicitor in that firm, was appointed in both John Pycock's and Margaret Candler's wills as executor and trustee. Margaret had also appointed her husband and son to be her executors but as John had already died this task fell to her son alone. She left her estate to her daughter Patricia, who was still under twenty-one and to her son, if she died before him. Margaret Candler had moved back to her home in Surrey from Brampton, after the War and died in another house in the same street.

Horace John Pycock Candler

John Pycock Candler and Margaret had a son named Horace John Pycock Candler, who was born in West Ham (*4a 401*) in the second quarter of 1911. Apparently Annie Candler, his aunt, a generous person who enjoyed spending money on the family, was responsible for naming Horace after her husband and Margaret was not pleased. In life he became known as John. John and Margaret also had a daughter named Patricia, born in 1921, who subsequently attended the Royal College of Music, played piano and studied singing. She took a secretarial course after finishing her music training, met her husband, John Turner, married and had two children and two grandchildren. Coincidentally, she lived in the same street in Eastbourne where Lady Emily Shackleton (*of whom more later*) lived when Ernest Shackleton died in 1922; there is a blue plaque on the wall of 14 Milnthorpe Road, Eastbourne. Equally coincidentally, John Turner used to play cricket with Laurence Dorman, one of the recipients of Annie Candler's will.

Like his father, Horace studied law at Cambridge University. He was known for his rowing and received two "*oars*" from St. Catharine's College. His father, John, was not much enamoured of Horace's lifestyle at Cambridge as the boy seemed to do a great deal of socialising and enjoyed going to parties.

> ***Horace John Pycock Candler*** Matriculated on 4th November, 1929, having been admitted to St. Catharine's College (Cambridge). He was placed in the third class in both parts of the Law Tripos in 1931 and 1932. He graduated BA on 21st June 1932, LL.B. in 1933 and M.A. (by proxy) on 11 December 1954. (source: UA Graduati 12/39)

In 1933 he announced his forthcoming marriage to Rosemary Roderick, the daughter of a surgeon. The marriage never took place as he then, on 12th December 1939, became engaged to Rachel Proud, the only daughter of Mr. and Mrs. E. B. Proud of Bishop Auckland. Horace was in the Royal Artillery and fought in the War but he might have been home on leave and staying with his mother at Brampton after his father died. The couple moved to Abergavenny in 1946 but both sons were born at their grandmother's home called "*Dellwood*" in Bishop Auckland, County Durham. Nicholas J.P. was born on the 5th September 1944 and Anthony Hugh Barton Candler in 1946. According to Anthony, the Barton name originated from his late mother's side of the family.

John Candler was working as a solicitor in a firm of solicitors in Bishop Auckland, Co. Durham, in 1946. He worked for a short time at his father-in-law's law firm, before making a new start in South Wales. According to Patricia, his sister, he had originally worked at Piers Ellis and Co., the solic-itors who managed the Candler wills, after being admitted to the Rolls in

London but he had not enjoyed his time there. At some point, he persuaded his mother to lend him £1000 to buy into the firm in Wales.

In 1946 he went to Gabb, Price and Fisher, solicitors in Abergavenny and both his sons, Nicholas John Pycock and Anthony Hugh Barton also became solicitors. He also had a daughter called "*Suki*". Not long after Anthony's birth, his parents moved to Llangattock Court, Penpergwm, near Abergavenny, where they lived until their respective deaths.

Anthony Hugh Barton Candler remained a consultant in his father's old firm, now Gabb and Co. and co-owner, with his wife, Judith, of the Pentre Court Guest House, Llanwenarth, Abergavenny, where they lived from 1980.

In 2001 Nicholas John Pycock Candler, died just after the death of his mother.

Portraits of the Candlers and Pycocks

Hugh Barton Candler has in his possession portraits of relatives of the Candler/Pycock families. Two are oil paintings and another a pencil drawing of quite an aged person, to which is attached the name of John Abbey. The oil paintings are not dated but an older, stern looking woman may be Mrs. Bateson, as the clothes are from the beginning of the nineteenth century. She was the great grandmother of Mary Louisa, John and Sarah Lavinia Pycock. The other portrait is of a beautiful, elegant and relatively young woman, who is dressed in clothes of the early Victorian period. She might be Mrs. Abbey, the grandmother of Mary Louisa, John and Sarah Lavinia Pycock. The portraits probably passed to Canon John Pycock from his mother, as the only son and then, when he died, to his wife, Mary Minshaw Pycock. Reference was made to the portraits in John Pycock Candler's will, although he did not have them in his possession at the time but knew that they were to be left to him by his aunt. He left them in trust for his son Horace, after his wife died. Reference is made to a portrait of the mother of John, Sarah Lavinia and Mary Louisa Pycock, who was the daughter of Mary Bateson and Phillip Abbey. The will refers also to a mirror from Mrs. Abbey, a pink Japanese vase, Crown Derby china, silver plate, salver, bowl and candlesticks which belonged, at the time of writing his will, to his aunt Mary Minshaw Pycock.

Mrs. Bateson was John Pycock Candler's great-great grandmother, who was married to Matthew Bateson, who left his estate to his four daughters. It was his will that led to action being taken against trustees to acquire a share of the estate. Mrs. Abbey, wife of Phillip Abbey whose estate was divided, on her death, into forty parts, was his great-grandmother. Mary Louise Candler was her grand-daughter.

Candler In-laws

Walter Herbert Cook, a timber merchant and son of John Cook, a farmer, at the age of twenty-six, on 2nd November 1880 married Helen French, Annie Candler's sister, in the Parish of Emmanuel at Maida Hill, in Marylebone, Westminster. The groom was living at 40 Hemingford Road and the bride, before the wedding, at 2 Clifton Road. Annie Candler was a witness, along with John Knight. The Cooks, from Frating in Essex will have known the Candlers, which is probably how the relationship was created.

Edith Nellie Constant Cook was born at New Southgate, Middlesex on 21st February 1883 and was baptised on 27th July of the same year. Helen and Walter Herbert Cook were living at 11 Springfield Cottages at the time of the baptism. Edith was the eldest child and Walter and Helen had two others, Dorothy Winifred Anne Cook, born in 1884 and John William Donald Cook, born in 1889. The family moved from Finchley after the birth of their son.

On the night of the census of 1881 Walter H. Cook and Helen Cook were staying with John W.C. Cook, at 74 Marton Road, Middlesbrough, York. John was head of the house, aged twenty-eight, a surgeon, born at Frating, in Essex; Walter was John's brother and Helen, aged twenty-eight, was his sister-in-law. Walter's place of birth was Alresford in Essex, not far from Frating. Walter by then was a retired timber merchant yet he was only twenty-seven. At the time of the census of 1891, the family was probably living at Moss Hall Crescent, Finchley. By the time of the census of 1901, Walter was a financial agent. The family was living at Cliff Road at Leigh-on-Sea in the Parish of St. Clement. By 1911, they reflected their success by having moved to "*Chadhurst*", Potter's Bar, a residence with twelve rooms.

Edward Scrivener Cox, a bachelor, aged twenty-five, a law stationer, married Edith Nellie Constant Cook, a spinster, aged twenty-three, on 18th April 1906. He was living at "*Wakefield*", Ballard's Lane in Barnet and she at Wood Grange, Leigh-on-Sea. They married at Christchurch in the district of Barnet, Middlesex. Both fathers were witnesses, along with Dorothy A. H. Cook, her sister, Margaret Walton and D. Cox. By the time of the census of 1911, when Walter was managing director of the Fastnut washer manufacturing company, Edith had two children born at Potter's Bar and the family was living at Barnet in Middlesex. One of her children was named Edward John Douglas Cox and was ten months old at the time.

The 1891 Census results reveal that when Edward was a child, his family was living at 102 Chancery Lane, with one servant. They had moved from Holloway in Islington before 1881, around the time Edward was born.

Table of occupants at 102 Chancery Lane in 1891.

Name	Relation	Age	Occupation	Birthplace	Disability
Edward H. Cox	Head	42	Law stationer	London St. Clement Danes	
Eleanor Cox	Wife	40		Northants Passenham	
Mary L. Cox	Daughter	17	Scholar	Middlesex Islington	
Grace E. Cox	Daughter	15	Scholar	Middlesex Islington	Hip disease
Alice M. Cox	Daughter	13	Scholar	Middlesex Islington	
Edward S. Cox	Son	10	Scholar	Liberty of the Rolls	
Douglas H. Cox	Son	6	Scholar	Liberty of the Rolls	Cataract from childhood

Edward and Douglas were born in the Liberty of the Rolls Parish in London. Their father was born in the vicinity of the Law Courts, near the

Church of St. Clement Dane is in the Strand. In 1901, the family was still at 102 Chancery Lane and *"living above the shop"*. The census showed:

Table of occupants at 102 Chancery Lane in 1901.

Name	Relation	Age	Occupation	Employer, worker or own account	Birthplace
Edward Cox	Head	52	Law stationer	Employer	London Strand
Eleanor Cox	Wife	50			Passenham Northants
Mary L. Cox	Daughter	27	Ancient records searcher	Own account	London Holloway
Grace E. Cox	Daughter	25	Paid worker (preach)	Worker	London Holloway
Edward S. Cox	Son	20	Law stationer's clerk	Worker	London Strand
Douglas H. Cox	Son	16	Auctioneers clerk	Worker	London Strand

There was one servant listed so the family was relatively well off. Everyone in the family was working, including Grace, their disabled daughter with a hip disease, who was a parish worker or preacher. The eldest daughters, Mary and Grace, were still single and living at home. Alice was the only member of the family who probably had married.

13

Charles Dorman 1829–1901

Charles Dorman was born in Canterbury in Kent, was admitted to the Roll of Solicitors in 1852 and became a law partner with James Kingsford in 1854. Charles' father was Thomas and his mother Julia Heritage. Thomas Dorman died on 10th July, 1856, aged 67, at his home, Castle House, Canterbury. According to his obituary in the *Morning Chronicle,* he was *"for many years distributor of stamps for the County of Kent"*.

13.1 Charles Dorman.

Kingsford, Dorman & Co.

At the time of the census of 1881, the elder James Kingsford lived at Sydenham Hill, The Wood, Lewisham, Kent, close to Charles Dorman and near to Crystal Palace. His eldest son, James Henry Kingsford, joined the firm in 1877. His other son, Frank, joined in 1890, after he was admitted to the Solicitors' Roll in 1888 and Frank is cited in some of the Memorials in the 1890s with his father. Kingsford had been admitted to the Roll in 1837 and in 1843 was part of Waterman, Wright and Kingsford at 23, Essex Street, the Strand. By 1877, the firm was renamed Kingsford, Dorman and Kingsford. The table below gives the various names of the firm's partners, courtesy of the Law Society archivist. The author has added dates of deaths, in some cases.

Table showing the firm and its partners compiled from Law Society data.

Year	Name of firm	Partners	Deaths
1843	Waterman, Wright & Kingsford	James Kingsford, William Waterman, William Harding Wright	
1847	Wright & Kingsford	William Harding Wright and James Kingsford	
1854	Kingsford Dorman	James Kingsford and Charles Dorman	
1877	Kingsford, Dorman & Kingsford	James Kingsford, Charles Dorman and James Henry Kingsford	
1881	Kingsford, Dorman, Kingsford, Candler & Moore	James Kingsford, Charles Dorman, James Henry Kingsford, Samuel Horace Candler and Arthur Chisholm Moore	
1886	Kingsford, Dorman & Co.	Charles Dorman, James Henry Kingsford, Samuel Horace Candler, Arthur Chisholm Moore, Charles Herbert Dorman	
1890	Kingsford, Dorman & Co.	Charles Dorman, Charles Herbert Dorman, Samuel Horace Candler, Frank Kingsford and Arthur Chisholm Moore	James Kingsford died 1895. Charles Dorman died 1901
1903	Kingsford, Dorman & Co.	Samuel Horace Candler, Arthur Chisholm Moore, Frank Kingsford, Francis Thomas Dorman, Charles Herbert Dorman	Samuel Horace Candler died 1903
1905	Kingsford, Dorman & Co.	Arthur Chisholm Moore, Frank Kingsford, Francis Thomas Dorman, Charles Herbert Dorman	Frank Kingsford died 9th November 1906
1910	Kingsford, Dorman & Co.	Arthur Chisholm Moore, Francis Thomas Dorman, Charles Herbert Dorman	Charles Herbert Dorman died 1915. James Henry Kingsford died 14th May 1915 Arthur Chisholm Moore died in 1921
1928	Kingsford, Dorman & Co.	Francis Thomas Dorman, Laurence Charles Dorman	Francis Thomas Dorman died 1931

In 1881 the firm became Kingsford, Dorman, Kingsford, Candler and Moore and in 1886 the name changed again to Kingsford, Dorman & Co. Various members of these families continued to join the firm and a second branch was opened in Sydenham. By 1890, James Kingsford, was no longer a member of the firm and he died in 1895. Charles Herbert Dorman joined the firm in 1882.

Kingsford, Dorman, Shepherd & Co. moved in 1940 from 23 Essex Street, Strand to 19-21 Hatton Garden. This is thought to be because the premises had been damaged by fire in that year. A picture from the National Monument Record taken in 1942 and provided by his great-grandson, Charles Dorman, nevertheless shows the Essex Street premises to be in good condition. They must have moved back to 23 Essex Street in 1951 as this address was given as the registered office of the *Woodberry Lodge Estate Company* in the Charge Deeds for 54 Vartry Road. The building in Essex Street itself had been built by the second most speculative builder of London after John Nash, Dr. Nicholas Barbon, otherwise known as *"Barebones"*. Barbon was a Doctor of Medicine and a notorious speculator at the time of Charles I. One of his first forays into developing was when in 1682 he bought Essex House, south of the Strand, from the executors of the Devereuxs. Charles II wanted to acquire the Tudor mansion but Barbon moved quickly to demolish it and built Essex Street. The pseudo-Roman arch at the south end of the Street leading to Temple Pier was built by Barbon to mask the brewers' and wood-mongers' wharves that he had created on the riverside. Some of the original houses survive and 23 Essex Street continues to accommodate practising lawyers. The firm's name continued with a succession of other partners, some of whom were related to Charles Dorman and after a series of mergers became DAC Beechcroft in 2011.

Dorman's background and family

Charles Dorman, a solicitor, married Jane (Janie) Swinford at Minster Abbey in Thanet, Kent on 25th March 1858. Janie was the third daughter of John Swinford, a direct descendent of Catherine Swinford, the wife of John of Gaunt, Duke of Lancaster, fourth son of Edward III (*historical note, Catherine Swinford, was a sister of Chaucer's wife*). The marriage was announced in The Morning Chronicle dated 29th March and gave the groom's address as Park Road, Haverstock Hill and also of Essex Street Strand. They had six children; their eldest son, Charles Herbert Dorman, was born at Park Road, Haverstock Hill, Hampstead on 30th March and baptised by S. Swinford; Julia was born on 9th April 1860. The family moved to "The Firs", Lawrie Park, Sydenham after that date; its members were recorded in the census of 1861 at Westwood Road, Lawrie Park. Electoral Registers show that Charles and his son, Charles Herbert were living at "The Firs" in 1885 and 1888. Janie Dorman died in 1892.

Charles Dorman was an important figure in the development of the area surrounding Vartry Road. His great-grandson, Charles Dorman, furnished a copy of a photograph (see figure 13.2), and information about him, giving a brief insight into his life.

Charles Dorman is seen, surrounded by a large group of men, holding the gavel and it may be that George Candler is one of the assembled, as he was in the area around this time. Charles Dorman and Charles Herbert Dorman, at different times, according to a relative, Patricia Reynolds, were masters of the Skinners' Company and she retained the trowel which she took to show the Headmistress when her youngest son became a member of the Skinners' Company. It is inscribed :

Trowel presented to Charles Dorman Esq.
Master
By the Worshipful Company of Skinners of London
On the occasion of his laying the Foundation Stone
Of their Middle School for Girls
Stamford Hill
June 6th 1889

13.2 Charles Dorman laying foundation stone of Skinners' Company's School for Girls, Stamford Hill in 1889.

The foundation stone on the front of the school building remains to commemorate the occasion and acknowledges Charles Dorman's involvement in the area.

The Worshipful Company of Skinners of London had its origins with the people who skinned or prepared skins or dealers in skins. Skinners or furriers in Medieval times were responsible for regulating the fur trade; costly furs from abroad such as sable and ermine were for Royalty and the aristocracy; furs of lesser value were for the middle classes and the poor were left with lambskin, rabbit and cat. Members of the Skinners' Company were wealthy merchants who often left charitable bequests and the Dorman ancestors had tanners in their ranks. Charles Dorman was admitted to the Skinners' Company on 11th June 1852. His son, Herbert was admitted, by patrimony, on 20th December, 1883.

Patricia Reynolds highlighted that Dorman Long, an engineering Company from Darlington and responsible for the contract to build the Sydney Harbour Bridge in Australia, was connected to Charles Dorman's family. Literature from the Company confirms that Arthur John Dorman was a founding partner of Dorman Long in Teesside, the firm that also built the Tyne Bridge. Arthur John Dorman died in 1930, just before the Sydney Harbour Bridge was opened. His grandfather, Mark was an elder brother of Charles Dorman's father, Thomas. Arthur John Dorman's father was also called Charles.

Charles Dorman was interested in orchids and had one named after him in 1880. He also was the first person to have their own private collection of orchids outside of botanical gardens.

The Orchid Resource
Highlights of Orchid History
1851-1899 A.D.
1879: Cattleya dormaniana: Discovered by H Blunt on mountains of Rio De Janeiro, Brazil. Blunt sent plants to the U.K. Described by Reichenbach in 1882 who first considered it to be a natural hybrid between C. bicolorxLaelia pumila. Mr. Charles Dorman of Sydenham flowered the species which bears his name in 1880.

Dorman's commercial activities

A letter to the editor of *The Times* on June 13, 1860, relating to The Smithfield Club, was written by Charles Dorman, solicitor for the Agricultural Hall Company, of 23 Essex Street, Strand, indicating that he was involved in business matters with one John Giblett.

In 1861, a John Giblet (*note, not Giblett*), was instrumental in finding and buying the three acres of land in Islington near St. Mary's Vestry and next to what was then the hospital, for a new permanent site to build what was then the *"Smithfield Club Cattle Show"*; the new Agricultural Hall was built in Islington in 1862. The capital for the project was raised by a joint stock company comprised of agriculturalists, agricultural implement makers and cattle salesmen. *"The ground plan and cattle fittings were designed by John Giblett an eminent Cattle Salesman of the Metropolitan market"* (*www.victorianlondon.org*). Mr. Giblett was the cattle salesman who had sold land in South Tottenham to James and Thomas Dorman in 1868 and also to Charles Dorman in 1870.

Charles Dorman was a first cousin to James and Thomas Dorman, who originally bought the land. Their fathers had been brothers and James and Thomas died respectively in 1856 and 1857. James was a tanner and Charles Dorman was the solicitor for his cousin and Giblett. Giblett was a member when the Smithfield Club had premises at 58 Baker Street. Giblett was the prime mover in structuring the move from the old site which they had outgrown and the Club, with offices in Barford Street just off Liverpool Road, had been formed in 1789; it included the King as a member. The *"fine"* for the land was £2000 and ground rent was £600 per annum. The grand, arched entrance to The Royal Agricultural Hall is on Upper Street and the building stretches all the way to the Liverpool Road.

The Royal Agricultural Hall was one of the most famous venues in Victorian London when it opened and Queen Victoria visited it during her reign. Charles Dorman appears to have been active in the management during the 1890s. Various shows that took place in those years at the venue including Cruft's Dog Show (the Cruft Family lived in Islington), bullfights, Motor Show (1890-1908), bicycle shows, confectionary shows, building trade shows, military tournaments and boxing fights. It also hosted a regular circus. Walter Sickert, the artist and his third wife were known to enjoy attending events at the venue. In 1894, when Dorman was managing director, it hosted a tightrope display by Charles Blondin, the person who successfully crossed Niagara Falls on a tightrope. At another time it held within it a walking marathon during which the contestants walked some 500 miles.

Documentary evidence shows that Charles Dorman, on 18th July 1896, was responsible for negotiating an agreement *"Re. Supply of electricity between the Royal Agricultural Hall hereafter called the 'Hall Company' and the Vestry of the Parish Saint Mary, Islington"* to take the electricity cables in the basement under the entrance of the Royal Agricultural Hall on Upper Street; the church may have owned the freehold in the land.

Kingsford, Dorman & Co. papers from the years 1891/92, when Charles Dorman was in charge until well beyond his death, up to 1937, have among them details of a legal case heard on 19th December 1892 when John Coleman and The Royal Agricultural Hall were in dispute at the High Court of Justice, Chancery Division. Another case on 13th February 1895, was between Powell, the freeholder of land in Charles Street next door, when they wanted to extend the site. Kingsford, Dorman & Co. represented the Royal Agricultural Hall. A Mr. Cockburn was cited in these documents and in the deeds relating to the sale of land in South Tottenham. The documents also refer to Harold Moore; Arthur Chisholm Moore was a partner at Kingsford, Dorman & Co. until his death on 3rd December 1921.

Two other cases are of interest. A workman on the site whose name was Mr. Williams, had an accident at the World's Fair, which resulted in his death. A clerk from Kingsford, Dorman & Co. attended the inquest at St. Bartholomew's Hospital and made *"voluminous notes"*. There were many meetings at which photographs were taken and interviews were taken from witnesses before the matter was settled. Under the Employers' Liability Act, the managing director, Charles Dorman, offered £50 to Williams' widow on condition that if she refused the offer of compensation, it would be withdrawn. She eventually accepted the offer in August 1895. There was also a much-publicised accident at the RAH on 31st December 1895; Mr. Beaumont, the lion tamer in Mr. Bostock's Menagerie, was attacked by a lion and killed; death by misadventure was recorded. The clerks at Kingsford, Dorman & Co. made many copious notes for posterity, recording the resolution of disputes. Some were for as much as £178 for individual cases, a sizeable amount in those days.

Charles Dorman had connections to the Northampton Institute, one of the first polytechnics in London and part of what is now City University on St. John Street in London. A plaque on the foyer wall commemorates the occasion on Monday, 19th July, 1894 at 5.00 p.m., when, as Chairman of the Governing body, he laid the foundation stone. The four sponsors of the Northampton Institute were the Worshipful Company of Skinners, the Worshipful Company of Saddlers, the Charity Commissioners and the Technical Education Board of London County Council. A Skinners prize was a feature of prize-giving events. Most courses at the Institute were of a technical and trade character, a selection on offer being bricklaying, tool-making, electrical engineering, woodworking, ornamental engraving, surveying, watch-making, clock-making, mechanical engineering and cabinet-making. Many workers were employed on sites during the day and studied to improve their skills and acquire qualifications at night. Charles Dorman is likely to have had many opportunities to find workers to employ on his building projects in South Tottenham but his interest in education gives some idea of the philanthropic nature of the man, beyond the law and his property portfolio. He worked in Islington at the Royal Agricultural Hall in the daytime, as Chairman of the Governing Body, in the evenings at the Institute on St. John Street and as a partner with his firm of Kingsford, Dorman & Co., while having the other interests that are mentioned in his obituary.

After Charles Dorman

An obituary from a local newspaper in Sydenham, from Saturday, October 26, 1901, explains the circumstances of Charles Dorman's death:

DEATH OF MR. DORMAN

We have much regret, which will be shared by our Sydenham readers, in announcing the death of Mr. Charles Dorman, late of The Firs, Lawrie Park, Sydenham, which took place on Monday last at his town residence 19, Wetherby Gardens, SW, in his 73rd year. Mr. Dorman met with an accident in August last and had been confined to his bed since the beginning of September. The cause of death was heart failure resulting from the shock to the system, due to the accident. The funeral took place yesterday (Friday) afternoon, the first part of the service being read at St. Bartholomew's Church, Sydenham and the interment being at Elmer's End Cemetery.

Mr. Dorman was born at Canterbury in the year 1829, and educated at the King's School, Canterbury. He was admitted as a solicitor in 1852 and from that date was in practice in Essex Street, Strand, where for many years he was in partnership with the late Mr. James Kingsford, who was also well known in Sydenham. Mr. Dorman came to reside in Sydenham in 1860 and lived at The Firs, Lawrie Park till 1900, when he moved to 19, Wetherby Gardens, SW. He also had a country house at Towngate, near Wadhurst, Sussex. Mr. Dorman took a great interest in the erection of Holy Trinity Church, Sydenham, and was one of the original churchwardens. Latterly he took a prominent part in the erection of the Sydenham Public Hall, and was Chairman of the Board of Directors. He was for many years Managing Director of the Royal Agricultural Hall, Islington, and was thus closely identified with the various shows and exhibitions which have been held there. He was also Chairman of the Governing Body of the Northampton Institute, a magnificent building in Clerkenwell, and one of the finest of the Polytechnics which have been established in different parts of London. He served the office of Master of the Skinners' Company, one of the twelve chief City Guilds, in 1888-9. Mr. Dorman was married in 1858 to Miss Janie Swinford, daughter of the late Mr. John Swinford, of Minster Abbey, Thanet, and leaves three sons and three daughters. Mrs. Dorman died in 1892.

Some of the contents of Dorman's home at Wetherby Gardens in Kensington were sold in 1902 at the auction house of Messrs. Christie, Manson and Woods, as advertised in *The Times*. The sale included important pictures and watercolour drawings, including landscapes with peasant girls, cattle, sheep and goats, woods, cornfields, river and coastal scenes of England, Scotland and Wales.

Elmer's End Cemetery, referred to in the obituary, is now called Beckenham Cemetery and is home to the headstones of Thomas Crapper, who did much to improve the popularity of the water closet, W.C. Grace, the cricketer and Wolseley, of motor car fame, in addition to those of Charles Herbert Dorman, who, aged 55, was buried on 6th February, 1915, and his youngest sister, Maude. A large headstone nearby, overgrown with ivy, is for Janie and Charles Dorman. Some of the other graves nearby are badly damaged with no headstones to identify them, so that other members of the Dorman family do not appear to be adjacent, although there are in the vicinity, Gaitskells, who were relations of Charles Herbert Dorman's wife.

Dorman's children, Charles and Julia

When he died, Dorman's son, Charles Herbert Dorman, had been living at *"Hillsboro"*, 23 Lawrie Park Road, Sydenham, to this day a large, detached, double fronted house. At the time of the census of 1901, his home was at 41 Lawrie Park Road, which was the last in a row of houses of a similar style. Saint Bartholomew's Church on Westwood Hill, which had been mentioned in his father's obituary, was situated at the end of Lawrie Park Avenue. The adjacent house at 12 Westwood Hill, the former Shackleton family home where Ernest Shackleton had lived as a child, now called St. David's, has a blue plaque dedicated to him. There is no visible evidence of *"The Firs"* Lawrie Park but modern flats with the same name are located at 44-46 Lawrie Park Gardens and probably occupy the site where Charles Dorman had lived before moving to 19 Wetherby Gardens, South Kensington. Lawrie Park Road was painted in 1871 by Camille Pisarro the famous Impressionist painter. The painting was called *"The Avenue, Sydenham"* and depicts a scene looking down Lawrie Park Avenue towards St. Bartholomew's Church. This would have been the view from Charles Dorman's house. The painting was bought by the National Gallery in 1984 for £560,000.

Charles Dorman's eldest daughter, Julia, married Charles Sarolea at Christ Church, Westminster, on 28th December 1905, when she was 46. He was a friend of the Shackletons and was born in Belgium; it was Sarolea who introduced George Bernard Shaw to Shackleton. Sarolea became a war correspondent in the First World War. He was also the political adviser for King Albert of Belgium and raised money for Belgian relief when Belgium was occupied by the Germans during the First World War. Sarolea was the Belgian Consular General for Scotland from 1901 to 1953 in Edinburgh. Julia was his second wife and they lived, from 1921, at 21 Royal Terrace in Edinburgh, a grand stone house with an impressive view, overlooking the Firth of Forth. He later bought 22 Royal Terrace, the house next door, to house his collection of books, estimated to be some quarter of a million in number, said to be the largest private library in the world. Julia Sarolea died in 1941 and one of her executors, as well as that of her husband, was her nephew, Laurence Charles Dorman. Julia left an estate valued at £5256.3.8. She was the last child of Charles Dorman to die.

Charles Sarolea was not afraid to put his point of view across through letters and articles. He wrote occasionally to *The Times* about issues close to his heart and particularly about Belgium and was a prolific writer in at least six languages. He was considered to be a Liberal, politically, when young, although his views changed over the years. However, he appeared to have a healthy suspicion of politicians, was particularly vehement in his opposition to Communism and often expressed controversial ideas. One of his letters to *The Times*, in the period between the Wars, might have been seen to be defending the Germans against the Czech Republic's Government invasion of Sudetenland along the borders of the two countries. He did, nonetheless, register his distaste of German militarism before the Second World War.

According to an advertisement in *The Times*, some of Sarolea's vast collection of books were sold on 14th July 1952 at Sotheby's & Co in an auction of valuable printed books, autographed letters and manuscripts. These included books on 18th-20th century French literature, including a first edition by Verlane. The remainder of his collection of books was given after his death to Keele University.

Sarolea was Emeritus Professor of French Literature at Edinburgh University when he died on 11th March, 1953 and he left an estate valued at £5737.4s.1d when probate was granted on 26th May that year. Charles Sarolea's will was administered by a number of Scottish notables, one of whom was William Beattie, the General Librarian for the National Library of Scotland. Another executor was Baron George Ernest Marchand, the Belgian Vice-Consul. A memorial service was held for him at St. Mary's Roman Catholic Cathedral in Edinburgh.

14

South Tottenham to South Pole
– The Shackleton connection

A throwaway comment from a local resident suggested that there was a connection between the South Tottenham area and Ernest Shackleton, the Antarctic explorer. The Poor Rate books for 1900 at Bruce Castle Museum were thought to reveal which houses, if any, were owned by George Candler but the names of C. Dorman and Kingsford, Dorman & Co. appeared as owning many of the houses in the area. The following table confirms the ownership of freehold land during the years 1882–1915, in records for Tottenham St. Ann's Parliamentary Polling District.

Table of land ownership 1882-1915.

Year	Polling district	Name	Ownership	Place
1882 1883	G	James Kingsford Charles Dorman	Share of freehold land	Woodberry Lodge Estate, Seven Sisters Rd.
1886 1887 1888 1889	B	James Kingsford Charles Dorman	Share of freehold land	Woodberry Lodge Estate, Seven Sisters Rd
1891 1895	I	James Kingsford Charles Dorman	Share of freehold land	Woodberry Lodge Estate, Seven Sisters Rd
1896 1900 1902	I	Charles Dorman	Share of freehold	Woodberry Lodge Estate, Seven Sisters Rd.
1904	D	Charles Herbert Dorman Francis Thomas Dorman	One sixth share of freehold houses	Woodbury Estate, Seven Sisters Rd. Vartry Rd, Richmond Rd, Franklin St, Manchester Rd, Heysham Rd, Berkeley Rd and St John's Rd.
1907	K	Charles Herbert Dorman Francis Thomas Dorman	One sixth share of freehold houses	Woodbury Estate, Seven Sisters Rd. Vartry Rd, Richmond Rd, Franklin St, Manchester Rd, Heysham Rd, Berkeley Rd and St John's Rd.
1915	G	Charles Herbert Dorman	One sixth share of freehold houses	Woodbury Estate, Seven Sisters Rd. Vartry Rd, Richmond Rd, Franklin St, Manchester Rd, Heysham Rd, Berkeley Rd and St John's Rd.

Charles Dorman was recorded as the shared owner of the freehold of the *Woodberry Lodge Estate* in 1902, although he died in 1901. In 1904 and 1907 Charles Herbert Dorman and Francis Thomas Dorman were named although

14.1 Francis Thomas Dorman (left) and Laurence Charles Dorman (right).

all the sons and daughters of Charles Dorman had a share. Note the different names as *Woodbury Estate* and *Woodberry Lodge Estate*. Charles Herbert Dorman was the only member of the family listed in 1915, the last year that the ownership category was included and also the year that he died. In a selection of years, George Herbert Candler appeared in the Polling District records in the occupation category in 1900, 1904, 1907 and 1915. Charles Dorman, the solicitor, was, of course, a professional partner of Samuel Horace Candler, the brother of George Herbert Candler. Samuel's wife, Annie Candler, left money in her will to Laurence Charles Dorman, among others. It is possible that Samuel Candler, owned a share as a partner of Kingsford, Dorman & Co. Annie Candler had a business relationship with Laurence and Kingsford, Dorman & Co. Laurence Charles Dorman, who was born in Chertsey in 1903 (*2a 43*), was the son of Francis Thomas Dorman. (The photographs above were made available by Charles S. Dorman, son of Laurence.)

Emily and Ernest

The 1901 Census shows that Charles Dorman and his daughter, Emily Dorman, spent the evening in question together with Ernest Shackleton, who was a visitor, described by the enumerator as a *"Master Mariner Seas"* at Towngate Farm, Wadhurst, in Sussex, his country house. Shackleton was soon to be Emily's fiancé. Their ages were given on the form as 63, 28 and 28, respectively, which were partially correct; Charles was 72, Emily was 33 and Shackleton was 28.

Emily was born in Lewisham in the third quarter (*1d 930*) of 1868. She was shown in the 1871 Census, aged two, with her family at Lawrie Park,

Sydenham. She became a quite conventional attractive, tall, dark-haired young woman and resembled her father. An educated woman, she was later to write a book with Laura Bennett, entitled the *"Corona of Royalty"* about the coronation ceremony and regalia, published in 1902. Emily was one of six children; her brothers, Herbert and Francis (Frank) Dorman were solicitors in the family firm; her other brother Arthur William was a minister and her sisters were Julia and Maude, the latter known as Daisy.

The Candler family clearly had connections with Shackleton through the Dormans. George's estate agency work had him looking after properties, whose freehold was owned by Charles Dorman and by his sons and daughters after he died. Lady Emily Shackleton became one of the trustees of her father's will during the 1930s with her nephew, Laurence C. Dorman, son of Francis, whose name appears regularly in documents referring to properties in South Tottenham.

Young Shackleton

Roland Huntford's book, *Shackleton*, gives a comprehensive account of the renowned explorer, his life and his expeditions. Shackleton was the son of Henry Shackleton and Henrietta Letitia Sophia Gavan, of Ireland, married in Ireland, in 1872. Henry was the fourth generation descendent of Abraham Shackleton, a Quaker, originally of Yorkshire, who moved to Ireland in the seventeenth century; Henry, however, was brought up an Anglican. He attempted to join the army, but failed, due to ill health and then became a farmer, living at Kilkea, County Kildare, Ireland, thirty miles from Dublin.

Ernest Shackleton was one of ten children, born on 15th February 1874, at Kilkea House. He had a younger brother, Richard Francis (Frank) and sisters Alice, Amy, Ethel, Eleanore, Clara, Helen, Kathleen, born 1884, and Gladys. In 1880, Henry Shackleton decided to study medicine and moved the family to Dublin, where he studied at Trinity College and after qualifying as a doctor in 1884, the family left Ireland and moved to England, partly due to the changing political situation and movement for Home Rule. His first practice at Croydon failed and then he moved to Sydenham, in the suburbs of London. In 1887, the young Ernest Shackleton went to Dulwich College, close to his home; the family had tried hard to eliminate the Irish accent but failed. At the age of 15, on holiday at St. Leonard's on Sea, his best friend, Petrises and his brother saved Shackleton from drowning as he could not swim. He was often late for school and insisted on making his excuses entertaining his class in the process. His father wanted Ernest to become a doctor despite his own interest in homeopathy but his son made it clear that he wanted to go to sea. Money was an issue as training was expensive but a cousin organised a placement for him on a full rigged ship named *Hoghton Tower*, owned by the Northwestern Shipping Company of Liverpool. In 1890, Shackleton left school and travelled to Valparaiso, in Chile, via Cape Horn, *"learning the ropes"* on the way. He wrote to friends saying that he was taking his life in his hands going up the rigging in all weathers.

By 1894, aged only 20, Shackleton was 2nd Mate but left *Hoghton Tower*. By calling in favours, an old school friend introduced him to the Welsh Shire Line, as 4th Mate, travelling to China, Japan and America. In 1896, he passed his exams for 1st Mate and in April 1898, aged 24, he was certified as master, qualified to command any British ship on the high seas.

One of his shipmates remembered Shackleton around this time, saying how he would like to make a name for himself and *"her"*. The person to whom he referred was Emily Dorman, whom he met in 1897 at his home. She was a neighbour in Sydenham and a friend of his sister, Kathleen. In a book by, Joan Alcock, entitled *"Sydenham and Forest Hill History and Guide"*, the author notes that the Shackletons lived at 12 Westwood Hill, Sydenham and Ernest Shackleton's father was a doctor. The daughter of Karl Marx, Eleanor Marx, lived at 7 Jews Walk, which runs off Westwood Hill. She committed suicide by poisoning herself in 1898 and Dr. Henry Shackleton attended to her.

At the end of 1898, while on leave from his ship, ostensibly to visit his father on his birthday at Sydenham, he called at his neighbour, Charles Dorman, to visit Emily. She recalled later that he told her that he loved her and how she let him out through the conservatory door after kissing her hand. Marriage was a distinct possibility for Emily. Ernest wrote to her from China while she was staying with her family at Lugano, in Switzerland feeling sorry for himself as they were apart. Perhaps as a sign of the seriousness of the relationship and to put himself in good standing with Mr. Dorman and Emily, Shackleton, through his friend, managed to find a placement on the Union Castle Line, the elite of the merchant service, travelling between England and South Africa. He was promoted to third officer in December 1899, a few months after the Boer War started. His ship, the *Tintagel Castle*, transported troops to fight in the War. His brother was commissioned to the Royal Irish Fusiliers and served there.

The relationship developed while Shackleton was on leave in London during the summer of 1900 and marriage was on his mind. Nevertheless, on 13th September 1900 Shackleton wrote to volunteer for the National Antarctic Expedition and was accepted.

Charles Dorman was no doubt charmed by Shackleton but it was a different prospect having him as a son-in-law. Dorman and his daughters had moved from Sydenham to 19 Wetherby Gardens, in the Borough of Kensington and Chelsea, allowing the relationship between Emily and Ernest to develop in person rather than by letter. Ernest wanted marriage but Emily was as yet undecided. She had other suitors but eventually she agreed to marry Shackleton.

Discovery sailed down the Thames on 31st July 1901 with Shackleton on board in readiness for the journey to the South Pole. At Stoke's Bay, near Portsmouth, on 3rd August, he wrote to Charles Dorman, his future father-in-law, stating his position, saying that although he had no money his intention was to make it quickly to be able to *"keep her as you would wish"* and he hoped that Dorman would give his permission for him to marry Emily when he had made money, if she still cared for him. His excuse for not speaking in person was that Emily had not given him a full answer. Shackleton probably had envisaged a rejection if he had made his request face-to-face. On 8th August

1901, Dorman replied wishing him a safe voyage and happy return some 2 or 3 years hence and said *"I can only say that if and whenever the time comes when you are in the pecuniary position you long for and that if you and Emmy are still of the same mind my consent to your union will not be wanting"*.

Shackleton arrived in New Zealand on 28th November and was there when he received the news that Mr. Dorman had died suddenly on 21st October 1901. Emily could now make her own decision to marry but he decided to continue on his travels.

Captain Robert Falcon Scott was the leader of the National Antarctic Expedition, 1901-1904 and Shackleton was a sub-lieutenant in the Royal Naval Reserve, serving as third officer. Shackleton first saw Antarctica, on 8th January 1902. They were ill-prepared for the journey and there was a certain amount of rivalry between the two men. Shackleton, with others, suffered from scurvy; some of the symptoms were inflammation of the gums, swollen joints, breathlessness and cough, dizziness and coughing up blood. It is also possible that Shackleton was suffering from a form of pneumonia; in intense cold, blood vessels become exceedingly brittle and microscopic ice crystals can tear the lining of the lung. He had contracted a mysterious illness, while working on the *Hoghton Tower*, possibly a form of malaria or rheumatic fever, which can affect the heart. Another possibility is that he was asthmatic but Shackleton had managed to secure a place on the expedition without a medical examination. However, Scott made the decision to send Shackleton home; he was twenty-nine years of age. On 25th March 1903, Emily Dorman received a cable which said *"Broken down in chest returning southern sledge journey suffering scurvy and overstrain don't worry nearly well coming home...."*. After convalescing in New Zealand, Shackleton arrived home on 12th June 1903, having been away for two years. Scott was not successful in achieving the goal of reaching the South Pole although he and Shackleton reached furthest south on 30th December 1902.

Shackleton and Dorman union

Emily's father, Charles Dorman, made his will on 2nd May 1901. The will was proved on 26th February 1902, the gross value of his estate being £164,450 13s. 8d. but the net value of his personal was recorded as nil. Emily's eldest sister, Julia Frances Dorman, then a spinster, along with Charles Herbert Dorman, a solicitor, the eldest son, were executors and all the sons and daughters were beneficiaries. The estate was worth in today's terms, approximately £16 million. The trustees had the discretion to sell and convert into money or postpone sale in the said real and personal estate and premises, including leasehold or other property, to pay funeral expenses, debts and legacies and to create a trust fund, the income of which was to be divided in equal shares among his six children, Charles Herbert Dorman, Julia Dorman, Arthur William Dorman, Emily Dorman, Francis (Frank) Dorman and Maude Dorman (Daisy).

Emily Mary Dorman received £700 a year in trust unconditionally for life. This amount was worth in today's terms around £50,000. She had by then made the decision to marry Shackleton. He was well aware that he had no money of his own and did not want to live off his wife but was hopeful of making a name for himself and a fortune. Emily by this time realised that her future husband was not going to make any ordinary living. Shackleton, according to Roland Huntford's book, before he married Emily, calculated that they would be able to live on her inherited trust. He listed housekeeping costs and calculated that it would take about £721 a year to keep a couple in an average middle class state, to include two domestic servants. Other costs were £24 a year for a trained cook, coals and light per year, £34, kitchen and three fires all year, £18. After food, washing, extras, £260, the largest single item was "*Clothes and personal for darling £150*".

On his return, Shackleton thought that he might make a career in journalism following his stint as editor of the *South Polar Times*, on the expedition and actually started on the *Royal Magazine* but soon realised that there was not going to be any easy route to success and started looking about for other sources of income.

A friend, Hugh Robert Mill persuaded him to apply for the secretaryship at the Royal Scottish Geographical Society in Edinburgh, despite his lack of qualifications for the job. On 11th January 1904, he heard that the job was his and wrote to tell Emily of his good news and immediate increase in social status. According to Huntford, Emily's eldest brother, Herbert Dorman, was the last member of her family to have misgivings about Shackleton's desire to marry, mainly for financial reasons because his salary at Royal Scottish Geographical Society was only £200 a year. Ernest went to Edinburgh to rent a home at £125 a year, using half his salary. Herbert Dorman had good reason to be nervous.

Ernest Shackleton married Emily Dorman on 4th April 1904 in Christchurch, Westminster, London. He persuaded Emily to do without a honeymoon as he was keen to start his new job. Ernest lasted at the RSGS for less than a year before he handed in his resignation in January 1905. On 2nd February 1905, at the age of 37, Emily had her first son, Raymond Swinford (named after her mother's family). Her daughter Cecily, was born on 23rd December 1906 in Edinburgh.

Early years of the marriage

Shackleton had a gift for public speaking, which he used to good effect when he was invited to stand for Parliament as a Liberal Unionist for the Dundee seat, travelling around Scotland on the campaign trail. However, he lost in the General Election in January 1906.

Emily Shackleton was included with her brothers and sisters in an indenture, held in the *Middlesex Deeds Registry* (*MDR/1906/7/594*), linked to her father's will, dated 22nd December 1905 and registered on 16th March 1906. Her address was given as 14 Learmouth Gardens in Edinburgh and both her sisters, Julia and Daisy, gave their address as Queen Anne Mansions, St. James Park, London. Julia went to live in Edinburgh after her marriage, on 28th December 1905. Daisy was still living at Queen Anne's Mansions in Westminster in 1908.

Ernest decided to return to London and tried through networking to get into the business world travelling back and forth to his wife in Scotland. He became involved in a Russian venture, through an old school friend, which he hoped would make him £30,000 profit. However he wrote to Emily to say that he didn't have enough money to go to Edinburgh to see her and the children. After the birth of their second child and worried about his health, Emily and the children returned to London and stayed with his brother Frank at 29 Palace Court, Bayswater, in London. She persuaded Shackleton to see a heart specialist but he still managed to escape a diagnosis; he was also smoking heavily.

British Antarctic Expedition

Shackleton hardly had the courage to tell his wife that he was planning another trip away. The race was on; he wanted to reach the South Pole before anyone else and he had only seven months to prepare before the weather would scupper his plans. He approached backers for the project and announced the British Antarctic Expedition on 12th February 1907. He hoped to be able to finance and repay the money from a book and talks on his expedition. He approached the crew of *Discovery* to go with him but for various reasons they declined so he set about finding a new crew. He secured loans guaranteed by William Beardmore, a Scottish ship builder, for £7,000, £1000 from Elizabeth Dawson Lambton, a wealthy elderly spinster and the promise of £4,000 from his cousin, William Bell. He bought *Nimrod* and had her refitted but needed more funds. He was forced to borrow a further £8,000 from Lloyds Bank, guaranteed by wealthy individuals and friends, among them the Duke of Westminster; he did not have royal patronage as this was a commercial venture. As if this were not enough to be organising, his brother Frank was interviewed by the police on suspicion of stealing the Irish Crown Jewels from Dublin Castle. It has been suggested that he stole the jewels in part to help his brother raise money for the British Antarctic Expedition.

In December, when Shackleton arrived in Australia, he discovered that the money from his cousin had not materialised. The Australian Government stepped in with a grant of £5,000 and the government of New Zealand, £1,000 but there was no money for wages for the crew. Shackleton wrote to Emily before he left New Zealand, on 1st January, 1908 hoping *"the conquest of the Pole ought to be enough for us to do and there will be money enough"*. Shackleton, Adams, Wild and Marshall did not reach the Pole but did manage to get to the furthest point south that any person had ever achieved. On 9th January 1909, when they were only 97 miles from the South Pole, after 120 days, with 90 days supplies depleted, all were suffering from starvation and exhaustion and lack of sleep. In extreme weather conditions they made the decision to turn back to meet *Nimrod* by the deadline of 1st March, before it was due to leave. They had covered over 730 miles and succeeded in beating Scott's record by 360 miles and this for him was a great achievement. They arrived back in England on 14th June 1909 to a heroes' welcome.

Shackleton family financial difficulties

Emily's brothers, Herbert and Frank, were both solicitors at Kingsford Dorman. While Shackleton was away, Herbert wrote to Emily on 29th December 1908 to say that "*I suppose Ernest must now be thinking of turning back. I often wonder how far he will have got. The time will soon slip by*". Herbert looked after Emily and had volunteered to act as solicitor for the expedition. He also represented Shackleton and did not charge him any fees. It was left to Emily to raise the money to bring her husband home although Herbert had to do all the work. Furthermore, he put up some of his own money, never repaid, to make sure that *Nimrod* sailed to relieve Shackleton and his crew. He expressed this sentiment to Emily on 15th November 1908, "*We Dormans stick together*". Herbert was still grappling with the financial disarray that his brother-in-law had left behind, still trying to find backers when the ship left. Shackleton did, however, persuade his brother-in-law to invest £3000 in buying shares in Maxim's, the Paris Restaurant.

On his return, Shackleton sold his story to the Daily Mail for £2,000 and over the next few years delivered 123 lectures all over the world. His achievements were acknowledged by Amundsen, the Norwegian, polar explorer. Shackleton decided to employ a young reporter, Edward Saunders, a New Zealander, to write a book about the journey, in amanuensis, allowing his companions to write their stories as well. Saunders was paid £10 a week and followed him around the world as he was giving lectures. *The Heart of the Antarctic: being the story of the British Antarctic Expedition 1907-1909 (2 volumes)* was published five months later, to great acclaim. Shackleton signed a copy for his brother-in-law with the inscription "*To Frank Dorman from the author in grateful remembrance of his kindness*". It was not just Herbert who supported Shackleton and his family; Emily's sister Daisy also joined the Shackletons on a tour of Europe when he was giving talks about his journey to the South Pole.

When *Nimrod* returned to England later that summer she was made into floating display of expedition relics and entrance fees made £2,000, all of which Shackleton gave to charity, much to the consternation of the members of the expedition, whose salaries still had not been fully paid. Shackleton published a statement in *The Times*, on 9th August, to quell speculation about the expedition's funding saying that he hoped that the money guaranteed could be paid back by the sale of his book and lectures and from "*the money that my wife's relatives and myself and friends have contributed*". He confirmed that he had not approached the government for a contribution since his return and therefore they had not refused him money. A week later, the government granted Shackleton £20,000, as they knew how much public opinion was on his side. He also named a mountain after the prime minister, Herbert Asquith. But in any case, most of the loans needed to be repaid and that was where a number of problems arose. The total costs of the expedition came to around £45,000, say £2.5m in today's values, though Shackleton never produced detailed accounts. In November 1909, Shackleton was knighted in recognition of his achievements and his wife became Lady Emily.

Theft of the Irish Crown Jewels

Back to Ernest's brother Frank, who was always trying to make money. He left school intending on a career in gardening and became interested in heraldry. He took an unpaid position in Dublin Castle, at the invitation of Sir Arthur Vicars, with a break until 1903 serving in the Royal Irish Fusiliers in South Africa. On his return, he went back to Dublin to work with Sir Arthur although Frank actually spent most of his time in London and Devon, where he started a rose growing business. All the shareholders were Shackletons.

In 1907, the Irish Crown Jewels were stolen some time between 11 June and 6 July, when the theft was discovered. There was no evidence of any break-in and Frank had been staying there at the time. They were never found and no one was ever charged. Their value today would be around one million pounds. Sir Arthur Vicars was dismissed as the Keeper of the Jewels after the subsequent investigation, which by all accounts was a half-hearted affair. Vicars was later assassinated by the IRA for entertaining British officers at his home in Kerry. He had been bitter about losing his job and in his will he stated his belief that Frank Shackleton was responsible for the theft (around that time Frank was able to buy himself a new car worth £850 and lived at Park Lane and Bayswater). The matter was somewhat suppressed by King Edward VII because, it is said, his brother-in-law, the Duke of Argyle, was involved and he was friendly with Frank Shackleton. He is alleged to have declared "*I will not have a scandal. I will not have mud stirred up and thrown about; the matter must be dropped*". Various goings-on at Dublin Castle were whispered and royals implicated. If Frank had been indicted for the theft, the scandal would have given the nationalists a golden opportunity to bring British rule in Ireland into disrepute.

Declining fortunes

By 1909, Frank's liabilities far outweighed his assets after yet another failed business venture. Emily and Ernest Shackleton were staying with Frank in Bayswater while looking for a house in London and were tainted by association. Ernest had bought shares in one of the companies his brother was involved with and evaded bankruptcy himself because Herbert Dorman, his brother-in-law and solicitor was there to help and guide him. In *The Times* dated 21ˢᵗ June 1911, it was reported that on 11ᵗʰ August 1910, Frank Shackleton, of 33 Park Lane, was declared bankrupt with debts of £85,000.

That summer, to distance themselves, Ernest and his family rented a house at Sherringham in Norfolk where the Dorman family used to go for holidays. They were there at the time of the census, on 2ⁿᵈ April 1911. On the form, Shackleton described himself as Polar Explorer, postal address 9 Regent Street. Daisy Dorman, his sister-in-law was then living with them along with six staff, Nurse Domestic, Nursery Nurse, Cook, Parlour Maid, Housemaid and Kitchen Maid. Lady Shackleton gave her age as 39, born in 1872, just two years older than her husband.

All the family moved to 7 Heathview Gardens, Putney Heath, in May 1911, just before Edward Arthur Alexander Shackleton was born on 15ᵗʰ July

1911, when Emily was 43. (*Alexandra Shackleton, the author and Shackleton historian, is the daughter of Edward Shackleton and Betty Homan, who married in 1939.*) It was Emily's income from her trust fund which ran the household. Her sister Daisy was still living with them, sharing costs from her own inheritance and Daisy kept Emily and the children company while Shackleton was away lecturing and on his expeditions.

The Dormans appear to have been a close and mutually supportive family. Emily kept her family together during Shackleton's expeditions, surrounded and supported by friends and family. Ernest spent much of his married life away on expeditions and saw little of his children during their formative years. He had many liaisons outside his marriage but Emily was always loyal to him. He remained dependent on Emily's trust fund for most of his life as many of his attempts to make a fortune failed due to his relative lack of business acumen.

Meanwhile, unknown to Emily, Ernest was borrowing money to repay his brother's creditors and to save face for the family; Frank had left the country. After Ernest's death, Emily admitted that if she had known that her husband had been borrowing from the bank she would have practised "*close economy*". On 21st January 1912, Shackleton wrote to Leonard Tripp saying "*I wish I could get another expedition and be away from all business worries.... all the troubles of the south are nothing to day after day of business*". He added that he would soon hear news of Scott if had reached the South Pole.

Escape from business worries – another expedition

The *Titanic* sank on 15th April 1912. Later that year, Sir Ernest Shackleton was called as an expert witness on ice navigation to the enquiry at Buckingham Gate in London. Although he did not make a great witness and was given a rough ride by defending counsel, Shackleton suggested that the *Titanic* went down because she was sailing too fast and did not enamour himself to ship owners by stating that when the owners were on board ship "*You go*". It was his opinion that they should have gone slowly, given the possibility of icebergs and poor visibility at night. The captain went down with 1,500 passengers including Thomas Andrews, the designer. The owner, J Bruce Ismay escaped into a lifeboat, of which there were enough for only half the passengers.

News reached England on 17th May 1912 that Captain Amundsen, a Norwegian, had reached the South Pole on 14th December 1911. It was not until February 1913 that news came that Captain Scott with Wilson, Oates, Bowers and Evans had also reached the South Pole, on 17th January 1912 but all perished on the return journey. The mother of Captain Oates, the one who famously left the tent and walked into a blizzard, blamed Scott and thought that her son's death was unnecessary. She later befriended Emily Shackleton and went on to pay her children's school fees.

Ever obsessed by ways of raising money to pay his debts, in a letter to Nansen, the Polar explorer, dated 12th September 1912, Shackleton wrote asking for his help in speaking to the King about receiving royal warrants to sell tobacco. He had invested in and started his own *Tabard Cigarette Company*. In the same letter he added that *"I have now after 3 years work paid off the £20,000 liability on my Nimrod"*. The company later went into liquidation.

Scotland Yard police arrested Frank Shackleton in West Africa, in December, 1912 and he was charged on 10th January 1913. It was Ernest who raised bail of £1,000 but in the name of his father, to keep himself out of the mess. Frank had written a cheque for £1,000, misappropriated from Miss Mary Josephine Browne, which he gave to his brother, for his last expedition, to replace the money promised by Elizabeth Dawson Lambton and perhaps implicating Ernest. Frank had met Miss Browne in 1907 at Tavistock in Devon and acting as her financial adviser, he defrauded her of all her savings. Frank was never charged with the theft of the Irish Crown Jewels but was indicted on 20th October 1913 for fraudulently converting Miss Browne's money for his own use. At the Old Bailey it became clear that Frank had defrauded other people. He went to prison for fifteen months and ended his days as an antique dealer in Chichester, using the name of Frank Mellor, ironically, with an interest in precious stones.

The failure of Captain Scott to reach the South Pole first was a great blow to British pride and Shackleton's ambition was to *"re-establish the prestige of Great Britain...in Polar exploration"* as described in *The Times* in December 1913. Ernest was nearly forty when he announced his intention to cross Antarctica from one side to the other by sledge with The Imperial Transantarctic Expedition. He had received a government grant of £10,000 from David Lloyd George in December 1912 and having to match that amount from other sources in order to receive the money, he worked to raise funds for the expedition. Emily acknowledged later that *"Ernest has to go"* and had to make it as *"easy for him as possible"*. After discussions with the Admiralty the expedition was allowed to proceed, despite the prospect of War.

Shackleton had new solicitors, Hutchinson and Cuff, as domestic tensions, due to his extra-marital relationships and financial problems, had made it awkward to continue using Herbert Dorman, his brother-in-law. Meanwhile, to try to hold the family together and ever-loyal to Ernest, Emily rented a more expensive house at 11 Vicarage Gate, South Kensington, which she paid for out of her own money. However, around this time, neither Emily nor the children saw much of their father. As before, he departed before he had secured all funding, leaving the solicitors to sort out the mess.

On 8th August 1914, *Endurance* set sail for South Georgia. Shackleton joined the ship later, having sailed separately to Buenos Aires after trying to placate his wife following a row. He was to use two ships for the trip, *Endurance* for the outward Journey from the Weddell Sea and *Aurora* for the return from the Ross Sea. The crew were to have newly discovered *"vitamines"*, as previous expeditions had failed due to malnutrition and scurvy. Shackleton also wanted dehydrated foods, which were less heavy to carry. He followed Amundsen's success, using dogs instead of walking, as in the ill-fated Scott expedition.

Endurance became trapped in the ice pack on January 19, 1915 and over the next few months she drifted, often trapped by ice floes. The ship was finally caught in a vice-like grip and buckled under the pressure from the ice and was crushed by 27 October. With the ship gone, the only objective was to get the men back home safely. They made their way by smaller boat to Elephant Island but Shackleton decided to take the best of them, the *James Caird* and some of the men back to South Georgia and obtain help; the journey took fifteen days. As they reached the wrong side of the island, Shackleton, Worsley and Crean took three days to cross it on foot. They left the rest of the men behind, in order to reach the whaling station and get help for the others. Then Shackleton had to return to the various places by ship to rescue the remaining men, which took more months. It was an astonishing, if perhaps somewhat insane test of leadership, endurance and heroism but remarkable that no one died. The headlines back home read *"Fifteen Months adventures in the Great Frozen South"*, which conveniently diverted the nation's attention away from the deadlock in the War.

Shackleton's final years

Shackleton arrived back in the Falklands in 1916 and was shocked to learn, in a letter from Emily, that her sister, Daisy had died in April 1916, aged 41, at that point still living with Emily and a great support to her and the children. His brother-in-law, Herbert Dorman, had also died suddenly in Eastbourne on 6th February 1915, at the age of 55. He returned to England in May 1917; he was 42 and too old to fight in the War, as conscription for all men between the ages of 18-41 had just been introduced. However Shackleton worked for the British Government in Russia and South America and received an OBE in 1919. In her will, Daisy left a picture to Sir Ernest Shackleton and three-quarters of her residual estate went to Emily, Lady Shackleton.

He returned to the Antarctic in late 1921 with the Shackleton-Rowett Antarctic Expedition. According to the expedition's geologist, Shackleton was hoping *"to find some mineral deposits that would get him out of his financial straits"*. Not long after he arrived at South Georgia, on 5th January 1922, at the age of 47, he died of a heart attack. His body was embalmed and taken to Montevideo, Uruguay, but Emily decided that he should be buried on South Georgia.

This is a summary of his will:

> **Shackleton**, Sir Ernest Henry of 14 Milnthorpe Road, Eastbourne, knight, died 5 January 1922 on board the steam yacht "Quest" at South Georgia. Probate London 12 May to Dame Emily Mary Shackleton widow. Effects £556 2s.2d. (Probate year 1922)

Although Emily was referred to as Dame, one of her relatives said that she was known as Lady Shackleton. At his death, Ernest owed some wealthy people around £40,000, which would be equivalent to around £1.5 million today.

Emily, after Ernest

As for Emily, despite the fact that she came from a wealthy family, she was to depend on friends, family and even her husband's women friends for financial support most of her life with him. Her brothers, Herbert and Frank, managed the property portfolio in South Tottenham, as trustees of her father's will. Frank appointed his son, Laurence Charles Dorman as a trustee in 1926 and Laurence joined his father in the firm in 1928. All the original partners, including members of the Kingsford family and Samuel Horace Candler had since died. When Frank Dorman died in 1931, Lady Emily Shackleton was appointed a trustee, with his son, Laurence Dorman. She died on 9th June 1936, aged 68. This is a summary of her will:

> *Shackleton*, Dame Emily Mary of Hampton Court Palace, Hampton Court, Middlesex widow died 9 June 1936. Probate London 9 July to Laurence Charles Dorman solicitor and Raymond Swinford Shackleton engineers representative. Effects £29,727 6s. 3d. (Probate year 1936)

She had been living, since 1929, in a set of apartments given to her by King George V at Hampton Court Palace and her financial situation had improved tremendously since the death of her husband. She is buried in the churchyard of St. Giles, at Coldwaltham, West Sussex in the same grave as her daughter Cicely. *The Woodberry Lodge Estate Company* still had unsold portions at South Tottenham, in 1951 but it was likely that tenants bought the flats and houses around this time.

One might speculate that rents and sales of properties and freeholds in South Tottenham may have partly funded or at least indirectly supported the expedition to the South Pole. Herbert Dorman acted as Shackleton's solicitor without charging fees, supported his sister financially and donated money to the expeditions.

Part Two

Early days of the land and those connected to it

15

The Lock, Martin and Candler families

The Victoria History of the Counties of England: A History of Middlesex, Volume 5, in its section on Tottenham *(pp.330-333),* explains how the largest monastic estate was held by the Canoness of St. Mary Clerkenwell. Henry of Scotland gave 140 acres in the *"hanger"* in Tottenham to Ughtred around 1152 and the nuns held the estate until the dissolution of the monasteries. By 1455 there were *"three crofts called Oatfields, land in a field called Great Hanger and woods and meadow at Snaresmead"*; Great Hanger and Oatfields were leased on the eve of the Dissolution and closes in Snaresmead and Thistlefield. Sir William Kingston bought the reversion of the lease to Great Hanger and Oatfields. On his death, in 1540, it passed to his stepson. Edmund Jerningham, who died in 1546 and it then passed to his step-brother, Sir Anthony Kingston. The latter passed 140 acres of Great Hanger to Henry Jerningham and Oatfields to Edward Pate. Henry Jerningham conveyed Great Hanger to Edward Pate in the same year. In 1553, Edward Pate conveyed Oatfields to William Parker, a London draper and 140 acres in Great Hanger to Augustine Hinde, alderman and after that to his infant son, Rowland. Most of the lands *"were granted in 1560 to Michael Lock, a London mercer, and Oatfields was conveyed by Parker to Thomas More, another mercer, in 1561"* (*a mercer is a dealer in textile fabrics, especially silk and other costly materials*). James and Joan Clay and Thomas, Richard and Robert Pate disputed with Thomas Etheridge and his wife Ann, in a claim by descent to freehold land in Tottenham between 1558 and 1603, *"late the estate of Richard Pate"* suggesting that the family still owned land in the area (TNA: *C2/Eliz/C16/60*).

In 1585, Richard Martin, described by the *ODNB* as a goldsmith and Warden of the Royal Mint, from 1572 until 1599, was the tenant who held the largest amount of land (279 acres). A document at TNA (*E 115/267/96*) confirms that during the year 1600-1601, he was liable for taxation in London and not in the hundred of Edmonton, Middlesex. He married Dorcas Eccleston, between 1552 and 1562, and a silver medallion was minted that year by Steven C. Van Herwicjk (*British Museum*) with a likeness of Richard on one side and Dorcas, aged 25, on the other. She is said to be the daughter of John Eccleston, a grocer in Cheapside and Tottenham.

Richard Martin was the person who defined what is now known as the Sterling Standard and he was knighted in 1589. He invested in the voyages of Sir Francis Drake and in an American salt works; his son, John Martin, lived in Virginia. By 1596, he owned a third of the shares in the Society of Mineral and Battery Works with two of his sons, Richard and Nathaniel, who also worked at the Mint. Sir Richard was joint governor of the Society of Mineral and Battery Works, with his son-in-law, Sir Julius Caesar, married to his daughter, Dorcas. His mother-in-law was Margery Locke, widow of Sir Caesar Adelmare and the second wife of Michael Locke, a wealthy traveller and translator who also owned land at Tottenham. Sir Richard Martin and his wife, Dorcas were committed Protestants. She was an educated woman, a translator and a publisher. Dorcas Martin died in Tottenham on 1st September, 1599 and was buried there the following day.

In 1602, Sir Richard Martin was declared bankrupt and was temporarily imprisoned when it was alleged that he owed £8,382 to the Crown. His accuser was the next incumbent to his wardenship at the Mint, Sir Thomas Knyvet. Sir Richard was forced to sell everything including his principal residence in Tottenham for £10,200, a messuage in Milk Street and other property and leases in town and country. At some time between 1599-1616, he married Elizabeth Bourne, sister of John Cottesford, goldsmith. When his son Richard Martin, goldsmith, died in 1616, in his will he left £3 each for a ring to his father and his lady. Sir Richard did not leave a will but his wife received a payment from the Mint after his death.

A most important source of early information on the triangle of land in the South Tottenham area and those people connected with it is William Robinson's book entitled *The History and Antiquities of the Parish of Tottenham in the County of Middlesex*, in two Volumes, published in 1840. Volume I of this edition includes a copy of a map of 1619, reduced from the original by T.T. Barrow and engraved by W.C. Walker made from a survey commissioned for Richard, Earl of Dorset, to prove ownership of the land. It gives a description of the lands belonging to the "*Mannors of Pembrooke Bruses Dawbneys and Mockings in the Parishes of Tottenham and Edmonton in the County of Middlesex*". Appendices I, II and III in Volume I have extensive information on land ownership and transfers in the Tottenham and Edmonton areas. Volume II includes a map of the Parish of Tottenham in the County of Middlesex from an actual survey engraved in 1818 by Bowler and Triquet. The same map of the Parish of Tottenham was included in the first edition of Robinson's book, published in 1818. That edition bore a slightly different title; it included "Tottenham High Cross" rather than "Tottenham" and was published in one volume.

The map of 1619 is invaluable in identifying most of the freehold, leasehold and copyhold land and ownership of land in the Tottenham High Cross area. Parts are coloured but the key only explains that the rivers are blue and that light brown areas designate the common land and highways. In some instances, by cross-checking from other documents, it has been possible to identify particular types of land. In 1605, Thomas, Earl of Dorset, purchased the land from Thomas Wheeler and the mortgage was vested to him. The lands continued in the Dorset family until 1625, when Edward, Earl of Dorset, conveyed them to Hugh and Thomas Audley. They were sold in the following year to Henry Hare, Lord Coleraine and he took over as Lord of the Manor; it was Charles I who in 1626 gave Henry Hare an Irish peerage. Dues were paid to the Lord or Lady of the Manor and the Church by the freeholders and copyholders. The following extract from *A History of Middlesex: Volume 5* (*Page 335*) is a list of the major tenants and owners of copyhold and freehold land in Tottenham, in 1619:

> The Chief tenants being Joseph Fenton with 179 a., John Burrough with 139 a., Sir Thomas Penistone with 86 a., Thomas Adams with 85 a. and Edward Barkham with 66 a. The largest freeholders were Edward Barkham with 174 a., Ambrose Wheeler with 141 a., Edward Osborne with 82 a., Bridget Moyse with 78 a., Lady Heyborne with 75 a. and the heirs of Michael Lock with 71 a. The chief copyholders were Elizabeth Candler with 345 a., Anthony Crewe with 80 a., Thomas Bolton with 63 a. and Erasmus Greenway with 62 a.

There are various spellings of the name in various documents in such forms as Candeler, Chandler, Chaundler or Candler. Richard Candelar hailed originally from Walsingham in Norfolk and was living in Tottenham in the late 1500s. For present purposes, the spellings *"Candler"* and *"Candelar"* are interchangeable. It has been suggested by Hugh Barton Candler, the great-grandson of George Herbert Candler, that papers and research produced by some of his relatives alluded to the distinct possibility that his branch of the family also came from Norfolk. There is reason to accept the view that even if George Herbert and Samuel Horace Candler from the late 19th century had no inherited land in Tottenham, they descended from a 16th century family that had held a great deal of land there, directly surrounding that which was acquired by Charles Dorman.

Elizabeth Candler, *née* Lock

Sir William Lock was the son of Thomas Lock and Joanna Wilcocks. Sir William Locke was an alderman for some years before he was knighted on 3rd October 1548 but died before taking office as Lord Mayor. Sir William married four times; he had nine children by his first wife, Alice Spencer and eleven by his second, Catherine Cook, who died in childbirth. The third was Eleanor Marsh and the fourth Elizabeth Meredith. Some of his wives were buried in the Mercer's Chapel, destroyed in the Great Fire and then bombed in the Second World War.

In 1547, according to Christine Protz, in her book, *Tottenham: A History*, Sir William and his sons, Thomas and Mathew Lock, owned upwards of 270 acres of land in Tottenham. Sir William Lock referred in his will, made in 1549, to all his surviving sons, they being Thomas, Mathew, John, Henry and Michael. Sir William was buried in the Mercer's Chapel on 27th August 1550. He was appointed mercer to Henry VIII, conducting many of the king's commercial affairs at home and abroad and was a favourite of the king, receiving him at his house. Records show that many of the materials used by the king and queen at the Palace were provided by Lock. He had travelled many times to Antwerp to source tapestries and was clearly a man of some importance. William Lock allegedly sent his youngest son, Michael, as a boy of 13, to travel and learn languages, which he continued to do for the rest of his life. Mathew was also a mercer and merchant. Sir William Lock died, possessed of land at Tottenham.

Thomas Lock was the eldest son of Sir William Lock. He had passed some of his land to trustees for the use for life of himself and his wife Mary and then to transfer to his son, William. Thomas died in 1556, four years after his brother Mathew. Thomas' son, William, died in 1558 and his heir was his brother Mathew, born in 1552. Mathew came to inherit properties belonging to the Lock family at St. Mary-Le-Bow. Mathew and his wife, Margaret, were possessed of these properties in 1598 but after his death, in 1599, they passed to his uncle Michael for the duration of his life. Mathew Lock, of Merton in Surrey, whose will was proved in 1599, was buried near his mother in the Church of St. Thomas of Aron; he identified his eldest daughter as Mary Lock. His widow, Margaret Lock, went on to marry Sir Thomas Muschampe and was living at Newington in Surrey when she died in 1624. She requested burial as near as possible to her first husband. Wills of her daughters, Ann Lock and Mary Threele help to explain the relationships and family living around that time. It was Michael Lock who paid homage for the land at Coombes Croft, at Tottenham, in 1576, as the only surviving son of Sir William Lock. In 1634, it was transferred from Thomas Lock, of Merton in Surrey, the great-grandson of Sir William Lock, to Tobias Massye and Thomas Wilcocks.

Mathew Lock was the youngest of eight sons of Sir William Lock by his first wife, Alice. He married Elizabeth Baker around 1550, the year that his father died and not much later he himself died; his will was proved on 27th May 1552. The names of some of his brothers, Thomas, John and Michael, his daughter, Elizabeth and Elizabeth Baker, are included in the will, as is a reference to his land at Tottenham. Elizabeth Lock was the daughter and sole heir of Mathew Lock of Tottenham, born around 1551. As Elizabeth Lock was an only child, she would have inherited her portion, that being the custom of the City of London. As her mother was not cited in her father's will, this might suggest that she had died before her father wrote it, perhaps in childbirth. Mathew's eldest brother; Thomas Lock, was named as executor. The name of Elizabeth Baker may have been a reference to another relative of his late wife with the same name. As Elizabeth was an orphan, it might be assumed that she was brought up by her uncle and executor, Thomas Lock or members of the Baker family.

The will of Elizabeth Lock, a widow, was proved on 27th February 1552. She was the fourth wife of Sir William Lock and step-mother to Mathew Lock. As Elizabeth Hutton, a widow, she married Robert Meredith, a widower, formerly the husband of Sir William Lock's only daughter, Jane, by his first wife, Alice. When Robert Meredith died, Elizabeth married her father-in-law, Sir William Lock. She made reference in her will to Robert Meredith, thereby confirming the existence of a marriage.

In 1561, Henry and Michael Lock were the only surviving sons of Sir William Lock but by a different wife, Catherine Cooke. Henry Lock married Anne Vaughan. She was the daughter of Stephen Vaughan and Margery Gwynneth *or Guinet*, his first wife. Lock was a mercer, like his father, with interests in Antwerp and he was a neighbour of Stephen Vaughan, a merchant adventurer and government agent who lived at Cheapside, in London. Anne was an educated woman when she married, with skills in many languages and was a prolific translator of religious writing. This was a time of religious revolution and she met and corresponded with John Knox, the Scottish reformer. With her husband's permission, at the request of Knox, she travelled to Geneva with two young children to translate Calvin's sermons. Her daughter, Anne, died shortly after their arrival; her son, Henry Lock, is known as a religious poet. Henry Lock, her husband, died in 1571 after a lingering illness. She was persuaded by her friend Dorcas Martin to marry Edward Dering but he died of consumption in 1576. She then married Richard Prowse and had two other sons, dying before her husband. Michael Lock (1553-1615) married twice. In a book on *John Dee (1527-1608)* by Charlotte Fell-Smith, published in 1909, there is a reference to Michael Lock, as a traveller and translator and to his sons, the eldest named Zachary and his brother Benjamin, who had an interest in alchemy. The author reported that Michael Lock had fifteen children. John Dee was a consultant to the Muscovy Company and famous as an astrologer and mathematician. His first wife, Jane Wilkinson died in 1571 and her will was proved on 6th April 1571. It referred to the names of some of their children as Elizabeth, Benjamin, Anne, Joanne or Jane and Ebenezer. He then married Margery *or Margaret* Adelmare, widow of Sir Caesar Adelmare, who died in 1569. Her maiden name was Perrient or Perin (*Annals of St. Helen Bishopsgate by John Edmund Cox*). Sir Caesar, an Italian immigrant and royal physician to Queens Mary and Elizabeth, was advised by Queen Elizabeth to take an English wife. Julius Caesar Adelmare, son of Margery and Caesar Adelmare, was born in Tottenham in 1557 and was baptised at St. Dunstan on 10th February 1557. Sir Julius Caesar, who adopted the surname of Caesar instead of Adelmare, married Dorcas Lusher, the young widow of William Lusher *(see above)*. Later known as Sir Julius Caesar, he became Chancellor of the Exchequer in the reign of James I and was the father of Sir Charles Caesar, who married Jane Barkham, daughter of Sir Edward Barkham, in 1626.

Records of a Michael Lock in the years 1576, 1577 and 1578 appear in a document at TNA (*C 47/34/6*), describing him in relation to voyages made by Martin Frobisher, the explorer "*as late treasurer of the Meta Incognita*". The voyages were planned to find new trade routes to Cathay (China) via the North-West passage. These attempts were of great interest to the Queen and Michael Lock, the latter being just one of the merchants and financial backers of the expedition at that time. He was Treasurer of the Muscovy Company, which had its headquarters at Muscovy House, Seething Lane, in London, until 1579/80 (*Survey of London Volume 15*). It was set up by a group of merchants and granted a monopoly by the Queen to search for new trading routes by the North-East passage to Russia. The Cathay Company was granted rights to the North-West passage. Frobisher's attempts in those three expeditions to discover new sources of minerals and mine ore, in terrible weather condition, and return it to England, did not produce gold as hoped and the ore turned out to be worthless. Both The Crown and Lock lost a great deal of money. Michael Lock and Sir Richard Martin, connected by marriage and both wealthy landowners at Tottenham, sponsored voyages of discovery and moved in the highest social circles.

At TNA, documents relating to *Michael Lock v. John Ellis* (*E134/4Jas1/Trin4*), dated 1606, state that Lock transferred ownership of tenements in Tottenham and lands at Cheapside and Lothbury to Richard Young. Then, in 1610, a document (*E134/8Jas1/Hil25*) declared that Young granted farms at Bow Lane land at Tottenham to William Powell, possibly seized for Crown debts and granted by the Crown to Susan Ellis, the daughter of Richard Young.

Elizabeth Lock

Elizabeth Lock married Richard Candler. In the *Calendar of State Papers*, a Richard Candler is recorded a number of times; in April, 1560, in a letter by Sir Thomas Gresham to Sir William Cecil, to say that his factor, Richard Candler, was to be at his disposal at 6.00 a.m. daily, as Candler was the person managing Cecil's business at Lombard Street; in June 1560, in relation to munitions in the Tower of London; and in a letter relating to a return journey of the Queen. In 1563 there was a further reference to him as a factor, in relation to delivery of gold and silver bullion. Again, in 1576, he was referred to in an answer to a bill of fees set down by certain aldermen and citizens, in respect of his making and registering of assurances. It might be presumed that he acquired the land, at Tottenham, during these years.

Richard Candler, Esquire, of Tottenham, was recorded in documentation held at TNA (*C2/Eliz/B2/32*) during the years 1558-1602 in a dispute with Robert Baker, son and heir of Robert Baker, a gentleman, by then deceased, formerly of Halstowe, St. Mary, Kent. Margery was given as the name of the mother of Robert Baker. These people may have been related to his future wife, Elizabeth Lock, whose mother was Elizabeth Baker. In the document, Candler was described as one of four tellers of the Queen's (Elizabeth I) receipt, at Westminster and it would seem that he moved in these circles.

There is a very large marble, wall mounted Memorial dedicated to the Candlers in All Hallows, Church Lane, Tottenham, close to Bruce Castle Museum and next to Tottenham cemetery. It depicts Richard Candler, Justice of the Peace, of Middlesex (died 24th October 1602, aged 61), his son-in-law, Sir Ferdinando Heyborne, also a Justice of the Peace (died 4th June 1618, aged 60), and their wives, Elizabeth Candler (died on 2nd January 1622) and Dame Anne Heyborne, their daughter (died on 24th June 1615, aged 44). The inscription declares that Richard and Elizabeth Candler had a son, Edward, who died in infancy and a daughter Ann and that they were married for 26 years, which implies the marriage took place around 1575. A certificate of residence at TNA shows that, between 1584 and 1585, Richard Candler was liable to pay taxes in London rather than in Edmonton, where he had previously paid, so this baptism in the City of London, may have been of his son, as an Edward Candler, was baptised on 8ᵗʰ March 1584, at St. Christopher Le Stocks (*www.familysearch.org*). Elizabeth Candler's age was not recorded on the Memorial. Anne Candler's birth year of around 1572, according to the memorial, does not quite tally with the length of her parents' married life. The memorial for Ferdinando and Anne also reported that they were married for twenty-three years. This would make the year of their marriage 1592.

An article in the Home Counties Magazine, entitled *The Candelers of London, Volume II*, suggested that after Richard Candler of Tottenham died in 1602, the grant of "*making and registering assurances on ships and merchandice in London*" went to his son-in-law, Ferdinando Richardson, *alias* Heyborne. Then, in August 1604, a grant was made to one Christopher Heyborne and to Candler's nephew, also named Richard Candler. Christopher Heyborne was a groom and gentleman of the Privy Chamber to Queen Elizabeth I and James I and by all accounts an accomplished musician, composer, dancer and poet, much favoured by the Queen. Ferdinando Heyborne is said to have been born around 1558 to John Heyborne and Margaret Dodd, at Waltham, in Essex. He received his knighthood in 1611. Apparently, Sir Ferdinando gave up his lucrative career in music in his later life to farm at Tottenham. Margaret Richardson, his mother, was buried in Tottenham, on 22ⁿᵈ February 1612.

The will of Richard Candler or Candeler, a citizen and mercer of London, was written on 12ᵗʰ December 1614 and proved on 20ᵗʰ March 1614 (*PROB 11/125/262*). He was the nephew of the late Richard. He requested that his estate was to be divided into three equal parts; he bequeathed one part to his loving wife, another third part was to go to his son Ferdinando and the remaining third to pay legacies, at the discretion of his executors. The following people received bequests: Mrs. Elizabeth Candler, his loving kinswoman (widow of his uncle); Lady Anne Heyborne; his brother-in-law, Richard Rydgedale; his brother-in-law, Richard Pulford "*to his wife her mother Mrs. Anne Smythe*" and to his mother-in-law, his father's wife (his stepmother but no name given); his half-sister Margaret Candler and another half-sister Sara Candler. He also bequeathed money to John Atkins of Bungay, Norfolk, as well as to servants and friends. (Bungay is now in the County of Suffolk but this confirms a connection to that area.) He gave to Christ's Hospital, the poor of Ludgate prison, St. Bartholomew's Church, Tottenham Church and £20 to the church at Little Walsingham, in Norfolk, where he stated that he was born. His executor and executrix were named as his good friend Sir Ferdinando Heyborne and his very loving wife and he remarked that Ferdinando had given him much fatherly love. The last reference was to a sum of money to bring up his son during his minority and his wife's widowhood and if his wife married again, his son was to be brought up by his other executor. If his son died before reaching the age of 21, the estate was to be divided in four equal parts; the first to his wife and her heirs; the second to Lady Heyborne and her heirs; the third to his brother-in-law, Richard Ridgdale, his wife and heirs; the fourth to his brother-in-law, Richard Pulford, his wife, Anne and heirs. If he left anyone out, his executors had the right to add them in. The will was proved by Sir Ferdinando Heyborne. It did not include the Christian name of his wife.

Ferdinando Candler, whose father was the younger Richard, was baptised on 4th November 1604, at St. Bartholomew by the Exchange and the father's will confirms relationships with other people in the Tottenham area. Edmund Traves, a merchant of St. Pancras, in London, married, by licence, Susanna Candeler, a widow, of St. Bartholomew by the Exchange, at All Hallows, Tottenham, on 30th May 1615 (the wife of Edmund Traves is identified in his will, written in 1636, as "Susanne"). She was probably the widow of Richard Candler. In 1616, in a conveyance, Traves is described as a haberdasher. Upon his death, his son Richard was sole executor and his daughters were identified as Elizabeth, Susanna, Jane and Martha Dethick, wife of John. Traves was buried at St. Michael, Cornhill. He left his property at Cornhill and a share of his land at Tottenham to Richard. Sir John Dethick, a mercer, as he was by then knighted, was living at Tottenham High Cross, when he died, in 1671.

The Christian name of Richard Candler's father is not recorded in the will but his father and uncle were born, like him, at Walsingham, in Norfolk. The local church records at Tottenham show that on 17th November 1600 Richard Ridgdale had married Susanna Candler, both of them single and servants to Sir Ferdinando Heyborne. She was the daughter of Simon Candler of Walsingham and Richard Candler was her brother; it is not unusual to find a relative in service. Richard Pulford, an ironmonger of St. Dunstan-in-the-East, married Anne Candler, of St. Bartholomew by the Exchange, another sister, on 16th February 1612, at Tottenham. Their son, Ferdinando Pulford, was baptised on 16th December 1616 at St. Bartholomew near the Exchange. Richard Pulford's name is shown in the Earl of Dorset Map of 1619 as an owner of copyhold land.

Sir Ferdinando Heyborne married Elizabeth More on 4th April 1616, less than a year after the death of his first wife, Anne Candler. This marriage produced a child named Ferdinando, born in 1617. Three of the children named in the wills, to add to the confusion, were called after Sir Ferdinando Heyborne. Sir Ferdinando Heyborne died a year after the birth of his son and the will was proved on 30th June 1618 (*PROB 11/131/823*). It explained that on 2nd June 1618, the date on which the will was made, he had surrendered his customary land and hereditaments at Tottenham, in Middlesex, to the hands of the Lord of the Manor, to the use of his "*cousin*," Richard Pulford and his heirs, to be sold for the best price, to pay a debt of £1,200 owed to Sir Anthony Crewe, John Kirby and one Lavender, for the portion of Ferdinando Candler, son of Richard Candler, *above*. He requested that his loving mother-in-law, Mrs. Elizabeth Candler, should have the use of attendants, chambers, lodgings and commodities "*in and belonging to his now dwelling house*," in Tottenham, for the length of her natural life and that because of the love and affection which she gave to him, he hoped that she would continue to give that love to his new wife and son and would be a second mother to them. Elizabeth Candler was living with her former son-in-law and his new wife. He appointed his wife, Dame Elizabeth Heyborne, as his sole executrix. He left all his manors, messuages land, tenements, and hereditaments in the counties of Middlesex and Essex or elsewhere to his son, Ferdinando Heyborne and his heirs and by default to Ferdinando Candler, son of the late Richard Candler, and his heirs, with the proviso that they pay his wife or her heirs, specified in her last will and testament, £3,000, to be released immediately after his death. By default, his land went to Ferdinando Pulford, son of his cousin or his heirs. He asked that his honourable friend, Sir Michael Stanhope, would give favourable respect to his wife and son, as he had given him.

The will of Elizabeth Candler *or Candeler*, made on 8th December 1622, was proved on 14th January 1623, a year later. Her will (*PROB 11/141/25*) was informative, particularly about her extended family. She left bequests or legacies of various amounts to her many cousins. Among the beneficiaries were Barbara, wife of George Preston and their daughter Elizabeth (George Preston married Barbara Locke, on 25th July 1615, at Tottenham, who was a cousin of Elizabeth Candler). Others included Barbara Preston's sister, Anne Locke, who was Mrs. Candler's servant, single and living with her at the time. Her cousin, Baker's wife, was a beneficiary. She gave thirty shillings to make a ring of gold to Susanna Traves, daughter of Edmund Traves of Tottenham and Mrs. Traves received £50, owed in a bond by her husband to Mrs. Candler, effectively wiping out a debt. Bequests were made to Anne Baker, daughter of Robert Baker, by then deceased and now the wife of a Mr. Tyroo, an apothecary. Her brother, Robert Baker, Ferdinando Baker (at the age of 21) and the other younger children of Robert Baker, by then deceased, were left gifts or money for their education and maintenance. It is not clear if Ferdinando was the son of her cousin, Robert Baker, or another relative but a person of this name, who matched the description, was born on 10th July 1608 and attended Merchant Taylor School. Elizabeth Candler left a diamond ring to Lady Heyborne, the widow of Sir Ferdinando Heyborne, her former son-in-law and a silver warming pan weighing fifty ounces, which, after Lady Heyborne's death, was to go to her son Ferdinando Heyborne. The latter was also to have the picture hanging in the room where she then lay. Mrs. Candler wrote the will in December and died on 2nd January, according to her memorial, so one might assume that she was ill for four weeks before her death.

She identified her friend as Elias Lavender, whose name appears above in relation to a debt owed by Sir Ferdinando Heyborne (Elias died in 1626). Then she named her relatives from her father's side of the family. William Lock, son of Mathew Lock, was to receive £100 plus her bedstead, *"wherein she usually lie with fine taffeta silk curtains of crimson colour"* and to her cousin, Robert Lock, £5. She cited her cousin, Susanna Crewe, then the wife of Anthony Crewe, Elizabeth Pulford, the daughter of Richard Pulford, the brother-in-law of her deceased nephew, Richard Candler and her cousin, Mrs. Genny, sometimes Jenney or Jennings. Anthony Crewe married Susanna Ridgdale on 29th May 1617, in Tottenham. Susanna was the widow of Richard Ridgdale and the sister of Richard Candler, the nephew.

All the children of her cousin, Thomas Lock, were to receive £20 apiece, except for Elizabeth, as she had already received a string of pearls worth £80, then an extraordinary amount of money. Her cousin, Thomas, then living at Merton Abbey, was to receive £400 and *"five pieces of tapestry and two pieces of bordering under the window and five curtains of purple and yellow taffeta and valance to them"*. She then appointed her friend, Arthur Robinson as sole executor of her will and overseers were her cousin, William Lock and Richard Pulford and if they should die before her, Elias Lavender. Robinson's wife was also described as her good friend. Pulford received a *"scrittory with drawing boxes"* a designated piece of furniture for writing. Christopher Heyborne, of Tottenham, a gentleman, received forty shillings to buy a ring for mourning as did her cousin Ferdinando Candler (actually the son of her late nephew Richard Candeler). Thomas Lock and his heirs were to receive the benefit of all her copyhold and customary lands and tenements in Tottenham, Middlesex, in the four manors. She made bequests to her cousin Charles Lock, Barbara Lock, the elder, presumably the mother of her cousin Barbara and wife of George Preston. Benjamin Jenney received money towards his schooling. Her cousins William and Thomas Lock were to have equal share of her goods, chattels and personal estate. Candler's reference may have been to second as well as first cousins. Her descriptions of the curtains and other items show that she lived in a luxurious house which showcased the wealth of its occupant.

The final Sentence following the will was made on 24th May 1623 and was contested by Arthur Robinson, the executor, against Thomas Lock, Robert Lock, William Lock and Elizabeth Genny, described as kin of the deceased. Benjamin Genny, referred to above, was the latter's son, born on 2nd February, 1611. It is assumed that the relatives won out. After Mrs. Elizabeth Candler died it has been said that her substantial house on Tottenham Green, beside the High Cross, became an inn but this may not be the case.

It was noted by the author of *The Candelers of London* that many of the beneficiaries of the will were owners of land of various sizes in the Tottenham area and many were related one to the other. Arthur Robinson held freehold land at Tottenham in 1619. Lady Heyborne held freehold land with the name of Langford Lands to the west of what is now Tottenham High Road and copyhold land at the corner of High Cross Green, next to copyhold land, then owned by Mrs. Candler. There was a cluster of parcels of land in the High Cross area under the names of Lady Heyborne and Mrs. Candler. They were, presumably, inherited by Lady Elizabeth Heyborne after the death of her husband in 1618, when her son was only one year old.

Dame Elizabeth Heyborne married Sir John Melton, of Petworth, at Tottenham, on 20th January 1623/4. Her will reveals that on 19th January 1623, the day before she married, she entered into an indenture tripartite among John Melton of the first part, Elizabeth Heyborne of the second part and George Moore, of Hackney, a clerk and Richard Pulford, a citizen and ironmonger, of the third part. The latter was described as the cousin of Sir Ferdinando Heyborne, deceased. The indenture was part of a marriage settlement.

John Melton and Elizabeth had four children; Anne was baptised on 21st March 1625; John and Francis were baptised on 27th September 1627, on the same day that their mother was buried; Elizabeth. John was buried on 27th January 1627/8. There is a monument to Sir John Melton and his wife in the same church as above at Tottenham. Dame Elizabeth Heyborne, then Melton, was his first wife. Her will was made on 9th March 1625, before the birth of her daughter, Anne and proved on 1st October 1627 (*PROB 11/152/412*). In it she referred to the arrangement made by her deceased husband, who had left manors, land, tenements and hereditaments in Middlesex to Ferdinando Pulford, son of his "*cousin*", Richard Pulford, for the bond to the Chamberlain of London, then £1,200. She made a bequest of £3,000 to Ferdinando Candler for the said manors and land, before-mentioned and said that said Ferdinando Pulford and his heirs should receive it on condition that he or his heirs pay her £3,000. This money was to go to her husband, John Melton, whom she appointed sole executor. Sir Ferdinando Heyborne had left his manors, land, tenements and hereditaments in Essex, Middlesex and elsewhere to his son, Ferdinando and his heirs and by default to Ferdinando Candler and his heirs and if they were deceased then to her and her assigns. Her will was signed in the presence of Edmund Traves. Ferdinando Heyborne was only 10 when she died. Sentences, a form of declaration, for both Sir Ferdinando Heyborne and his wife Elizabeth, were added in November, 1630.

Christopher Heyborne was buried in Tottenham on 20th September 1630. A form of will was made for him in 1633. Ferdinando *Candeller* was buried at All Hallows', Tottenham, on 26th July 1632. Ferdinando Heyborne, Dame Elizabeth's eldest son by her first husband, died at the age of 21, in 1638/9 (Sentence was proved 2nd December 1640, sometime after his death). Presumably any land held in his name would have gone to his step-father, Sir John Melton and his children

The will of Richard Pulford, an ironmonger, was proved in 1630. He was living in the Parish of St. Gabriel, Fenchurch and was buried at St. Bartholomew by the Exchange on 15th March 1630. It explained that he had bought land in Tottenham from Thomas Locke, which was to go to his youngest son, John Pulford. Records show that, in 1638, some of the land at Edmonton and Tottenham, owned by Sir Ferdinando Heyborne, was then owned by Ferdinando Pulford and his mother, Ann. Sir John Melton, still owned other land in the area, which he sold in 1638. The will of Ferdinando Pulford, a gentleman, of Tottenham, was proved in July, 1640. He requested that he be interred with his father, Richard. He left land in Essex, to his mother, Anne Pulford but the land at Tottenham was not named. He made reference to his brother, John and his sister, Hannah. Church records show that the son of Mr. Pulford, of the Insurance Office of the Royal Exchange, was buried between 19th April and August 1640.

Sir John Melton married Catherine Currance and had a further three sons and a daughter. When Catherine died, he married Margaret Aldersey, a widow and she outlived him, as did his four children by his second wife. He was buried on 19th December 1640 and his will proved on 11th March 1641

(*PROB 11/185/372*). His will explains that his eldest son, Francis, had been left £100 by his half-brother, Ferdinando Heyborne and reference was made to his daughter, Elizabeth. They were the only surviving children by his first wife, Elizabeth. Sir John still held land at Willoughby, in Tottenham as well as being Keeper of His Majesty's Signet at York. Dame Margaret Melton died in London, in 1662.

Ferdinando Candler was the last person with that surname from the Tottenham branch of the Candler family. If George Candler, born in 1850, was descended from Richard Candeler, who died in 1614, it was through brothers of the latter from Walsingham, in Norfolk.

16

The Barkham family

The Earl of Dorset map of 1619 indicates that Edward Barkham was the owner of the largest freehold estate in the Tottenham area, which comprised 174 acres of freehold land plus 65 acres of copyhold land. In the triangle of land at South Tottenham were Great Gallow Field and Little Gallow Field; land marked as leasehold lying in several demesnes; Oat Fields in three parts; Thistly Field in two parts (one was freehold land owned by Edward Barkham; the other half was labelled "P.A. Lock."); Little Snares Field; Great Snares Mead and Hatchers, also known as Sergeants Field. A little further north was a mixture of copyhold and freehold land with the name of Crooks Grove, beside Blackhope Lane. In 1597, Barkham was liable for taxation in London and not in the hundred of Edmonton, as he was in 1601, which might suggest that he already held land in that area. It is possible that in 1602 Barkham acquired land from Sir Richard Martin after the latter was forced to sell his land. Figure 16.1 is a detail adapted from the map of 1619 showing land owned by Edward Barkham, Mrs. Candler, Anthony Crewe, Lock and Bolton.

Sir Edward Barkham (1571-1634)

According to Fisk's book on Tottenham, Edward Barkham was a leather-seller, alderman and in 1621-1622, Lord Mayor of London. Other documents suggest that he was a mercer. Edward married Jane Crouch and they had four daughters; Susan married Robert Walpole in 1619; Margaret was the third wife of Sir Anthony Irby (Lady Margaret's death, in 1640, is commemorated on a brass plaque at All Hallows' Parish Church in Tottenham); Elizabeth married John Gerrard in 1621; Jane married Charles Caesar in 1626. The Barkhams had two sons, Edward and Robert and two others who died young.

Sir Edward Barkham died in 1634. He was succeeded by his elder son, Sir Edward Barkham (1597-1667) of Tottenham and Southacre, in Norfolk. In his will (*PROB 11/165/39*), proved in January 1634, Sir Edward Barkham requested burial on the north side of the chancel at Southacre Church, Norfolk, which is dedicated to St. George. In summary, the will, written in 1632, records that Sir Edward gave to his beloved wife Dame Jane Barkham all his copyhold lands in Tottenham and all his tenements, leases and hereditaments in Wainfleet, St. Mary and All Saints and Friskney in the County of Lincoln, for the course of her natural life and then to his second son Robert and if he were to die, to his male heirs. He also referred to Elizabeth Mallory, recorded in the accounts in the Tottenham Manorial Court Rolls and her right to an

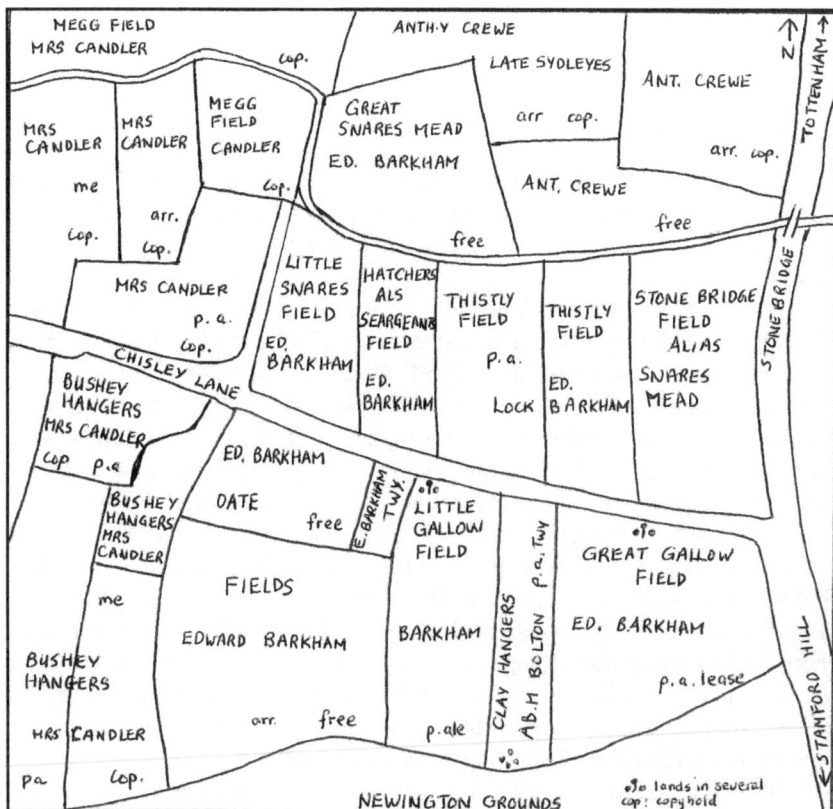

16.1 Section of 1619 map adapted by the author, showing ownership of land in Tottenham.

estate for life (Elizabeth Mallory's own will was proved in 1637). He left many bequests to churches in Norfolk and London as well as to hospitals. There was also a request that he be remembered on the Coat of Arms of the City of Londonderry, which was colonised and so named by the Drapers' Company. From his lists of bequests for mourning, it might be deduced that his daughters Susan Walpole and Elizabeth Garrard (or Gerrard) had already died. He made bequests to his other daughters, Jane, Margaret and his sons-in-law, Sir John Garrard, Sir Charles Caesar, Sir Anthony Irby and Robert Walpole, among others; there were also many grandchildren. He insisted that his son Robert had to agree to make no claims on his land or personal estate except for the annuities out of his land to be paid annually by his mother to him. If he did not comply with this arrangement, it became null and void and everything was to go to his elder brother, Edward. Probate was granted to his widow, Jane and eldest son, Edward, executrix and executor of his will, on 17th January 1634. Tapestries and other family pieces were settled on his widow for her use for life and then to his eldest son. Sir Edward Barkham's eldest son, of the same name, was to receive no land, except by default. He may have already had land settled on him before the death of his father, possibly when he married.

Dame Jane Barkham

Original wills at *The National Archives* (copies are recorded on Layston Church website) build up a picture of the Barkham family and trace a sequence of events. The information that follows was compiled from both sources.

Dame Jane Barkham, mother of Edward and Robert, made her lengthy will on 22nd February 1653 and added two codicils, the last in May 1654. Her will was proved on 26th June 1654 (*PROB 11/240/634*) and it served to explain the family relationships. She requested burial in the tomb of her husband at Southacre. She left money for mourning in favour of her eldest son, Edward, his wife and their children and "*a border with diamond buttons*". She also gave her second son Robert and his children, money for mourning and gave him her "*border of buttons of goldsmith work beset with diamonds rubies and pearls*". At a more practical level, she gave Robert all the bedding and wall-hangings and furniture in the chamber over the parlour called the King's Chamber in her house at Tottenham. Perhaps the King had stayed there at one time, hence its name. She also bequeathed funds for mourning to her daughter, Jane and her two sons, Charles and Henry and her son-in-law Robert Walpole and his son, Edward. She added that Walpole was not to receive any further legacies as he had had much from her already.

She then explained that her eldest son, Edward Barkham was bound to her since 20th June 1652 for the sum of £3,000, which was to have been paid back during her lifetime with a further £25 to be paid every 1st March. Edward was to pay legacies out of this money; to his own children, £100 each and the same to his brother Robert and his children; a total of £1,800. Jane's granddaughter was identified as Elizabeth Huxley, the only one of Robert's children married when the will was written in 1652 and proved in June 1654. Dame Jane stipulated how the money was to be paid back in the year following her death, to cover the legacies. They were to be paid to her grandsons when they achieved the age of 21 and 18 for her granddaughters or whenever they married. The remaining £200 was to be paid to her executor. When her son, Edward paid the legacies, the bond to her for £3,000 was to be cancelled and made void. If either son did not fulfil her conditions, then they and their children were to receive nothing.

It was then that she explained that her son-in-law, Sir Charles Caesar (Adelmare), then deceased, had left a debt to Dame Jane for the sum of £1,000 with interest, which he had been unable to pay back before his death. She had much love and affection for her daughter and had decided that the bond or debt was to be cancelled for her daughter's benefit and that of her youngest grandson, Charles Caesar. Her daughter Jane received her best jewels. Each of her sons, Henry and Charles Henry Adelmare, received £100.

Jane's will requested that her son Robert should agree in writing, within 28 days, to any decisions made by the executor, by the custom of the City of

London, as well as such provisions as were set down in the will of her deceased husband, Sir Edward Barkham, in respect of chattels, rights, credits, mortgages and personal estate held in trust for him, except for any gifts legacies or bequests due to him from his mother. This included having, taking, removing and carrying away, within 40 days, anything from her house.

The next section of the will was practical and related to the house at Tottenham. Jane's executor was to continue housekeeping and maintain the house for four weeks after her death. She wrote about the hay in the barn and woods. In it, she confirmed that as her second son Robert was to have her house, he had the right to fell the wood in the yard, for his own benefit and not for the maintenance of the house or housekeeping. Then followed a list of people, the poor women in Tottenham Parish, who were to receive money, among them John Pickering and other servants, and churches, She made a bequest to a grammar school in the Parish of Layston in the County of Hereford.

After debts and legacies were paid, all Dame Jane's goods, chattels, cattle, plate, household stuff, rights, credits and personal estate left, were to be divided equally among Edward Barkham, the eldest son of her son, Sir Edward Barkham, Sir Robert Barkham and her daughter, Dame Jane Adelmare, also known as Caesar. She then named her cousin, Thomas Crouch, of Cambridge, a gentleman, as executor and gave him a further £50 for his trouble; she revoked any other wills, legacies or bequests. There were a number of codicils made giving her feather bolsters, bed linen, sheets, pillows, tablecloths, napkins, towels etc., to various people. All her wearing apparel was to go to her cousin and the "*worst cloaks*" to her servants. Jane Barkham was obviously very much in control of family finances.

Sir Edward Barkham (1597-1667)

The younger Edward was born in 1597 and was created a baronet of Southacre by James I, on 28th June 1623. He lived in Norfolk and Tottenham and married Frances Berney in July 1622 at All Hallows' Church, in Tottenham.

Sir Edward had estates in Norfolk and it was there that Frances Barkham, his wife, was buried on 25th July 1667, at the Church of St. George, Southacre, followed by her husband on 2nd August, the day his will was written. The will of Sir Edward Barkham, of Tottenham High Cross, was proved on 6th August 1667 (*PROB 11/324/466*), upon which event his land at Westacre, in Norfolk was settled on his eldest son, Edward. It was the father's wish that some of that land be disposed of to pay his debts and any surplus to be divided between his sons, William and John. The Mansion House at Tottenham High Cross, with all his lands at Tottenham and Edmonton, went to his second son, William (who was baptised at Tottenham, on 26th February 1639). His youngest son, John, received his houses at Little Moorfields in London and his daughter Elizabeth, still unmarried, received £1,500 and land at Newton. His daughters, Lucy received £1,200 and Juliana, £1,200. The Manor of Walton in Norfolk went to both William and John Barkham. His executors were John Allen, William Barkham and John Barkham.

John Barkham (died *c.*1670)

John Barkham wrote his will on 7th July 1670. He was buried at Southacre and his will was proved on 9th May 1671 (*PROB 11/336/40*) by his brother, William and Anthony Smithson, his brother-in-law. All his goods and stock in partnership with his brother, William Barkham, messuages in Cheapside and in the Parish of St. Lawrence and among others, a tenement in Little Moorfields in the Parish of St. Giles without Cripplegate. Any other messuages in the City of London bequeathed by his father, Sir Edward Barkham, were to go to William Barkham and his heirs. He made bequests to his brother-in-law, Anthony Smithson, sister Frances White, a widow, sister Dame Margaret Jennings, wife of Sir Edward Jennings, sister Jane Deane, wife of Anthony Deane, sister Mary Curtis, wife of Norton Curtis, sister, Susanna Smithson, sister Ann Jennings, wife of Jonathan Jennings, and sister Elizabeth Lister, wife of John Lister. Lucy and Juliana Barkham each received a share of messuage built by Brook, Clark and Nelthrop. William was the main beneficiary; his eldest brother, Edward, benefited very little.

Sir Robert Barkham (1598-1661)

Robert Barkham (1598-1661), knighted by Charles I in 1641, of Wainfleet, St. Mary, Lincolnshire, married Mary Wilcox (known also as Wilcocke, Wilcocks or Wilcoxe), on 24th November 1625, when she was seventeen. Her father, according to marriage records at All Hallows, Tottenham, was Richard Wilcox, already deceased. Richard Wilcox was a citizen and haberdasher of London and was living in the Parish of St. Magnus the Martyr when his will was proved on 9th March 1625. In May, 1623, Richard Wilcox and his wife Alice had acquired from Arthur Robinson a number of small fields, messuages, cottages, gardens and forge, situated in various parts of Tottenham. The heirs of Michael Lock owned 71 acres of freehold land in 1619.

The children born to Robert Barkham and Mary were Edward, baptised in 1630/31; John, who died 3rd April 1638; Margaret, born in 1629, who died 20th January 1652; Elizabeth; Mary; Jane born in 1632; Alice born in 1634; Dorcas born on 29th September 1636; Susanna, who died on 24th September 1649; Robert, who died in 1641, a second son with the name of Robert, baptised on 10th September 1643 and another daughter. Mary, their mother, died aged 36, in 1644. All Hallows Church displays a large monument, representing Robert, Mary and their eight girls, one of whom died as a baby, and four sons. Information concerning Sir Robert appears in the Appendix III of Robinson's book in connection with an indenture made on 19th May 1648. He secured for himself and his family a burial place *"in fee"* in All Hallows Church. In return for this arrangement, he assigned a rent charge from two acres of land near Blackhope Lane; the parish was to receive 10 shillings a year for the poor of the parish and the sexton received 2 shillings. The monument is still in the church and depicts Sir Robert in a suit of armour.

When Sir Robert Barkham died in 1661, it is said that he ordered his mansion to be sold for the benefit of his second son, Robert but it was in fact acquired

16.2 Monument to Sir Robert Barkham at All Hallows, Tottenham.

by the testator's elder brother, Edward and not sold, as was requested. In 1664, Sir Edward Barkham was living at Crooks Farm, by all accounts a substantial house, in a lowly populated parish, next to Tottenham Street. The house, opposite the vicarage, had twenty-one hearths and was the second largest in the area. In the Earl of Dorset Map of 1619, the parcel of freehold land on which Crooks Farm stood is described as *"late Dalbys-Edward Barkham"*. The farm was a good deal further north within the borough and closer to Edmonton, to the left of what is now Tottenham High Road. Edward, the son, was said to have had a substantial income of £1,600 a year and that he was something of a drinker.

Documentation held at Lincolnshire Archives suggests that it was Robert Barkham who was administering financial affairs after the death of his mother. In 1657, he made a conditional surrender of some customary land at Wainfleet, St. Mary, in the Manor of Ingoldmells with Addlethorpe and declared that it was for Sir Robert Barkham's own use and then the use of his son Edward and then the use of the male heirs of Edward and his wife Ann.

Sir Robert Barkham died between 27th February 1660, when he made his will, and 3rd May 1661, when he was recorded as deceased in the Tottenham Manorial Court Rolls. By 1666, the only children surviving were Edward, Robert, Dorcas, Elizabeth, Mary, Jane and Alice. The will of Sir Robert Barkham, of Wainfleet, St. Mary, Lincolnshire, was proved on 18th July 1661 (*PROB 11/305/127*). He requested burial as near as possible to his wife in the church at Tottenham High Cross. He left money for mourning only to his grandchildren, children, brother, Sir Edward, his sister, Dame Jane Caesar, his only surviving siblings and to Thomas Thornley and his servants. Lady Jane

Adelmare alias Caesar died in November 1661 and portraits survive of her and her husband, Sir Charles, who died of smallpox in 1642, as did his daughter and eldest son.

Sir Robert left his bedding, linen and other household goods in his houses in the Parish of St. Mary, Wainfleet and Langton to his son Edward. Edward was in debt to his father and he received bonds and counterbonds. He had married Anne Lee in Westminster in 1655. The intention to marry was declared at Tottenham, although Edward may additionally have kept a house at his father's estate at Wainfleet as he had received his linen and other commodities from his father's dwelling house in Lincolnshire.

Sir Robert bequeathed to his executor and his heirs all his messuages, lands, tenements, marshes and hereditaments in the Parish of Friskney in the County of Lincolnshire, to sell as required to the value of £1,600. From this sum he then left £300 to his son-in-law, John Alured, Jane, his wife, sons and children the balance and any rents and profits from the land not sold to go to his son, Edward. He wrote:

> I give and bequeath onto my executor and his heirs all that my capital messuage or mansion house at Tottenham High Cross in the County of Middlesex and all singular messuages lands tenements meadows pastures and hereditaments with free and copyhold with their every appurtences situated at Tottenham High Cross aforesaid and in Edmonton in the said County of Middlesex.

Barkham's intention was that his executor, James Huxley, had the right to do as he thought fit to achieve the best performance of his will by absolute sale, lease or mortgage before his son, Robert, reached the age of 24. Any profits from the land was to go to Robert or his heirs. He had already made it clear in the will, recorded in the Tottenham Manorial Court Rolls, that the land and house at Tottenham was to go to his second son, just as his father had done for him.

He gave his daughter Dorcas and her heirs £100, which was her portion left to her by her late grandmother, Dame Jane Barkham as well as his tenements, land and hereditaments at Brough, Wainfleet, All Saints, and Thorpe, in the County of Lincolnshire.

Robert Barkham then bequeathed various parcels of land, including Pinfold, Crone Hill, at Wainfleet, St. Mary, Kingsground, Kingsmarsh, Saltergate which he had demised to Thomas Thornley, who occupied the land, among other parcels of land. Any profits were to go to his son, Robert, having formerly settled it on his eldest son, Edward. The yearly rent was to be paid on feast days to James Huxley, his son-in-law and sole executor named in his last will and testament until his son came of age. Barkham requested that James Huxley was, during the child's minority, to bring his son, Robert Barkham, *up to learning and use his best endeavour to make him fit to be a lawyer*. Any other profits from the land were to be divided equally among all his surviving children. In a rather morbid yet pragmatic bequest, he left his death bed, bed sheets, in which he was then lying and furniture to his daughter

Dorcas and his serge bed, in the upper chamber, where "*he lately lay*" with his bedstead, bedding and all other furniture, to his son Robert; both children were unmarried at that time. His other daughters, Mary and Alice, were probably already settled in their respective marital homes and had each received a marriage portion.

There is a diversion here linking Oliver Cromwell, his son Henry and his grandson, also Henry, among others, to the Barkham family. *British History Online* explains that by a deed dated 17th July 1651, Cromwell, *alias* Williams, conveyed the manor of Broughton, in the county of Huntingdon, with capital messuage and the messuage of Horley Farm, occupied by John Disbrowe, brother-in-law of Oliver Cromwell, to Sir Robert Barkham of Wainfleet, in the County of Lincoln and Anne Huxley, spinster, of Edmonton in Middlesex, for the sum of £4,650, paid by James Huxley of London. This was around the period of the Civil War. It is suggested that it was only a mortgage as the name of Henry Cromwell, son of Oliver, was still on the Manorial Court Rolls in 1666. James Huxley, Sir Robert Barkham's son-in-law by virtue of the former's marriage to Elizabeth Barkham appeared, however, to have acquired the Manor, possibly by foreclosure because, in 1678, his daughter and co-heir, Jane, the wife of Sir Nicholas Pelham and Elizabeth the wife of Robert Cresset, conveyed the manor to Robert Jenkinson. Anne Huxley is likely to have been the sister or aunt of James Huxley.

Sir Edward Barkham (1630-1669)

The eldest son, Sir Edward and his wife, Anne, had four children, Robert, Edward, Margaret and Ann but only Robert, born in 1656, survived. In 1664, Sir Edward was Sheriff of Lincoln but he died intestate, aged 38, on 14th September 1669, leaving his widow and son. He was buried at St. Mary, Wainfleet. An entry in the Manorial Court Rolls of Ingoldmells, dated 1st October 1669, recorded that Sir Edward Barkham, a baronet, a free tenant "*seized of one messuage and 55 acres of pasture in Whinthorpe*", had died since the last court. His son Robert Barkham, then under 21 years of age, was named as his next heir. His widow later married John Hodges. Robert, eventually inherited his father's estate and acquired the title.

Sir Robert Barkham (1656-1701)

Sir Edward's son Sir Robert Barkham acquired other land when he married Hester Jeffery on 20th May 1679. In January 1694, an Act of Parliament entitled Barkham's Estate Act, was initiated for vesting the Manors of Earl's Croome and Baughton, in the County of Worcester, held in trust, to be sold for settling the manor of Wainfleet, St. Mary, worth a greater amount, for the benefit of his younger children. The lands were formerly owned by Hester Jeffrey and the trustees gave their consent. It was the same scenario as that initiated by the daughters and heirs of Sir William Barkham after he died in 1695. Robert and Hester had three children, Edward, born in 1680, Mary and

Hester. Sir Robert Barkham, died intestate around June 1701. The administration of his estate was completed in June 1702 by Edward Barkham, Baronet "*the natural son of Sir Robert Barkham of Wainfleet, St Mary, in the County of Lincolnshire*". Hester had died in 1691 and was therefore not cited in the administration.

Sir Edward Barkham (died 1710)

The will of Sir Edward Barkham was made on 19th January 1709 and proved on 13th June 1711 (*PROB 11/521/289*). He died on 1st February 1710 and was buried at All Hallows, Tottenham. He was the son of Robert Barkham (1656-1701) and Hester Jeffrey (1660-1691). The will explained that Edward had two sisters; Mary was married to Samuel Newcomen and received £2,000. Hester married James Smallpiece and received £1,000. Edward did not appear to like either of their husbands as he stated that they had to have no control over their wives' inheritance and asked that they were not to interfere in money matters. He made reference to his dear wife's estate, which was to be sold; Mary was buried at South Thoresby, Lincolnshire, in linen, on 19th December 1709. Sir Edward made a bequest to Mrs. Mary Wooley, the daughter of Charles Wooley, obviously a relative of his deceased wife.

Sir Edward Barkham left his estate to his cousin, Robert Barkham of Wainfleet or his heirs but his title did not transfer. If his cousin, Robert, named as his sole executor and beneficiary, were still abroad, then Sir William Massingberd and Dymoke Walpole were to act as overseers and if Robert Barkham was dead, then his male heir was to be executor and take the estate. Robert was the eldest son of Frances Lister and the late Robert Barkham.

Robert Barkham (1643-1691) and Frances Lister (c.1644-1711/12)

A record of the Barkham family was compiled by the chaplain of Bethlem Hospital, Reverend Edward Geoffrey O'Donoghue (1892-1930) and recorded for lectures in lantern slides made during his lifetime. They are held by the Bethlem Royal Hospital Archives and Museum, Beckenham, in Kent. These include family trees, portraits and photographs. They show that Robert Barkham was baptised in Tottenham on 10th September 1643 and joined Gray's Inn on 5th February 1661.

Robert Barkham (1643-1691), was the second son of Robert Barkham (1598-1661) of Wainfleet, Lincolnshire, Knight. Gray's Inn was commonly used as an educational facility by the landed gentry but it would appear that he did not take up a career in law. An Edward Barkham, possibly his uncle, had been admitted to Gray's Inn on 27th February 1607 or 1608.

Robert married Frances Lister, second daughter of Sir Martin Lister, at St. Michael, Burwell, Louth, Lincolnshire, on 29th January 1667. Frances was born around 1644 and was given the same Christian name as her half-sister, Frances Thornhurst. She had sisters Jane and Susanna Lister and brothers Richard, Michael and Martin Lister (1639-1712), the last who was well-known as a naturalist. Her great-uncle was Sir Matthew Lister, physician to Anne of Denmark, wife of James I and later Charles I. Francis Thornhurst married Richard Jennings, a gentleman from Sandridge, in Hertfordshire and their daughter, Sarah, secretly married John Churchill, Duke of Marlborough in 1677. Sarah Churchill was a close friend of Princess Anne, later Queen Anne.

Sir Martin Lister was the member of Parliament for Buckley in Northamptonshire, from 1640 to 1648 and was a farmer and landowner. In 1646, according to the *ODNB*, the family moved to Thorpe Arnold, in Leicestershire. He also had an estate at Radcliffe in Buckinghamshire but moved to the home of Sir Matthew Lister at Burwell in 1656, to where his uncle had retired. He owned land at Muckton, Burwell and Authorpe. Sir Matthew had no children and in his will he also left houses in Covent Garden to his nephew, Sir Martin Lister, his sole executor. Sir Martin Lister himself was buried at Burwell, on 29th August 1670.

Frances Lister was a daughter by his second wife, Susanna Thornhurst, *née* Temple, widow of Sir Gyfford Thornhurst, who died in 1627 (they had a daughter named Frances Thornhurst). When Susanna married Martin Lister, around 3rd December 1633, her half-brother, Sir Thomas Penniston, acted for her in the marriage settlement (*Yorkshire Archaeological Society: MD335/1/1/33/1*). Susanna was the only daughter of Sir Alexander Temple and the widow, Mary Penniston but she had two brothers, one of whom was James Temple; Mary Temple died in 1607. Susanna Temple was maid of honour to Anne of Denmark and her portrait was painted by Cornelius Johnson (or Jansen) in 1620 posing in her wedding gown, before her marriage to Sir Gyfford Thornhurst. The painting is in the Tate Collection, previously having been in the possession of George Gregory, Esq., of Harlaxton, in Lincolnshire, a relation. A line engraving, dated 1626, of Sir Martin Lister by Robert White, is in the National Portrait Gallery collection.

Sir Thomas Penniston, whose name is recorded on the 1619 map of Tottenham and Edmonton, leasing land and occupying Lordship House, now Bruce Castle Museum, married Martha Temple, a niece of Alexander Temple. He married three times and lived in Oxfordshire and Cornwall. Despite the family connection to the Tottenham area, it was more likely that Frances met Robert Barkham at Burwell, in Lincolnshire, where her family was living, some fifteen miles from the Barkham estate at Wainfleet St. Mary and All Saints.

Robert and Frances' children were Frances, baptised on 8th October 1667, at Burwell, who died 6th December, 1667; Susanna baptised on 15th December 1668, at Burwell; Mary baptised at Burwell on 7th May 1670 and buried on 8th May; Robert born on 12th July 1672 at Louth, in Lincolnshire; Edward born on 6th November 1673 at Kelstern in North Lincolnshire; Michael born on 2nd April 1679 and baptised on 16th April 1679 at St. Mary Magdalene, Lincoln. Susanna was named after her grand-mother, Mary after her great-grandmother, Michael after an uncle and Edward after his great-grandfather, Barkham.

Robert Barkham died on 19th May 1691 and church records show that *Barcham*, of Lincoln, was buried on 22nd May at St. Michael, Burwell; the church has been saved by the Churches Conservation Trust. The tomb is situated outside the church, on the south side, against the wall. It is decorated with a skull and crossed branches on both ends and drapery on the other side. The inscription is in the same words as the following statement that was recorded in the *Lincolnshire Monumental Inscriptions (LI/MI), Volume I, S.O.G., 1674-1979*:

> 77: Here lies the body of Rob:t Barkham, Esq. second son of Rob:t Barkham of Tottenham [High] Cross in ye County of Middlesex, K:t married to Frances ye second daughter of S[ir Martin], of Burwell in the County of Lincoln Frances Susan Mary, aged 47.
>
> *(The information added in square brackets is by the author)*

As an aside, another inscription (*106*) was recorded for one Hugh Alington, of Stenigot, in the County of Lincoln, also buried at Burwell on 3rd June, 1674, aged 39. He also had land at Harrington, in Lincolnshire. He is described as the husband of Jane Lister, also the daughter of Sir Martin Lister. Jane was Hugh's second wife and they had two children, Hugh and Barbara. His son, Hugh, died before his father and was buried with him. Barbara Alington married Richard Pye *(the large monument is inside the church, next to the altar along with those for other members of the Lister family)*. Jane then married John Thynne, of Egham in Berkshire. She was described as a widow, lately of Acton but living in the Parish of St. George, Hanover Square when she died in 1727. In her will she requested burial with her second husband in the vault at Egham. She bequeathed her Manor of Authorpe, Lincolnshire, to George Gregory of Nottingham. In 1750, George Gregory, of Harlaxton, son and sole executor of George Gregory, lately of Nottingham, was involved with the lease and release of a mortgage, on a lease of 1000 years (*1 PG/3/4/2/1 1750*), held at Lincolnshire Archives, taken out, in 1678, by his grandfather, George Gregory.

Frances may have been the executrix or beneficiary of Robert Barkham's estate until her sons reached the age of 21; their eldest son, Robert was only 19 when his father died. The Bethlem Hospital historian described him as of Lincoln, which implies that he spent most of his time there and not at Tottenham. As Robert Barkham had died in 1691, it was probably his heirs and administrators who transferred the land to the younger Robert Barkham. The land or part of it was then transferred from Robert Barkham, in 1694, to one Henry Hayter.

The names of William Barkham, a soldier and Robert Barkham both appeared in the *Defalt Tenentium Liberorum* section (*page 237*) in the copy of the Tottenham Manorial Court Rolls of 19th April 1692. On the same page is the obituary of Robert Barkham, as recorded in the previous court account in October, which recounted (in approximate terms) of:

> Death of Robert Barkham – At this court it was presented by the aforesaid Homage that Robert Barkham, armiger, who held for himself and his heirs certain free lands within this manor of the Lord of this Manor for payment of rent, fealty and suit of court,

has since the last court and before this court died so seized of the said lands and premises by which a relief fell due to the Lord, and since no-one came here to the court to pay the relief fell due to the Lord, therefore the bailiff is ordered to distrain for the said relief and to answer thereto at the next court.

Normally a relief was paid after the death of a free tenant. On 17th April 1694, Robert Barkham, presumably the son, was recorded in the copy of the court rolls (*page 245*) in the *Defalt Liber Tentium* list, with his uncle, Sir William Barkham.

Frances Barkham, wrote her will on 20th October 1711. Frances was then living at "*The Close*" Lincoln. She explained that her late son, Robert, had left to her and her heirs all his land at Wainfleet St. Mary, Wainfleet All Saints, North Holme and Thorpe, in Lincolnshire. Her son had had a mortgage on his land from John Elsington, Esq. She noted that her late son was also indebted to her for the sum of £500 on a mortgage for his said estate and for many years' interest. She gave the £500 plus interest to her friends Margaret Dales, a spinster, of the Parish of St. James, Westminster and John Walpole of Gray's Inn, in London, so that her son's debts be paid. She requested that her friends Dymoke Walpole, of Louth and George Gregory, of Nottingham, sell some land, for the best price, to settle her son's debts and pay the mortgage to John Elsington, Esq. The interest on the remaining sum of money was to be paid to her daughter Astry "*for her sole and separate use and maintenance*" during the course of her natural life. She instructed that, even if her daughter were married or to marry anyone else in the future, she was to receive the bequest as if she were "*sole and unmarried.*"

The will provided further evidence that there was a daughter named Susannah. It was administered on 9th May 1712 (*PROB 11/526/371*). In the accompanying statement, Susanna Astry was described as the wife of Jacob Astry and the natural and legitimate daughter of Frances Barkham. A further statement, in Latin, added in the margin, included the date of 21st January 1719 and in the will described Daniel Leighton as the guardian of Edward Barkham, in his minority, the legatee of Frances Barkham, citizen of London, widow, Susanna Astry being also a legatee. The inclusion of this date may have been due to the death of Susanna Astry. Mrs. Astry was buried in Sir Robert Barkham's vault, on 21st March 1718 at All Hallows, Tottenham). Frances was described in this statement as a citizen of London and not Lincoln.

Frances also specified that Miss Dales and Mr. Walpole were to pay interest to her grandson, Edward Barkham, the only child of her deceased son, Michael Barkham, for his maintenance and education, until he was 21. If her daughter Astry were to die, the principal sum was to go to Edward. If her grandson died before the age of 21 then the sum was to go to someone in the Barkham family: She suggested her "*niece Thornicroft, widow, her executors or administrators*" (Mary Thornicroft was Mary Delaune before her marriage and the widow of Lieutenant-Colonel Edward Thornicroft who was killed in an explosion in Spain in 1709. Mary was the daughter of Dorcas Barkham, elder sister of Robert Barkham, the late husband of Frances). She hoped that her dear son would understand why she chose to bestow her estate on her daughter and grandson. She left £50 for mourning to her son as he had a good estate of his own *"besides the remainder of my nephew Sir Edward Barkham's bequest"*. She hoped that he would be very kind to his sister Astry and his nephew Edward Barkham. Margaret Dales was appointed sole executrix. Frances gave £10 for mourning to *"my daughter"* Jane Barkham and her grandson Edward. George Gregory was also a trustee in her son, Michael's will. Frances Barkham did not state if Gregory was her brother-in-law or nephew as both had the same name; Edward, her only surviving son, was out of the country when she died.

Robert Barkham (1672-1711)

The will of Robert Barkham of Wainfleet, Lincolnshire was written on 10th June 1709 witnessed by John Walpole and others and proved on 8th September 1711 (*PROB 11/523/53*), a few months after his younger brother's death. He left his manors, lands and tenements at Wainfleet, St. Mary and All Saints, North Holme and Thorpe to his widowed mother, Frances and nominated her as executrix. He stated that he owed money on a mortgage to John Elsington. It was Robert who, most likely, transferred the land at Tottenham, to Henry Hayter in 1694.

Lincolnshire Archives Committee (Report 22) helps to explain the situation surrounding the death of Robert Barkham. His cousin, Sir Edward Barkham, died in 1710. The latter's will had devised all his lands to trustees, who were to sell all or part of them to pay his debts and legacies. Any residue of his estate was to go to his cousin Robert Barkham and his the latter's heirs or those of his great-grandfather, Sir Robert Barkham. Attempts were made to contact Robert Barkham, which took some time. Pressure was put on one of Edward Barkham's trustees, Sir William Massingberd, to resolve the issue as Sir Edward Barkham had let his finances descend into a terrible state. His friends risked ruin and he had debts of £12,000. He had not paid any tradesmen and his steward had no accounts. Furthermore, Sir Edward, before his death, had hoped to settle his debts by selling half of the estate inherited by his wife from Robert Boswell of Thoresby, her uncle but before the *"fine"* was completed Mary Barkham, *née* Woolley, died.

Mary Woolley was the daughter of Anne Boswell and John Woolley, though Edward, in his will, referred to her as the daughter of Charles Wooley, late of Alford. William Marwood, on behalf of his wife, the sister of Robert Boswell, claimed the other half of the Boswell estate and went to court to settle the matter. As late as November 1716 there was an assignment of term for 1000 years of the Manor of Dalby when Edward Barkham of Wainfleet, executor of the will of his late cousin Sir Edward Barkham, himself the administrator of the goods of his deceased wife Dame Mary, along with William Marwood of South Thoresby and Mary his wife, Frances, wife of William Smithson, Doctor of Physic, and Alice, late wife of Dymoke Walpole of Louth, all administrators of the late Robert Boswell of South Thoresby were all parties to the deed.

Edward Barkham (1673-1732)

Robert Barkham, Sir Edward Barkham's cousin and beneficiary, had been killed in Spain. Robert's brother, Michael had also died and their brother, Edward Barkham, as next male heir, was far away in India and it would have taken some time for a message to reach him by ship. Then his mother, Frances Barkham, died. In the prevailing circumstances, the two sisters of the late Sir Edward, Mary Newcomen and Hester Smallpiece, took the view that as their brother's heir had actually died before him, in law, he had died intestate and they presented a suit declaring themselves to be co-heirs to their brother's estate. In the background were the creditors standing to lose everything because of their unpaid debts, so they initiated a Bill in Chancery, against the trustees to recover the money owed to them. Edward Barkham eventually arrived back in London from India in the summer of 1714. He was unhappy about the handling of the situation by the trustees, in particular Massingberd and demanded that a stop be put to the lawsuits, which culminated in Edward Barkham eventually taking Chancery proceedings against Massingberd in 1715. Finally, in 1717, the matter was settled when the Lord Chancellor decreed that the estate was to go to Edward Barkham, the plaintiff, after all debts were paid.

In the *Diaries and Consultation Books of the East India Company* (British Library), during the years 1709-1714, Edward Barkham was cited a number of times. In 1710 and 1711, he was listed as a freeman at Fort St. George, India. He was obviously a religious man as there was also an account of him as a signatory to a petition, as a churchwarden of St. Mary's Church, Fort St. George, Madras, complaining about the activities surrounding the coconut tree in the churchyard. There were, according to the petitioners, noisy drinking sessions by the buffalo keepers in the evening. The latter were allegedly stabling buffalo using makeshift shelters of the tombs in the churchyard, creating a great mess and causing many complaints for their irreverence to a hallowed space. Barkham was still there in January 1714, being declared absent from a meeting in February but back again later. He may have left after this time to return to address his family's affairs.

In 1721, around ten years after the death of Robert Barkham and his mother, some of the freehold estate at Wainfleet was advertised for sale in the *London Gazette* in the issue of May 21, 1723-May 25, 1723:

> Notice is hereby given that pursuant to an order of the High Court of Chancery such of the creditors of Robert Barkham, late of Wainfleet in the County of Lincoln, Esq.: deceased son of Frances Barkham, late of Lincoln, widow deceased (who has not already proved their debts) that they do come in and prove the same before John Borrett, Esq. one of the masters of the said Court at his chambers in Symons Inn, Chancery Lane, in six weeks time from the date thereof otherwise they will be excluded the benefit intended them thereby

On 9th July 1728, Edward Barkham, Esq., of the Parish of Wainfleet, in the County of Lincoln, stated in person that he was above forty years of age and a widower. He announced his intention to marry Mary Wheeler, a widow of St. Anne's, Westminster, in the County of Middlesex (*Faculty Office Marriage Allegation*). They married at St. Andrew, Holborn, in London, on 11th July 1728, by licence. He had been, by his own declaration, at Fort St. George, working in the East Indies, before his marriage (*document at TNA: C11/263/36*). This document, dated 1730, included a copy of his brother's and mother's wills.

A further document at *TNA* (*C11/245/16*), dated 1731, explained a legal action entitled *Gregory v. Barkham*. George Gregory, of Nottingham and his heirs, Gregory being one of the trustees named in the will of Frances Barkham, who, along with Mary Thornicroft, a widow, of the Parish of St. George the Martyr, Middlesex, had been instructed to sell land to pay off her son's debts. Mary Thornicroft, niece of Frances, was the member of the Barkham family who would inherit the estate if Frances' daughter Astry and grandson, also Edward, were to die. This had apparently happened. Edward argued that he should have inherited the estate by "*tenant in tail*" as his "*said brother Robert Barkham had no power to dispose of the same by will or any other ways to his said mother Frances Barkham or any other person*" and he alleged that £2,000 had been left for "*the younger children of said marriage who were three in number*". This may have been a reference to the as yet undiscovered will of his father Robert Barkham, Esq., who had inherited the estate from his father, Sir Robert Barkham, in 1661. The three younger children of the marriage were Robert, Edward, Michael and/or Susanna. It would appear that Edward won the case as the land was in his possession at the time of his death in the following year.

Edward Barkham died on 6th March 1732, aged 59. He had married late in life, at the age of fifty-four; there were no children. An entry in the *Daily Courant*, dated Tuesday 27th March 1733, reported that he had died a few days previously at Lincoln. It went on to describe how Edward Barkham was formerly a director of the East India Company who had resided for many years in India and that he had left the bulk of his estate to charitable uses, in particular an estate worth, in rental income, £900 per annum, to the directors of the Bethlem Hospital. The estate, of some 3000 acres, was primarily in the Parish of Wainfleet, St. Mary.

His will was proved on 19th May 1733 (*PROB 11/659/167*). He requested burial in the chancel at the Church of St. Mary, Wainfleet, Lincolnshire. Edward Barkham named his cousin as Samuel Newcomen and Mary, the latter's wife and Edward's sister-in-law Jane, as the wife of Major Leighton (she was the widow of his late brother Michael, living at Queen Street, in Westminster. There was no mention of Michael's son and his nephew, Edward Barkham). Barkham's bequest to the governors of Bethlem Hospital in Moorfields was to help improve the:

> ...deplorable condition and circumstances of my poor fellow crea-
> tures who labour under the extreme affliction of insanity of mind

... for the further and better support, reliefe and maintenance of
poor incurable lunaticks...

Edward's wife, Mary, his cousin Samuel Newcomen, Robert Harr, the
elder and Thomas Marwood were executrix and executors of his estate.
Thomas Marwood was the steward of the estate and may have been the son
of William Marwood, referred to above, in one of the legal disputes. Thomas
Marwood was born at Laughton, Gainsborough, Lincoln on 10th December
1688. Edward wrote his will in 1729 and added a codicil on 14th February
1732. He left his wife their house at *The Close* in Lincoln, for the term of
her natural life as a widow. A description of the property included outhouses,
brew houses, stables, yards, gardens, orchards and the contents of the house.
If she married again it was to go to the hospital. *The Close* was probably the
house in which his mother lived. His estate included the manors of Hanby
and Anderby, Wainfleet, St. Mary and All Saints with Firsby in Lincolnshire.

Edward Barkham was buried at St. Mary, Wainfleet. This church is situated quite some distance away from the village of Wainfleet All Saints, in
open countryside. *Volume 37, of Lincolnshire Monumental Inscriptions* (LI/
M37: SOG) includes a description of the monument to Edward Barkham decorated with his coat of arms and pillars. There are two tablets on either side of
the chancel walls dedicated to Edward Barkham. One describes all the items
in the church for which he paid. When Edward Barkham died, the Bethlem
Hospital was situated at Moorfields near Bishopsgate but was moved south of
the Thames in 1815 to a new building at a St. George's Fields, Southwark, off
Lambeth Road, on what is now the main part of the Imperial War Museum.
The bequest supported the *"Incurable department"* at Bethlem Hospital. In
1919, the governors disposed of the land at Wainfleet and in 1930 the hospital
was moved out of London.

Mary Newcome, a cousin of Edward Barkham, took a legal action against
the governors of the Bethlem Hospital in 1735 to try to recover some of
her cousin's inheritance. She was obviously unhappy about his decision to
bequeath it for the benefit of others, although his great-grandfather had made
generous donations to the same hospital. She was a widow, living also at *The
Close*, Lincoln, at the time of her death in 1741. Her will referred to her late
brother, who chose to give his estate to his cousin.

The Barkham Estate at Wainfleet, which had once belonged to the younger
Robert Barkham and then to his brother Edward, was listed again in the press
on 15th December 1741. It was described as a *"freehold estate lying near
Wainfleet in the County of Lincoln, part of the estate of Robert Barkham, late
of Wainfleet aforesaid deceased"*. It may have been the trustees of Bethlem
Hospital who put the land up for sale. In the village of Wainfleet All Saints,
there are streets named Barkham and Bethlem.

Michael Barkham (1679-1711) and Jane Thurrold (1687-1759)

Michael Barkham was the youngest son of Robert and Frances Barkham. The
marriage of Michael Barkham, of Wainfleet to Jane Thurrold, of Lincoln,

was recorded in the *Lincolnshire Register of Marriages, 1562-1837,* on 13th November 1707. Jane was baptised at St. Peter, Eastgate, Lincoln, on 8th November 1687. Her parents were Nathaniel Thorold and Elizabeth Lascelles, of Lincoln. Her father died in 1693 and her mother in 1705. Jane's brother, John Thurrold married Eleanor Lister, sister of Mathew Lister.

Michael wrote his will on 22nd April 1710, and was living at that time at Kingston upon Hull, Yorkshire. The will was proved on 15th June 1711 (*PROB 11/521/308*). He explained that he had been involved in a Chancery suit against Mrs. Darwin, a widow, contesting the will of Elizabeth Thorold, his mother-in-law, for the recovery of £1,000. (*A case report, Barkham v. Thorold, dated 1709, indicated that the couple were already married.*) When he wrote the will, his wife was not pregnant so the child was born in late 1710 or early in 1711. Michael nominated George Gregory and Sir William Burnett of *The Close,* Lincoln, to assist his wife, who was the sole executrix. He is likely to have been buried on 9th February, 1711 and was only 31 when he died. George Gregory, of Nottingham, had married Susanna Lister on 21st January 1663. She was the sister of Frances Barkham. George Gregory was probably a cousin of Michael Barkham. At the time of her death in Nottingham in 1713, Susanna Gregory was a widow. Her son George, named in her will with other members of her family, was also married to a woman named Suzanna.

Jane Barkham, Michael's widow, married Daniel Leighton, second son of Sir Edward Leighton, on 8th June 1717 at Lincoln's Inn Chapel, Holborn, in London. Daniel and Jane Leighton had children named Herbert, Edward, Elizabeth Ann and Jane, born between 1725 and 1731. Her son by her first husband, Edward Barkham, may have died young. An entry in the *British Gazetteer* dated 1st May 1736 reported that the Honourable Mrs. Leighton, wife of Major Leighton of Horseguards and the son of Sir Edward Leighton of Wattlesborough, Salop, became a Lady of the Bedchamber to the Princess of Wales. Following in his mother's footsteps, according to the *Whitehall Evening Post,* on 11th February, 1748, Herbert Leighton was appointed as a gentleman usher to the Prince of Wales.

The *Universal Chronicle or Weekly Gazette* for the week 9-16 June 1759 announced the death of the Lady of Colonel Leighton, woman of the bedchamber to the Princess of Wales, on 10th June 1759 at Boreham, in Essex. The will of Daniel Leighton, written in 1759, of the same place, was proved on 29th January 1765. He named his son, Herbert Leighton and daughters, Jane Cope and Elizabeth Ann Sabine, of Brussels, along with grandchildren Harriot and Francis Leighton (Jane Cathcart, *née* Leighton, widow, married Jonathan Cope around 1752). The Honourable Jane Cope, widow of Sir Jonathan Cope, died in Bath in 1770 and Herbert Leighton, in 1772.

Jane Barkham (born 1632) and her husband John Alured (Allured)

Jane Barkham married John Alured (also known as Allured). The couple had two children prior to 1658. John was the son of John Alured, a member of a Puritan family from Hull in Yorkshire, who inherited the family estates in 1628.

John, the father, died in 1651, as evidenced by a legal case in the Court of Chancery that year, held at *TNA (C10/14/3)*, initiated by Mary, his widow, then living at Preston in Yorkshire. The father was a parliamentarian during the Civil War and is noted as one of the signatories to the death warrant of Charles I, in his capacity as a member of the High Court of Justice, to which he had been appointed in 1648. The elder John Alured, by then deceased, after the restoration of the monarchy, was charged with regicide by Charles II and as a result the Crown had the right to confiscate any property belonging to his beneficiaries. The *ODNB* states that John Alured, senior, married twice. In 1631, he married Mary Darley, with whom he had two or perhaps three sons but she died in 1635. He then, around 1640, married Mary Arnold, with whom he had one son and two daughters before he deserted them.

The elder John Alured may have died before his son married Jane. Later, Jane Alured's name appears in a document at TNA (*E/134/ 28 Chas 2/East 11*) from January 1676 to January 1677 as the administratrix of the goods and chattels of John Alured, Esq., deceased, described as the son of John Alured and his wife Mary Darley, daughter of Richard. A dispute with one George Coatsforth related to rectory land in the Parish of Sculcoats, at Kingston upon Hull, addressing the receipt by her deceased husband of an income during the years 1657 to 1667, partly during the reign of Charles II. It has been suggested that the son died fighting in Ireland in 1659. Another document, from 1661, would appear to suggest that he was still alive at that time. Jane Alured's daughter Jane married William Pincke and their son, Alured Pincke married Mary Faunce. The Shorsted Estate in Kent, of Jane Delaune, a widow, who remarried Edward Dering, found its way to this branch of the family.

Mary Barkham (died 1662) and Richard Nelthorpe

Mary Barkham had married Richard Nelthorpe. There is evidence of their marriage settlement dated 3rd May 1654, for land at Scawby and Bradley, now in Humberside. The marriage licence, dated 13th July 1654, declared that both were living in the Parish of St. Andrew's Holborn, in London. It may be that Robert Barkham had a house there. Mary died in 1662 and her husband may have remarried.

Alice Barkham (1634-1676) and Robert Coney

Alice Barkham, married Robert Coney in 1655 and died in 1676.

Dorcas Barkham (1636-1720), William Delaune and Edward Dering

Dorcas Barkham married William Delaune *(spelt in a variety of different ways)*. The licence was dated 10th May 1662 and the marriage took place either at St. Gregory or Clement Danes, in London. He was a widower, aged 30 and she was a spinster, aged 22, living in the Parish of St. Margaret, Lothbury. Her parents were deceased. Other records suggest that she was born on 29th September 1636 which would have made her 26 at the time. On 5th May 1662, a lease for a year was granted from Dorcas Barkham, described as the daughter of Sir Robert Barkham, of Wainfleet, to William Delaune of Sharsted in Kent for lands at Winthorpe, Burgh and Wainfleet, All Saints. The witness was John Nelthorpe, presumably a relation of her brother-in-law, Richard Nelthorpe. This was part of her marriage settlement.

Delaune was the grandson of a Huguenot refugee, Gideon Delaune. William had a daughter, Anne, from his first wife, Anne. Dorcas and William had two children, William and Mary. Sir William Delaune died in 1667 and is buried at Doddington. His son, William Delaune married a widow, Anne Swift and his daughter, Mary Delaune, at the age of 22, married Edward Thornicroft, aged 24, of the Parish of St. Andrew, Holborn, Middlesex. A marriage licence was granted on 7th January 1687. When the younger William Delaune died in 1739, the estate went to his nephew, Gideon Thornicroft, son of his sister, Mary.

There is a record of another marriage on 2nd September 1669, between Dame Dorcas Delaune, of Sharsted in Kent, widow, aged about 25 (which appears inaccurate), to Edward Dering, of London, a bachelor, about 30, at Camberwell, in Surrey. Edward was an M.P. like his father but the elder Sir Edward died in London in 1684. He was buried at Pluckley in Kent although his will described him as living at St. Martin-in-the-Fields. His son and heir died intestate five years later. A House of Lords Estate Bill, dated 13th January 1693, would appear to confirm that when he died, his trustees and executors applied to sell his land to pay his debts. Dame Dorcas Dering is said to have died on 31st October 1720.

Elizabeth Barkham and James Huxley (Died 1672)

A History of the County of Oxford, Volume 11, Wootton Hundred (northern part) indicates that the earliest record of James Huxley, in 1640, was in connection with a mortgage for a number of years on the estate of Dornford in Wootton, in Oxfordshire, once owned by Francis Gregory and sold by his son Thomas to Edmund Goodyer of Heythrop, to discharge his debts. James Huxley apparently acquired the estate in 1653 and the transaction was later disputed. However, in 1660, Huxley was living at Dornford and was the M.P. for Oxford for a very short time. He died in 1672 but his will was not proved until 1673. In it, he listed the Manor of Broughton, the Manor of Dornford and Wedmore in Somerset. They were to go to his wife Elizabeth and his daughters. His wife received £2,000 and the residences were to be divided between his two daughters. Jane received £800. Dornford passed to his two married daughters, Jane Pelham and Elizabeth Cresset. Sir Nicholas Pelham and his wife lived there for a number of years but in 1679 they were forced to sell the estate by order of Chancery to pay off their father's debts. One might assume that the estate at Broughton, to which reference is made above, was sold for the same reason in 1678, to Sir Robert Jenkinson, who may have been related by marriage to the Barkham family.

The will of Nathaniel Wilcocke of Tottenham High Cross confirms that James Huxley had married Elizabeth Barkham before 1st November 1658, when the will was made. It was dated 17th June 1659 and the name of Wilcox was written on the back. Nathaniel cited his nieces as Mary Willis, Elizabeth Huxley and Jane Alured. Mary Willis received his freehold and copyhold land at Tottenham High Cross; Elizabeth received freehold and copyhold land at Fryarin, in Essex, which was then to go to her daughters Jane and Elizabeth; Jane Alured received a messuage and lands at Ingatestone, in Essex, which was then to go to her daughters, also named Jane and Elizabeth. He left £20 for mourning to Sir Robert Barkham, his brother-in-law and Wilcox identified his nieces and nephews as Edward Barkham, Robert Barkham, Mary Nelthorpe, Anne Coney and Dorcas Barkham. His diamond ring, already in the possession of his niece, Elizabeth Huxley, was to be delivered to the younger Jane Alured at the age of 12 or if she died it was to go to her sister Elizabeth and if she died to the younger daughter of Elizabeth Huxley. Mary Willis and Elizabeth Huxley were his executrices. In October 1659, in the Manorial Court Rolls *at page 99*, the reversion from Nathaniel Wilcocke to Mary Willis was recorded. It also confirms that Mary Willis was the daughter of Thomas Wilcocke and the wife of John Willis of the University of Oxford.

Elizabeth and James Huxley's daughters, Jane and Elizabeth, married after 1659. The will of Elizabeth Cressett, a widow of Holton, Oxfordshire, was proved on 21st January 1692. Her will helps to explain who among the other relatives were still alive and where they were. She bequeathed to her daughter, Katherine, her houses and land in Shropshire for 99 years and then to her brother-in-law, Sir Nicholas Pelham, of Catsfield in Sussex and Sir Robert Jenkinson of Walcot in Oxford and their heirs, her daughter to take all the profits. In a convoluted way, she explained how it was to be handed on. After her daughter Katherine's death it was to go to her eldest son and then to her mother Elizabeth Huxley, her son Edward, his first son and then to her sister Katherine Cressett for life and to the right heirs of the testatrix. Obviously, her mother, Elizabeth Huxley was still alive. She left her diamond ring to her son Edward. Sir Nicholas Pelham, Sir Robert Jenkinson, her father-in-law, Robert Cressett and her sister Katherine Cressett received £10 for mourning. Robert Barkham (her cousin or son of her cousin), her aunt Lady Deering, living at Red Lion Street in Holborn, London, Mr. and Mrs. Pinck, Jane Knight and Mrs. Katherine Sheppard, possibly relatives, were each to receive a gold ring. Jane Alured's daughter, Jane, married William Pinck. Elizabeth Cressett explained that her son Edward was to inherit his grandfather's estate (Robert Cressett) and that she had spent a considerable sum on his education and clothing for him to be a gentleman. His guardians and executors were Sir Nicholas Pelham, Sir Robert Jenkinson and Frances Wheate. As a memento she gave a ring worth 20 shillings to her uncle Thomas Huxley, to Mr. Wheate and his wife, Mrs. Mary Willis and her daughter, Margaret, of Oxford, rings worth 12 shillings. One might assume that her sister, Jane Pelham, was already dead as she received nothing in the will.

Documents at the *LMA* confirm that she was indeed the same Mary Willis mentioned as the niece of Nathaniel Wilcocke, *above*. Mrs. Willis, of Oxford, was involved in mortgaging, bargaining and selling, for various amounts, a freehold messuage, freehold cottages with orchards and gardens, 20 acres of freehold land at Tottenham High Cross with all other freehold property belonging to her between 1688 and 1690. She died around 1708. She did not leave a will and one Pickering, who may have been a relative of John Pickering, one of the beneficiaries in Dame Jane Barkham's will, acquired her land.

17

Sir William Barkham and Barkham's title

William Robinson, in Appendix 111 to Volume I of his book, *The History and Antiquities of the Parish of Tottenham, Volume 2* (*edition printed in 1840*), prefaced the account of *"Barkham's title"* by writing that the land, including that at Tottenham High Cross, had been sold or mortgaged at different times in separate parcels. As Sir Edward Barkham (1571-1634) had two sons, Edward and Robert, it may be that the estate was split other than as suggested in the account by *British History Online,* as *BHO* intimates that Robert Barkham, his grandson, was to inherit only Crooks Farm. The purpose of this chapter is to seek to explore what land was held by Sir Edward's grandson, Sir William Barkham, whose father, Sir Edward Barkham and mother, Frances died in 1667 and how it eventually passed to Ephraim Beauchamp. The passing of the greater part of the land is dealt with elsewhere.

In Robinson's book, an indenture is referenced, dated 10th October 1683, among Sir William Barkham of East Walton in Norfolk and his wife Dame Judith, Thomas Halsey of Great Gaddesden, Hertford, Sir William Franklin, of Malvern, in the county of Bedford, of the one part and Martin Folkes and Andrew Card, gentleman, both of Gray's Inn of the other part. It states that by indentures of lease and release dated 17th and 18th April 1764:

> ...the release being of three parts and made between the said Sir William Barkham (by the name of William Barkham, citizen and brazier of London, one of the sons of Sir Edward Barkham, Knight and baronet, deceased) of the first part, said Dame Judith Halsey, then the wife of William Barkham (by the name of Judith Halsey, one of the daughters of Sir John Halsey deceased) of the second part, and Sir Edward Barkham, of Westacre, in the county of Norfolk, Baronet, and Thomas Halsey, the said Sir William Franklin and Anthony Smithson, Roger Gillingham and John Franklin, Esq. of the third part. In consideration of a marriage then intended between William Barkham and Judith Halsey.

William Barkham conveyed and assigned the messuages, closes, farms and land at Tottenham to Thomas Halsey and Sir William Franklin, to:

> ...the use of William Barkham for life, without impeachment of waste-remainder... to trustees... to said Dame Judith Barkham for life in bar of dower"... remainder to the first and all the

sons of Sir William Barkham on the body of said Dame Judith…
in tail male-remainder to said Sir Edward Barkham, the father,
Anthony Smithson, Roger Gillingham and John Franklin, their
executors, administrators and assigns for 500 years…and reciting that the said marriage had taken effect and there were no
sons then begotten.

It was witnessed and agreed that the said parties and Sir William Barkham
did grant and agree with Folkes and Card and their heirs to levy a fine before
Micklemas. (*A dower was a widow's right to one third of her late husband's
property by the custom of the City of London.*) The remainder referred to the
person to inherit the estate and his heirs and if there were no heirs, then the next
person in line inherited. There were a number of discrepancies in certain of the
dates, which may have been transcription errors (17th and 18th April, 1764 were
more likely to have been in 1674) as the date of the other indenture was 1683.
William Barkham married Judith Halsey before 1683. He was in possession of
some of the land that his grandfather owned in 1619, possibly inherited from
his father or bought or mortgaged from someone else. Table 17.1 outlines the
land described in the indentures relating to the marriage settlement.

To sum up, all the parcels of land included in the indenture, at Tottenham
High Cross and Edmonton were two messuages, three gardens, four orchards, 70
acres of land, 20 acres of meadow, 50 acres of pasture and 25 acres of marshland
amounting to over 175 acres. There was no reference to *Oatfields, Great or Little
Snares Mead, Thistly Field* or *Great or Little Gallow Field* owned by Sir Edward
Barkham in 1619. The land had been divided after that date.

Sir William Barkham (1638-1695) and Judith Halsey had at least six
daughters and one son. Some of the children's births were registered at All
Hallows, Honey Lane, in London. Dorothy was born in 1678, Jane in 1683,
Mary in 1686, Theodosia in 1687 (named after either her aunt, Theodosia
Halsey or her grandmother), Anne in 1688 and Edward in 1692. His birth
was registered at St. Andrew's Church in Holborn, where the family were
living at the time. There was also a daughter named Frances. She was listed
in Robinson's book as the second child, possibly born between 1678-1683.
Robinson records in a footnote to his book that in 1683 there were no sons
of the marriage and there was further investigation around 1790 to prove if
there was a son, because of the original controversy when the will was written
and the land was being sold by the then owner, William Beauchamp Proctor.

A further indenture, dated 14th July 1694, was reported in William Robinson's book between Sir William Barkham of the first part and Luke Robinson,
of Gray's Inn, of the second. It recorded that:

…in consideration of £1,000, paid by Luke Robinson did demise,
grant bargain and sell all that said messuage….to Robinson, his
executors and assigns, subject to a redemption on payment of
£1,000 by Sir William Barkham to Robinson.

This was a 500 year lease. Sir William Barkham borrowed £1,000 on a mortgage.

Table 17.1 The Barkham land in 1683.

Description of land	Location	Occupier
Capital messuage or tenement, with gardens, orchards, yards and pasture ground (6 acres) This was copyhold land on 1619 map.	Tottenham High Cross	Then or late in tenure or occupation by Lady Coleraine or her under tenants
Messuage lying near outhouses of one above	"	Samuel Randall
4 closes of pasture called "Hawkin's Field" (16 acres)	"	Samuel Randall
1 little close of pasture beside one above (2 acres) (In 1811 known as "Holloway Piece")	"	Samuel Randall
6 closes lying near the Parsonage, called "Crookes Grove" (30 acres)	"	Samuel Randall
Marsh land in the Wild Marsh (9 acres)	"	Samuel Randall
Marsh ground at "Clendish Hills" (3 acres) (Now known as Glendish)	"	Samuel Randall
Arable land in the common field called the "Languidge" (7 acres)	Edmonton	Samuel Randall
1 close of pasture (6 acres)	Tottenham High Cross	Widow Bray
Marsh land (3 acres)	Edmonton	Widow Bray
Garden ground called "Trotter's Garden"	Tottenham High Cross	Thomas Holloway
Close or pasture ground "Slyfield" (6 acres)	"	Thomas Wythered
Little wood called "Dolbys" (18 acres)	"	Edward Bridgeman
Little wood called "Little Raynald's" (3 acres)	"	Edward Bridgeman
4 closes of enclosed arable and pasture ground (19 acres)	Tottenham High Cross/ Edmonton	John Parrett
I little close called the "Grove" (11.5 acres)	Tottenham High Cross/ Edmonton	John Parrett
Marsh ground (3 acres)	Edmonton	John Parrett
Arable land in common field called "The Hyde" (1 acre)	Edmonton	Edward Salter
Arable land in field called "Mill Field" (1 acre)	Edmonton	Edward Salter
Arable land in common field called "Oakfield" (6 acres) All premises called "Crook's" Farm on the south side of White Hart Lane.	Edmonton	Joseph Salter

Sir William Barkham, of East Walton in Norfolk, died in December, 1695. Both he and his only son Edward were buried on 28th December 1695, at the Church of St. George, Southacre, in Norfolk, alongside many other deceased relatives of the Barkhams and Coneys. Edward was only four when he died. Barkham had been living at Great Kirby Street, near Hatton Garden, in the Parish of St. Andrew's, Holborn but he also had the estate at East Walton in Norfolk. The codicils explain that Sir William's will was written when he was very ill and the executors were witnesses to this fact. They show that he owed £4,000 on a mortgage to Sir John, Samuel and William Lethieullier on the land he held in Norfolk. The executors of the will were given instructions to sell such properties in Middlesex and the City of London owned by William Barkham to pay the outstanding mortgage on *"his manors messuages lands and hereditaments in Norfolk"* which he had wanted to remain with the family. The trustees, Coney, Walpole and Gilbert were to pay any surplus to the Barkham heirs after debts were paid. More funds would be raised for the remaining Barkham children by the rents on land in Norfolk than on those in London. Dame Judith was to receive jewels, rugs, watches and ornaments and her *"wearing apparel"*. Dorothy, her daughter, was to receive £500 when she achieved the age of consent or married. The estate was to be divided among them equally at the age of consent or when they married. If they died before achieving the age of consent at twenty-one, their share was to be divided equally by the surviving daughters. Funeral expenses, legacies had to be paid.

An account that related to the Act of Parliament, making good the last will and testament of Sir William Barkham was written in the *House of Commons Journal, Volume 11 (1693-1697)*. It explained the situation surrounding his death. The Archives at the House of Lords record six Bills amended a number of times before finally passed. The first was on 10th February 1695, two months after his death. According to the Bill, the executors had renounced their executorships in favour of the suppliant, *viz.* Dame Judith, maker of the petition, who was the relict, as the children were of tender years. The petition stated that the *"interest and charge of debts will greatly waste and eat up all of the same (inheritance) to the great damage if not the ruin of the said children"*.

Thomas Gilbert testified that he had been called to the house of Sir William Barkham on 21st December and was requested by Sir William to write his will, which he dictated. Barkham asked Gilbert to call in Robert Walpole, who was in the next room, so that he could read it through again. Gilbert confirmed that Barkham was of good understanding and memory. There were three other witnesses in the other room. When Gilbert asked Barkham if he wanted them to witness the will, the testator raised himself up in the bed and the will was placed on a book to sign but then, with the pen in his hand to sign, his *"spirits sunk"* and he fell into a slumber. Three hours later he died.

Colonel Walpole, trustee and kindred of Barkham gave his account. He stated that if the Lady Barkham *"should have a son"* the Norfolk estate was to be preserved for the child. This suggests that Judith Barkham was pregnant when her husband died but that her child must have died, as there is no record of another birth. The Bill was for the advantage of the son if any were to be born. Mr. Fowkes explained the financial situation. The rent on the estate in London and Middlesex was £300, whereas the Norfolk estate was worth £1,500 per annum. Sir William Barkham had debts of £11,000 but he had cleared all but £4,000 before his death. One of the issues raised related to a lease for 500 years for messuages and premises lying in the County of Middlesex and the City of London. Reference was made to Tottenham and Edmonton, as it was to land in the Parish of Saint Giles without Cripplegate. The Bill declared that:

...by and out of monies raised by such sales should pay and discharge all his debts legacies and funerary charges (other than and except the debt of £4000 owed by him to Sir John Lethieullier, Knight) upon a mortgage of some of the manors and messuages in the County of Norfolk.

The Bill was read a third time, was passed and went to the House of Lords. The main papers held by the House of Lords of the amended Act were delivered on Wednesday 10th April 1696. Probate was granted on 24th January 1696 *(PROB 11/433/205)*. The land was to be sold by the trustees for the purposes expressed in the will of Sir William Barkham.

Dame Judith Barkham, by then a widow, married John Holworthy on 19th June, 1697 at Westminster Abbey. It was eighteen months after the death of her first husband. The courtship of Holworthy may have been conducted as the Bills, Acts of Parliament and petitions were being made for the resolution of Barkham's will. One Bill was presented to the Court of Chancery on 21st June 1697, just two days after Dame Judith married John Holworthy. She and the trustees were at odds with her daughters' action as they were on opposing sides and indeed Judith's financial situation may have been somewhat insecure, with considerable debts. It was the case that, according to wills of the City of London, normally the estate was divided in three portions after debts were paid, the first to the wife, the second among the children and then the third as requested by the donor. As some of the children were under-age the capital would have been held in trust by the City of London and not paid by the City to the children until marriage or they came of age. The inference is that Dame Judith, as the widow, did not appear to receive the share which should have been hers by right. It was common in wills that the wife is described as *"loving"* or discussed in an endearing way but it was not the case in this will. Perhaps her relationship with her husband was not a good one and that it is what is excluded rather than included that might lead to this conclusion.

The trustees became free to sell that part of the estate, in London and Middlesex, to the best bidder to be apparent to Dr. Edisbury, an official of the Court. Ephraim Beauchamp made the highest bid at £3100, confirmed on 4th May 1699 and his was accepted. It was agreed that the sum of £421 was to be paid to Luke Robinson for outstanding principal and interest on the mortgage from 1694 and £2,678 went to the heirs of William Barkham. A footnote in William Robinson's book stated that £600 had been paid back to Luke Robinson in Barkham's lifetime but there was still an outstanding debt. The remainder was to be paid to Thomas Gilbert, one of the trustees and the nominal sum of five shillings apiece to Walpole, Coney and Halsey. It was granted in *"pursuance of said Act of Parliament"* to Beauchamp, his heirs and assigns and a receipt was issued for £2,678 12shs.

This legal action was resolved by an indenture of bargain and sale, dated 23rd May 1699, enrolled in Chancery between Walpole, Coney, Gilbert and Halsey of the one part and Ephraim Beauchamp of the other part. An indenture of assignment, dated 23rd May 1699 made between Walpole, Coney, Gilbert and Halsey of the first part, Luke Robinson of the second part and Ephraim Beauchamp, Robert Barker of London, gentleman and Lawrence Spencer, a gentleman, of the third part, recited the indenture of mortgage made on 14th July 1694, stating that Beauchamp had purchased of Barkham's executors the *"above mentioned messuages, &c., and the money due on the mortgage was agreed to be paid off out of the purchase money and the mortgage was to be assigned in trust to protect"*. Beauchamp paid Robinson the principal and interest of £421 and the said messuages, land etc., originally mortgaged by Sir William Barkham were passed to Barker and Spencer and their executors, administrators or assigns for the remainder of the 500 year lease that was unexpired. The daughters were not mentioned but Coney, Walpole, Gilbert and Halsey were the trustees of the will. It was recorded in Chancery that Robert Walpole, Robert Coney, Thomas Gilbert and Thomas Halsey of Great Gaddeston in Hertford and their heirs, were to sell the land, in trust, for purposes of the will to Ephraim Beauchamp, a mason of London, for the benefit of the daughters of William Barkham, Dorothy, Frances, Jane, Mary, Theodosia and Anne.

The indenture was the formal handing over of the land to Ephraim Beauchamp following Bills, Acts of Parliament and the Court of Chancery ruling, a long drawn out process taking some four years. The trustees of Sir William Barkham had sold the land at Tottenham in May 1699 but there was still a mortgage on the land in Norfolk. The money raised from the sale of the land did not clear the mortgage to Sir John Lethieullier and his two brothers on his estate in Norfolk.

In 1699, Ephraim Beauchamp became the new owner of Sir William Barkham's land at Tottenham and acquired the main house opposite the Rectory. The original house, shown on the Earl of Dorset Map of 1619, had been owned by Sir Edward Barkham and passed to his son, Sir Robert and then to his brother, Sir Edward. When the Barkham family owned it, it was called *"Crooks Farm"* but it was rebuilt and renamed *"White Hall"*. Today, the only reference to this house is Whitehall Street, opposite the Tottenham Hotspurs Football Ground in North London.

Documents at Norfolk Records Office provide relevant financial information. In August 1699, £1,000 was paid back to Sir John Lethieullier and his brothers, Samuel and William, though there would appear still to have been an amount outstanding. Roger Lawrence and John Wyberd were witnesses to the signing of the document on 11th August 1699 at Bread Street Hill in London at the home of John Widgely, a scrivener. The original document explained that two amounts of £100 and £4,100 had been paid in 1695, presumably before the death of Sir William Barkham. Sir John Lethieullier would have known of the situation and the location of the land in Tottenham, sold for the benefit of the daughters of Sir William Barkham but he chose not to buy it from Barkham's trustees and heirs. The original Indentures, dating from 1679/80 relating to Sir Edward Barkham and his ownership of the land in Norfolk, included the names of Robert Walpole and Robert Coney, who were also the trustees for Sir William Barkham, when he died in 1695. Robert Walpole was the son of his cousin, Edward Walpole and Robert Coney, the husband of his cousin, Anne Barkham, daughter of his uncle Robert,

Documentation held at Cambridgeshire Archives, from the Holworthy family of Elsworth *(279)*, suggests that as late as 11th August 1701 the legal matters relating to Barkham and his daughters were still not completely resolved. A report of the Master in Chancery states:

> ...in suit was given among Dorothy Barkham, Frances, Jane, Mary, Theodosia and Ann Barkham, daughters of William Barkham baronet, deceased being infants, through Sir Jonathan Jennings, knight, their next friend, versus Lady Judith Barkham, now wife of John Holworthy, Esq. and Robert Walpole, Esq., Robert Coney, Esq., Thomas Halsey, Esq. and Thomas Gilbert, gentleman, trustees under the will of Sir William Barkham concerning the administration of his estate including lands in Tottenham and Edmonton, Middlesex and Moorfields, Saint Lawrence Lane, Moore Lane, Butlers Alley, Oyster Shell Court and elsewhere in St. Giles, Cripplegate, in London.
>
> *(Sir Jonathan Jennings was married to the daughters' aunt, Anne Jennings, née Barkham, Sir William's sister.)*

This document referred back to the original Bill, dated 21st June 1697, when it was proposed that the land was to be sold to the highest bidder.

William Barkham's daughters still held land at Norfolk. Estate and family papers of the Halsey Family of Gaddesden Place, Great Gaddesden show that in 1703-4 an agreement was made related to their estate in Norfolk.

An agreement was made *(DE/HL/12302)*, held at Hertfordshire Archives, dating from 20th February 1703/4 relating to the sale of the manors at Southacre and Bockine in Norfolk and property at Southacre, Castleacre, East Newton, Sporle, Palgreave and Newton next to Castleacre, owned by the Barkhams and others, to Andrew Fountaine; these papers belonged to the heirs of the Halsey Family. The parties to the agreement were John Mercer of London, a gentleman, and Dorothy, his wife, Frances Barkham and Jane Barkham, spinsters, daughters of Sir William Barkham, late of East Walton, Norfolk, of the first part, Robert Coney of Walpole, Norfolk, Thomas Gilbert, a citizen and cloth worker of London and Thomas Halsey of Great Gaddesden, Hertford, Esq. of the second part, Sir John Lethieullier of London, Samuel Lethieullier and William Lethieullier of London, merchants of the third part and Andrew Fountaine of Narford, Norfolk. of the fourth part. Coney and Gilbert were the surviving executors of Sir William Barkham as Walpole had died in November 1700. The land may have been sold or mortgaged to finally pay off debts or the mortgage to the Lethieulliers.

Dorothy Barkham, the eldest daughter of William Barkham, had married John Mercer between the years 1701 and 1703. Frances and Jane were spinsters but over twenty-one, which suggests that Frances was born around 1681; Thomas Halsey was their uncle. There is a conspicuous absence in the document of Dame Judith, their mother but it appears that the daughters were to sell the land in Norfolk, with the help of the surviving executors of Barkham's will, though some of the daughters were still not twenty-one or married in 1703. Sir John Lethieullier still was involved financially with the trustees and Sir William Barkham's daughters. There is evidence of legal wrangling among the trustees, Coney, Gilbert and Walpole, Dame Judith and the daughters, further complicated by the Acts of Parliament and the consequent remarriage of Dame Judith to John Holworthy in 1697.

The House of Lords Library holds documentation relating to John Holworthy, the second husband of Judith Holworthy; this is also recorded in the *Journals of the House of Lords, Volume 18: 1705-1709*. On 10th January 1705, the petitioners asked to *"bring in a Bill for the vesting a legacy of two thousand pounds, given by the will of his mother, Mrs Anne Holworthy, in trustees, to be applied for the payment of the debts of the said John Holworthy, pursuant to an agreement made with his creditors"*. Again, on 14th and 17th January 1705, the bill was ordered to be considered by the Lords. It was *"an act for vesting the sum of two thousand pounds in trustees for payment of the debts of John Holworthy gentleman"* made for the benefit of Holworthy, of the Parish of St. James, a gentleman and of Henry Neale of London, a merchant, one of the creditors of the said John Holworthy. The document explains that the said Anne Holworthy who was living, at the time of her death in 1702, in the Parish of St. Andrew, Holborn, left £2000 in her will in a trust for her son's children; her son was identified as John Holworthy. The trustees of the will were her cousins, John Proby, of the Middle Temple and Matthew Holworthy of Shacklewell in Hackney, who made the petition to release this money for the benefit of John Holworthy so that he could pay his main creditor, John Neale. The documents explain that as John had *"no issue of his body"*, the money should be released from the trust for the children to enable him to pay off his debts incurred with the *"misfortunes that had befallen him"*. It is evidenced in Court Session papers that Dame Judith Barkham was still Holsworthy's wife during the years 1712-1714. Her choice of husbands was not good, as both had considerable financial problems.

Matthew Holworthy was Anne Holworthy's nephew and a trustee of her will; John Holworthy was his cousin. Matthew's father, Sir Matthew Holworthy of Hackney made provision in his will of 1678 for his nephew, John, son of his brother John Holworthy, among others. Sir Matthew made a bequest of £1,000 to the College of Cambridge, New England (now Harvard) for the promotion of learning and promulgation of the Gospel. The will of John Holworthy, the father, was settled in 1687. If it is the case that John married her for her money, the complicated nature of her first husband's financial affairs and debts may have scuppered these plans. It is unlikely that he benefited financially by the marriage.

In James W. P Campbell's book, *Building St. Paul's*, there are references to Thomas and Edward Strong and Ephraim Beauchamp in his chapter on the wealth of masons. Joshua Marshall and Thomas Strong operated two teams of masons on the construction of St. Paul's Cathedral, under the direction of Sir Christopher Wren. According to Campbell, *"Thomas Strong joined the*

Masons Company in 1670, paying by redemption to avoid having to wait seven years for his freedom". Thomas Strong (1634-1681) and master carpenter, John Langland laid the foundation stone at St. Paul's on 21ˢᵗ June 1677 at which time Marshall and Strong started work on the east end and dome of the cathedral. Thomas Strong had inherited from his father quarries at Tinton in Oxfordshire and Barrington in Gloucestershire. When Marshall died in 1678, his team was taken over by Edward Pearce and Joseph Latham. When Thomas Strong died in 1681, his younger brother, Edward Strong (1652-1724) took over his lucrative contracts at the cathedral, working on the east side and parts of the west side. Edward was apprenticed to Thomas at the age of nineteen and came to London to work with his brother. Thomas left most of his estate to his brother as he had died unmarried. Edward Strong became a master of the Masons Company in 1696.

Thomas Strong started on the east end of the building in 1675 and then Edward took over his team of masons working on the building, after his brother died in 1681 and continued on to the dome until 1714. In 1690, Edward Pearce was replaced by Christopher Kempten and Ephraim Beauchamp who worked on another section at the east end and the dome from 1690 to 1707. According to Campbell, most of the master masons working at St. Paul's made their living from building work and in most instances worked for Wren in other places. Beauchamp, like many of the other masons, was a member of the Masons Company, buying his freedom by redemption and did not serve an apprenticeship. Ephraim Beauchamp is likely to have been a substantial merchant, earning in the region of £5,000-£10,000 p.a. It took thirty years to build the Cathedral and Beauchamp was working on it for 17 years from 1690 to 1707. According to a census taken by the Masons Company on 26ᵗʰ September 1694, Edward Strong had 66 masons on site and Kempten and Beauchamp had 24.

Edward Strong and Ephraim Beauchamp worked together, were close friends and brothers-in-law. Edward Strong had married Martha Beauchamp around 1700 and had three children, one of whom was also named Edward (1676-1741) and he too became a mason. Ephraim Beauchamp died on 16ᵗʰ September 1728 at the age of 68. In his will he left instructions for the creation of a monument to his family in All Hallows Church, in Tottenham. The monument is made of black and white marble, decorated with Ionic pilasters, cornices and pediments and is situated against the north. It has the following inscription:

> Near this place lies interred the body of Ephraim Beauchamp, citizen and mason of London and many years one of the Governors of Christ Church Bethlehem and Bride well Hospitals which offices he discharged with Honour and Integrity. He was a loving husband, a tender father and a kind master. Pious and charitable without ostentation and in all his dealings without reproach. He departed this life the 16ᵗʰ day of September, 1728, in the 68ᵗʰ year of his age and here also lies interred his three children Thomas,

Mary, and Letitia. This monument is erected, to his memory, by his mournful wife, Letitia, daughter of John Copping, of Pull ox Hill, in the County of Bedford, Esq. Who after a life of exemplary Piety and Charity went to receive her Eternal Reward the 16th day of March, 1739, in the 72nd year of her age.

18

Evidence of the Hayter legacy
in Manorial Court Rolls

The land at Tottenham High Cross was identified, in the Earl of Dorset Map of 1619, as freehold, leasehold or copyhold. Freehold land can be held indefinitely, leasehold is held for a specified period and copyhold is special tenure from the Lord of the Manor. Other than manors being bought and sold, some owners acquired land as a result of past favours to monarchs. To this is added the effects of the political upheaval of the Civil War after the beheading of Charles I, in 1649, the restoration of the monarchy and return of Charles II to England.

Conflicts did arise between family members and sometimes Acts of Parliament were presented to the King to clarify ownership if a person died intestate or there were unusual circumstances surrounding the will. This was the case with Barkham and his heirs. In the 17th century, it was customary for copyhold land to be inherited by the youngest son or if there was no male issue, to any daughters.

Information relating the day-to-day running of the land at Tottenham High Cross was recorded in the Manorial Court Rolls, copies of which are held at Bruce Castle Museum. The originals Rolls are on long, rolled parchment but copies have been made and are now on microfilm, sometimes in Latin with parts in English. It was not until 1733 that they were entirely written in English. The stewards or clerks who transcribed the information made mistakes in recording names and their competence was variable.

The land owned by Sir Edward Barkham in 1619 and after that by his sons and grandsons was a mixture of freehold and copyhold and was outlined in maps, deeds and other documents. Freehold land is held in "*fee simple*" and could be sold, passed on or settled on whomever the freeholder chose to do so. Freehold tenants were largely independent of the Manorial system and such transfers were not acknowledged in the Manorial Court Rolls. Thereby, transfers of freehold land to new owners are more difficult to pinpoint. In theory, the Lord of the Manor owned the copyhold land; lessees paid a "*fine*" to the him and then, normally, after a certain number of years the land reverted back to him. Not all manors operated to the same customs and people named may have been the owners of the copyhold, freeholders or just tenants and under tenants. Every transfer of land had to go through the Lord of the Manor and he had the right to take fees from new tenants and receive a payment called a "*hereto*" from owners of cattle, on the death of previous one. The land served the Lord or Lady of the Manor well.

Smaller landholdings were held by copyhold tenure but could not be let for more than a year and a day without permission. The transfer of copyhold land was written into the Manorial Court Rolls and then an official copy was made by the steward of the Manor, as proof of title, for the owner. Copyhold land could still be bought and sold, inherited, left in a will and mortgaged just as with freehold land. When land was leased, sold or inherited, copyholders could not lease it for more than twenty-one years but terms of fourteen and seven years were common.

Not all copyholders and freeholders are recorded in the copies of Manorial Court Rolls. The court entries were usually recorded twice in the year, in October and April but early entries did not always list them. In later years, the term *"Defalt Libri Tenens"* and *"Defalt Customan Tenen"* were the two categories given at the sitting of the court; the first the freeholders and the second copyholders or tenants of the custom of the Manor. The people listed, in both sections, were taken to task for not obeying the rules of the manor and had to pay a fine to the Court. The jury passing judgment included copyholders, freeholders and sometimes the Bailiff. The Lord of the Manor could also be fined by the court for not looking after land. The freeholders and copyholders who lived in the area were probably more likely to look after their land. Copyholders had to ask permission to make changes with their holdings. There were reports of the day-to-day management of the manor and records show longer accounts of disputes and transfers of land to do with wills. Ditches had to be maintained, bridges and fences had to be repaired and this gave some indication of the nature of the land in question. Some names appeared frequently, often of people in trouble continuously for not repairing ditches and suchlike.

An entry in the Tottenham Manorial Court Rolls, dated, 3rd May 1661, concerns Robert Barkham and handwritten in the margin is the name of Huxley, an armiger. The long account refers back to a special court on 14th April 1657, when Robert Barkham, a knight, a customary tenant of the manor, had appeared personally at the Court and admitted that he held, possessed and occupied customary land, tenements and hereditaments including all those 11 acres of meadows, divided in two parts and situated near Clendish Hills within the Manor and tenure of Mocking. He also held those enclosures of pasture, known by the name of *"Hatchcroft"*, estimated at four acres and more, abutting a lane in the south called *"Chisley Lane"* and meadows called *"Snares Mead"*, on the west and north. He held fifteen acres and one rood of land in the tenure of the manor of Dawbneys in a place called *"Redlands"* (in 1619 Redlands was marked as owned by Lock) and all the singular tenements in the possession and occupation of Robert Barkham. This land was recorded in the Manorial Rolls because it was customary land, with fees due to the Lord of the Manor. By 1798, Chisley Lane was renamed Hanger's Lane and is now known as St. Ann's Road. There was a field at this location called *"Hatchers"* sometimes known as *"Sergeants Field"*. Snares Mead was identified as freehold land owned by Edward Barkham in 1619.

The following passage, in the Court Rolls, originally in Latin and said, in approximate terms, that:

...the aforesaid Robert Barkham, Knight, had died a little before the said court with all the premises and other things seized entirely to him and his heirs and it is found that Robert Barkham, Esquire, of the age of 17 years and more, is the son and heir of the aforesaid Robert Barkham, Knight, deceased and that the aforesaid Robert Barkham, son, not any other person, came to the said court to take the aforesaid premises out of the hands of the Lord of the manor, a proclamation having been first made. However it was sufficiently agreed at this court that before this court (viz) on 27th February, 1660, the aforesaid Robert Barkham, Knight, then being seized of the premises among other things, being of sound mind and memory, made his last will in writing bearing date above said, and by his said will and testament, made and appointed James Huxley, Esquire, executor thereby [...] and gave to the said James Huxley and his heirs, the full power by the said will to alienate, lease, pledge and dispose of the premises aforesaid and other parcels amongst other things in [...]

...with the following words (in English) – *"I give and bequeath unto my executor and his heirs:*

All that my capital messuage or mansion house at Tottenham High Cross in the County of Middlesex and all singular other my messuages lands tenements meadows pastures hereditaments whatsoever both freehold and copyhold with their and every of their appurtences situated and being in Tottenham Highcross aforesaid and in Edmonton in the said County of Middlesex to the intent and purpose that he may sell or convey the same or any part thereof for the better raising of moneys for performance of this my last will at any time before my son Robert shall or might attain his age of four and twenty years by absolute sale lease mortgage or otherwise in his discretion and the surplus of the moneys arising by such sale grant or mortgage / if any shall be / as also the rents and profits of all the said premises / if any shall be / after the performance of this my last will and the lands and tenements remaining unsold shall pay deliver convey and assure onto my said son Robert Barkham his heirs executors or administrators at such time as he shall or might attain his said age of four and twenty years (with respect the said will was produced here in court).

Sir Robert Barkham, bequeathed to his executor, James Huxley and his heirs his freehold and copyhold land at Tottenham until such time as Robert Barkham, the son, received the land unusually as 24 and not 21 years of age.

Later in the same account, the history of land ownership of other properties and parcels of land were declared by James Huxley, Robert Barkham's executor. It said that on 21st October in the 17th year of the reign of James I, of England (1620), in the presence of Richard Amhurst, armiger, of that manor, Robert Barkham, a soldier, known as Robert Barkham, the father,

surrendered to Edmund Sharpe, to admit, hold, possess or occupy the hereditaments and assigns until the death of Elizabeth Mallory, widow and relict of
the late Andrew Mallory, one quarter part of a cottage, barn and orchard by
estimation three acres, situated in the northern part of Tottenham Street and
another orchard, by estimation ten acres, two roods of meadow in a common
meadow called *"Michley" (there are 4 roods in an acre)* and also four acres of
pasture situated in a place called *"Baldwins"*, near a lane some distance from
Highcross Street, near the Hale. There were also ten acres of land situated
in a field called *"Downe and Halefield"*. The account continued to say that
on the 21st day of October, in the 20th year of the reign of James I (1623),
Robert Barkham accepted that Thomas Meeke, an attorney, surrendered it to
John Ralph, to admit and hold the hereditaments of another quarter; it was
then passed to Peter Dancer. Then on 16th February, in the 13th year of the
reign of Charles I (1638) in the presence of Peter Pheasant, sub-steward of the
manor, the court declared that William Cotton was admitted to hold another
and last quarter after the death of Elizabeth Mallory. The last quarter was
held jointly by William Cotton and Jane Barkham, during the course of her
lifetime and when she died it was declared that Sir Robert Barkham, her son,
was admitted to hold the last quarter. The account referred again to the fact
that Robert Barkham had appeared personally at the court on 27th February
1660 with James Huxley, the sole executor of the will of Sir Robert Barkham.
The land outlined in the Manorial Rolls was customary and therefore transfer
of ownership, even for a short period, was recorded. Freehold land would not
have been included.

In another entry in the Court Rolls, on 4th June 1666 *(page 107)*, again there
is a statement outlining the customary land and tenements at Clendish Hills,
Hatchcroft, Redlands, the cottage, barn and orchard at Tottenham Street, land
behind the orchard called Michley, Baldwins, Down and Halefields, which
was formerly held by Sir Robert Barkham. The court entry referred back to
the entry of May, 1661 when the land had been held in good faith and trust
by Jacob Huxley, who had presented the last will and testament of Sir Robert
Barkham to the court. Robert Barkham the son, his heirs and assigns, named
in his father's will, was now free to take over the running of the estate from
Huxley, as he had reached the age of majority. Barkham appeared personally
before the court, to be admitted to the court and said that he would pay all
fines, revenue, debts, in good faith. In the margin there are statements roughly
translated as *"Barkham copyhold: fees or fines paid"*. This entry recorded
the formal handing over of ownership, called *"Virgam"* (the rod), from James
Huxley, as executor, to Robert Barkham, the son and heirs.

On 8th May 1675, Robert Barkham was recorded as the customary tenant of
copyhold land of some 3 acres, north at Tottenham Street, including a cottage,
barn, stables and orchard, along with three closes of pasture, situated behind
an orchard, estimated at 10 acres, in the occupation and possession of Thomas
Bolton and John Russell, together, with 11 acres of meadow called *"Clendish
Hills"*. These were assigned to Charles Dyson, of Tottenham, a gentleman. All
those hereditaments and land, from Robert Barkham, his heirs, executors and

administrators transferred on 17th October 1675 to Charles Dyson, his heirs and administrators. As the item was entered in the court rolls, the land was copyhold or a mixture of both.

Again it is shown that on 8th July 1676, the same 3 acres, north at Tottenham Street, including a cottage, barn, stables and orchard, along with three closes of pasture, situated behind an orchard, estimated at 10 acres, in the occupation and possession of Thomas Bolton and John Russell, altogether, with 11 acres of meadow called Clendish Hills altogether with 10 acres of arable land at Downfield and Halefield, along with half an acre of land at Mitchley Marsh in the possession of Thomas Raymond, 4 acres called Hatchcroft, occupied by Henry Cocking and 15 acres called Redlands, occupied by Alice Bishop, were in the possession of Charles Dyson, a confectioner, the document being dated 14th July, 1676 *(page 168)*.

An item dated 17th April 1694 *(page 245)*, written in Latin, says, in approximate terms that:

> Robert Barkham, Gentleman, who held certain free lands of this
> manor, since the last court, has sold and alienated the aforesaid
> land to a certain Henry Heater, whence a relief fell due to the Lord
> of the Manor which Henry Heater was present here in this court
> and paid the aforesaid relief.

Robert Barkham thereby transferred his land to Henry *Heater,* who became the new owner of the freehold land. Heater acquired the land before the death of Sir William Barkham. This was not the land described in the chapter dealing with Barkham's Title. The name of "Henry *Heater*" appears among the freeholders on 28th April 1696 *(page 253)*, the year after Sir William Barkham died. In October 1699, an entry recorded that Ephraim Beauchamp had acquired that part of Sir William Barkham's estate that was in Tottenham, Middlesex, from Sir William's heirs, together with an annual rent.

In April 1701, the Tottenham Manorial Court Rolls entry cited Matthew Holworthy with George and Sarah Ballard, Francis Milles and George Moyse. Frances Milles was the steward for Lord Coleraine, Lord of the Manor of Tottenham. Matthew Holworthy was the cousin of John Holworthy, who married Judith Barkham, widow of Sir William Barkham. Holworthy's role in these affairs was as executor and administrator of the will of the late George Moyse, Sarah Ballard's father. The last dates on which Sir William Barkham or his heirs were mentioned in the Tottenham Manorial Court Rolls were in 1702 and 1704.

Heater appeared in the freeholder section again on 21st April 1707 *(page 302)*, on 11th October 1709 *(page 319)* and on 16th April 1711 *(page 326)*. Henry *Heater* appears again on 17th October 1711 *(page 329)*. One might assume that Henry *Heater* was Henry Hayter as the transcriptions of many of the names varied in the translation from Latin into English and they are likely to have been transcribed by different people. For purposes of this work he will be referred to as Henry Hayter.

An entry on 16th October 1716, for *Henricus Hayter (page 357),* written in Latin says, in approximate terms:

> Death of Henry Hayter, free tenant – At this court the aforesaid Homage presented that Henry Hayter, who held certain free lands within the Manor of the Lord of the Manor aforesaid by free grant, fealty and an annual rent, before this court has died so seized by which a relief fell due to the Lord of the Manor and because no one came to the court to make fealty and to pay the aforesaid relief, therefore the Bailiff is ordered to distrain for the relief at the next court.

In summary, the late Henry Hayter, had owned freehold land, with permission to take annual rent and as a result owed money to the Lord of the Manor.

Hayter was cited in the *Default Libre Tenens* section in 1717 *(page 359).* An entry in the Court Rolls, dated 16th October 1717 *(page 363)* recorded that a Mr. Drew, on behalf of Thomas Hayter, described, in parenthesis, as the next heir of Henry Hayter, came to the court and paid a certain relief due to the Lord of the Manor for his freehold at six shillings per annum, quit rent. This confirms that it was Henry Hayter who owned the freehold land in South Tottenham and that Thomas Hayter had inherited it from his brother.

19

Samuel Pepys and Tom Hayter

Thus far, an account has been given of the fact that Sir Edward Barkham acquired the land at Tottenham in the early seventeenth century, which passed to his sons Sir Edward and Sir Robert Barkham. Different parcels of land there were acquired by their sons, Sir William Barkham and Robert Barkham. The latter's son, also Robert Barkham acquired his father's portion on his death, around 1691; it was he who sold the land to Henry Hayter in 1694. In 1716, on the death of Henry Hayter, it was inherited by his brother Thomas Hayter who with other relatives, later sold it to William Lethieullier, son of Sir John Lethieullier.

Claire Tomalin's book, entitled *Samuel Pepys – The Unequalled Self*, makes reference to Pepys' clerk, Tom Hayter, father of Henry and Thomas Hayter *(above)* and this chapter seeks to provide a background to the arrival on the scene of the two sons.

William Lethieullier lived close to the Navy offices, where Samuel Pepys worked, when the latter was writing his diary. Sir John Lethieullier and two of his brothers had been financially involved with Sir William Barkham as the latter had borrowed money from them. This money was repaid after William Barkham's land at Middlesex and Tottenham was sold to Ephraim Beauchamp in 1699.

It was not until around 1721 that William Lethieullier, son of the late Sir John Lethieullier, acquired the various parcels of land identified in a later chapter in the indenture of 1721, at Tottenham High Cross from the heirs of Henry Hayter.

Tom Hayter, Clerk to Pepys

Insight regarding the early life of one Thomas Haiter/Hayter is contained in the *Calendar of State Papers, Domestic Series, Tables and Indexes*, for the years 1654 -1661, stored at the British Library. The period in question was six years before Pepys and Hayter began to work together. Tom Hayter, is cited in a letter, dated 30th May 1654, written by Edward Pateson, from Plymouth, to the Navy commissioners. The following compassionate statement gives a flavour of the consequences of the Civil War at the time. It starts:

> ...having had large experience of your willingness to hear the cries of the fatherless and widows. I beg you to remember those about whom I laboured with you when in Scotland and order

Mr. Hayter to write to the captains of the fleet to send you up the tickets for the wages due to such as were slain so that their wages might be received and something for their deaths. Hayter promised me, on receipt of the tickets, to get the money for the wages and pay it where I could appoint but I hear of no progress nor any hope of getting for these distressed families the money purchased by the price of blood. My endeavour in their behalf are from their continued tears and cries to me and from my tender bowels towards them. Pray get the tickets before the captains go off to remote places and so the families will be left to perish.

P.S. Pray remember Widow Ashwell and her family who was wronged of her husbands wages by a women from Southwark representing she was dead.

Another relevant entry for Tom Hayter was a letter written by him from Portsmouth on 18th December 1654 to Edward Hopkins at the Navy Commissioners, when he stated that he *"had been detained by illness and is now ordered to remain to assist M. Portman in paying ships when they are fitted out in the bay. The Torrington and her squadron have taken in all their soldiers and will sail tomorrow"*. Although in Portsmouth, he may have been visiting rather than working there full-time but he certainly had friends in that city. Then, a series of letters were written during the month of August 1656 that confirm that Hayter was moving around the country on his business for the Navy Office. The first, dated 8th August 1656, was from Little Dean to Edward Hopkins at the Navy Office. It describes how he *"has been much delayed by the confusion and intricacies of the accounts occasioned through the death of one and the grievance of others and though engaging from 6a.m. to 8p.m. has not completed them"*. By 25th August 1656, he was back in London when he and Richard Kingdom wrote to the Admiralty Commissioners that they *"have proposed the enclosed instructions for the better keeping of the States Accounts in connexion with the iron works in Dean Forest; not withstanding leave it to their better judgement"*. The following day the Admiralty Commissioners gave an order to the Navy Commissioners *"to make out a bill to Captain Richard Kingdom and Thomas Hayter for £12 for travelling expenses to and from Dean Forest to take the accounts to Major Wade in the management of the iron works there as also for Mr Aldridge for felling and converting lumber for the state; also £10 for their pains in the business"*.

Tomalin's book begins with the diaries of Samuel Pepys written between the years 1659 and 1669. She makes reference to Tom Hayter, one of Pepys' two principal clerks; the other principal clerk was Will Hewer. Pepys, who lived from 1633 to 1703, during the period of the diaries, had four clerks, Hayter, Edwards, Hewer and Gibson. Will Hewer became closest to Pepys and remained his trusted friend until his death. The ten volumes of Samuel Pepys' diary themselves provide references to Thomas Hayter and his wife as primary evidence. For purposes of this section the Thomas in question will be called Tom.

The Unequalled Self, by reference to the source material, offers a mine of information regarding Tom Hayter. Pepys was first appointed as Clerk of the Acts with the Navy Board in 1660, at a salary of £350 a year. He secured the job through his relation, Montagu, who had been appointed first Earl of Sandwich and was an advisor to the King. The King appointed the members of the Navy Board, which consisted of four principal officers; treasurer, comptroller, surveyor and clerk of the acts as well as three commissioners. According to J. D. Davies in his book *Gentlemen and Tarpaulins* (1991), the Navy was then the largest employer in the country. The Navy Offices were situated at Seething Lane, near Tower Hill where there were, by all accounts, five large residences with other office accommodation and a secure gate. Pepys, in his diary, relates the occasion and describes his dismay when someone came to take possession of one of the larger residences after he had been in the job for only a few weeks and was worried that he might lose his chance of a house in the enclosure. Pepys and Tom Hayter arrived with some sheets and knocked at the door of the house that Pepys coveted and, after staying two days in the house, he asserted his right to the house.

Of course, in those days overt nepotism was the norm, full of corruption in the way work, jobs, trade and contracts were awarded. Clerks in positions of power, having been bribed or given favours, were able to reward certain people with contracts. They were also able to choose with whom they worked and arranged jobs for other people, such as family and friends. Pepys chose his two clerks at the Navy Board when he arrived in 1660, although Hayter was already working as a clerk in the office at the time and had seniority. One might assume that Hayter was some years older than his colleague. William Hewer was the nephew of one Robert Blackborne, who was a friend of Pepys. Hewer was only seventeen when he was appointed as a personal servant and clerk to Samuel Pepys. Hewer eventually became one of his closest friends, although they did not always see eye-to-eye when he was first employed by Pepys and refused to allow himself to be treated disrespectfully. He refused to go to church, got drunk and was perhaps excessively friendly with the maids. When Hewer was taken on by the Pepys family, Samuel was only ten years older than his clerk and Elizabeth, his wife, was only two years older than Will. Tomalin suggests that there was a degree of jealousy between Pepys and Hewer and that Will was clearly smitten with the charms of Elizabeth. Despite earning a small salary as a clerk, he was able to supplement his income from his job, as on one occasion he bought a gift for Elizabeth Pepys, which cost more than a year's wages. Hewer himself became quite wealthy and Samuel Pepys and Mary Skinner were living with him at Clapham when Pepys died in 1703.

The second half of the seventeenth century was also a time of great reorganisation of the Navy, partly instigated by Samuel Pepys in a bid to rationalise and make people accountable for their actions and to reduce corruption. The scale of the Navy was such that it was tremendously crucial for trade, its influence and importance at this time being reflected upon its employees. During Pepys' lifetime, war was waged against the Dutch and French and political power derived from this. It was a time of great social upheaval, conspiracy and religious intolerance in the country.

During the time that Pepys and Hayter were working at the Admiralty, countless deals were made for clothing for the sailors, food, wood for the construction of ships, tar, metal fittings, etc. and there were perks of the job. Pepys made his fortune through these lucrative arrangements and not from salary. It might also be assumed that Tom Hayter was able to supplement his income as a clerk, to provide well for his family.

Among Samuel Pepys' very close friends were James Houblon, son of a rich merchant and his wife Sarah. Houblon met Pepys in his dealings with the Navy. After Elizabeth Pepys died, the Houblons welcomed Samuel into their home and Sarah Houblon shared an interest in music and the theatre. James Houblon, on at least one occasion, put up £5000 for bail when Samuel Pepys was imprisoned in the Tower of London in 1679 and then again in 1690. Later in his life they shared a summer house together in Parson's Green. Houblon sat on the board of the Bank of England, as did members of the Lethieullier family; Houblon was related to William Lethieullier.

The first reference in the diaries to Mrs. Hayter, Tom's wife, is on 30th April 1661, when Samuel Pepys met her for the first time. Samuel and Elizabeth Pepys and a Mr. Creed took the coach to Fish Street to pick up Tom and his wife to set off on a trip to Petersfield and Portsmouth, combining business with pleasure. Mrs. Hayter was wearing a travelling mask to protect her complexion and Pepys thought at first that she was an old woman. When she removed the mask, she was uncovered as "*a very pretty, modest black woman*" which might mean either that she was a brunette or of a dark complexion. Perhaps she was very sun-tanned or may have come from a country where the weather was much hotter than in England.

On 2nd May, Hayter, Pepys and their wives went to visit the ship, *Montague* and also admired the room in which the Duke of Buckingham had been killed by Felton in 1628. The next day, Mrs. Hayter went to stay with her husband's friends while Pepys and Hayter continued with their work and their visit.

Hayter's wife is not cited again in relation to this outing. The fact that the two couples took the trip together implies that Tom had a valued relationship with Samuel and Elizabeth Pepys, to be able to embark on a journey lasting a few days. Of relevance may be the fact that Tom Hayter had a connection with the Portsmouth area, the possibility being that his family originally came from there or that the friends to whom reference was made were connected to his work at the Navy Office.

On 9th August 1661, we find a reference in the diary to Elizabeth Pepys, who was called by Tom Hayter to his home to help his wife, who was in labour. Samuel Pepys, when he returned home at the end of the day, remarked that Mrs. Hayter still had not delivered her baby. So, a child was born to Tom Hayter and his wife after this date in 1661. A baptism of a child with the name of Thomas Hayter was recorded at St. Leonard, Eastcheap, in the City of London, on 30th August 1661. The register showed the name of the father as Thomas Hayter of St. Margaret, Fish Street. This is most likely to have been Tom Hayter. No other births of any other children named Hayter were recorded in the registers at St. Leonard's in the next ten years.

Tom Hayter was a Nonconformist. Despite the Declaration of Breda by Charles II on 4th April 1660, which signalled the restoration of the monarchy and recommended that other sects, outside of the authorised Church, should be allowed to practice their religion, in May 1663 Hayter found himself in trouble for his views. He had attended a meeting with friends on the Lord's Day (3rd May) and he was *"taken to the counter"*, the equivalent of an arrest. He told Pepys about the incident on the 9th of May. Claire Tomalin believes that he had attended a Quaker Meeting. Pepys drew on a favour from William Coventry, secretary to The Duke of York, who spoke to the Duke and sorted out the affair. Other references later in the diary suggest that Tom was an *"Anabaptist"*, normally educated people whose doctrine stated that baptism should only be administered to believing adults. On 22nd September 1666, Pepys wrote that Tom was unhappy about working again on the Lord's Day but nevertheless he submitted to the order to work. Pepys records in his diary on 17th June 1667 that he had lunch alone with Mr. Hayter, who expressed his opinion that the only thing that would save the nation was the reconciling of the *"Presbyterian party"*. Hayter was considering moving to Hamburg, as were other Nonconformists. At that time, England was at war with the Dutch, who were close to London. Talk in the streets was that *"the country was being bought, sold and governed by papists"* (Tomalin). Whatever evolution of his religious affinities, Hayter had attended services at Quaker Meeting Houses, which may explain why no records are shown on *www. ancestry.com* for baptisms of any other Hayter children after Thomas at St. Leonard, Eastcheap.

Finding evidence concerning certain people during the period in question can be challenging, in part due to the possibility that some records may have been destroyed in the Great Fire of London in 1666 and after the fire many families were forced to flee the city whilst rebuilding took place. Tom Hayter's family appears to have been, at least for a time, Nonconformist. Nonconformist registers, prior to 1837, for births, baptisms, marriages, deaths and burials (*BMD registers, in association with the TNA*) include Quakers, although this particular Hayter family is not in evidence.

According to Tomalin, regarding the marriage of Samuel Pepys to Elizabeth Marchant De St. Michel in December 1655, *"religious ceremonies had been declared invalid since August 1653, but churches were still used for the civil ceremonies that replaced them"*. Puritans and Nonconformists believed that, of necessity, marriage was a contract between people, with no religious connotations. Normally, the event happened in front of witnesses and did not have to be in a church or a consecrated place. Relatives had to give permission for the marriage and once the engagement was announced it was common for sexual relations to take place. Likewise, burials also did not always take place in consecrated ground. In the country, bodies would sometimes be buried in fields, though this was not possible in the city. Spa Fields and Bunhill Fields, on the edge of the City of London, were burial grounds for Nonconformists from a wide variety of religious backgrounds. Some groups were lain adjacent to permanent memorials to loved ones while others did not object to memorial plaques. The latter believed that graves honoured the body rather than the soul and therefore were unimportant. Records of Baptisms are sometimes not particularly easy to find although the Established Church did record some of them. The Quakers did record baptisms, deaths and marriages in the accounts of the quarterly meetings.

According to the diary, Hayter had lunch with Pepys many times, often worked late and made arrangements on behalf of his superior, being able to combine making music with keeping shipping lists up to date. Tom was a highly valued colleague. According to Claire Tomalin, when Pepys wanted to prove how much more expensive it was to buy ship building supplies on credit in 1668, he asked Hayter to provide the evidence. Moreover, he gave credit to Tom Hayter for his efficiency and his efforts. The thoroughness of the diary is such that it indicates prices paid by the King and by merchants for items such as door handles, screws, etc. However, despite their efforts to save money, Pepys being the first person to organise the records of officers and ships and running an efficient office, things continued as before.

Working with Pepys in Seething Lane, Tom Hayter's residence in Fish Street, which was the street running north from London Bridge, was prior to the Great Fire of London; the Fire caused his house to burn down in September 1666. In consequence, Elizabeth Pepys suggested that Will Hewer and Tom Hayter come to live with them at Seething Lane but this idea was not pursued. On 30th October, Hayter apologised to Pepys for his lateness at work, as he had been *"looking out for a little house for his family, his wife being much frightened in the country with the discourses about the country of troubles and disorders likely to be and therefore durst not her from him…… therefore he is forced to moving her to town so that they be together"*. *"The country"* may have been in villages such as Islington, Kingsland or Chelsea, which were considered to be rural, though only a few miles from the City. It is likely that the family's next residence will have been close to the offices at Seething Lane, as his work required him to be available at all hours. As for Samuel Pepys, although well educated, he had worked his way up from humble beginnings so it is understandable that there was a degree of trust and loyalty with his clerk and the support he gave the latter's career. When Elizabeth was dying, in November 1669, Pepys recorded that Tom and his wife attended her deathbed. Upon his own death, Pepys himself was buried at 9 o'clock at night, as he requested, in a vault underneath the memorial to his wife in St. Olave's Church, at Hart Street.

Of Tom Hayter, we see reference to his salary records for his job at the Navy Board, outlined in J. M. Collinge's book, *Navy Board Officials 1660-1832* (1978). In his introduction to the jobs identified in all the offices of the Navy Board, the author states that the number of clerks employed fluctuated with the amount of business in each office, particularly when war was declared. Besides the upheaval of the Civil War, England had been at war with France, Holland and Spain as well as in the Colonies. Hayter had been a Clerk to the Clerk of the Acts from 1660 to 1664, after which he was appointed as Chief Clerk to Clerk of the Acts from 25th June 1664 until 25th March 1672. Samuel Pepys was promoted to Secretary of the Admiralty in June 1673. Tom Hayter, jointly with John Pepys, brother of Samuel, took Samuel's job as Clerk of the Acts from 19th June 1673, to May 1679. John Pepys died suddenly in 1677 at the age of 37 and was buried at St. Olave, Hart Street.

Hayter left the office of Clerk to the Acts in May 1679, on appointment as Secretary of the Admiralty, the job previously undertaken by Pepys, when the latter was committed to the Tower. Tom Hayter was Secretary at the Admiralty from 22nd May 1679 until 3rd February 1680. John C. Sainty, in his book on *Admiralty Officials 1660-1870* (1975), states that a Secretary was the senior official at the Admiralty. Hayter was Controller from 28th January 1680 and surrendered the office on 14th January 1682 when he was replaced by one Richard Haddock. A letter in the Herrick Family Papers dated 10th January 1682, held in the Bodleian Library at Oxford University, confirms that Mr. Hayter was dismissed from his position as Comptroller of the Navy; Hayter was the only civilian ever to hold the office of Controller. He was then appointed to a new position as Assistant Controller but doing the same job as Controller from 4th February 1682 to 26th March 1686, earning a salary of £400 a year. Then he became Assistant to the Commissioner for Old Accounts from 26th March 1686 to 25th December 1688. The entry *(ADM 20/49 No. 1541)* records:

> To Thomas Hayter, Esq. 25th December, 1688 for his salary as assistant to the Commissioner for examining and adjusting the accounts of his Majesty's Navy before 25th March 1686 from 13th October, 1688 to day above said at £400 per annum sum £85.

The record of his salary for the quarter, ending 25th March 1689 *(Adm. 20/54 Nos. 287 Page 60)* is as follows:

> To Rebeccah Hayter widow of Thomas Hayter Esq., ...for his salary for one quarter ending 25th March 89 (in which quarter he dyed) at 400 £s per annum the sum of £100 a quarter.

He is likely to have died around New Year's Day 1689. The entry in the church register of St. Olave, Hart Street, reads *"Thomas Hayter Esq.: was buried 3 Jan in the new vault"* in the year 1688/9. (*The Register of St. Olave Hart Street London 1563-1700, published, in 1916, in a Harleian Society Publication, Register Section, recorded the burial as that of Thomas Hayton.*)

Although Tom Hayter had been in trouble with the authorities for his religious beliefs as a Non-Conformist while working with Samuel Pepys, it would appear that at the time of his death he was a member of the established Church. When Hayter died in 1688/9, his position was not filled. Tom Hayter was buried in the same church as Samuel and Elizabeth Pepys.

Rebecca (Rebeccah or Rebekah) Hayter, Tom's widow *(There are various spellings of her Christian name)*

In *Calendar of the State Papers, Domestic Series, William and Mary, May 1690 – October 1691*, an entry dated April 23, 1691, Whitehall, on page 344, records:

Proceedings upon the petition of Rebecca Hayter, widow of Thomas Hayter, showing that her husband, having spent his whole useful time, being above 36 years in the service of the navy, and it being universally known that his assiduous pains and care in that employment have shortened his days, has left her, with many children unprovided. Prays that she may have something allowed her from the navy, as a great many others enjoy". Referred to the Lords of the Admiralty. [S.P. Dom. Petition Entry Book 1, p118]

This pleading took place approximately six months after her husband died. It may be inferred that Tom, if he had worked for the Navy for 36 years and was at least 16 years of age when he joined, would have been no less than about 52 years of age when he died, being born probably around 1637. The full extent of Mrs. Hayter's family was not recorded and there was an implied hint of unfairness in her plea that others were receiving the benefit of financial compensation upon the loss of life and income and it had been denied to her. Her attempt was to stand up for what she thought was fair and just. She believed that her husband had been conscientious, overworked and under stress for most of his working life. He had not left her provided for as he died intestate and there was no administration.

Again, in the *Calendar of State Papers, Domestic Series, William III, May 1699 – October 1700*, on November 28, 1699, *page 300-301*, an entry records:

Proceedings upon the petition of Rebeccah Hayter, widow: showing that she represented to the late queen the service of her deceased husband, Mr Thomas Hayter, who had long served as one of the commissioners of the Navy and the great necessity she was under, having many to provide for: that the Queen, according to what had been practised in the Navy, granted her a pension of £300 per annum which since Midsummer 1698 was reduced to £150. This retrenchment has brought the petitioner under sorrowful circumstances. She prays that her full pension may be restored. Referred to the Admiralty.

The late queen in question was Mary, daughter of James II and wife of King William III. Queen Mary reigned in her husband's absence, when King William was fighting the war in Ireland and then in the Netherlands. Mary died from smallpox, in 1694 and King William died on March 8, 1702.

Mrs. Hayter's pension of £300 a year was quite a substantial annuity but it would suggest that she had still many of her family at home to take care of and the *"sorrowful circumstances"* certainly underpinned a dramatic declaration.

In *Calendar of State Papers, Domestic Series, William III, 1700–1702*, on February 10, 1702, page 508, at Whitehall, there is an entry:

James Vernon to the lord high Admiral. H.M. commands me to transmit the enclosed petition for your opinion. The petition of Rebecca Hayter, with a list appended, of persons in the Navy whose pensions were entrenched in 1698 and were afterwards restored.

The appended list included titled people such as Sir Richard Haddock, Sir Robert Robinson, Captain Christopher Mason, and Elizabeth Wren among others. Mrs. Hayter was diligent and forthright in her research into the financial situation of the other people in receipt of pensions and her impression that she was being unfairly treated was sustained.

The matter was raised again on February 18, 1702, at the Admiralty, *on page 518*, when it was reported:

> Report of the earl of Pembroke, lord high admiral to the king upon the petition of Rebecca, widow of Thomas Hayter, esq., setting forth that in consideration of the long services of her husband and her necessities, her late Majesty (in his Majesty's absence) granted her a pension of £300, which at midsummer 1698 was reduced to £150, as others were in proportion retrenched at that time. [The report concludes] I humbly submit it to H.M. great goodness whether the petitioner, in consideration of her circumstances and of the long services of her husband, as secretary of the Admiralty and one of the principal officers and commissioners of the Navy, may not be a fit object of H.M. compassion [Signed Pembroke].

The position, as it affected Mrs. Hayter, remained constantly under review, as in *Calendar of State Papers, Domestic Series, Queen Anne, 1702-1703*, on July 17, 1702, *page 189*, in which another entry stated:

> Transmits Mrs Rebecca Hayter's petition. Unless there is some objection, the Queen desires it to be granted in recognition of her husband's faithful service.

The reference to Queen was to the late Queen Mary, who had originally granted Rebecca Hayter's request, as Queen Anne having acceded to the throne after March 8, 1702. Rebecca's perseverance by presenting her petition to the Prince's Council, was duly rewarded.

Other evidence of Rebecca Hayter, as the widow and relict of Thomas Hayter, was found in volumes of the *Calendar of State Papers, Treasury Books*.

In *Volume 21.1, Oct. 1706-Dec. 1707, covering December 31, 1705 to December 31, 1706, page clxxxiv*, in a section headed with:

> Declared Accounts: Navy Treasurer Account for the Navy and Victualling (Dame Anne Littleton, widow and executor of Sir Thomas Littleton), Salaries and entertainment to the Admiralty Commissioners, Navy Commissioners, clerks, etc...... pensions to Officers and others of ships and for services: Rebecca Hayter, 225L.

On the same document as Dame Anne Littleton and others, Rebecca Hayter was only one name out of many shown on that document who received a pension. In *Volume 27.1, covering January 1, 1712 to December*

31, 1713, page clxviii, in *Declared Accounts: Navy and Victualling,* under pensions, was recorded *"Rebeccah Hayter, relict of Thomas Hayter, a late Navy Commissioner"* but the amount is not shown.

In *Volume 29.1, covering January 1, 1714 to December 31, 1715, on page cxiv,* in *Declared Accounts: Navy and Victualling,* included in pension payments, was *"Rebeccah Hayter, relict of Thomas Hayter"* although the amount is not shown.

In *Volume 31.1, covering January 1, 1716 to December 31, 1717, on page clxxvii (177),* in *Declared Accounts: Navy,* under pensions, was a payment of £150 made to *"Rebecca Hayter, relict of Thomas Hayter, late a Navy Commissioner, half year to Michelmas, 1716"* (September 29). This was the last entry in her name and might confirm that she died around this time.

Rebecca Hayter claimed her right to a pension on grounds that she had many for whom to provide. Her husband's long-standing service to the Navy Board, she claimed, had resulted in his premature death.

Mrs. Hayters daughters and her family

A document *(M/093/271)* dated 1691, held at the *London Metropolitan Archives,* provides evidence of a link between the Hayter and Whitfield families and James Disbrowe, nephew of John Disbrowe, himself a brother-in-law of Oliver Cromwell. Written on the back was the statement *"The Counterpart of the assignment of the house on Stepney Causeway To Capt. John Wilmott 1691- Lease 1688- 60 years -1748".*

The Indenture tripartite of 9th July 1691 in London, Middlesex, was among three parties. They were Mary *Whitfeild* (Whitfield), of the Parish of St. Olave, Hart Street, a spinster, Elizabeth and Rebecca Hayter, also of said parish, spinsters, of the first part, Captain John Wilmott of St. Paul, Shadwell, a mariner, of the second part and Joseph Marsh, of Garston, in the County of Herts., administrator of the will annexed of James Disbrowe, late of the Parish of Stepney, Middlesex, Doctor in Physic, *"Lord",* of the third part. Francis Barnefield, a carpenter and his wife Mary had leased the Stepney property in the first year of their marriage in March 1689. The indenture describes the house on land called *"Pondfields".* It had marble hearths, wainscots and chimney pots, width twenty-two feet, north to south and eleven feet, east to west, lying on Church Street, Ratcliffe, abutting Stepney Causeway; the plot was one hundred feet wide. The couple transferred the lease of all the customary lands to James Disbrough (also written *"Disborrow"* in same document) for his benefit and that of his executors and administrators. The sum of £160 was paid by John Wilmott to Mary Whitfield and Elizabeth and Rebecca Hayter for the *"absolute purchase of lease and premises".* The document records that *"also the said Rebecca Hayter when she shall attain to her full age of one and twenty years or her husband in case she intermarry".* At the time of the transaction she was under 18 years of age and in 1691 Elizabeth Hayter must have been over the age of 21.

It explains that when James Disbrowe wrote his will on 26th November 1690, he left the property at Stepney Causeway to his wife, Abigail and if she were to die before him it was to go to Mary Whitfield, a spinster, for the remaining years of the lease and then to be divided equally between Elizabeth Hayter and Rebecca Hayter. Abigail Disbrowe was the sole executor of James Disbrowe's will and after her death it became his father, Samuel Disbrowe. Abigail Disbrowe died before her husband, James, who died only a short time after her. The Indenture included *"and whereas the said Samuel Disbrowe the executor though he survived the said James Disbrowe yet he happened to depart this life before he had proved the said will and whereby the said James became intestate and whereupon letters of administration of the goods chattels and estate late of James Disbrowe together with his will annexed hath been committed to Joseph Marsh"*. As a result of the sequence of these deaths, Joseph Marsh, became the executor of James Disbrowe, Doctor in Physic, of Stepney in Middlesex, whose will was proved on 14th January 1691 (*PROB 11/403/80*). Included in the will was the following statement:

> I devise the guardianship and tuition of my said daughter Elizabeth and her estates until the age of twentyone years or day of marriage which shall first happen unto my said wife Abigail if she shall so long live and after her decease to my said father and after his decease unto Joseph Marsh gent.

Joseph Marsh was nominated as guardian of Elizabeth Disbrowe, James Disbrowe's daughter, until she reached 21, she being then a minor, after the death of James' wife Abigail Disbrowe and Samuel Disbrowe, James' father. Marsh was the brother-in-law of James Disbrowe. Elizabeth Disbrowe was to inherit the Manor of Elsworth when she reached the age of 18.

The Faculty Office marriage allegation with the name of Abigail *Marshall*, shows that James Desbrowe, of St. Neots, Huntingdon, then a bachelor aged 30, had announced on 27th February 1678 his intention on 27th February 1679 at All Hallows-in-the-Wall, London to marry Abigail Marsh of Stepney, Middlesex, a maiden, aged 23 and daughter of John *Marsh* of Garston, Herts. The *ODNB* records that in fact they married on 9th March 1679.

James Disbrowe died at his house at Stepney Causeway. His burial, at St. Dunstan All Saints, Stepney (Tower Hamlets) on 11th December 1690, recorded that he was a physician, of Ratcliffe *(Church Register)*. Abigail Disbrowe, his wife, was buried there on the same day. (However, *Memoirs of the Protectoral House of Cromwell, Volume 2, by Mark Noble, written before 1877,* suggests that James Disbrowe resided at Cheshunt in Hertfordshire and was buried there.)

His father, Samuel Disbrowe of Elsworth, Cambridgeshire had also died around that time and was buried at Elsworth Church on 18th December, where there is a large black memorial stone, on the floor of the chancel, dedicated to him alone. It records simply *"Samuel Disbrowe died 10 December 1690 aged 71"*. Samuel's will was written in September 1680 and proved in April 1691 (*PROB 11/404/236*). He asked that his son James should take care that my *"said dear wife may enjoy without interruption or molestation from him"* suggesting that there may have been difficulties in the relationship between James and his stepmother, Rose Disbrowe. Samuel left 1,500 acres in County Meath, Ireland, granted by the Company of Drapers in London, with a lease for thirty-one years from the death of his wife, Rose, to his son and heir, James. He gave £20 to each of his grandsons, Christopher, Samuel and James Milles, sons of his late daughter, Sarah and Christopher Milles. That couple married at Elsworth on 18th October 1666; Samuel Milles was born in 1669 and died in December 1727 aged 58; James Milles was buried at Herne in Kent on 29th March 1682 and Mr Christopher Milles (his brother) was buried at Elsworth on 15th August 1684 (*Church registers*).

James and Sarah may have had an elder sister as Samuel Disbrowe of Elsworth gave his consent to the marriage of a daughter, Elizabeth Disbrowe, a spinster, aged 19, to Richard Bland, a bachelor and silkman, aged 24, of the Parish of St. Dunstan-in-the-West, London. It was their intention to marry at St. Peter, Paul's Wharf, London. The licence was dated 31st March 1663/4 *(Faculty Office Marriage Allegations)*. Elizabeth was born around 1645 and was probably the first child of Dorothy and Samuel Disbrowe. A certificate of residence at TNA dated 1663 confirms that Samuel Disbrowe was liable to pay taxes in Cambridgeshire. Elizabeth died before her father.

The will of John Marsh, of Watford, Hertfordshire, was proved in 1681, in which he named as beneficiaries his wife, Rose, son, Joseph and daughter, Sarah, wife of Samuel *Sheaffe*. The will of Rose Marsh, a widow of Highgate in the Parish of Hornsey, Middlesex, written in 1690, made reference to her son Joseph, her *"loving daughter"*, Abigail, wife of Dr. Disbrowe and Rose's grandchild, Elizabeth Disbrowe. Other beneficiaries were her grandchildren Elizabeth and Mary Taylor, daughters of Elizabeth, her own late daughter and her husband John Taylor and her daughter, Hannah, wife of John Raymond and their children, Hannah, Mary, Samuel, Elizabeth, John and Joseph Raymond. Her son-in-law, John Raymond, received copyhold land in Hendon and freehold land in Finchley. Rose Marsh was buried on 29th November 1690 at St. Dunstan and All Saints, Stepney, as were her daughter Abigail and son-in-law, James Disbrowe. Her will was proved on 13th January 1691 *(PROB 11/403/76)*.

The Faculty Office marriage allegation, dated 1st September 1697, confirms that Matthew Holworthy, Esq. of Hackney, Middlesex was to marry Elizabeth Disbrowe of Hornsey, Middlesex, aged 16, with the consent of her guardian, Joseph Marsh, of Watford, Hertfordshire and that John Raymond, of Highgate, Middlesex was her trustee, as her parents were dead. They were to marry at Hornsey Church. This suggests that Elizabeth Disbrowe was brought up in Highgate by her maternal grandmother, Rose Marsh and then, after the grandmother's death, by her aunt and uncle, Hannah and John Raymond. When the will of Rose Disbrowe, widow of Samuel Disbrowe, was proved in April 1699 *(PROB 11/450/175)* she gave Elizabeth Holworthy her grandfather Samuel's picture set in gold and if she were to die it was to go to his grandson Samuel Mills. She gave Samuel Mills his grandfather's ring that bore a coat of arms and if he died it was to go to Matthew Holworthy and his wife Elizabeth. Rose Disbrowe wanted her brother, Joseph Hobson to have their father's picture and that of her first husband, Richard Lacey. Her sister Sarah White was to receive a picture of Richard Lacey's father.

Rose Disbrowe, who was the daughter of William Hobson of Hackney, a haberdasher, was baptised at St. Martin Ludgate on 24th March 1615. She married three times; a marriage allegation dated 26th January 1633 was made between Richard Lacey, a haberdasher, aged 24 and with the consent of her father, Rose Hobson, aged 18, both of the Parish of St. Martin Ludgate. Richard was, according to the parish register, a captain who died at the fight at Brentford and was buried on 17th November 1642 at St. Martin, Ludgate. The battle, which the Royalists won, was fought on 12th November. Captain Lacey was in one of the first regiments, consisting of six companies on foot, raised by Parliament in the summer of 1642. Lacey had written his will in Buckinghamshire on 14th August 1642, in anticipation of his possible death. He appointed Rose as executrix and his father-in-law Hobson and his brother Nathaniel Lacey as overseers. Rose and Richard had had a son, William, born in 1638 and buried in 1639. She buried two stillborn children at St. Martin, Ludgate on 10th May 1643 *(Parish register)*.

Rosamond *Hobson*, not Lacey, married *Samuell* Penoyer (Penoier), a merchant from London, on 1st April 1645 in the Collegiate Church of St. Katherine by the Tower. He was buried on 5th May 1654 at St. Olave, in the liberty of the Tower. In the will of her father, William Hobson, written in 1661 and proved in 1662, Rose was acknowledged as the wife of Samuel Disbrowe. She died in 1698.

Mary Whitfield, Elizabeth and Rebecca Hayter

The will of Nathaniel Higginson, a merchant, refers to his aunt, Mary Whitfield, "*if living*", suggesting that she was known to be close to death when he wrote his will some time before probate was settled on 13th November 1708 (*PROB 11/504/248*). Appointed by the East India Company, Higginson was a former Governor of Madras who had returned with his family around 1699. Having survived his stay in the East Indies, he died from smallpox in the Parish of St. Pancras, Soper Lane, on 1st November and was buried in St. Mary Le Bow Church, Cheapside on 13th November 1708. Mary Whitfield and Nathaniel Higginson died within days of each other. His aunt Mary would then have been around 77 years of age. The records of St. Olave, Hart Street, confirm that Mary Whitfield died around 5th November 1708 and was buried in Bunhill Fields, which was a burial ground of the Nonconformists. Her niece, Elizabeth Hayter, died on 19th September 1712 and was buried in the new vaults under the vestry at St. Olave; Tom Hayter was also buried in the new vault. An *"admon"* (*PROB 6/90, Page 120 Number 78*) for Elizabeth Hayter, in Latin, taking the place of a will, was administered in July 1715, around six months following December, when the application was made. In approximate terms, it describes Thomas Hayter, the natural and legitimate brother of Elizabeth Hayter, of the Parish of St. Olave, Hart Street, she being deceased and unmarried, having to administer grants, rights and credits of said deceased well and truly sworn. Rebecka Hayter, widow and mother of the deceased had first renounced the administration in favour of her son, Thomas. It further confirms that Rebecca Hayter, wife of Tom Hayter, was still alive in July 1715.

Tom and Rebecca Hayter's daughter Rebecca married William Hubbald. Evidence of a marriage exists in *Marriage Licences-Faculty Office:1632-1714,* between William Hubbald, and Rebeccah *Hayler sic.,* held at Lambeth Palace, Library. It was dated 12th June 1696 and said:

> Which day appeared personally Samuel Pelling of the Tower of London Gent under oath that there is a marriage intended to be solemnicised between Wm: Hubbald of the Tower aforesaid widower and Rebeccah Hayter of Crutched Fryers London aged above 22 years spinster with the consent of her mother ___ Hayter of the same place widow not knowing of any impediment by reason of any prior contract consanguinity affinity or otherwise to hinder ___ marriage of its truth of those present made oath prayed licence for them to be marryed in the parish church of St Olave Hart Street London. (Pg 137)

The notice was signed in person by "*Sam:* Pelling" and "*Wm:* Oldys", the latter an official. Rebecca and her mother were living at Crutched Friars, which is close to Hart Street and Seething Lane. The marriage took place after the date of the notice but probably not at St. Olave, Hart Street as there were only four weddings recorded there in 1696 and none for the couple. It was not unusual, with a marriage licence, for couples to marry in churches other than that specified as the purpose was to marry quickly, without fuss and dependent on availability.

That William was a widower at the time of his marriage is borne out by a letter written by him from the Tower on 12th November 1692 to his father, Edward Hubbald, at Stoke, near Guildford, in Surrey, saying: *"Tower Nov. 12th 1692:*

> Honoured Sir
> We have had no Office today. Mr Bertie came out finding none did not stay, I told him what you ordered me, he is very well satisfied and said you have not been wanted and further that you kept the office the time he was in the country and that it was but reasonable you should take your turn
>
> I have persuaded Mr Gardiner to stay till you come to town as I was going to Sir Henry Sheeres about what I had intimated in my last meet with his servant which he discloses here is [___] extraordinary, All is well and give you their duty and service especially Mr Parker. My sister Hickman hath been ill but is now much better. My wife with myself gives you and my mother our duty and service to brother and sister.

I am Your dutiful son Wm: Hubbald

I kept George till now expecting to have sent him with some writings from my Brother Hickman but he disappointed me.

(New York State Library, Albany, Edward Eggleston Estate Purchase, No. 1308)

William Hubbald was married at this time and had a brother and sister staying with his parents at Stoke, probably Edward and Mary Hubbald as his other sister, Elizabeth Hickman, was staying with William and his wife at the Tower of London.

The records of St. John the Evangelist Church, at Stoke near Guildford, show that Rebeccah was buried there on 2nd February 1699:

Febr 2 Mrs Rebekah Hubbald wife of William Hubbald Gent of the Parish of S. Peters in the Tower of London 'Jane' day a certificate.

St. John was the church nearest the estate which was owned by Edward Hubbald, William's father. The entry also confirms William Hubbald's connection to the Parish of St. Peter's within the Tower, close to where he probably lived. *The Natural History and Antiquities of the County of Surrey,* by John Aubrey and Richard Rawlinson, published in 1718, volume 3, pp. 273 and 277 and *A History of Stoke next Guildford by Lynn Clark,* provide several references for members of the Hubbald family. The former states that there was a white grave stone in St. John the Evangelist Church, which said *"Here lieth the body of Rebeckah, wife of Mr. William Hubbald, Esqr. who departed this life the 26th day of January, in the year of our Lord God 1699. And in the 27th year her age"*. This is reasonable confirmation that she was Rebekah Hayter before her marriage and that she was born around 1672. Likewise, she was the person who in 1691, under the age of twenty-one, inherited a share of the house, once owned by James Disbrowe. She was probably the last of the Hayter children to have been born.

William's burial was recorded on 10th December 1709 at the same Church as his wife at Stoke, near Guildford. He had died on 8th December.

The will of William Hubbald, Esq., was made on 1st December 1709, in which he described himself as *"weak in body but of perfect mind and memory"*. He referred to *"controversies about the advowson of the Church of Stoke"* and to a problem that *"having bin cashier under Sir Thomas Littleton, Treasurer of the Navy"* may have caused. He bequeathed £1000 to Edward Hubbald, his youngest son and all his real and personal estate was to be divided equally between his two sons named as executors. He ordered his eldest son, William, to act in the said executorship *"or else that he shall take no benefit by this my will"*. The will was witnessed by Henry Durley, Mary Shaw, Nathan Hickman and *Jer:* Holt; Durley and Hickman being his brothers-in-law. Probate was not granted to his sons and executors until the 13th February 1709/10, *"English style" (PROB 11/513/296).* Written alongside the will was a statement which said that probate was granted on 2nd July 1724 to William and Rebecca's son, Edward Hubbald, *"other executor"*.

The names of the young Edward and William Hubbald arise in connection with an Act of Parliament of 1711, following the death of their father. The petition is summarised in the *House of Lord's Journal Volume 19*, of 7th February 1711 and was brought by Henry Durley and Nathan Hickman. The next friends and guardians named were Mary and Henry Durley, Elizabeth and Nathan Hickman and Edward Hubbald, the brother of the deceased who acted on behalf of the two infant sons, the elder brother, William who *"was but 18 years of age"* and the younger brother, Edward. Elizabeth Hickman and Mary Durley were the daughters of Edward Hubbald, the children's' grandfather (this suggests that the elder son William was born around 1693 and provides proof that he was a son of William Hubbald by his first wife). The petition brought before the judges was to enable the estate to be sold *"for discharging an annuity of £189 to Henry St. John out of money raised by the sale of Merton Abbey and applying the surplus for Edward and William Hubbald"*. The amount of £12,777 was raised, which was paid to Dame Anne Littleton, the widow of Sir Thomas Littleton, to clear the debt to the Crown.

In Manning's and Bray's book, other memorials and inscriptions for the Hubbald family were recorded at Stoke Church. The church dates back to the sixteenth century although some parts are from an earlier period. It retains a black marble memorial in the floor to Edward Hubbald, at that time, Lord of the Manor of Stoke. He died at the age of 70, on 5th July 1707, having been born around 1637 and was buried before the high altar in Stoke Church on the 10th July. Near him is his wife Elizabeth. whose black marble memorial describes that she had died on Sunday night on 28th December 1701 in her seventieth year and was buried on 3rd January 1701. She was born in 1631 and was thereby older than her husband. In *Some Account of the Parish of Stoke near Guildford* by Thomas William Graham M.A. Rector, published in 1933, the author describes a silver paten *(a shallow dish used for the bread at the Eucharist)*, some eight ounces in weight. Engraved on it was *"The gift of Edward Hubbald, Esquire 1702"* and the same inscription was repeated on a much bigger silver flagon, also used for wine for the Eucharist and weighing some sixty-three ounces and hallmarked with the year 1631. The information, originally taken from Surrey Archaeological Collections, listing church plates of Surrey, explains that Mr. Hubbald was Lord of the Manor and patron of the living.

20

Henry and Whitfield Hayter

Henry Hayter

J. M. Collinge's book on *Navy Board Officials* is a revealing source of information on Henry Hayter, who was Clerk to the Controller from 26th March 1681 while Tom Hayter was the Controller. Henry is recorded as being one of six Clerks to the Commissioners for Old Accounts from 26th March 1686, along with one Nathaniel Whitfield. He then became clerk (Bills and Accounts) from 25th June 1689 to 25th December 1692. The entries in the Admiralty books *(ADM 20/54 nos. 299,350,1025,1598)*, covering the period 1st April 1690–13th March 1691, show that he received £7. 10s. per quarter as a clerk "*belonging to accompt*" (controller) in HM Navy. Henry was Tom's son. Compared to his father, his remuneration was quite low but he would have been in his twenties during the period in question. Then Henry's career in the Admiralty ended.

A letter dating from 8th July 1696, when management of the Ticket Office was attached to the Controller of Treasurer's Accounts and held among Admiralty records at The National Archives *(ADM 106/488/125)*, was sent by Henry Hayter from the Treasury Office where he had become employed to Mr. Jeremy Gregory, Clerk of the Cheque, Chatham. Hayter explained that he had been out of Town, preventing him from replying sooner. The letter was not in itself especially significant but the signature was identical to that of Henry Hayter in later documents, proving that Hayter was working there in July 1696.

An entry in the *Calendar of State Papers, Treasury Books, Volume 13, on March 24, 1697-1698, page 281*, in the Treasury Warrants, stated that:

> ...same to George Dodington Esq. the Petition of Henry Hayter shewing that he was employed under Mr Anthony Stephens, the Deputy to the Navy Treasurer, for several years and that there remained under the care of the said Stephens at his death near 800,000L in tallies and money and petitioner has ever since Stephens' decease been employed on his accounts and in paying and issuing the said sum, which trust he has discharged very faithfully and has been at constant attendance therein but has received no allowance or salary for the same: therefore praying consideration and reward. (Reference Book VII Pg 260)

Dodington was sometimes Doddington, when transcribed. Henry Hayter was dealing with substantial amounts of money and was obviously a well-respected and trusted employee. An entry in the *Calendar of State Papers, Treasury Books, Volume 15, on May 22, 1699-1700, page 86*, in the Treasury Minutes, referring to a meeting in the Treasury Chambers Cockpit said:

> Sir Thomas Littleton [the Navy Treasurer] and other Commissioners of the Navy are called in. My Lords direct Mr Doddington and Mr Hayter (who are present) to give an account of the money and tallies in the hands of Mr Doddington and Mr Stephens respectively for the public service and for what particular uses the same remain. Mr Hayter will go to the books in the Navy [Office] and see what part is assigned and what not.

The issue was not resolved as again, as reported in *Volume 17.1, 1702, on June 24, page 459*, there was recorded:

> June 24 – Henry Hayter [petition read] Referred to the Commissioners of the Navy.

In the Treasury warrants, in the same volume, on June 30, *page 273*, was written:

> Same to the Navy Commissioner to report on the enclosed petition [missing] of Henry Hayter for reward for his services in paying away near 800,000L which remained in the hands of Anthony Stephens late Cashier of the Navy at the time of his death and returning certificates of the raid payment.

The last such reference to Henry Hayter was in *Volume 20.2*, on June 6, 1705, *page 127*, reporting:

> Hen[ry] Hayter [clerk to the late Navy Treasurer, his petition for reward is read] Speak to the C[ommissioners of the] Navy about this at the next attendance [June 6, Treasury Board Papers.

Volume 20, records that there was a payment of £80 made some time during the year January 1, 1705 to December 31, 1705 in *Declared Accounts Audit Office Bundle 1725, Roll 147* in the name of Dame Anne Littleton, widow and sole executrix of Sir Thomas Littleton, baronet, late treasurer of the Navy. There are no further references in the Treasury Books to Henry Hayter, so this may have been the end of the matter.

Henry Hayter would by then have acquired a reasonable standard of living and wealth from his job, contacts and family and may have given up his job as clerk. John Carswell, in his book on *The South Sea Bubble* (revised edition. 1993, Alan Sutton Publishing), explained that in this period, built on the expansion of business in the City, there was an increase in demand for literate clerks and tellers both in government and for accounting and business documents. The wages may have been modest but for some it was a way to commence their money-making careers and engage in trading themselves as they were at the heart of the process. It would appear to have been a time of significant self-interest. This may have been the case with Henry Hayter. The evidence is that his father, brothers and uncle had friends in high places.

Such was his position that, according to *The Calendar of State Papers, Treasury Books, Volume 10.2, 1693-1696, on page 911,* on January 4, 1695, Henry Hayter (Haytor), made a loan of £1,000 to the King. On the same page was recorded a loan of £700 from William Lethieullier, the brother of Sir John Lethieullier. In the same volume, *page 914,* on January 19, Lady Lethieullier loaned £5,500 and on January 22 Henry Hayter loaned a further £1,000. This William Lethieullier was the uncle of a younger William Lethieullier, who appears later in the book.

It is difficult to comprehend why Rebecca Hayter was pleading hardship when clearly her sons were involved in financial and property transactions of enormous magnitude. It may be that their father had many debts or invested heavily and in complicated ways in order to set his sons up in business.

Whitfield Hayter

Whitfield Hayter was the youngest brother among Tom and Rebecca Hayter's children. Nevertheless, his relevance to the overall activities of the Hayter family is of importance.

The Goldsmiths' Company confirms that Whitfield Hayter was a member by apprenticeship. He was apprenticed to Stephen Evance in 1679 and became *"free"* in 1689/90. Apprentices were taken on between the ages of 13 and 16, suggesting that Whitfield Hayter was born between the years 1663 and 1666, the years of the Plague and Great Fire. In the Pepys Diary there were accounts of Hayter's wife staying in the country during this difficult and dangerous time, during which it may be that the births were not registered in the normal way.

The Freedom of the City Admission Papers 1681-1925 *(database on-line, source LMA COL/CHD/FR/02/0027-0033)* includes an indenture for Whitfeild Hayton [Hayter], son of Thomas Hayton [Hayter] of London who was apprenticed in April 1679 for eight years to Steven [Stephen] Evance, a citizen and goldsmith of London, in order to learn the latter's art. The master was to instruct, feed, clothe and provide lodgings and the apprentice was forbidden to marry during his apprenticeship. Goldsmiths would not enter a mark until apprentices were freemen; it might be presumed that Hayter had a mark, working as he did with a well-established goldsmith. In the same database in 1690, is a memorandum of Robert Barkham, son of Robert Barkham of Lincoln, who was apprenticed for seven years to Stephen Evance; Barkham was eighteen at that time and was described in an attached note as *"Robert Barkham Goldsmiths' Company by service"*, indicating apprenticeship. Goldsmiths' Company confirms that he appeared in their index of apprentices and freemen but that there is no record of his freedom. His father died in 1692 and Robert inherited the land at Tottenham. Whitfield's brother, Henry Hayter, bought it in 1694.

The name of Whitfield Hayter appears in Appendix A of Moshe Milevsky's book, *King William's Tontine'* (*A tontine is "an annuity shared by subscribers to a loan, the shares increasing as subscribers die until the last survivor gets all,*

or until a specified date when the remaining survivors share the proceeds" –
Concise Oxford Dictionary.) The purpose of the scheme was to raise £1,000,000
for King William and Queen Mary to carry on the war against France. The sum
raised by midsummer 1693 was £108,100, made up of 1081 shares each of
£100; it did not reach the target expected. A printed list of nominees known as
"the Heyrick List" (1694) is held by the British Library. It states:

> A particular Accompt of the Moneys paid into the Receipt of the
> Exchequer, upon the late Million Act for the benefit of Survivor-
> ship: containing the names of the several Nominees their Ages,
> Places of abode, the sums paid upon each Nominees life ….. BL
> 514.k.2. (23)

The document, printed for Samuel Heyrick at Grays-Inn-Gate, Holborn,
in 1694, was examined by Sir Robert Howard, Kt., Auditor of the Receipt of
Exchequer. It was recorded that Whitfield Hayter of St. Edmond, Lombard
Street, London, a goldsmith, who was aged 27 years in 1693 and therefore
born around 1666, contributed the sum of £100. A later document, printed
by Henry King, gives in alphabetical order with a separate list of nominees
who died prior to 1730 (*BL 8285.ee.48*) "a *list of the surviving nominees on
the Fund of Survivorship; at Midsummer 1730 and their descriptions to that
time*". *Witfield* Hayter's name appears in the list of 499 nominees who had died
(*page 19*). In another article, written in 2014, Milevsky suggests that as the
list of dead nominees was not in alphabetical order, it might be assumed that
it was recorded in the order in which they died. According to his calculations
Hayter lived for 57 years, making his year of death 1723.

In the book *John Dryden: Tercentenary Essays* edited by Paul Hammond
and David Hopkins, in a chapter by John Barnard, "Dryden, Tonson and the
Patrons of *The Works of Virgil* (1697)", Whitfield Hayter was included as one
of its eighteen patrons, some of whom were merchants, on incomes of more
than £600 a year. The information was included in *London inhabitants inside
the City Walls 1695,* introduced by D.V. Glass, published by *London Record
Society 2 (1966)*. Hayter was described as a bachelor and goldsmith, living
at Lombard Street, which was where his partner, Stephen Evance had a business. Whitfield Hayter had been obviously a man of culture as well as wealth.

Whitfield was a bachelor in 1695 but went on to marry Martha Whatton.
A baptism of Martha Whatton, daughter of William and Martha, took place
on 28[th]April 1680 at St. Margaret, Westminster, suggesting a connection to
that area. The earliest that Martha and Whitfield Hayter are likely to have
married was around 1695, at which time, assuming there is no other Martha
Whatton, she would have been 15 years of age. At the same church is a record
of a William Whatton, who married Mary Flood on 5th September 1652; they
are likely to have been her parents or grandparents. If Whitfield Hayter was
a wealthy man one might assume that his wife would have also been from a
similar background.

A picture of the life and business activities of Whitfield Hayter has been
constructed for present purposes from the documents at The National Archives

and other sources. Documents *(C111/184)*, covering some twenty years, relate to Whitfield Hayter, Peter Percivall and Sir Stephen Evance. They include original wills, draft agreements, conveyances and indentures and other documents. An indenture, dated 27th February 1688, indicates that Whitfield Hayter became involved with Peter Percivall and Stephen Evance at that point or earlier. An extract from the draft document, with the name of a third party missing, outlines the relationship:

> Shall and will for and during all the said term of three years wholly truly faithfully and diligently to the utmost of his power, knowledge, and skill employ and apply himself in onto and about the said trade and dealings aforesaid and the affairs and business thereof to and for the utmost benefit and advantage of the said Stephen Evance and Peter Percivall [...] out of stock and trade aforesaid [...]. of all such bonds bills, speciality notes and other assurances [...] for any money plate jewels, gold, silver, goods declared within [...] for the benefits of Stephen Evance and Peter Percivall [...] will take him (Whitfeld Hayter) into partnership if still alive, one quarter part.

After three years, if all partners were still alive, Hayter would be taken into partnership with one quarter of the business, for which he had to pay £150 in four instalments per annum *"in trust"* to Stephen Evance and Peter Percivall, citizens and goldsmiths. On the back of the indenture is the following statement:

> I Whitfeld Hayter within mentioned do hereby declare and agree that during the life of the within mentioned Peter Percivall wherein I acted on my name... was used as partner with Peter Percivall and Stephen Evance within mentioned, now Sir Stephen Evance, Knight, that I so acted and my name was so used only in trust and for the proper use and benefit of the said Stephen Evance and Peter Percivall and that ever since...Peter Percivall's death wherein on any account I have stated or shall...or my name hath been or shall be used as partner then...of Sir Stephen Evance, the same as shall be in trust only for ye paper [proper] use and benefit of the said Stephen Evance, his executors administrators and assigns for the said Stephen Evance his executor administrators and assigns having allready allowed or bring to allow and pay to me the sum of lawful English money per annum for so long time as I have acted or shall continue to act with him as partner for my pains and troubles therein until some other agreement to ye contrary hereof shall be concluded on between us and made in writing executed by us under our hands and sealed in the presence of two or more credible witnesses and witnessed whereof I have hereunto sealed my hand this witness
>
> Sealed and delivered in the presence of us Nathan Whitfeld H. Hayter Laur. Hatsell.

The witnesses to the agreement were Nathan Whitfield, an uncle of Whitfield Hayter who died in 1696, Henry Hayter, elder brother of Whitfield Hayter and Lawrence Hatsell, a step-brother of Stephen Evance. Peter Percivall died in or around 1693. A second witnessed statement, supplementary to the original agreement, written after Percivall's death, suggests that Whitfield was expecting to continue to receive money from the partnership as the three years had elapsed. It also suggests that the partnership was not equal and Hayter was beholden to Sir Stephen Evance. Included in the collection of documents at The National Archives is the will of Peter Percivall, which was proved on 2nd November 1693 (*PROB 11/417/11*). Sir Stephen Evance was given £60 for mourning and Whitfield Hayter and Mrs. Hatsell, the mother of Sir Stephen Evance, 40 guineas each for mourning. Peter Percivall's cousin, Samuel Percivall, Ebenezer Sadler and Thomas Lake were executors of the will. Thomas Lake received £300 for himself and his children. Percivall had a sister by the name of Mary, a brother called Andrew and nephews, Andrew, James and Peter Percivall. The Peter Percivall mentioned in Whitfield Hayter's administration is likely to have been the other nephew in question as the heirs and assigns continue to have responsibility for debts and agreements. Andrew Percivall's will was proved in 1696. Ebenezer Sadler of the Parish of St. Martin-in-the-Fields died in 1714.

Whitfield Hayter's name appears in the *Journals of the House of Commons, Volume 10,* on 11th October 1690 *(pages 437 and 438)* in detailed accounts of expenditure incurred in the War on armaments, ships and other costs. The King and Queen (William and Mary), acknowledged that they had borrowed:

> ...principal monies borrowed by way of loan upon the public revenue and taxes between November 5, 1688 and June 27, 1690.

Hayter had loaned £40,000 in February 1689; he was one of a number of people who lent sizable amounts. It was recorded that the money had been repaid to Hayter between the two dates in question.

The following entries relating to Whitfield Hayter's loans were also recorded in the *Calendar of State Papers, Treasury Books, Volume 9, William and Mary, 1689-1692.* For the purpose of these transcriptions, *Whitfield* is used in place of *Whitfeld* and *Hayter* for *Hater.* From a meeting, which took place at the Whitehall Treasury Chambers, the following statement was recorded in *Volume 9.2, on December 19, 1689, page 337:*

> ...same to same the following sums will be lent into the Exchequer on the credit of the 12d. Aid, viz. 600L. by Justice Dolbin; 100L. by Richard Marriot; 150L. by Cassandra Harrison and 100L. by Whitfield Hayter, making 250L.; 2,000L. by Lancelot Burton and 23,000L. by Whitfield Hayter making 25,000L.

Volume 9.2, February 14, 1689/90, page 369, included the statement:

Sir Samuel Dashwood, Mr Duncombe, Mr Foche and Mr Evans do agree to advance the King, 40,000L. on the Excise to be repaid at 5,000L. a week, the first payment to commence the first week in April. The money will be lent on Mr Whitfield Hayter's name. *(Treasury Minute Book VII, Pg 221-222 [out letters] (general) XII Pg 198)*

A further reference in the same volume to the loan, on *February 14, page 501*

Same to same to receive from Whitfield Hayter, the 40,000L. which he has agreed to lend on credit of the Excise and to give him tallies of loan on said revenue for same.

In *Volume 9.2, on February 19, 1689/90, page 509*:

Treasury warrant to the Receipt for tallies of pro on the Excise for the several sums as follows, amounting to 30,000L., lent into the Exchequer by Whitfield Hayter, Esq. (as by tallies of loan for respectively 5,000L., 5,000L., 5,000L. and 5,000L. on Feb 14 and 5,000L. and 5,000L., on Feb 15) on credit of the Excise: taking care that when the tallies of pro are levied the said tallies of loans be taken in and vacated.

In *Volume 9.2, on March 4, 1689/90, page 524*:

Treasure warrant to the Receipt for tallies of pro on the Excise for 10,000L. to Whitfield Hayter, he having lent said sum into the Exchequer, viz. 5,000L., Feb 19 and 5,000L., Feb 25, on the credit of the Excise. When the tallies of pro are levied the tallies of loan for same are to be taken in and vacated.

In *Volume 9.2, on March 14, 1689/90, page 540* :

Same dormant to the Excise Commissioners to pay (out of the revenue of Excise) to Whitfield Hayter from time to time 6 per cent interest on the 40,000L., which he has lent into the Exchequer on the credit of the Excise (to wit 20,000L. lent Feb 14, 10,000L. lent Feb 15, 5,000L. lent Feb 19, 5,000L. lent Feb 25).

In *Volume 9.4, on July 27, 1692, page 1742*:

Whitfield Hayter: 5,000L.: tally of loan dated July 22 inst.
Whitfield Hayter: 1,000L.: 22 July: payable after 15,500L.

On *page 1744,*

Whitfield Hayter: 4,000L. 22 July: payable after 29,662L.

These were huge amounts of money to lend, particularly as Whitfield Hayter was still a young man and not yet a partner with Peter Percivall and Sir Stephen Evance.

The following table is compiled from the *Calendar of State Papers Treasury Book, Volume 9.5, 1689–1692*, Appendix II and outlines the extent to which Whitfield Hayter, Sir Stephen Evance and other family members and business associates were involved in various financial matters.

Calendar of State Papers, Treasury Book, Volume 9.5 1689-1692, Appendix II. Not all names are included. Amounts are given in Pounds and are rounded up. Some of the larger sums are made up of smaller amounts.

Year	Date	Loans on the Present Aid	Amount in £	Page
1689	Aug 9	Peter Percivall	5,000 (3,000, 2,000)	1975
	Aug 16	Peter Percivall	10,000 (4,000,3,000,2,000, 1,000)	"
	Sep 5	Christopher Lethieullier	2,000	"
		Thomas Frederick	4,000 (2,000, 2,000)	"
		Stephen Evance	2,000	"
		John Ward	4,000	"
		Whitfield Hayter	2,000	"
	Sep 18	Stephen Evance	3000	"
	Oct 25	Stephen Evance	10,000 (5,000, 5,000)	"
1689	Date	**Loans on the First Poll**	Amount in £	
	May 24	Sir John Lethieullier, kt	500	1976
	July 10	Whitfield Hayter	5,000	1977
		John Ward	5,000	"
		Thomas Frederick, esq.	7,000	"
		Stephen Evance	7,000	"
	July 26	Stephen Evance	7,200 (3,000, 4,200)	"
	Aug 6	Stephen Evance	1,500	"
	Aug 17	Stephen Evance	2,000	1978
		Whitfield Hayter	2,000	1978
	Aug 27	Stephen Evance	2,450	"
		Thomas Frederick	327	"
	Sep 18	Stephen Evance	2,417	"
		Stephen Evance	2,000	"
	Sep 27	Whitfield Hayter	2,000	"
		Stephen Evance	2,000	"
	Sep 28	Stephen Evance	5,000	"
1689	Date	**Loans on the 12d Aid**	Amount in £	
	Jul 29	Sir John Lethieullier	500	1980
	Dec 10	Nathaniel Whitfield	1,200	1987
	Dec 19	Stephen Evance	3,125	1987
		Whitfield Hayter	23,100 (small amounts)	1987
	Dec 20	Sir John Lethieullier	500	1988
		Stephen Evance	3,000	1988
1690	Date	**Loans on the 2s Aid**	Amount in £	
	Apr 17	Thomas Frederick	2,000 (700, 1,300)	1995
	Apr 26	Nathaniel Whitfield	1,000	1995
	May 30	Stephen Evance	10,341 (small amounts)	1996
	Sep 26	Stephen Evance	1,019	1999
		Stephen Evance	1,100	1999
	Oct 2	Stephen Evance	1,528	1999
		Whitfield Hayter	10,054 (small amounts)	1999
		Stephen Evance	4,622	1999
		Stephen Evance	2075	1999

1689/90	Date	Loans on the Additional 12d Aid	Amount in £	Page
	Jan 23	Sir John Lethieullier	500	2001
	Jan 27	Stephen Evance	4,000 (1,000, 1,000, 2,000)	2001
		Stephen Evance	8,000 (3,000, 3,000, 2,000)	2001
	Feb 1	John Lethieullier, esq.	500	2001
	Feb 10	William Hooker	5,000	2002
	Feb 11	John Lethieullier	1,000	2002
	Feb 12	Thomas Frederick	1,300	2002

William Hooker was the father-in-law of Sir John Lethieullier. Christopher and William Lethieullier were brothers of Sir John Lethieullier. Thomas Frederick and Peter Percivall were business associates of Stephen Evance. John Ward was the brother-in-law of Stephen Evance. Nathaniel Whitfield was the uncle of Whitfield Hayter.

In Volume 10.1, of the *Calendar of State Papers, Treasury Books, 1693-96, on April 3, 1693, page 141*:

> Same to same for tallies of pro on the Excise for 2,500L. to Whitfield Hayter, gent., in repayment of so much lent by him Mar 28 last, on the Excise.

In *Volume 10.1, on April 11, 1693, page 152*:

> Treasury warrant to the Receipt for tallies on the Excise for 2,000L. to Whitfield Hayter in repayment of so much lent by him thereon April 4 inst.

In *Volume 10.1, on April 28, 1693, page 174*:

> Same to Mr Knight, Customs Cashier, to pay 46L. 14s. 8d. to Whit[field] Hayter for 2 per cent. gratuity on 4,000L. lent by him.

In *Volume 10.1, on May 30, 1693, page 219*:

> Henry Guy to the Auditor of the Receipt to reserve for my Lords' disposal the 300L. which is or will be paid into the Exchequer by Mr Hayter on credit of the Hereditary and Temporary Excise.

In *Volume 10.1, on June 8, 1693, page 231*:

> Henry Guy to the Auditor of the Receipt to issue 300L. to the Duchess of Buckingham out of the like sum lent by Mr Hayter on the Hereditary and Temporary Excise, which was appointed to be reserved for the Treasury Lords' disposal.

In *Volume 10.1, on June 11, 1693, page 238*:

> Same to the Receipt for tallies of pro on the Hereditary and Temporary Excise for 300L. to Whitfield Hayter in repayment of so much by him lent on credit thereof the 2nd inst.

In *Volume 10.1, on October 4, 1693, page 35*:

Royal sign manual for 188L. 5s. 1d. to Lancelot Burton and 39L. 19s. 6d. to Whitfield Hayter: making together 228L. 4s. 7d. without account, in reward for good and acceptable services (Money warrant dated Oct 9 thereon) (Money order dated Oct 11 thereon).

In *Volume 10.1, on October 11, 1693, page 362*:

Same to same to issue as follows out of the Hereditary and Temporary Excise,viz.188L. 5s. 1d. to Lancelot Burton: 3L. 19s.6d. to Whitfield Hayter.

In *Volume 10.1, on December 18, 1693, page 429* :

46L.14s.8d. to Whitfield Hayter.

In *Volume 10.1, on March 26, 1693/4, page 549*:

Treasury Commission to Richard Lascells of the parish of St Martin-in-the-Fields, goldsmith, to be a Receiver for the Act [5 William and Mary c 7] for duties on salt, etc. for securing 1,000,000L. loans. The like commissions severally to:
   Whitfield Hayter, Richard Hoare of London, goldsmith.....

In *Volume 10.2, 1693-1696, on April 20, 1694, page 595*:

Henry Guy to the Auditor of the Receipt to issue104,000L. to the Earl of Ranelagh on account for the service of the Forces; out of loans to be made at the Exchequer by Sir Joseph Herne and Sir Stephen Evance or on their procurement, on credit of the Exchequer in general. This sum is intended to pay one year's subsidy to the Duke of Savoy and the exchange thereof to Turin. (Same dated April 23 to said Earl. This sum is ordered to you out of loans on the Exchequer in general which are made in the name of Mr Whitfield Hayter. It is the King's pleasure that you pay same to Herne and Evance, 96,000L.. thereof for 12 months' subsidy to Oct. 10 next to said Duke at 8,000L. a month and 8,000L. for the exchange thereof to Turin.)

The loan was made in the name of Whitfield Hayter and not Herne and Evance.
   In *Volume 10.2, 1693-1696, on April 23, 1694, page 597*:

Royal sign manual for the issue of 143L. 12s. 7d. viz., 91L. 17s. 4d. to Sir Stephen Evance, 19L. 3s.10d. to Henry Furnace, 2L. 3s. 0d.to Whitfield Hayter and 30L. 8s. 3d. to Josiah Ordway, without account: in consideration of good and acceptable services.

In *Volume 10.2, 1693-1696, on May 8, 1694, page 610-611*:

Treasury warrant to the Auditor of the Receipt to repay to Whit-field Hayter of London, goldsmith the 104,000L. (lent on April 21 last on credit of the Exchequer in general) out of the first moneys arising by the Poll [5&6 William and Mary c 14] in such course and order as the [repayment] orders for the said loan are already entered or numbered: paying the agreed 6 per cent interest thereon out of the unappropriated moneys of the fourth of the Customs.

In *Volume 10.2, 1693-1696, on July 3, 1694, page 688*:

Treasury warrants to the Receipt for tallies to persons as follows for repayment of loans made by them respectively on credit thereof:
910L. to Whitfield Hayter: lent June 30.
Whitfield was only one of many lenders listed.

In *Volume 10.2, 1693-1696, on July 6, 1694, pages 694-5*:

Treasury warrant to the Auditor of the Receipt to enter and charge upon the Register of the present Quarterly Poll the following principal sums which have been lent on credit of the Excheq-uer in general and for which orders were drawn for repayment thereof with 6 per cent interest payable quarterly: the repayment thereof to be hereby made out of the said Quarterly Poll in the following manner, viz. the sums lent between May 31 last and June 4 inst., amounting to 281,435L. 9s.6d. are to begin to be paid next after repayment of 104,000L. principal money lent in the name of Whitfield Hayter of London, goldsmith [and which is charged on the said Register], as by a Treasury Warrant, supra, p.610.The interest on the said loans [as follows] is to be paid out of the unappropriated fourth part of the Customs.

Appending: schedule of said loans on the Exchequer in general:
1694- April 21- Mr Hayter.................... 104,000L. 0s.0d.

The list included others lending amounts of 87,135L. down to 100L.

In *Volume 10.3, 1695-96, on January 10, 1695/6, page 1279*:

Treasury order for the renewal of a lost money order of loan No.1,346, on the two thirds of the Additional Excise: same being lost as appears by the affidavit of Mr. Whitfield Hayter.

In *Volume 10.3, 1695-96, on January 22, 1695/6, page 1288*:

Treasury order for renewing a lost order of loan No. 520 for 200L. on the Quarterly Poll, afterwards transferred to the first 4s. Aid [being drawn in favour of Edward Russell, but assigned to Whitfield Hayter and] the loss thereof being sworn to by said Hayter.

In *Volume 10.3, 1695, on June 14, 1695, page 1386*, the entry, as part of the business covered, in the afternoon, included the statement:

Write to Mr Hayter to be here on Monday afternoon.

(presumably Whitfield Hayter)

In *Volume 17.2, 1702*, an entry for Whitfield Hayter, detailing Secret Service payments, dating back to August 11, 1691, *page 631*:

...paid Whitfield Hayter in satisfaction of so much money remitted by Sir Joseph Herne to Hamburg to be there disposed of by William Duncombe, Esq., their Majesties Envoy at Stockholm for their Majesties service: clear [of fees] 2,300L.

Whitfield Hayter was involved in giving financial support to the King and Queen in matters of state in different countries.

The last entry recorded for him in the *Calendar of State Papers, Treasury Books, Volume 31.3,1717*, was dated *September 14, 1717, page 579* and said:

Treasury warrant to the Auditor of the Receipt, the clerk of the Pells et al to draw a[dormant money] order for paying to Sir Caesar Child et al as assignees in a commission of bankrupt a Banker's annuity of 6L. 8s.1d. standing in the name of John Hoyle as an assignee of Sir Robert Viner: all in conformity with the certificate as follows taking care such proper memorandums be made on the former certificate and in all your Books and entries of the said annuities as may effectually secure his Majesty from any double payment on the said annuity.

Prefixing: certificate by Lord Halifax, Auditor of the Receipt, dated 22 May 1717, of the assignment as above. By a certificate made to the late Lord Treasurer Godolphin, John Hoyle is certified to be the proprietor of an annuity of 6L.8s.1d. as in lieu of the principal sum of 213L. 9s.9d. as in the certificate of the assignees of Sir Robert Viner or his executors or those claiming under him. By the entries of deeds and other assurances since produced, the said annuity does now appear to be vested in Sir Caesar Child, Elihu Yale, Thomas Gibson and Roger Braddyll, assignees in a commission of bankrupt awarded against Sir Stephen Evance, deceased, and William Hales of London, goldsmith, as assignees of Whitfield Hayter, who was assignee of Samuel Brockenborough, who was assignee of the said Hoyle.

Whitfield Hayter was still financially involved with the creditors of Sir Stephen Evance through that agreement preceding partnership set up in 1688. Brockenborough was a creditor of Sir Robert Viner.

Whitfield Hayter and Stephen Evance

Whitfield Hayter was active in business matters, in addition to banking deals, as evidenced by several documents relating to him held at The National Archives. In 1695, he was named in a document *(C111/192 Packet 41)* outlining an agreement between Don Mario Plati and himself for a process for cleaning pearls and diamonds. In the same year, Henry Hayter was cited in a document for a matter involving Sir Stephen Evance and Whitfield Hayter. On 28th October 1695, in the records of the Hudson's Bay Company, £100 of stock was acquired by John Nicholson from Whitfield Hayter. (*Nicholson was Deputy Governor of the Hudson's Bay Company, between the years of 1701-1710.*) In 1696, document (*C111/192 Packet 42*) shows evidence of a mortgage between Michael Newman of Iver, Buckinghamshire to Whitfield Hayter of London, goldsmith, in relation to land at Trelights, Trewint and Endillion, in Cornwall. In the same year, the case of Evance *v.* Whitfield (*C10/246/26*) reveals that Peter Percivall died around 5th April, 1693 and speaks of the elder Hayter having "*put his son Whitfield Hayter as an apprentice*" to Percivall and Evance. In 1698, document (*C111/191 Packet 36*) from Sir Stephen Evance concerns a release of bonds relating to the sale of shares in an invention. Whitfield Hayter was referred to as the previous owner of the machine for cutting and polishing glass and stone using a mill wheel invented by Thomas Savery. It would appear that Whitfield Hayter was still involved as a jeweller and goldsmith around this time.

In 1698 there was a Bill of Complaint (National Archives – *Browne v. Hubbald* – *C9/253/38*) whose parties included William Hubbald, Comptroller and Phillip Wightman against Richard Browne, relating to land at Whetstone, near Leicester, which Phillip Wightman had purchased and a bill of exchange for the sum of £537, which was unpaid by Whitfield Hayter. It included the statements on 4th May 1696 that Hayter was insolvent, that Sir Stephen Evance was an M.P., that he had lent money to the government and that Whitfield Hayter and Sir Stephen Evance were partners jointly in the trade of goldsmith. The inference seems to be that Evance was a man who could well afford to pay the debt in question. The dispute continued over a number of years as evidenced by relevant documents in 1699 and earlier.

Stephen Evance

Stephen Evance, son of John Evance, born on 8th May 1652 at New Haven Connecticut (*New Haven Vital Records, Part1*), became Member of Parliament for Bridport in 1690. On 14th October 1690, he was knighted at Kensington, partly as a reward for his usefulness to the Crown. Evance, Child and Herne, in 1692, advanced £50,000 to the King to meet the expenses of the government in Ireland. Evance was involved in many government contracts after the year of his election. The Calendar of Treasury Books gives several examples of contracts entered into by Stephen Evance, including those relating to copper mines in New England and silver mines in Ireland. These were businesses about which he persuaded others of his knowledge. He made contracts to provide copper for coins to the Royal Mint and was, with many goldsmith bankers, opposed to the setting up of the Bank of England around this time because the competition would have limited their ability to profit from loans and deals. Much of his fortune may have been made from trading internationally, in which context many deals would have seen little supervision and would have avoided tax liabilities. However, it brought him into conflict with the English Establishment and others of importance, some taking the view that Evance's business and financial tactics may have been improper. He was paid a salary of £800 a year as a Commissioner of Excise and is said to have made on one deal alone the sum of £50,000 by melting down coinage to give to Holland. He became a Commissioner of Wine Licences, which provided one among other sources of income. He supplied clothes to the troops and stores to the Navy. He was involved in a number of questionable deals when, for example, timber he had imported from New England for the Navy was deemed to be unfit to use. Although re-elected as an MP at Bridport in 1695, he did not stand again in 1698.

The *Oxford Dictionary of National Biography*, in a listing for Sir Francis Child, founder of the Bank of England, states that Sir Stephen Evance held the post of jeweller to the King after Sir Francis Child resigned from the position in 1697. In 1702, Evance was responsible for looking after a large diamond which had been found in India in the previous year. It was bought by Thomas Pitt, Governor of Madras, some said, for £20,400. Evance was the custodian of it and other jewels belonging to Pitt, which he kept in a trunk in his shop at Lombard Street. Pitt referred to it as "*his great concern*". In 1707, when rumours circulated that Evance was in financial difficulty, Robert Pitt, Thomas Pitt's son, removed the diamonds from Evance's care. In 1717, Pitt sold the large diamond in its rough state to the Prince Regent, the Duke of Orleans, for the vast sum of £80,000, and the stone later became known as the *"Regent diamond"*. With its tinge of blue, it was originally 410 carats but was cut down to 144 carats in a process taking two years and costing £5,000, the offcuts remaining the property of the former owner, Mr. Pitt. In 1791, the year before it was stolen but later returned, it was valued at £480,000, According to Max Baeur, in his book, *Precious Stones*, it was then included in the jewels of France and used in the coronation of Louis XIV and Napoleon. Today the jewel is on permanent display at the Louvre in Paris.

Evance employed his career skills as a goldsmith and jeweller to make large sums as commission for procuring diamonds for clients. He was still trading in diamonds and looking for business and ways of making money right up to the end of his life but was declared bankrupt early in January 1712. His debts are said to have amounted to the remarkable sum of £100,000. Unable to "*keep shop*", he is alleged to have committed suicide by shooting himself in the head. The more likely account was recorded in the *British Mercury* 5-7th March 1712, where it was reported that he hanged himself from an attic window at the home of Sir Caesar Child at Woodford in Essex; Child was married to Evance's niece, Hester Evance.

Stephen Evance may have been married, as certain documents at The National Archives suggest that he was a widower. He died intestate and was buried at St. Edmund King and Martyr, Lombard Street, which was adjacent to his premises. The church entry reads "*Sir Stephen Evans (Evance) by order of [....] was buried in woollen March 8th 1711*". A copy of the register includes "[blank] sic", signifying a mistake in the recording. It was unusual, given the circumstances of his death, for him to have been buried in consecrated ground.

The National Archives' papers relating to Stephen Evance and his business affairs (*C111/207 Goodere v. Lake*) include a document concerning a survey of the Province of New Hampshire, in New England, in which it outlined that a parcel of land, some 60 miles by 36 miles, covering 1,709,490 acres, was valued at £23,452. This was land that had been owned by the indigenous population and which the settlers had divided up. Related documents include indentures, bills and accounts concerning Stephen Evance, Whitfield Hayter, Peter Percivall and Thomas Lake. They include lists of people and transactions, debits and credits written following Evance's death and linked to the bankruptcy proceedings. Numerous small scraps of paper record money lent or paid to Evance. Some of them were signed by his niece, Hester Evance, who may have played a role as a book-keeper for her uncle. Some referred to are dated during the period 1710-1712, although some dates might not be entirely accurate as they were made after his death and copied; some items are not dated. Accompanying notes in brackets describe actual or possible relationships to Sir Stephen Evance. Some documents were signed by Mr. Hayter and Mr. Barkham or by business associates and/or clerks. The following entries are selected from the account books of Sir Stephen Evance (1700-1711), shown to Philip Booth on July 13, 1731 and November 26, 1733. Many of these people cited were relatives or related by marriage:

Evance Ward: £2765.17.3, 27th August, 1711 (*son of John and Elizabeth Ward, née Hatsell, the half-sister of Sir Stephen Evance*);

Executors of Peter Percivall: £9,788.12.4 (*former business partner died in 1693*);

Thomas Hatter (Hayter): £206 (*brother of Whitfield Hayter, partner of Stephen Evance*);

Madam Hassell's house in Southwark: £88.8.6 (*possibly the mother of Stephen Evance, Suzanne "Hatsell" who died in 1707 or another member of the Hatsell family*);

Stephen Evance: diamonds £173;

Captain John Evance: £384.2.11 and £500;

Caesar Child: £793.19.2 and £3,000 (*husband of Hester Evance, niece of Stephen Evance and daughter of his brother, John Evance*);

Hester Goodere: £2,831.2.6 (*widow of John Goodere and John Evance, and sister-in-law of Stephen Evance*);

John Goodere: £1,128.0.11 (*John Goodere, father, married Hester Evance, widow. Their son was also John Goodere*);

Elihu Yale: £6,665.11.2 (*his father David Yale would have known John Evance, senior, father of Stephen Evance, in New England*);

Elizabeth Higginson: £40 (*Widow of Nathaniel and cousin of Whitfield Hayter*);

William Hatsell: £4.14.6 (*Step-brother of Stephen Evance who died in 1700*);

Whitfield Hayter: £30,000 due from; also interest payment, in 1708, of £171 (*previously his partner and significant debtor*);

William Hubbard (Hubbald): Bills of sale for one sixteenth of ships, Caesar and Loyal Cook in 1707: £450 and £475 (*husband of Rebecca Hayter, the sister of Whitfield Hayter*);

William Hubbald: £12,074.15.11 and £8,000 + interest due from the estate of Mr. Hubbald deceased (*he died in 1709*);

Several large sums of money due from the late King William and present Queen Anne exceeding £6,300;

Thomas Evance: £526.3.0;

Thomas Evance (senior): £100 (*this might suggest that there was a son by the same name*).

Further notes

Whitfield Hayter was apprenticed to Stephen Evance, a goldsmith and then partner of Sir Stephen Evance. In the Poll Books and Electoral Registers of 1710 for Lombard Street in the City of London, under the heading of "Goldsmiths", Sir Stephen Evance, Whitfield Hater (Hayter) and William Hales were among those listed (page 177).

John Evance and Susanna, his wife and their children, Daniel, John and Stephen Evance, born in New England, were known to the Whitfield family in America, before returning to England to live.

Susanna Evance, widow, married Henry Hatsell and had a daughter, Elizabeth, half-sister of Stephen Evance.

Whitfield Hayter's mother, Rebecca, grew up in New England as did her sister, Sarah Higginson, wife of John Higginson.

Thomas Higginson, the son of John and Sarah Higginson, who was born in America, was apprenticed to the Goldsmiths' Company, in England, around the same time as Stephen Evance, on 13th April, 1670.

Whitfield Hayter was the cousin of Thomas Higginson. This may have been a factor in Hayter choosing this career path.

Tom Hayter, husband of Rebecca Whitfield, was working in the Navy Office before his death and may have been useful to Stephen Evances' business interests. It would be fair to suggest that an American connection is common to both families.

William Hubbald married Rebecca Hayter, sister of Whitfield Hayter, who was also financially involved with Sir Stephen Evance.

Decline of Whitfield Hayter

Other documents at The National Archives contain references to Whitfield Hayter during the next decades. A 1710 paper (*C5/355/59*) shows that he was a party in a long-running Court action against Elizabeth Higginson, the widow of his cousin, Nathaniel Higginson, who died in 1708. A lengthy document (*C10/416/1*) shows that in 1720, Thomas Frederick, whose will was proved on 3rd June 1720, on his return from the East Indies, disputed alterations in books and accounts. The critical names were Caesar Child, John Goodere, Peter Percivall, Thomas Frederick and Whitfield Hayter.

Documents show that in July 1720, Whitfield Hayter, previously a man of some standing and wealth, sold his share in the ship the *"Larke"* to the Honourable Philip Bertie. Thomas Hayter, Whitfield Hayter's brother, also knew Philip and Charles Bertie, having been involved with Philip in a conveyance on land in Lancashire in 1717. Charles Bertie was Paymaster and Treasurer of the Ordnance and had worked with William Hubbald at the Tower. Whitfield was cited with his brother Thomas in an indentutre *(MDR/1720/2/302)* in December 1720 *(discussed in a later chapter)* in relation to the land at Tottenham High Cross.

A document *(PROB 5/2476)*, concerning probate at The National Archives, dated 26th June 1722 records:

> ...instead of a declaration and inventory of all the goods and chattels and credit of Whitfield Hayter late of St. Margaret's Westminster and come into the possession of John Fitzgerald......the deceased at his death had a horse and a pair of silver spurs and furniture for a horse which were appraised at the pound and seized by the stalemates for money due to him for housekeeping......... some old clothes linen and wigs the value of which this exhibitant knows not and the declaration that the deceased had at the time of his death several mortgages bonds and notes but in whose hand the arrears or from what person or for what money............ but when the name of any other part of the said deceased affects shall become to his hand or possession... his wife charge himself therewith and accountable for the same.

It was signed by Fitzgerald, who stabled Whitfield Hayter's horses. Martha Hayter was held accountable for the debts of her husband. If there were any of the deceased's effects found, Fitzgerald was due the money owed, other than the saddle and silver spurs and possibly the horse, items already taken. Whitfield Hayter had, at his death, mortgages, bonds and notes which were in arrears. It would appear that Fitzgerald's relationship to the deceased was purely a business arrangement. Indeed, Fitzgerald made a claim from the estate of Whitfield Hayter and his widow, to cover outstanding debts, in June 1722, six months after Whitfield Hayter died.

Some of the realities of life at the time are indicated in the document above, with details of horses, old clothes, linens, the silver spurs and the expensive but obligatory wigs. If Whitfield Hayter had once loaned huge amounts of money to the King, the circumstances surrounding his death seem surprising. The document gives the impression of a once wealthy man who had fallen on hard times. Whitfield Hayter was already disposing of his assets in 1720 and it might be inferred that Whitfield Hayter had lost most, if not all, of his money by the time of his death.

Papers at The National Archives confirm a subsequent sequence of events. In *Child v. Fitzgerald (C 11/43/36)*, dated 3rd November 1722, the complainants were Sir Caesar Child, a baronet, Hester Child's husband, John Goodere, Hester's half-brother and Peter Percivall taking action against John

Fitzgerald. The lengthy document indicates that Fitzgerald had pretended to be a creditor of Whitfield Hayter when he had applied for the letters of administration, to secure what was left of Hayter's estate. The complainants further alleged that in 1696 Sir Stephen Evance, was still in partnership with Hayter, perhaps thereby hoping to retrieve any surplus as they were creditors of Sir Stephen Evance. The document, in passing, named the executors of Thomas Frederick's will as John Borrett, of the Inner Temple, William Peer Willis of Gray's Inn and Richard Chapman. Frederick's and Hayter's estates may have been linked by Hayter being owed money by Frederick.

Document (*C11/151/3*), *Goodere v. Borrett*, dated 1742/3, records that Thomas Frederick died in 1720 and the dispute over his estate was still ongoing. It would appear that soon after Thomas Frederick died, so too did Whitfield Hayter and some time after this, John Fitzgerald replaced Hayter in the action. A claim was then made against John Fitzgerald, as the representative of Whitfield Hayter, by default, to pay his outstanding bills, as Fitzgerald had claimed the belongings of the deceased. Ultimately the action was not continued against John Fitzgerald. According to this account, Hayter died after June 1720 and before January 1722. The document suggested that Whitfield Hayter in 1696, *"did assign and release all his rights and title to the joint estate and trade and all his interest in the joint stock and partnership to him the said Sir Stephen Evance to his separate use and benefit"*. John Goodere was said to be the only surviving assignee and creditor.

The personal circumstances of the widow of Whitfield Hayter were explained when Thomas Hayter added a codicil to his will, dated 29th March 1722. He stated that he had *"lately made his will"* on 8th February 1721. The codicil was in fact written a few months after the original will, as 1722 started on 25th March. Thomas Hayter described his compassion for his sister-in-law, Martha and her deplorable circumstances and lunacy. He set aside money to be used to care for Martha and named the carers as her mother, Martha Whatton, a widow and Samuel Horsley.

Whitfield Hayter may have died naturally or have taken his own life. Either way, the death must have been quite sudden as he had died intestate and had made no provision for his wife, perhaps because he had nothing to leave and was ruined or bankrupt. At the time of his death he had been living in the Parish of St. Margaret, Westminster. There were no children from his marriage. He was buried at St. Martin of Tours, in Epsom on 21st December 1721; his family had not deserted him, despite his circumstances.

Whitfield Hayter died at the time of the most famous financial scandal of that era, the South Sea Bubble Crash. It ruined many people, from the exceptionally rich to small investors. Whitfield Hayter's one time partner, Stephen Evance, was already dead by this time, having faced financial ruin and taken his own life in March 1711/12.

Whitfield lived and died in Westminster. The administration (*Westminster City Archives – Probate papers – 2206/5/15*), dated 23rd April 1722 stated, in Latin, that Whitfield Hayter was from the Parish of St. Margaret, Westminster. Other names to which reference was made, other than to officials, were of Sir

Caesar Child, Baronet, John Goodere and Peter Percivall, these having been among his creditors. Hayter's business partner, Peter had long since died, earlier than November 1693.

Thomas Hayter or his sister, Mary Morland, were not cited in these documents relating to their brother, Whitfield Hayter and his belongings and debts, despite the fact that Martha, their sister-in-law, was described as a *"lunatick"* and clearly unable to look after herself. Perhaps Thomas was distancing himself from Whitfield Hayter's financial situation, all the brothers being traders, merchants and property owners. Henry had died in July, 1716. Their sister, Mary Morland, in 1722, was described in the will of Thomas Hayter as a widow. Whitfield Hayter died around 21st December, 1720 and Mary Morland in 1723. When Thomas Hayter died in 1724, shortly after the death of his sister, the only member of his immediate family still alive was his sister-in-law, Martha Hayter, one nephew, Edward Hubbald and some cousins.

As to Martha and her family, a letter of administration (*Westminster City Archives-Act Book 10 Fol. 45*), written in Latin, exists for *Guilimus* (William) Whatton. He was living at the time of his death in the Parish of St. Margaret and the letter was filed in January 1714 by his widow Martha and granted in April. A will (*Westminster City Archives – Acc. 120 Piece No. 1902 Will*) for Martha Whatton, a widow, in May 1725, was written on 6th April 1725 and proved on 6th May 1725 by Samuel Horsley, one of the executors. The elder Martha was still living in the Parish of St. Margaret, Westminster when she died. She gave rings valued at twenty shillings each to her brother-in-law, Robert Moubray, the elder, to his son Robert Moubray, the younger, to the widow of her late brother, John Skingell and to any of his children living at the time of her death.

She expressed her confidence that her good friend, Samuel Horsley, a woodmonger and coal dealer and his wife and very good friend Ruth, should take care of her only daughter and child, Martha Hayter, a widow, *"who is now a lunatick"*. She bequeathed all her goods, chattels and money to Samuel and Ruth Horsley so that they could take care of her daughter. She explained that Thomas Hayter, a gentleman, late of Epsom, had made comfortable provision for her only child by way of a codicil to his will. Samuel and Ruth Horsley were named as executors of her will. Thomas Hayter had died a year before. Of the beneficiaries, a Robert Moubray married Elizabeth Skingell on 28th June 1702, in Edinburgh (*familysearch.org*). He was either Martha Whatton's brother-in-law or her nephew, as both had the same Christian name.

An administration for Martha Hayter dated May 1733 (*Westminster City Archives-Act Book 11, Fol.62*) indicates that it was written in April 1733 and it was granted in August. It said:

> Martha Hayter. On the second day of May administration of the goods of the said Martha Hayter, late of St Margaret's Westminster in the County of Middlesex, widow, deceased was granted to Thomas Skingell, the cousin and next of kin being first sworn duly to administer and so forth.

Thomas Skingell is likely to have been one of the sons of Martha Whatton's brother, John. The original administration document (*Westminster City Archives- Probate Papers 2206/8/18*) indicates that it was signed and dated in Westminster on 2nd May, 1733. It explained that the deceased had died in the month of January, intestate, without making a will. She was described as a *"widow without children, father, mother, brother, sister, uncle, or aunt"* The name of William Whatton had been struck from the document and replaced with the name of her cousin and next of kin, Thomas Skingell, who appeared in person, under oath, to attest his right to her inheritance. By implication, William Whatton and Thomas Skingell were both her cousins but William Whatton must have also died around that time. Her estate was valued at less than £40. Records at St. Margaret, Westminster, show that Martha Hayter was buried there, on 5th January 1732 and not with her husband at Epsom.

At The National Archives, there are two further administrations recorded for Whitfield Hayter. The first was in June 1722, *Middlesex* (*PROB 6/98 Page 94/130*). It was written in Latin and mentioned the name of John Fitzgerald as the principal creditor of the deceased of the Parish of St. Margaret's Westminster in Middlesex. Martha Hayter was described as a widow and relict and to Thomas Hayter, a brother, with reference to the lunacy of Martha Hayter. It was granted in January 1723. Also written in the margin was *"ceased and a new grant in February 1740"*. The second administration was dated February, 1740/1 (*PROB 6/117 Page 25*) and confirmed the link between *"Whitfeld"* Hayter and Edward Hubbald. It said:

> Whitfeld Hayter – On the twenty-fifth day (August 1741 written in margin) admon of the goods chattels and credits of Whitfeld Hayter late of the parish of St Margaret's Westminster County of Middlesex deceased was granted to Edward Hubbald the nephew by a sister deceased being first sworn duly to administer. The letters of admon of the goods, chattels and credits of the deceased granted in June 1722 to John Fitzgerald, the principal creditor of the said deceased for the use and behest during the lunacy of Martha Hayter, widow, the relict being ceased and expired by reason of the death of the said Martha Hayter and Thomas Hayter the natural and lawful brother of the deceased having formally renounced the admons of the goods of the deceased as appears by the Act of Court and Mary Morland widow the natural and lawful sister of the deceased dying before she had taken the admons upon her.

This administration was granted in 1741, nearly twenty years after the death of Mary Morland, Whitfield's sister. The document did not provide the Christian name of Edward Hubbald's mother, who was again proven in this legal document to be a Hayter. In 1733, Thomas Skingell, Martha Hayter's cousin and not her nephew, Edward Hubbald, had been granted letters of administration on her estate. As to what was left of Whitfield's Hayter's estate, perhaps Edward Hubbald acquired personal items belonging to his uncle, taken by John Fitzgerald, as the principal creditor, following the petition in 1722. There is the possibility that other funds materialised from interest or other sources which had not been declared in the original administration or the goods had been left not administered.

21

Mary and Joseph Morland
and the Hackney connection

Given the likelihood that Tom Hayter had doubts about his relationship with the Church and may have at one time allied with Protestant Nonconformists, it seems unsurprising that his daughter, Mary, married into a family well-known for their dissenting views.

Mary was the wife of Joseph Morland and the daughter of Tom and Rebecca Hayter and therefore one of the six siblings of the family. As Mary Hayter was not included in the will of James Disbrowe, one of her known relatives, written in 1690 and discussed elsewhere, it might be that her marriage to Joseph Morland was not her first. Perhaps she had previously married, later becoming a widow. It seems unlikely, however, that Joseph was married before 1699.

Joseph Morland

Joseph Morland F.R.S., was included in *"Bulloch's Roll"*. (William Bulloch collected biographical information on members of the Royal Society, which remains an organisation promoting research into scientific, medical, botanical, anatomical, astronomy and philosophical issues.) Bulloch's handwritten notes show that Joseph Morland was a relation of Sir Samuel Morland. According to *The ODNB* and Venn's *Alumni Cantabrigienses*, Samuel Morland was born around 1625-1627, educated at Magdalene College, Cambridge, became a Fellow in 1649 and received his M.A. around the same time as his brother, Martin, in 1652. He was a foreign envoy and intelligence expert during the time of the Commonwealth, although he worked as a double agent and was knighted by Charles II in 1660. He was an accomplished linguist, mathematician, inventor of water pumps and adding machines, *inter alia*. Samuel Morland was a tutor to Samuel Pepys and recognised the potential of the young Pepys, setting him to make ciphers. Morland was cited a number of times in the diary of Pepys and must have known Tom Hayter. Despite his many inventions, his finances were not always healthy but nor was he unsuccessful in those terms. He worked in France for some time during the 1680s on a project to bring water from the Seine to the Palace of Versailles; he turned to religion in his later years. Sir Samuel Morland married four times and divorced his last wife on grounds of adultery. He was blind when he died in 1695 and so made his mark on his will. He left his estate to Mrs. Zenobia Hough, possibly his mistress, having disinherited his only son by his first wife, Samuel; the younger Samuel also attended Cambridge.

Bulloch wrote of him:

> In the British Museum catalogue is the ref. Morland, Joseph (see Sir Samuel Morland, Bar.) "Hydrostaticks or instructions concerning waterworks collected out of the papers of Sir Samuel Morland edited by Joseph Morland, London 1697.12". He died 1716. Royal Society records. Not in D.N.B. Innes Smith's English speaking students at the University of Leyden 1932, Joseph Morland inscribed at Leyden, on 19 June, 1699, aged 28, being already a medical doctor. The day before viz. 18 June, 1699, when he graduated M.D. Leyden. His thesis "De Asthmatic" is at British Museum. He was inscribed at Utrecht 1687. In 1713 he published "A disquisition on the force of the heart and circulation".

Sir Samuel had already given his papers to his nephew, Joseph, before his death. Joseph Morland's entry here and elsewhere confirm that he was studying at Utrecht, in Holland in 1687, that he was in England around 1695 when his uncle died and back in Leyden, in Holland in 1699. The date of his application to practice medicine indicates that he was abroad before 1703 as he wrote to the Royal Society in February 1703 and did not appear in person. It might be deduced that his year of birth was 1671 and his death in 1716. The British Library website displays the book by Sir Samuel Morland, published for John Lawrence, at the Angel, in the Poultry, in 1697. The preface was written by Joseph Morland and said:

> The following tables I received from Sir Samuel Morland amongst the rest of his mathematical papers all of which kind he was pleased to bestow on me not long before his death. As for these which I now publish he told me particularly that they contained the Mystery of that Art and nimble Dispatch, which he was master of, in the making and managing (more especially) such mechanical engines as relate to the water; in the improvement of which sort he was so much happier than the rest of mankind. He thought that it might be an acceptable and useful piece of service to the world to arrange these materials in good order; and where there should be occasion, to add so much light as might make them intelligible to a common reader. How I should do this, he gave me large directions from his own mouth and I have punctually observed them, in the completing of this piece; so that here are plain and easy rule and directions delivered in a perspicuous manner that guide the practitioner into the concisest way of calculation in these matters; and almost infallibly secure him from mistakes and errors which are so veracious and expensive, and I think it is not necessary to give any longer account of this treatise, which other of his papers may hereafter be made published, must be left to further enquiry and consideration.
>
> Joseph Morland

The book was filled with tables, equations and diagrams on instructions for waterworks.

An entry in the minute book of *The Journal Book of the Royal Society, Volume XI, 1702-1714,* dated 10th February 1703 includes the following statement:

> A letter from Mr Moreland concerning secretions in animal bodies was read. He was ordered the thanks of the Society.

Regular meetings of the Royal Society took place at that time at Crane Court, off Fetter Lane, London. It was usual for people to present papers by letter or to be invited to appear in person before admission to the Society. On 30th November 1703, Dr. Moreland, Dr. Mead, Dr. Areskine and a number of others were proposed, balloted and chosen as members of the Royal Society. A month later, on 8th December, 1703, Dr. Moreland was admitted to the Society, when he appeared in person.

Before Joseph Morland could practice medicine it was necessary to apply for a licence from the Archbishop of Canterbury. The licence (*Vicar General Series Licences 1576-1775-VX1A/10/379, Lambeth Palace Library*), written in Latin, was processed by John Michell of St. Mary le Bow, London. It was applied for on 31st December 1703 and granted, on 4th January 1703. It was co-signed by Robert Areskine, M.D., J. Morland, M.D., Lionel Wafer, *Chy* (surgeon) and *Rich:* Hardmett, *Chy*.

Years later, in the minutes of the Royal Society, dated 20th December 1710, was the following entry:

> Dr Moreland presented a new method in investigating the law of attraction by the planets revolved about the sun here applied to the conic sections and easily applicable to other curves. It was referred to the President and Dr Halley to examine and report their opinion to ye Society. Dr Moreland was thanked for the communication of this paper.

The president in question was Isaac Newton, who held the post from 1703 to 1727 and Dr. Halley was he of Halley's Comet.

The Wellcome Library retains a copy of a book, written by Joseph Morland, M.D. and F.R.S., scrutinised and approved by his learned friends and published in 1713, its title being *"Disquisitions concerning the force of the heart, the dimensions of the coats of the arteries and the circulation of the blood"*. He wrote in his preface, that *"I find I am better qualified as I flatter myself I am to ease pain and cure diseases. This alone will be sufficient for me."* He continued *"What follows is part of a letter written to Dr Mead some years ago and then published in the Philosophical Transactions."* The article was about movement of blood through the heart and the size of the arteries, veins and the movement of other fluids, e.g. urine, into smaller canals in the body. He gave an example of the experiment by Dr. Areskine, who had injected wax into arteries and veins. Dr Areskine was a signatory to Morland's licence to practice medicine in 1703 and was accepted as a fellow of the Society at the same time as Morland.

At the end of the book is an article entitled *"Of the secretions of the animal body"*, to which reference had been made in the minutes of the Royal Society.

In *"Never at Rest: A Biography of Isaac Newton"*, by Richard S. Westfall, Joseph Morland's letter to Isaac Newton, is included, writing about Morland's faith. The letter said:

> Sir, I have done and will do my best while I live to follow your advice to repent and believe I pray often as I am able that god would make me sincere and change my heart. Pray write me your opinion whether upon the whole I may dye with comfort. This can do you no harm written without your name god knows I am very low and uneasie and have but little strength.

Westfall believed that Morland wrote the letter in 1716, shortly before he died.

Joseph Morland wrote his will on 28th June 1715 but gave no indication that he was in poor health. It was not proved until 2nd March 1716. He did not specify where he was to be buried and asked that as little as possible be spent on his funeral. He gave his occupation as Doctor of *Phisick*. Joseph made reference to his good friend John Brand, a merchant and his house at *Ebsham* (Epsom). He also referred to the children of his late cousin, Nathaniel French (more of whom later). His brothers Benjamin and Samuel Morland were executors and were asked to take care of everything. He left £100 stock in the South Sea Company to his wife Mary and the same to each of his brothers, Benjamin and Samuel Morland. He instructed that Benjamin should receive *"£100 of South Sea Company upon condition that my said brother shall not challenge or demand out of my estate any debt or debts which I owe him otherwise my will and meaning is that he shall have only the remainder of such £100 stock after the said debts shall be paid"* Joseph left his beloved wife a mare *"in hope that she may be serviceable to her health"* He left his books to his brother, Benjamin, although they were already in his possession in Hackney and Samuel was to inherit the books at his house in Epsom along with his saddle, bridle and other horse furniture. Doubtless the books had great value and were prized possessions. Joseph left nothing to any members of his wife's family but of course Joseph and Mary Morland were clearly not as wealthy as her brothers, Thomas, Henry or Whitfield Hayter.

Mary Morland

Mary Morland wrote her will on 30th September 1717, six months after the death of her husband. It was a short will followed by a statement dated 26th March 1723, verifying that it was written by her. One of the witnesses was a servant who had lived with her. The will was proved by Edward Hubbald on 28th March 1723 (*PROB 11/590/213*).

Mary was described as a widow living at Epsom. Like her late husband, she too did not specify where she wanted to be buried. Her nephew, Edward Hubbald was the sole executor, which suggests that he was above or close to the age of 21. He was instructed to pay Mary's cousin, Rebecca Whitfield, daughter of the late Nathaniel Whitfield, £8 a year out of an annuity of £50 a year, held in the exchequer and to Elizabeth Higginson she gave the interest on £100 held in South Sea shares. However, by the time of Mary's death these shares were probably worthless or worth very little as that Company crashed in September 1720.

Mary Morland left her brother Thomas Hayter six silver spoons, forks and silver handled knives and to her brother Whitfield Hayter, some silver items. She left to the eldest daughter of her cousin Milles, probably Mary Milles, daughter of Samuel Milles, her diamond earrings. She left to her *"cosin"* Holworthy's eldest daughter, her silver teapot and lamp with six gilt tea spoons. The beneficiary in question, was probably Elizabeth Holworthy, daughter of Matthew and Elizabeth Holworthy, formerly Elizabeth Disbrowe, daughter of James Disbrowe, Mary Morland's first cousin. She left to her *"cosin Hubbald"* (*"Edward" was scribbled in the margin*) the remainder of her plate. This may have been a mistake in the transcription, when she meant her nephew or it may have been a reference to her brother-in-law's child, also by the name of Edward Hubbald. She left her cousin, Rebecca Whitfield, her *"grave"* calico and white *"tabby"* suit (*"tabby" referred to a watered or striped weave fabric, usually a silky poplin, made originally in Attab, Baghdad, in the seventeenth century, although it may have still been in fashion; "grave" may refer to an outfit to be worn on sombre occasions*). To Elizabeth Higginson, she bequeathed her black suit of cloth and a pair of sheets. To her *"Cosin Smith"*, she gave her red suit and her suit of chintz (*now more commonly known as a furnishing fabric but then printed calico from India, sometimes glazed, with exotic and colourful bird motifs and flowers*). To her *"Cosin Otway"*, probably the wife of John Otway who, a month earlier on 29 August 1717, had married Rebecca Whitfield, she gave her yellow satin suit. All household linen was to go to her nephew Edward Hubbald. Mary left £5 to the poor of Epsom. All in all, she did not have a large amount of money to leave and did not appear to own a home or land.

These descriptions of the clothes offer an impression of the wearing apparel of the period. Clothes, particularly black cloth, were expensive at that time, so this was not just a case of *"hand-me-downs"*. Each of the women received an equal share of Mary's wearing linen and laces. In her will. Mary Morland did not refer to any of her husband's family, which might suggest that, besides the fact that they lived in Epsom, his family was not especially close. With the account of her personal wardrobe, it was, however, an intensely pragmatic will.

"Madame" Morland's burial was recorded at St. Martin of Tours, Epsom, on 8th March 1723. Her husband, Joseph probably died in late February 1716 and it is likely that he too was buried there.

Joseph Morland's Family

The family of Joseph Morland was a well-educated one. Entries in the *Alumni Oxonienses, 1500-1714*, listed a number of Morlands. His grandfather was Thomas Morland, from Westmoreland, in the north of England, who attended

Queen's College, Oxford and left in 1605 with an M.A. Thomas was rector at Bright Waltham in 1615 and then, by 1625, at Sulhampstead, Abbass, Berkshire. He was the father of Thomas, who attended the same College, matriculated in 1632, aged 16 and in 1637 received his B.A. from New Inn Hall. The youngest son was Samuel, who went on to become the noted Sir Samuel Morland. A middle son of the elder Thomas was Martin Morland, whose entry in *Alumni Cantabrigienses, Part 1, Volume III*, below records:

> **MORLAND, MARTIN. M.A.** 1652 (Incorporated from Oxford), S. of Thomas, R. of Sulhampstead, Berks, School, Winchester, Matric, from Wadham College, Oxford, June 26,1644, age 20: B.A. (Oxford) 1648: M.A.1651, Minister at Weld, Hants, ejected 1660. Died June 13,1685, aged 60: "a school master," Will (P.C.C.) 1685.Brother of Samuel (next) and father of Benjamin (1676). (Vis. of Berks, 1665: AI Oxon)

Entries appear for Martin Morland in both Cambridge and Oxford Alumni records and there appears to have been controversy over his status, as Martin did not attend all his classes and owed money to the College. He depended much on the influence of his brother, Samuel, a fellow of Magdalene College, Cambridge, to remedy his difficulties (*ODNB*). The entry in Alumni Oxonienses reveals that he was incorporated at Cambridge and ejected from his ministry at *Weld*, now Upper and Lower Wield, in Hampshire for his religious differences at the time of the Restoration. According to the dates given in these entries, Thomas was the eldest brother, born in 1616 and Martin was born in 1624. Samuel, the youngest brother, was born in 1625.

There is evidence in the Church register of a marriage on 22nd July 1656 between Martin *Moreland,* a minister from Chilton in Kent and Lidia Lee, a spinster, of the Parish of St. Leonard, Eastcheap, at St. Giles Cripplegate, Middlesex. (*Morland and Moreland are interchanged as surnames.*) A baptism was recorded for Lydia Lee, daughter of Samuel, on 12th October 1638 at St. Leonard, Eastcheap. Assuming this entry to be correct, Lidia was only eighteen when she married. She had a brother, Samuel, baptised, on 29th August 1627 and a sister, Mary, baptised on 18th November 1636, also at St. Leonard, Eastcheap. Although the marriage took place in London, it would appear that Martin Morland had been living at Chilton, near Dover, prior to the wedding.

Boyd's Index and other sources confirm that Lidia was Martin's wife, her father was Samuel Lee and their children were Benjamin, born in 1657, Martin in 1660, Samuel in 1666, Joseph in 1669 and Lidia in 1672. The birth of Benjamin Morland was recorded on 29th July 1658, with baptism on 4th August at Cliddesden, Hampshire as was the case for Martin Morland, baptised on 20th April 1660 (*www.ancestry.com*). According to *the IGI*, Samuel Morland was baptised on 1st June 1665 at Sulhamstead, Abbot's, Berkshire and Joseph Morland on 15th August 1667. This baptism, for Joseph, conflicts with his date of birth, recorded as 1671 in *Bulloch's Roll*. The family was at Cliddesden, Hampshire between 1658-1660 and Martin Morland was ejected from his ministry at Weld in 1660. By 1665, the family members were living with their grandfather, Reverend Thomas Morland, at Sulhamstead. The distances between these places were not substantial; Cliddesden is ten miles south of Sulhamstead and Weld (Weild) is about five miles south from there.

The historian, Edmund Calamy, wrote that Martin Morland spent his later life setting up and running a school in Hackney (*The non-conformist's memorial, Volume 2*). In 1672, Martin Morland owned a house in Hackney, which was licensed as a Presbyterian meeting place (*British History online*).

Martin Morland, then of the Parish of St. John at Hackney, a clerk, was buried at that church, aged 60, on 13th June 1685; his will was proved on 2nd July 1685. He named as beneficiaries his wife, Lydia, sons Martin, Benjamin, Samuel and Joseph (the latter two were under the age of 21) and daughter, Lydia. The younger Samuel and Lydia, Martin's wife, were executors of the will. He made bequests to each of his children. He explained that he and his wife had bought a tenement at Westbrook, in the Parish of Boxford in Berkshire, from which they received rent. His wife was to receive the rent during her lifetime and then it was to pass to his sons, Samuel and Joseph. His daughter, Lidia, was to receive £200 when she reached the age of 21. He made a bequest of £6 to his sister, Elizabeth Morland and £10 to his cousin Mary Skinner. John Ballard of Ramsbury in Wiltshire received twenty shillings (*in 1682, an Ambrose Ballard was baptised at Ramsbury, he being the son of John and Sarah Ballard. John was related to Jarvis Ballard, who married Mary Lee, in 1656. Mary was Martin Moreland's sister-in law*).

The elder Lidia Morland's brother may have been Samuel Lee. In *The ODNB*, he is described as the only son of Samuel Lee, a haberdasher, of Fish Street. Samuel Lee, the son, was a scholar at Oxford before he took up a position at St. Botolph, Bishopsgate in 1655, at the request of Oliver Cromwell. He owned an estate close to Bignal, near Bicester, Oxfordshire, where he sometimes lived and he preached in other churches in London. He was joint pastor with Theophilus Gale at Baker's Court, Holborn but after Gale's death, in 1678, Samuel Lee moved to the independent Newington Green Church, in Hackney, where he was minister until 1686 (*Theophilus Gale, referred to elsewhere in the book, took over preaching at Winchester Cathedral, after Henry Whitfield died*). In 1685, Samuel Lee wrote his will naming his then wife, Martha and daughters, Rebecca, Ann, Lidia and Elizabeth but did not make provision for any other relatives. In 1686 he migrated, with his wife and daughters, to America. Three of his daughters married there, though not all unions were approved by their father. He decided to return to England after William and Mary came to power but his ship was seized by a French pirate and Lee was separated from his wife and daughter, Elizabeth. He became ill and died in 1691 in St. Malo, in France, without seeing his family again; his will was proved in April, 1692.

Martin Morland's eldest son, Benjamin Morland appears in *Alumni Cantabrigienses: Part 1 Vol. III, Venn* :

MORLAND, BENJAMIN. Adm. Pens, at Jesus May 18,1676.Of Hampshire. Son of Martin (1652), clerk, minister of Weld Hants,

Of Hitchin, Herts: age 30 in 1687. F.R.S, 1707 Schoolmaster at Hackney and afterwards High Master of St Paul's, 1721-33. Died Oct. 9,1733, aged 80. Buried at Hackney, M.I. Will P.C.C.. Father-in-law of Henry Newcome (1706). (Vis. of Berks, 1665.)

The entry shows that he was enrolled at Cambridge but he may not have acquired his degree. The minutes of the Royal Society show that Benjamin Morland was proposed, balloted and chosen on 12th March 1706. A few weeks later, on 26th March 1707, he sealed a bond, subscribed to the statutes and was admitted as a member of the Royal Society. Venn noted that he was 30 in 1687 and was 80 when he died in 1733 but these dates might not be accurate. If he was 80 in 1733 this indicates that he was born in 1653. As his parents did not marry until 1656 and there is evidence of his birth in 1658, it suggests that it was more likely he was 75 when he died.

In the *Register of Marriages (1653-1710)* there is evidence at All Hallows Staining, attached to St. Olave, Hart Street, in the City of London, of a marriage on 3rd March 1684/5 between Benjamin Morland and Elizabeth Cruttenden. Sarah and Elizabeth, the latter born around 1661/2, were the daughters of Thomas Cruttenden, a clerk, of Hackney, whose will was proved in 1674. In his will he gave half of what little he had to his wife and the other half for his children. A baptism for Elizabeth, daughter of Thomas Cruttenden and his wife, Sarah, was recorded on 7th July, 1663 at St. John at Hackney. Earlier, Thomas Cruttenden assisted at one of the first schools for girls set up, in 1650, by his mother-in-law, Mrs. Salmon, a Presbyterian. As noted above, Martin Morland, the father of Benjamin Morland, taught in school in Hackney from 1672, some years before his son went on to set up an academy in 1685; many private schools had been set up by dissenters, supported by rich sympathisers (*A History of the County of Middlesex – Vol.10*).

Benjamin Morland had many children during his marriage, including Sarah, baptised on 7th January 1685, Elizabeth, on 24th January 1694 at St. John at Hackney, Lydia and Hester; many did not survive. Elizabeth and Hester never married.

The will of Benjamin Morland, a gentleman, of the Parish of St. Faith, under St. Paul's, in the City of London, was proved on 6th November 1733 (*PROB 11/662/42*) and explained that he had four daughters, two of whom were married. After various bequests, he left money for mourning to his sisters-in-law, Mary Morland, a widow and Margaret Reddall. (*Margaret Cruttenden married Ambrose Reddall on 19th December, 1720, at Woburn (IGI). Cruttenden was the maiden name of Morland's wife.*) A codicil, dated 7th February 1730, added that his daughter Lydia Newcome had died. However, there was no amendment to acknowledge that Mary Morland had died in 1723. He first signed his will in 1729 but he may have drafted it earlier. His late brother Samuel, whose wife was named Sarah, had died in 1721.

Other members of Benjamin's extended family were involved in education. From 1685, Benjamin Morland was the original owner of one of the largest private educational establishments in Hackney. He was named in documents (*LMA*) in 1703 concerning premises belonging to Francis Tyssen.

Benjamin's daughter Lydia married Henry Newcome in December 1714. Henry Newcome was born in 1689 at Gawsworth in Cheshire. His grandfather was Henry Newcome, a non-conformist preacher; his father was Peter Newcome and mother was Ann Hooke. Peter Newcome was vicar of Hackney for thirty-five years until his death in 1738, aged 80. It was Peter who, in 1717, gave an account of the funeral of Francis Tyssen, a wealthy landowner and local resident. After Benjamin Morland was elected to the position of High Master at St. Paul's School, London in 1721, the academy was taken over by his son-in-law, Henry Newcome and then by his grandson, Peter Newcome. It is sometimes referred to as *"Newcome's Academy"* The school was situated near the site of what is now the London Orphan Asylum on Lower Clapton Road, London.

Henry Newcome was a minister in Clapton. With Lydia he had children, Peter, born in 1715, Henry in 1716, another Henry in 1718, Benjamin in 1717 and Lydia born in 1720. Lydia Newcome (his wife), was buried on 13th February 1730 and then Henry Newcome married Anne Yalden and had yet another son named Henry, baptised in 1734. Some of these grandchildren were cited in Benjamin Morland's will but not Benjamin and Lydia. When Henry Newcome died in 1756, he was a wealthy man owning substantial property, some of it at Clapton, in Hackney.

In 1710, Benjamin Morland's daughter Sarah married Seth Partridge, described as a citizen and goldsmith, who died in 1748. Seth was one of the executors of Benjamin Morland's will along with Henry Dry and Lydia French. Benjamin's brother, Joseph Morland, in his will, had made reference to the children of his late cousin, Nathaniel French, who had married Lydia Clerke at St. James, Duke's Place, Middlesex, in 1693. Their daughter, Lydia French, went on to marry Richard Newcome in 1734 (*IGI*).

The Church Register for St. John at Hackney shows that Benjamin's wife, Elizabeth Morland, was buried there on 12th November 1719 and Benjamin on 18th October 1733. Written alongside his entry were the words *"High Master of St Paul's London was buried this place in the church yard 18 October"*

Martin Morland, a haberdasher from Clapton, second son of Martin and Lidia, was buried at St. John at Hackney on 12th December 1692. Martin's maternal grandfather, Samuel Lee, had also been a haberdasher.

In an article on the Morlands in *Notes and Queries,* published in June 1919, Benjamin Moreland was described, with words taken from a monumental inscription at St. Augustine's, Hackney, which included an inscription for his late wife, Elizabeth, who died on 7th November 1719, aged 58, as the natural and eldest son of Martin Moreland; the Memorial no longer exists. The same article referred to the youngest son of Martin Morland as Samuel, a strict Non-Conformist, said to be a brilliant scholar and a master at The Blind Beggar's House School at Bethnal Green where, according to Bulloch, he was resident in 1718. This description of him as the youngest son conflicts, however, with evidence that suggests that Joseph was born in 1667 and the fact that Samuel was old enough to be named as executor of his father's will in 1685. Martin's son, Samuel Morland of Clement Danes, was married to Sarah Wright of St. Mary Aldermanbury, on 23rd July 1695 at St. Nicholas Cole Abbey *(www.ancestry.com)*.

The *Journal Book of the Royal Society, Volume XI, 1702-1724*, has the following entry, on 20th October 1703:

> A paper was read from Mr Morland wherein he gives an account of his observations upon vegetables. He thinks the farina in the flowers of plants is the male seed which renders the female seeds fecund (fertile). He was ordered the thanks of the Society.

In February 1704, Samuel Morland was recorded in the minutes but it was not until 30th November 1704 that he was proposed, balloted and chosen as a member of the Royal Society and thereby admitted. He played an active part in the proceedings of the Society and was elected to Council many times until he died in 1722. An entry was noted on 20th December 1710 when *"Mr Morland said it had been observed that those at Stockholm who drank wine and eat plentifully escape ye plague which now rages there"*

Venn's *Alumni Cantabrigienses,* for Samuel Morland's son, notes:

> *MORLAND, SAMUEL*. Adm. Pens. at Clare College, May 16, 1716. B. at Stepney, Middlesex.

This confirms that the family was living at Stepney and the son was born before 1700. The younger Samuel was elected Fellow of the Royal Society on 24th May 1722.

The will of Samuel Morland, a gentleman of the Parish of St. Leonard, Shoreditch, was proved in December 1721. His wife, Sarah, was executor and he named as beneficiaries his sons Martin and Samuel and his cousins Benjamin and Samuel Skinner and Elizabeth Cooke.

The elder and late Samuel's son, Martin Morland, of the Parish of St. Albans, Hertfordshire, a bachelor, married Anne Thorne, a spinster, of the Parish of St. Mary Woolnoth, London in 1727 at St. Christopher Le Stocks, London. Their daughter, Mary, was baptised at Christchurch, Spitalfields on 20th October 1730.

When the elder and late Samuel's son, Samuel wrote his will in 1732, he was described as a Doctor of Physic and he too had been living in the Parish of Christchurch, Middlesex. His burial was listed in records there on 19th June 1735. His will was proved in January 1735 by James King, his cousin, rather than by his wife, Jane. Samuel did not refer in his will to his brother, Martin, his sister-in-law or his niece, Mary.

22

The Reverend Henry Whitfield and his family –
Guilford, New Haven

Henry, Thomas and Whitfield Hayter were brothers and the nephews of Nathaniel Whitfield. Whitfield Hayter was named after his paternal grandfather as it was then common to give the surname of a family member as a Christian name. Whitfield is the most common spelling of the surname but for the purpose of wills the spelling may vary.

Robert Whitfield's descendents

Henry Whitfield was the second son of Thomas and grandson of Robert Whitfield. The names of Robert and Thomas were recorded in licences to purchase land on 12th April, 1567, when Thomas was a law student and again on 26th March, 1575, when he was fully qualified. Robert Whitfield had another son called William, who was a rector at a church at Emmington, near Thame in Oxfordshire. Robert was a wealthy Sussex man and it was said that his own father had set up the iron forge at Rowfant, near Worth in Sussex, where he also built for himself a large manor house on the site of a previous one.

Robert, upon his death, was buried in the chancel of the church at Emmington. His will, describing him as a *"gentleman of Worth"* in Sussex, was written on 6th December 1594 but was not proved until 16th February 1598 (*PROB 11/91/170*). He left ten shillings each to Mildred, wife of Thomas, to Mary, wife of William and to his married daughter, Johan Baker (possibly Joanna or Joan), the wife of Robert Baker. Robert Whitfeld left the same amount to his other daughters Margaret, Sara, Jane and Fraunces. He also gave money to the poor of the Parish at Wadhurst and Worth. His elder son, Thomas, was the main beneficiary and sole executor of the will and received all his copyhold land at Wadhurst, as well as goods. In his will, Robert referred to his eldest grandson, John.

John Whitfield had married Elizabeth Culpepper on 25th May, 1611. She was the daughter of Sir Edward Culpepper of Surrey and was baptised on 13th December 1584. A marriage settlement was made between Thomas Whitfield and Sir Edward in exchange for land and services over a period of seven years following the marriage. Sir Edward paid £1200 and was to convey marsh lands at Hoe Marsh in Sussex, which Sir Edward had bought from William Jordan. John, like his father, was to follow a career in the law and by 1611 was training at Lincoln's Inn to be a barrister; it was stated in the settlement that John should complete his training by 1616. Elizabeth Whitfield died on 23rd May 1624. The names of her surviving children, Thomas, John, Robert, Elizabeth, Anne and Mary are recorded on a commemorative plaque for Elizabeth at the Rowfant chapel at the church at Worth.

Mildred Whitfield died, aged 67, at Rowfant, Worth in Sussex on 1st September 1627. Following this, in 1628, Thomas wrote his will and he died on 1st May 1629. Probate was granted on 23rd March 1631, wherein he was described as a *"gentleman of Worth"* (*PROB 11/159/385*). He made bequests to his grandson, John Whitfield and if he died before the age of 22 it was to go to his grandson Robert and if he died to Thomas' son John, an executor and finally to the sisters of Henry Whitfield. He made reference in the will to his son and to his daughter, Southcote. Henry did not receive a bequest in the will but other members of the family received items of clothing, linen and furniture.

Evidence of John Whitfield's death in 1636 is to be found in the Sussex Coroner's inquests records dating from the period 1603 to 1688. He had died after a tragic accident; his horses ran out of control on the way to church. John had urged his children to jump from the runaway carriage and when he followed them, he was fatally wounded, dying a few days after the accident; probate was settled in February 1637. His will had been written in 1635 and refers to his *"beloved brother, Bachelor of Divinity, Henry Whitfield"*, one of his executors. He left his estate to his eldest son, Thomas but made the proviso that in the event of Thomas' death, it was to go to his other sons, John followed by Robert and then to his brother Henry and Henry's male heirs. He described land that he owned in Somerset. Henry's daughter, Dorothy Whitfield, was referred to by name but she was the only member of his family specifically identified. This might confirm that Dorothy was in fact the eldest daughter of Henry Whitfield.

Henry Whitfield (1590/1-1657)

Published in 1911, in *Historical Papers relating to Henry Whitfield House Guilford Connecticut,* Reverend Hereford B. George suggested that Henry Whitfield or Whitfeld was born at Greenwich although his father was owner of the manor at Mortlake in Surrey. Henry was elected a scholar in Winchester School and around 1610, at the age of 17, Henry went to New College Oxford and was awarded a fellowship as a Winchester man; the Oxford Dictionary of National Biography suggests that Henry arrived at Oxford on 6th June 1610 at the age of 19, thereby creating minor uncertainty as to his age. Information provided by the Henry Whitfield State Museum indicates vagueness about his exact date of birth and educational achievements. The Museum believes that Henry started out at New College Oxford to study law but changed course and was awarded a Doctor of Divinity. The ODNB suggests that there is no evidence to support the view of Cotton Mather, who wrote about Henry's life, that he studied at the Inns of Court after his degree. As to his fellowship, there are two ways in which these may have been given; one was that there is a presentation of a benefice, which was a living from a church office, for example, as a rector; the other was by succession to landed property. The former is more likely as Henry's father was still living at the time.

There is evidence that Henry Whitfield "*contracted his hand*" in marriage to Margaret, the daughter of Henry and Elizabeth Hardware, some time before 1616; however, she died before the marriage took place. Probate relating to Elizabeth was settled on 17th March, 1617 in Poole in Cheshire, where Margaret had been living (*PROB 11/129/304*). She described Whitfield as a loving friend and wrote in her will that because of the love and friendship she had for him, she left £140 from her estate, to him. She left small sums of money to various people, as well as her brother and his wife and to a niece. She made reference to her minister, Nicholas Byfield and to a Miss Frances Whitfield. Henry had a sister by the name of Frances so it is conceivable that the couple had originally met each other through a friendship with his sister. Alternatively, it may be that the reference was to a member of the Byfield family, such being its similarity to the Whitfield name. There was a touching account of the list of items in her trousseau, prepared for her marriage, which she left to Whitfield. It included two down pillows, four towels, a pair of valances, a feather bed, three pairs of best flower linen pillowcases, a flower blanket, flower tablecloth, one dozen fringed napkins and some other needlework. She may even have embroidered them herself.

By 1618, Henry Whitfield was ordained as a minister and at the age of twenty-seven he married Dorothy Sheafe. Around the time of his marriage, he settled as a minister in the church at St. Margaret's, in Ockley, in Surrey. Dorothy, born around 1600 in Berkshire, was the daughter of Thomas Sheafe, from Cranbrook in Kent. Sheafe studied at Cambridge and was awarded a Doctor of Divinity; her mother was Mary Wilson. In 1597, her father had become the vicar of Welford in Berkshire and was a canon at St. George, Windsor between 1614 and his death in 1639.

Henry and Dorothy Whitfield had at least nine children, some of whom died young. Church records of St. Margaret, Ockley, in Surrey, held at Surrey archives show that the children were baptised on the following dates, with any other information being added where known:

- Dorothy, baptised 25th March 1619 (married Samuel Disbrowe or Desborough in America);
- Sarah, baptised 1st November 1620 (married John Higginson; died 1675, in America);
- Abigail, baptised 1st September 1622 (married James Fitch; died 1659, in America);
- Thomas, baptised 28th December 1624 (date of death unknown);
- John, baptised 11th February 1626 (date of death unknown);
- Nathaniel, baptised 28th June 1629 (died 16th September 1696, London);
- Mary, baptised 4th March 1631 (buried 5th November 1708 at Bunhill Fields, London);
- Henry, baptised 9th March 1633 (buried 28th February 1634, Surrey);
- Rebekah, baptised 20th December 1635 (died after 1716, England).

The journey to America

In 1639, after twenty years of the ministry at Ockley, Henry Whitfield sold his house and left a comfortable living to take his family to America where he could practise his religion without fear of persecution.

Ockley village in Surrey is situated amid wonderful countryside on a beautiful, very straight, single street with a large common surrounded by houses, some from the sixteenth and seventeenth centuries. St. Margaret's Church, Ockley is about half a mile from the main road. Just inside the door there is a commemorative plaque, which lists twenty-four people, some from the local community, who, with their families, accompanied Whitfield on the voyage. The plaque was erected in 1977 by John B. Threlfall of Madison, Wisconsin, one of Whitfield's descendants.

The ship, the *St. John,* left for America on 26th April 1639 and arrived on 10th July in the same year. The first covenants were signed on board ship on 1st June 1639. All the names printed on the plaque were those of the witnesses to the covenant. The group pledged to join the Plantation; they promised not to desert each other, without the consent of the others in New England and with God's help *"to be helpful according to every man's ability and as need require"*. Samuel Disbrowe may also have travelled to America with Reverend Henry Whitfield. Not all the ship's passengers are listed but Disbrowe was in New Haven in July 1639. He may have gone to Connecticut on another ship at a different time or simply may not have been recorded on that voyage. In 1639, Samuel Disbrowe, along with John Higginson, Reverend Henry Whitfield, Jacob Sheaffe and possibly another relative of Dorothy Whitfield were among the first named members of the Church at New Haven. That Samuel Disbrowe did not sign the covenant may have been because he was under the age of consent at the time. Only three of the families who signed the covenant were specifically from Ockley. The others were friends and contacts from Dorothy's family home not far from East Guldeford, at the mouth of the estuary at the River Rother, near Rye, in Kent. William Chittenden came from Cranbrook in Kent and had married Joanna Sheaffe, a cousin of Dorothy. After Chittenden's death, Joanna married Abraham Cruttenden, who also accompanied them on the voyage. Margaret Sheaffe, another relative, married Robert Kitchel. John Jordan and his wife, Anna, had a daughter named Joanna, who later married Thomas Chittenden, the son of William Chittenden and Joanna Sheaffe. Some of the couples were already married before embarking on the voyage.

When the Whitfield family set off on the voyage, the children ranged in age from Dorothy, who was twenty, to Rebekah, who was only three at the time. Whitfield is said to have subsidised the other people who accompanied them.

Establishment of the colony at Guilford

Henry Whitfield and his party arrived at the new plantation at Quinnipiac (New Haven) but after consultation decided to move up the coast half-way between New Haven and Saybrook, the distance between the two being approximately twenty-five miles. When Henry Whitfield had studied at Oxford, he became friends with George Fenwick, later Colonel George Fenwick, who became the Governor of Saybrook Colony between the years 1639 to 1645; Fenwick had been instrumental in encouraging Whitfield to go to America. The Governer married Alice Boteler, a widow and the daughter of Sir Edward Apsley. After she died in childbirth in 1645, her husband returned to England and threw himself into politics, represented in Parliament Berwick, Edinburgh and Leith; he also strongly supported Oliver Cromwell. Fenwick remarried and died in April 1657 at Warminghurst in Sussex, coincidentally in the same year as did Henry Whitfield.

Said to be the richest person in the settlement, Whitfield was one of six wealthy settlers who bought the land from the Native Americans. An agreement was made with a Sashem squaw, named Shaumpishuh, the leader of a small tribe of Menunkatuck (Menumkatuck) Indians which solely owned the designated land lying between the East River and Stoney Creek and the tribe agreed to leave; the agreement was signed on 29th September 1639. Items included in the sale were 12 coats, 12 pairs of shoes, 12 glasses, 12 knives, 12 hats, 12 spoons, 12 hatchets, 12 fathoms of Wampum (shells), 12 pairs of stockings and 4 kettles; Shaumpishuh was fully satisfied. The Settlement was named Guilford, after the village in Kent, which is not far from Ockley and not after Guildford in Surrey. The American Guilford is sixteen miles north of New Haven, now in the State of Connecticut, close to the sea and an area of natural and wooded beauty. The landscape has been said to resemble that at East Guldeford, in East Sussex, England. Some of the streets remained named after their former inhabitants.

Many of the first settlers initially lived in temporary shelters as it was late in the year and winter snow was expected. Four stone houses and a church were planned and constructed and work was concentrated on their pastor, Henry Whitfield's house, begun in 1640. The style of architecture has much in common with that of the north of England and a carpenter had been employed by the settlers to work for three years. The three floored building was constructed from local granite, the floor joists and rafters were made from hand hewn oak and flooring made from wide planks of pine. The house has five large fireplaces.

The first houses were constructed around a square or common. Henry Whitfield's house is now a museum and the only stone house remaining; the oldest one in New England. Today the house has been restored inside and out and sits in a large plot, with only the lower walls of another stone house nearby, just off Old Whitfield Street. His house was not the grandest but was certainly big enough to accommodate Henry, his wife, possibly nine children, man-servants and maids. British Library documents describe the "old stone house," as a fort, probably, in addition to serving as a home, to defend the settlers from attacks and to protect them from the ravages of winter. Some of the first settlers were farmers and most were well educated but there were few skilled craftsmen in the party. Records suggest that there was one carpenter but no blacksmiths or masons. Considering those limitations it was quite an achievement to have built a house which still stands today.

Henry Whitfield's return to England

Despite his signature on the covenant in 1639, which committed Reverend Henry Whitfield to stay in the community, he made the decision to return to England in 1650. Aged around 60, he set sail on 25th August 1650, via Boston, at the start of his journey home and the whole community was there to wave him on his way and was saddened greatly by his departure. The younger children, it would seem, returned with him at this time. Steiner, in *A History of the Plantation of Menunkatuck and of the original town of Guilford Connecticut,* states that in General Court held in 1649 Whitfield had requested that two sons be excused from *"watching"* for that year; later in his book he said that Nathaniel and John stayed behind for a few more years after their father's departure. He also suggested that Henry Whitfield's estate was much depleted. Whitfield settled back in England, in Winchester, in Hampshire. Perhaps he found the severity of the winters too intense and/or, according to an account in the *Dictionary of American Biography,* Guilford still being much of a *"wilderness".* As a man of religion and learning he may also have found life in the colony difficult and not meeting his intellectual expectations. He had received letters from his friends in England and was encouraged to return home after the death of Charles I, when Oliver Cromwell came to power. Although a period of great political change and upheaval, it would then have been safer for non-conformists to follow their religious beliefs without fear of retribution.

In the *Massachusetts Historical Society Collection (Transcript and foot notes for Winthrop Papers, Volume VI, 1650-54, edited by Malcolm Freiberg, M.H. S. 1992)* there is a letter written by John Higginson to John Winthrop. In it, he asks if his father-in-law Whitfield's house and lots were *"yet to be sold".* The original date on the letter from Guilford was the sixth day of the week and had "Sept" crossed out, the suggested date being 29th September 1654 or thereabouts. Higginson wrote that *"my brother Nath and Cousin Jordan are to take their journey to England"* so that if Winthrop was interested in buying the house, Higginson would ask his *"brother"* not to sell it until Thursday of the following week. The sale could not take place after *Nath* and his cousin had gone to England. *Nath* was Nathaniel Whitfield, actually Higginson's brother-in-law and Cousin Jordan may have been Thomas Jordan, also a brother-in-law of Higginson, as suggested in Steiner's book. Jordan was a lawyer, who held positions of responsibility at New Haven and acted as a deputy in the court, sitting with the magistrate. He was certainly in New Haven in 1653. Thomas Jordan made various journeys on behalf of the others in the colony as an elected representative. Thomas Jordan had arrived in Guilford sometime between 1639 and 1643 but was not a signatory to the covenant, nor was his brother, John, perhaps because he was under 21 at the time.

References appear in *Ancient Town Records, Volume I, New Haven Town Records, 1649-1662,* produced by the New Haven Colony Historical Society and edited by Franklin Bowditch Dexter, Litt. D. In November 1652 (*page 150*), in a court entry about selling cows, Edward Hitchcocke related that he had sold one to Mr. Evance before *"Nathaniel Whitfield came to dwell with*

Mr Evance" Nathaniel was 21 at that time and not living with his mother Dorothy, at Guilford, some sixteen miles along the coast.

Henry's daughter, Dorothy Whitfield, became the wife of Samuel Disbrowe some time between 1639 and 1649, the year in which Sarah was born; the most likely date of the marriage was 1645. Samuel Disbrowe and his family were still in Guilford in early November 1650, so his wife and children returned to England after that date. If Rebekah Whitfield had returned with her father she may at different times have lived with him or her sisters, Mary Whitfield or Dorothy Disbrowe. Rebekah would have been about fifteen years of age in late 1650. As Henry Whitfield's wife, Dorothy, stayed behind in America, it is also possible that Rebekah remained with her mother and returned to England at a later date, perhaps in 1654, with her brother Nathaniel. In 1659, Dorothy Whitfield was referred to in the records of Guilford as managing the estate. Steiner recorded that Samuel Disbrowe was sent to Scotland immediately on his return and wrote a letter asking if he might expect a permanent position there for himself, his wife and children. Disbrowe was chosen to represent Edinburgh and at a council held at Whitehall, on 4th May 1655, was appointed by Oliver Cromwell as one of the nine councillors for Scotland. Dorothy Disbrowe died of smallpox around this time (ODNB). A particular letter among the *Papers of General Desborough 1651-1659 (BL Egerton MS 2519)* dated 11th October 1654, from William Leete at Guilford to his worthy friend Samuel Disbrowe in Leith, Scotland makes reference to John Whitfield, Mr. Jones and Samuel Disbrowe's *"brother"* Nathaniel (Whitfield); John was Nathaniel's brother. Samuel Disbrowe was the brother of General John Desborough *(Disbrowe)* who married Oliver Cromwell's sister, Jane. Other letters confirm that on 4th May 1655 Oliver Cromwell appointed Samuel Disbrowe as Keeper of the Great Seal of Scotland and on 24th October 1660 he was given a pardon *"for all such offences with restitution of lands and goods"* when Charles II returned to the throne. In 1656 Samuel Disbrowe had acquired the Elsworth Estate from the Wendy family (*Daniel and Samuel Lysons, Magna Britannia: Cambridgeshire Vol. 2, Part 1, pg. 183*).

The *Dictionary of American Biography* records that Henry had been unable to sell the house at Guilford and left his son, Nathaniel and his wife behind to finalise arrangements. The mother apparently suffered poor health and fortune. If the sale was first mooted in 1654 and was still owned at the time of Henry's death in 1657, then it was not an easy property to sell; the Henry Whitfield State Museum has evidence which outlines the history of the land ownership of the Museum, confirming that in 1657, Dorothy Whitfield had received the house and lots in a bequest from her husband. After the sale, Dorothy probably departed *"the Fort"* at Guilford. She may have left with her daughter Sarah and son-in-law, John Higginson, with the intention of returning to England. Many members of Dorothy Whitfield's family had by then left Guilford and were in England. It is known that another of Henry Whitfield's daughters, Abigail, married Reverend James Fitch and died at Saybrook, Connecticut, in September 1659.

The relatives remaining in England

Back in England, the will of Thomas Sheaf (or Sheafe), a Doctor of Divinity, then living in the Parish of Welford, in Berkshire was proved on 2ⁿᵈ March 1640 (*PROB 11/182/338*). He named his sons Thomas and Edmund as executors. His son Grindall received all lands at Hungerford and Inkpen in Berkshire, all the books in his studies at Windsor and Wickham, near Welford and the lease of a house at Newbury. Thomas received a coppice and cottage in Benenden, Kent. His daughter, Dorothy Whitfield, received a pair of fustian blankets from his house at Windsor. His family was described as sons, Edmund, Grindall and Edward Sheafe, daughters, Whitfield, Westley, Norwood and Hesilrige. The residue of the estate was to be divided equally among these seven children. Dorothy, wife of Henry Whitfield was his eldest daughter and the youngest was Rebecca, wife of Mr. Hesilrige; Rebecca had married Thomas Hesilrige on 6ᵗʰ September 1632 in St. Luke's Chelsea. Thomas Sheafe died in Wickham, near Welford but was buried in St. George's Chapel, Windsor. He made reference to books chosen by his "*loving wife*". Henry Whitfield's father-in-law, Thomas Sheafe, died after Henry and his family left for New England.

Thomas Sheafe's daughters, Isabel and Dorothy were as yet unmarried when in 1617 they received small bequests by way of the will of David Rawson. Rawson had married Margaret Wilson and her sister, Mary Wilson, had married Thomas Sheafe. Margaret and Mary's father was William Wilson, Canon of the King's Chapel of St. George at Windsor Castle, who died in 1615. Mary Sheafe had died around 1613. A marriage was recorded at Holy Trinity the Less in London on 11ᵗʰ November 1613 between Doctor Thomas Sheafe and Ann Woodward. Edmund Wilson, a Doctor in Physic of the Parish of St. Mary at Bow, in his will of 1633, confirmed that Rebecca Hesilrige was a cousin, along with cousins, Whitfield, Norwood and Westley, Grindall, Thomas and Edmund Sheafe. Their father, Thomas Sheafe was an overseer of Edmund Wilson's will. Edward Sheafe was not a beneficiary, suggesting that he was a son by a wife who was not connected to the Wilson family.

Edmund Sheafe, a mercer, died in 1649. His will benefited, among others, his wife, Elizabeth, his mother-in-law Elizabeth Cotton, his daughters, Elizabeth and Rebecca and his son, Sampson Sheafe. He then referred to his brother, Doctor Thomas Sheafe and his daughter, Mary, his brothers, Grindall and Edward and sisters Westley and Bale; Rebecca Hesilrige may have already died. His sister Dorothy and Henry Whitfield were still in America at the time.

Thomas Hesilrige, who had been a soldier, was buried on 30ᵗʰ October 1651 at St. Margaret's, Westminster. His estate was administered in July 1652 by his brother-in-law Dr. Thomas Sheafe on behalf of his nieces Dorothy and Frances Hesilrige, who were at that time minors. Hesilrige was described as a mercer of the Parish of St. Martin, Ludgate. His remains were disinterred after the restoration of the monarchy and put in a common grave in the churchyard and his name appears on a plaque at the church. The younger Dr. Thomas *Sheaf* (1607-1657), a fellow of the College of Physicians (*Munk's Roll*), married Mary Wright at St. Martin Ludgate on 18ᵗʰ December 1638. He was buried on 10ᵗʰ August 1657 at the Church of St. Benet and St. Peter in London as was his wife in May 1659. Her will was proved in October 1659 (*PROB 11/295/957*). Dorothy Hesilrige married John Grimstone and administered her father's will in 1658.

Grindall Sheafe, Doctor of Divinity, married Ann Munday. As Mrs. Ann Sheafe, the wife of Dr. Grindall Sheafe, archdeacon of Wells, she was buried in St. Catherine's Chapel, on 1st May 1673. Grindall died in 1680. Below is the monumental inscription on a floor slab inside the Cathedral of St. Andrew's, Wells:

> Hear lyeth y body of Grindall Sheafe Doctor of Divinity arch-
> deacon of Wells and Canon residentiary of this Cathedral church
> who died 27 day of April 1680 statis sua 72.

Of the female members of the Sheafe family, when Grindall died, few members of his immediate family were still alive. In his will, he left various bequests to his sister-in-law, Elizabeth Barker, his nephews Samuel Westley, a woollen draper and John Bale, son of Dr. John Bale of Canterbury; to nieces Mary Whitfield, Mary Vivian and her sister Martha Vivian and to Dorothy Grimstone, among others. Mary and Martha were daughters of Dr. Thomas Sheaf. Presumably they had married brothers. It might also be presumed that Mary Whitfield was the only unmarried daughter of his sister Dorothy and Henry Whitfield, by then deceased. As the father of John Bale was also John from Canterbury, it may be that there was a marriage between Isabel Norwood and John Bale, parents of John, born on 29th March 1646, at St. Mary Magdalene in Canterbury. Thomas Norwood, a clerk, of St. Michael Harbledown, Kent had died in November 1638 leaving his wife Isabel and three daughters, Mary, Rebecca and Isabel. Elizabeth Barker, widow of Edmund Sheafe, was then the wife of Mathew Barker, a clerk of St. Giles Cripplegate. They married at All Hallows, London Wall on 22nd September 1653.

Henry and Dorothy Whitfield's deaths

Henry Whitfield spent his last few years in England writing pamphlets and preaching. He was clearly a devoutly religious man; his name was recorded in the burial register at Winchester Cathedral on 17th September, 1657. Lambeth Palace retains a record of Theophilus Gale taking over Whitfield's position as a preacher there from 1657 until 1660.

At The National Archives, a short memorandum (*PROB 11/272/502*) for Henry *Whitfeild* is followed by letters of administration and states:

> Memorandum that on or about the seventeenth day of September, one thousand six hundred fifty seven or thereabouts Henry Whitfeild of the City of Winchester in the County of South-ton Clerke with an intent to make his will and dispose of his estate, being of sound good and disposing memory and understand-ing, did utter nuncupate and declare his last Will and Testam-t

in manner and form following, or the lyke in effect, vizt., I doe give and bequeath all my estate whatsoever unto my wife to be disposed of by her to, and amongst my children as she shall see cause. In testimony whereof we the witnesses present when the said dec-ed uttered the same words or the lyke in effect have here-unto sett our hands/Nath: Whitfeild, Mary Whitfeild.

The twenty ninth day of January, one thousand six hundred fifty seven l-res of ad-ion issued forth unto Dorothy Whitfeild widdow the relict and universal legatary named in the Will of Henry Whitfeild late of Winchester in the County of South-ton de-ced to ad-ster the goods chat-ls and debts of ye s-d de-ced with the said will annext according to ye manner and effect of ye s-d Will she being first by commission sworn truly to administer or there being no ex-tor therein named.

(Abbreviated words: testament, letters, administration, Southampton, deceased, chattels, annexed, said, executor.)

Henry Whitfield made an oral will to his son and daughter, Nathaniel and Mary, confirming that Nathaniel was in England when his father died. It is probable that Dorothy Whitfield returned from America around the time the letters of administration were granted or it may be that her son acted on her behalf.

A deed of sale document from the *Massachusetts Historical Society Collection*, included the following statement:

All the lands and allotments with all the appurtances of other or after divisions lately belonging to Mr Henry Whitfield or his heirs in Guilford are acknowledged by letter from Mr Nathaniel Whitfield to be sold and alienated unto Major Robert Thompson merchant of London in old England from the nine and twentieth of September in the year of 1659 to be and remain for him and his heirs for ever.

There were a total of two hundred and seventy six acres, some marsh and meadow, upland and plain, identified in various locations in the Settlement. It was Nathaniel who arranged the sale of the house to Major Robert Thompson, a puritan and he did so by letter, which would suggest that he was in England by this time. Thompson was the head of the Society for the Propagation of the Gospel in New England and lived in England. He had no intention of living in the house and probably bought it to help the Whitfield family. Thompson and his heirs rented the house and land to tenant farmers for over a century and sold it in 1772.

A burial was recorded for Dorothy Whitfield at St. John of Wapping, Middlesex on 5th September 1668; the cause of her death was given as old age. It is probable that she lived with her son or daughters on her return to England, as Nathaniel, Mary and Rebecca were all living in London. Nathaniel was given power of attorney as the executor of her will. He was the youngest son of Henry and Dorothy Whitfield, which might suggest that he was the only surviving son when he dealt with the financial affairs following the deaths of his father and mother.

On many occasions Nathaniel represented the interests of his extended family. For example, Francis Higginson, whose burial from Mr. *Hayton's* house was recorded at St. Olave's, Hart Street, London, on 24th February, 1684, was interred in the churchyard. He was the son of John Higginson and Sarah Whitfield and would have been twenty-four when he died of smallpox. The administration of the estate of Francis Higginson was granted to his uncle Nathaniel Whitfield. Written in Latin, it confirms that Francis died in the Parish of St. Olave, Hart Street and was granted to his uncle, the first creditor, on 30th April 1686 (*PROB 6/61*).

Nathaniel Whitfield

Nathaniel Whitfeld, son of Henry, was born in 1629. The *Vicar General Marriage Allegations 1660-1850* of 23rd June 1666 records an intended marriage between Nathaniel Whitfeld, aged *"about 34"* to Sara Biggs of Portsmouth, a spinster, aged 19. The marriage was to take place with the consent of her mother, Donsabell Biggs, a widow of Southwick, Southampton in Southwick, near Portsmouth or Southampton in Hampshire. Nathaniel *Whitfeld* was living then in the Parish of St. Margaret's, New Fish Street, in London, that street being from where in 1661 Samuel Pepys collected Tom Hayter, his clerk and his wife, to go on a trip to Portsmouth. Rebekah Hayter was said to have visited her husband's friends at Petersfield and Portsmouth in 1661. Tom was still living there in September 1666 when the Great Fire of London began; the monument to the Fire now stands on the site of St. Margaret's Church.

A bible in the collection of The National Trust at Blickling Hall, Norfolk, printed around 1663, which had been translated into Massachusett Algonquin by the Puritan, John Eliot (1604-1690) with an English title page, was one of twenty copies sent to England. The anonymous sender was identified as John Higginson and it included the following inscription in its end papers: *"For my loving brother Mr Nathaniel Whitfeld to be sent unto my loving brother Mr Francis Higginson Minister at Kirby Stephen in Westmorland. Enquire of Mr Nathaniel Whitfeld at ye Navy Office he lives at Bell Court in Fish Street Hill. Shew this also to my brother Mr Charles Higginson"*. Within the same bible is another inscription on an end paper with the name of Daniel Whitfeld and the date *20th March 65*. The bible may have been delivered to Francis Higginson but he died in 1673. It may have come back to London in 1684 with John Higginson's son, also Francis Higginson.

Elizabeth Whitfield, daughter of Nathaniel and Sarah was buried at St. John of Wapping on 20th May 1668. The cause of her death was recorded in the register as measles. A record of a baptism *(ancestry.com)* for Samuel Whitfield on 13th January, 1669 at St. Katherine Coleman, in the City of London, the son of Nathaniel and Sarah Whitfield, may be the child of the marriage described above. The church escaped the Great Fire of London but has since been demolished. It is close to St. Olave's, Hart Street.

In his diaries, Pepys recorded Whitfield (Nathaniel) a number of times. The first entry was on 12th July 1663, when Whitfield walked with Pepys to the docks at 11p.m. on a moonlit evening and they took a boat. On 25th June 1665, Sir George Carteret had told him, out of kindness, that the Council intended to render *Hater* and Whitfield (Tom and Nathaniel) "*incapable of ever serving the King again but that he had stopped the entry of it*", which caused Pepys to be troubled. J. M. Collinge's book, *Navy Board Officials 1660-1832* offers details from salary records on the job history of one Nathaniel Whitfield. He was working as a Clerk to the Commissioners on 27th June 1665 and resident at Chatham. Collinge noted that no Clerks were employed exclusively in the Ticket Office until 1666. He was a clerk at the Ticket office from 26th December, 1666 to 31st December 1667. Whitfield was a clerk to the Storekeepers' Accounts from 25th June 1672 until 25th March 1674. While he was paid as a Clerk to the Commissioner in 1665 and 1672 and also as a Clerk to the Controller of Storekeeper's Accounts in 1672, he was resident at Chatham in Kent, which is some distance from London. The salary for a clerk was normally £30 per annum but it was possible for some to earn up to £50 with special payments for examining Tickets. Tickets concerned wages rather than supplies; they were promissory notes for wages due. They were negotiable and seamen could, when desperate for money, accept cash against the Ticket without waiting until they could claim their wages; this was often at heavily discounted rates. There were many problems for seamen and for the Treasury arising from this system of wages, primarily because the Tickets could be forged. The likelihood was that the clerks could make money on Tickets to supplement their salaries.

Nathaniel was reappointed as a clerk to the Ticket Office on 3rd March 1673 and then appointed to a newly created position as Chief Clerk at the Ticket Office, paid from 26th March 1674 seemingly by a retrospective order of 31st October 1674; the salary was initially £80 a year and he was appointed by the Admiralty on the recommendation of the Navy Board. He was discharged by order from this position on 24th January 1682 but Collinge believed that Nathaniel probably remained in the Ticket Office as a clerk after this date. Whitfield was paid as a Clerk to the Commissioners for Old Accounts from 26th March, 1686 until 1688 along with M. Hale, who died in office in 1688. Coincidentally, on the same date, Henry Hayter was appointed as a Clerk in the same office and Tom Hayter was appointed as Assistant to Commissioner for Old Accounts. Nathaniel Whitfield and Henry Hayter were both earning salaries of £30 a year and were working with Tom Hayter as their superior. Nathaniel Whitfield was paid as a Chief Clerk to the Ticket Office from 25th June 1689 until December 1692. The salary of a Chief Clerk had been increased to £100 in 1688. Hc was paid as a Clerk at the Ticket Office from 26th December 1692 until 10th September, 1696. An Admiralty document (*ADM. 20/60, no.798*), shows, in a page entitled "*Services to the seas*" that a payment was made:

To Nathaniel Whitfield another clerk to the aforesaid comptroller
25th March 1693 for his salary for one quarter then 50 per annum
in sum twelve pounds and ten shillings.

It would appear that Whitfield was working as a clerk until his death in
1696. His salary and position varied significantly over the years but he was
only earning £50 per annum during the last few years of life. Document
(*AO 1/1721/138*) for 1696 (*page 9*) contains the entry: "*Nath: Whitfield late
clerk in ye ticket office*". However another document at TNA suggests that
Whitfield was a merchant. The case of Wharton *v*. Whitfield (*C 6/295/65*)
1690, outlines a dispute over debts between Andrew Wharton and Nathaniel
Whitfield of London, a merchant and Samuel Read of Hackney, a merchant.
Whitfield and Read were executors of the will of Richard Wharton from
New England, who died in London; his considerable estate was valued at
£2,000. Nathaniel and Samuel were looking after the interests of Wharton's
five daughters as they were under the age of 21. Wharton was the husband
of Nathaniel's late niece Sarah, daughter of John Higginson and Sarah
Whitfield, his sister.

In 1689, Nathaniel Whitfield made a loan of £1,200 recorded in the Calendar of State Papers; Stephen Evance, Sir John Lethieullier and Whitfield
Hayter also made loans in varying amounts.

The will of *Nathaniell* Whitfeld (*PROB 11/446/92*) was proved on 8th June
1698. His son Samuel received £700 and his daughters Sarah and Rebecca,
both not then 21, £600 each. His executors were his son Samuel, his brother-
in-law Isaac Ash, a linen draper and his nephew, Henry Hayter. Further
evidence in the register for wills for that year, show that *Nathaniell Whitfeld*,
with a slightly different spelling, is recorded as a gentleman of London; in
square brackets following the description is written "*St. Olave's, Hart Street*".
The original will (*PROB 10/390*) was signed by Nathaniel Whitfield and it
confirmed that his death was in 1696. Below is an approximate and incomplete
copy of the writing:

Testator mortem obijt infra ...sain St Olaves Hart .... di Londis
middx Sept 1696

Nathaniel Whitfeld's burial was recorded in the register for St. Olave's, Hart
Street on 16th September 1696; he was buried at Duke's Place.

His will was written in October in the sixth year of the reign of William and
Mary (1694). Witnesses to the signing in Exchange Alley were John Clapham
of Gray's Inn, Richard Blamirley and Peter Gunby. Admiralty documents
(*ADM 106/314 – 248, 250, 252, 254, 156 and 158*) dated 1675, refer to ticket
books and cover various topics to do with faults in accounts, etc. Number
252 records that the Book was in the hands of Tom Hayter and 254, from
29th August, 1675, reports defects in the Deptford Ketch "*books*" On the back
is written "*for Thomas Hayter Esq. one of the commanders of his Majesty's
Navy*". The distinctive signature on these letters for Nathaniel Whitfeld, as the

clerk at the Ticket Office, was the same as the one on the will signed in 1694 and as a witness to the document of 1688 (*C/111/184*) with Whitfield Hayter and Henry Hayter.

Further accounts of Nathaniel Whitfield working at the Navy Office are contained in a Memoranda, in the Collection of the Massachusetts Historical Society Sixth series, Volume 1 (1886), in *The Letter-book of Samuel Sewall*. It was dated 29th February, 1691/92 and was addressed to him there. There are other references in letters to Nathaniel and Samuel Whitfield. In a letter dated 4th February 1689/90, Sewall sent greetings to Mr. Whitfield, Madame Mills and all friends as named; it is most likely that Madame Mills was the fourth wife of Christopher Mills, who was formerly married to the late Sarah Disbrowe, the daughter of Samuel Disbrowe and Dorothy Whitfield. Again in a letter from Sewall to Edward Hull, dated 30th May 1691 he sent greetings to his cousins Mr. and Miss Perry and Mr. Whitfield, probably Nathaniel. The last reference in the letter book of Samuel Sewall was dated 10[th]June 1700 when he wrote to John Love. He enclosed with his letter a bill of exchange for the sum of 9L. 6s. 7d. *"drawn by a young merchant James Taylor on Mr Samuel Whitfield"*; Samuel was the son of Nathaniel Whitfield.

Samuel Whitfield, his spinster sister Rebecca and his son Henry received bequests from Thomas Hayter in 1724. There was a baptism for Henry Whitfield, son of Samuel and Alice, at St. Andrew, Holborn on 12th June 1709, which gave their address as 12 or 17 *Grevil* Street (*Greville Street crosses Leather Lane and Hatton Garden*), in that parish. On 7th October 1712, there was a baptism of Samuel, to the same parents but this time at St. John the Evangelist, London. If these were the children of Samuel Whitfield, his second son, Samuel, may have died before 1721 as he was not cited in the will of Thomas Hayter. An Alice Whitfield was buried at St. Andrew, Holborn, in July 1728.

An administration *(PROB 6/109)* for Rebecca Whitfeld, who died in 1733, was granted on 27th April 1734, there having been normally a period of six months before the administrations were processed, to Samuel Whitfeld the *"natural and lawful brother and next of kin of Rebecca Whitfeld late of the Parish of Islington in the County of Middlesex"*. She is likely to have been the sister of Samuel Whitfield, himself identified in Thomas Hayter's will as a cousin. In the *London Gazette* of 28th February 1738, the name of Samuel Whitfield, late of Gray's Inn Lane in the Parish of St. Andrew, Holborn, Middlesex, a haberdasher, appeared as a prisoner of debt in the King's Bench Prison in Southwark.

Who was Daniel Whitfeld?

Daniel Whitfeld, whose name was included in the Blickling Hall Bible, was also recorded as a clerk to the Clerk of the Acts at the Navy Office from 25th June 1678 to 24th June 1680. He appears next as Clerk (Treasurers Accounts) from 15th September 1691 and then as a Clerk (Ticket office) from 25th June 1693 until he was discharged on 25th November 1700. However, in 1679

Daniel Whitfield's name appears in a letter from the King to New England appointing him as Collector of Customs. However, the letter was not sent, nor was he appointed *(Calendar of State Parers Colonial, America and West Indies, Volume 10, 1677-1680, in Miscellaneous 1679, No. 1248)*.

Daniel Whitfeild was named in the will of Nathaniel Higginson, who died on the last day of October 1708. He gave £10 each to the two daughters of his uncle, Daniel Whitfeld, then deceased. A statement was added to the will in November 1708 which explained that the date of the original will was incorrect: it confirmed that Higginson had made it on 31st July 1703. If Daniel's career path terminated in 1700 and Higginson's will was written in July 1703, one might assume that Daniel died prior to that year. The burial of Daniel Whitfeld, a yeoman, was recorded on 26th August 1702 at St. Giles, Cripplegate *(ancestry.com)*. The administration of Daniel Whitfeld of the Parish of St. Aegidy (St. Giles) Cripplegate, applied for in November 1702, was granted to Marie Whitfeld, his widow, on 30th November 1703 *(PROB 6/78)*.

It may be that Henry Whitfeld and Dorothy had another son born in America. It may also be that Rebecca Whitfeld, born around 1694, who married John Otway in 1717, was one of the daughters of Daniel Whitfeld.

23

Tom Hayter's son, Thomas Hayter and his legacy

Tom Hayter, once clerk to Pepys, who died in 1689, was not the person who had owned the land in South Tottenham, as recorded in 1720 but it is probable that it was owned by his son, Thomas, who had in turn inherited it from the latter's brother, Henry. Tom Hayter's wife Rebecca had a child, born in August 1661, as recorded in the diary of Samuel Pepys; he may have been Thomas, son of Thomas (Tom), the child having been baptised in 1661 at St. Leonard, Eastcheap. The couple had others as well, including Henry, Whitfield, Elizabeth, Mary and Rebecca.

Henry Hayter was recorded as owner of the land in Tottenham High Cross from 11th April 1694 and then his brother Thomas inherited it in 1716. In 1720, Thomas and his brother Whitfield Hayter mortgaged the land at South Tottenham to Charles Turner.

A reference to a Thomas Hayter appears in the *Calendar of State Papers, Treasury, Volume10.3, 1693-1696,* on March 28, 1696, in an entry, which records:

> Treasury reference to same of the petition of Edward Buck, a
> King's waiter in London Port but much disabled, praying that Mr
> Thomas Haytor may be constituted in his place.

The spelling Haytor and not Hayter was used but it is likely that these were interchangeable and indeed that this reference was to the son of Tom Hayter, clerk to Pepys. The role of a King's waiter was to inspect cargoes as they arrived and in 1694 the office holder earned £52 a year. The wage would not have been large but the position was one of some responsibility. In 1720, Thomas Hayter, a merchant, is listed in *Strypes Survey of London (on-line)*. Perhaps the role of King's waiter led Thomas to become a merchant of London, as he was described in a document at TNA (*C111/187*).

More is revealed about Thomas Hayter from his will and the wills of his friends and relatives. His was written on 8th February 1721, with a codicil in 1722 and probate was granted on 19th June 1724. Thomas gave instructions to be buried in the same vault as his brother Henry in the Parish Church at Epsom. Henry had died in 1716 and Thomas was referred to as his heir in 1720 and 1721 in the Indentures for the land in Tottenham and Edmonton; both brothers had lived in Epsom. On the floor, in a little chapel at the front of the church of St. Martin of Tours, Epsom, there is a large black slate memorial plaque with the information that follows recorded on it; a small corner has been broken off.

23.1 Henry Hayter's memorial at St. Martin of Tours, Epsom.

"Here lyeth interred ye body of Mr Henry Hayter who departed this life July ye 14th 1716 in ye 53rd year of.........."

Henry died, aged 53, in 1716; his date of birth was 1663. This is a transcription of the will of Henry Hayter *(PROB 11/553/113),* which records some of the same people identified elsewhere in other documents:

I hereby appoint Mr Thomas Hayter my sole executor and administration giving to him all I possess of houses goods land tenements annuities funds and rendering him out of the promises to pay one hundred pounds to Whitfield Hayter out of the 200 on order the same 100 to be paid him quarterly as grows due at the exchange annuities I order him also to pay cousin Rebecca Whitfield 50 per annum during her life out of the exchequer annuity order I also order him to pay Mrs Morland 50 pounds during her life not to commence till after my mother [.......] Signed 6th June 1716 at Epsom.

Henry's will was written less than four weeks before his death. He chose Thomas Hayter as his executor and left explicit instructions but unfortunately he did not specify the nature of all the relationships. Some of the same names appeared in the indentures; Mary Morland, Whitfield Hayter and a cousin called Rebecca Whitfield. He made reference to his mother, so one might assume that she was still alive when he wrote the will in June 1716 but the will was ambiguous because there were no words following the word "*mother*". It is possible that Mary Morland's mother was living with her at Epsom, hence the reason why the inheritance would not be paid to her until after her death. The mother may have died after Henry Hayter's will was written in June and before the will was proved on 17th July, 1716. This was also around the time of the last entry for Rebekah Hayter in the Declared Accounts of the Navy Office. When Mary Morland wrote her will in 1717, she made no mention of her mother, which might suggest that Rebecca Hayter was by then dead.

The Hayter family was important and wealthy enough to have a memorial placed inside the church at St. Martin of Tours in Epsom. Nevertheless, there is no presently visible memorial stone for Henry's brother, Thomas Hayter inside it. Thomas Hayter did say in his will that he wanted to be interred in the vault that he had built in the churchyard for his late deceased brother, which might suggest that the memorial slab to Henry Hayter inside the church is all that survives and that Thomas was buried with his brother. The church was built in the fifteenth century and according to a church official, was remodelled entirely in Victorian times and many of the early memorials were destroyed. Some of the old headstones and memorials had been moved to different places inside and outside it. If there had been a vault outside the original church, the exact location was said to be unknown. The gravestones outside are in various states of disrepair and some of the inscriptions are still visible but many are completely worn away by the weather. A memorial to Henry Hayter was recorded on *page 696* of *The Graveyard and Church Monuments of Epsom* (including St. Martin of Tours) *(SOG: SR/M1.)* It was compiled in 1963, at a time when there was less erosion of the headstones, from drawings and notes of headstones and vaults made in the nineteenth century and from other sources. Under a section headed *"Particulars as to grave, gravestones and tombs disturbed in building operations 1907-1908" on pages 208-209*, it advised that there had been an ordinary grave with headstone, presumably in the churchyard, with the name of Hayter, disturbed during the building work.

Thomas Hayter, in addition to having become quite a wealthy merchant, had owned other land at Lindsey Level, Lincolnshire, which he sold in 1708-09 to Thomas White of St. James, Westminster. Thomas Hayter was certainly a landowner in his own right although he inherited land from his brother. White had bought some 500 acres of drained land and 500 acres of undrained in late February 1708. These acreages were part of some 25,000 acres originally granted for draining to the Earl of Lindsay. In documents relating to Lindsey Level, up to 1712, Sir Cleave Moore (sometimes More) was cited and he obviously had known Thomas Hayter for some time before the former bought the land in Lancashire. Hayter's brother, Whitfeld, had been a witness to the sale of the land in 1708/1709 along with Thomas Lynge of Gray's Inn and a Mr. Gerard.

The extent of Hayter's land ownership is evident from various documents which survive today. He had mortgaged land in Lancashire and Lincolnshire. How he came to be involved in transactions in these areas may have been connected to the activities of his brother or his Navy Office father. Liverpool, as a port, would have been a centre of trading with the New World and Thomas Hayter's career as a merchant may have been connected. His brother, Henry, had died in 1716, so his involvement in the following land deal may have been connected to or in consequence of his death. Henry may have originally owned the land or Thomas may have bought it with the proceeds from his brother's estate. The pieces of land in question were in Liverpool and the surrounding area. The conveyance, held at Lancashire Record Office (*Ref. DDK/471/231 & 232*) dated 27th January, 1717, included property at Bootle. They were *"conveyed upon trust for sale .....as should raise money wherewith to discharge a bond for £5000 and interest wherein the said Plumbe, Earle and Gildart then stood bound with George Prickett and then the remainder of the premises to stand as security for £6000 and interest owing by the said Sir Cleave Moore to the said Thomas Hayter"*. A note on the deeds and conveyances shows that Hayter's share of land, mentioned above, was assigned by Edward Hubbald and others, his trustees, on a deed endorsed by Deed Poll on 31st March and 1st April 1724 to James, Earl of Derby and paid in full by the Earl of Derby with the consent of Sir Cleave Moore (*DDK/471/254a and 254b*). The amount agreed to be paid was £6000 plus £700. Thomas Hayter was still alive in April 1724 but his nephew was obviously acting on his behalf. The conveyances took place with these same people over a number of days.

Plumbe, Earl and Gildart were rich merchants and landowners in the Liverpool area. In fact, Gildart was also known to be a slave trader. George Prickett was responsible for developing the Liverpool docks at the start of Liverpool's long history of trading in slaves and merchandice. Sir Cleave Moore, at the age of fifteen, had inherited the land in question from his father when the latter died in 1678. Another document *(DDK/471/233)* at Lancashire Record Office, shows that the son was responsible for introducing the supply of water to Liverpool from the springs of Bootle, having made an agreement with Philip Bertie to do this in August 1718. It was brothers Philip and Charles Bertie who had been reported in Parliament in 1695 because they appeared to have appointed themselves as members of Parliament for Stamford in Lincolnshire without going through the correct electoral process. Philip Bertie, in 1711, married Lady Elizabeth Brabazon, the former wife of Sir Philip Coote, with whom he had had an affair. She became and was described in her will of 1719 as Elizabeth Bertie, Countess of Lindsey, in Lincolnshire. After Philip Bertie died in 1728, he left an interest in Sir Cleave Moore's Waterworks to charity and his estate in Liverpool, land in Lincolnshire and Somerset to his brother, the Honourable Albemarle Bertie. The Honourable Charles Bertie and his wife, Mary also mortgaged land at Lincolnshire in 1721 to Albemarle Bertie, for the sum of £9,500. Charles Bertie died in 1727 and he and his wife were buried at Theddlethorpe. Unfortunately for Sir Cleave Moore, he was increasingly in debt and around the time of the death of Thomas Hayter, in 1724, the Earl of Derby bought what was left of Moore's estate.

Thomas Hayter's death was recorded in the burial records for St. Martin of Tours, Epsom, on 15th June 1724. He made no reference in his will (*PROB 11/597/397*), dated 19th June 1724 or in any of the later documents to his mother, which might suggest that by then she was already dead. Thomas drafted his will on 8th February 1721, shortly after the indentures were registered. He may have been reflecting on the death of his brothers or his own mortality as he wrote in his will *"the uncertainty of this life and how certain we are to die"*. Upon his death, Thomas had an estate greater than the sum of £6,700 in value. The executors of his will were his good friend Matthew Holworthy, Edward Hubbald, his nephew and Samuel Whitfield, his cousin. Matthew Clark, his minister received £20 and Matthew Holworthy also received a payment and a *"picture of the Resurrection standing in his parlour"*. Hayter left £2000 to his nephew, Edward Hubbald, a gentleman of the Parish of St. Thomas the Apostle, which is near College Hill in the City of London. Hubbald being a nephew of Thomas Hayter, his mother would have been a Hayter, namely Thomas' sister, Rebecca. Edward Hubbald was a witness to the signing of the indentures already mentioned, which might suggest that he was actively involved in the business of his uncle. His mother and father were already dead and therefore were not included in the will. Hayter also left Edward and his heirs his freehold messuage or tenement and garden with appurtances at Wood Cott Green in the Parish of Epsom in Surrey.

In Epsom, a road still exists called Woodcott Green and Thomas Hayter may have been referring to this place or the village of Woodcote, which is close to Sutton and not in Epsom. Woodcott Green Road contains some very grand houses and it is most likely that this was what Hayter was describing. There has been horse racing at Epsom since the time of King Charles II and the town derives its name from the medicinal qualities of the salts found there. One might imagine that it was a pleasant and convenient place to live, close to London but still far enough away from the dirt and squalor of life and disease in the city.

Thomas Hayter referred in his will to a mortgage *"subject nevertheless to the mortgage I have made thereof to my sister Mary Morland of Epsom aforesaid widow for securing the payment of an annuity of fifty pounds to her during the term of her natural life"*. The reference to the mortgage is ambiguous because prior to this statement he discussed his freehold messuage at Woodcott Green, which he may have mortgaged. It may also have been a reference to a mortgage on his land at Tottenham or Lancashire, discussed below.

Mary Morland is identified as Thomas' sister in documents relating to the land in South Tottenham. What is unusual is that Thomas Hayter did not leave his sister a larger annuity. One might speculate that she was in poor health and thought unlikely to survive him and/or well provided for by her husband's will.

The will explains that Hayter was owed by Sir Cleave Moore £6000, a substantial sum of money, with a further surety of £700, for land that Hayter had owned in Lancashire. There was no reference to the land in South Tottenham, which serves to confirm that he had already relinquished ownership in 1721. Most of his assets were in land and not shares in companies or as loans to the Exchequer. Other beneficiaries of his will were named as Abraham Fell and the latter's sister Elizabeth Jones, who received some thirty pounds each. Abraham was a gun-lock maker of Goodman's Fields, an area close to the Tower of London. The fact that Hayter left funds to him suggests a close relationship besides any business dealings in which they may have been involved together. Hayter also had a servant named Sarah Fell, a spinster, probably related to Abraham Fell and Elizabeth Jones (*above*), to whom he left £100. He left £50 apiece to his servants, Joseph Kingham and Elizabeth Gubbins, obviously holding them in a high regard.

Thomas Hayter made better provision, in the sum of two hundred pounds, for his sister-in-law, Martha Hayter, the widow of his brother, Whitfield. The record of it was confirmation that Whitfield Hayter died between the writing of the indenture, registered on 30th December 1720 and when Thomas Hayter wrote his will. Codicils to Thomas Hayter's will, written on 29th March 1722, offer insight about Martha. The following passage explains that:

> in compassion to the present deplorable circumstances of her the said Martha Hayter as being a lunatick and for the natural love and affection which I have and do bear unto my said sister in law and in order to the making a more comfortable and competent provision for the necessary support and maintenance... I am now minded and desirious to make some alteration....

He had agreed to set aside more money to Martha Whatton of Westminster, Martha's mother and Samuel Horsley, a woodmonger and possibly a Non-Conformist, also of Westminster, to make provision for her welfare and care. The younger Martha, although a lunatic, was obviously expected to have a longer life than Thomas' sister Mary as he left his sister-in-law more money. Both Martha and Whitfield Hayter lived in the Parish of St. Margaret's, Westminster prior to their deaths. Thomas Hayter, was also listed in certain documents as living in the same parish but at the time of his death was living in the Parish of Epsom.

Samuel Whitfield, of the Strand, a haberdasher and Hayter's cousin, was given £1500 and his son Henry, £500. A Nathaniel Whitfield, cited above, worked with Henry Hayter at the Navy Office and was almost certainly related, offering documentary evidence that the Whitfield and Hayter families were linked by marriage. Samuel Whitfield's spinster sister, Rebecca, received £800. Another cousin by the name of Rebecca Otway, wife of John Otway, received £200. He also left £40 to his spinster cousin, Elizabeth Higginson.

Rebecca Otway, née Whitfield, married John Otway on 29th August 1717 at St. Nicholas, Cole Abbey in London. A copy of the marriage allegation, dated 28th August, is archived at Lambeth Palace Library (*Index of Faculty Office Marriage Allegations, 1701-1725*). It explains that when it was made, John Otway was living in the Parish of Ashstead in Surrey and that he was 28 years of age. His future wife was 24 and described as being from Epsom in Surrey. Otway was born in 1689 and Rebecca in 1693. John was the son of James Otway deceased and had inherited substantial freehold and copyhold messuages and land from his uncle, John Otway of Ashstead in Surrey, whose will was proved in April 1716 (Ancestry). Rebecca may have been living with Mary Morland or Thomas Hayter at Epsom before she married. It is ever possible that Rebecca was not technically Thomas Hayter's *"cousin"* but otherwise related, perhaps the daughter of a first, second or third cousin.

The will of Rebecca *Olway* (Otway) of Eckington in the County of Derby, a widow, proved on 24th May 1758 (*PROB 11/838/214*), confirms the connection with the Whitfield, Hayter and Hubbald families. She gave *"to my old friend and acquaintance Grace Waterman and her daughter Betty one guinea for a ring"* and her estate was left to her kinsman Edward Hubbald, a gentleman of Milk Street, London and his heirs. He was appointed her executor; Hubbald died the following year. The will of Edward Hubbald, a gentleman of Milk Street in the City of London was proved on 19th November 1759 (*PROB 11/850/333*). He left his estate to his good friend, Betty Waterman who was also his executrix. Edward Hubbald was buried at the Church of St. Martin of Tours, Epsom. The entry states that *"Edward Hubbald from London buried on 14th November 1759"*. Henry Hayter, Thomas Hayter, Mary Morland and Edward Hubbald were all buried at St. Martin of Tours at Epsom. It is probable that Mary's husband, Joseph Morland and Rebeccah Hayter, their mother were also buried there.

Matthew Holworthy was one of the executors named in Thomas Hayter's will. His presence serves to explain in more detail the relationships among the Hayter, Holworthy, Disbrowe and Whitfield families and how they are all connected to the land at Tottenham High Cross. The two may have known each other through Matthew's cousin, John Holworthy who in 1697 married Dame Judith Barkham, *née* Halsey, the widow of William Barkham. Alternatively or in addition, the relationship may have been in consequence of Matthew marrying Elizabeth, whose father, James Disbrowe was the cousin of Thomas Hayter.

Matthew's daughter, Elizabeth Holworthy married Samuel Heathcote on 3rd May 1720, at Gray's Inn Chapel. A year later, a child was born to Elizabeth's sister, Susanna, then 16 years of age. The circumstances leading to this birth were explained in *The Post Boy*, dated 4-6th July 1721 (*17th and 18th Century Burney Collection Newspapers*). Heathcote, of Queen's Square, London and Anne Fletcher, Susanna's maid, were charged with betraying, seducing and corrupting Susanna Holworthy, then aged 15. Heathcote stood accused of taking advantage of his sister-in-law on visits to her home at Clapton and when it became obvious that she was pregnant, Samuel removed Susanna from her friends and transferred her to lodgings at Covent Garden, where she was delivered of a son. She fell ill and was visited a number of times by Sir David Hamilton, physician to the Queen, who testified that Samuel used the name of Stephens; other witnesses confirmed that the couple were cohabiting as husband and wife. (*The illegitimate son, named Samuel Smith, was given this surname because he was born out of wedlock, as church and civil law prohibited the child from taking the name of Holworthy or Heathcote.*) Susanna died on 2nd June 1721, aged sixteen, not long after the birth and was buried in the churchyard at Covent Garden. Her father, Justice Matthew Holworthy, on hearing of her death, removed the corpse for burial to the church at Elsworth, Cambridgeshire and immediately initiated proceedings against their son-in-law and his accomplice, Anne Fletcher. Heathcote and Fletcher were found guilty of the charge in July but in October it was noted in the *Daily Journal* that they had been included in the King's Act of Indemnity. It has been suggested that this pardon was granted because Samuel Heathcote was the nephew of Sir Gilbert Heathcote, a wealthy banker and former Governor of the Bank of England, whose influence and power helped rescue the King from the mess created when the shares in the South Sea Company crashed around 1720-21. The *"Bank Contract"* drawn up by Robert Walpole, the politician and later first English prime minister, made three proposals, one of which transferred South Sea stock to the Bank of England (*The South Sea Bubble,* by John Carswell). The Bank of England, East India, Sword Blade, South Sea Companies and others were involved as they were funding the government. Elizabeth Heathcote, Suzanna's sister died on 6th May 1726, aged 27 (*Monumental inscription Holy Trinity Church, Elsworth, Cambridgeshire*), the children died before their father. The memorial at Elsworth includes Matthew Holworthy, Esq., who wrote his will in Hackney and died on 18th May 1728, aged 54 and his wife Elizabeth Holworthy, daughter of James Disbrowe, Esq., Doctor of Physic, who died 19th August 1748, aged 67. Samuel Smith took the Holworthy name after the death of his grandmother and he died in 1765.

Part Three

The Lethieullier era 1721–1798

24

Memorials, deeds and indentures

Besides building development and rebuilding after the Great Fire of London, the period around the turn of the 17th century saw a great expansion in banking, share ownership and investment in international trading; the Bank of England was established in 1694. Some of the people owning land in Tottenham were extremely wealthy individuals who were investing and trading in commodities from the East and West Indies. Others were investing in the infrastructure for what are today's towns, with the need for water supplies and in the drainage of land in various parts of the country to make the land more productive.

Mortgaging and leasing land was a form of financing and a way of borrowing to fund projects or pay debts. Many such arrangements were temporary transfers of land for these purposes. The new class of speculator included merchants, professional people and skilled craftsman, such as stonemasons, wood merchants and brewers. Sometimes the buying and selling of land occurred when individuals were in debt. At other times, mortgages were raised by individuals to provide marriage settlements for their sons, daughters or relatives.

Among the many reasons that land exchanged hands was to increase holdings in a particular area and to consolidate or release other land held further afield, which was difficult to manage. Sometimes it was to achieve a better return on investment, depending on the type of land held. For example, in the cities there was a need for more homes. Great amounts of timber were imported from Sweden but English woodland was much in demand, as was land for brickworks. London had the greatest population of any European city in 1700, standing at over half-a-million people, even though the death rate was greater than that of birth. London stretched from Millbank to Stepney and northwards towards a new development at Seven Dials, in what is now Covent Garden. At one end was the centre of government and at the other were the merchants. There were few houses in the Tottenham area in 1699, except those dotted along Ermine Street, going north, beyond Middlesex to Essex.

Freehold and copyhold land could be mortgaged. Copyhold mortgages were recorded in the Manorial Court Rolls but sometimes when the mortgaged estate was part freehold and copyhold, copyhold land was included in freehold mortgage deeds. When a house or land was mortgaged, it was not occupied by the new owner as, in the seventeenth century, the law stated that the mortgagor could continue to live in the land or administer the mortgaged estate. If the mortgagor did not pay the annual interest on the mortgage, just as today, then the mortgagee could take steps to recover the money owed. At any time, the mortgagor could pay back the money taken on the mortgage and again take full ownership of the land. The term used to describe such a situation was *"equity of redemption"*. When someone wished to leave leasehold property before the end of the term originally taken, the lessee asked permission from the lessor to do so and then assigned the lease to the other person. The new lessee had to accept the original conditions of the lease.

Nottingham University's *Deeds in Depth, Manuscript and Special Collections* is an accessible source of information on these matters. Deeds are the legal documents which prove the ownership of land and show *"title"* and were written on parchment. Property or land was held in three different ways; freehold was for an indefinite time, leasehold was for a specified length of time and copyhold was a special tenure as the land was held by the Lord of the Manor. Among the types of deeds are bargain and sale, abstract of title, leases and releases, marriage, mortgages, wills and other settlements. An *"abstract of title"* is a document which explains how the title arrived to the present owner and often includes a summary of previous deeds. Indentures are a type of deed which had an indented top, cut in a wavy line. If there were two parties to the transfer of land, each had a copy and sometimes the two parts matched up. The lawyers who drew up the deeds were paid by drafted lineage, hence, to a certain extent, sometimes the length and level of repetition within documents. Key words suggest the gist of the transaction.

There were differing types of leases. If the lease was for five hundred or a thousand years it usually signified that the documents were related to family settlements or mortgages. A lease for six months or a year, for a small consideration (five or ten shillings) or a nominal rent of one peppercorn or a rose, per year, was probably not a real lease. A lease and release were two separate documents relating to the same transfer. The lease took place one day and the release, the next day, when the freehold was then handed over to the new owner and when the true value of the land was paid. They are sometimes separated but when they are copied into the Deeds and Memorial Books they follow each other. The original leases could be sewn together. An assignment of lease occurred when a lessee decided to leave the leasehold property before the lease had elapsed and with the permission of the lessor he assigned the lease to someone else. In 1814, the laws concerning land changed and long leases became the norm, reverting back to the landlords or freeholders after they expired. In 1841, the lease/release format finally disappeared to be replaced by the Conveyance by Release Act and then in 1845, releases were replaced by a *"grant"* or what is now known as a conveyance.

The Middlesex Registry Act 1708 set up a registry in the county of Middlesex for deeds, conveyances wills, encumbrances, etc. on freehold land or on land held by lease of over 21 years.

> Deeds and documents brought to the registry for registration were initially copied onto pieces of parchment called memorials and then into large volumes or registers The memorials from 1838 to 1890 were destroyed in 1940. From 1891 the original memorials were bound into volumes to form the registers.

The documents copied into the registers are not complete copies of the originals. Only certain information was abstracted from the original. This included the date of the transaction, the names of the parties and a description of the property. Covenants and other restrictions contained in the original document were not always recorded in the registered version. From the middle of the nineteenth century plans of the property concerned were frequently included in the entries and from 1892 a separate series of plan tracings of larger maps and plans bound into volumes were made. *(LMA Information Leaflet Number 38)*

After 1709, the rather haphazard system of recording transfers of land was rationalised. Land ownership was recorded in the Middlesex Deeds Registry, 1709-1938, now held at the London Metropolitan Archives, which were initially set up to keep track of mortgages between parties to avoid any secret mortgages or fraud at a time when there was great expansion and building development. According to Stella Colwell in her book *Family Roots: Discovering the Past in the Public Record Office,* all parties were able to inspect the record to check leases of 21 years, sales, gifts and wills of freehold land, memorials or mortgages. As to transfers of land identified in South Tottenham, between the death of Sir William Barkham in 1695 and 1709, when the registers were started, some of the deeds in Robinson's book were from that period and as the book was written close to the events, his information is probably correct. Some, after 1709, can be confirmed from other original documents or copies, held at the London Metropolitan Archives.

Not all those involved in the indentures (sealed agreements) are always declared and the names are not recorded in alphabetical order, with writing style and the spelling of the names being of that time. For the period after 1718, for present purposes, every reference connected with the area of Tottenham, Tottenham High Cross and Edmonton, as well as known names, were examined to find any that included land in South Tottenham. Land was sometimes identified as Tottenham High Cross and sometimes as Tottenham, Edmonton and Enfield. Not every deed identifies clearly the parcel of land. The Deeds record any assignment or surrender of a lease, transfer of a mortgage, further charge, conveyance or re-conveyance. They were sometimes the result of wills and affected freehold land and land held by a lease, for over 21 years, within the county of Middlesex. The memorials have, written in the margins near the beginning of the document, the names of the main parties involved with the number of the Indenture, for example, Giblett to Dorman. The name or names are usually those of the person or people from whom the property or land is being transferred. On occasion, there were many parties involved in conveyances. If there was more than one person involved, for example, members of the same family, parties were identified as the second, third or fourth part depending on the number of people. The last name is usually the one to whom the land passed.

25

The Lethieullier connection

One of the earliest Indentures of demise or mortgage (*MDR/1720/2/301*) archived at the Middlesex Deeds Registry, that makes reference to Thomas Hayter and Tottenham, was dated 8th June 1720, in the sixth year of the reign of George I (between 1st August, 1719 and 31st July, 1720). The lengthy document explains that Thomas Hayter of All Hallows Steyning (Staining) within the City of London, a gentleman, of the one part, had granted a mortgage to Charles Turner of Staples Inn, of the Parish of St. Andrew's, Holborn, in the County of Middlesex, a gentleman, of the other part. The description of the land in the Indenture was as follows:

> All those three closes of meadow or pasture ground commonly called or known by the name of the Oat Fields formerly two closes contained together by estimation twenty six acres more or less lying and being in the Parish of Tottenham High Cross in the County of Middlesex in a certain place there called by the name of Stamford Hill and abutting south upon the lands now or late of Sir Robert Smith Knight and north upon Hangers Lane And also all that messuage cottage or tenement stables shop loft and coach house yard and well with all and singular the appurtenances there unto belonging in any wise pertaining in all containing twenty eight perches be the same more or less late in the tenure or occupation of John Russell deceased and lying and being in Tottenham aforesaid adjoining to the parish of Edmonton near the messuage or tenement called the Blue Boar And also all those four acres of meadow land lying in the Wild Marsh in Tottenham aforesaid late in the tenure or occupation of John Russell And also those two acres of arable land be the same more or less lying and being within a certain field called the Downfield late in the tenure or occupation of Thomas Raymond Yeoman his assigns or undertenants and All those two acres of meadow pasture or ground be the same more or less lying and being at or near a place called the Clendish Hill late in the tenure or occupation of the said Thomas Raymond And all that one other acre of meadow pasture ground more or less lying and being in a certain meadow called Broadmead late in the tenure or occupation of the said Thomas Raymond his assigns or undertenants And also one half acre of meadow or pasture ground be

the same more or less lying and being in Mitchley Marsh late
in the tenure or occupation of the said Thomas Raymond his
undertenants or assigns And all that one other acre of arable
land be the same more or less lying and being in Langua also
Languish Field [.....] late also in the tenure or occupation of the
said Thomas Raymond his undertenants or assigns And also all
those two acres of meadow or pasture ground be the same more
or less lying and being in a place called the Wild Marsh late
also in the tenure or occupation of the said Thomas Raymond
his assign or undertenants All which said two acres of arable
land and other the said last mentioned grounds and premises
are lying and being in the several parishes of Tottenham and
Edmonton aforesaid or in one of them And also all those eight
acres and three roods of meadow or pasture ground be the same
more or less called Crookes Grove lying near Blackhope Lane
in the said parish of Tottenham And also all that close or parcel
of meadow or pasture ground containing by estimation two acres
be the same more or less lying and being at West Green in the
parish of Tottenham aforesaid abutting eastupon the land now
or late of John Pulford Esquire west upon lands now or late
of John Barnes gent and north upon West Green aforesaid And
also those two closes of meadow or pasture ground containing
together by estimation twelve acres be the same more or less
commonly called or known by the name of Snares Meads or
adjoining south upon Hangers Lane aforesaid All which said last
mentioned two closes and premises are lying and being in the
parish of Tottenham aforesaid And also all that close or field of
meadow or pasture containing by estimation eight acres be the
same more or less abutting south upon Hangers Lane aforesaid
which said close or field then was in the occupation of Henry
Cocking and is lying and being in the parish of Tottenham aforesaid And all and singular other the messuages land tenements and
hereditaments whatsoever of him the said Thomas Hayter situate
standing lying and being in Edmonton and Tottenham aforesaid
either of them in the said County of Middlesex and all ways
casement libertys priviliges profits commodities and appurtences
whatsoever to the said messuages lands and tenements hereditaments premises belonging or in any wise appertaining which
said Indentures of demise or mortgage was witnessed by Joseph
Williams of the Middle Temple London gentleman and Richard
Saunders servant to Mr Benjamin Wilcock of the Middle temple
London aforesaid also gentleman and is hereby required to be
registered pursuant to the same late Act by me the said Thomas
Hayter the grantor in the said deed as witnessed my hand and
seal the twentieth day of December Anno Dom one thousand
seven hundred and twenty by Thomas Hayter

Signed sealed and delivered in the presence of (this parchment being first duly stamped) Richard Saunders Jos: Baron.
(City of London, Metropolitan Archives.) *"Hereditaments" refers to property that can be inherited.*

It included Oat Fields and Snares Mead, near Hangers Lane, Tottenham and the land comprised seventy two acres. The indenture was witnessed, sealed and delivered by Joseph Williams of the Middle Temple and Richard Saunders, servant to Mr. Benjamin Wilcock, of the Middle Temple, a gentleman on 20th December 1720 (which was actually the seventh year of the reign of George I as six months had elapsed between writing and completion). Hayter was living at the time of this indenture in the Parish of All Hallows, which is at the corner of Hart Street and Mark Lane, close to St. Olave Middlesex.

An Indenture (*MDR/1720/2/302*) in the same book, recorded as *Turner and Lethieullier*, written on 20th December 1720, on the same day that the previous one had been signed, was an Indenture of Assignment or Mortgage tripartite, pursuant to the said late Act among Charles Turner of Staples Inn, in the Parish of St. Andrews, of the first part, *"Thomas Hayter of All Hallows Steyning brother and heir and also devisee of Henry Hayter late of Epsom in the county of Surrey, gentleman deceased and Whitfeild Hayter citizen and goldsmith of London brother of the said Thomas Hayter of the second part"* and William Lethieullier of Beckenham in the County of Kent, of the third part. There was a lengthy description of the land as in the previous Indenture. This one was witnessed, on 30th December 1720, by Mr. Benjamin Wilcock, of the Middle Temple, a gentleman, Humphrey Brent, of the Parish of Trinity Minories, a scrivener and Josiah Baron, London, clerk to Mr. Brent. Neither this or its sister document contained information on the sum paid. This indenture was unusual to the extent that all three brothers, Henry, Thomas and Whitfeild Hayter were cited in the same document.

An original document *(ACC/0026/064)* at the City of London, London Metropolitan Archives, shows how the Lethieullier family came to acquire lands from Thomas Hayter. Below is a transcription of the agreement made in 1721:

Articles of Agreement made concluded and fully agreed upon this fourteenth day of December Anno Dm one thousand seven hundred and twenty one in the eighth year of the reign of Lord King George Er between Thomas Hayter of the Parish of St. Margaret's Westminster in the County of Middlesex Gent of the one part and William Lethieullier, of Beckenham in Kent Esq. of the other part in manner following /viz/.....

Whereas the said William Lethieullier hath already advanced and lent the said Thomas Hayter the sum of eight hundred pounds upon the mortgage of the land and hereditaments hereinafter mentioned and whereas the said William Lethieullier hath contracted and agreed with the said Thomas Hayter for the purchase of the said land and hereditaments for the sum of two thousand seven hundred and fifty pounds and is also agreed to advance and lend the said Thomas Hayter the sum of five hundred pounds more until such purchase can be made and perfected now in pursuance to this agreement the said Thomas Hayter doth for himself his heirs and assigns covenant and promise to and with the said William Lethieullier his heirs and assigns by these present as follows/ viz/ that he the said Thomas Hayter his heirs and assigns and also John Otway of Epsom and Rebecca his wife cozen of him the said Thos Hayter and Mary Moreland of Epsom aforesaid widow sister of the said Thos Hayter and George Wanley of Edmonton Middx and all other person and persons having or lawfully claiming any estate or interest of and in the lands and hereditaments hereinafter mentioned shall and will for the consideration hereinafter expresst by or before the last day of January now next ensuing at the proper costs and charges in the Law of the said William Lethieullier his heirs and assigns make do execute Levy and Acknowledge or cause to make done levied Executed and acknowledged all and every such Act & Acts Deed and Deeds fine and fines assurances and assurances or other Conveyances in the law whatsoever as the said William Lethieullier his heirs and assigns or his or their Counsel learned in the Law shall advise or require for the same conveying and making a good and sure title unto the said William Lethieullier his heirs and assigns of all the several pieces or parcels of Land and Hereditaments with their and every their appurtences containing by estimation seventy two acres more or less situate lying and being in the several parishes of Tottenham and Edmonton in the County of Middx now in the possession of Henry Bootes Michael [piece of parchment missing] their undertenants or assigns Which premises are now in mortgage to the said William Lethieullier as above is mentioned To hold to the said William Lethieullier his heirs and assigns from the feast of the birth of our Lord Christ now next ensuing and that the premises shall at the time of the making & executing such Conveyances or assurances be free from all manner of Encumbrances except the aforementioned mortgage In consideration whereof the said William Lethieullier doth for himself his heirs and assigns Covenant & promise & agree to with the Thomas Hayter his heirs & assigns by these present as follows/viz/ that the said William Lethieullier shall & will not only forthwith advance & lend to the said Thos Hayter the said sum of five hundred pounds on the further Mortgage of the premises and also accept such Conveyances of the same in manor as aforesaid but shall & will upon the completing and perfecting such Conveyances of the premises in manner as aforesaid well and truely pay or paid to the said Thomas Hayter his heirs or assigns the further sum of one thousand four hundred & fifty pounds which together with the said several sums of eight hundred pounds already lent and five hundred pounds more now agreed to be lent in full payment of the Consideration Money hereby agreed to be paid for the Purchase of the Premises to the true performance of all and every the Covenants and Agreements above herein Contained on each of the partyes to be kept and performed each of the said partyes bindeth himself his Heirs and Assigns unto the other of them his heirs and assigns in the total sum of four thousand pounds truely to be paid by these present In witness whereof the said Thomas Hayter and William Lethieullier have hereto set their hands and Seales the day and year first above written.

On the reverse was the following statement:

Sealed and delivered in the presence of us the paper first duly stamped and these words [further but & shall be paid and fifty pounds] were interlined on the other side hereof before the executing of these present.
(*City of London, London Metropolitan Archives*)

The agreement was sealed and delivered in the presence of Samuel Whitfeld, Edward Hubbald, Humphrey Brent, and Roger Laurence. Thomas Hayter's signature was scratchy but William Lethieullier's was neat, flowing and elegant. It was a covenant and agreement binding on the parties involved in consideration of the total sum of four thousand and fifty pounds (£2750, £500 and £800) agreed to be paid, transferring the ownership from Hayter *et al.* and his heirs to Lethieullier and his heirs; the land was not described in detail. The agreement referred to forthcoming Christmas and January and had the date of 6th February written on it but December seemed the most likely month of its drafting. The eighth year of the reign of George I was between 1st August 1721 and 31st July 1722. Hayter's address was different to that given in the previous agreement so he may have moved from the Parish of All Hallows, Staining, London to St. Margaret's, Westminster, in Middlesex between December 1720 and December 1721. The Rebecca, to whom reference was made, was possibly the child of a cousin.

This would appear to be the only indenture in which George Wanley was included with Hayter. Wanley, who married Mary Watson in 1712, was apprenticed to James Chambers, his uncle, in 1703, "*Free*" in 1711 and "*livery*" in 1712, according to The Goldsmiths' Company records; in 1684, Chambers had premises at 19 Fleet Street, London called "*The Three Squirrells*". Between the years 1713 and 1720, George Wanley, by then a goldsmith and banker and George Craddock operated a business at the "*Three Squirrels*" (Frederick George Hilton Price's book *A Handbook of London Bankers*). Wanley may have been involved in the sale of land at Tottenham in his capacity as a banker.

In 1728, when his daughter, Dorothy Wanley, married, her father was described as *"a wealthy banker on Fleet Street"*. Wanley was also a churchwarden and retained a pew in the local church at Tottenham. Daniel Defoe wrote in the 1720s, after one of his walks in the area, that the banker Wanley's small villa and gardens, on the west of the High Road, around Tottenham Green, was one of the most beautiful as one left London. Wanley died in 1729 and his will requested that he be buried in the churchyard at Tottenham High Cross. He asked that his six principal tenants at Tottenham High Cross were to be pall-bearers at his funeral. They were named as Mr. Cooper, Mr. Hogg, Mr. Hunt, Mr. Clark, Mr. Holt and Mr. Knight. The only other person requested to attend the interment was his uncle, Chambers.

According to William Robinson's book on the *History of the Antiquities of the Parish of Tottenham,* Henry Hare (Lord Coleraine), George Wanley, Ralph and Thomas Harwood, Abraham Loeffs and Hugh Smithson were recorded in the Tottenham Manorial Court Rolls as chief parishioners during the early years of the eighteenth century.

Three further deeds relate to this same land at Tottenham High Cross. The first (*MDR/1721/6/262*), bearing date 1st February 1721, was an Indenture of Assignment, tripartite among William Lethieullier, Esquire, of Beckenham in Kent of the first part, Thomas Hayter of Epsom in Surrey, a gentleman, brother and heir and also devisee of Henry Hayter, late of Epsom, a gentleman, deceased, of the second part and Edward Missenden of Walbrooke, London, a merchant, of the third part. It was a transfer from Lethieullier and Hayter to Missenden. It provided a long description of the land as described above in (*MDR/1720/2/30*). The Indenture of assignment was witnessed by Henry Bouts of Stoke Newington, Middlesex, a yeoman, Edward Hubbald of St. Thomas the Apostles, London, a gentleman and Humphrey Brent of the Parish of Trinity Minories (Holy Trinity) in London, a gentleman. It included the statement that the transfer was required to be registered *"pursuant to late Act"* and granted by Thomas Hayter, one of the grantors and stamped before Edward Hubbald and Josiah Baron, London, clerk to Mr. Brent. The indenture of Assignment was registered at 4.00p.m. on 5th February 1721 by Edward Hubbald. It recorded the fact that Henry Hayter had been living at Epsom before his death. Thomas may have moved into his brother's home, as this was a new address for Hayter, not noted elsewhere. Edward Missenden was a relative of Lethieullier's first wife, Mary Manning. Her mother, also called Mary, née Missenden, had a brother named Edward.

The second Indenture in the same register (*MDR/1721/6/263*), was also written on 1st February 1721, naming Hayter *inter al.* as the grantor, to Lethieullier *et al.* It was a lease for one year registered for three messuages, lands, tenements, hereditaments and premises in Tottenham High Cross and Edmonton *"which are more particularly mentioned and expressed in a certain Indenture of Release Tripartite bearing date the second day of February Anno Domini one thousand seven hundred and twenty one"* (*MDR/1721/6/264*). It was made among Thomas Hayter of Epsom in the County of Surrey, Gentleman, brother and heir and also devisee of Henry Hayter, late of

Epsom, in the County of Surrey, a gentleman, deceased of the first part, Mary Moreland, of Epsom, widow and sister of Thomas Hayter, John Otway of Epsom, a gentleman and Rebecca his wife, the cousin of Thomas Hayter of the second part and William Lethieullier of Beckenham in Kent and Roger Laurence of St. Giles, Cripplegate, Middlesex, a gentlemen, of the third part. A memorial was registered and Indenture witnessed by Henry Bootes of Stoke Newington, a yeoman, Edward Hubbald, of the Parish of St. Thomas, a gentleman and Humphrey Brent of the Parish of Trinity Minories, a gentleman. The parchment was stamped, sealed and delivered in the presence of Edward Hubbald and Josiah Baron, clerk to Mr. Brent and registered on 5th February, 1721 as required to be registered by Act of Parliament by Thomas Hayter, one of the grantors. Thomas Hayter *inter al* granted it to William Lethieullier and Roger Laurence. Roger Laurence, named in the will of Sir John Lethieullier, William Lethieullier's father, who died in 1719, was Sir John's financial adviser.

The third Indenture of Release Tripartite (*MDR/1721/6/264*), was dated 2nd February 1721. It again gave a full description and included the 26 acres in South Tottenham known as Oat Fields, Snares Mead, messuages and tenements, cottages, stables, shop, yard, coach house and well. It was among Thomas Hayter of the first part, Mary Morland, John and Rebecca Otway of the second part and William Lethieullier and Roger Laurence of the third part. The indenture of release was witnessed by Henry Bouts of Stoke Newington, a yeoman, Edward Hubbald of St. Thomas the Apostle, London, a gentleman and Humphfrey Brent, a gentleman, of the Parish of Trinity Minories. Again, it was required to be registered by Thomas Hayter, one of the grantors and was signed sealed and delivered, the parchment being fully stamped, on 5th February 1721 in the presence of Edward Hubbald and Josiah Baron, London, clerk to Mr. Brent. A lease and release was a means of conveying property, in most cases being a lease for a year, with the following day the grantor's rights of ownership, in this case, members of the Hayter family, being released, for a consideration.

Another original document at the London Metropolitan Archives links Hayter and members of his family with Lethieullier and Laurence. The Indenture Tripartite (*ACC/0401/033*), bearing the date 2nd February 1722 in the eighth year of George I, was between Thomas Hayter of Epsom in the County of Surrey, a gentleman, brother and heir and also devisee of Henry Hayter, late of Epsom, in the County of Surrey, a gentleman, deceased of the first part, Mary Moreland of Epsom, widow and sister of Thomas Hayter, John Otway of Epsom, a gentleman and Rebecca, his wife, the cousin of Thomas Hayter of the second part and William Lethieullier of Beckenham in the County of Kent and Roger Laurence of St Giles, Cripplegate, Middlesex, a gentlemen, of the third part. The sum of £2,750 was paid in full for the absolute purchase of the lands, tenements and hereditaments. In consideration, William Lethiullier paid to Mary Morland and John Otway five shillings apiece, a nominal amount to acquit, release and discharge, grant bargain and sell to William Lethieullier and Roger Laurence, their heirs and assigns. It included all the land:

...situate standing lying and being in Tottenham and Edmonton aforesaid or either of them in the said County of Middlesex together with all timber and other trees woods underwoods ways casements libertys privileges profits commoditys and appurtences whatsoever to the said messuages lands tenements hereditaments and premises all which said bargained premises are now in ye possession of Hen: Boots and Mich: Arm.

Written on the reverse side of the parchment was the following statement signed by Thomas Hayter, witnessed and signed by Henry Bouts, Edward Hubbald and Humphrey Brent Senior:

Reced the day and bear within written by me the within named Thomas Hayter of and from the within named William Lethieullier the sum of two thousand seven hundred and fifty pounds of lawful money of Great Britain in full payment of the consideration money within mentioned to be paid to me I say reced.

It was sealed and delivered in the presence of Bouts, Hubbald and Brent, the parchment being first stamped with a five shilling stamp. The names of Hen: Boots and Mich: Arm had been amended in the document but the signature was Bouts so there were a number of inconsistencies. One might assume that Bouts was a witness because he was in possession of the land. A statement written on the back of the same document, in Latin, advised, in approximate terms, that the land was registered, as required by Act of Parliament passed during the reign of William and Mary. In 1694, Stamp Duty was introduced on the transfer of ownership of land as a way of raising money to pay for the war against France. This document was almost identical to the previous one except the word "*release*" was not included. The previous one had no mention of five shillings to be paid to Mary Moreland, John Otway and his wife Rebecca.

A further original Indenture *(ACC/0401/034)* written on 22nd June 1726 (in the twelfth year of the reign of George I) confirmed that William Lethieullier was then the landowner as he, the grantor, of the one part, bargained and sold a lease for a year to Samuel Winder Junior, a merchant of London and Thomas Motley, of Beckenham, a gentleman, of the other part, which included all those three closes of meadow known as Oat Fields amounting to 26 acres, 12 acres known as Snares Mead, a messuage, cottage or tenement, stable, shops, loft, coach house, yard and well and other land in Tottenham High Cross and Edmonton. It was "*in consideration of the sum of five shillings*", a peppercorn rent. Samuel Winder was related to Lethieullier's wife and Thomas Motley was a close and trusted friend and neighbour from Beckenham. On the reverse side of the parchment was written:

Lease for a year
I do hereby certify that a memorial of the within written Deed was registered (pursuant to an Act of Parliament made for the

purpose) at four of the clock in the afternoon of the 27th day of June 1726 1 & No 144" *and also the statement* "17 leases for a year September 1831".

Some of these parcels of land described in 1726 may have been leased again over a century later, in 1831. The document was sealed and delivered in the presence of Roger Laurence, Thomas Prime and Francis Beyer. The Deed *(MDR/1726/1/144)*, cited in the quotation bearing the date 22nd June 1726, registered on 27th June 1726, confirmed the information above. Roger Laurence gave his address as St. Saviours, Southwark and Thomas Prime and Francis Beyer were both of the Parish of St. Peter Cornhill; all were gentlemen.

Another Indenture Tripartite *(MDR/1726/1/145)*, bearing the date 23rd June 1726, was made among William Lethieullier of Beckenham in the County of Kent and Mary, his wife of the first part, Samuel Winder of London, a merchant and Christopher Lethieullier of London, of the second part and Samuel Winder Junior, described as the son of Samuel Winder and Thomas Motley of Beckenham, of the third part. It was an indenture of release made following the one the day before by William Lethieullier, of the one part and Samuel Winder and Thomas Motley, of the other part. Presumably this was Samuel Winder Junior. Christopher Lethieullier was, most likely, the cousin of William Lethieullier.

In the *Defalt Libri Tenen (freeholder section)* of the Tottenham Manorial Court Rolls, the following people were recorded over the next few years, confirming the names of the parties referred to above and the details of the ownership of the land: on 16th October 1721 (*page 385*) the name of Thomas *Playter,* probably Hayter; in April 1722, the name of *John* Lethieullier (possibly the brother of William Lethieullier as his father of the same name was deceased) and George Wanley (*page 387*); on 15th October 1722, the name of Laurence (*page 388*) without a Christian name; in April 1723 the name of Lethieullier (*page 392*), without a Christian name; on 15th April 1724, Lethieullier, armiger (*page 395*), again without a Christian name.

Thomas Hayter's brother, Whitfield Hayter, recorded in Indenture *(MDR/1720/2/302)* on 30th December 1720, was not named in the Indenture *(MDR/1721/6/262)* dated 1st February 1721. This is explained by his death in the interim period.

As the calendar year did not start until 25th March, a whole year had elapsed before the death of Whitfield Hayter. Until Phillip Stanhope, Earl of Chesterfield, introduced the Calendar Act for Great Britain and Ireland, passed in March, 1751, the Julian calendar applied, when the first day of the calendar year was 25th March, commonly known as Lady Day. The Calendar Act decreed that the first day of 1752 was to start on 1st January and that the 2nd September would be followed by 14th September, dropping eleven days of the calendar year, which, it being 1752, was a Leap Year. The Julian calendar had been at the mercy of the Spring Equinox which fluctuated between the 10th and 25th of March. The official start of the new year, for legal purposes, had been 15th March. The Catholic countries of Europe were already following the Gregorian calendar from October 1582 when Pope Gregory changed from the previous calendar. The Protestants delayed changing because it was initiated by Roman Catholics. Britain was one of the first Protestant countries to adopt the Gregorian calendar to resolve the legal and religious anomalies regarding the changing start to the year. Other countries continued to follow the old calendar until 1900s.

The Earl of Dorset Map of 1619 shows the then ownership of land in Tottenham. Some parcels were marked as freehold, copyhold and *"p.a. lease"*. Other parcels of land were not given names and described by their size. Some of the land identified in the deeds, in the following table, was owned by Sir Edward Barkham in 1619. Unfortunately few names of places at Tottenham High Cross and Edmonton, in the indentures, correspond to the fields and places owned by Henry and then Thomas Hayter identified at South Tottenham in later deeds. Below is a table describing the land outlined in indenture (*MDR/1720/2/301*) with their names, description of their locations and occupiers, as and where known at the time of the transfer. The names of Tottenham High Cross, Tottenham and Edmonton are often interchangeable and described in a general way. In 1721, the Articles of Agreement (*ACC/0026/064*) measured the total land as seventy two acres but it only contained a summary of the land then in the possession of Henry Bootes or Bouts and Michael Arm.

Table describing land Thomas Hayter owned in 1720 (MDR/1720/2/301).

Size	Description	Location	Occupier
26 acres	3 closes of meadow or pasture once 2 closes known as Oat Fields	Tottenham High Cross Stamford Hill, north upon Hanger Lane and south of it on land now or late of Sir Robert Smith	John Russell (deceased)
28 perches*	Messuage, cottage or tenements, stable, shops, loft, coach house, yard, well and land	In Tottenham, adjoining Parish of Edmonton, near the Blue Boar	John Russell (deceased)
4 acres	Meadow land in the Wild Marsh	Tottenham beside River Lea close to Edmonton	John Russell (deceased)
2 acres	Arable land lying within a certain field called Downfield	Possibly part of "The Downe" next to Clendish Hills	Thomas Raymond his assigns or under tenants
2 acres	Meadow pasture or ground called Clendish Hill	Clendish Hills beside River Lea next to Michley	Thomas Raymond
1 acre	Meadow pasture ground in a meadow called Broad Mead	Beside Michley Clendish Hills and the Wild Marsh	Thomas Raymond
half acre	Meadow or pasture in Mitchley Marsh	Beside River Lea	Thomas Raymond
1 acre	Arable land at Langua also "Languish" field	Location unknown	Thomas Raymond
2 acres	Meadow or pasture ground called the Wild Marsh	Next to River Lea and Parish of Edmonton	Thomas Raymond,
2 acres	Arable land or pasture	Edmonton and Tottenham	
8 acres & 3 roods	Meadow or pasture ground called Crookes Grove	Near Blackhope Lane Tottenham	

Size	Description	Location	Occupier
2 acres	1 close of meadow or pasture (not named)	At West Green abutting east on land owned by John Pulford and west on land now or late of John Barnes (or Barons) and north upon West Green	
12 acres	2 closes of meadow or pasture ground called Snares Mead	Adjoining south upon Hanger Lane in Tottenham	Henry Cocking
8 acres	1 close or field of meadow or pasture ground	Abutting south upon Hanger Lane at Tottenham and possibly "Thistley" Field	Henry Cocking

There are four roods in an acre and forty perches in one rood. A perch is unit of measurement of five and a half yards.

The name of John Russell, deceased, is recorded in deed (*MDR/1720/2/301*) as the occupier of the land in 1720, along with Thomas Raymond. The names of John and Mary Russell appeared together, in the *defalt libri tenen* section of the Tottenham Manorial Court Rolls. Henry Bootes held land near Stonebridge and Hanger Lane. Henry Cocking's name appears in different places, spelt as Cockayne and Cockain.

In 1619, Edward Barkham owned some 174 acres of freehold land and 65 acres of copyhold land. Around 1670, the land in "*Barkham's Title*", which William Barkham had inherited from his father and grandfather, amounted to 175 acres of land, which was sold in 1699, after Barkham's death, to Ephraim Beauchamp. Jane Barkham, the spinster daughter of Sir William Barkham, when she died in 1725, left three tenements to be rented out by the parish for the benefit of the poor, which might suggest that all the land was not sold to Ephraim Beauchamp in 1699. There are few similarities in the descriptions of the parcels referred to in "*Barkham's Title*" in Appendix III of Robinson's book in 1683, as between the land described in *the deeds and mortgages around 1720 held by Thomas Hayter and sold to* William Lethieullier in 1721. The only place names that featured in both bodies of documentation were those of Languish Field and Wild Marsh and these were large areas of land with many smaller parcels of land within them. Crooks Grove, north of Blackhope Lane, was described in 1619 as a mixture of copyhold and freehold land; it was a large field of approximately 8 acres. Three closes named Oatfields were 26 acres in size. In 1619, a number of fields close to Hanger Lane including the word "*Snares*" in their descriptions. There was Stonebridge Field, known as Snaresmead, Little Snares Field and Great Snaresmead, which was freehold land. The indentures around 1720 did not include all of them. Clendish Hills was not identified as freehold or copyhold land. Clendish Hill, freehold land, was owned in 1619 by Mrs. Moyse and was passed down to Sarah Moyse, who married George Ballard. His name appears as a freeholder in the Tottenham Manorial Court Rolls in 1707.

26

The Lethieullier Family – merchant traders

It was described earlier, the context in which Sir John Lethieullier was cited in 1695 in the will of Sir William Barkham, who had owned the land at Tottenham High Cross and how, when Barkham died, he owed Sir John £4,000 on a mortgage on his estate in Norfolk.

Various sources including the Museum of the Bank of England explain that William Lethieullier, who bought the land in Tottenham High Cross in 1721, was the son of Sir John Lethieullier and a descendant of a Huguenot martyr, Jean Le Theuiller, his great-grandfather, who was killed at Valenciennes in 1568. James Granger, in his book *A Biographical History Of England: From Egbert the Great to the Revolution,* published in 1824, in the Appendix on page 109 of Volume 3&4, under a heading of *"Foreigners"* includes the name of Catharine Lethieullier. Sir John's grandfather, Jean Lethieullier died in Cologne around 1593, leaving a widow, Jane, daughter of John Frappè of Tournay. She then married Jan De Weez of Frankfurt, who died in 1604, two years after they married. The following July, in 1605, Jane came to England from France with her daughter Catherine, born on 8th January 1587 and her son John Le Thieullier (1591-1679) born two years before his father's death.

Another record in the Walloon Registry in Canterbury in 1630, in part, provides an account of Jacob Desbouverie of Killeghorn in Holland, an evangelical minister and native of Canterbury, who on 9th September 1630 married Catherine Lethieullier, daughter of the late Jean Lethieullier. Jacob was the second son of Laurens Desbouverie, who settled in Canterbury. Granger suggests that Catharine was around 43 when she married and is unlikely to have had children. She died in 1664, aged 77 and was buried with her mother at St. Helen's le Grand. *The Harleian Society Register, Volume 31, of St. Helen Bishopsgate* contains details of a burial for Jane Du Wees, a widow, on 27th July 1631 and one for Catherine *Leathhaliere* on 14th April 1664, who was buried in the church behind the pulpit. Unusually, her maiden name and not her married name was used. The National Portrait Gallery exhibits an etching of Catharine Desbouverie (née Lethieullier), made in 1656, a half-length portrait of her sitting in a chair, after T. Luttichuys.

According to the *Registers of Marriages of St. Dunstan Stepney, 1609/10-1631/2 at LMA (P93/DUN/265)*, on 12th June 1627 a marriage was recorded between *"John Le Thulier of the parish of St. Margaret Lothbury London and Jane Fortery of the parish of Gracechurch London married by the minister of the French Church"*. John's surname has been written with various spellings such as le Thulier, Lethieullier and Lethieulier and Jane as Fortery, Fortrye,

Fortrey, de la Fort, de la Fortree or de la Forterie. She was the daughter of John de la Fortrey and Anne Francqueville; the Fortrey family left France and moved to England. John Fortrey, a merchant, was buried on 30th July 1633 at All Hallows, Lombard Street. When Jacob de la Fortree, a merchant of East Greenwich died in 1655, his will referred to his brother John de le Thullier and his wife.

John and Jane Lethieullier had at least eight children. There were six sons, John, Peter, Christopher, Samuel, William and Abraham, whose baptisms were recorded in the Barking Parish Registers in 1646. (*It has been suggested in an article by Chown in the Essex Review Volumes 36, 37 and 38 that William and Abraham Lethieullier were in fact twins, born in 1646 and the births registered in the Parish of Barking in Ilford. A further piece of evidence to corroborate this assertion is recorded in a family tree at Breamore House in Hampshire, the country house of the Hulse family, when William was described as first born and Abraham as 2nd born.*) Among their daughters were Jane and Leonora. The death of Peter Lethieullier (1636-1646) is recorded at Barking; Samuel was born in Holland in 1643. In a *1911* publication of the Huguenot Society, entitled *Aliens in England and Ireland, 1603-1700,* John Le Thieullier's name appears twice; the first entry, dated 13th July 1632 stated that he was "*born in foreign parts with proviso that he shall pay custom and subsidy as strangers do*"; the second entry was in relation to naturalisations which received Royal Assent on 29th December 1660, when it was recorded that Samuel Lethieullier, son of John Lethieullier, born in Amsterdam in Holland, became naturalised. At the outbreak of the Civil War in England, John took his family to Holland but the family returned to England around 1646 and at that point settled in Lewisham. The Lethieullier family had a house at Low Leyton in Essex, where some of the children were baptised; they also had a house at Greenwich. According to Claude Henry Iyan Chown, in an article on the Lethieullier family in the *Essex Review* of 1927, there is a memorial to all the family in Barking. John Lethieullier died at the age of 88 and was buried at the Church of St. Peter le Poer in the City on 2nd November 1679. His wife Jane died in 1693 at the age of 83.

Sir John Lethieullier (1632/3-1718/9)

John Lethieullier, born in 1632/3, in England, was the eldest son of John Lethieullier (1591-1679) and the person who was involved in indentures relating to William Barkham and the land in Tottenham High Cross. An entry in a transcription of the *Charlton Parish Register 1653-1753, Volume 2,* by Francis Ward *(S.O.G.)* shows that "*Mr John Lethevnier and Amee Hoocker*" married at St. Luke, Charlton, Kent on 18th May 1658. An intention to marry was recorded in the *Registers of St. Clement Eastcheap and St. Martin Orgar 1539-1839 (Harleian publications)* which stated that the banns were read on 25th April and 2nd and 9th May 1658; a footnote confirmed that the marriage took place on 18th May 1658 but obviously not at that place. This was during the Commonwealth period when civil registration was the norm. Anne was the eldest daughter of a wealthy merchant by the name of Sir William Hooker and Lettice Coppinger, who had married in 1640. The church was close to Greenwich, where the Hooker family lived. References are made in the Greenwich Rates Books for the years 1674-5 both to Lethieullier and Hooker; Sir William owned a walled residence called *"The Grange"* on Croom's Hill, built in 1665, a visit to which Samuel Pepys records in his diary. This is the oldest house in the road and according to Ben Weinreb and Christopher Hibbert in the London Encyclopaedia, some of the timbers in this house date from the beginning of the 12th century. In 1672, William Hooker had a gazebo built to the designs of Robert Hooke, which overlooks Greenwich Park and survives today. This offers some indication of Hooker's wealth and status. John may have come into an even greater fortune as a result of the marriage to Anne as Sir William Hooker was Sheriff of London during the time of the Great Fire of 1666, in which year he was knighted; he held the position of Lord Mayor of London in 1673-1674. There is a marble plaque at St. Alfege, with a figure above dressed as an alderman, dedicated to Hooker. In his will, proved in 1697, he described himself as *"late Lord Mayor of London"* and made reference to his then wife Dame Susan, whom he married in 1673 and to his daughters Anne Letheiullier, Letitia Vaughan, his son William and to his grandchildren.

John and Anne had three daughters, Anne, born in 1662, Letitia, born in 1663, Leonora born in 1678 and two sons, John, born in 1659 and William, born in 1671. The elder John Lethieullier is recorded in the first Directory of Traders in 1677, trading at Mark Lane but he also had a house at Mincing Lane.

Samuel Pepys refers in his diary to John and Anne Lethieullier; this is cited in a 1999 article in *Proceedings of the Huguenot Society XXV II (2)*. On Sunday 3rd December 1665, Mrs. Pepys and the Huguenot, Elizabeth St. Michel, had returned to London from Greenwich and Pepys refers to a meeting at St. Alfege, Greenwich, where the local Huguenot community worshipped in the pre-Hawksmoor Church. He wrote of a meeting with a *"fat brown beauty of our Parish, the rich merchant's lady"*, whom he and his wife admired, who was Anne Lethieullier, daughter of William Hooker and wife of John. On another occasion, Pepys is invited to William Hooker's other house at Eastcheap for dinner, about which he writes that his host, a very rich, silly man, kept the poorest, mean table in a dirty house, although Mr. Lethieullier seemed a very understanding merchant. On Christmas Eve, he once again hoped and wished that he would meet Mrs. Lethieullier when he went to Sir William Hooker's house. He eventually spoke to her at the house at Eastcheap and Pepys described her as *"a most beautiful fat woman and had a salute of her and after dinner good discourse"*.

Sir John Lethieullier was initially apprenticed to a barber surgeon named Sir John Frederick (1601-1685). Lethieullier became a master of The Barber Surgeons' Company in 1676 but it would appear that he did not spend a great deal of time in that practice. Sir John was knighted on 29th September 1674 and was Sheriff from 1673 to 1674 and was nominated by the Lord Mayor and

Sir John Frederick as an alderman in the City of London on 15th June 1676. It was Thomas Frederick who married Lethieullier's niece, Leonora Maresco. Sir John Frederick never practised his trade as a barber surgeon but instead became an immensely wealthy merchant and ship-owner in the Mediterranean and New World. He had a mansion in what is now Frederick Place (Old Jewry, City), near the Guildhall. When he died in 1685, he left much of his fortune to charity but there was still enough left to make his children wealthy. In 1741, his grandson bought the manor of Paddington.

John Lethieullier, like his father before him, made his fortune from trading and was particularly familiar with the southern European markets. In H.G. Roseveare's article on Lethieullier in *The Oxford Dictionary of National Biography*, the author explains that:

> Lethieullier specialized initially in the export of English textiles to Southern Europe and the Levant, buying extensively from East Anglian and West of England manufacturers and superintending the dyeing and finishing in partnership with his brother in law, Charles Maresco, but his interests became diversified. In 1669, for example, he was importing sugar from Portugal and iron from the Netherlands while exporting lead and tin to Venice and Rotterdam. He became a member (and later director) of the Levant Company and by 1673 was also a director of the East India Company. At the same time he was involved with the Hamburg trade in English textiles and German linens carried on by the declining Company of Merchant Adventurers, of which he became a governor, and with the new Royal African Company of 1671, in which he served as a director after 1681.

Roseveare records that in 1666, after the Great Fire of London, the Lethieullier family shared its home with members of the Maresco family. The home at Low Leyton was rented from William Bowyer and in 1668 John Lethieullier paid £100 expenses to Maresco, who recorded later in the same year that he paid £125 for rent, housekeeping and warehousing to John Lethieullier, on behalf of his servants and his family.

Sir John Lethieullier and his family lived for a time in a house at Hylord's Court, off Mark Lane, in the same parish as Samuel Pepys. Then he moved to a house at College Hill, adjoining Clark Lane in the City. The street was close to Mansion House and Pudding Lane, where the Great Fire of London began. Prior to Lethieullier, the house had belonged to the Duke of Buckingham who gave up this business address at College Hill in 1696. Sir John took on the house and lived there some of the time, as well as at his other house at Lewisham, until his death in 1718/19. A plaque on the wall of the present building indicates that Buckingham had a house on the site.

Lethieullier kept houses in Essex and Greenwich like his father before him and the family worshipped at St. Alfege, Greenwich. It had been shortly after his father's death in 1679 that Sir John built a new home for the family called *Lewisham House*. The mansion was at the junction of Ladywell Road and Lewisham High Street and was built in brick but later covered in stucco. Evidence of the building survives today at Lewisham Local Studies and Archives in the form of photographs taken in the nineteenth century before it was demolished in 1894, although by then it had been converted into two houses. A photograph depicts a lead water spout with the date 1680 and initials *"J"* and *"A"* embossed on it.

The death of Sir John Lethieullier, on Sunday, 4th January 1719, was announced in the Whitehall Evening Post. Sir John Lethieullier had lived for 86 years and was buried at St. Alfege, Greenwich with his wife, Anne and other family members. In his will he requested burial in the vault bought by his father-in-law, Sir William Hooker who described the location in his will as *"the vault by me built leading out of the parish church into the churchyard at East Greenwich"*. The memorial is situated in a relatively sheltered position outside the church and is grand, with inscriptions inserted with metal on two sides that are still legible today, despite weathering. The memorial is said to have been funded by Sir John Lethieullier's grandson, Smart, although the inscription might suggest otherwise. Below is a transcription of the memorial. Smart may have restored or looked after it before his death in 1760, given his keen interest in antiquities. This inscription explained that Leonora had died in 1717, before her father

> In a vault below this monument lies the body of Sir John LETHIEULLIER of Lewisham in the County, Knight, Sheriff of London in the year 1674 departed this life January 4th Anno Domini 1719 at the age of 86. He married Anne, eldest daughter to Sir William Hooker, Knight, Lord Mayor of London in the year 1673 by whom he had 2 sons and three daughters viz. John Lethieullier of Aldersbrooke in the County of Essex William Lethieullier of Beckenham in this County of Kent, Anne formerly married to John De Leau of Whaddon in the County of Surrey, Esq. thereafter to Sir William Dodwell of Sevenhampton in the County of Gloucester, Knight, Letitia and Leonora.

> Dame Anne Lethieullier died January 3rd Anno Domini 1702 and lies here interred. Here lies also Leonora Lethieullier, their youngest daughter who died November 20th Anno Domini 1717 to whose memory's this monument is erected by Letitia Lethieullier the only surviving daughter Anno Domini 1737 who departed this life the first day of January 1739 age 76 years and is here interred. Here also is deposited William Gosselin of London Esq. who being connected by blood and friendship to this family requested that his remains might rest with theirs. He died 26th day of January 1743 aged 77 years.

John Deleau's surname is recorded in different places as Deleau, Delean, De Leau or De Lean. The style of writing of that period and even his signature leave the spelling ambiguous but for purposes of this work it is referred to as Deleau. Although the family had left France in 1605, its members did not maintain close ties with the French Protestant community. However, Sir John Lethieullier did leave a bequest in his will to the French Church at Threadneedle Street. He also gave £5 towards the rebuilding of St. Paul's Cathedral after the Fire, by which time he had become a respected and generous member of the English Establishment.

Many of the members of the Lethieullier Family are cited in an indenture dated 18th October 1829, regarding title of Kent House Farm, Beckenham (A62/6/61); it is archived at Lewisham Local History and Archives Centre. The Lease and Release was made originally on the 6th & 7th April 1709, between John Reynolds of the first part and John Lethieullier. The same day, an Indenture of assignment was made among John Reynolds of the first part, William Peere Williams (a member of the Inner Temple and the owner of large areas of land) of the second part, William Williams (possibly his father) of the third part, John Lethieullier of the fourth part, Samuel Lethieullier, a merchant, of the fifth part and John Lethieullier of Aldersbrooke of the sixth part. The lease was to Samuel Lethieullier for 500 years and John Lethieullier for 1000 years. The document gave details of deaths and wills, explaining how the land was to pass from one family member to another during the next one hundred years, as its various members died and passed the lease to relatives along two strands of the family, commencing with John and Samuel Lethieullier.

In April 1709, Samuel Lethieullier, whose will was written in 1690, appointed his brothers William and Abraham as his executors. In Luttrell's approximately contemporary account from 7th February, 1710, he explains that *"Samuel Lethieullier an eminent merchant of this city is dead and the said has left an estate to the value of £100,000"*. Samuel, by some accounts, died in Holland around January/February 1709 but his burial was recorded on 8th February, 1709, located in a very prominent position in the chancel between the Reader's desk and the Communion table, at the Church of St. Peter le Poer. William Lethieullier proved the will as Abraham had died in 1705 and William died on 17th September 1728. William's wife, Mary, wrote her will in 1739 to which she added a codicil in 1741 but it was not proved until 29th October 1741. She was buried in the parish church at Clapham. Her three daughters Mary Tooke, Sarah Loveday and Dame Anne Hopkins were named as executors. A share of the farm passed to Sarah Loveday who produced her will in April 1738, appointing her son John Loveday as her heir. She died in January 1761 and was buried on 9th February 1761 at Caversham. John died on 27th May 1789. He appointed his son John Loveday as sole executor but he died on 20th April 1809. Anne Loveday, his wife, made the decision to sell the farm having inherited the 500 year lease originally owned by Samuel Lethieullier and passed to his brother, William Lethieullier as Samuel had no children.

Sir John's will was written in 1709 and was proved on 23rd January 1719 (*PROB 11/567/161*). Most of his estate went to his children. Leonora and Letitia, received £10,200 each as well as other bequests. He made a bequest of £1,000 to his daughter Anne, the wife of Sir William Dodwell and formerly the widow of John Deleau, a merchant. His grandchildren received £100 each. His eldest son, John, inherited freehold, copyhold and leasehold land in Essex and property in the City of London (the Essex estate, bought in 1693, was formerly owned by Francis Osbaston and called *"Aldersbrooke"*). This included the contents of Sir John's then dwelling house formerly called Buckingham House, which was to be used and enjoyed by all the family and servants for a year after his death in order to carry out instructions of his will. Two houses on *"Colledge Hill"* near what is now College Hill, were given to Letitia and Leonora; one was occupied by Sir Henry Furnese, a baronet and the other was occupied by Sir Alexander Cairnes. They also received the house at Lewisham which he had bought from his father and other houses there purchased from Francis Norman. William, his second son, inherited land at Beckenham, Lewisham, Battersea, Manors at Sutton-at-Hone, Wilmington and Dartford in the County of Kent. In June 1714, Sir John bought the Manor of Rowhill at Wilmington and other parcels of land from George Ward of Dartford in Kent and it was recorded in a codicil. Sir John asked that Roger Laurence, his faithful servant, be employed after his death, by the executors, to handle any of the monies and transactions and any sale to convert property into monies. Laurence would no doubt have been well respected and trusted with the financial aspects of Sir John's business and inheritance. Sir John's wealth at death was estimated at £100,000, much of it being in property.

Laurence was a student of divinity and decided in 1708, as a result of his studies, to doubt the validity of his baptism. He was re-baptised at Christ Church, Newgate Street and joined the *"non jurors"*. causing a great stir in the Established Church, particularly by the Bishop of London. He then entered non-juring orders, being ordained on 30th November 1714 by Bishop George Hicks. He became a minister in an oratory on College Hill, near to where Sir John Lethieullier had a house. Laurence was subsequently consecrated as a bishop by Bishop Archibald Cambell and Thomas Deacon, which appointment was not accepted by other non-jurors. He wrote books and articles explaining his views on various subjects including his own baptism.

R. Borrowman, in his book, *Beckenham Past and Present,* provides further information on Roger Laurence, sometimes written as *Lawrence.* He was buried at Beckenham on 11th March 1736, The *Universal Spectator,* in an issue dated 13th March 1736, confirmed that Reverend Roger Laurence, aged 65, died on Saturday 6th March, after a long fit of the palsy, probably at Kent House, the home of William Lethieullier, although Borrowman wrote that Laurence was with Sir John Lethieullier at the time of his death. As the latter had died in 1719 it is more likely to have been with William. Borrowman explained that Laurence had been born of dissenting parents and was a *"Blue Coat boy"*. He had been taken on by Sir John Lethieullier as a young man, working in Spain as a factor and later in Lethieullier's counting house. It was later in his life, that he pursued his interest in religion.

Letitia Lethieullier's Legacy

When she died in January 1739, Letitia Lethieullier, a spinster of Lewisham and the Parish of St. Olave, Hart Street, in the City, left her estate to members of her family. The executors of her will were her brother William Lethieullier, her cousin William Gosselin and her nephew, Smart Lethieullier; and if her brother died, John Lethieullier, the eldest son of her brother William Lethieullier, was to take his place. This suggests a close relationship between Gosselin and the Lethieullier family, confirmed by their burial together. A statement under oath explained that her brother, William, died after her will was written. William was buried in December 1739 and she died in January 1739.

The other living recipients of Letitia's will were her nephews, Smart and Charles Lethieullier and her niece, Elizabeth, all the children of John Lethieullier and Elizabeth Smart of Aldersbrooke in Essex. Charles Lethieullier, also her godson, was given £500 and paintings of his father, grandfather and grandmother, which had hung in the house which Letitia had occupied in Lewisham. A picture of William Gosselin, which also hung in her house at Lewisham, was given to his relative, Sarah Trinquand. Her god-daughter, Letitia Lethieullier, the daughter of her brother William, received £500 which was to be held in trust for her until she reached the age of 21. Her cousin, Christopher Roffey, received £150. The house and out-buildings at College Hill were to go to Smart, Charles and Elizabeth Lethieullier. The house at Lewisham, then occupied by the testatrix, with orchards, gardens, land and remaining contents went to her brother William Lethieullier and his heirs. There was also other land which she rented in Lewisham. The residue of her estate was to be divided in two parts; one share went to Smart, Charles and Elizabeth Lethieullier and the other to William Lethieullier and his heirs, John, William, Manning, Mary, Samuel, Letitia and Leonora for them to *"share alike"*.

Some indications are that Letitia left the house at College Hill to Smart, Elizabeth and Charles Lethieullier who were to be given equal shares but some texts suggest that it was demolished around 1730 and new small merchant houses were built on the site, which then became known as New Castle Yard; it may be that there was another house on the site. The general area of College Hill was, in its day, the centre of the merchant classes with houses, banks and warehouses, as described in *The London Encyclopaedia*, edited by Christopher Hibbert and Ben Weinreb.

27

William Lethieullier (1671-1739),
barber surgeon and his heirs

The Estate in Tottenham was bought by William Lethieullier and Roger Laurence in February 1721, two years after William's father's death.

William Lethieullier, whose baptism was registered at St. Olave, Hart Street, in the City of London on 17th May 1671, was the son of John and Anne Lethieullier. Sir John Lethieullier's son followed his father into the profession of Barber Surgeon as he described himself as such in his will (*PROB 11/699/368*), written in 1736 and proved in 1739. Joseph Foster, editor of *London Marriage Licences 1521-1869,* records that *"John Lethieullier of Little Ilford, Essex, esq., alleges the marriage of William Lethieullier of the city of Hamburg, bachelor, about 28 and Mrs. Mary Manning, spinster, about 19, daughter of Nicholas Manning, of said city of Hamburg, merchant, who consents attested by John Smith, servant of Sir John Lethieullier, Knight – to marry in the chapel of the English Factory at Hamburg aforesaid. 18th March 1700/1"*. This appears in the *Index of Faculty Office Marriage Allegations, 1701-1725;* a copy of the licence is held at Lambeth Palace Library. *Boyd's Genealogy Index* alleges that William Lethieullier married Mary Manning in 1709 but this conflicts with Foster's account and as their children were born before 1709, the later date would appear unlikely. Evidence indicates that on 18th March 1700, it was John Lethieullier of Little Ilford, who appeared personally to allege that a marriage was to take place between his brother and Mary Manning. Mary's father consented as she was under the age of 21. The spouses' ages suggest that she was born around 1681 and William in 1671/2. There is, however, evidence of a baptism for Mary Manning in June 1683 at St. Mary, Cray, in Kent.

Lethieullier had followed in his father's footsteps and was also regarded by various sources as a *"Turkey merchant"* being someone who had commercial links with Turkey. His father, Sir John, was trading English textiles for German linen as a member of the Company of Merchant Adventurers and it may be that William spent time abroad trading on behalf of his father.

A family tree at Little Ilford Church, near Aldersbrooke in Essex, published in the *Essex Review* in 1927, indicates that Nicholas Manning, Mary's father, was originally from Hamburg and he had a brother called John and two sisters called Mary and Catherine. Nicholas, with the consent of his bride's father, married Mary Missenden; both were from Hamburg but living in London; the licence was dated 16th April 1677; he was 25 and a merchant and she 20.

Nicholas was the son of Thomas Manning. Monuments and inscriptions from St. Mary's, Westerham, in Kent, record that Thomas Manning, Esq. died in 1695, aged 80 and that his wife, Susan Dacres, who died in 1654, was the daughter of Sir Thomas Dacres. Thomas, in his will, written in 1692/3 (*PROB 11/427/224*), named Elizabeth as *"my late wife, deceased"* suggesting that he had married again. He referred to an indenture from March 1668 when he agreed to give his eldest son, Thomas, income from the Manor of Heavers at Brasted in Kent. He also gave him land at Whitechapel, near London and in the County of Bedford. His second son, Ranulph was to receive the mansion house known as *"Valence"* with the orchards and mill, freehold and copyhold land at Brasted and Westerham in Kent, as well as land and tenements at Edmonton, Middlesex. Thomas made bequests to his sons Nicholas and John, his grandsons Ranulph and Thomas, sons of Ranulph and his grand-daughter, Susannah, the wife of John Aynsworth. Susannah was the daughter of Anthony Earning, a draper, who married Susannah Manning, both by then deceased; Ranulph was the sole executor. In Thomas' will, he described Ranulph as his eldest son, which might lead to the supposition that Thomas was dead. Included in the will was the statement *"I give and bequeath to my daughter my son Thomas his wife ten pounds and to my granddaughter her daughter Susannah Manning ten pounds"*.

An entry in *Alumni Cantabrigienses* confirms that Thomas was the son of Thomas Manning, Esq., from Westerham in Kent. The younger Thomas was admitted to Lincoln's Inn around 1659 and married Mary Oldfield of Islington in 1666/7. The marriage licence (*Vicar General*), dated 8th January, confirms that Mary's parents were deceased and that he was about 24 and she 21. The couple were to marry at St. James's, Clerkenwell or Islington. The entry in *The Records of the Honourable Society of Lincoln's Inn: Volume I, Admissions, from A.D. 1420 to A.D. 1799*, on 12th January 1658/9 show that Thomas Manning was the son and heir apparent of Thomas M., of Westerham, Kent, arm (armiger). The indenture between Thomas and his eldest son Thomas may have been a marriage settlement. From the records, it would appear that two years earlier, in December 1665, Thomas, of Lincoln's Inn, had been licensed to marry a widow aged 40, from Essex. The will of Ranulph Manning, a gentleman of Edmonton, proved in 1663, who was the brother of Thomas, the father, confirms the order in which the sons were born; it was Thomas, Ranulph, William, Nicholas and John Manning.

The marriage of Ranulph Manning of the Parish of St. Stephen, Coleman Street, London, aged 30, to Catherine Missenden of Islington, a spinster, aged 20, took place at Westerham in Kent, in September 1681, with the consent of Catherine's father. Ranulph died in September 1712, aged 69 and Catherine in 1732, aged 72. It was their eldest son, also Ranulph, who erected a monument to their memory. He died in 1760, aged 76. His sister Bridget died in 1734, aged 45. Bridget had been living at Great Marlow, Buckinghamshire and in her will named *"her loving cousin Samuel"*, also of that place.

Nicholas Manning died in 1723, aged 74 and his wife Mary in 1735, aged 78. In an inscription in the church at Westerham, she is described as the daughter of Samuel Missenden. Nicholas, in his will, proved on 23rd October 1723 (*PROB 11/593/403*), included land and tenements at Westerham in Kent, purchased from Dame Catherine Reeves and her sisters. They were to pass to his wife and after her death to his son Samuel and his wife, Mary and their sons, his brother John Manning and then to his grandson, Manning Lethieullier and his heirs. Other land at Westerham was identified; Mary and his brother John Manning were executrix and executor. In a codicil he made further bequests of £500 to his grand-daughter Mary Manning, only daughter of his son Thomas, deceased, £500 to the children of his son by Mary, Samuel, his present wife and £500 to be disposed of by his executors, to include bequests to his grandchildren John, Manning, Mary and William Lethieullier, his brother John Manning and Edward Missenden, his brother-in-law. The codicil added Edward Missenden as an executor.

A few years later, John Manning was buried at Great Marlow with his wife, Alice. Samuel was also living at Great Marlow when he died in 1745 (*PROB 11/738/58*). He named Mary, John, Manning and William Lethieullier, as the children of William and Mary Lethieullier "*who was my sister*" and Mary, daughter of Thomas "*my brother*". His estate went to his wife and then his daughter, Sarah Manning. His then living wife, Mary and his daughter Sarah Manning were executrices with Samuel Remnant, a gentleman of Woolwich, executor. When Remnant died in 1752, he was described as a glover of Bread Street Hill in the City of London. Sarah Manning, of Great Marlow, aged 23, was licensed to marry Stephen Remnant, aged 24, son of Samuel, in June 1747 (*Faculty Office*), the marriage having taken place at St. Luke's, Charlton, in Kent. Sarah died in 1778, aged 55; she had been born around 1723/4.

The link to Hamburg, as indicated in the Lethieullier family tree held at Breamore, may have related to both the Missenden family and the Mannings. Mary Manning, who married William Lethieullier, was the grand-daughter of Samuel Missenden, Esq., the Deputy Governor of the Right Worshipful Fellowship of Merchants Adventurers of England, residing in Hamburg. In his will, written there in 1688, he explained that his children Edward, Mary and Catherine, all of whom probably were born in Hamburg, had already received their portions of his estate. His other children, Samuel, Thomas and Bridget were provided for after the death of their mother, Bridget. Samuel Missenden also made reference to his grandsons, Samuel Manning, son of his daughter Mary and Nicholas Manning and Thomas Manning, son of daughter Catherine and Ranulph Manning; Edward received all his father's books. The will (*PROB 11/318/101*) was proved in January 1690 by his wife Bridget and son, Edward Missenden. His "*son*", Nicholas Manning and Octavian Pulleyn, in Hamburg, were to oversee his affairs there. An inscription at Westerham Church confirms that Edward Missenden was the husband of Susanna Manning, only daughter of the late Thomas Manning, of Lincoln's Inn, when, aged 37, she died in 1706. Edward died, aged 68, in 1727 and his son Thomas, who had been baptised in January 1694 at St. Margaret Pattens, in the City of London, administered his father's estate that year.

There are records of baptisms at St. Olave, Hart Street for John, Manning, William and Mary, Samuel, Letitia, Leonora and Ann Lethieullier, who died in infancy. At the times of the christenings, the ministers were John Turner and Edward Arrowsmith. Manning Lethieullier was born on 11th July 1705, although there is a record of a burial of an infant also called Manning on 8th November in the same year, at St. Olave's; he was buried in the pen next to the Belfrey. If the first child by the name of Manning died, it is likely that a second Manning Lethieullier was born after his sister, Mary, who was born on 16th February 1706. Yet Manning was described in his father's will as the second son and William as the third son to his father's first wife, Mary Manning. An infant by the name of William was christened on 23rd April 1704, at St. Olave, Hart Street, but according to records at St. George, Beckenham, he was buried on 28th March 1708. The second Manning may have been born between the years 1707-1710. A child named William Lethieullier was baptised on 25th October 1711 at All Hallows, Staining, Mark Lane, to parents William and Mary.

At St. Olave, Hart Street, there is a carved memorial in the church, indicating how long it has existed on the site. It is noted that Samuel Pepys and his wife Elizabeth are buried there, with memorials to them high up on the wall, in addition to Elizabethan family memorials. The church survived the Great Fire but was extensively bombed during the Second World War and was restored subsequently. Built in stone, it resembles a medieval church, with similarities to the Tower of London.

The burial records from St. George, Beckenham indicate that there were two other babies born to William and Mary Lethieullier with the name of Samuel. Samuel Lethieullier was baptised on 21st June 1709 and was buried on 4th May 1711 and another Samuel, a child of William and Mary, was baptised on 14th January 1713 at St. Stephen, Walbrook *(IGI)*. The second Samuel was buried at Beckenham on 12th February 1713. Ann, whose baptism was recorded at St. Andrew, Holborn on 11th April 1715 *(IGI)* was buried on 22nd April 1716 at Beckenham.

William and Mary may have had a house at Beckenham as early as 1708 as the child William was buried in the churchyard of St. George's. The family may have moved among Beckenham, Mark Lane, near St. Olave, Hart Street, in the City, College Hill, where his father had a house, the house at Lewisham and Westerham in Kent, where the Manning family lived. *Hasted's History and Topographical Survey of the County of Kent (Volume 2)* suggested that the manor of Sutton was left to William Lethieullier by his first wife, Mary daughter of Nicholas Manning.

Mary Lethieullier, wife of William, was buried at St. George, Beckenham, on 29th August 1717 and William, then around 47 years of age, married by licence, on 9th July, 1719, Mary Salkeld, daughter of John Salkeld, she of the Parish of St. Botolph Bishopsgate, at St Mary, Abchurch, Abchurch Yard, London *(Parish Register)*. They were married by Mr. Thomas Clerke and a copy of the allegation is held among the records of the *Faculty Office Marriage Allegations, 1701-1725* at Lambeth Palace. William Lethieullier appeared personally on 26th June 1719 and stated that he was above 30 years of age and a widower, intending to marry Mary Salkeld, a spinster, above 21 years of age and living in the Parish of St. Botolph, Bishopsgate. The marriage was intended to take place at St. Botolph, Bishopsgate but the venue was changed and it did not happen for another two weeks.

St. Mary Abchurch, a short walk from College Hill, is a remarkable example of a Wren church, built between the years 1681 and1687, after the Great Fire of 1666. It survives much as it was when William and Mary married there. It has an unusual square design, with plain brick walls, stone dressing and a spire to one side but with a slated pyramidical roof on the main part of the church. There is a large painted domed ceiling inside covering the seated area, above the pews, with a Hebrew inscription, meaning "*I am God*", in its middle. It contains the only wooden carvings or "*reredos*" by Grinling Gibbons (*1648-1721*) who worked on the alter panels carved out of lime wood. Gibbons worked on St. Paul's Cathedral and many other churches and royal buildings and his signature is an open peapod. The church, with its original organ, has a wonderful atmosphere, with its dark wooden panelling, some of which is beautifully carved, at the base of the walls.

Samuel, Letitia, Ann, Leonora and Thomas were the children by William Lethieullier's second wife, Mary Salkeld. She was pregnant within months of her marriage and the children were born in quick succession. The first four were baptised at St. Olave, Hart Street. Thomas was baptised at St. Andrew's Undershaft but was buried at Beckenham on 12th February 1726. Ann was buried in silk on 10th May 1731. Under English law bodies were normally wrapped in wool, a much cheaper alternative. The parents paid the "fine" to the church of fifty shillings for the privilege of wrapping the child in the more expensive material.

Mary Salkeld and her Family

Mary Salkeld through her mother, a sister of John, Samuel and Jonathan Winder *(below)*, was their niece. Jonathan and Samuel Winder may well already have known William Lethieullier and his father, Sir John Lethieullier, as they living in the same neighbourhood. Mary Salkeld may have lived with her uncle Samuel Winder at Mark Lane, perhaps an explanation as to how she met William. William Lethieullier later identified in his will one of his godsons as John Williams, likely to be a relative of Mary on her maternal grandmother's side.

A large, ornate marble memorial to members of the Winder family adorns the wall, next to the altar of All Hallows by the Tower, Byward Street. The church was known in earlier times as All Hallows, Barking, by the Tower. It is close to Mark Lane and St. Olave, Hart Street, where William Lethieullier traded and lived. The memorial was erected by the executors of Jonathan Winder's estate and tells of a number of people. John Winder a barrister of Gray's Inn (he died 1699, aged 41) had married Lettice Williams, daughter of William Williams of Johnby Hall in Cumberland. John was the eldest son and heir of John and Mary Winder of Lorton Hall in Cumberland. John Winder, the son, who was born in 1658, had two children, William born in 1690 and Mary, born in 1693, both at Kenwich, in Cumberland. Jonathan Winder, his third brother, born around 1669, who was unmarried and a sometime East India Agent in Bengal, died on 12ᵗʰ January 1717, aged 48. In fact, all three brothers, John, Samuel, and Jonathan were buried there.

John Winder, eldest son and heir of John Winder, died in 1699. His will was made on 22ⁿᵈ July 1699 and was proved at York, on 6ᵗʰ January 1700 on the oath of Lettice Winder, his widow, relict and sole executrix. His mother, Mary Winder, was still alive as were his brothers, Samuel and Jonathan. Their mother died in 1709. Lettice Winder, then a widow, married Joshua Blackwell and lived until 16ᵗʰ November 1730, aged 63.

Mary's uncle Jonathan Winder had bequeathed to her on his death a gold watch, to which reference was also made years later in William Lethieullier's will. Jonathan's will was proved on 25ᵗʰ January 1718 (*PROB 11/562/182*) and it included in a codicil a reference to a watch and chain. He also gave his niece "*Mary Salkeld daughter of John Salkeld deceased*" £3,000. Later in the will Winder made reference to Mary's brother John Salkeld and hinted that John owed money to his uncle and consequently only received the small sum of £60. Jonathan placed responsibility for certain arrangements on William Williams and Mary Salkeld, whom he trusted. Mary gave the watch and chain to her husband, William Lethieullier after their marriage and on his death he left it for the benefit of his son Samuel, to be given to him when his mother "*saw fit*". In his will, Jonathan Winder also named his brother Samuel Winder and his children, Beake, Jonathan, Samuel, Elizabeth, John and Anna Maria. His other nephew and niece, William and Mary Winder, children of his late brother, John also received bequests as did his niece, Mary Jefferson, a sister Rebecca Stephenson and her two children, John and Deborah Stephenson. Other members of the family received bequests.

The London and Surrey, England, Marriage, Bonds and Allegations, 1597-1921, held at *The LMA* confirm that Samuel Winder, aged 30, of All Hallows, Barking (by the Tower of London), announced his intention to marry Elizabeth Beake, aged 21, whose parents were deceased, of the Parish of St. Dunstan in the East at St. Benedict, near Paul's Wharf, on 29ᵗʰ August 1692. By 1695, Samuel Winder was living on the west side of Mark Lane, London, in a house owned by the Drapers' Company, together with his wife Elizabeth, son Beake, daughter Mary with four servants. A later-born child, Samuel Winder (junior), was recorded in an indenture of 1726 at Tottenham with William Lethieullier; Samuel was born after 1695. In the letters of the *English Company* from the directors in London, dated 21ˢᵗ January 1698, it was noted that Jonathan Winder had recommended his brother Samuel for a position. As for Elizabeth, although left without parents at a young age, she was well connected. One Abraham Beake, in his will of 1710, left £300 each to Beake, Mary and the other children of his niece, Elizabeth Winder.

In *Journals of the Board of Trade and Plantations, Volume 3, covering the period March 1715 to October 1718,* Samuel and Beake Winder, with John Adams and others were described as traders to Barbary. Later in the same account the Lords asked Samuel Winder, who also traded with Leghorn, his opinion on fish. He responded that the price was low because the merchants at Falmouth had not cured the pilchards with enough salt and sent them at unseasonable times.

In September, 1721, in the *Post Boy* newspaper, there was an account of an incident reported when John Salkeld, William Lethieullier's brother-in-law, was bound over for good behaviour, for assaulting Sarah Trinquand at the house of her uncle, William Gosselin. It reported that Salkeld *"came home with her from receiving the sacrament and drew out two pistols, one to shoot her and the other himself"*. This suggests an intense relationship between Trinquand and Salkeld and of course Mr. Gosselin was extremely close to the Lethieullier family.

William Lethieullier's business transactions

William Lethieullier appears to have been a more serious person than other members of his family and may have retained a much lower profile, living quietly in Beckenham. Documents held at the British Library, including an indenture tripartite (*IOR/L/L/2/371*) created on 26th April 1704, between William Lethieullier of London, a merchant, of the first part, Edward Gilbert of London, a scrivener, of the second part and William Sayle of London, of the third part, provide insight into William's business arrangements. Attached to this document was a note, handwritten on a scrap of paper (*L/L/2/371/1*):

> In the register of the Parish of Beckenham Kent I find as fol-loweth May 4th 1695 Mrs Dorothy Rawlins in wool witnessed by my hand this first day of August 1735 – Thomas Clerke, rector of Beckenham aforesaid (and below it written).
>
> Upon my further search, Mr Watford an aged man and clerk of the said parish conducted me this first day of August 1735 into the church of the said parish and there shew'd me the very spot of ground at the south side of the chancel where Mrs Dorothy Rawlins, widow of Anthony Rawlins, Esq. was he well remembers buried in her husband's grave: just one year after her said husband was buried: but he says there never was a gravestone with their names thereon. Signed Roger Laurence N.B. Her husband was there buried Anno 1694.

Also included on another scrap of paper (*L/L/2/371/2) is the following:*

> 1st Query- When did Mrs Rawlins, widow of Mrs Anthony Rawlins die? Where she lived to search – to bring a certificate from the register signed by ye minister if find it not there go to the Commons.
>
> 2nd Query-whether he made any settlement on his first wife or whether it was any part of this estate. If he died ye cour... Must see it if he did not... suffices in writing and witnessed.

On the back of the note there is written:

> Mr William Lethieullier copy of his letter to his father Sir John Lethieullier dated Hamburg, May 1695 has these words "Honoured Sir, I am now to acknowledge ye receipt of yours of 26th past. Mrs Rawlins poor woman has not long enjoyed what was left her to God's good pleasure we must submit, who trust will enable us all well to follow. I observe Sir what you are pleased to write concerning my now coming in possession of what my worthy friend Mr Rawlins left me and gratefully acknowledge the care and trouble you are pleased to say you will take of it in my absence" (copied out of William Lethieullier's copy book of letters this 1st August,1735 by me Mr Roger Laurence).

These writings concerned the fact that William had inherited land after the death of Anthony Rawlins and his widow Dorothy, which later was bought by the East India Company. Rawlins is said to have died in the house of Sir John Lethieullier. William Lethieullier had to prove when the couple had died so that the conveyance could proceed. The first indenture was dated 26th April 1704, which was some eight years after Rawlins died. The transfer was effected on 26th May 1704, from William Lethieullier to Edward Gilbert, the tenant of freehold premises and his heirs. It included four messuages and tenements, six vaults, two warehouses at Pump Court, Crutched Friars in the Parish of St. Olave, Hart Street, occupied by William Lethieullier, Robert Shaw, Thomas Smith, Henry Middleton, Ralph Harwood, Philip Nesbitt, Peter Albert, Thomas Stiles and Major Noble, with three messuages and twenty acres of arable meadow and pasture at Beckenham, in the County of Kent, including a house, outhouses, barns, stables, buildings, yards, gardens and orchards occupied by Edward Clubb, Thomas Towne, Valentine Aldridge, Richard Bygrave and Widow Smith. A lease for a year (*IOR/L/L/2/372/1*) dated 21st October 1735 was recorded for the freehold messuages and ground in Pump Court "*between William Lethieullier of Beckenham devisee of the messuages and heriditaments therein....and by virtue of the last will and testament of Anthony Rawlins, late of Beckenham aforesaid dyer, deceased, of the one part and the United Company of Merchants of England trading to the East Indies of the other part*". Lethieullier had to prove ownership again before he could sell the warehouses. On 22nd October 1735, the release (L/L/2/372/2) of the messuages and ground in Pump Court, including dwelling houses, warehouses, outhouses, cellars, vaults and a parcel of ground transferred from William Lethieullier and his wife Mary to the East India Company. Drawings of the land in the City of London with measurements were attached to the indentures. On the back of the last indenture was the following statement:

> Received the day and year first within written of and from the within named United Company of Merchants of England Trading

to the East Indies the sum of four thousand seven hundred and
sixty pounds being the consideration money within mentioned to
be paid to me I say received by me William Lethieullier.

The land at Beckenham was not included in these last two indentures, so
Lethieullier may have acquired that separately.

The will of Anthony Rawlins, written on 20th February 1693 and proved
on 7th May 1694, confirms that he had bequeathed to his wife and then to
William Lethieullier and his heirs, his property at Pump Court, Crutched Friars
and a farm at Battersea and then to Leonora, the youngest daughter of Sir
John Lethieullier. The whole Lethieullier family comprising Sir John, his wife
Elizabeth, John, William, Leonora and Letitia were beneficiaries. William was
also to receive the residue of Rawlins' estate, both real and personal. When
the will of his wife, Dorothy Rawlins, was proved on 21st May 1695, she
named her cousins as Sarah Marshall, Suzanne and Ann Smith and appointed
as her executors Thomas Richards and Mary Smith of Beckenham. She did not
specify that her deceased husband's estate was to go to William Lethieullier,
after legacies, so this may have been the reason for the requirement of proof
of ownership in 1735.

Documents (*IOR/L/L/2*) that are the property of the East India Company
and the India Office from 1734-6, show that the Company erected warehouses
in two stages commencing in 1734, at Fenchurch Street in the City of London
on ground purchased from Charles Gore, Moses Helbut, William Lethieullier
and John Smith. Charles Gore may have been the brother of Mary Gore, who
married Charles Lethieullier in 1746.

Essex Record Office retains a group of relevant files. Document (*D/DC
23/775*) dated 1st December 1737 records an indenture of partnership for a loan
of £2,000. The arrangement was among William Lethieullier, the father, of the
first part, William Lethieullier, the son, of the second part and Thomas Challenor,
a grocer of the third part. The younger William had decided to become a grocer
in partnership with Thomas Challenor and he had borrowed £2,000 from his
father for this purpose. Document (*D/DC 23/782*) relates to this loan and is a
declaration of trust and release, dated 31st July 1740. It explains that William
Lethieullier, by then the deceased father had, according to the custom of the City
of London, given one third, described in his will as the "*orphanage portion*"
to his seven children in equal parts. Mary Lethieullier did not have enough
money to pay the legacies so this declaration was by way of a resolution of the
problem. Manning Lethieullier had waived the claim on his share in a document (*D/DC 23/781*), dated 31st July 1740 as he had already received a portion
greater than his share of the legacy, when his father was still alive. William
Lethieullier had advanced two sums of £1,000 and £500 to his son, William,
though in fact the father, still owed his son the sum of £325. Document (*D/DC
23/783*), concerning legacies, was dated 18th May 1741, when the final outcome
was that the six children were to divide "*the orphanage*" portion.

The will of William Lethieullier was written on 8th December 1736 and
proved on 13th December 1739 (*PROB 11/699/368*). Most of it was dominated

by matters concerning his eldest son, John. It was the custom of the City of London to divide the estate into three separate parts; Mary Lethieullier, the widow, received a third and all seven children (in order of their birth dates), John, Manning, William, Mary, Samuel, Letitia and Leonora shared a third. Mary and her brother William Lethieullier were given a further part of the remaining third of her father's personal estate, which was at his own disposal to give, to the value of £2000 for each of them. Manning was not included in this section. In 1719, William Lethieullier had inherited from his father Sir John Lethieullier, extensive properties and land at Beckenham, Lewisham, Battersea, Manors at Sutton-at-Hone, Wilmington and Dartford in the County of Kent, occupied at that time by John Marshall. However, the land in South Tottenham, Middlesex, was not included in William's will. Indeed, there may also have been estates in Essex. William's eldest son, John was left the property at Sutton-at-Hone in Kent.

William's family, at least in part, had already benefitted from inheritance. In 1735, when Mary Manning, mother-in-law of William Lethieullier, died at Westerham in Kent, she made reference in her will to her grandson John Lethieullier and her grand-daughter, Sarah Manning, to whom she left two fine damask tablecloths, twenty-four napkins and a figure of Adam and Eve. To Mary Lethieullier she left a parcel of linen tied up in a course tablecloth. She made bequests only to her blood-related Lethieullier grandchildren by her daughter, namely John, Manning (*also her godson*), Mary and William Lethieullier and not those children by their father's second wife. Other members of her family who were beneficiaries were Mary Manning, her grand-daughter and only daughter of Thomas, her son, the latter by then deceased. Mary Manning made reference to her son Samuel and his wife Mary and also to her sister, Bridget Baron.

The *Gentleman's Magazine* referred to William Lethieullier's sudden death, at about 70 years of age, after supper on 2nd December 1739. He was described as being formerly a great *"Turkey merchant and immensely rich".* Another notification of his death, in the *Daily Post,* said that he died on Sunday evening and that he had left his estate *"as every honest man ought to his wife and children".*

He asked in his will to be *"interred by his late dear wife and children at Beckenham".* There is a record of his burial on 10th December 1739 at St. George, Beckenham. Indentures, after he died, relate to Beckenham and Kent and to his widow. A map of Beckenham marks Mrs. Lethieullier's house at the edge of the village and it would appear that it had formal gardens and an orchard opposite the site on the other side of the road, with a farm at the rear of the property. The surrounding land appears mainly to have been agricultural.

After the death of William Lethieullier

At Bromley Public Libraries, Local Studies and Archives, near Beckenham, various documents are held relating to leases taken out by William Lethieullier and managed by his second wife, Mary, after his death in 1739. An agreement, originally entered into in 1717, explains that William Lethieullier, late of London, a merchant, and now of Beckenham, sold land which he owned to William Davies. The witnesses to this agreement were Thomas Clerke, Edward Vigeris and Roger Lawrence, the trusted servant of Sir John Lethieullier. Henry Batt and William Lethieullier entered into a lease of twenty-one years from 1727, for land at Penge Green in Battersea. Indentures were made by William Lethieullier in 1729 with the Knapp family prior to the marriage of Grace King to John Knapp. Joseph, George and Robert Knapp, the only son and heir of Joseph Knapp, were also cited. Additionally, Mary Lethieullier and the Knapp Family made mortgage agreements in 1740 and 1743. The land in question, at Lewisham, belonged in 1711 to Sir William Courtney and covered 143 acres. William East, of the Inner Temple, was the grantor. The sum of £6,800 was paid to Mary Lethieullier, half of which was to be paid, as was the custom of the City of London, to the Guildhall as part of the settlement of her husband's estate to her children. Her husband's nephew, Charles Lethieullier, of Lincoln's Inn, was one of the parties. Thomas Clerke and Parmenter are recorded as witnesses to some of these agreements.

Mary Lethieullier was buried on 13th January 1746/7 in Beckenham. It was announced in the *St. James Evening Post* that Mrs. Lethieullier, an ancient widow gentlewoman and relict of William Lethieullier, many years a Turkey Merchant, had died on 8th January 1746/7 at her house at Beckenham. She had written her will in 1745, proved in 1746/7 (*PROB 11/752/140*) and asked to be buried near her husband. Her daughter Letitia received one shilling, £500 was to go to Leonora and her jewels except for her "*best jewel*" in a necklace, were to go to her son Samuel, along with his father's picture and china with the family crest. All the rest of her china, without arms, was to go to Leonora along with her body linen and her choice of her wearing apparel; the remainder to go to the servant. Her uncle's watch and chain were cited and she added that it carried family arms, presumably those of the Winder family. The residue of her estate was bequeathed to Samuel and his heirs, he being named as executor.

John Lethieullier (1703-1760): City of London official and farmer

Venn's Alumni Cantabrigienses lists William Lethieullier's eldest son John, indicating that he was born around 1703.

> **LETHIEULLIER, JOHN**. Admitted Fellow – Com. (age17) at PEMBROKE, Nov. 9, 1720. Son and heir of William, of Beckenham and Sutton, Kent, Esquire Matriculated, 1720. Admitted at the Inner Temple, April 1, 1723. Of Sutton Place, Esquire. Died May 3, 1760, s.p. Buried at Sutton. Brother of the next. (G, Mag.; Hasted.239)

William Lethieullier, in his will, wrote that, at the request of his eldest son John, he had purchased from John Preston, for the sum of £2900, the office of Remembrancer of the City of London, which his son had enjoyed for some considerable time. He then explained that his son had recently made a further request for £2500, which he had borrowed from William Gosselin, a relative and close friend of his father. This amount he had raised before he wrote his will in 1736 by mortgaging the Manors of Sutton-at-Hone, Wilmington and houses at Roughill, Dartford and Marsh Street, near Dartford.

Further evidence of John's position at the Office of Remembrancer at the Guildhall is in the manuscripts of the Earl of Lancaster at Lincolnshire Archives, by way of a piece of paper containing John's signature, wrapped about some documents (*1-ANC/9/D/6*). A letter from John Lethieullier to Sir Gilbert Heathcote outlines the City's action regarding bills for the recovery of small debts. The note was dated 10th March 1729/30 from the City Remembrancer. Chown, writing in the *Essex Review* of 1926, believed that John held the position from 1726 to 1746. *British History Online* confirms that John Lethieullier was admitted and sworn on 10th January 1726 and surrendered the position on 15th November 1743. It was an important position, created in 1571 and was the chief means of communication among the Lord Mayor, City of London and Parliament. The Remembrancer dealt with reports to the courts on all Bills through Parliament relating to the administration of justice, licensing and other subjects affecting the Justice of the Peace. It also had a ceremonial element and responsibility for protocol.

John Lethieullier of Sutton-at-Hone, a bachelor aged around 30, married Mary Butler on 9th September 1740 at the Guildhall Chapel. She was recorded as a widow of St. Bennet, Paul's Wharf, London (*London Marriage Licences 1618-1828*). The marriage took place after the death of John's father and the groom was obviously financially secure. His wife died in 1748 and on 20th June 1752, at Lincoln's Inn Chapel, he married Anne Garrett, a spinster of the Parish of St. George, Bloomsbury.

At the British Library Manuscripts section, the *Hill Family Papers* contain a diary *(Add MS 5488 Fols. 68-72, pages 28-32)*, which is a copy of John Lethieullier's accounts of life on the farm at Sutton Place, Sutton-at-Hone, Kent, between the months of April and June in 1756. The diary records that John went with his wife on the 3rd of April to Dartford and dined with "*Brother*" Scrimsour and came home late. Thomas Scrimsour was, in fact, his brother-in-law since his sister Mary had married Scrimsour in the previous year on 1st May 1755, at Wilmington. On 12th April, he notes that a postboy was killed by two officers while going up Shooter's Hill, although there is no explanation of why the event took place. Lethieullier reports that there was a soldier stood in the pillory for abusing a girl after an attempt at rape. The 16th of April was Good Friday and he makes reference to "*Waller's Field*", recording that he had gone to the wood with Mrs. Lethieullier. He records that the Wilmington Fair was on 28th April that year, Wilmington being quite close to Sutton-at-Hone. He went to London on business on 25th May and mentions that his wife had policies on properties in Foster Lane, so she may have been wealthy in her own right. His diary shows that he grew hops and planted wheat. He worked on the farm along with his employees but he "*can't hold stooping long*". Wine growing was possible at that period, as he describes nailing the vines up in the garden, confirming that he was not averse to doing some of the work himself. He was engaged in making a fountain in the garden. He kept sows but he may have had other animals and he reports that "*his spare man*" ran away but he does not explain why or whether he ever returned.

From Sutton-at-Hone it is possible even today to see the church spires of the City of London. The local church is dedicated to St. John the Baptist. *Hasted* records that the churchyard had a vault and monument to John Lethieullier and to both his wives. John would have been a prominent member of its community.

John Lethieullier died in 1760 at Sutton Place and his wife, Anne was his sole relict when his will was proved on 16th May 1760 (*PROB 11/856/166*). All his manors went to his wife and when he wrote his will in 1755, he wrote of his love and affection for her although they had only been married for three years. He left minimal amounts to his sister Mary Scrimsour and to his brother William Lethieullier but nothing to other members of the Lethieullier family. Edward Hasted's *The History and Topographical Survey of the County of Kent (Volume 2)*, produced in 1800, suggests that his will was contested by Mary Browne and that the estate at Sutton-at-Hone passed to Nathaniel Webb in 1766.

The will of his widow, Anne Lethieullier, then of Great Russell Street, in Bloomsbury, was proved in 1772. She does not make bequests to any of the Lethieullier family. She names her sister, Mary Finch and great-nieces by the name of Schoen. In the will of Mary Finch, a resident of Bloomsbury who died in June 1790, she makes reference to her grandsons, one of whom was George Lethieullier Schoen. Mary Garret, born in 1700, married Daniel Finch in 1726. They had a daughter, Dorothy who married John Henry Schoen on 14th June, 1752 at Mortlake and died in 1778.

Mary Lethieullier/ Scrimsour (1706-1782)

Mary Lethieullier was baptised on 16th February 1706 at St. Olave, Hart Street, London. She married Thomas Scrimsour relatively late in life, at the age of 49. Their intended marriage was recorded in the *Vicar General Marriage Allegations, 1751-1775,* on 29th April 1755 and they married on 1st May 1755 at Wilmington, in Kent. The licence presents a degree of conflicting information. Thomas Scrimsour described himself as a bachelor, aged 30, formerly living at Dartford in Kent. His stated intention was to marry Mary Lethieullier of the Parish of Wilmington, also aged 30. It is likely that the ages were described incorrectly and they both were around 50.

The Reverend Samuel Denne wrote a letter dated 18th January 1797, published in *Illustrations of the Literary History of the Eighteenth Century: Consisting of authentic memoirs and original letters of eminent persons* by John Nichols in 1831, which refers to Scrimsour. Denne knew him at Darenth as a parishioner who married a Lethieullier, she being described as an "*old maid with a competent fortune*" Scrimsour was a surgeon at Dartford but retired from his practice after he married Mary Lethieullier and moved to Darenth and then to North Cray where the two *"now sleep"* in the churchyard. This account was written just twelve years after Thomas Scrimsour died so it was a living record.

Mary Scrimsour did not have any children or natural heirs and in her will, written in 1775, she left part of her estate to Matilda and Thomas Clerke, the children of her half-sister, Letitia Clerke, *née* Lethieullier, Letitia having married Thomas Clerke in 1755, the latter in 1775 being still alive. Most of the estate of Thomas and Mary Scrimsour went to her nieces Rachel Waller and Margaret Lethieullier, the children of her brother William. James Waller, husband of Rachel and James Beddell were executors. Margaret married Richard Pinckard in 1791.

Mary was buried on 9th July 1782 in the churchyard of St. James, North Cray, which is a village south from Dartford, where she had been living. Her husband was buried on 10th December 1784 and in the register, written in pencil beneath his name, is scribbled *"doctor at Ls Li Cottage"*. The wills were not proved until 1786; Thomas on 12th February 1786 (*PROB 11/1139/90*) and Mary on 14th February 1786 (*PROB 11/1139/105*). An account in the *North West Kent, Family History Society, Volume 1, Autumn 1978-1980*, on the Lethieullier family, quotes the following inscription on a gravestone in North Cray Churchyard.

> In a vault underneath lies the body of Mary Scrimsour, wife of Thomas Scrimsour, gent and daughter of John Lethieullier, Esquire, late of London, Merchant. She died July____ 1782, in the_____ year of her age. Also in the same grave is buried Mr. Thomas Scrimsour, her husband, who died <u>Dec.1st 1781</u>, aged____ years. They were religious conscientious and just persons. He was formerly Surgeon of the Luxenborough Galley, burnt on her passage from Jamaica, in the year 1727, and was the last survivor of her unfortunate Crew, sixteen of whom perished in the flames, or were drowned in attempting their escape, sixteen of twenty-two who with himself had crowded into a small boat, utterly destitute of every kind of provision, were overcome by hunger and fatigue and died most of them delirious and seven only were by divine Mercy preserved to reach a distant shore but not without having been first driven to the shocking extremity of subsisting themselves on the remains of their famished companions.

Mary was about 76 when she died and some accounts from the crew after the events of the *Luxborough* suggest that Thomas Scrimsour survived until his eightieth year. There are a number of discrepancies within the information in the memorial, perhaps a question of inaccurate transcription or that it was a memorial other than from family members. The date of Thomas' death was 1784 and not 1781. Mary Scrimsour was not the daughter of John Lethieullier. Sir John Lethieullier was her grandfather and he was a wealthy merchant.

Her father was William Lethieullier, a merchant and barber surgeon who had a brother called John Lethieullier. Mary Scrimsour's brother was also John Lethieullier but a farmer and an official in the City of London and not a merchant. The Ship was the "*Luxborough*" and not *Luxenborough*, more of which later. Mary and Thomas were both living, at the time of their deaths, at North Cray, near Dartford in Kent and Thomas Scrimsour gave instructions that the portrait of Sir John Lethieullier and his wife, Anne, was to be given immediately to Reverend Curry of Dartford for safe-keeping. Thomas wrote the will and dated it on 4th November 1782, dying in 1784. Reverend John Currey, A.M., was cited as rector of the Blessed Virgin of St. Mary's at Dartford in 1778 in *Hasted's History of Kent, Volume 2*. The portrait was obviously important to Thomas, his wish being that it should be preserved for future generations as his wife Mary was the last member of William Lethieullier's immediate family to die.

The National Maritime Museum holds a series of paintings relating to the fire on the *Luxborough* Galley, painted after it was lost in 1727. It maintains references in other documents and books, some of them connected to the family of William Kellaway, who was the captain, confirming that the incident took place. William Boys was the second mate on Captain William Kellaway's Galley. Boys published a book in 1787, shortly after Thomas Scrimsour died, outlining the events leading up to the loss of the ship.

The *Luxborough* Galley was used by the South Sea Company for slave trading. It left England in 1725 on one leg of the journey to West Africa. It then carried some six hundred slaves, captured or traded from Cabinda in West Africa, now Angola, for sale in Jamaica. According to Boys, the Captain had been attacked before his departure from Africa by an African King because one of the white crew had slighted the King. Of the total number of slaves on this particular voyage, some two hundred and three died of smallpox on the journey, along with eight of the crew. When they reached Jamaica, they despatched the slaves and loaded up the Galley with a cargo of rum and sugar and set sail for England in May 1727. On 25th June 1727, the Galley went up in flames. Some of the black slaves were still on the ship and it was said that it was they who, partly due to their curiosity, decided to test whether, by lighting it, a wet patch on the deck was rum or water. The liquid caught fire and immediately set the leaking barrel alight. The two boys in question were reluctant to tell anyone about the fire in case they were implicated and it raged out of control and either set alight the powder kegs stored on board or the rest of the barrels of rum. The crew had to abandon the ship after the resultant explosion and twenty-two of the officers and crew piled into one of the lifeboats of the Galley to escape death by fire; others of the crew were killed. As the days progressed, a number of cruel methods were practised to enable the crew to survive. It was suggested that two of the slaves were to be thrown overboard to allow the remainder more space, which was not an uncommon experience on slaving ships when slaves were ill, diseased or "*wasting*" precious food resources. They agreed to draw lots, without the approval of the captain but before they were thrown overboard one of the slaves died as did a crew member. The remaining survivors were forced to drink their own "*water*" and sea-water to stay alive. When it rained they licked the water from each other's clothes to keep their lips moist and stay alive. Thomas Scrimsour, Kellaway and Boys apparently refused to drink salt water. All, according to Boys, ate some of their dead colleagues but decided that the heart was the only edible part and drained the blood of the dead into a container and drank it to stay alive. They rigged a sail from some of their clothes and eventually were rescued and landed on Newfoundland. Kellaway, the captain, only survived for a day on land but another boy with the same surname survived. Of the twenty-two who left the *Luxborough* on 25[th]June 1727, only five survived and Thomas Scrimsour was one of them. As surgeon, he may have been the person who performed the odious task of cutting up the bodies and draining the blood.

Manning Lethieullier (c.1705/1711 – 1752) – Merchant trader

Manning Lethieullier was born between 1705 and 1711 and was described by William Lethieullier in his will as his second son. There are records of Manning Lethieullier during the years 1727-1739 in the East India Company documents at the British Library, in general correspondence and in orders and instructions. Anthony Farrington's book, *A Biographical Index of East India Company Maritime Service Officers, 1600-1834,* lists Manning on the *Prince Augustus* in 1726/7, which is likely to have been at the start of his trading career, following in the footsteps of his merchant trader grandfather, father, uncles and brother. Manning was one of a number of supercargoes who travelled to India and beyond at that time, supercargoes and captains being those instructed to keep their ships together for protection against pirates, aided in some cases by soldiers. He was obviously quite an adventurer, choosing to travel under most dangerous conditions, subject to serious risk to life and limb.

In *Volumes × of Despatches to England, page 28,* correspondence held at the British Library for the years 1733-35, records that Mr. Lethieullier (Manning) had returned from China to India on the ship *Prince Augustus,* rather than go to Europe. It was also noted that he had entered into a marriage contract at Fort St. George, on the Coromandel Coast, Tamil Nadu, India. Manning Lethieullier was in a poor state of health and wanted to stay at Fort St. George. On 24th June 1734 in Madras, he married Anne Gyfford, born on 6th October 1714 at Bombay, Maharashtra (*N2/1/277*) with a Mr. Howard officiating. A copy of the register is held at the British Library in the East India section. Anne's father most likely was William Gyfford, a merchant of Anjengo in the East Indies, whose will was settled in 1725. He refers in his will, written in 1719, to his daughter Anne, his wife Catharine and "*son-in-law*" Thomas Chowne. This was an unusual description of his stepson as the child would only have been about 5 or 6 years of age at the time.

William Lethieullier, Manning and Anne's son, was baptised by a Mr. Howard on 24th October 1735 at Fort St. George, Madras. A few months later, the Minutes of the Council meeting explained that Manning Lethieullier had sent a letter asking permission for him and his wife and their effects to return by ship home to England as his *"affairs were calling him home"*; he did not mention a baby.

A Faculty Office marriage allegation, dating from 14th January 1742/43, shows that Manning Lethieullier, of the Parish of Lewisham, in Kent, a widower, appeared personally to announce his intention to marry Anne Green, of the Parish of Stepney, Middlesex, a spinster, aged *"upwards of twenty years"*, with the consent of Elizabeth Green, a widow, her natural and lawful mother, *"she being guardian by her father's will and not being a ward of court of Chancery"*. The marriage was to take place in the Chapel at Guildhall, London, where Manning's brother John had married. Ann's father, Joseph Green, who died in 1739, had been a Quaker.

Manning had two daughters, Elizabeth, baptised on 18th October 1744 at St. Olave, Hart Street and Anne, who was baptised on the same date exactly one year later at St. Mary, Lewisham, near to where the family was living at the time. Elizabeth died before her father, who died in the same year as his half-brother, Samuel Lethieullier. His burial was recorded on 14th July 1752 at St. Alfege, Greenwich. *Musgrave's Obituary* gives his date of death as 9th July 1752, reported from the *Gentleman's Magazine*. Manning wrote his will on 22nd June 1752 and it was proved on 23rd July 1752. He left, *inter alia*, a coach, a collection of wine, books, corn and hay, the last of which might suggest that he was an active farmer. He left to his wife his house in Beckenham *"which his wife liked best"*, where he was living prior to his death and the one in Lewisham; this was probably *Kent House Farm*. His will made provision for his daughter Anne and any son born within ten months of his death. Perhaps when he wrote the will he did not know for certain whether or not his wife was pregnant. His son, John Green Lethieullier, was baptised at St. Andrew's, Holborn on 20th February 1752. The father's name was shown as Manning Lethieullier, Esq. and the mother's name as Anne. Their address was given as Bartlett's Building in the Parish of St. Andrew's, Holborn.

Anne Lethieullier, a widow, in December, 1753 married Samuel Henry Pont and had a daughter, Henrietta Maria Pont in the following year. In London, in April 1755, Anne Pont's mother, Elizabeth Green, a widow, married George Drummond, Lord Provost of Edinburgh and one of the Commissioners of Excise in Scotland. He had travelled to London from Scotland in January 1755 (*Whitehall Evening Post*). Samuel Pont died in 1758 and Elizabeth Drummond died in November 1759. In September 1764 Anne Pont married George Drummond, her stepbrother. On 16th June 1777 at St. Alfege, Greenwich, Anne Drummond was buried in the same grave as her first husband, Manning Lethieullier.

28

Samuel, Letitia and Leonora Lethieullier

Samuel Lethieullier (1720-1752)

Samuel Lethieullier was baptised on 1st July 1720. He was 18 when his father died in 1739 and he inherited the farm formally known as Dalton's Farm and later as Hartley Farm, described by his father as Hartley's Wood, in the Parish of Haxtley (*sic*) in Kent. This farm was occupied in 1726 by tenants Robert Batt of Longfield for 21 years at an annual rent of £50 and then by Thomas and Rachel Fielder in 1748. William Lethieullier had bought Hartley Wood Farm in 1726 from Ralph Egerton. Samuel was given one seventh share of one third of his father's other assets, according to the custom of the City of London. He also received the watch which had once belonged to his mother's uncle Winder and given first to his mother and then his father as a present by his wife.

A series of documents at Essex Record Office relate to the financial dealings of the Lethieullier family. The first (*D/DC 23/777*), dated 17th July 1740, is a declaration of trust among Mary Lethieullier, the widow and executrix of William Lethieullier of Beckenham in Kent, Charles Lethieullier, her nephew and Thomas Motley, to William Gosselin, Smart Lethieullier and John Lethieullier, the eldest son of William Lethieullier, reciting the will of Letitia Lethieullier, late of the Parish of St. Olave, Hart Street, who had bequeathed money to her niece of the same name. A document (*D/DC 23/778*) dated 29th July 1740 was an agreement and release concerning legacies, stocks and shares following wills. The parties were William Gosselin, Smart Lethieullier, executor of his aunt Letitia's will, of the first part, along with his brother and sister, Charles and Elizabeth Lethieullier, of the second part, Manning, William and Mary Lethieullier, the elder children of William Lethieullier by his first wife, of the third part and Mary Lethieullier, the second wife and executrix of his will, Charles Lethieullier and Thomas Motley, trustees for Samuel, Letitia and Leonora, the youngest children by his second wife, of the fourth part. All parties had signed the agreement and the signatures were good and clear. Elizabeth Lethieullier recorded her address as Princess Street, near Hanover Square in Middlesex.

A document (*D/DC 23/784*) dated 17th August 1744, was a release of Right (*quitclaim*) of all actions. It explains that Samuel Lethieullier was under the age of 21 when his father had died. He had also been left money by his aunt Letitia, who died in 1737. His mother, Mary Lethieullier, had managed his real estate and the farm at Hartley Wood in Kent and acted as guardian to all the younger children. Thomas Motley and Charles Lethieullier, Samuel's cousin, had invested his fortune. As Samuel had come of age, he was entitled to look after his own affairs. Samuel wrote that he was full of *"duty and gratitude to my said mother for her great care and tenderness"*.

Venn's Alumni Cantabrigienses notes, of Samuel Lethieullier:

> **LETHIEULLIER, SAMUEL.** Adm. pens. (age 19) at St. John's Nov.1,1738. Son of William, Esquire, of Middlesex. Born in London. Educated at home (Mr Craddock) and by Mr. Grigman. Matriculated 1738. Admitted at the Inner Temple, August 5th, 1737; 4th son of William, of Beckenham, Kent. Brother of John above.

An entry in the *Index of Vicar General Marriage Allegations, 1751-1775* offers evidence of the marriage of Sarah Painter to Samuel Lethieullier. A copy of the licence, archived at Lambeth Palace Library, explains that Samuel Lethieullier, a bachelor of Beckenham in Kent and Sarah Painter, a spinster of the Parish of St. Mary's, Whitechapel, were both upwards of twenty-one years. They announced their intention to be married in the Parish Church of St. Mary's, Whitechapel or St. Giles, Cripplegate, London. An almost illegible entry in the marriage records of St. Mary's, Whitechapel confirms that Samuel Lethieullier married Sarah Painter by licence on 24th May 1751. Miss Painter's place of residence was Wellclose Square, sometimes called Marine Square. Other churches identified in various documents in connection with her family were St. John's, Wapping and St. Paul's, Shadwell. Sarah had been living with her mother in the Whitechapel area before the marriage. By September the following year, 1752, Samuel was dead.

Samuel Lethieullier was buried on 10th October 1752 at the Church of St. George, Beckenham, having died at only 32 years of age, later in the same year in which his half-brother Manning, had died. His will (*PROB 11/797/240*), in which he stated that he wanted to be buried in a *"decent but not expensive way"*, was proved on 12th October by his wife and sole executrix, Sarah Lethieullier. His sister, Leonora, was to receive his diamond sleeve buttons and £20 for mourning. Letitia was also to receive his gold watch and chain with his father's picture, in case he had no children, in addition to £20 for mourning. Everything else was to go to his wife, her heirs and executors. If he were to have any children, his executrix was to choose to whom who to distribute his remaining assets.

Letitia Lethieullier/ Clerke (1721– *c.*1779 +)

Letitia Lethieullier was baptised on 27th July 1721 and went on to marry Thomas Clerke. An entry in the *Vicar General Marriage Allegations, 1751-1775,* as at 19th August 1755 shows the marriage licence of Thomas Clerke and Letitia Clerke, formerly Lethieullier. He was over 21 years of age and had lived for the previous four weeks in the vicinity of the Chapel of the Savoy, within the Liberty of the Rolls. However, for *"greater serenity and assurance"* the marriage was to be solemnicised in the Church of St. Andrew, Holborn or St. Dunstan-in-the-West in the parish adjoining the extra-parochial place of the Liberty of the Rolls. It took place on 20ᵗʰ August 1755 at the Church of St. Dunstan-in-the-West with Dr. *"Deverell"* officiating and confirming that both were living in that parish.

It was Thomas Clerke or his father, also Thomas, who was the witness cited in the above indentures. Thomas Clerke, the father, was the rector of Beckenham in 1711, when Epiphany Holland was a curate and he remained there until his death. Records at the church identify Elizabeth, daughter of Thomas and Sarah Clerke, who was baptised on 29ᵗʰ September 1715 and buried 14ᵗʰ August 1716. Abel Clerke, their son, was buried 29ᵗʰ August 1718. The elder Thomas Clerke was buried in the churchyard at Beckenham on 26ᵗʰ May 1765, his wife Sarah having been buried on 23ʳᵈ February 1753.

John Clerk, a Doctor of Physic, married Jane Brome by licence at St. George, Beckenham on 8ᵗʰ February 1753. Henry Clerke, son of Dr. John and Jane Clerke was born 14ᵗʰ March and baptised 17ᵗʰ March 1756 at St. Gabriel, Fenchurch Street, London. Charlotte was born and baptised at the same place a year later, on 24ᵗʰ March 1757. Henry's burial was recorded on 4ᵗʰ December 1759 at Beckenham.

Jane Clerke, when she was buried on 4th May 1757, was described as the wife of a physician in Epsom where records show her husband, John Clerke to have been living. Rachel Notley's book on St. George's Church, Beckenham, identifies a memorial to Jane Clerke on the west wall of the north transept, to the left of the St. George window. The following passage, from the monument, *"EPITAPH ON MRS CLERKE"* by Thomas Gray, suggests that she was a mother.

> Jane Clerke died April XXV11 MDCCLV11 AGED XXX1
> Lo where this silent marble weeps
> A friend, a wife a mother sleeps

In a book of correspondence with Thomas Gray, edited by Paget Toynbe and Leonard Whibley (*1971*), they declared that John Clerke was born in 1717 and was the son of Thomas Clerke, a rector.

The younger Thomas Clerke died before his father and was buried at Beckenham on 17ᵗʰ January 1761. Letitia did not marry again, as she is referred to in various wills in 1779 and 1782 as the widow of Thomas Clerke. She may have died before her brother-in-law, John Clerke, as her daughter was his executrix.

Both Dr. John Clerke and Thomas Clerke were recorded in the *Alumni Cantabrigienses*.

CLERKE JOHN: Admitted pens. (age 20) at St. Katherine's April 29th, 1734. Of Kent. Migrated to Peterhouse November 11th 1735. Matriculated 1735; Scholar1735; B.A.1738-9; M.A. 1742; M.D. 1753, Fellow1740. For many years a physician at

Epsom. Died 1790. (Will P.C.C. T.A. Walker 272 Admissions to Peterhouse 1615-1912)"

CLERKE THOMAS: Admitted pens. (age 16) at St. John's April 14th 1730, son of Thomas, clerk of Berkshire, Farringdon School, Reigate, Surrey. Matriculated 1730; B.A.1733-4;M. A.1737. Fellow 1735-44 Admitted at the Middle Temple June 18th 1743, son and heir of Thomas, clerk of Beckenham, Kent, Barrister, 1744. (Scott-Mayor; 111 426 from Admissions to St. John's College)

There are references to Thomas as the son and heir of Reverend Thomas Clerke, Clerk of Beckenham in the records of the Middle Temple. Thomas Clerke, husband of Letitia Lethieullier, was referred to in *Hasted's History of Kent* as a Counsellor at Law. Furthermore, in the *Gentleman's* and *London* magazines, Thomas Clerke's death was recorded on 9th January 1761 with reference to him being a Counsellor of Law and on 10th January 1761 as Counsellor and Clerk of Chancery Lane. Thomas Clerke died intestate. An administration was dated February 1761 and 1762.

THOMAS CLERKE, 6th day of August, late of the parish of St Dunstan-in-the-West, London, Esquire, was granted to John Clerke, Doctor of Physic, the uncle and curator or guardian lawfully assigned to Thomas Clerke and Matilda Clerke, infants, the natural and lawful and only children of the said deceased for Thousand benefit of the said infants until they or one of them shall attain the age of 21 years (Letitia Clerke, widow, the Relict of the said deceased) first renouncing having been first sworn duly to administer.

The application of the administration usually occurred six months after the death so this might explain the two dates. Both children were cited in the will of Mary Scrimsour, written in 1775 and their mother, Mrs. Letitia Clerke, then a widow, in the will of Sarah Holland in 1779, suggesting that Letitia was still alive around that time.

John Clerke's short will was written before his niece married, as he left his estate to Matilda Clerke, his niece and sole executrix. He was buried at Beckenham on 24th December 1790. By the time probate was settled on 14th January, 1791, she was the wife of William Sanxay. Matilda married Sanxay on 19th January 1786 at Epsom in Surrey before which time she may have been living with her uncle John Clerke at Epsom when and where she met her husband. William Sanxay's family came from Cheam in Surrey; his father was called John and his mother, Catherine. William's uncle was Edmund Sanxay, who had a substantial house at Cheam. William was christened at Sutton in 1757 (*parish records*).

The will of Matilda's brother, Thomas Clerke, of Hammersmith, a gentleman, written on 22nd October 1787 identifies his wife, Margaret and children at that time, Thomas and Matilda. Louisa Clerke was baptised on

29th January 1794 at All Saints Fulham, Middlesex. Thomas, the father, died in 1799 and his will was proved by Margaret Clerke on 18th February 1799.

William Sanxay died in 1813, when he left his freehold estate at Derby and copyhold land in Stoke Newington to his wife. In 1815, *The Times* advertised a sale by auction by Matilda, then executrix of William Sanxay, of a large brickbuilt, copyhold residence at Stoke Newington, with three to six rooms on every floor, offices and iron railings at the front, on the west side of Stamford Hill, close to Stamford Hill Bridge and including a detached coach house and stables. The exact location may have been marked on John Roque's map of 1745.

By the time that Matilda Sanxay died on 4th June 1816, she was living at the stone house at Woodcote Green, Epsom in Surrey. In her will (*PROB 11/1581/45*), she referred to an agreement dated 4th January 1786 which may have been part of her marriage settlement as she married on 19th January 1786. She identified her farm of 151 acres at Dalton's Wood, Hartley, in Kent. Hasted, in *The History and Topographical Survey of the County of Kent, Volume 2, 1797,* identified Hartley Wood with 150 acres in the Parish of Hartley. Samuel Lethieullier, in his father's will in 1739, had been left the farm at Hartley Wood in the Parish of Hartley and Sarah Lethieullier, his widow, acquired the farm on the death of her husband in 1752. Sarah Lethieullier went on to marry Stephen Holland in 1756. Hartley Wood Farm appears not to have been highlighted in Sarah Holland's will of 1779 but it has been suggested in other sources that she left it to Dr. John Clerke, as the guardian of his nephew and niece, as confirmed in their father's administration, in trust for them; it thereby passed to Matilda. Alternatively, it may be that Sarah Holland had already disposed of the farm by 1779. Matilda Sanxay named her nieces Louisa Clerke, late of Kentish Town parish and Matilda Newbolt as her main beneficiaries. She explained that her nephew, William Clerke, was "*labouring under a mental derangement*" and he should only benefit if, in the opinion of her trustees, William Hill Newbolt, Mr. Cholmley and Alexander Radcliffe, he were ever to recover his understanding. If her nephew were to die, his share was to be divided equally between her nieces. Matilda Sanxay also left stocks and her house to her husband's spinster sisters, Katherine and Caroline Sanxay. When Katherine Sanxay died at the age of 88 in 1850, she was living at Woodcote Cottage, Epsom in Surrey.

Matilda Clerke married Reverend William Hill Newbolt on 15th October 1805 at the Old Church, St. Pancras, Middlesex. Her husband had graduated from Oriel College, Oxford in 1799 and became a Doctor of Divinity in 1813. He was the rector of Morestead in Hampshire and was a minor Canon of Winchester Cathedral. William and Matilda had a son named William Henry Newbolt, born in 1806. Their daughter, Matilda Hill Newbolt was baptised on 26th November 1808 at St. Thomas, Winchester in Hampshire. The will of Louisa Clerke, a spinster, was settled on 25th July 1832 at Winchester, Hampshire. She left her estate to William Hill Newbolt, whose obituary was recorded in the *Gentlemen's Magazine* on 25th February 1833.

Leonora Lethieullier/ Holden (1724-1754)

Leonora Lethieullier was baptised on 24th May 1724. Her brother, Samuel, referred in his will to his sister, Leonora Holden. On 7th May 1748, Leonora Lethieullier was married to Henry Holden at St. Luke's, Old Charlton, in Kent, quite close to Greenwich. The church records show that Henry Holden was living at the time of his marriage in the Parish of St. Clement Danes, Middlesex and Leonora at Beckenham in Kent. An Anne Holden married Edward Colyer at the same Church in 1752, so they were probably related. Edward Colyer died in 1797 at Southfield in Kent.

A document (*D/DC 23/785*) dated 5th May 1748 at Essex Record Office relating to the marriage settlement, describes the movement of stocks and shares between Leonora Lethieullier, a spinster of Beckenham and Henry Holden, of the Six Clerks Office, London, described as a gentleman. Samuel Lethieullier and Stephen Holland were the trustees for both parties. The settlement referred to jewels and china, which had belonged to Leonora's aunt Letitia and to the purchase of £1,000 of stock in Bank of England annuities, £2,000 in new South Sea Stock and stock in the East India Company. Samuel Lethieullier was acting for his sister as both parents were deceased. Stephen Holland may have been acting on behalf of Henry Holden. It also confirms that Stephen Holland knew Samuel Lethieullier, the community at Beckenham being quite small.

The burial records of St. George's Church at Beckenham record that Mrs. Leonora Holden died on 19th August 1754, following the deaths of her two infant children, Robert Holden, on 13th December 1751 and Leonora on 22nd June 1753.

29

Sarah Painter and her family

John Painter: Mariner (father of Sarah Holland, née Painter)

The will of John Painter, in life a wealthy man from Marine Square in the County of Middlesex, was proved on 24th October 1728 (*PROB 11/625/222*), it having been written on 26th March of that year.

Marine Square, known originally as Wellclose Square, then Marine and then Wellclose Square again, is described in Ed Glinert's Book, *East End Chronicles*. It is sandwiched between what is now Cable Street and the Highway, in Tower Hamlets. It was the first residential estate in East London, created after the Great Fire of London of 1666, built on the site of an ancient well and sacred territory from Roman times, close to the Tower of London. It is said that it was developed by Nicholas Barbon around 1682-3, with grand houses set around a square. In the beginning, many of the occupants of the houses were shipmasters and Scandinavian timber merchants whose fortunes were much enhanced by the lucrative trade in timber, as the City of London was rebuilt after the Fire, even though the houses which replaced the earlier timber ones had to be built with brick. A church was built in 1696 for the Danish merchants in London, paid for by the Danish King Christian V and designed by the Danish sculptor and architect, Caius Gabriel Cibber, an assistant of Nicholas Hawksmoor, himself an assistant to Sir Christopher Wren. Cibber had also designed and executed the relief on the Monument to commemorate the Great Fire. Later, the places of merchants in Marine Square were taken by intellectuals and professionals of whom John Painter may have been one. The whole area had an unusual character in that it was outside the jurisdiction of the City of London, Middlesex and all except that of the Lord Chancellor.

The names in the will confirm that John Painter's wife was Elizabeth and his sister was Hannah. He had a brother, Andrew, whose wife was also named Elizabeth and a married sister, Ann Kinson. His son was John, who at the time of his father's death was under the age of twenty-one. The executors of the will were his wife Elizabeth, his dear friend Thomas Motley, a gentleman of Beckenham in the County of Kent, John Prudom of Wapping, in the County of Middlesex and Captain John Colvill. He asked that they, their heirs and assigns, should be directed to administer his estate and after funeral charges and legacies were paid, to dispose of all his lands, tenements and heredita-ments, goods and chattels in the performance of this will. He requested that his shares in lead and ships were to be sold and the profits of his personal estate were to be invested in bank stocks and annuities of three to four per cent, at the discretion of his executors, in order to pay annuities to his children. His son would receive an annuity from his lands at Ramsholt in Suffolk until he was of age. The family remained connected to the area because John's father left him land there. He owned other land at Hemingstone and Henley in Suffolk, which are just north of Ipswich and at Thenfield in Essex. He also owned two leasehold messuages on Wapping Wall in Middlesex, running alongside the River Thames, income from which was to pay out an annuity for the natural life of his sister Hannah, if she remained unmarried. He specified that after his wife died, all the land would go to his son John, then to his other sons and then to his daughters. After his wife's death, the leasehold messuages on Wapping Wall were then to be passed to his brother Andrew and sister Ann Kinson. Sarah, his daughter, received £400.

Essex Record Office retains documents relating to the family of John Painter. The probate will (*D/DC 23/847*) of Elizabeth Davis, a widow, of Hornchurch in Essex, was dated 2nd April and was proved on 11th August 1725. It explains that Elizabeth Painter, wife of John Painter, was her daughter. Mrs. Davis granted legacies to her daughter and grandchildren John, Elizabeth and Hannah, to her sister Ann Batts, Mrs. Ann Smith and the remainder of the estate was to go to her daughter, Elizabeth and her son-in-law, John Painter, who were executors.

Documents relating to two of the children include one (*D/DC 23/774*) for Elizabeth Painter, the daughter of the John Painter, deceased, of Marine Square in London. It addressed the release of a right to legacies from her grandmother, Elizabeth Davis to Elizabeth Prudom, Thomas Motley and John Colvill, names that were cited in the will of John Painter. The document recited the will of Elizabeth's grandmother, Elizabeth Davis, devising legacies to her grandchildren and stocks and shares following the death of their father in 1728. One might assume that as Elizabeth came of age she was entitled to her inheritance.

A further document (*D/DC 23/776*), dated 22nd August 1738 explains the release of right to legacies for Hannah Painter, a spinster of Swincombe, in County Oxfordshire, also the daughter of John Painter. Shares in lead and ships belonging to her father as well as stock in the Bank of England had been sold since his death and the money had been invested in bank stock or annuities at three or four percent, as instructed in his will. Elizabeth Painter, the daughter, since her recital of legacy, in 1736, had become the wife of Samuel Greenhill. According to their father's will, the ages at which the children were to receive their fortunes, were, for the son at the age of twenty-one and for the daughters at the age of nineteen. By the time of the documents, there were four children living; John, born around 1716/1717, Elizabeth, Hannah and Sarah. Baptismal records of the church at St. Paul's, Shadwell indicate that Elizabeth was baptised on 1st March 1715, when she was eighteen days old, making her birth date around 10th February; Hannah was baptised on 23rd July 1717, when she was fourteen days old, making her birth date 9th July and Sarah Painter was baptised on 18th March 1721, when she was fifteen days old, making her birth date 3rd March.

An entry for John Painter, son of John, of St. Paul's Shadwell, Middlesex in Joseph Foster's *Alumni Oxonienses 1715-1886*, describes him as a gentleman, educated at the Merchant Taylor School. His date of birth was shown as 10th April 1717 but he may have been born in 1716; it is recorded in a memorial slab at Ramsholt Church. He attended St. John's College, Oxford, having matriculated 14th December 1733, aged 17, receiving his B.A. in 1737. St. John's College indicate that he remained until June of 1738 before leaving, which in those days was quite common. His studies would have consisted of classics, history and a little science. St. Paul's overlooks what is now Shadwell, New Basin, close to the River Thames and is called *"The Sea Captain's Church"*. It was built originally in 1657 but rebuilt in 1820 after the Battle of Waterloo when it became known as one of the *"Waterloo churches"*. Some seventy captains are buried in the churchyard; Captain James Cook's son was baptised there, as was Jane Randolph, the mother of Thomas Jefferson. John Wesley preached his last sermon there a few days before he died.

The elder John's widow, Elizabeth, had since married John Prudom, one of the executors in Painter's will but Prudom himself was dead by 1738. Hannah, who was living in Swincombe at the time, probably with her sister and brother-in-law, asserted that she was now entitled to a share of her legacy of approximately £1,700. The total of their father's estate amounted to £6,900, made up of £5,000 of bank stock, £1,000 of three per cent annuities and £900 in South Sea stock. Her share of the legacy was a *"handsome fortune"* referred to in press, when Hannah married John Keeble.

In the will of Elizabeth Prudom, of the Parish of St. John, Wapping, which was proved on 1st May 1753 (*PROB 11/800/192*), she requested burial at *"Shadwell Church by the remains of her former husband John Painter"*. She described herself as the widow of John Prudom, a grocer and referred to an indenture tri-partite from 27th May 1730, when she made a marriage agreement with John Prudom, her intended husband, of the first part, herself of the second part, and Thomas Motley and William Martin of the third part. The contract was concerned with shares in capital joint stock in the company producing lead and smelting with pit and sea coal. Her second husband had died intestate and she explained that they had a son together, who died at under the age of one. Her son John had already received funds from the trust set up for the children of John Painter. Her daughter was her still unmarried executrix when Elizabeth wrote her will on 18th December 1747 but by the time it was proved, Sarah was the widow of Samuel Lethieullier. Sarah Painter had married Samuel Lethieullier in 1751.

The will of Samuel Greenhill, of Swincombe, was proved on 23rd January 1750. His beneficiaries were his son John Russell Greenhill by his first wife and his present wife, Elizabeth. It was drafted in 1741, with additions in 1742 and 1747. The circumstances surrounding Greenhill's death were explained in a codicil which revealed that the will had been hidden in an envelope and discovered among papers after his death. The person who verified that it the will was written by the deceased was John Greenhill of Lincoln's Inn, who confirmed that he was well acquainted with Greenhill *"late of Swincombe and Antigua in the West Indies but in the ship Mary Gally at sea deceased for many years"*. The *Mary Galley* was rebuilt in 1744, which suggests that Samuel Greenhill died at sea between the years 1744 and 1749. A ship of that name was recorded transporting people from Germany to the West Indies around that period. It might be that Greenhill had dealings with the West Indies as a merchant. John Greenhill, who made the statement in the codicil, wrote his own will on 3rd October 1749 and died 15th May 1752.

Samuel Greenhill was first married to Elizabeth Russell, the youngest daughter of John Russell, Governor of Bengal and Rebecca Eyre, sister of Sir Charles Eyre of Kew, born in 1704. Elizabeth was the grand-daughter of Sir John Russell and Frances Rich, daughter of Oliver Cromwell and widow of Robert Rich. John Russell died in December 1735, aged 66, and his wife in 1713. Elizabeth gave birth to John Russell Greenhill in 1730 but died some time before 1736. It was in that year that at St. George in the East, Middlesex, on 22nd January 1736, Samuel, then a widower, married Elizabeth Painter, a spinster of Wellclose Square. Samuel was significantly older than Elizabeth, as she was born in 1715.

John Russell Greenhill, LL.D studied at Oxford and married Elizabeth Noble, daughter of Matthew Noble of Sunderland. John became rector of Fringford in Oxfordshire and Marsh Gibbon in Buckinghamshire and lived at Cottisford. He inherited the estate at Chequers from his cousin Mary Russell after a succession of relatives died. His son, Robert Greenhill was born in 1754, like his father, attended Oxford and trained to be a barrister. A second child, Charles died young. Robert became an M.P. representing Thirsk for many years. After the father's death in 1813, Robert inherited Chequers. In 1815 he changed his name by Royal Licence to Robert Greenhill Russell and in 1831 became Sir Robert Greenhill Russell, Baronet of Chequers Court. When he died without issue in 1837, the title lapsed. The estate at Chequers was eventually donated to the nation in the twentieth century and is the country residence of the UK prime minister.

In 1758, Elizabeth, the widow of Samuel Greenhill, died at Isleworth. She left £20 to her nephew, Jonathan Keeble, the son of her sister Hannah and her husband John Keeble of Hanover Street, in the Parish of St. George, to be enjoyed when Jonathan reached the age of 21. She also gave him *"plate"*, two pictures, one of her mother, another of his grandmother, Elizabeth Prudom and one of herself. She bequeathed a bracelet containing a picture of Jonathan to Hannah her sister. The remainder of her estate went to her brother-in-law John Keeble, who was also the sole executor.

Baptismal records at St. George's, Hanover Square, offer evidence of other children of the marriage of John and Hannah Keeble, besides Jonathan and Sally. Ann was baptised on 24th December 1749; Henry John Keeble was born on 3rd December and baptised on 14th December 1753; Jonathan was born on 16th April and baptised on 12th May 1756; Sally was born on 21st May and baptised on 15th June 1759. Sally was born after her aunt, Elizabeth Greenhill, had died, hence the reason that she was not named in Elizabeth's will. Indeed, Jonathan was only two years of age when he received a bequest.

As Ann and Henry John were not beneficiaries, it may be that they had died earlier.

An entry in the news from the country section of the *Public Advertiser*, dated 28th August 1764, included the death of John Painter, Esq. at Alderton, in Suffolk. John, the son, whose simple memorial is at Ramsholt Church, died intestate in 1764.

At All Saints Church at Ramsholt in Suffolk, on the floor, in front of the altar, there is a stone-carved memorial:

> Here lieth the body of John Painter, Esq. ob. 16th August 1764
> aged 48.

John's lack of a will might explain the Indenture of 1765 when Frances Austen of Sevenoaks, Stephen and Sarah Holland, Hannah and John Keeble and Thomas Gregory of Clifford's Inn were involved in a transaction relating to an estate in Suffolk. Frances Austen was the son-in-law of Thomas Motley, the good friend of John Painter, the father, and executor of his will. Sarah had been named in her father's will but his other daughters, Hannah and Elizabeth, were not, in specific terms.

Thomas Motley was one of the witnesses when Sarah (*Painter/Lethieullier*) married Stephen Holland. Stephen had family friends called the Brudenells, who lived at St. George's, Hanover Square, close to the Keebles, who lived at Conduit Street. Stephen Holland may have met his future wife when she was visiting her sister or at Beckenham, where his father at one time had been a curate.

Stephen Holland and his relatives

Stephen's father was Reverend Epiphanius Holland and his mother was Susannah Colt, widow of Stephen Colt. Dr. Thomas Clerke, discussed above, was rector of Beckenham and one might assume that Epiphany Holland, as curate there, also lived for a time at Beckenham. The name of Mr. Holland or Epiphany Holland *(sometimes Epiphanius or Epiphanus)* was recorded as officiating many times at services at St. Helen's, Bishopsgate. Epiphany, clerk of the church and his wife Susannah were recorded as parents when their first son, Epiphany, was baptised there on 1st April 1711. In the same year, Epiphanus, an infant child, was buried in the churchyard. Another child named Epiphany Holland was born on 12th March 1719 but a burial for Epiphany at St. George's Beckenham was recorded on 1st October 1721. An infant named Mary Holland was buried there on 18th May 1717 and two others, both named William Holland, were buried on 18th December 1719 and 19th April 1730. It is likely that they were children of Epiphany and Susannah, who died before their father, as his only son Stephen and his stepdaughter, Susanna, were named in his will, dated September, 1730. The records of St. George, Beckenham, show that Stephen Holland was born there on 7th June 1721. Epiphany was in his late forties when Stephen was born.

An entry for Epiphanius Holland in the *J.A. Venn Alumni Cantabrigienses from the earliest times to 1900 (Cambridge University Press: Cambridge, 1922-54 (10 Volumes))* reads:

> HOLLAND, EPIPHANIUS. Admitted sizar at JESUS, June 29, 1693. Son of Edward (1656). Rector of Waltham-on-the-Wolds, Leicester. Exhibitioner from Charterhouse. Rustat scholar, 1693; Matriculated, 1694; B.A.1696-97; M.A.1700. Ordained deacon (Peterborough) September, 24, 1699; priest (London) December, 22, 1700. Probably Curate of St Helen's London 1711-13. Brother of Edward (above). (J.Ch. Smith)

A sizar is a student who receives assistance of some kind such as meals, fee support or accommodation while studying, occasionally in return for doing certain work. Epiphanius received a scholarship from Tobias Rustat, who during his life-time, paid for seventeen scholarships, worth some £40 to £50 for the sons of clergymen, deceased or living, to study at Jesus College, Cambridge. This entry suggests that Epiphany was officiating at St. Helen's, Bishopsgate during the years 1711-1713. He is likely to have moved to Beckenham as a curate in 1713.

At the *LMA London,* Epiphany Holland is recorded in memorials in 1724 as having property in Ashford and Stanwell. In 1729, he is identified with property and land at Artillery Lane, between Spitalfields and Bishopsgate in Shoreditch. This indenture refers to earlier indentures among Nicholas Barbon (described earlier in this work in connection with Charles Dorman's law offices), George Bradbury (who shared a surname with Epiphany's mother) of the Middle Temple, Edward Noell of the Inner Temple and John Parsons.

Epiphany Holland –East India Company correspondence

The Chaplains of the East India Company, by S.J. McNally, 1976, a record held at the British Library in the Asian and African Studies collections, includes reference to Epiphanius Holland, appointed on 13th December 1700 as chaplain at St. Helena, off the coast of Africa in the Atlantic but it notes that he did not serve there. The East India Company operated on St. Helena and their ships sometimes used it as a stopover for fresh food and water on the long journey to India and China. John Humphreys was appointed as chaplain on St. Helena on 30th November 1698 but was dismissed by the Company and was back in England by 1700/1.

In the East India Company *Court Minutes 1699-1702 (IOR/B/43) page 186,* dated 13th December 1700, records that the Court of Committee had confirmed Mr. Epiphanius Holland MA on the recommendation of Sir William Langhorne, a baronet and Committee member, who appointed him to serve the Company as chaplain at St. Helena. He was to receive fifty pounds a year and fifty pounds gratuity. Humphreys, described as late chaplain of St. Helena was gone by February 1700/1 *(page 197)*. The same Court Minutes (*page 207*), on 11th April 1701, record that the Court was "*pleased this day to approve of Mr Epiphanius Holland as chaplain at Surat*". Holland had already been deemed qualified for that employment by the Committee of Shipping that issued a warrant for payment of twenty pounds for his fresh provisions to take passage on the ship *Loyal Bliss*. The Letter Book *(10), 1698-1709 (IOR/E/3/93)* by a letter (*ff 217v-20*), dated 11th April 1701, from the directors in London to the President and Council at Surat, reported:

> 19. We have entertained Mr Epiphanus Holland to be your minister at Surat he is very well recommended to us for his learning piety and virtue. We hope he will fully answer his character and prove to your entire satisfaction he is to have the usual salary of fifty pounds a year & fifty pounds gratuity

Chaplain Epiphanus Holland is recorded as a passenger, with factors and writers, on the *Loyal Bliss*, captained by Robert Hudson and sent to Bombay in May 1701 (*ff 235v-36*). Epiphany arrived in Bombay and then in Surat some time after that time. He never took up his position on St. Helena; perhaps Surat was a more prestigious appointment

In *Selections from the letters, despatches and other state Papers, preserved in Bombay Secretariat: Home Series, Volume 2*, in *Selections from the Surat Diary, 1660-1781 (page 247)*, Sir John Gayer, General, the Honourable Stephen Colt, President, the Worshipful Ephraim Bendall, Bernard Wyche, accountant and purser marine and Epiphanus Holland, chaplain, were listed as Company servants at the Factory in January 1703 (*a Factory was a merchant company's trading station*). Gayer and his wife, Dame Mary had been seized from Swally by native troops and they, Colt and others were confined at Surat, in the Factory between 1700 and 1710, although some members of the Council and servants had free movement and letters did get through to the Court in England. These were difficult and dangerous times, for in addition to the weather, illness and pirates, threats, accusations, attacks and mischief-making was being made among the leadership of the Old and New Companies, with the Mughal Government benefitting from the rivalry.

Correspondence contained in Letter Book *(10) 1698-1709 (IOR/E/3/93)*, in item 20 (*ff 321v-25*), dated 4th June 1703 to "*our General & Council of Bombay and Surat*", Captain Owen, on behalf of President Colt, requested that the latter be allowed to return home, as was his wish, after settling his accounts with the Company. Stephen Colt was then, it would appear, unmarried.

The *Factory Records Surat (G/36/118)*, entitled "*Surat letters received 31st July, 1704, to 15th September, 1705, received per Albemarle 11th February, 1708*" give an account of Stephen Colt and his wife being imprisoned with Sir John Gayer and others in the Factory and confirm that by 30th November 1705 he had married (*pages 51&52*). On 3rd December 1705 Colt concluded his letter, with hopes that he might get "*mine and wifes clearance from this perplexive place*" and described Surat as "*troublesome*", again pleading his case to the Council to be given his arrears of salary as well as his liberty from his *"so unjust detention"*. He declared that in July the Company had promised leave for him and his wife to embark on a ship to England, when his accounts were settled. As Colt was confined to Surat, it might be supposed that he married there. Stephen Colt died at Surat in May 1708. His will, proved in January 1710 (*PROB 11/513/126*), was administered by his widow, Susannah and sole executrix on 8th January 1711, on her return to England. The following statement suggests that his wife was pregnant when Colt made the will a month before his death, as he hoped she would *"happily go out her time with the present or any child lawfully begotten by me"*. Sir John Gayer, Captain Nathaniel Owen and Epiphany Holland each received £20 as overseers to the will. Some time after 1708, Stephen's widow, Susannah Colt, married Epiphany Holland.

In the index to the *East India Company Court Minutes* for the years 1699-1712 (*IOR/B/43-51*), Epiphanius Holland was cited three times between 1710 and 1712 (*IOR/B/51*). The first was in an account of a meeting at a Court of Directors held in London on Wednesday, 30th May 1711 *(page 451)* which minuted:

> Mr Epiphanius Holland, the Company Chaplain at Surat who returned on the Abingdon, presentd himself to the Court and praying his and familys wearing apparrell and necessaryes may be delivered them. Ordered That the Committee of Shipping be desired to examine the said necessaryes and give directions for delivering the same or such part thereof as they think fit
> (Written in the margin is *"Holland Epi: necessaryes delivered"*.)

This entry confirms that Epiphany Holland was the chaplain at Surat, had married before leaving there, as he had a family and had returned to England on the *Abingdon*. Epiphany Holland was a witness to the making of the will of Daniel Evance, a purser on board the *Abingdon*, in July 1710 but that will was not proved until 28th May 1711. It is likely that the ship arrived shortly before that date as the above entry was also made two days later on 30th May 1711. The second entry *(page 455)*, in relation to Epiphany Holland was in the minutes of a meeting the Court of Directors held on Friday 1st June 1711, reporting:

> Bills of Exchange drawn on the Company, one from the Governor and Council of St Helena, dated the 30th November last for £372 payable at twenty days sight to Mr Epiphanius Holland.... One from the General and Council of Bombay dated 11th April 1710 for £1,500 payable at ten days sight to the Reverend Mr Epiphanius Holland Ordered That the Committee of Accompts be desired, to examine the said Bills, whether they are advised off; and ought to be accepted and make report.
> (Written in the margin is *"Holland Epi:Bills referred"*.)

Holland's fortune was not acquired as part of the estate of Stephen Colt, the late husband of Susannah Colt, she now married to Holland, as the will cited above was not proved until 1711. The next and third entry in the Court Minutes dated Friday 26ᵗʰ October 1711 (*page 619*) reported:

> That the goods mentioned in the Accompt of Mr Epiphanius Holland amounting to £47. 1s. 4d be delivered him on his paying into the Treasury £21. 4s. 8d.
>
> (Written in the margin is "*Holland Epip: Goods to be delivered.*")

Documents at Hoare's Bank suggest that as early as 1712 there was an Assignment absolute (*HE/3/C/1*) dated 8ᵗʰ October 1712 from Epiphany Holland, a clerk, to William Gayer of London, a gentleman, of...

> ... all that capital messuage called the Manor House of Beckenham, situate in the parish of Beckenham, in the county of Kent together with.... the gardens orchards courtyards.... to contain by estimation 8 acres more or less.....meadow land called or known by the name of Court Mead.....to contain by estimation 12 acres.... and arable and pasture land, commonly called or known by the several names of Pound field containing by estimation 7 acres and a half ...Church Fields containing by estimation 16 acres...Broomfield containing by estimation 14 acres...some of which said parcels of ground ....have been divided into a greater number of closes by new hedges therein made and are also situate lying and being in the parish of Beckenham aforesaid. Consideration L 90.

On 23ʳᵈ June 1726, the same land as above, more or less, including the fishpond, which was then in the tenure of Epiphany Holland and his undertenants was leased (*HE/3/C/2*) for three years for the sum of £77 15s per annum from the Right Honourable Henry Lord Viscount St. John Baron of Battersea to Epiphany Holland of Kent, a clerk.

On 27ᵗʰ April 1731 Susannah, as Epiphany's widow and executrix, assigned a lease (*HE/3/C/3*), taken out by her late husband on 13ᵗʰ April 1730, to Richard Acland of Devon, for the remainder of the term of seven years, for the same rent. When Richard Acland died on 29ᵗʰ September 1747 his widow, Ann, took over the lease, formerly in the tenure or occupation of Epiphany Holland and his undertenants, presumably his son, Stephen, as both his parents were dead, for an increased rent of £95.15s.

Other members of the Holland family

Entries for both Edward Hollands in the *J.A. Venn Alumni Cantabrigienses from the earliest times to 1900 (Cambridge University Press: Cambridge, 1922-54 (10 Volumes)* read:

HOLLAND, EDWARD. Admitted sizar at EMMANUEL, May 22, 1656. Son of Richard of Salop. Born in Gloucestershire. Matriculated 1658; B.A.1659-60 Incorporated at Oxford 1664. Ordained deacon (Lincoln) February 22, 1661-62; priest (Peterborough) September 20, 1663. Vicar of Weekley, Northamptonshire, 1663-70. Rector of Waltham-on-the-Wold, Leicestershire, 1670-87. Prebend of Lincoln 1670-87 Rector of Stibbington, Hunts.,1678-80. Married, at St. Helen's, London, July 14, 1683, Honora Orson, widow. Died 1687. Father of Edward (1683) and Epiphanius (1693). (Al. Oxon.; Nichols, II 385,424;J.Ch. Smith)

Records at St. Helen's, Bishopsgate, London, show that Edward Holland, a widower, married Havarah (*sometimes Honora*) Orson, a widow on 11th July 1683. He was described as a rector of Waltham in Leicester and she as living in the Parish of St. Dionis Backchurch, London; he died intestate.

HOLLAND, EDWARD. Admitted pens. at EMMANUEL, July 3, 1683. Of Northamptonshire. Son of Edward (1656), Rector of Waltham-on-the-Wolds, Leicester. Matriculated 1685; B.A. 1687-8; M.A.1692. Ordained priest (London) December, 20, 1691. Rector of Waltham in Leicester 1692-1722. Died July 23, 1722 aged 56. M.I. at Waltham. Brother of Epiphanius. (Nichols, 11.386)

Edward studied at the same college as his father and became rector in the same church at Waltham, after the elder Edward died in 1687. It was common to hold positions in various churches. These entries suggested that Edward was older than his brother; Edward went up to Cambridge in 1685 and Epiphany began at Jesus College, Cambridge in 1693.

Epiphany's and Edward's father was Edward Holland, who married Grace Bradbury on 17th September 1661 (*Weekley Parish Registers Northamptonshire Notes and Queries Volume VI, 1896 edited by John Taylor*), although Venn's listing above for the elder Edward suggested that as from 1663 he was vicar of Weekley. Edward's elder son was born at the earliest in May 1662. The three sisters who shared the same parents, identified in Epiphany's will, were Dorothy, Grace and Mary. Church records show that Mary was baptised at Waltham-on-the-Wolds on 3rd February 1676; Epiphany was also baptised there on 14th January 1674. Dorothy married James Aston on 5th March 1695 at St. James, Duke's Place, London (*familysearch.org*).

Edward Holland, Epiphany's brother, died intestate. An administration (*PROB 6/98*) for Holland, rector of Waltham, Leicestershire, written in Latin and dated 14th August 1722 indicates that Catherine Scott, widow of John Scott and natural daughter of Edward was granted her father's estate. Her mother was, it might be presumed, dead.

Catherine, daughter of Edward and Ann Holland was baptised on 31st January 1694, at Waltham-on-the-Wolds, Leicester (*familysearch.org*).

Catherine married John Scott on 13th October 1715 at Christ Church, Greyfriars, Newgate in London. Their children were Grace, born 7th August 1716; Mary, born 18th September 1717; Catherine, born 19th July 1720 (all baptised at St. Margaret, Lothbury). The younger Catherine married Henry Willoughby Pennell on 14th February 1743 at St. George's, Mayfair, in London. Grace Scott married Michael Honnor on 19th January 1741 at St. Anne and St. Agnes, Aldersgate. Mary Scott died in 1782 and left her estate to her widowed sister, Catherine, who died in 1792. Both Mary and Catherine were living in the Parish of St. Mary, Newington in Surrey. The latter left her estate to her married daughter, Catherine Trottman and son William Pennell.

Death of Epiphany Holland

Mr. Epiphanius (Epiphany) Holland was buried on 6th January 1730/1 at St. George's Beckenham. His short will was written in September 1730 and proved on 26th January 1731 (*PROB 11/642/147*). Epiphany was connected to *Goadby* through his father and brother, Edward; the latter died in 1722 and both were ministers at Waltham-on-the-Wolds, Leicestershire; there is a village named *Goadby* Marwood close by. He left his share of *Goadby*, to his three sisters and niece Scott, on the bond of his mother (presumably Grace Bradbury). His wife, Susannah Holland was his sole executrix. All the income from his estate was to go to his wife to provide a "*handsome maintenance to his son*". He left £2000 to her to give to her relations on her demise and the residue was to go to his son, Stephen, in trust, as he was not 21. If Stephen died, one share was to go to Epiphany's wife and another £3000 was to go to his "*daughter*" Susanna (his stepdaughter and half-sister of Stephen, brought up from the age of two) and the residue was to be divided among his three sisters, Mrs. Dorothy Warren, Grace Holland, Mrs. Mary Seayer and his niece, Catherine Scott. He asked that his friends Henry and Susannah Hoare, John Robinson and Peter Wyche should assist his wife. In addition to the will, there was a statement added on 26th January 1730, after Epiphany was deceased, to assert that John Seayer and John Robinson, both of the Parish of St. Helen's, London appeared personally to confirm that the will was in the handwriting of Epiphany Holland. In the margin, beside this statement there was a further statement, added on 20th August 1817, relating to a 1000 year lease, originally dated 7th March 1722, on land at Paglesham and Little Wakering, in Essex. Then it was part of the estate of the late Epiphany and afterwards the late Susannah Holland. These documents suggest that Epiphany did not have all his affairs in order before his death as draft bills of complaint and legal opinions continued until 1817.

Mary Holland married John Seayer at St. Helen, Bishopsgate on 15th February 1707, when they were both living in that parish. Seayer's first wife, Dorcas Gedney, was buried at St. Helen's on 28th July 1704. Epiphany's sister, Grace Holland, never married and was buried at St. Helen's on 4th January 1745. She left her estate to her nephews and niece, *viz.* Reverend Langhorne Warren, Stephen Holland and Ann Smyth, who were also executors and executrix of her will.

The Wyche family

Gray's Inn records show that in January 1734 Peter Wyche was described as the only son of Bernard Wyche, deceased, of Surat. In February 1752, Wyche was recorded in an assignment of mortgage (*MD/259/K/4*), held at Yorkshire Archaeological Society as "*late of Gray's Inn and now of Goadby, Leicestershire*" He had acquired *Goadby* in 1739, before in that year he married Elizabeth Brown, only daughter of Mary and John Brown, the father a merchant from Boston in Lincolnshire. Peter and Elizabeth Wyche had a son named Peter, born on 3rd March 1740 but the boy died before his father, the family history having been recorded by the minister at Goadby. Peter Wyche was appointed a sheriff in Lincolnshire in 1741 and he may have bought Goadby from Epiphany's relatives.

Susannah Holland and her relatives

In 1731, Epiphany's wife, Susannah Holland and mother of Stephen Holland was recorded in memorials shortly after her husband's death with land at Essex Street, Strand and along with Ralph Harwood, whose name was mentioned many times in memorials at the beginning of the eighteenth century, with properties in Tottenham.

Original documents (*D/DC 23/819,820,821*) are held at Essex Record Office and include letters of administration of Epiphany Holland granted to George Nelson, a gentleman of Essex Street, Strand, London. They include the names of Susannah Holland, as executrix of Epiphany and Stephen Holland, her son, in 1758, long after her death.

Susannah Holland was buried at St. George's Church, Beckenham on 7th February 1741. She made a lengthy will, proved on 10th February 1741/2 (*PROB 11/716/111*), which appointed John Robinson of Bridlington in the County of York and Peter Wyche, of Gray's Inn, Middlesex, as executors. Wyche was appointed guardian of her son, Stephen, "*for maintenance and his education*" and to hold money in trust and pay legacies (her late husband, Epiphany, had asked Robinson and Wyche to assist his wife, Susannah, in carrying out the instructions in his will). Epiphany had stipulated that Susannah could dispose of £2,000 to her relations. She bequeathed £500 to her "*cousin*" Mary Sumpter, a widow and if she died to her children, William, Peter, Samuel and Mary. Mary Sumpter's brother, Richard Marshall received £20. Mr. Henry Batt and his wife Elizabeth and their children, Henry, Michael, Elizabeth and Mary also received bequests. The sister of Henry Batt (the father) and Mary Pugh, a widow, also received £25 for mourning (when Henry's mother Mary Batt, née Kinsey, died in 1722, she had made bequests to Reverend Epiphany Holland and her kinswoman, Susannah Holland, his wife). Susannah bequeathed £100 to her first husband's sister, Mrs. Mary Shaller. She made a bequest of £150 to her "*cousin*", Stephen Colt, of Chatham and £50 to her "*cousin*", Joanna Colt. Her late husband's sisters received the following: Grace Holland, £400, Dorothy Warren, £200 and Mary Seayer was to receive interest from £1,000 and after her death, the principal sum was to be divided and distributed to her children. Mrs. Dorcas Seayer received £10 if she was still living (suggesting that she was old or ill). Furthermore, Reverend Langhorne Warren, son of Dorothy and his sister, Mrs. Anne Smyth, each received £100. Susannah bequeathed to the three children of her late husband's niece, *Grace* Scott, Katherine, Mary and Grace, £400 apiece (*here there was an error as Catherine Scott was the Christian name of her husband's niece and not Grace, evidenced from other documents*). She gave the interest on £800 to her "*niece*" Susanna Barrett and after her death to her daughter, also Susanna Barrett. She bequeathed money and personal belongings, including all her rings, plate, jewels and quilts to her son, Stephen Holland, when he came of age. The residue of £2,000 was to be invested by the executors, in trust for her son, to achieve the best return. If he died, it was to go to his children and if he died without issue to her daughter, Susannah Hoare. A further £4,000 out of her husband's personal estate was to go to her daughter, Susannah. She asked her son-in-law, Henry Hoare, to assist Peter Wyche with his duties. The will named her grandchildren as Henry Hoare, Colt Hoare and Susannah Hoare. Servants received various items and clothes, as well as money. The will, dated 1st October 1737, was witnessed by Anna Lane and Thomas Fox. A week later she added a codicil. A second codicil was dated 11th September 1740 and cancelled a debt to her cousin, Mary Sumpter, née Mary Marshall, of Beckenham, who had married William Sumpter of St. Andrew, Holborn, on 29th October 1713 at St. Helen's Bishopsgate, with Epiphany Holland officiating.

Church records show that William Sumpter was buried at St. George, Beckenham on 12th August 1737 and his daughter, Mary, on 13th May 1752. When the will of William Sumpter, prior to his death living at Great Russell Street was proved on 20th August 1737 *(PROB 11/ 684/368),* it confirmed that he was possessed of an annuity to be paid to Epiphany Holland, deceased and then to his widow, Susannah Holland. Its consequences were explained in a number of subsequent documents. The first, dated, 7th February 1752, was when the goods and chattels of William Sumpter, left not administered by his widow and relict, Mary Sumpter, were granted to Mary Sumpter, the elder Mary's spinster daughter, as the mother died intestate. The second repeated much of the same information and was dated 15th August 1752, six months after the inheritance had been granted to the younger Mary Sumpter. It explains that she too was then deceased and that their father's estate was granted to her brother, Peter. The third, dated 23rd February 1759, indicated that by this time Peter Sumpter was also deceased and his father, William Sumpter's estate was granted to his son, also William Sumpter.

The reference in her will to Mrs. Mary Shaller, described as her first husband's sister, appears to suggest that Susannah was a widow when she married Stephen Colt. After her son and daughter, her closest relative appears to be her "*niece*", Susannah Barrett, married, with a daughter also named Susannah Barrett. This suggests that Susannah Holland's sister or brother were dead.

Susannah Colt, Henry Hoare and his family

Susannah Colt, the daughter and an heir of Stephen and Suzannah Colt, was born after her father died in 1708 but there was no baptismal record in Surat or Bombay, as church records there did not commence until 1709. She was the half-sister of Stephen Holland, sharing their mother.

Documents held by C. Hoare & Co, who have been private bankers since 1672, confirm that a marriage settlement (*HE/1/A/27*) was agreed on 5th July 1728, among Henry Hoare of the first part, Epiphany Holland and his wife Susannah, widow of Stephen Colt, a merchant of East Indies and Susannah Colt, sole daughter and heir of Stephen Colt, of the second part and Simon Michell, Esq. of Lincoln's Inn, Middlesex, of the third part. The settlement included the castle at Stourton, dairy, malthouse and other land, referring also to leases and releases of 10th and 19th February 1722, made by Henry's father before his death in 1724. After Epiphany died, there was a further covenant (*HE/1/A/30*) dated 25th January 1730/1 between Henry Hoare and his wife Susannah to Susannah Holland, Epiphany's widow and Simon Michell, which confirms that £8,622 was part of the marriage settlement and that "*all the purchase money that will arise from the sale of the lands in Kent will be laid out in the purchase of lands in Southampton, Wiltshire, Dorset and Somerset*". This land in Kent may have been once owned by Stephen Colt. Simon Michell and his partner Charles Wood were responsible for much of the development of Spitalfields and parts of Clerkenwell (*British History Online*).

Susannah Colt was the second wife of Henry Hoare II, distinguished from his father by the nickname "*Henry the Magnificent*". The marriage of Henry Hoare of the Parish of St. Martin-in-the-Fields, London, to Mistress Susannah Colt was recorded on 5th July 1728 at the Church of St. George, Beckenham, Kent. The children of Henry and Susannah Hoare were Henry, born and died in 1729, Henry, born in 1730, Susannah, born on 15th April 1732, Colt Hoare, born on 11th November 1735 and died on 6th May 1740 and Ann Hoare, born on 27th June 1737. Only three of the grandchildren were cited in Susanna Holland's will, written on 1st October 1737; they were Henry, Colt and Susannah Hoare. She did not include Ann, the youngest child to have been born.

Stephen Holland

Stephen Holland of Beckenham in the County of Kent, Esquire, a bachelor and Sarah Lethieullier of the same place, a widow, were married on 31st August 1756 by special licence from the Archbishop of Canterbury in Oxenden Chapel, St. Martin-in-the-Fields, Westminster, by Langhorne Warren, a minister from Hampstead, in the presence of Thomas Motley and Stephen Brown, a clerk. Sarah's surname was recorded as *Lethieullier*. They were married in the summer months and may have been visiting relatives. Sarah's mother was already dead. Langhorne Warren was Stephen Holland's cousin and Thomas Motley may have acted in place of her father. Motley was a good friend of her late husband's father, William Lethieullier, also deceased and an executor of his will, as he was of the will of Sarah's own father.

In 1750, there was a decree of the Attorney General in suit of Reverend Langhorne Warren and Edward White, a schoolmaster, pleading against Stephen Holland and John Jackson in relation to money left by Sir William Langhorne for a rectory and charity school. It was, therefore, a dispute between cousins, Stephen Holland and Langhorne Warren.

Joseph Foster's *Alumni Oxonienses 1715-1886* lists:

WARREN, LANGHORN: Only son of Robert, of Charlton, Kent, Doctor. Matriculated from Brasenose College on 11[th]April, 1728, aged 17:B.A. 1735, Rector of Charlton, 1736, vicar of Hampstead 1740, until his death in 1763.

Langhorne Warren's daughter, Anne Warren married Christopher Horsfall on 20th October 1766 at St. Nicholas' Cathedral, Newcastle upon Tyne. The death of Christopher Horsfall was reported in *St. James' Chronicle* on 12th January 1793, at Blackheath. He was then a Lieutenant Colonel in the 58th Regiment of Foot and the family moved frequently because of his military career. Samuel Weyman Wadeson, *attorney at law*, whose name appears later in the narrative in connection with the land at South Tottenham, was a witness to his will, proved on 23rd March 1793.

Stephen Holland farmed at Beckenham. He is seen in documents in 1758, a few years after he married, when two men were committed to the new gaol at Southwark for stealing seven fowl, the property of Stephen Holland of Beckenham.

At Hoare's Bank, Fleet Street, there is an original letter from many years earlier, dated 30th January 1755, written by Henry Hoare, from Fleet Street, to his nephew, Richard at Stourhead, in which he gave his consent for the younger man to stay there as long as he wanted. The letter continued:

I rejoice to hear Dear Lady Ann is recovered to all and well enough for a dance and that you and Mr. Holland had so fine a day at Stourhead and that what is there in creation struck you, those are the fruits of industry and applied to business and shows what great things by it, the envy of all the indolent who have no claims to temples, grotts, bridges, rocks, exotick pines, ice....

Lady Ann was Richard Hoare's daughter and he showed concern for her well-being. She was to marry her cousin Richard Hoare a year later. This letter was written over a year before Sarah Lethieullier, as she then was, married Stephen Holland.

Stephen banked with Hoares, and the ledgers containing details of his bank accounts are still at the bank in Fleet Street. Customers' accounts were not recorded alphabetically to prevent other family members being able to find out information about monies in and out of accounts but there are indexes at the front of ledgers. Once or twice a year, the customer would visit to check that his or her account was in order. Some of the names are familiar, such as

Thomas Motley, Frances Austen and Captain Thomas Baddison. Baddison paid Stephen Holland two sums each of £1,000 in 1765 and thereafter the running balance of his account reduced. Holland was receiving interest and sometimes paying large amounts to himself and receiving money from Lord Oxford. On 1ˢᵗ June 1768 (*Volume 69, Folio 231*), Mr. Holland paid on a bill to Mr. Barker. This was the last entry for him, as below it was written "*Mrs. Sarah Holland, widow £3,722.10., sole executrix*". Others identifiable within *Hoare's Bank, A Record 1672-1955, Appendix IV* who were clients of Hoare's Private bank between 1673 and 1718 include Samuel Pepys (1680), John Holworthy and John Ward (1694), Sir John Lethieullier (1698), Sir Stephen Evance (1699), Charles Yallop (1701) and Elihu Yale (1714).

At the London Metropolitan Archives, references to Stephen Holland relate to title deeds for a lease of one year for property in Collingbourne in Kingston in 1766, involving Thomas, Lord Bruce, the Right Honourable Robert Brudenell of St. George's, Hanover Square, Middlesex and Stephen Holland. Further references in 1790 indicate that Stephen Holland had been an executor of the Brudenell's will but he was by then deceased. The original document related to a marriage settlement. On 17ᵗʰ February 1761, Susanna Boyle, a widow, daughter of Henry Hoare II and a niece of Stephen Holland by his half-sister, Susannah Colt, married Thomas, Lord Bruce.

Stephen Holland was buried at St. George, Beckenham on 29ᵗʰ June 1768. The parish church, where he was buried, was demolished and replaced in 1885 and some of the original monuments have been replaced in the newer church building with many of the headstones in the churchyard being damaged in the War by two bombs. Joan Conway has been especially diligent in collecting information on the headstones from old records compiled at the beginning of the twentieth century. A large memorial, high up on the wall in St. George, Beckenham, has the following touching inscription dedicated to Stephen Holland.

To the memory of Stephen Holland who died June 22nd 1768 aged 47
Could virtue prolong life
His family friends and the poor had not mourned the early loss of so truly
valuable and good in a man
His very amiable disposition rendered him engaging to his superiors
His sincerity and sociability to his friends and equal
His kind charity and condescension
to the poor and the distressed
The rewards follow him.

Next to his memorial plaque are others related to the Colt Hoare family from Nine Elms from a later period.

Probate was granted on 30ᵗʰ July 1768 (*PROB 11/941/198*) and Stephen Holland left his estate to his "*beloved wife, Sarah and her heirs*".

Susanne Baddison was a witness to Stephen Holland's will. She was the daughter of Edmund Smyth and Stephen's cousin, Anne Warren and the god-daughter of Stephen's mother, Susannah Holland. The will of Edmund Smyth was written in February and proved on 6th March 1767. It might be presumed that his wife, Anne, was dead as she was not cited in the will and he referred to his daughter as the wife of Thomas Baddison. Susanne Smyth had married Thomas Baddison on 14th April 1759 at St. George, Stepney and they had one child also named Susanne. A will was proved on 7th July 1770 for Thomas Baddison, then living in the Parish of St. George the Martyr. The elder Susanne Baddison wrote her will in 1768 and added codicils in October 1770, Sarah Holland, widow of Stephen Holland, being a witness to her will. When her will was proved on 26th February 1771 Susanne was shown to have been living prior to her death at Devonshire Street, near Regent's Park, in the Parish of St. George the Martyr. She bequeathed money to her worthy friends Sarah Holland, John and Hannah Keeble of the Parish of St. George, Hanover Square and Erasmus Warren, among others. By then a widow, her beneficiaries included her mother-in-law, Mary Baddison, her brothers-in-law, Edmund and Phillip and her only daughter, Susanne. She left £2000 to Erasmus Warren and £500 to Sally Keeble, the daughter of John and Hannah Keeble. Thomas and his widow Susanna Baddison were buried in the churchyard at Hampstead, along with her uncle Langhorne Warren and her grandfather and grandmother, Robert and Dorothy Warren. The names of various members of the Warren family appear in the wills of Epiphany, Susannah, Stephen and Sarah Holland, as executors and beneficiaries. They were related to the Holland family through marriage because Epiphany Holland's sister was Mrs. Dorothy Warren.

Sarah Holland's Legacy

Sarah Lethieullier and Stephen Holland gave their addresses as being in Beckenham in Kent, when they married in 1756 and Sarah's will (*PROB 11/1055/94*), proved on 8th July 1779, listed a house in Beckenham, which she gave to Erasmus Warren, the son of Stephen's cousin, Langhorne Warren. However, among this family and its circle, many of the properties and locations included in wills, such as Wilmington, Charlton, Beckenham, Greenwich and Sutton at Hone, are relatively close together.

Sarah Holland left a farm in the Parish of Tottenham in Middlesex to Rachel Waller and Margaret Lethieullier as "*tenants in common and not as joint tenants*". She was quite specific in her instructions regarding the landed estates. There were three pieces or parcels of land identified in the will, *viz.* the farm in the Parish of Tottenham, Middlesex, the farm at Battlebridge in the County of Essex with all land and the meadows adjoining Hatfield Mill and the copyhold lands and hereditaments in the County of Suffolk. The estate at Battlebridge, Essex was left to Erasmus Warren, the father. Hannah's daughter, Sally Keeble was left the landed estate in Suffolk that had reverted to Sarah after the death of her brother, with a reversion to Erasmus Warren, Stephen Holland's cousin, once removed.

Sarah bequeathed £500 to Colt Hoare, grandson of Henry Hoare II and Susannah Colt and son of Richard Hoare and his first wife, Ann and £200 each to Lady Frances Bruce and the Honourable Charles Bruce, children of Richard Hoare's second marriage to Frances Acland. Susannah Hoare/Colt was Stephen Holland's half-sister, who died in 1743.

Samuel Sumpter of Rochester in Kent, a relative of her mother-in-law, received a bequest of £200.

Sarah Holland bequeathed significant sums of money and annuities to her relatives and those of her deceased husband, many of whom were women. She left bequests to Mrs. Anne Warren, wife of Reverend Erasmus Warren of Hampstead, Anne Horsfall, wife of Captain Horsfall and Eleanor Lynne, a widow. The latter two were the daughters of Langhorne Warren. Stephen Holland's cousins once removed, the three daughters of Edward Holland, received annuities and bequests. Catherine Pennell, a widow, inherited £200; Mary, a spinster, £100; Grace Honnor, a widow, £100. Sarah gave £200 to her servant Claudius Pinot.

Many members of the family of Susanna Siggurs, then a widow, received in Sarah's will sizeable amounts ranging from £100 to £200. Susanna Barrett, mother of Susanna Siggurs, was described in her will by Stephen Holland's late mother, Susannah Holland as her "*niece*". Stephen Holland and Susanna Siggurs' mother, Susanna Barrett, were cousins. William Siggurs, a bachelor and baker of Ware, married Susanna Barrett, a spinster, in the Sun Coffee House, London, on 3rd January 1743, under the rules of the Fleet (*in 1710 there was a Sun Coffee House on Threadneedle Street*). The wedding was recorded by Walter Wyatt in his Fleet notebooks in a register of non-conformist marriages, located at The National Archives. The groom's abode was Hertfordshire, as was the bride's. Susanna Siggurs' children were Susanna Thorpe, Thomas Holland Siggurs, Elizabeth Boot and Mary Siggurs. "*Sukey Barrett*" Siggurs was baptised on 16th October, 1743, Elizabeth Siggurs on 19th July 1749 and Thomas Holland Siggurs, on 24th April 1752 all at Ware, Hertford and all children of William and Susan or *Sukee* Siggurs. Susanna Siggurs, one of the daughters, married a Mr. Thorpe and her will was proved on 22nd July 1805, prior to which she was a widow living at Corsham in Wiltshire. Elizabeth Siggurs married James Boot in 1772 at Saint Leonard, Shoreditch and her daughter was identified as Sarah Holland Boot. Thomas and Lydia Siggurs named their daughter Susanna, who was baptised, on 14th May 1777 at Ware in Hertford.

A will at Essex Record Office (*D/ABW 98/2/33*) archived in the Archdeacon records of the Commissary of Bishop of London, indicates that Thomas Siggurs of Ware in the County of Hertford, a baker, asked that his wife, *Clim* Siggurs, should continue the trade at his house at Ware, for the remainder of his lease and if she gave that up it was to go to his son William Siggurs, with his tools, troughs, scales and weights. All his wearing apparel was to go to his son. He specified that his grandson, Thomas Holland Siggurs, who would have been only three years of age, was to receive forty shillings and a further four pounds and forty shillings, to be paid within three months of the testator's death. All the rest of his personal estate was to go to his wife, Clim Siggurs and Jonathan Brown, who were appointed executors. The will was proved in Essex on 21st

April 1755, with the mark of the executors. Clim Stevenson married Thomas Siggurs, at Ware, Hertford, on 19th June 1739 (*familysearch.org*) suggesting that Clim was his second wife, as his son, William, married in 1743.

The will of William Siggurs, of Ware, in Hertfordshire, then a gardener, was proved in the Commissary Court on 11th January 1780, approximately six months after it was written on 22nd July 1779 (*LMA: DL/C/426/197*). He left his stocks and shares along with his goods and chattels to his wife, Susanna, named as sole executrix. William was a baker in 1743, working for his father and mother and a gardener in 1779. Sarah Holland wrote in her will, first written in April 1779, that Susanna Siggurs was a widow but there may have been be a mistake in the transcription.

Sarah's will was dated 17th April 1779, followed by a codicil in May 1779 and proved on 8th July 1779. The value totalled some £7,000 at annuities of 4%.

John and Hannah Keeble

Musgrave's Obituary confirms that John Keeble lived between the years 1711 and 1786. He was an organist, born in Chichester around 1711. He was encouraged as a chorister at Chichester Cathedral by Thomas Kelway, the organist there from 1720 until his death in 1744 and harpsichord maker to the Queen.

The *Oxford Dictionary of National Biography* describes how John Keeble arrived in London around 1736, when he applied unsuccessfully to be the organist at St. Bride's Church, Fleet Street, the first of Wren's new churches in the City of London. He was acquainted with various notable people who were well-known in the field of research into Greek music theory. It was their interests that were to influence his own music in years to come. Keeble produced a number of books, including *Theory of Harmonics and An Illustration of the Grecian Harmonica,* published in 1784, shortly before his death. Another was *Forty Interludes to be Played between the Verses of the Psalms in Organ Music,* which is still consulted today. His works were reviewed, some unfavourably, in the *European Magazine.*

He was also by all accounts a successful harpsichord player and teacher, who had wealthy and talented pupils, notably John Burton and Jacob Kirkman, who went on to become renowned in their own right. As early as 1738, Keeble was one of the first people to subscribe to the *"Fund for the Support of Decay'd Musicians"* probably in consequence of his own humble background. This was to become the *Royal Society of Musicians*. He was the first organist at the *Rotunda* in Ranelagh Gardens, opening in 1742 and playing there until 1772. Various sources give the dates 1737 or 1744, when he became an assistant to Thomas Roseingrave, who was the official organist at St. George's, Hanover Square. Roseingrave was, according to some, *"insane"*. They initially shared the salary for the job, until Roscingrave's death, given in different accounts as 1759 or 1766. In 1750 it was increased from £20 to £30 and as recorded in the Vestry minutes, was £50 when Roseingrave died. John Keeble became the sole organist by 1750, due to the indisposition of his partner. It is said that George Frederick Handel, who worshipped at St. George's Church, recommended Keeble for the job over another applicant called Mathieson.

Around 1751, Canaletto, who stayed in England for ten years from 1746, painted two views of the riverside of both Ranelagh Gardens in Chelsea, where John Keeble played the organ and the Tyers' family's Vauxhall Pleasure Gardens, where Mozart played in 1764. These paintings were subject to a bar on export until 2006 as there are so few depictions of this important part of the history of the leisure activities of eighteenth century London. They were saved from export in May 2006 by the heir to the *Littlewood's* business, Sir Peter Moores, who shows the paintings, as part of his collection, at his own gallery at Compton Verney, a Grade I listed 18th Century country house in Warwickshire.

On 1st September 1747, John Keeble married Hannah Painter of New Bond Street, at St. Botolph without Bishopsgate, which at that time had no organ. The event was recorded in the Whitehall Evening Post and Hannah was said to be *"a very agreeable young lady with a handsome fortune"*.

John Keeble died on Sunday evening, 24th December 1786 and his will, dated 27th July 1786 was proved on 16th January 1787 (*PROB 11/1149/168*). It referred to a marriage settlement on 25th July 1786, between Sally and Captain Thomas Hamilton, his daughter and son-in-law. Keeble's address was in Conduit Street in the Parish of St. George's, Hanover Square, where he had been organist for forty years. His daughter married by special licence on 26th July 1786, in St. George's, even though she was a resident of the parish. The two witnesses were John Keeble, her father, as her mother had already died and Jane Ponsonby, possibly a friend or perhaps the sister of her husband. John Keeble wrote his will a few days after his daughter's marriage.

Keeble's will named Reverend Dr. John Russell Greenhill, son of the late Samuel Greenhill by his first wife. Samuel Greenhill had died in 1749. John Keeble left shares in and money loaned to the Mines Royal and Mineral and Battery Works Company to his son-in-law, Thomas. The remainder of his real and personal estate went to John Russell Greenhill and Augustus Pechell, his executors, based on several earlier trusts made for purposes of his daughter's marriage settlement. A residue went to his only daughter. He also left money to his nephews, John Roche Heaums and Peter Heaums. John Roche Heaums, a bachelor, lived in Lambeth and *"Old Change"*, College Hill in London before his death in 1815 at Richard's Place in Bath. Peter Heaums who was an apothecary, married Catherine and they lived at Saint Mary's Lambeth. He died in 1818; his wife in 1832. Peter and Catherine had at least one daughter called Frances. A Sally Keeble Heaums, obviously connected to the Keeble family, who married Edmund Hacon at the Old Church, St. Pancras in 1824, was a beneficiary. Other nieces who were beneficiaries in his will were Elizabeth and Mary Kitching. Keeble probably had two sisters who married men with the surnames of Heaums and Kitching.

John Keeble requested in his will to be buried in the same place as his wife at Ramsholt in Suffolk. All Saints Church at Ramsholt in Suffolk sits alone and isolated, overlooking the River Deben on a small estuary. It is an old, flint building with a Norman circular, some say oval-shaped tower but certain parts, such as the pews, were added in the nineteenth century. Inside, at the front on the right hand side, overlooking the alter, is a large marble plaque high on the wall, erected by their daughter, Sally, dedicated to John Keeble and his wife. The plaque reads:

> Near this place are interred the remains of John Keeble, Esq. who died 24th December 1786 aged 76 years and of Hannah his wife who died 21st May 1774 aged 56 years. To their honoured memory this monument was erected as a tribute of filial affection.

In the churchyard there are headstones dedicated to the Waller family. Hannah Keeble died intestate.

At the age of 27, Sally Keeble was married to Captain Thomas Hamilton, the son of Dr. William Hamilton of Dublin. He had risen through the ranks to be Rear Admiral of the Blue, 1809, White, 1810 and Red, 1812 and was appointed Vice-Admiral of the Blue on 4th June 1814. He was also late Commissioner of His Majesty's Navy, at the time of his death, a position held by Horatio Nelson in 1801. This title was sixth in the Navy hierarchy and promotion usually came after the death of the person of an existing holder of the rank. Thomas Hamilton died on 27th June 1815 at Southampton, aged 60 and his death was reported in *Jackson's Oxford Journal* and in the *Caledonian Mercury* in early July. His will was proved on 6th July 1815. It was short and simple and he left everything to his wife. The family was living at Newman Street in London.

Sally Hamilton's will was proved on the 30th September 1835 at Marylebone in London. She left her house and part of her estate, first to her daughter Elizabeth Fitzgerald and her son-in-law Colonel Edward Fitzgerald, secondly to her daughter-in-law, Susan Hamilton and thirdly to her other daughter-in-law, Emma, who was the widow of her son, William Augustus Hamilton. She also left funds to her friends, Lady Onslow, widow of Admiral Richard Onslow and Robert Greenhill Russell of Chequers, the only son of John Russell Greenhill, who was named in the will of Sally's father and had taken the name of Russell when he inherited Chequers. Sally's other son was not named in the will, which was written originally in 1825 but a codicil was added on 4th October 1833 when her daughter-in-law, Susan Hamilton, had remarried and changed her name to Carr.

Sally Hamilton's eldest son was John Leveson Hamilton, born on 17th July 1788, either at Much Hadham or Little Hadham in Hertfordshire, as the couple had moved from London shortly after their marriage. *Volume 2 of Clerical and Parochial Records of Cork, Cloyne and Ross compiled by W. Maziere Brady D.D. from Parish Registers and Family Papers,* in 1863 explains that John was the son of Admiral (*he was in fact Vice-Admiral*) Hamilton of the Royal Navy and Sally Keeble. John Leveson Hamilton graduated in 1810 with a first class degree in Mathematics, from Christ Church Oxford, coincidentally at the same time as Henry Hatsell, a relative of Stephen Evance. Hamilton married Susan Woodward and they had a daughter named Elizabeth Sally born in 1821 and a son named Leveson Russell Hamilton, born in 1822. The father wrote and published books of sermons. He was admitted to Holy Orders and was the rector of the Church of St. Peter and St. Paul at Ellesborough from 1823 to 1825, where he died on 5th August 1825 at the early age of thirty-seven. Shortly after that, Susan's father, Dr. Woodward, died at Nice on 11th December 1828 and his burial place, on 8th January 1829, was in the Cathedral of Cloyne, where there is a tablet to his memory. His father was the Bishop of Cloyne and he too is commemorated in the Cathedral.

On 9th September 1829, Susan Hamilton, then a widow, married Reverend Thomas William Carr, at South Stoneham, Hampshire. Although he was born on 6th June 1801 in the Parish of St. George's, Bloomsbury, he ended his life at Southborough in Kent and his will was proved on 3rd October 1840. They had three children together; Thomas William, Lucy Emily and Frank Culling Carr. Susan's daughter by her first husband went on in 1842 to marry Reverend Henry Mengden Scart. Susan Carr died on 8th July 1834, not long after the birth of these three children and before her mother-in-law, Sally Hamilton.

William Augustus Hamilton, the second son of Sally and Thomas Hamilton, was born on 9th February 1790 and baptised on 19th March in that year at Buriton in Hampshire, near Petersfield. The son's marriage was recorded in the *Asiatic Journal Monthly Miscellany* in 1824, which reported that W. A. Hamilton, son of the late Vice-Admiral Thomas Hamilton, was married to Emma, third daughter of J. Clegg of Liverpool. They were married for less than a year and there were no children. He died before his mother wrote her will in 1825. His widow, Emma Hamilton died on 19th May 1866 at Silverdale, near Lancaster, aged 67.

30

William Lethieullier (1711-1775): grocer

It was Rachel Waller, daughter of William Lethieullier, who in 1779 inherited from Sarah Holland, her aunt by marriage, half of the estate in South Tottenham.

William was the third surviving son of William Lethieullier of Beckenham, after John and Manning and the second son of that name born to the parents. The first William, baptised, on 23rd April, 1704, was buried in St. George's churchyard at Beckenham on 21st March 1708. There is a record of a second William Lethieullier born to William Lethieullier and Mary at All Hallows, Staining on 25th October 1711.

William Lethieullier, a bachelor and merchant of the Parish of Welbrook, London married Rachel Farmer of Ironmonger's Place, Bermondsey, on 8th November 1730, at Fleet Prison, under the rules of the Fleet. Their marriage was conducted by a minister but it was not performed in a normal church.

The Fleet records show that William Lethieullier, son of William Lethieullier and Rachel, was baptised at "*Mr. Farmers*" on 25th June 1732. Mr. Farmer was his grandfather and the father of Rachel. The same entry includes the statement that the child's parents were "*married by me*" (a Mr. Horne) on 29th December 1730, which is at odds with the their marriage records. All the other children of William and Rachel Lethieullier were baptised at St. Andrew Undershaft in Leadenhall Street, near his business, so it is likely that the family kept a house in London. Of the children, Rachel was baptised on 29th November 1738, Letitia on 3rd January 1741, Mary on 26th April 1743, Margaret on 13th October 1747 and Challenor on 29th September 1749, the last being named after his uncle Thomas Challenor; Mary Farmer had married Thomas Challenor on 8th January 1739 at St. Anne and St. Agnes, Aldersgate, in London. Rachel and Margaret were the only children to survive to adulthood. When the grandfather, William Lethieullier of Beckenham, died, he left his third son his messuage and tenement, then in the occupation of Bassett, at Dartford Heath and two woods called "*Haxells and Death Springe*".

William seems to have been involved in property acquisitions connected to his trading activities in the City. He and his brother-in-law, Thomas Challenor, bought a lease for 21 years for the "*Pewter Pot*" at St. Andrew, Undershaft in 1752. William Lethieullier was, *inter alia*, a "*Turkey merchant*" at Suffolk Lane, Cannon Street as was his cousin Benjamin Lethieullier, who was a director of the Bank of England from 1734 to 1760. It is likely that Challenor and Lethieullier were trading in herbs, spices, and other goods from Constantinople in Turkey, Italy, Sweden, Barbados and the West and East Indies. Around that time *"grocers were powerful merchants because they traded in oriental spices and drugs essential for alleviating the medieval diet"* according to Gillian Bebbington in her book *London Street Names* (*Batsford, 1972*). Henry Roseveare's *Markets and Merchants of the Late Seventeenth Century, The Maresco-David Letters (1668-1680) published for The British Academy, 1991* offers an immensely thorough and interesting account of every aspect of that business.

Sir Thomas Challenor and his wife, Dame Mary were buried in the Church of the Virgin Mary, Walthamstow. He was described as an alderman of the City of London and living at Walthamstow. His will was proved on 2nd June 1766 and that of his wife on 16th January 1770. She was then living at Ashstead in Surrey. Dame Mary's will was witnessed by her brother-in-law, William Lethieullier and the latter's son-in-law, James Waller. She left the bulk of her estate, including a coach house and stables at Billiter Lane, off Fenchurch street, to her sister Rachel and her nieces Rachel and Margaret Lethieullier. Mary did not have any children.

William Lethieullier died at Charlotte Street, Bloomsbury. His death was recorded in the *Daily Advertiser* on Thursday as 13th April 1775 but the *London Magazine* published it as 19th April 1775. Church records show that William Lethieullier, Esq., of Bloomsbury, was buried, in linen, in a vault under the churchyard at St. Mary Magdalene, Bermondsey, on 19th April 1775. His age was shown to be 64. Records show that there was a charge for opening the vault, suggesting that he was buried with other members of his family, possibly his children and many members of his wife's family (Farmer) were also from the Parish of St. Mary Magdalene, Bermondsey. When his will was proved on 16th May 1775 (*PROB 11/1008/82*), William was shown to have been living at East End, Finchley and working as a grocer at Leadenhall Street in the City of London. He had first written his will in 1769 and asked his nephews, Jonathan and Thomas Tyers to be the trustees of *"all his estate both real and personal"*, declaring that they should each have for their troubles a ring to the value of thirty guineas. He made bequests to his son-in-law James Waller, his sister-in-law, Lady Mary Challener, his sister Mary Scrimsour and god-daughter Mary Farmer, a spinster; his daughter Margaret Lethieullier was to receive £3,000 when she married. William instructed the trustees possibly to sell parts of his estate to invest in Government stocks and parliamentary funds and to pay rents and profits from other land to his wife and daughters in equal proportions; he identified the house at Dartford Heath, Kent and the two woods which he had inherited from his father; his wife was sole executrix and the estate was undoubtedly substantial. A codicil was added in October 1773. William withdrew his legacy and bequest to his nephew Jonathan Tyers as the latter had *"refused to accept of the said trust"* and he increased the amount he gave to his sister, Mary Scrimsour.

Rachel Lethieullier died intestate two years later, aged 73, at her home at Kensington Square, where she may have been living with her daughter Rachel, as her son-in-law, James Waller, was at one time a minister at St. Mary

Abbot, Kensington. She was buried with her husband at St. Mary Magdalene, Bermondsey on 6th February 1777. If ages given at death are correct, they indicate that Rachel Lethieullier was seven years older than her husband and was born in 1704. In March 1806, Rachel Waller, made a claim upon her late mother's estate, valued at £450, in the form of an administration.

William Lethieullier had already settled £3000 on his daughter Rachel for her marriage to the Reverend James Waller of St. Andrew, Undershaft, at Leadenhall Street in the City of London. James Waller was the clerk and rector of that parish when he married the younger Rachel Lethieullier on 19th November 1767. Angel Chancey, the previous rector of the parish was buried in May 1761 so Waller took over the parish after his death. Her father and James Waller were witnesses at the wedding, James Waller being, most likely, the bridegroom's father. The church still stands on the corner of Leadenhall Street, close to the Lloyds building and near to her father's grocery business at Leadenhall.

Jonathan and Thomas Tyers, named as trustees of the estate of William Lethieullier, were the sons of Jonathan Tyers (1702-1767), William's brother-in-law. Jonathan Tyers, of the Parish of St. Mary Magdalene had married Elizabeth Langley, a widow, at St. Edmund the King and Martyr in 1722. Anne Tyers married Edmund Farmer, the brother of Mary Farmer and of Rachel Farmer, the latter who married William Lethieullier. The elder Jonathan, Elizabeth and Anne Tyers were the children of Thomas Tyers, who died in 1721 and whose home address was White Gardens, in the Parish of St. Mary Magdalen, Bermondsey, in Surrey. Church records show that Anne Tyers was born on 13th February 1701 and Jonathan, around 12th April 1702. In his will, Thomas' beneficiaries were his second wife, Anne and his children Jonathan, Elizabeth and Anne.

Anne Tyers and Edmund Farmer had at least four children named Anne, born in 1735, Mary, born in 1739, Sarah and Richard, born in Wandsworth in 1742. Edmund Farmer was a calico printer, involved in the clothing industry. This may have been his connection to the Tyers family, who were in the booming leather business, being Bermondsey *fellmongers* – dealers in skins and hides. When Edmund died in Wandsworth in 1770, his will included a bequest to William Farmer, whose mother was Margaret and his late father was John Farmer, who had lived in Portugal. It might be presumed that John Farmer was Edmund Farmer's brother. (It might be noted that Sarah Holland, in her will, bequeathed £50 to Mary Farmer, the wife of a William Farmer of Beckenham.) Other recipients were Elizabeth Wood, Edmund's niece and Richard and Mary, his own children. Anne and Edmund's daughter, Anne may have died by that time. The last bequest was to Daniel Farmer whom he oddly described as his *"brother-in-law"* from Mile End and whose children were Daniel, Sophia, Elizabeth, Edmund and Titus Farmer.

Jonathan Tyers' sister Elizabeth married William Hall in 1737 at Westminster. His daughter, Elizabeth Tyers, married John Wood on 12th May 1749 at St. Margaret, Westminster, the church beside Westminster Abbey. Their children were George Rogers Wood, John William Wood, Mary Challenor

Wood, Margaret Tyers Wood, Rachel Wood and Emily Wood. Mary Challenor Wood was named after Dame Mary Challenor, formerly Farmer, the wife of Sir Thomas Challenor.

Edmund and Anne Farmer's daughter, Mary Farmer, a spinster of Kennington Lane and the god-daughter referred to in William Lethieullier's will, died in 1789. She left some of her estate to Margaret Lethieullier, the youngest daughter of William and Rachel Lethieullier. Another recipient was Elizabeth Barrett, wife of Bryant Barrett and the grand-daughter of Jonathan Tyers. A third recipient was Rachel Waller, the wife of Reverend Doctor Waller of Kensington and the eldest daughter of William Lethieullier. She was to receive an income of £200 a year.

Jonathan Tyers died, aged 58, at his house at Spring Gardens, Vauxhall at the end of June, 1767. The *London Evening Post* reported that he was buried on Sunday evening in the family vault at St. Mary, Magdalen, Bermondsey. His burial was recorded there on 5th July 1767. (In the same edition it was reported that ladies were to be fined £5 for wearing painted and dyed calicoes, commonly known as chintz. The Farmer family were in the calico business.) Jonathan referred in his will to his brother-in-law, Edmund Farmer, the husband of Anne Tyers. The will was witnessed by William Lethieullier, also his brother-in-law. William Lethieullier chose to be buried in the Tyers vault at St. Mary Magdalen, so clearly they were close.

Elizabeth Tyers, the widow of Jonathan Tyers, died at the house of her son-in-law, in Southampton, in February 1771. She did not leave a great inheritance to her children and grandchildren, though her sons had inherited the business. In 1785, Tom, a great friend of Doctor Johnson, sold his share to his brother Jonathan and changed its name to Vauxhall Gardens. Jonathan Tyers died in 1792 at an advanced age. According to an account in Manning and Brays *The History and Antiquities of the County of Surrey*, his only daughter and heir was then married to Bryant Barrett, who ran the business until his own death in 1809. It then passed to one of his sons, George Roger Barrett, another being Reverend Jonathan Tyers Barrett, until the former's death.

It was the elder Jonathan Tyers who was famous for his involvement with the Vauxhall Pleasure Gardens and his establishment of the *"Wits' Club"*. The Gardens had existed from around 1660 and were managed by Tyers before he bought a share of the business in 1729 and the remainder in 1758. They were situated south of the River Thames, near what is now Lambeth Palace Road, the site being now bordered by Goding Street on the west, St. Oswald's Place on the east, Leopold Street and Vauxhall Walk to the north and Kennington Lane on the south. Today, Tyers Street and Jonathan Street in the Vauxhall area recall the legacy of the family. Sculptures and other artworks were commissioned by Tyers one of which was of Handel by Roubiliac. Originally on the site there had been a single building but Tyers added supper boxes and commissioned paintings for the walls by Francis Haymen. One of them was a portrait of the Tyers family in 1740 which is now at the National Portrait Gallery. Other attractions included ruins, arches, statues, a cascade, music room and Chinese pavilions. William Lethieullier and John and Edmund Farmer had season passes, in the form of medallions, to the Vauxhall Pleasure Gardens and Wits' Club. The Gardens were a successful enterprise, considered to be beautiful and the place to be seen. People used to walk around enjoying orchestras, refreshments and other entertainment.

Tickets cost a shilling and season tickets were sold for a guinea. Even the Prince of Wales partook of the Garden's entertainment and Samuel Pepys attended on many occasions before his death in 1703, he having moved to Clapham at the turn of the century. In 1732 there was a special event called "*Ridotto al fresco*" when the entrance fee was one guinea, an enormous amount of money in those days and tokens are now collectors items, some of them quite rare, especially the gold and silver ones. The high entrance fee was a way of ensuring that only those with enough wealth could enjoy the entertainment and food. Access was by boat from the north side of the river at Westminster, which apparently was quite dangerous, hence adding to the excitement of the occasion. A fireworks display in 1749, arranged to complement a performance of music composed by Handel, with 100 musicians taking part, was attended by some 10,000 people and caused London Bridge to be closed for three hours. It was reported in a newspaper in 1784, that twenty years before, old Jonathan Tyers shut up the business early in August, giving as his reason that he had tired of collecting money. It was estimated that he had made profits in excess of £12,000 for that season. The Pleasure Gardens continued to be operated by the family for over a hundred years. One might speculate how Rachel Waller (Lethieullier) and her husband, a minister, reconciled the fact that her father, William Lethieullier, was a grocer with a taste for pleasure.

31

Heirs of Stephen Holland – Rachel Waller and Margaret Pinckard

The *Rent Charge Books for Tottenham*, at Bruce Castle Museum, show that in 1779 and 1780 parcels of land were recorded as being owned by Sarah Holland or "*Madam Holland*". Rachel and Margaret Lethieullier, daughters of William Lethieullier and grand-daughters of William Lethieullier of Beckenham, were the heirs of Stephen Holland. Rachel and Margaret were also beneficiaries of the will of Sarah Trinquand, a relative of William Gosselin, when she died in 1790. This will offers further evidence that Rachel's husband was Reverend Doctor Waller, then the vicar of Kensington. Sarah Trinquand also made reference to Rachel's eldest son, Richard Waller, who received no bequest and to other children but not by name. Rachel's sister, Margaret Lethieullier was then living at Portman Street, near Portman Square in London, in the Parish of St. Marylebone.

James and Rachel Waller had eight children, some identified in various wills. Rachel was born on 8th January 1769 and Richard Waller on 12th March 1770 (their births were registered at St. Andrew, Undershaft in the City of London). Among them were Ann, Margaret, Mary Anne and Susannah. Rachel's eldest son, Richard, became a minister and ended his days as the rector of Great Birch, Essex, where he died in 1848. Details of male family members are included in the passages below found in the J.A. Venn *Alumni Cantabrigienses from the earliest times to 1900* (Cambridge University Press; Cambridge 1922-54):

> **WALLER, RICHARD**. Adm. pensat Jesus, May 15, 1787. Of Middlesex. Matriculated Michelmas 1787; Scholar; B.A. 1791; M.A.1794. Ordained priest (London) September 20, 1795. Rector of Great Birch, Essex, 1795-1842. Disappeared from Clergy list, 1843. (Clerical guide)

...and his father:

> **WALLER, JAMES**. Admitted (age 17) at King's, a scholar from Eton, Dec.10, 1757. Son of James (and Anne). Born June 27, 1739, at St. Giles-in-the-Fields, London. Baptised there, July 23, 1739. Matriculation Michelmas, 1757; B.A.1762; M.A. 1765; D.D.1777. Fellow, 1760-5. Ordained deacon (Peterborough)

1762. Rector of St. Andrew's Undershaft and Rector of St. Martin's Ludgate. Vicar of Kensington, 1770-95. Archdeacon of Essex, 1770-95. Prebend of St. Paul's, 1766-95. Killed November 10, 1795, at Great Waltham, when in bed, by the fall of a chimneystack. (Eton College Register; Northants. Clergy; G. Mag., 1795II.972; J.D.G. Scott, Story of St. Mary Abbots, Kensington, 148-9)

James Waller's death was a dramatic one. He may have been staying at Great Waltham to perform his duties as Archdeacon of Essex. This would explain the reason for his death intestate as he died unexpectedly. The Church of St. Abbots is next to Kensington Palace and was used by their royal occupants as a place of worship before a chapel was added to Kensington Palace. Waller performed a number of roles at various churches, including St. Paul's Cathedral and was a cleric of some importance. His death warranted a special mention in the parish magazine of St. Mary Abbots, Kensington.

The burial records at Great Waltham explain the circumstances of his death. He was buried there on 11ᵗʰ November 1795. The statement said:

> James Waller was accidentally killed at the Parsonage house in this parish by the falling of a chimney in the high wind on Friday morning November 6ᵗʰ· Thus died universally regretted and to the irreparable loss of his family and friends in the fifty-seventh year of his age. The Reverend James Waller, Doctor of Divinity and Archdeacon of Essex, in him the character of the Divine and Gentleman imminently portrayed his affability and cordiality to his friends. loss immeasurable and his humanity to the Poor was boundless.

He was obviously much respected and loved by many. The *Gentleman's Magazine (Vol. 65, 1795, Pages 886, 961 & 972)* provides further details on the events of the night in question, with stories about its inclement weather. After outlining his career, the account explains that Waller was staying at Bromfield Parsonage. Mrs. Waller had just risen from her bed to take care of her eight children because of the storms, when the chimney fell. If she had been in bed, her life may also have ended that night and the ownership of the land in South Tottenham would have taken a different direction. The article also reveals that James Waller's mother died intestate in the same year, at the age of ninety.

An indenture (*MDR/1799/3/669*) of lease and release, bearing the dates 19ᵗʰ & 20ᵗʰ July 1799, was registered 28ᵗʰ August 1799; it included members of the Lethieullier and Waller families. It was between Bryant Barrett of Vauxhall and Elizabeth, his wife *"only child and heiress at law of Jonathan Tyers late of Vauxhall aforesaid Esquire deceased"*, who was the surviving devisee in trust named in the last will of William Lethieullier, formerly of Finchley, deceased and his daughters and co-heirs, Rachel Waller and Margaret Pinckard. The lease was between Rachel Waller, then a widow of Mark

Tey, Richard Pinckard of Mortimer Street, Cavendish Square and Margaret, his wife, of the one part and Reverend Stephen Eaton, of the Parish of St. Ann, Soho, a clerk and rector and George Wilson of Upper Gower Street, Middlesex, of the other part. The release was in four parts; Bryant Barrett and his wife, Elizabeth of the first part, Rachel Waller, Richard Pinckard and Margaret, his wife of the second part, Reverend Richard Waller, rector of Great Birch, Essex, Rachel, Ann, Suzanne, Marianne and Margaret Waller, spinsters of Mark Tey, only children of Rachel Waller, of the third part and Reverend Stephen C. Eaton and George Wilson of the fourth part. The people identified in the first three parts "*in consideration of ten shillings apiece*", released to Stephen Eaton and George Wilson and their heirs "*among other hereditaments in the County of Kent*", a messuage and tenement, stables, brewhouse, garden, houses, orchards, fish ponds with a close or meadow, home field, adjoining kitchen garden (3 acres) and 6 acres, in the Parish of Finchley, belonging to William Lethieullier, deceased.

Rachel Waller died in 1815, aged 72 in the Parish of St. James, Colchester in Essex, where a daughter was living at the time. Her will, written in 1813, was proved on 6th March 1815 (*PROB 11/1566/95*) and she bequeathed £3000 to her beneficiaries. Rachel gave a small amount of money to her sister, referred to only as the wife of Richard Pinckard and not by her Christian name. Rachel was nine years older than her sister. One of the female children was left a ring with diamonds surrounding a portrait of her mother. Rachel gave her son Richard a picture of her unspecified *Aunt Lethieullier*, which had previously belonged to Mrs. Trinquand.

In her will, Rachel refers to her children as Rachel, Richard, Mary Anne, Susannah Bird and Mrs. Kersteman (Margaret). The remaining two of her eight children may have died before 1813. She makes a reference to the fact that, in 1809, she had lost her daughter Ann, the wife of George Round. George Round lived at East Hill near Colchester and was a significant landowner in Essex, as the various farms and areas of land that he owned were described in his will, when he died in 1824. Ann Waller and George Round had three children, George, Eliza Ann and Edward John. Their son, George, was a banker who married Margaret and at his death in 1857 he was also living at Colchester. They appear not to have had children, as in his will he referred only to Edmund/ Edward Round, who was also a banker. This is likely to have been his married brother. His sister, Eliza Ann Round, married John Thompson.

Susannah Waller married Reverend Godfrey Bird on 21st October 1806 at St. Paul's, Covent Garden. She was his second wife and they had one son together named James Waller Bird. Geoffrey had children by his first wife, Susanna Greaves, on whom he settled much of his estate. James Waller Bird was her sole executor when she died at Brinton in Norfolk.

Margaret Waller married Reverend Andrew Kersteman some time before 1801. The *Alumni Cantabrigienses* explains that he was admitted to Christ's College, Cambridge in 1778. He was the son of William Kersteman and was born in Chelmsford in 1760. He was awarded his B.A. in 1783 and his M.A. in 1786 and was ordained deacon of Lincoln in 1784 and then became the vicar of Brenchley in Kent as well as the rector of St. Mary, Bermondsey between the years of 1814 and 1827. He died at Brenchley on 4th June 1827, aged 65.

A birth was recorded for Isabella Frances Kersteman on 14th December 1801 at Marks Tey in Essex, confirming a family connection to that area. George was baptised in 1804, Margaret in 1808 and Julia in 1812, at Brenchley in Kent, all children of Margaret and Andrew Kersteman.

The will of William Kersteman, a merchant and then gentleman of St. James Colchester, who died in 1790, clarified that he and his wife Ann had four children, one of whom was Andrew. His other children were William, Mary and Ann. Ann became the wife of Benjamin Craven and William, the son, was married by the time the will was written. The father had land at Colchester, where his wife continued to live until her death in 1797. Notes written in the margin of the will explained that Ann Kersteman, the late William's wife, had died without naming executors and that executorship was granted to one of her sons in March 1797. Then both sons, William and Andrew, had died without leaving wills and on 15th April 1829 Margaret Kersteman, the daughter of Reverend Andrew Kersteman, who had since married, following administration, became the sole beneficiary of the estate. There was no further reference to sisters Mary Kersteman, the spinster sister and Ann Craven, so they may have already died by 1822. When Benjamin Craven died, his three children, Anna Maria, Isabella and Clara were not shown to receive any legacy, so they may not have survived.

Margaret Kersteman may have been the only surviving relative or relict. She married Robert Algeo, a widower, at St. James, Westminster on 1st January 1829 and another ceremony took place at St. Mary the Virgin in Dover. Algeo died of cholera in June 1837, aged 32, when in Naples, without leaving a will. Margaret then married Sir Robert Edward Wilmot, a baronet, on 20th March 1842, who took the name of Wilmot-Horton after the death of his mother in 1872. He owned homes at Osmaston and Catton Hall, both in Derbyshire, the Catton Hall estate having been inherited from an earlier ancestor. *The Times* on Friday 25th February 1881 recorded that Sir Robert had died on 22nd September 1880 and his will had been proved by Dame Margaret Wilmot-Horton, his widow and sole executor. In Sir Robert Edward Wilmot-Horton's will, dated 18th December 1857, with a codicil added on 10th November 1874, he bequeathed his entire estate, valued at under £30,000, to his wife Margaret. Dame Margaret died on 20th September 1893, aged 85 at her home at 63 Sloane Street. Previously she had been living with her husband in Albemarle Street in London. She had no sons and the title passed to her husband's brother.

Mary Anne Waller, a daughter of Rachel Waller, never married. Probate was granted on 25th November 1829 and her will refers to a "*sister*" Mrs. Algeo and a nephew by the name of Charles Kersteman. Frances Isabella Cheval was described as a great-niece. She left her cottage in Sunning, where she had lived, to her sister Susannah and her other cottage in Westmoreland to Rachel Waller, her spinster sister. There is memorial evidence in the church at Windermere that Mary Ann Waller died at the age of 57 and was buried in the north aisle, east floor, of the church. Rachel Waller's daughter, also called

Rachel, died a spinster at 38 River Street, Bath, in the Parish of St. Saviour, in 1842. In her will she left her estate to Susannah, her sister who was living at that time in Gray's, Chadwell in Essex. The younger Rachel's nephews were identified as Reverend James Waller Bird and Charles Kersteman, a surgeon and her brother as Richard Waller.

James Waller Bird probably made his living as a rector in a number of parishes, hence the reason he was recorded in different places. At the time of the census of 1861, James Waller Bird, then aged 52, was living at the Rectory in Foulsham, along with his wife Sarah E. Bird, aged 30. They had a young family; Margaret was the eldest, aged 6 and the other children ranged in age from Emily 4, George E.G.W. 3, Richard 1 and Beatrice, one month old. Margaret was born at Briton in Norfolk but the rest of the children were born at Foulsham in Norfolk. James' wife Sarah was born at Price Reading in Berkshire and James Waller Bird's own birthplace was Little Waltham in Essex.

At the time of the census of 1871 James Waller Bird and his family were living at Contra Park, Croydon, together with five servants:

Table of occupants at Contra Park, Croydon, as per the census of 1871.

Name	Age	Birthplace
James W Bird	62	Little Waltham Essex
Laura E. Bird	41	Hampshire
Margaret E.S. Bird	16	Briston Norfolk
Frances E. Bird	14	Foulsham
Henry R. Bird	9	Reading in Berkshire
Belinda Bird	7	Foulsham
Robert Bird	6	Foulsham
Edward B. R. Bird	4	Foulsham
Ellen G.M. Bird	1 month	Bayswater, Middlesex

He was still Rector of Foulsham in Norfolk but Sarah, his first wife, was not included in the census return. James had a different wife. It is likely that Henry was Sarah's last child, born in 1862 at her mother's home at Reading in Berkshire. She had three children in quick succession; George E. G. W. Bird and his brother Richard were not shown at home, nor was their sister, Beatrice in 1871. It may be that the boys were at boarding school when the census took place and Beatrice may have died in childhood.

The next child born to James Waller Bird's family was Belinda, born in 1865. Frances E. Bird was probably Emily recorded in the 1861 Census as she was the same age. By the time of the census of 1881 many of the children were away at boarding school in various parts of the country. Henry was a student at Shepton Mallet School at Batcombe in Somerset, boarding at the Rectory; Robert was boarding at Haileybury School at Ware Hoddeston; Ellen was receiving an education and boarding at Collingwood College.

A notice of the death of Reverend James Waller Bird of Foulsham Rectory in Norfolk, and of 8 Leinster Square in London, was included in *The Times* dated Friday 5th May 1876. It was by way of a notification by his widow Laura Emily Bird, to advise anyone who had a right to make a claim on his estate. His will was proved on 1st April 1876. He had died on 20th February 1876 and his effects amounted to £7,000 in value.

On 26th April 1890, Laura Emily Bird, widow of Reverend James Waller Bird, died in London. Her will, confirming that her maiden name was Beauchamp, was proved on 30th May of that year. Her address was shown as 135 Ledbury Road but late of 7 Nottingham Place, Marylebone, where she had died. It was proved by Reverend Robert William Beauchamp of Wickmere in Norfolk, a clerk, Laura's brother, a retired Lieutenant in the Madras Native Infantry and George Edward Henry Beauchamp, nephew of the deceased, of Tyford. Her effects were valued at £2,000.

A child of the Waller/Bird family was Lieutenant Richard Sidney Bayley Bird, described as the second son of Reverend James Waller Bird of Foulsham Rectory, in Norfolk. He was the son of James Waller Bird's first wife, Sarah. After his death, an obituary in *The Times* of 14th December 1892, recorded that he had died of typhoid on Sunday 11th December at the Royal Navy Hospital at Hasler, at the age of thirty-three. His will revealed that he was a Lieutenant in the Royal Navy on Her Majesty's ship "*Marlborough*" at Portsmouth. He had died at Gosport in Hampshire, leaving £1,975 and his administration, with will, was proved at London on 25th March 1892 by his elder brother George Edward Godfrey Waller Bird, an army captain.

The Pinckard Family

In 1791 the elder Rachel Waller's sister Margaret Lethieullier married Richard Pinckard. The marriage was recorded on 18th September 1791 and showed that Richard Pinckard, a bachelor, who was at the time living in the Parish of St. Anne's, Westminster, married Margaret Lethieullier, a spinster, living in the Parish of St. Mary, Marylebone. The church is on Marylebone Road in London, close to where she was living at Portman Street. Edward Hadfield, Nathaniel De Vaux and Betsy Holland were witnesses to the wedding. Richard Pinckard was born on 15th March and baptised on 30th May 1765. When he married Margaret he was 26 and Margaret was 44; she was baptised on 13th October 1747.

Poor Rate records at Westminster City Archives show that Margaret was not living at Portman Street during the years 1783-87 but she was recorded there from 1788 until 1793. She was a next door neighbour of Edwin Lascelles, later Lord Harewood, who obviously kept a large residence, rated at £400 compared to Margaret's house, valued at £60. She was there for two years after her wedding and then in the year 1793-1794. Later, William Pinckard, Richard's brother, came to live in her house. In the indenture of 1798, when the land in Tottenham was sold, Richard Pinckard gave Great Russell Street as his address and Dr. George Pinckard is said to have lived there in 1797.

Margaret came from a wealthy family and she had acquired a substantial portfolio of property by way of inheritance. Her parents, William and Rachel Lethieullier, deceased by the time of her marriage, had owned houses in Finchley and at Charlotte Street in the West End, where Margaret was living when her father wrote his will in 1769. Furthermore, the sisters were left land by their aunt, Dame Mary Challenor. William had settled £3,000 on his daughter, as her dowry, although Margaret did not marry for another twenty years. Both sisters received bequests from various relatives as well as the farm at Tottenham from Sarah Holland, widow of Stephen Holland and Samuel Lethieullier.

The Pinckard family had a connection with Handley Hall, near Towcaster in Northamptonshire and several members had their births and deaths registered around the period 1750-1770 in old church records at St. Lawrence Church, Towcaster. It would appear that Henry, the father, married twice. His first wife was Ann (née Flesher), as evidenced in deeds and documents in the Grant-Ives Papers in Archives at Northampton, which refer to the three sons of Henry Pinckard by his wife Ann, then deceased, she having died between the years 1761 and 1765. The Flesher family lived at Greens Norton which is relatively close to Towcaster. The table below provides some of the detail:

Table of information on the Pinckard children.

Parents	Children	Birthday	Baptised Towcaster	Died
Henry & Ann	Henry	21.6.1757	27.6.1757	c.1836
	John	5.4.1759	30.5.1759	c.1796
	Thomas	11.6.1761	7.7.1761	c.1790
Henry & Rachel	Richard	15.3.1765	30.5.1765	10.4.1835
	Joseph	13.7.1766	13.9.1766	16.2.1839
	George	14.2.1768	27.2.1768	15.3.1835
	William	17.9.1769	27.2.1769	c.1851
	Ann	26.4.1772	3.6.1772	
	Rachel	9.4.1778		c.1852

The birthdays were confirmed and recorded in a diary by Dr. Richard Pinckard, son of Joseph Pinckard.

Dr. George Pinckard

Dr. George Pinckard is one of a number of Pinckards who are listed in the *Oxford Dictionary of National Biography*. He was born on 27th February 1768 at Handley Hall near Towcaster, son of Henry and Rachel Pinckard and was tutored by a clergyman relative. He studied first at St. Thomas' and Guy's Hospital, then at Edinburgh University and at Leiden, where he finally graduated in medicine in July 1792. He then travelled to visit hospitals in Paris and Geneva before going to live for a short time with his brother and sister in Switzerland. George was living at Copet, near Geneva, when the French General Montesquieu captured the city. George returned to Britain and became a licentiate of the College of Surgeons on 30th September, 1794.

In 1795 George Pinckard was appointed a physician to the Army and sailed to the West Indies and Guyana under the supervision of Sir Ralph Abercromby. During this visit he visited South America, the West Indies, Barbados and the United States. Some of his observations on the places and conditions suffered by the indigenous population were published in *Notes on the West Indies: Written During the Expedition Under the Command of the Late General Sir Ralph Abercrombie (1806)*. It was as an army officer, during the following years, that he gave accounts in letters home to his friend of the brutality meted out to slaves on the plantations. His testimony helped the cause of the abolitionists, which had been weakened by the Napoleonic War when some reacted against ideas of freedom and equality. He saw slaves wearing instruments of punishment, such as heavy iron collars with three long spikes projecting out about a foot from the collar. Their bodies were also covered in welts on their loins, from flogging. Dr. Pinckard then went to Ireland and served during the Rebellion of 1798 under General Hulse, who was related by marriage to the Lethieullier family.

He wrote on several matters and many of his writings, particularly about the treatment of slaves, are reprinted today in America. With his interest in public health issues, there can be found a number of references in a range of medical journals referencing papers he wrote about the development of such diseases as yellow fever and hydrophobia and where he outlined the course of events following three cases of men bitten by dogs. Dr. George Pinckard was responsible for the establishment of a dispensary at Bloomsbury.

There is evidence that Richard Pinckard too was involved, as an advertisement in *The Morning Chronicle* announced that the *First Anniversary Dinner of the Friends and Governors of the Bloomsbury Dispensary* charity, at 62 Great Russell Street, was to be held on Thursday 29th April 1802 at the *Crown and Anchor* on the Strand, with tickets on sale at 10s. 6d. Richard Pinckard and Julius Angerstein were among the stewards for the event.

The following announcement in April 1802, in *The Times* newspaper, was made by the Bloomsbury Dispensary at their offices, under the patronage of the Duke of Bedford.

> We give notice that all persons desirous of being inoculated for the cow-pox without any expense or letter of recommendation do attend the Dispensary on Saturday. We recommend to all who regard the health of their children, the safety of their friends and neighbours to avail themselves of the opportunity now offered as experience has shown that the cow-pox is effectual in preventing the smallpox.

It showed what an invaluable role the Dispensary played in the fighting of disease. Dr. Edward Jenner was the superintendent of inoculation and was involved in the work of the Dispensary prior to his death in 1823 (it was Jenner who developed the Smallpox vaccine, after his research was published in 1796). He was a doctor of international repute, knighted after his Smallpox vaccine discovery. Napoleon was an ardent admirer and thought that he could do no wrong. As a result, Napoleon had all his troops vaccinated against Smallpox. Among other diseases that the Bloomsbury Dispensary staff addressed were Syphilis, Tuberculosis and Chronic Bronchitis, due to the poor air quality. It was around this time that an association was made between Cholera and dirty drinking water. Living conditions at the time, including sanitation, were not necessarily always the first priority of the rich but living so close to the poor, it was in their interests that airborne disease should not spread. This view was reinforced by Roma McAuliffe in her pamphlet about the Bloomsbury Dispensary. St. George, Bloomsbury, she argued, was built because *"respectable"* people did not want to travel to St. Giles Church, situated a few hundred yards away, because of the many poor people they would encounter on their way to worship. The rich would also have had domestic staff who posed a threat of infection. During the 1850s a great many impoverished Irish people descended on the area because of the Potato Famine. *The Lancet* opined in 1857 that one house in 60 was said to be a brothel and one woman in sixteen, a whore.

Ever the visionary, George Pinckard recognised a need for an assurance company, set up solely for the needs of medical and clerical people. Following a meeting of interested parties in a tavern, it opened for business on 24th January, 1824 with Joseph Pinckard, George's brother, appointed as secretary at an annual salary of £300; Joseph later became the chairman. It was called the *Medical, Clerical and General Life Assurance Society*. It later became known as the *Clerical Medical* and continues to operate as part of the Lloyds Banking Group. The original shareholders included two Richard Pinckards, one a doctor and the other the husband of Margaret Pinckard. The building from which they operated was originally at 32 Great Russell Street but the offices moved to larger, grander premises at Lichfield House, 8 St. James Square, in 1855, its registered address now being at 33 Old Broad Street, London.

The will of Dr. George Pinckard of Bloomsbury Square was proved on 24th July 1835. When he had made his will in 1831 he added a codicil which stated that *"I give to my brother Richard Pinckard all the monies, which he is indebted to me"* He also said the same of his other brother, Joseph. There was no reference to his sister-in-law, Margaret Pinckard.

Death of Margaret Pinckard

A record of the death of Margaret Pinckard, aged 87, is contained in *Foreign Registers and Returns of Deaths Overseas*. She died on 18th December 1833 and her place of residence, at the time, was at Rue Des Vieillards, Boulogne. Richard Pinckard died on 10th April 1835, aged 70, also in Boulogne. The deaths were both recorded at the British Protestant Chapel, Upper Town, Boulogne.

Part Four

Closing the circle 1799–1952

32

Owners and occupiers of land
at Hanger Lane after 1798

A *Survey of the Parish of Tottenham in the County of Middlesex* (*CLC/270/ MS 12700A*) taken for Henry Piper Sperling, Esq. in 1798 and compiled by James Wyburd, is held at the LMA. It contains an index and abstract with details of "*owners, occupiers, fields, closes, houses, statute measure with general remarks in pencil*"; only one copy was made. A map of the Parish of Tottenham, held at Bruce Castle Museum, accompanies the survey, compiled from an actual survey by Wyburd, engraved by Bowler and Triquet appears in William Robinson's *History of Tottenham,* in 1818 and 1840 editions and provides the numbers and sizes of the parcels of land.

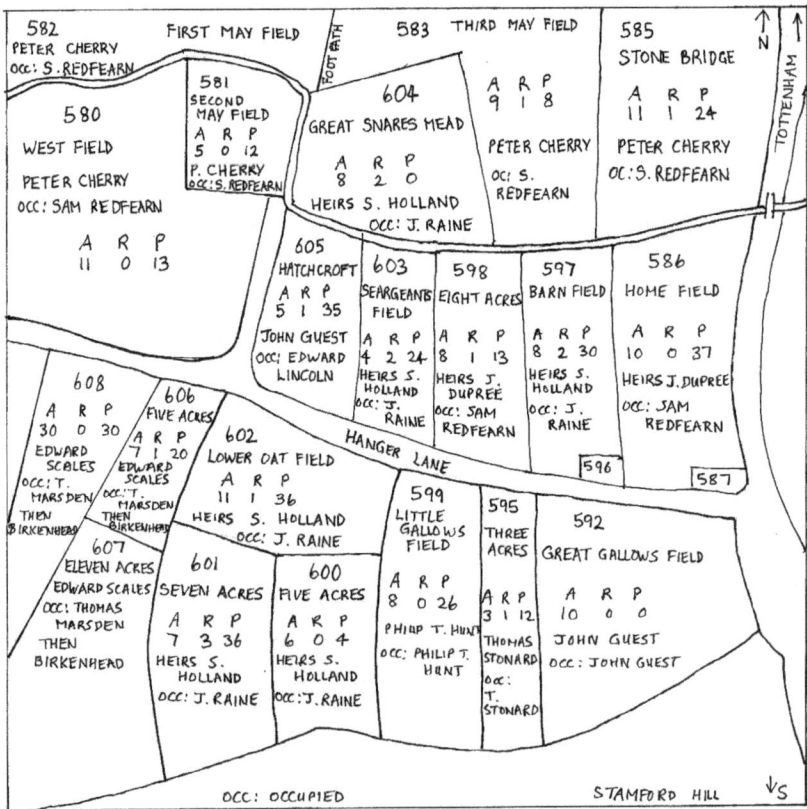

32.1 Author's map based on 1798 Survey of Tottenham by Wyburd.

The table below shows this information for the Hanger Lane area and other relevant parts of Tottenham:

Table of owners and occupiers in 1798.

Occupier/Pg	Owner	Nos.	Fields & Closes	A	R	P	Remarks
Jonothan Raine	Heirs of S. Holland	596	House, barns, stables, yard	0	1	7	
"	"	597	Barn Field	8	2	30	Hay
"	"	600	Five Acres	6	0	4	Wheat
"	"	601	Seven Acres	7	3	36	Hay
"	"	602	Lower Oat Field	11	1	36	Hay
"	"	603	Seargeants Field	4	2	24	Potatoes
"	"	604	Great Snares Mead	8	2	6	Hay
"	"	384	Wild Marsh Yolkford Shoot	3	2	35	
Page 55			Total	51	1	18	
Edward Lincoln	John Guest	605	Hatchcroft	5	1	35	Hay
Page 80			Total	5	1	35	
Thomas Marsden	Edward Scales	606	Five acres	7	1	20	Hay
crossed out and replaced with name Birkenhead	Edward Scales	607	Eleven acres	11	1	16	Hay
written in ink	E. Scales	608		30	0	30	Hay
Page 54			Total	48	3	26	
Sam Redfearn	Heirs of John Dupree	586	Home Field	10	0	37	Hay
"	"	598	Eight acres	8	1	13	Hay
Page 57			Total	18	2	10	
Philip Thomas Hunt	Philip T. Hunt	599	Little Gallows Field	7	0	26	Hay
Page 49			Total	8	0	26	
Thomas Stonard	Thomas Stonard	595	Three Acres	3	1	12	
Page 55			Total	3	1	12	
Sam Redfearn	Peter Cherry	580	West Field	11	0	13	Hay
"	"	581	Second Mayfield	5	0	12	Hay
"	"	582	First Mayfield	6	1	4	Hay
"	"	583	Third Mayfield	9	1	8	Oats
"	"	584	Third Mayfield, part	1	3	8	Hay
"	"	585	Stonebridge Field	11	1	24	Hay
Page 56			Total	44	3	29	

Occupier/Pg	Owner	Nos.	Fields & Closes	A	R	P	Remarks
John Guest	John Guest	592	Great Gallows Field	10	0	0	Hay
"	"	590	House, yard & garden	1	2	0	
"	"	591		0	2	0	
Page 80			Total	12	0	0	
William Rugman	Heirs of S. Holland	556	Nine acres	8	3	11	Hay
"	Mr Warren	653	Two acres	1	3	37	Hay
"	Written in ink	187	In Down Field	1	2	16	Oats & Barley
"	"	274	In Glendish Hill Marsh	2	0	24	
"	"	282	In Mitchley Marsh	0	1	34	
"	"	351	In Harp Rood Shoot Wild Marsh	1	2	36	
Page 85			Total	16	2	38	

The plots of land in the Tottenham area, occupied by Rugman, were in the north and west of Tottenham. The total land owned by the heirs of Stephen Holland, in 1798, occupied by Raine and Rugman was 68 acres and 16 perches. The *Rent Charge Books* of 1798 record the name of William Rugman for land of Stephen Holland and *"ditto land of Lethieullier"*. In 1800, in the Poor Rate Books also *"William Rugman for Home Hall £30 land of Reverend Edward Warren, £48 and land Lethieullier £30"*. Coincidentally the name of Mr. Warren was written below those of the heirs of Stephen Holland in the Tottenham Survey. Sarah Holland was related through her deceased husband to the Warren family.

The remarks were added in pencil in 1798 and in 1804, alongside the entries 600-604, were the words *"sold to John Wood Esq"*. In 1804, the crops were wheat and hay but no potatoes. In 1805 oats were grown instead of wheat. Additionally, the plots numbered 394, 654, 658, 662 and 663 were owned by Henry Causton but also written in ink below his name were the names of John Wood and Thomas Parker. Some of the plots had changed their names, borders and been combined since 1619. Samuel Redfearn occupied other parcels of land but these were the only ones in the area identified.

Samuel Redfearn, a horse dealer of Tottenham, Middlesex, died in 1798. John Guest (*above*) died before October 1799. Jonothan Raine, late of Woburn Court in the Parish of St. George, Bloomsbury, a broker, dealer and chapman, had a Commission of Bankruptcy awarded against him, dated 5th December, 1810 (*London Gazette*).

In 1813, according to Robinson's *The History and Antiquities of the Parish of Tottenham, Volume 1*, under a heading entitled *"An Account of the lands in the Parish of Tottenham subject to the Rectorial or Great Tithes"*, the tithes held by the lease under the Dean and Chapter of St. Paul's were put up for sale by auction in five lots. Of them, *"Lot 1 – The Rectorial tithes of 715 acres, 3 roods and 19 perches of land extending from Stamford Hill to Hanger Lane and on the east of the turnpike to Stonebridge, abutting upon a rivulet down to the Barge River....*" The Table below is compiled from this information (*pages 227–229*). The letter denotes the name of the parcel of land, where available.

Table for Hanger Lane area in 1813, compiled from Robinson's book.

Nos.	Fields & Closes	Comment from author	Acre	Rood	Perch
581w	Megg Field		5	0	21
587		House			
592 b	Great Gallow Field		10	0	0
595 c	Clay Hanger		3	1	12
596		House			
597 y	Thistley Field		8	2	30
598			8	1	13
599 d	Little Gallow Field		8	0	26
600 e	Oatefield		6	0	4
601		Part of Oatfield	7	3	31
602		Lower Oatfield	11	1	36
603 z	Hatchcroft	In 1619, this was named Hatchers or Sergeants Field	4	2	24
604 a	Great Snares		8	2	6
605 b	Little Snares Field		5	1	35

The land was subject to a rent of £3 per annum with Land Tax of £9 per annum to the Dean and Chapter, being redeemed by them. In the Wyburd Survey of 1798, No.581, called "*Second Mayfield*" had 5 acres and 12 perches. According to the Tithe Maps of 1813, it had 5 acres, 21 perches and was called Megg Field. In 1844 it was then 5 acres 24 perches and called Little Mayfield. The names and the measurements changed over the years.

The names of the following people were shown to be occupying the land in question: Messrs. Hobson, William Rhodes, Driver, Gray, Jones, Hargraves, Scales, Samuel Rhodes, Hancock (William), Stevens (Thomas Coxhead), Burnand (Louis or Lewis), Larken, Anderson, Stonard (Thomas), Babington and others. (*William Hobson was responsible for building the Martello towers at the time of the Napoleonic War: William Rhodes may have been the brick manufacturer.*) Samuel Rhodes died in 1815. The will of William Hancock, a farmer from Tottenham, was proved in December 1820. On his death, a plot of his land, around two acres at Blackhope Lane at Tottenham High Cross, was sold at auction. This had been part of Sir Robert Barkham's gift of an annuity to the parish dating from the reign of Charles I, for the relief and sustentation of the poor, in return for a burial plot (17 feet by 7 feet) in the north chancel of Tottenham Church and for a vault with monument for Barkham and his heirs.

33

The new owners and occupiers
of the land and property

The land was described in an indenture at the LMA *(ACC/1028/109 Weath-erall Family Collection)*, made on 16th November 1798 and according to the wording of the indenture, registered the following day, 17th November. It was leased for a year by Rachel Waller, Richard Pinckard and his wife Margaret to Josiah Messer, a chemist of Holborn, who paid a peppercorn rent of one shilling each to Waller and Pinckard. The indenture in four parts was between Rachel Waller, a widow of the first part, Richard Pinckard and his wife, Margaret, of the second part, George Stacey and Mary his wife, a chemist, of Lambs Conduit Street and Josiah Messer, of Holborn.

The *Middlesex Deeds Registry* recorded an indenture *(MDR/1798/4/475)*, Holland to Waller (an office copy of the last will and testament of Sarah Holland) registered on 23rd November 1798. It confirmed the last will and testament of Sarah Holland, late of Beckenham, dated 17th April 1779, in which she bequeathed the farm in the Parish of Tottenham to Rachel Waller and Margaret Lethieullier and their heirs to take as tenants in common. It was required to be registered by Rachel Waller, one of the devisees, in the presence of George Wilson of Upper Gower Street, in the Parish of St. Pancras on 17th November 1798.

An indenture *(MDR/1798/4/478)* dated 15th & 16th October, also registered on 23rd November 1798, was a lease for one year of freehold land at Tottenham High Cross with a release involving five parties. These were Rachel Waller of Mark Tey, in the County of Essex, a widow, of the first part, Richard Pinckard of Great Russell Street in the Parish of St. George, Bloomsbury in the County of Middlesex and Margaret, his wife, of the second part, John Wood, of Austin Friars in the City of London, of the third part, Samuel Weyman Wadeson of Austin Friars, a gentleman, of the fourth part and George Wilson of Upper Gower Street in the Parish of St. Pancras, Middlesex, of the fifth part. John Wood was to pay £495 to Rachel Waller and £495 to Richard and Margaret Pinckard and then two sums of £985, secured, to make a total of £2960. Waller and Pinckard "*did grant, bargain, sell, alien, release and confirm unto*" Samuel Weyman Wadeson and his heirs. The land was to be held by Samuel Weyman Wadeson for the use of George Wilson for 1000 years and then to John Wood and his heirs, for a lease of 1000 years at a rate of five pounds per cent per annum. The land included two/three closes, by estimation 26 acres, called Oat Fields and two closes or meadows known as Snares Mead, by estimation 12 acres. Thereby, John Wood was to become the new owner of Oat Fields and Snares Mead after the death of George Wilson, the indenture having been signed and sealed on 19th November 1798.

An indenture (*MDR/1798/4/544 & ACC/1028/110*) of appointment and release of four parts, dated 17th November, was registered on 1st December 1798 and was a lease for one year. The parties were Rachel Waller of the first part, Richard Pinckard and his wife, Margaret of the second part, George Stacey, a chemist and his wife, Mary, of Lambs Conduit Street, Holborn, of the third part and Josiah Messer, a chemist, of Holborn, Middlesex, of the fourth part. It included all that messuage, cottage or tenement, stable, shop, loft, coach house yard and well formerly occupied by John Russell, deceased, near to the Blue Boar at Edmonton (28 perches) and eight acres north of Hanger Lane, together with all the houses, outhouses, edifices, buildings, barns, stables, yards, gardens, orchards, paths, passages, water courses, fences, trees, saplings and pollard works(*"pollard" can mean a tree which has had the branches removed so that it encourages the growth of new young branches*), formerly occupied by Henry Cocking. George Stacey acquired the eight acres adjoining to the south on Hanger Lane, known as Barnfield, with Barnfield House.

An indenture *(MDR/1798/4/565 & ACC/1028/107* as among three parties, dated 12th July 1798 was registered on 4th December 1798. Below is a transcription of part of the document confirming the participants, relationships and events preceding the transfer made, as follows:

> Rachel Waller of Mark Tey in the County of Essex, widow (late Rachel Lethieullier, spinster the relict of the Reverend James Waller, Doctor in Divinity deceased and a devisee in fee as to one moiety of the hereditaments herein after mentioned under the last will and testament of Sarah Holland, late of Beckenham in the County of Kent widow deceased who was formerly the wife of Samuel Lethieullier her first husband thentofore of the same place Esq., deceased and a devisee named in the last will and testament the said Samuel Lethieullier having been the only son of William Lethieullier formerly of the same place, Esquire, by Mary his second wife both also deceased and which the said Sarah Holland was the relict of Stephen Holland Esquire her second husband deceased) of the first part, Richard Pinckard, Esq., of Great Russell Street in the parish of St George, Bloomsbury in the County of Middlesex and Margaret his wife (late Margaret Lethieullier, spinster, the sister of the said Rachel Waller and also a devisee in fee as to one other moiety of the hereditaments thereinafter mentioned under the said will of the said Sarah Holland deceased) of the second part and George Wilson of Upper Gower Street in the parish of St Pancras in said County of Middlesex of the third part.
>
> *(City of London, London Metropolitan Archives)*

In summary, William Lethieullier, the son of Sir John Lethieullier, had bought the land around 1721 and wrote his will in 1736. Ownership transferred, on William's death in 1739, to his widow, Mary Lethieullier and she left it to their only son, Samuel, when she died on 29th August 1747. Samuel Lethieullier married Sarah Painter and on his death in 1752, it was left to his widow, Sarah Lethieullier. In 1756, she married Stephen Holland and he acquired the estate but he died in 1768. As his widow, the estate returned to her and she made a bequest in her will of the farm at Tottenham to Mrs. Rachel Waller and Margaret Lethieullier, as she had no children of her own.

Rachel and Margaret Lethieullier were the daughters of William Lethieullier's son, William, by his first wife, Mary Manning; Samuel Lethieullier was William's half-brother. Margaret Lethieullier had, since the bequest, married Richard Pinckard. Mrs. Rachel Waller, by 1798, was the widow of Reverend James Waller. Their son, Richard Waller, described as Rector of Great Birch in Essex, was named in the indenture as a witness to the proceedings.

The "*deed of covenant for levying a fine*" was made by Rachel Waller, Richard Pinckard and his wife to George Wilson and his heirs. The land in this indenture was described as three closes of meadow or pasture known as Oat Fields (26 acres), south of Hanger Lane, a messuage, cottage or tenement, stable, shop, loft and coach house, yard and well (28 perches) in Tottenham, adjoining the Parish of Edmonton, four acres of meadow in the Wild Marsh once in the tenure of John Russell, deceased, two closes of meadow or pasture (12 acres) known as Snares Mead adjoining south on Hanger Lane and a close or field of meadow or pasture (8 acres) also adjoining south on Hanger Lane, formerly occupied by Henry Cocking. Of the fourteen parcels of land outlined in the Table describing land owned by Thomas Hayter in 1720, eight in various parts of Tottenham had been sold, amounting to some twenty acres, leaving some fifty acres. By the time this indenture was registered, George Stacey had acquired the eight acres at Hanger Lane with Barnfield House along with the cottage, stable, etc. measuring some 28 perches, near the Blue Boar at Edmonton.

Shortly after this time, another parcel of land originally outlined in the sale (*MDR/1798/4/565*) was sold. An indenture of lease and release bearing the dates 16th & 17th November 1798 (*MDR/1798/4/607*), was registered on 8th December 1798. The lease was between Rachel Waller, Richard Pinckard and his wife Margaret, of the one part, to Joseph Osborne, of Enfield, of the other part. Osborne paid £210 (£105 to Rachel Waller and £105 to Richard and Margaret Pinckard) for four acres of meadow land in the Wild Marsh, Tottenham. The release in four parts was made by Rachel Waller of the first part, Richard Pinckard and his wife, Margaret of the second part, Joseph Osborne of the third part and George Stacey of the fourth part. The document recorded that George Stacey had bought it at auction (*Lot 5*), that he and his heirs owned it at the present time and he did covenant it from him and his heirs, presumably to Osborne.

As was the case with indentures, many of the parties involved were related by marriage. Josiah Messer married Elizabeth Wilson and on 21st December 1781; her sister, Mary Wilson, married George Stacey. Therefore, Josiah Messer and George Stacey were brothers-in-law. Mary and Elizabeth Wilson were daughters of Isaac and Rachel Wilson, Quakers from Kendal. An obituary in *The Annual Register (Dodsleys)*, dated 1st October 1804, explains that George Wilson of Upper Gower Street died of a *"paralytic disorder"*, aged 77. He was described as an eminent solicitor in the High Court of Chancery. His wife, Sarah Cox, from Kent, died in 1796, and only one of his four children, Mary, wife of Sir Hugh Inglis, survived him. George Wilson left his estate, in trust, to his daughter, Lady Mary Inglis and made a bequest to his friend Mrs Rachel Waller among others. As George Wilson died, John Wood took ownership of Oat Fields and Snares Mead.

George Stacey featured in an article entitled *The Rise of the English Drugs Industry: The role of Thomas Corbyn in Medical History* (1989), by Roy and Dorothy Parker. In 1781, Thomas Corbyn, John Brown, John Beaumont and George Stacey were business partners. In 1787, the partnership comprised John Corbyn, John Beaumont, George Stacey and Josiah Messer. In 1794, it was John Corbyn, George Stacey and Josiah Messer in the partnership and in 1801 they were joined by Edward Swaine. By 1834, the members of the partnership were John Corbyn, Abraham Beaumont (who married George Stacey's daughter, Rachel), George Stacey II and Josiah Messer II. In 1847, after the death of John Corbyn, the remaining members of the partnership were Abraham Beaumont, George Stacey II and Josiah Messer II (*Wellcome Library Catalogue*).

Josiah Messer was living in Hampstead when he died in 1830. His son, Josiah Messer, was listed in the Electoral Rolls in 1847 as the leaseholder of a house on the High Street, Tottenham.

George Stacey of Tottenham was buried there, aged 66, on 17th January 1816. His will (*LMA ACC/1028/113*) was made in 1813 and proved on 20th March 1816. Probate was granted to Mary Stacey, his widow and relict; John Daubeney and Josiah Messer were executors. Abraham Beaumont was identified as George's son-in-law and George Stacey as his son, who also lived in Holborn. There were three daughters. The younger George Stacey received *"freehold hereditaments and premises situated in Hangers Lane in the parish of Tottenham, Middlesex"*. George's second son, Isaac was to be provided for under the terms of the will as he could not care for himself (Isaac lived until he was 63).

George Stacey, the son, married Deborah Lloyd, the eldest daughter of Samuel Lloyd, Esq. of Birmingham, at Friend's Meeting House, Birmingham (*The Derby Mercury, 23rd April 1818*); George was living at Bruce Grove, Tottenham before his marriage. George Stacey was a Quaker and a leading abolitionist and his wife was a member of the Lloyd's banking family, also Quakers. In his will, proved in 1857, he identified his then wife as Mary Barclay, widow of John Barclay and his two stepsons.

John Wood (-1813) and his heirs

William Robinson's book on Tottenham acknowledged, in its list of contributors, the help given by a John Wood. John Wood, Esq. owned the freehold but did not occupy the land, leasing it to other parties. Some fifteen years after buying the land at Tottenham, on 11ᵗʰ September 1813, Wood, a stockbroker, died. His death at Walthamstow, Essex was announced in *The Morning Post*. His will was written on 8ᵗʰ June 1812 and proved on 3ʳᵈ November 1813 (*PROB 11/1549/181*). It identified the freehold estate at or near Hanger Lane, Tottenham, Middlesex, copyhold and freehold land in Walthamstow in Essex, freehold property at Albany House, Piccadilly, a freehold estate at Brixton, Surrey and his office at Austin Friars in the City of London. The estate was left to his dear wife Frances. Frances Wood, William Varden, an ironmonger, Edward Owen and John Brown, a coal merchant from Walthamstow were executors. He made reference to his son Edmund and his other children but the trustees were responsible for looking after the estate.

An additional statement, copied alongside the will, confirmed that John Wood died on 11ᵗʰ September 1813 and noted that Frances Wood, his widow, survived the other testators and died intestate on 17ᵗʰ July 1858. Her death was registered at West Ham in Essex. It also acknowledged that on 10ᵗʰ March 1860, the administration of the estate of John Wood was granted to Edmund Heysham Wood, *"one of his children"*, as Edward Owen, William Varden and John Brown, the other executors, were then also dead. Frances Wood died at Woodford in Essex in her 81ˢᵗ year and her obituary was recorded in *The Gentleman's Magazine*. She was described as the relict of John Wood and the daughter of Reverend Edmund Heysham of Little Munden, Hertfordshire. Letters of Administration for her effects, valued at under £2,000, were granted on 15ᵗʰ October 1858 to Edmund Heysham Wood, her eldest son.

An indenture of lease (*MDR/1815/5/480*), dated 26ᵗʰ December 1807 but not registered until 8ᵗʰ August 1815, was made between John Wood of Austin Friars in the City of London, of the one part and Thomas Coxhead Stevens, a merchant, the lessee, of the other part. Wood had released the 12, 5 and 6 acres known as Oat Fields (*c.*26 acres) and Snare's Mead (12 acres) in Tottenham for the occupation of Thomas Coxhead Stevens. The lease for 96 years had commenced in 1807 and the transfer was witnessed by Archer Moore Barlow and Samuel James Wadeson, both of Austin Friars. The indenture was signed on 4ᵗʰ August 1815. Samuel James Wadeson, born in 1790, was the son of Samuel Weyman Wadeson cited in the 1798 indenture, above. The unusual lengthy period time that had elapsed between the original date of the lease in 1807 and this indenture recorded in 1815, may have been because John Wood died in 1813. Samuel Weyman Wadeson died on 18ᵗʰ May 1822. Another Memorial (*MDR/1815/5/481*) dated 24ᵗʰ June 1815, was registered on the same day, 8ᵗʰ August, 1815. The parties were Thomas Coxhead Stevens of Union Wharf in the Parish of St. John's, a stave and timber merchant, of the one part to Thomas Coxhead Marsh, of Russell Square, Middlesex, of the other part. Thomas Coxhead Stevens *"did grant bargain, sell, assign and transfer"* to Thomas Coxhead Marsh and his heirs the 12, 5 and 6 acres known as Oat Fields (*c.*26 acres) and Snares Mead (12 acres) at Tottenham High Cross and the lease was for the remainder of the ninety-six years. The indenture made reference to the previous indenture (*MDR*/1815/5/480) and *"redemption of the said premises upon payment of £4,000"*.

Information on the wife of John Wood, Frances Heysham, is held at the *"Thornton Heyshams"*, web site *http://shissem.com/Hissem_Thornton-Heyshams.html*. She was born on 11ᵗʰ June 1778, one of nine children and was christened on 8ᵗʰ July at Little Munden, Hertford. The records at the Guildhall in London of births, deaths and baptisms from St. Peter le Poer at Old Broad Street confirm that John Wood married Frances Heysham on 25ᵗʰ October, 1800. Apart from the minister, the witnesses were Sarah and Edmund Heysham, who may have been her parents or her elder brother and sister. Frances' father was the Reverend Edmund Heysham LL.D, who was installed as rector in All Saints Church, Little Munden in 1771, when his elder brother inherited the patronage of the church and most of their father's estate. Edmund's wife was Anne Maria Smith of Watford in Hertfordshire and they married in 1772. Reverend Edmund Heysham died on 23ʳᵈ January 1819, at the age of 79. He had been rector at Little Munden for 47 years and is recorded on a monumental inscription there. An obituary from *The Gentleman's Magazine* confirms that his widow, Sarah, died on 26ᵗʰ January 1838, aged 91. She may have been known before her marriage as Sarah Anne Maria Smith.

The Clothworkers' Company confirms that John Wood was made *"free"* by redemption, that is, he purchased his freedom on 2ⁿᵈ July, 1794, when he was a stockbroker at 41 Royal Exchange, in the City. To become *free* means to be an ordinary member of the Company and Freedom requires that the individual be over 21. It is likely that John Wood became *free* for sociability and networking. He worked in the Fenchurch area of London, Austin Friars and the Stock Exchange was adjacent thereto. It was more expensive to become *free* by redemption so it is suggested that probably his father and grandfather were not members of the Company.

John Wood, a wealthy and successful man, either by family or his endeavours, lived for a time in Walthamstow. He became the owner of the land at Tottenham around the time he married Frances Heysham. His son, Edmund Heysham Wood, was christened on 17ᵗʰ May 1804 at the Church of St. Peter le Poer, close to Austin Friars. George Wood was baptised on 4ᵗʰ May 1807, Herbert William Wood on 30ᵗʰ October 1808 and Frances Ellen Wood on 31ˢᵗ October 1813, all at the same church. The Wood family had also, through the Heyshams, connections with the Church of St. Botolph's, Aldgate in the City of London. After his death in 1813, the heirs of John Wood, including his widow and relict, Francis Wood and a number of trustees, managed his estate.

Edmund Heysham Wood of Elm House, Clay Street Walthamstow, eldest son of John Wood, married Sophia Branton on 25ᵗʰ October 1828. She was the third daughter of the late John Branton, from Higham Hill in Walthamstow. In 1832, Edmund Heysham Wood was recorded in the Electoral Registers at Colney Hatch Lane, Muswell Hill. William Morris, the designer and social activist, was born at Elm House on 24ᵗʰ March 1834. The Morris family had moved to the leafy countryside near Epping Forest from his father's premises at Lombard Street in the City, where the father was a discount broker in Sanderson & Company, some time after the birth of William's sister in 1832. In 1840 the family moved across the Forest to a larger Georgian Mansion called Woodford Hall, rented for £600 a year. His father was buried in the churchyard of St. Mary the Virgin at Woodford and William Morris was baptised there.

Edmund Heysham Wood, son of John (*Free* 1794) was made *Free* on 10th August 1825 by Patrimony, when he was described as "*of the Stock Exchange and a broker*". George Heysham Wood, also cited in the Memorial as a son of John, was made *Free* on 1st April 1829, by Patrimony, when he was described as "*of Woodford and a Drug Broker*". Edmund was elected Master of the Clothworkers' Company of London in 1870 but he was excused service in 1872. Another son of John, Herbert William Wood, was made *Free* by Patrimony on 7th June 1876, when he was described as a "*Lieutenant-Colonel in the Indian Army, retired, of 35 St. Stephen's Road, Shepherd's Bush*". His father was described as "*late of Austin Friars, stock broker and deceased*". An entry for his son Frederick Arthur Wood, son of Herbert, who was made *Free* on 4th December 1878 by Patrimonial Redemption *i.e.* he was born before his father had become *Free*, when he was described as "*of Brisbane, Queensland, Australia*".

Edmund and his wife were still living at Colney Hatch Lane at the time of the census of 1841. When the census of 1851 was conducted, Edmund Heysham Wood, then a merchant, was at New House, Watford. When his mother, Frances, died in 1858, he was still living at the same address. The death of his mother may have brought about the sale of Woodberry Lodge (*MDR/1859/10/574*). While in 1859 he was one of the owners of the Woodberry Lodge Estate, the census of 1861 places him in Watford at 12 High Street (New House) and he is registered as a member of the Stock Exchange. The 1871 Census confirms that Edmund Heysham Wood was born at Austin Friars, London and his wife Sophia at Walthamstow in Essex. The church where he was christened was in Old Broad Street, which meets Austin Friars. By this time he had retired and was living at 37 Kensington Square in London. Sophia Wood died on 18th February 1873. Her husband and two nephews were executors. At the time of the census of 1881, Edmund was lodging at 15 Regency Square, Brighton, but as the census took place around Easter, he may have been on holiday.

Herbert William Wood, a bachelor, served in India and married Maria Louisa Conwell, a spinster, in Bangalore on 1st September 1836 (*B.L. N/2/17/137*). Some of their children were born at Madras. They were Herbert William Wood, born on 17th July 1837; Fanny Isabella Wood on 10th January 1839; Henry Conwell Wood on 5th July 1840; Sophia Ellen Wood on 2nd March 1842. By the time of the census of 1851 there were others at Cheltenham. These were Edmund, Charles and Reginald; Frederick Arthur Wood was born on 3rd January 1855. In 1881, Herbert was recorded at 49 Godolphin Road, in Hammersmith. His wife, Maria L. Wood (67), born in Ireland, was staying with Frederick L. Schuster, a merchant and his wife, Sophia Ellen at their home at Alderley Edge, Chorley in Cheshire, with Sophia's brother, Reginald W.H. Wood, aged 32.

On 20th September 1882, Edmund Heysham Wood of 37 Kensington Garden Square, married Frances Caroline Sarah Besly, born in 1835. His brother,

Herbert William Wood, late Lieutenant Colonel in the Army at Madras, at that time retired, died on 5th June 1883, aged 75. His death was registered at Cheltenham. His son of the same name, a major in the Royal Engineers, had died in Madras on 8th October 1879, aged 42. He has an entry in the Oxford Dictionary of National Biography.

It was reported in *The London Gazette* on Friday 5th September 1890 that on 23rd August, the Queen had granted Edmund Heysham Wood of Kensington Gardens Square, in the Parish of St. Mary Abbot, Kensington and Frances Caroline Sarah Wood, his wife and eldest of four daughters of William Henry Besly of Dunmore, Bradninch, in Devon, *"her licence in compliance with a clause in the last will and testament of John Besly"*, uncle of Frances Caroline Sarah Wood, to take and use the name of Besly after Wood and for any issue of this marriage to take the surname and arms. The Royal concession and declaration was to be recorded at Her Majesty's College of Arms, in order to take effect. Edmund died a few months later. A legal notice in *The Standard*, dated 29th October, said that the will of Edmund Heysham Wood-Besly, formerly Wood, late of 37 Kensington Gardens Square and the Stock Exchange was proved on 19th November 1890 (he died 27th October 1890). The net value of his estate was £26,536. Wadeson and Malleson, solicitors, of 11 Austin Friars in the City of London, acted on behalf of his widow.

George Wood worked at the Stock Exchange. He married Caroline Charlotte Connor of the Parish of St. George, Hanover Square; the marriage licence was dated 17th March 1857. At the time of the census of 1861, George (54) and his wife Caroline (37), were recorded with Henry Cornwall Wood (20), their nephew, who was a clerk in the Stock Exchange. At the age of 21, Henry, son of Herbert William Wood, who had been educated at Cheltenham College, went to Australia, where he had a town named after him (Woodford, in Essex, was where his grandmother had lived for most of her life). Henry and his business partner imported the first Hereford cattle into Queensland. When he died, at the age of 86, his obituary was published in the *Brisbane Courier* dated 19th June 1926. His brother Frederick also went to Australia and died there.

At the age of 84, George Wood and his wife, Caroline Charlotte (67) were recorded in the census of 1891 at 85 Westbourne Terrace. George died at 15 Farquhar Road, Upper Norwood on 1st October 1894 when he was 88. Caroline died on 11th October 1896, leaving her effects to Frances (Fanny) Isabella Arbuthnot (wife of George Alexander Arbuthnot) and Sophia Ellen Schuster (wife of Frederick Leo Schuster). Frances and Sophia were daughters of Herbert William Wood. Herbert was the only brother to have children.

The Coxhead connection

Thomas Coxhead Stevens married Mary Catherine Henley, with the consent of her father, on 29th October 1789, at St. George in the East, Tower Hamlets in London. Mary Catherine, born on 29th July 1770 and baptised at St. John, Wapping, was the daughter of Michael and Mary Henley.

The land owned by Rachel Waller and Richard and Margaret Pinckard, once occupied by Jonathan Raine, had been acquired by John Wood, who leased it to Thomas Coxhead Stevens. Steven's name was written on an indenture (*LMA: ACC/0489/004*) as owning the parcel of land next to meadow and gardens surrounding Albion Lodge in 1806, proving he was there from that time.

Reference was made to Thomas Coxhead Stevens with Thomas Coxhead Marsh in an indenture (*MDR/1815/5/481*) regarding land at Tottenham. Thomas Coxhead Marsh (1780-1847) and William Coxhead Marsh were the illegitimate sons of Sir Thomas Coxhead, M.P. and Sarah Marsh of Ashwell, Hertfordshire. Sir Thomas Coxhead was described as a cooper in 1770, a timber merchant in 1774 and a stave merchant, when he became an M.P. in 1790. On 2nd December 1783, Thomas Coxhead Stevens, son of Joseph Stevens, a miller, of Remenham in Berkshire, was apprenticed for seven years to Thomas Coxhead, a citizen and cooper of London (*Freedom of the City Admissions 1681-1925*). In 1790, Thomas Coxhead Stevens, then a livery man and a Middlesex freeholder, entered into a partnership with Thomas Coxhead and is recorded in 1796, in the *Poll Books and Electoral Registers (1538-1893)*, as a cooper in Wapping. The Coxhead and Stevens timber merchant partnership of Union Wharf, Wapping was dissolved on 5th April 1800, as confirmed in *The London Gazette*. The business was to be carried on by Thomas Coxhead Stevens and Thomas Coxhead Marsh. In 1813, Thomas Coxhead Marsh was described in *The Gentleman's Magazine* as a goldsmith.

The will of Joseph Stevens of Henley-on-Thames, Oxfordshire, was proved on 20th October 1808 (*PROB 11/1487/116*). He identified his wife Mary as sole executrix, his sons Henry and Thomas Coxhead Stevens and his daughter Frances Chadwick, a widow. Rents from the freehold properties were to go to his wife and then to Henry after her death. Henry received two houses at Henley, Thomas four leasehold houses at Nightingale Lane in the Parish of Limehouse and Frances a house at Hurst.

In his will, made on 11th April 1810, Sir Thomas Coxhead had made good provision for his wife, Lady Deborah, née Healey, who died on 2nd November 1810 (*History of Parliament on-line, http://www.historyofparliamentonline. org/*). He died on 4th November 1811, aged 77 and left his considerable fortune to his two natural sons, who were named as executors. Their mother, Sarah was deceased. Sir Thomas made many bequests to his extended family in his will, proved on 6th December 1811 (*PROB 11/1528/82*). To his sister, Mary Stevens, he left £2,000, "*three per cent stock*". She was the widow of Joseph Stevens above. Thomas Coxhead Stevens and Henry Stevens, Frances Chadwick and Margaret Stevens, widow of the late Joseph Stevens received £1,000 "*a piece three per cent stock*". These were the sons, daughter and daughter-in-law of Joseph and Mary Stevens, although neither the younger Joseph or Margaret had been acknowledged in the will of Joseph Stevens. The six children of Thomas Coxhead Stevens received £200 stock each; they were William Stevens, Michael Henley Stevens, Charles Stevens, Mary Ann Stevens, Elizabeth Stevens, Maria Stevens. So also did their mother Mary

Catherine Stevens and their aunt Elizabeth the wife of Henry Stevens. Henry and Elizabeth's son, the younger Joseph Stevens also received the same. The four children of the deceased Joseph Stevens, Joseph, Thomas, Elizabeth and Mary Ann Stevens also received £200 in stock each. Sir Thomas gave £2,000 three per cent stock to his sister Frances Nichols, wife of Lesiter and bequests to her five children and other members of the Healey and Marsh families.

Coxhead Stevens' father-in-law, Michael Henley, of the Parish of St. John, Wapping and Derby died in Wapping in 1813 and left a considerable fortune to his children, Joseph, Mary Catherine and Elizabeth. Mary Catherine was to receive the dividends and interest on £20,000. His son Joseph Henley and grandson Joseph Warner Henley were executors. The will was proved by his son, Joseph on 19th October, 1813 and by his grandson, Joseph Warner Henley on 15th March 1814, when the boy attained the age of 21. According to the *History of the County of Derby, Part 2* by Stephen Glover, published in 1829, there is a memorial on the north aisle of St. Werburgh Church, Derby, which records:

In memory of Michael Henley. Esq., who died 11th September 1813, aged 71 years. Mary Catherine, widow of Thomas Coxhead Stevens, Esq., of Stamford Middx, daughter of the late Michael Henley, Esq., who died 27th February 1826, aged 56.

Presumably the reference on the memorial should have read "*Stamford Hill, Middlesex*".

Thomas Coxhead Stevens wrote his will on 23rd September 1815. According to the Vestry minutes for Tottenham Church (*14th January 1817 to 26th January 1836*) dated 16th April 1818, Stevens was appointed as an overseer for High Cross Ward, receiving 24 votes. In the same book on 22nd September 1818, it was recorded that "*in consequence of the death of Thomas Coxhead Stevens*" a new overseer was appointed. His death is recorded in *Jackson's Oxford Journal* on Saturday, September 5, 1818. He died in Stamford Hill, Middlesex, aged 52 and was buried on 11th September 1818 at St. John's, Wapping. The administration, with will, proved, on 1st April 1819 (*PROB 11/1615/12*), was granted to Thomas Solly and John Bainbridge, creditors of the deceased, being sworn to administer. (*Solly and Bainbridge were named as committee members, in an account of The London Infirmary for curing diseases of the eye, at Charterhouse Square, London.*) Thomas Coxhead Marsh and Richard Bowman, the elder of Union Brewhouse, Wapping, a brewer and Charles Stevens were named as executors. Marsh and Bowman were universal legatees acting in trust for Mary Catherine Stevens, widow and the natural and lawful mother and guardian of Charles Stevens, a minor and the son of the deceased. Any interest from freehold property was to go to Mary Catherine Stevens. When Charles reached 21, his mother's portion was to be reduced to one third and the rest was to be divided among all the living children. Sometime later was added a statement which included the names of the mother and sons and daughters; Mary Ann Stevens, a spinster, Michael Henley Stevens, son, Elizabeth Henley Stevens,

Maria Henley Stevens, Amelia Henley Stevens and William Stevens. This was before 1827 when Elizabeth and Mary Ann Stevens married.

The following advertisement, which appeared in *The Morning Chronicle*, on Thursday, 20th May 1819, proves that Thomas Coxhead Stevens built and occupied a house at Tottenham prior to that time. The description of the house at Hanger's Lane was:

> Hanger's Lane-Stamford Hill – Capital leasehold Residence-Offices-Gardens and about twenty-three acres of Meadow land – Land Tax redeemed – By Winstanley & Sons at the Mart on Tuesday June 8 – at twelve- By order of the Administrators.
>
> A very superior detached RESIDENCE, delightfully situate on the south side and preferable part of Hanger's Lane, in the immediate vicinity of Stamford-Hill commanding retirement within little more than three miles of the Metropolis, surrounded by shrubberies, excellent fruit and kitchen gardens, with well clothed walls of the choicest trees in full bearing, and 23 acres of very fine meadow land, the late residence of Thomas Coxhead Stevens, Esq., deceased, by whom it was erected in a substantial manner, and at a very considerable expense: the house is approached by a lawn and gravel carriage sweep, and possesses ample accommodation for a family of the first respectability, in five bedrooms and two dressing rooms on the principal story, and three secondary chambers, a breakfast parlour, drawing room, elegant eating room, morning or gentleman's room, spacious entrance hall, housekeeper's room, and every requisite domestic office; the detached office consists of a double coach house, chaise ditto, stabling for six horses, lofts and every other necessary outbuilding; the whole premises are held on a building lease, whereof 84 years will be unexpired at Christmas next – To be viewed by cards only, which, with particulars, may be had of Winstanley and Sons, Paternoster Row; Particulars also of Messrs. Rooke and Coe, Armourers' Hall, Cannon Street; and at the Mart.

The building lease had eighty-four years unexpired. The ninety-six year lease was granted in December 1807 as confirmed by the reference in the indenture above. Beside this entry is another for waterside premises at Fore Street, Limehouse, fronting the River Thames, which included a cooperage, newly erected warehouses above a mast-maker's shop and dwelling house, to be sold by order of the administrators of Thomas Coxhead Stevens. The property at Stamford Hill was still being advertised for sale in March 1821. This advertisement proves that Stevens had acquired 23 acres of fine meadow land from John Wood and his heirs, which may have included the house and other buildings.

Among the children of Thomas Coxhead Stevens and Mary Catherine were Charles, Mary Ann, Elizabeth Henley, Maria Henley, Amelia Henley, William,

Michael Henley and Louisa Crawford Stevens, baptised at Tottenham on 26th August 1813; Louisa died seven weeks after her baptism. She was buried at St. John's, Wapping on 22nd September 1813. Mary Catherine Stevens, then a widow, was living at Burton Crescent, Middlesex when she drafted her will on 14th December 1820. She identified only daughters as Mary Ann Stevens, Elizabeth Henley Stevens, Maria Henley Stevens and Amelia Henley Stevens; Her executors were Joseph Warner Henley (1793-1884), her nephew, son of her brother Joseph Henley (1766-1832) and George Greaves, brother-in-law of Joseph Warner Henley. One of her daughters, Maria Henley Stevens, aged 15, was buried with her father at St. John Wapping, Middlesex on 11th August 1821. She had been living with her mother and sisters at Tonbridge in Surrey when she died. Mary Catherine Stevens died in 1826 but her will was not proved until 8th July 1827.

The death of Thomas Coxhead Stevens was not without consequences. Two years elapsed before his house was sold and his creditors paid in full. The original documents concerning the transfer at the City of London, London Metropolitan Archives, in bundle *MDR/MB/3890*, are transcribed below. The first is dated 1816 and was registered in 1821 (*MDR/1821/5/538*):

> A Memorial to be registered of an Indenture of assignment bearing date the first day of August one thousand eight hundred and sixteen made between Thomas Coxhead Stevens of Union Wharf in the Parish of St. John Wapping in the County of Middlesex stave and timber merchant of the first part Thomas Coxhead Marsh of Russell Square in the County of Middlesex Esquire of the second part and Joseph Henley of Waterperry in the County of Oxford Esquire of the third part Whereby (after reciting as therein recited) in consideration of two thousand five hundred pounds of lawful money of Great Britain paid lent and advanced to the said Thomas Coxhead Stevens by the said Joseph Henley and of the sum of five shillings to each of them the said Thomas Coxhead Stevens and Thomas Coxhead Marsh paid by the said Joseph Henley He the said Thomas Coxhead Marsh at the request and by the direction and appointment of the said Thomas Coxhead Stevens testified as therein mentioned did grant bargain sell assign transfer And the said Thomas Coxhead Stevens did grant bargain sell assign transfer and set over ratify and confirm unto the said Joseph Henley his executors and administrators and assigns All those several pieces or parcels of land with the messuage or tenement and premises with the appurtenances which are severally mentioned and described in and by a certain Indenture of Lease bearing date the twenty sixth day of December one thousand eight hundred and seven and made between John Wood therein described of the one part and the said Thomas Coxhead Stevens of the other part a Memorial whereof was registered the eighth day of August one thousand eight hundred and fifteen.

(B5 No. 480). To hold the said pieces or parcels of ground messuage or tenement and all and singular other the premises with the appurtenances unto the said Joseph Henley his Executors Administrators and assigns from thenceforth for and during all the rest residue and remainder of the Term in and by the said Indenture of Lease thereof granted and then to come unexpired subject to the payment of the rent and performance of the Covenants and Agreements in and by the said Indenture of Lease reserved and contained and also subject to a Proviso for Redemption as therein mentioned which said Indenture of Assignment as to the Execution thereof by the said Thomas Coxhead Stevens is witnessed by Thomas Young clerk to Messieurs Rooke and Coe Armourers' Hall London and as to the Execution thereof by the said Thomas Coxhead Marsh is witnessed by Thomas Rooke of Armourers' Hall London Gentleman and as to the Execution thereof by the said Joseph Henley is witnessed by James Coe of Armourers' Hall in the City of London and James Berriman Tippetts his clerk And is hereby required to be registered by the said Joseph Henley As witnessed his hand and seal the twenty ninth day of June one thousand eight hundred and twenty one.

(*City of London, London Metropolitan Archives*)

This action was retrospective. It was dated 1st August 1816 when Thomas Coxhead Stevens was alive but signed on 29th June 1821 by Henley, after Stevens had died. Stevens and Marsh transferred ownership to Joseph Henley when the latter registered the Indenture on 5th July 1821. The copy of the indenture in the MDR Book also stated that the amount paid was £2,200.

The next indenture in bundle *MDR/MB/3890*, dated June 1821, registered on 5th July 1821 (*MDR/1821/5/539*), was between Solly and others to McGhie:

A Memorial to be registered of An Indenture of Assignment bearing date the twentieth day of June one thousand eight hundred and twenty one and made between Thomas Solly of St Mary Axe in the City of London Esquire and John Bainbridge of Bread Street Cheapside in the said City of London Esquire the administrators with the will annexed of Thomas Coxhead Stevens late of the Parish of Tottenham in the County of Middlesex deceased of the first part Joseph Henley of Waterperry in the County of Oxford Esquire of the second part Thomas Coxhead Marsh of Holles Street Cavendish Square in the County of Middlesex Esquire of the third part and Brodie Augustus McGhie of Edmonton in the County of Middlesex aforesaid shipbroker of the fourth part Whereby (after reciting as therein recited) for the consideration therein mentioned the said Joseph Henley at the request and by the direction and appointment of the said Thomas Solly and John Bainbridge and with the privity and consent of the said Thomas

Coxhead Marsh testified as therein mentioned did grant bargain sell assign transfer and set over And the said Thomas Solly John Bainbridge and Thomas Coxhead Marsh did according to their several and respective estates rights and interests grant bargain sell assign transfer set over ratify and confirm unto the said Brodie Augustus McGhie his executors administrators and assigns All those several pieces or parcels of land with the messuage or tenement and premises with the appurtenances which are severally mentioned and described in and by a certain Indenture of lease bearing date the twenty sixth day of December one thousand eight hundred and seven and made between John Wood therein described of the one part and the said Thomas Coxhead Stevens of the other part a Memorial whereof was registered on the eighth day of August one thousand eight hundred and fifteen.

(B5 No. 480). To Hold the said several pieces or parcels of ground messuage or tenement and all and singular other the premises with the appurtenances unto the said Brodie Augustus McGhie his executors administrators and assigns from the twenty fifth day of March then last for and during all the rest residue and remainder of the Term in and by the said Indenture of Lease thereof granted then to come and unexpired subject to the payment of the rent and Performance of the Covenants and Agreements in and by the said Indenture of Lease reserved and contained And also subject to an Underlease of part of the said Premises as in the now memorialising Indenture mentioned Which said Indenture of Assignment as to the Execution thereof by the said Thomas Solly is witnessed by Thomas Dennis of 13 Gray's Inn in the County of Middlesex Gentleman and James Berriman Tippetts hereinafter mentioned and As to the execution thereof by the said Thomas Coxhead Marsh is witnessed by John Kirth and William Bond servants Bettisons Library Cheltenham in the County of Gloucester And as to the execution thereof by the said John Bainbridge Joseph Henley and Brodie Augustus McGhie is witnessed by James Coe of Armourers' Hall in the City of London solicitor and James Berriman Tippetts his clerk and is hereby required to be registered by the said Brodie Augustus McGhie As witness his hand and seal the twenty ninth day of June in the year of our Lord one thousand eight hundred and twenty one.

(City of London, London Metropolitan Archives)

Brodie Augustus McGhie, a ship broker, was now the leaseholder. There were significant omissions from the proceedings, notably Mary Catherine Stevens, widow of Thomas Coxhead Stevens, her son Charles, named in his father's will as an executor and Richard Bowman, a brewer. The reference to an underlease in both these memorials may have been to an agreement made between Thomas Coxhead Stevens and Louis Burnand, both of Hanger

Lane, dating from 7th April 1817 but not registered until 17th August 1825 (*MDR/1825/9/539*), some years after Stevens' death in September 1818. The lease, for 86 years, for a long parcel of land, south of Hanger Lane, 60 × 30 poles and six feet wide, to be rented for £1,12s. per annum, began on 1st January 1817 (*ACC/0489/006*). A marginal plan showed an area of land, outlined in red, stretching from Hanger's Lane in the north, down towards Stamford Hill in the south. The house and land (known later as Albion Lodge) on one side, was occupied by Lewis Burnand and the occupier of the house built on Oat Fields, to the west of this land, was marked as that of Thomas Coxhead Stevens. This parcel of land was identified in later indentures.

Mary Stevens, a widow, of Henley on Thames, made her will in 1824, leaving her personal estate to her daughter Frances Chadwick, when it was proved on 14th May 1825. Frances was the sister of the late Thomas Coxhead Stevens. Mary's nephew Thomas Nichols was sole executor.

The marriage of Thomas' eldest daughter Mary Ann Stevens, late of Stamford Hill and William Swinton, of the East India Company, took place at St. Pancras New Church, London on 27th July 1827 (*The Times*). It was noted that she was the niece of Joseph Henley, Esq., of Waterperry Park, Oxford, a farmer. Elizabeth Henley Stevens, second daughter of Thomas Coxhead Stevens, had been baptised at Tottenham on 18th January 1804, suggesting that by that time the family had already moved to the Tottenham area. She married John Danby Christopher, a solicitor, at St. Werburgh, Derby on 27th December 1827. In the census of 1851 they were recorded living at 30 Penton Street, London, where her husband died on 23rd March 1859. In the census of 1861 she was living at 6 Titchfield Street, St. John's Wood, London. She was living at Broadstairs in Kent when she died on 17th February 1864, aged 60. She was buried at St James Swains Lane, Highgate, on 24th February 1864.

By way of an aside, the will of Frances Chadwick, of Henley on Thames, written 19th July 1832 and proved 22nd January 1834 named various members of the Stevens family. Her mother also died at Henley. Frances left £400 to her nephew, Joseph Stevens, the son of her late brother, Henry, £200 to her nephew Michael Henley Stevens and £50 apiece to her three nieces, Mary Ann Swinton, Amelia Henley Stevens and Elizabeth Henley Christopher. She also made reference to Thomas, Mary Ann and Elizabeth Stevens, children of her late brother Joseph, her sister-in-law Margaret Stevens and Ann, widow of her late nephew Joseph.

It was reported in the *Edinburgh Gazette* on 19th October 1830 that Michael Henley Stevens, dealer and chapman, of James' Place, Princes Road, Lambeth in Surrey was bankrupt. Michael Henley Stevens was living prior to his death in the Parish of Christchurch, Surrey. He was buried at St. John Wapping, on 15th June 1839, aged 43. He was born around 1796 and died intestate.

A burial was recorded on 16th January 1853, also at St. John Wapping, for Charles Stevens of 9 Upper Ebury Street, Pimlico, London. Born in 1798, he was 55 when he died. Coincidentally, at the time of the census of 1851, Charles Stevens was a visitor at Upper Ebury Street, in the Parish of St. George, Hanover Square. He was born in Wapping, was unmarried and of independent means. It seems likely the brothers were buried with their sisters and father at Wapping.

Amelia Henley Stevens never married. She died on 27th November 1864, aged 54 in Eastbourne (*The Times*). Letters of administration were granted to her sister, Mary Ann, wife of William Swinton, on 20th April 1865. Her effects were valued at under £3,000.

The new road in 1833 – Seven Sisters Road

Accounts of life in the 17th and 18th Century record, in *A History of the County of Middlesex, Volume 5,* that most of the land west of the High Road, from Stamford Hill to Page Green, was farmland. Ermine Street, the Roman Road to York running through Stamford Hill, was the oldest road in the area. William Robinson wrote that the new road was made under provisions of an Act of Parliament. It commenced at Gloucester Gate, Regents Park and went through Camden and Holloway to Tottenham. Seven Sisters Road was named after a group of elms surrounding a walnut tree and it was the first new road in the area since medieval times, having been started around 1831 and completed around 1833. Robinson gave a summary of the accounts which show that £40,000 in total was paid for the road, of which £24,000 was for the section from Holloway to the Stamford Hill turnpike road; there was one turnpike. The sum included the cost of purchasing the land, conveyances, fencing, bridges, redirecting part of the New River, labour costs, materials, etc.

In 1833, the Middlesex Deeds Registry *(MDR/1833/2/379)* record that Brodie Augustus McGhie was resident at Hanger Lane. He did "*bargain sell assign transfer and set over*" to the Commissioners for the Metropolis by an Act of Parliament, some parcels of land for the purpose of a new road "*for the residue of the term of ninety-nine years by the said indenture of lease granted subject to the payment of the yearly sum of £12 and also to the observance of the covenants provisoes and agreements contained in said indenture of lease*". There were three parcels of land identified on a plan in the margin. The first parcel of land crossed Oat Fields and was 1 acre and 7 perches; the second crossed the lower part of Snares Mead, closer to Hanger Lane and was 1 acre and 30 perches; the third crossed the larger part of Snares Mead and was 1 rood and 5 perches in size. The indenture, registered on 8th March 1833, referred to an indenture dated 26th December 1807 made between John Wood, Esq. and Thomas Coxhead Stevens and registered on 8th August 1815 *(MDR/1815/5/480)*. McGhie was leaseholder of these parcels of land.

Two years later, an indenture *(MDR/1835/6/225)*, dated 11th & 12th August 1835, between John Lucas of Tooting in Surrey, Esq. and his wife Sarah, of the one part and the Commissioners for the Metropolitan Turnpike Roads of the other part was registered on 29th August 1835. The couple leased and released for one whole year to the Commissioners parts of three closes of land, known as Bushey Hangers in Tottenham, containing altogether 2 acres and 38 perches, shaded in pink on the plan in the margin. It was witnessed by Joseph William Thrupp of 160 Oxford Street. The parcels of land for the road were south of Hanger Lane and adjacent to Oat Fields cited above. In 1835, Lucas was not the owner of Oat Fields *(see below)*.

Later the same year an indenture (*MDR/1835/7/239*) was registered on 21st October 1835. This was an Indenture of lease and release dated 26th & 27th April 1833 between the Wood family and executors and Road Commissioners. Frances Wood of Woodford, Essex, a widow, William Varden of Gracechurch St in the City of London, an ironmonger, Edmund Heysham Wood of Muswell Hill, Middlesex, George Wood of Woodford, Essex, Herbert William Wood, a Lieutenant in the 4th Regiment of Native Infantry in the Honourable East India Company Service and Frances Ellen Wood of Woodford, Essex, a spinster, all of the one part and the Right Honourable William Lowther, John Joseph Austin, Esq. and Richard Lampert Jones, Esq., of the other part, for the use of the said Commissioners for carrying into execution certain acts of Parliament for consolidating the Trusts of certain Metropolitan Turnpike Roads. Frances Wood and William Varden, of the first part, Edmund Heysham Wood, George Wood, Herbert William Wood and Frances Ellen Wood, of the second part, Frances Wood, of the third part, did release, bargain and sell to William Lowther, John Joseph Austin and Richard Lampert Jones, Commissioners, of the fourth part. Included in the indenture was the following statement:

> Described from all her right of dower therein and from a certain annuity or yearly sum charged thereon bequeathed to the said Frances Wood during her widowhood in and by the will of her late husband the said John Wood dated the eight day of June 1812 and a memorial registered on 26th March 1814 (B2 No. 605).

This indenture was for the purpose of *"discharging the lands and heredits hereinafter mentioned"* and described as all those parcels of land at Tottenham High Cross, part of a new road and listed as 1 acre 7 perches, 1 acre 30 perches and 1 rood 5 perches. A plan was drawn in the margin. There were also references in this indenture to the indenture of release dated 26th December 1807 and another relating to John Wood and Thomas Coxhead Stevens, registered 8th August 1815 (*MDR/1815/5/ 480*). It was witnessed by Robert Spiller Wadeson of 11 Austin Friars, a solicitor. The heirs of John Wood were the owners of the freehold in 1835.

The memorial cited above (*MDR/1814/2/605*) was registered on 26th March 1814. It involved probate and the last will and testament dated 8th June 1812 of John Wood of Austin Friars and Walthamstow, a stock broker.

> ...he charged his freehold estate at or near Hanger Lane at or near Tottenham in the County of Middlesex in the first place with the payment unto his wife Frances Wood of such annual sum of money as therein mentioned and subject thereto the said testator devised unto his said wife and to Edward Green of Strangewell near Ware, William Varden of Gracechurch St., London, ironmonger and John Brown of Walthamstow, Essex, coal merchant and to their heirs.....all above and freehold Chambers part of Albany

House, Piccadilly in County of Middlesex all other his freehold and copyhold lands and heredits.

It was witnessed by Archer Moore Barlow (died 1818) of Austin Friars, London, a gentleman, John Warsop Sandys (died 1823) and James Faulkner. The will was proved by Frances Wood and William Varden on 3rd November 1813 (on 20th October 1813, Edward Green and John Brown renounced the probate and executors of said will). A memorial of the will registered by William Varden, witnessed by clerk, Edward Duke of Wadeson Barlow and Grosvenor of Austin Friars. The land was held in trust. This deed proved that John Wood owned the freehold and thereafter it passed to his heirs.

The following indenture (*MDR/1814/2/606*), registered 26th March 1814, was a Deed Poll, dated 26th January 1814. Edward Green and John Brown recited the will of John Wood giving freehold Chambers at Albany House, Piccadilly, London and freehold at Hanger Lane, devised unto them, to Frances Wood and William Varden. Green and Brown, by this deed poll, renounced and disclaimed "*all and singular the gifts, devises and bequests*" given to them in the will of John Wood and gave to Frances Wood and William Varden all "*trusts, directions and authorities*".

The heirs of John Wood were again listed in the Middlesex Deeds Registry (*MDR/1839/3/214*) in an Indenture of lease and release dated 14th & 15th March 1839 and registered on 28th March 1839. The lease was between Edmund Heysham Wood of Muswell Hill, of the one part and George Wood of Woodford and Herbert William Wood of the Fourth Native Infantry, stationed in India, of the other part. The release was between Edmund Heysham Wood of the first part, Frances Wood, a widow of Woodford, of the second part and Edmund Heysham Wood, George Wood and Herbert William Wood, of the third part: "*Which said lease in pursuance of the statute made for transferring uses into possession and in conson of ten shillings* ". For the nominal sum of 10 shillings, Edmund Heysham Wood "*did bargain and sell unto*" George Wood and Herbert William Wood, for one whole year and then release to same:

> All and singular the estate part share, right and interest of Frances Ellen Wood, of Woodford, spinster deceased, all those the chambers and heredits situate in the Albany, Piccadilly in the City of Westminster and also all those the houses lands and heredits situate at Stamford Hill in the County of Middlesex of to which the said Frances Ellen Wood was seized and entitled at the time of her decease and all other real estate which had descended upon him the said Edmund Heysham Wood as her heir at law to hold unto the said George Wood and Herbert William Wood their heirs and assigns...to the use of Edmund Heysham Wood, George Wood and Herbert William Wood in equal shares and proportions as tenants in common and not as joint tenants for their respective absolute benefits.
>
> Witnessed by Robert Spiller Wadeson, 11 Austin Friars, Solicitors and J. Friend, clerk.

Frances Ellen Wood's share of her fathers estate, with the consent of her mother, was divided among her brothers. She had died intestate but there was an administration (*PROB 6/215*):

> ...on twentieth day of February 1839 admon of the goods chattels and credits of Frances Ellen Wood late of Woodford in the County of Essex spinster deceased was granted to Edmund Heysham Wood the natural and lawful brother of the said deceased having been first sworn duly to administer Frances Wood widow the natural and lawful mother and next of kin having first sworn the letters of admon of the goods chattels of deceased.

She was only 26 when she died but her estate was valued at £7,000. In 1839, the heirs of John Wood still owned the freehold land at Hanger Lane, Tottenham High Cross. The will of Robert Spiller Wadeson of Austin Friars was proved in 1848. The heirs of John Wood still owned the land at Stamford Hill in 1839.

34

Hanger Lane

Poor Rate Books 1820-1876

Much of the evidence of owners in the Hanger Lane area is found in the Tottenham High Cross Ward Poor Rate Book (*D/PT/SE/7*), held at Bruce Castle Museum. This includes details of the inhabitants of houses and land at Hanger's Lane as from 10th October 1820. Four large detached houses with land on Hanger Lane were recorded on the *Old Ordnance Survey Map of Stamford Hill of 1868*; they were Gothic House, Barnfield, Albion Lodge and Woodberry Lodge. The following records are in evidence:

Table of owners in 1820.

Name	Description	Rental value
Thomas Bridges	Land	£70
	Land on common	£2
John St. Barbe	House and 7½ acres (Barnfield House)	£60
Charles Stevens	25 acres of land house empty	£120
Louis (Lewis) Burnand	House & 6 acres Little Gallow Hill (Albion Lodge)	£200
	6 acres Dupree	£24
	4 acres John Wood	£16
	For part of the field of Stonard	£10
	For 8 acres of Wood	£40
	Land of common	£2
James Collins	House garden & 5 acres of land	£140
	6 acres at Hanger's Lane	£25
	Common land	£2
William Hobson	House, garden & 18 acres of land (Markfield House)	£250
	11 acres of land	£30
	19 acres of land Wharf Lane	£76

The house names in brackets are added by the author.

On 16th March 1799, at St. Stephen's, Coleman Street in London, Louis Burnand, Esq., of St. Botolph, Bishopsgate, a bachelor, married Jane Antoinette Louise Sapte of the same parish, a minor, with the consent of her father, Peter Anthony Sapte. In the electoral register, in 1832, Louis or Lewis Burnand was shown to be living at Church Row, in the Parish of St. Mary, Stoke Newington.

Little Gallows Field (*sometimes Hill*) had been acquired around 1790 by Philip Hunt of Tottenham High Cross, a farmer, from Henry Hare Townsend Esq., eldest son of the late James Townsend. It was formerly part of the estate of Henry Hare, Lord Coleraine, sold by his son and others, after his son came of age, to clear the debts of James Townsend.

On 6th September 1791, records show that Philip Thomas Hunt of Tottenham, a farmer and son of Richard Hunt, a carpenter and citizen, was made *"Free"* by patrimony. Richard Hunt, in his will, proved in 1796, identified his son, Philip Thomas Hunt, daughter-in-law, Mary Frances Hunt, widow of Richard Hunt, son-in-law, Anthony Henry, grandson John Philip Hunt and referred to Little Gallows Field, south of Hanger's Lane, which he had purchased from James Townsend. Around 1804/05, the mansion house and other buildings were leased by Phillip Thomas Hunt to Richard James at a rent of £60 annually. In 1811, Richard James leased it to Lewis Burnand for £2,550 and in the same indenture it can be seen that Ralph Nicholson leased it to Burnand for a further £5,000. In 1826, Burnand leased the land with mansion house (*MDR/1826/10/415*) to Ebenezer Johnston, an ironmonger. The Poor Rate Book of 1820 shows that Major John Hunt and Philip Hunt held land in other areas of Tottenham.

William Robinson, in his book on Tottenham, records that James Collins was given permission to enclose some waste land at Tottenham in 1800. William Hobson lived at Markfield House, east of the road from Stamford Hill to Tottenham.

In October, 1820, Charles Stevens, appears as the owner of land and a house which was empty with a rental value of £120. He was the son of Thomas Coxhead Stevens, who had died in 1818. His mother had drafted her will in December 1820 and her son Charles was not included in it.

John St. Barbe was living at Barnfield House, owned by George Stacey.

Poor Rate Book (*D/PT/SC/18*) 1837 identifies inhabitants at Hanger's Lane. The only premises with a rateable value of £120 (see Stevens *above)* were those of Elizabeth Bayley (her own) and the house and garden occupied by Brodie Augustus McGhie. John Lucas of Tooting in Surrey was said to be the owner of this land. A Mrs. *Bailey* is recorded, by way of an indenture of 1833, north of Hanger Lane, next to Snares Mead. She was probably, in fact, Elizabeth Bayley.

Table of owners and occupiers in 1837.

Owner	Occupier	Description	Rental
George Stacey	Thomas Gibson	House & garden (Barnfield) Land	£50 £28
Miss Collins	Green	House & garden at corner	£35
Miss Collins	Frederick Cook	House & garden adjoining High Rd.	£30
John P. Hunt	Ebenezer Johnston	House & garden (Albion Lodge) Land	£160 £28
John Lucas Tooting, Surrey	B A. McGhie (Brodie Augustus)	House & garden Land (2 parcels)	£120 £86, £45
John Townsend	John Townsend	House & garden, land	£90,£8

By comparing entries in the Poor Rate Books for High Cross Ward for Hanger Lane, from different years, a pattern emerges, as the properties were similarly numbered in the books between the years 1837 to 1842. Gross estimated value is abbreviated to G.E.V. In some instances page is given instead of number.

Table of rateable value 1837-1870.

Date	No.	Occupier	Owner	Description	G.E.V.
Nov. 1837	261	B A. McGhie	John Lucas Tooting	House & garden Land (two parts)	£120 £86, £45
March1838	260	B A. McGhie	Lucas	House, garden and land	£120, £131
June 1840	262	B A. McGhie	Lucas	House, garden, cottage and land	£120 £131
May 1841	259	Late McGhie G.A. Walstab	Lucas	House, garden, cottage and land	£120 £131
May 1842	260	Walstab A J G Jerram J. Jerram John	Lucas Jerram John	House & Garden, Land Lodge	£140 £131
March Nov. 1844	262 259	John Jerram John Jerram	John Lucas	House, land, lodge House, land, lodge	£140, £10 £131
June 1845	Pg. 38	John Jerram	John Lucas	House, garden, premises, lodge Land	£140 £10 £131
June 1850	Pg. 33	John Jerram	John Lucas	House, garden, lodge Land	£140, £10 £131
June 1853	284	John Jerram	John Lucas	House, garden, lodge Land	£140, £10 £131
April 1854	Pg. 22	John Giblett	John Lucas	House, garden, lodge and land (39 acres)	£140, £10 £131
May 1857	366	John Giblett	John Lucas	House, garden, lodge Land	£140, £10 £131
June 1858	370	John Giblett	John Lucas	House, garden, lodge Land	£140, £10 £131
June 1859	Pg. 23	George Stacey Giblett (John)	John Lucas	House, garden, lodge Land	£140, £10 £131
June 1860	413 414	Samuel Stacey John Giblett	John Lucas	House garden lodge Land	£140, £10 £131
May 1861	443 444	Samuel Stacey John Giblett	John Lucas	House, garden, lodge Land	£128, £10 £131
May 1862	Pg. 31	James Black William John Giblett	John Lucas	House, garden, lodge, Land and cattle lairs	£168 £10 £148
June 1870	639 640	John Giblett John Giblett	John Lucas Executors of Collins	House, garden, lodge, land and cattle lairs Land St. Ann's Rd.	£168, £10 £130, £18 £18

The owner in the first instance was shown to be John Lucas of Tooting in Surrey. Brodie Augustus McGhie occupied the house and land owned and occupied by Thomas Coxhead Stevens. The entry for May 1842 has a number of amendments added in pencil; John Jerram appears in the *Owners* column beside the land as well as next to the Lodge. The rateable value for the house and garden is shown to have increased from £120 to £140. The additional £10 may have been for the lodge. References to A. J. G and G. A. Walstab are both to Arend George John Walstab.

George Stacey died in 1857 so it was his son, Samuel Lloyd Stacey who took over the rental of the house. In 1861, the amount for the house was less but written beside the gross estimated value is "*too little*". In 1862 it was John Black and not William James Black who occupied and rented with Giblett and the estimated rateable value was increased to £168 for the house and garden and £148 for land and cattle lairs. In 1870 the "*situation*" was described as St. Ann's and Seven Sisters Road, as Hanger Lane was renamed. The "*executors of Collins*" referred to Mary Ann Collins who inherited this land from her father, James.

Electoral Registers 1832-1836

The following information is collated from the Electoral Register 1832 for the Parish of Tottenham, with reference to Hanger's Lane. "**Situation**" describes "*the street, lane or other like place where the property is situate or name of the property or name of the tenant*". "**Qualification**" refers to category to vote.

Table of voters in 1832.

Name of voter	Place of abode	Qualification	Situation
John Austin	Hanger's Lane Tottenham	House as occupier	Himself
Thomas Gibson	Hanger's Lane Tottenham	House & land as occupier (Barnfield)	Hanger's Lane Tottenham
William Howard	Hanger's Lane Tottenham	Leasehold house as occupier	Himself occupied
Ebenezer Johnston	Hanger's Lane Tottenham	Freehold land (Albion Lodge)	Himself occupied
John Lucas	Upper Tooting, Surrey	Freehold house & lands	Mr Howard tenant
George Press	Tottenham Hanger's Lane	Freehold houses	James Coyons, E. Firth, Tomas Gray James Perriman
John Scales	Hanger's Lane Tottenham	Freehold land & house	Himself occupier

The following information was collated from the Electoral Register, 1836, for the Parish of Tottenham.

Table of voters in 1836.

Name of voter	Place of abode	Qualification	Situation
Frederick Clarkson	Hanger's Lane Tottenham	House & land as occupier	Himself tenant
Thomas Gibson	Tottenham	House & land occupier	Hanger's Lane
Ebenezer Johnston	Hanger's Lane Tottenham	Freehold land	Himself tenant
William Kirby	Hanger's Lane Tottenham	Leasehold house	Himself tenant
John Lucas	Tooting Surrey	Freehold land	Mr Howard tenant
Brodie Augustus McGhie	Tottenham	Leasehold house & land	Hanger's Lane
Henry Isaac Neild	Tottenham	Rental above £50 per annum	Hanger's Lane
Richard Dawkins	Tottenham	Farm and land above £50 per annum	Himself occupier
George Press	Hanger's Lane Tottenham	Freehold houses	Mr Cousins E. Firth and other tenants
John Scales	Hanger's Lane Tottenham	Freehold house & land	Himself tenant
John Townsend	Tottenham	Freehold house & land	Hanger's Lane
William Wansey	Tottenham	Rental above £50 per annum	Hanger's Lane

An Indenture (*MDR/1835/5/474*), dated 24th June and registered on 27th July 1835, confirms that William Howard, formerly of Hanger Lane and later of Hartley House near Plymouth in Devon, had assigned the lease to Henry Isaac Neild of 3 King Street, Cheapside, Middlesex, for the residue of the term of 31¾ years, for the messuage, outhouses, stables, yard, garden and paddock adjoining it. By 1836 Howard was the tenant of only the freehold land owned by John Lucas. John Lucas appears in the electoral registers for Tottenham, as the owner of freehold land occupied by Mr. Howard for the years 1847 to 1861, although John Lucas died in 1852. Lucas recorded in his will that he owned land of late or now occupied by William Howard.

William Howard was the son of Robert and Elizabeth Howard, a Quaker couple who lived in Tottenham. His elder brother was Luke Howard, known as *"namer of clouds"*. William was born in 1774, was apprenticed to his father as a tin manufacturer and had his own workshop. Like his brother, he was notably studious. William married Anna Maria Bell and had four children and was living at Hartley House, Plymouth when he died aged 86 in 1860. Some of his sisters continued to live in Tottenham long after he left it (*Elizabeth Howard web site*).

Henry Isaac Neild, a solicitor of Euston Square, married Sarah Kent in 1823 and most of their children were baptised at St. Mary Le Bone, Middlesex. However in 1838, the electoral register still showed Henry Isaac Neild in residence at Tottenham. In 1839, when their son Thomas was baptised, the family was living at Windsor Terrace, Maida Hill. Neild may have occupied the house that William Howard had leased from John Lucas. By 1848, Henry Isaac Neild was shown to be an insolvent practitioner, then living at Worthing in Surrey (*The London Gazette*). He died in 1860, aged 63.

William Kirby was a silk manufacturer and William Wansey, a fishmonger. Brodie Augustus McGhie was not registered to vote at Tottenham in 1832, but was in 1836. The Electoral Register for 1838 shows the same people at Hanger's Lane, including McGhie, who was registered to vote in two places. His place of abode was shown as Tottenham and he qualified to vote there because he had a leasehold house and land at Hanger's Lane. His place of abode in the electoral register for the Parish of St. Mary, Islington Middlesex was shown as Hanger's Lane, Stamford Hill but he qualified because he had a freehold house at Highbury Park, Islington. The Rate Books suggest that McGhie leased the land from John Lucas.

Records indicate the eligibility of liverymen to vote by reason of occupation in the City of London. In 1831, Brodie Augustus McGhie was recorded as a haberdasher at Exchange Alley. In 1834 and 1835 he was listed in the haberdasher's section but with an address at Hanger's Lane, Stamford Hill.

The Lucas Family

Related documents from the same period make reference both to John and Joseph Lucas. Joseph Lucas, of Upper Tooting in Surrey, died in 1807 leaving a will of some twenty-seven pages in length making bequests of money and property to many members of the Lucas family. He outlined his intention to bequeath to his nephew John Lucas, son of his brother, Rudd Lucas...

> ...all that farm of land with the heredits, rights and appurts thereunto belonging situate standing lying and being at Hanger Lane in the parish of Tottenham High Cross in the County of Middlesex and now in the tenure or occupation of Birkenhead as tenant thereof under lease lately granted by me and which said farm and estate I lately purchased of Edward Scales Esquire to hold the same unto and to the use of said John Lucas his heirs and assigns.

Birkenhead was named in Wyburd's Survey of Tottenham in 1798. He also passed to his nephew John Lucas, copyhold land, messuage, tenements and farm in the Parish of Hornsey known as Stapleton Hall. Joseph, John, William, James and Lawrence were sons of Rudd Lucas and they all received bequests; James Lucas was a significant beneficiary from his uncle of buildings and equipment. Joseph Lucas never had children and made his fortune, which he promptly put into property, from whaling in the South Seas. It is said that he and his partner, Christopher Spencer, were ship-owners and managers rather than on the whaling side of the business. However a document at the LMA dating from 1791 describes Lucas as an oil merchant. In 1806, again at the LMA, insurance documents (*Records of Sun Fire Office*) describe Joseph Lucas, Christopher Spencer and Samuel Hodgson as oilmen and lamplighters for whom, given the nature of their business, it would have been imperative to have insurance against fire.

Rudd Lucas had married Sarah Lawrence and was living at Hitchin, Hertfordshire when he died in 1810. He confirmed in his will that his five sons had been well provided for by his brother Joseph so he announced his intention to leave his freehold estate to his two daughters as tenants in common. Their father was buried in the Society of Friends Quaker ground at Hitchin.

The will of Rudd's son, Joseph Lucas of Upper Tooting, Surrey, made in 1812, was proved in 1821. Joseph left his brother John, of South Villa, Surrey, all his freehold estate at Hitchin, Hertfordshire, which he had lately purchased from his sisters, Elizabeth Peacock and Sarah Judkins and all of his fixtures and fittings, plate and silver at his dwelling house at Upper Tooting. He bequeathed to his brother, William, then living in Stapleton Hall, Stroud Green, Hornsey, Middlesex, all his copyhold and leasehold estates; Lawrence, his youngest brother, received £2,000 and all his clothes. His sisters, Elizabeth and Sarah each received £500. James Lucas was also cited but he had already received a bequest from his uncle. Joseph gave instructions for burial along with his late uncle Joseph at Streatham Church, Surrey.

Elizabeth, Joseph, Ann and Rudd Lucas, children of William Lucas, were all baptised on 20th July 1815 at St. Mary, Hornsey when the parents were living at Stroud Green. Other members of the Lucas family were baptised as children and adults, perhaps as some of the family were Quakers. William Lucas died in 1832, aged 55 and was buried at St. Mary, Hornsey. His widow, Sarah, his eldest son Joseph and William's brother, John Lucas were executors of his will. He identified his six younger children as Anne, Rudd, Sarah, William, Mary and Emma and he made a bequest to his nephew, John Lucas, son of his brother Lawrence. Sarah Lucas, widow of William, was buried in 1836, aged 56, with her husband. A statement in her will indicated that she *"was late of Cross Street"* in Islington, suggesting that she had moved from Stapleton Hall; an Indenture (*MDR/1838/5/477*) followed the proving of the will. The freehold messuage at Stroud Green in Hornsey was to go to William's wife and after her death to his son Joseph, as did his leasehold estate at Castle Street and Brownlow Street, Cirencester Place, Pentonville and Deptford. As both parents were dead, Joseph inherited this land. Joseph William Thrupp of 160 Oxford Street, a solicitor, was present at the signing of this document.

Sarah Lucas, wife of John Lucas, aged 82, of Upper Tooting, was buried on 4th May 1847 at St. Leonard's, Streatham. In the census of 1851, John Lucas (75), a widower, was recorded at Heene in Sussex near Worthing. His place of birth was Hitchin in Hertfordshire and his occupation had been that of a land and house proprietor. His nephew, James Lucas (26) and his nieces Maria (38) and Mary Ann Lucas (36) were living with him. They were all fund holders and land proprietors, actively involved in the property business. Mary Ann was already involved by 1839 (*see indenture above*). These were the son and daughters of his deceased brother, James Lucas, a captain in the Merchant Navy, who died in 1839. Their mother, Mary Ann, according to research on the Lucas Family of Hitchin, had died in 1825, leaving five daughters and a young son, James John Seymour Spencer Lucas, who was only two years old when she died.

John Lucas died on 23rd October 1852, aged 77 (*The Times*) and he was buried with other relatives at St. Leonard's, Streatham on 30th October. In his lengthy will, written in 1851, John described his land held in various parts of the country, which he granted to various family members; these included Clapham, Lambeth, Lewisham and Kent. Lucas was still in possession of freehold and copyhold land at Stapleton Hall in Hornsey. He wrote, *"I give devise and bequeath all that my freehold estate situate at or near Tottenham in the County of Middlesex and now or late in the occupation of William Howard and all other my estate at or near Tottenham aforesaid"* and in relation to other land at Clapham, which the trustees were instructed to pay during the lifetime of his brother-in-law, Samuel Judkins, *"the rents issues and profits of the said last mentioned freehold and leasehold estates and hereditaments"*. The will made specific reference to the freehold land once occupied by Howard at Tottenham but Lucas also held other land at Tottenham. John Lucas appointed his nephews, Joseph Lucas of Trinity Place, Charing Cross, eldest son of his late brother William Lucas and Rudd Lucas, a surgeon from Somerset, the second son of William Lucas, as well as his cousin, Joseph Lucas, a brewer, of Hertfordshire, as executors. John, the son of Lawrence Lucas, also received a bequest. Joseph Lucas studied at Edinburgh University and qualified as a solicitor in 1833. He had offices at the Strand and later at Surrey Street in Central London. In 1835, Joseph Lucas had married his first cousin, Sarah Lucas Judkins and had 16 children. Joseph Lucas moved in with his uncle John and lived at Stapleton

House, Nos. 78 and 79 East Side in Upper Tooting. Samuel Judkins, once a corn merchant, died in 1866, aged 86 and according to the censuses of 1851 and 1861, was living at 82 East Side in Upper Tooting before his death. For many years he had lived at No. 71 Tooley Street, Southwark, Surrey.

In 1853, a record appeared in the Electoral Register of James John Seymour Spencer Lucas, living at Heene House, Worthing in Sussex, where he had lived with his uncle. James J.S.S. Lucas was also the owner of Nos. 43 to 58 Rupert Street (inclusive), near Piccadilly Circus, Middlesex, as indeed John Lucas, in his will, recorded that he owned a fourth-part share of houses at Rupert Street. James never married and when he died at Burfield Priory, near Bristol, in 1873, his estate went to his sisters and nephews.

Lawrence Lucas, a farmer of Irthlingborough, Northants, died in December, 1857. By his will he explained that his son John was already provided for and he left a trust fund for his two daughters, Sarah Foster and Elizabeth Woods and for his grandchildren.

William's second son, Rudd Lucas, a surgeon, died in 1865 and his will was proved by his widow and his brother Joseph, the solicitor. Joseph Lucas (92) and his wife Sarah (88) died within months of each other in 1903, at Stapleton House, Upper Tooting, in Surrey. The couple had been married for 68 years.

Joseph Lucas, nephew of John and his cousin, also Joseph Lucas, continued to act as executors for the estate of John Lucas, who had died in 1852 and were involved in land deals in Tottenham in 1866, 1867 and as late as 1876. John Lucas had held freehold land south of Hanger Lane and the Rate Books suggest that he, rather the heirs of John Wood, was the owner of the land, even though John Lucas died in 1852 and continued to be recorded as the owner of the land known as Oatfields and Snares Mead.

Information from the *Tottenham Tithe Map and Tithe Award Book (1844)*, prepared during the summer months but not finalised until September that year, is compiled in the table below and identifies some owners, occupiers, plots, description of land and sizes in acres, roods and perches. It relates to the *"apportionment of the rent charge in lieu of tithes in the parish of Tottenham in the County of Middlesex"*. The new Seven Sisters Road crossed Hanger Lane and split some of the parcels of land identified in *Wyburd's Survey of 1798*. (*There are four roods in one acre and forty perches in one rood.*)

Table, from tithes, of owners and occupiers in 1844.

Owners	Occupier	Plot	Description of land & premises	A	R	P
Wood John executors	Francis Herrington	1470	nine acres meadow	8	1	6
			Total	8	1	6
Wood John executors	John Jerram	1463	Seven acres	6	2	26
	"	1465	Twelve acres	13	0	1
	"	1466	Acre piece	1	2	6
	"	1467	Lodge and pasture	0	1	37
	"	1468	Three acres	3	2	2
	"	1469	meadow	0	3	0

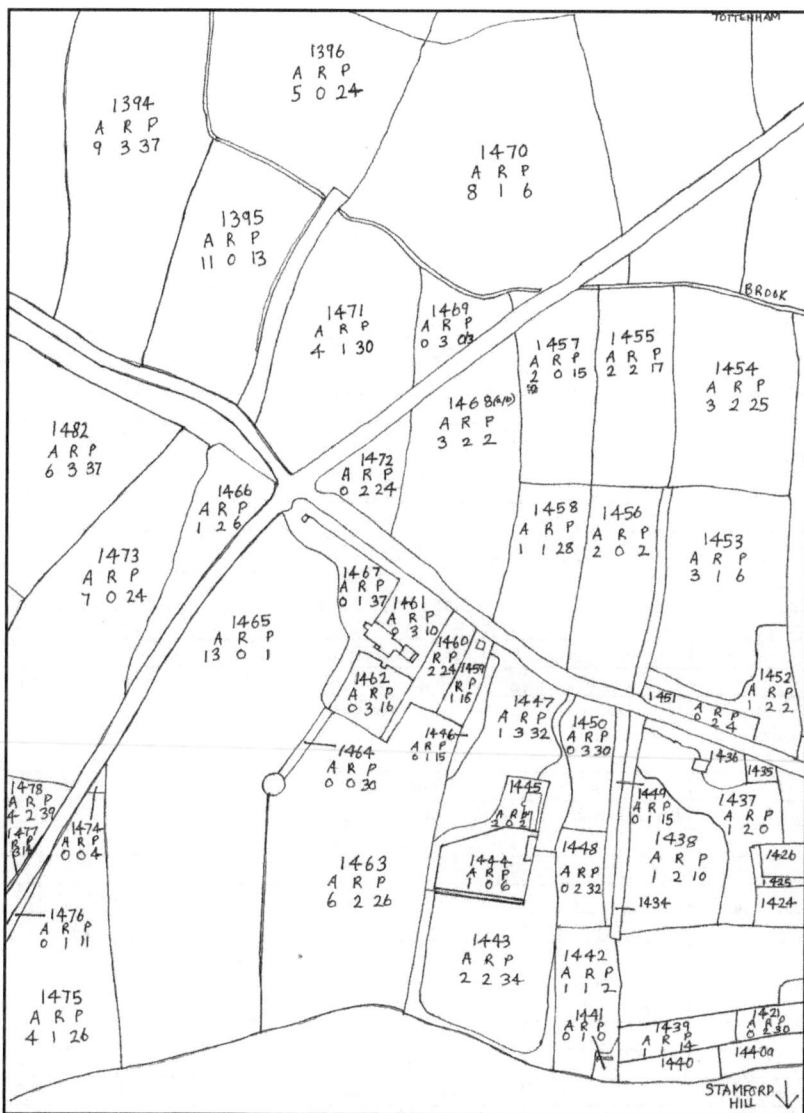

34.1 Section of Tottenham Tithe Map (1844) adapted by author.

Owners	Occupier	Plot	Description of land & premises	A	R	P
	"	1459	Sheds stables & yards	0	1	16
	"	1460	Kitchen garden	0	2	24
	"	1461	House Buildings & pleasure ground	0	3	10
	"	1462	Kitchen Gardens & water	0	3	16
	"	1464	Pleasure Ground	0	0	30
			Total	28	3	8
George Stacey	Henry Gregory	1453	Meadow	3	1	6
	"	1454	Meadow	3	2	25
	"	1451	Kitchen garden	0	2	4

Owners	Occupier	Plot	Description of land & premises	A	R	P
	"	1452	House buildings cottage & pleasure ground	1	2	2
			Total	8	3	37
Mary Ann Collins	Edmund Mills	1471	Meadow	4	1	30
	"	1472	Meadow	0	2	24
			Total	5	0	14
Ann & Elizabeth Dupree	John Maddan	1455	Meadow	2	2	17
	"	1456	Meadow	2	0	2
	"	1457	Meadow	2	0	15
	"	1458	Meadow	1	1	28
			Total	8	0	22
Philip Thomas Hunt	Ebenezer Johnston	1443	Meadow	2	2	34
	"	1447	Meadow	1	3	32
	"	1450	Meadow	0	3	30
	"	1444	Kitchen garden	1	0	6
	"	1445	House buildings yards pleasure ground & shrubbery	2	0	2
	"	1446	Wood	0	1	15
	"	1448	Garden & orchard	0	2	32
			Total	9	2	21
Trustees of Metropolitan Roads	James Dawkins	1476 1477	Slips of pastures	0 0	1 3	11 14
			Total	1	0	25
Joseph Lucas	James Dawkins	1474	Arable	0	0	4
	"	1473	Meadow 7 acres	7	0	24
	"	1475	5 acres	4	1	26
	"	1478	3 acres	4	2	39
	"	1479	18 Acres	18	3	34
			Total	35	1	7
Joseph Lucas	George William Lenox	1481	Part of 9 acres	2	2	13
	"	1482	Meadow	6	3	37
	"	1480	Wood	0	0	14
	"	1483	Kitchen garden	0	2	37
	"	1484	House buildings & pleasure grounds	0	3	15
			Total	11	0	36

Francis Harrington was recorded in the census of 1841 with his wife Esther, both aged 40, at 6 Tottenham Hale at "*Down Row*". He was a dairyman, so he may have used part of Snares Mead to graze his cattle. By the time of his death on 14th January 1871, he was living at Church Lane, Cheshunt and was described as a gent. His wife died in April that year, at 5 Robert Street, Hampstead, Middlesex, where she had been staying with her nephew John Herrington Parks.

Philip Thomas Hunt, a farmer, died in 1851. His will, written in 1842, made reference to Gallow Hill, then in the occupation of Ebenezer Johnston, to his wife Sally (married in 1807), nieces and to his nephew Lieutenant Colonel John Philip Hunt. A codicil explained that Sally had died. Lieutenant Colonel Hunt also owned land in Tottenham when he died in 1858, aged 78.

John Lucas was recorded as a freeholder of land in Tottenham in 1839/40 (*William Robinson's Book*). Various members of the Lucas family are shown as owners of land in Tottenham High Cross and Wood Green Ward in the Rate Books. The Tithe Map recorded that it was Joseph Lucas who owned land on the west of Seven Sisters Road, going towards Hornsey, occupied by George William Lenox. James Dawkins occupied land on either side of Seven Sisters Road, owned by Joseph Lucas and the Trustees of the Metropolitan Roads. This land was in Wood Green Ward, despite its proximity to Hanger Lane. On the 1844 Tithe Map, the parcels of land, then numbered 1474, 1475, 1476, 1477 and 1478 showed two banked areas on either side of Seven Sisters Road as it reached the border with Hackney. This was adjacent to the land owned by the executors of John Wood, occupied by John Jerram (1465 and 1466).

In the Rates Book for Wood Green Ward (1837) John Lucas of Tooting was recorded as the owner of a house and garden at Hanger Lane occupied by Henry Isaac Neild, with land occupied by G. W. Lenox. A Memorandum acknowledged that Mr. Neild's house was occupied by G. W. Lenox, with eight acres of land, the notes followed by *"John Lucas 34½ acres of land £112 Richard Dawkins £103"*. An Indenture dated 23rd December 1837 (*MDR/1838/1/96*), registered on 4th January, 1838, explained that Henry Isaac Neild of King Street, Cheapside in the City of London, a gentleman, assigned his house and land to George William Lenox of Mill Hall, Poplar, in the County of Middlesex, Esq., in consideration of £400, for the remainder of the lease.

An entry in the *London Gazette* of October 1840 declared that James Dawkins of West Green, Tottenham, Middlesex, a cattle dealer and chapman was insolvent. In the census of 1841, James Dawkin, a farmer aged 35, was living at Green Lanes, Tottenham. In the census of 1851, he was recorded at West Green Road, aged 47, with his wife Elizabeth; he had married Elizabeth Steeden in 1826. He was still there in 1869. James was the son of Richard and Priscilla Dawkins and was baptised at All Hallows, Tottenham in 1804.

George William Lenox was baptised at All Hallows, Tottenham on 8th May, 1800. In 1824, he entered into a partnership with Samuel Brown, Samuel Lenox and James Thomas Walker; Brown, while in the Royal Navy, had originally patented a stud-link chain. The company had premises initially at Millwall, near Deptford and then additionally at Pontypridd in Wales. For many years the it made chains for the Navy and expanded rapidly with the industrial revolution, making cables and equipment for the iron and coal industries, bridges, merchant shipping; it created many other inventions. In August 1838, Lenox, then of Angler's Lane Tottenham, was named in *Proceedings of the Old Bailey* in connection with the theft of his horse. He married Rosa Ross Wilkinson in Guernsey in 1839. In the census of 1841, he was recorded at Hanger Lane as a merchant, with his wife Rosa and in 1851 as an iron cable supplier. In 1843 he appeared in the Electoral Register, living in Millwall, East London and in 1846 and 1852 in Wales. Lenox died in 1868, leaving under £50,000 in his will, with residences in the City of London, Portland Place, Middlesex and Wales.

The *Tithe Award Book* (1844) records ownership of land at Hanger Lane by the heirs of John Wood, with *Joseph* Lucas as the owner of adjacent land. In the same year, in the Rate Books and electoral registers for High Cross, *John* Lucas is recorded as the owner of the same land. The Poor Rate Books for Wood Green (*March 1844*) show that John Lucas owned a house and garden at Hanger Lane, occupied by G.W. Lennox and land occupied by James Dawkins, whose name is crossed out and replaced by that of John Lowe.

Both sources indicate that the land was occupied by John Jerram. As to why was Lucas said to be the owner, there are two possible explanations for the name of Joseph Lucas being shown. One is that he was the nephew of John Lucas and both were living at the same address; Joseph looked after his uncle's business affairs as his solicitor. Another possibility is that part of Bushey Hangers, which had been acquired from Edward Scales by Joseph Lucas before he died in 1807, was then left to his nephew, John Lucas. In 1839, when Frances Ellen Wood died, her share of the freehold estate at Stamford Hill passed to her brothers, which might suggest that John Wood was the owner and not John Lucas, as indicated within the Middlesex Deeds Registry. It was the heirs of John Wood who sold Oat Field and Snares Mead in 1859 and not John or Joseph Lucas.

35

Leaseholders of Woodberry Lodge after 1821

Brodie Augustus McGhie (1766–1841)

Brodie Augustus McGhie, baptised at St. Botolph Aldgate, Middlesex on 6th July 1766, was the son of Brodie Augustus McGhie and Elizabeth of Little Burr Street (this may be Burr Close, near St. Katharine's Way and Hermitage Wall in London). His father was a mariner, then living in the Parish of St. George in the East, London. In his will, the elder Brodie referred to his property on the north side of Great Hermitage Street, Middlesex which he had bought from John Beaston. He also owned a quarter share of a brigantine of 140 tons, called *Elizabeth*, under his command, travelling from England to Holland. Elizabeth and then his children were to receive a share of his estate. His will was proved on 14th August 1780. Elizabeth was the eldest daughter, baptised on 19th July 1761 and the second daughter was Ann baptised on 3rd July 1768 at St. George in the East. Elizabeth married Watton Willcox the younger on 25th July 1781 (*Willcox is sometimes written as Wilcox*).

Elizabeth Kent, formerly McGhie, the widow of the elder Brodie Augustus McGhie, was living in the house of Elizabeth, the widow of Watton Willcox, in Ostend when, from her sickbed, she made her will, dated 5th May 1792. She described the goods and services that her daughter had given her for several years as an expression of "*extraordinary love*". She left her silver and furniture to her widowed daughter and requested that the latter take care of her burial and organise a "*funeral by a Protestant parson of this town*". Her second daughter Ann, wife of John Robert Sherman and her son Captain Brodie (Augustus) McGhie were also named in the will. She gave £20, to be used for their education, to each of her grandchildren, Bartholomew Kent Willcox and Brodie McGhie Willcox, who were fatherless. It was scribed by notaries and translated and administered in July 1792 by her daughter, Ann Sherman, who lived in England. It might be inferred from this will that Watton Willcox died abroad if Elizabeth Willcox was living there. Ann's husband, a ship owner of Ingram Court, Fenhurch Street appeared in a list of bankrupts in November 1803 (*Morning Post*).

Captain Watton Willcox is reported many times in newspapers, travelling from Horsleydown on the River Thames to Rotterdam from 1749 to 1789. Watton Willcox the elder, was described as a mariner, living in the Parish of St. John, Horsleydown, Southwark, in Surrey, when his will was written in September 1890 and it was proved in June 1791. His part-share of the ship *Duke of York* was to go to his wife, Ann Mary. He recorded that his son Watton Willcox junior, who lived in the Parish of St. George in the East,

Middlesex, was a co-partner with Sampson Coysgarne and that anything due from that partnership was to go to his wife and to his daughters, Elizabeth, Sarah, Ann Mary and Suzanne. Coysgarne married Rebecca Willcox in 1781, suggesting that he was related by marriage. In 1791, a Watton Willcox was listed as a joiner in a Livery Directory for London. Watton Willcox the younger and Sampson Coysgarne, both ship's chandlers, chapmen, dealers and co-partners and both living at Little Hermitage Street in the Parish of St. George in the East, were declared bankrupt in 1783 (*London Gazette*). Walton, the eldest son of Watton and Elizabeth Willcox, aged 9, was buried in Northumberland in August 1791 (Memorial Inscription in the Church of St. Nicholas, Newcastle on Tyne). It may have been this Sampson Coysgarne, a former purser in Admiral Nelson's flagship "*Foudroyant*", when he died in 1822, who left in his will to his children and grandchildren various items of jewellery, buttons and other trinkets.

The younger Brodie Augustus McGhie was also a ship-owner and builder. He was in partnership with William and John Beatson, the latter of whom Brodie's father had named in his will. At their large yard at Rotherhithe, McGhie and Beatson were in the business of breaking up warships and ships from the East India Company. By a Bill of Sale dated 1791, Brodie McGhie, master mariner and commander, living at Hermitage Street in the Parish of St. George, Wapping, bought an eighth part of the ship *Eagle* from William Clappeson, a merchant, also of that parish. In August 1791, Brodie McGhie insured his premises at 3 Torrington Street, Ratcliff Highway, Stepney (*LMA Records of Sun Fire Office*). McGhie was in partnership with Beatson and Thurgood, ship and insurance brokers, until 1817 when the partnership was dissolved (*London Gazette*). The McGhie and Willcox families were involved in all aspects of shipping and lived near the river at Hermitage Street.

Pallot's Marriage Index confirms that Elizabeth Addison married Brodie Augustus McGhie at St. Nicholas, Newcastle upon Tyne in 1796 and his name appears in various documents after this time. In 1798, B. A. McGhie appeared in land tax records at Mile End, Middlesex, Tower Division in the Parish of St. George. He occupied property owned by Thomas Bradshaw. McGhie insured property near Wapping at Hermitage Street in November 1801 and at 31 Henry Street in Pentonville, London, in 1802.

Bartholomew Kent, of Newcastle-upon-Tyne, an upholsterer, died on 27th January 1803. His abstract of administration TNA (*IR 26/425/476*) named his executors as Robert Rankin and John Robert Sherman, of Pentonville in London. The legatees were Mrs. Elizabeth Willcox, a widow, who was his niece, John Robert Sherman and his wife Ann, Bartholomew's nephew and niece and £100 was to go to Elizabeth McGhie, daughter of his nephew, when she would reach 21. According to a newspaper report (*Newcastle Courant*) in March 1803, Elizabeth Willcox had assisted Mr. Kent for some considerable time, managing the old-established business but the stock and premises were to be sold. She was going to run it until a buyer was found.

The reference in Kent's will to Elizabeth McGhie, the daughter of his nephew, was to the child of Brodie Augustus McGhie and Elizabeth Addison.

The table below, compiled from BMD Nonconformist records, gives details of their family.

Table of baptisms and burials of children of McGhie family.

Name	Relation	Year	Event	Place of abode
Elizabeth	Mother Elizabeth	1797	Baptism	Ratcliff Highway
Brodie Augustus	Mother Elizabeth	1800	Baptism	Ratcliff Highway
Brodie Augustus		1801	Burial (14 mths)	Torrington Street
Elizabeth		1803	Burial (5½)	Pentonville
Eleanor	Mother Elizabeth	1805	Baptism	Wentworth Place Mile End Road
Elizabeth	Daughter of B. A.	1814	Burial (3)	Edmonton
Elizabeth	Wife of B.A.	1814	Burial (36)	Tanner's End Edmonton

In 1805, Eleanor McGhie was recorded in the *Register of Births and Baptisms* at the Presbyterian Chapel in Great Alie Street at Goodman's Fields (*RG4 4512*). Eleanor's birth was also registered in 1809 at Dr. Williams's Library, Redcross Street, near Cripplegate, London and signed by two witnesses in the following words:

> These are to certify that Eleanor M:Ghie daughter of Brodie Augustus M:Ghie and Elizabeth his wife, who was daughter of Joseph Addison, was born in Wentworth Place, Mile End in the Parish of St Dunstans Stepney in the County of Middlesex the first day of October in the year one thousand eight hundred and five at whose birth we were present. (RG5 039)

In the census of 1851, Ellen's place of birth was recorded as Mile End, Middlesex. She was baptised for a second time at All Saints, Edmonton some years later, on 25th July 1822, and these records show her birth date as 1st October 1805. Presbyterians were Nonconformists, hence the second baptism in the established Church of England. The deaths of Brodie Augustus McGhie's daughter on 30th March 1814 and wife on 27th July 1814, appeared in the *Register of Burials at the New Gravel Pit Presbyterian Meeting House at Paradise Fields in the Parish of Hackney, St. John, London.*

Brodie McGhie Willcox grew up in Newcastle but was sent to London to work with his uncle, Brodie Augustus McGhie. In 1808, the latter appeared in land tax records at Mile End Road, Stepney. Willcox married Sophia Ann Vandergucht, the daughter of a Belgian merchant around 1812. In the census of 1851 it was declared that he was a ship-owner, a British subject, born in Belgium, of English parents and that his wife was born in the Parish of St. George, Hanover Square. Willcox was born in 1784. His son, Brodie Augustus Willcox, also listed, was described as a ship agent.

Brodie Augustus McGhie, a widower of Hammersmith, married Eleanor Smith, a widow of Wantage in Berkshire on 5th August 1815 at All Saints, Fulham. Augusta Sherman McGhie, their daughter, was born on 15th July 1816 and was baptised by D. Warren on 6th August 1816 at All Saints, Edmonton. The couple then lived at Tanner's End, near Silver Street, Edmonton.

Bartholomew Kent Willcox died at sea on 20th September 1815 at the age of 27, while on his way to Malta. His death is commemorated on a memorial plaque at the Church of St. Nicholas, Newcastle-upon-Tyne, where he had lived in his youth. On 19th December 1816, the estate, which was below the value of £3,000, was administered by two of his executors, Brodie McGhie Willcox, Esq., of Seymour Place, Middlesex (his brother) and Brodie Augustus McGhie, of Tanners End Edmonton (his uncle). Bartholomew Kent Willcox, prior to his death lived in Marchmont Street, Brunswick Square, in London. It was around this time that Brodie McGhie Willcox started in the shipping business so, advised by his uncle, he may have used the money inherited from his brother's estate.

In the Vestry Minutes for Tottenham Church (*14th January 1817 to 26th January 1836*), McGhie is cited on 21st June 1821. He acquired the lease for the house at Hanger Lane officially on 29th June 1821 although the Indenture (*MDR/1821/5/539*) stated that he had taken it from March; he was described then as a shipbroker. Eleanor McGhie, wife of Brodie Augustus McGhie, died in Edmonton, Middlesex, aged 36 and was buried at St. Mary Magdalen, Reigate, Surrey, on 4th December 1822 (*church records*). William Robinson, in his book on Tottenham, provides an account of the funeral of Reverend Thomas Roberts, who died in October 1824 having served twenty-six years in the Parish of Tottenham. In one of a fleet of carriages that followed the funeral procession from Tottenham to St. George's Middlesex was William Howard Esq., with companions. In carriages solely occupied were James Collins, Miss Dermer, Thomas Rhodes, Esq., Ralph Nicholson, Esq., Brodie McGhie, Esq. and others. McGhie appeared in the Vestry Minutes on 1st March 1825 and again on 22nd September 1826, when he was nominated to the office of Surveyor of the Highways for the High Cross and Wood Green area.

Ellen McGhie married Thomas Bridges at All Hallows, Tottenham on 3rd April 1830, in the presence of Augusta and Brodie Augustus McGhie and Louise and M. A. Bridges. It is possible that Ellen had raised Augusta as the former was born some ten years before her half-sister. Ellen McGhie Bridges was baptised at the same church in July 1831. Her father's occupation was shown to be that of a solicitor and the family was living at Laura Place, off Lower Clapton Road in London. Thomas, born on 11th December 1805 and baptised at St. John at Hackney, was the son of Thomas Bridges and Mary Ann Knapp.

The elder Bridges were married on 30th December 1802 at St. Maurice, Winchester, in Hampshire. Thomas Bridges was then living in the Parish of St. Olave, Hart Street, in London; Mary Ann was the widow of Edward Knapp junior, from Winchester, a merchant and banker. Edward's father, also Edward, a coal, corn and salt merchant, in 1786 set up a private bank, known as the Winchester Bank. Mary's first husband died in 1801. The couple had two daughters, Susan and Emma Knapp, brought up in Tottenham, who respectively married James and Philip Cazenove of Hornsey, the latter of the stockbroking dynasty. The step-daughters had received substantial amounts from their grandfather, Edward Knapp, arising from his will in 1819.

Thomas and Marie Ann Bridges had three daughters. The eldest, Marie Ann, in 1825 married Gustavas Evans, a commander in the Royal Navy and they lived at Headley Grove in Surrey. Frances, who was born in 1807, in 1828 married Joseph Lidwell Heathorn of Stafford. In October 1831 Ann Louise, at All Hallows, Tottenham, married Carey Bonham Hopkins, a solicitor from Wilmington, near Dartford in Kent but following his premature death, married John Groves in December 1833 at the Parish church of St. Thomas, Clapton. It was the elder Thomas Bridges who was recorded in the Tottenham Rate Book of 1820. Thomas Bridges was living at Stamford Hill when his youngest daughter married Carey Bonham Hopkins.

Thomas Bridges, the father, died on 4th November 1834, aged 61 and his wife died in Clapton within hours of hearing of his death. A Mary Ann Bridges, of Sutton Place, London, was buried at St. John at Hackney on 12th November 1834. Thomas Bridges, described as being late of Stamford Hill, was living at Langham Lodge, Epping, in Essex. By his will, he gave each of his four children £2,000 but left nothing to his wife or step-daughters. He named as executors his son, Thomas, of 20 Kings Arm's Yard, Coleman Street in the City of London and his sons-in-law, John Groves and Gustavas Evans.

John Robert Sherman, the brother-in-law of Brodie Augustus McGhie, died on 17th March 1838. Letters of administration at LMA (*DL/C/0514/010/001-003*) were granted to his widow, Ann Sherman. His address was recorded as Stamford Grove, Clapton, Middlesex (off Old Hill at Clapton Common) and his estate was valued at under £100.

In April 1839, Brodie Augustus McGhie of Hanger Lane, Tottenham wrote his will. He identified his daughters as Augusta Sherman McGhie and Eleanor (Ellen), wife of Thomas Bridges and referred additionally to an Ann Montgomery. His household goods and furniture were to go to his daughter Augusta. McGhie's house at Highbury Park was to be held in trust in equal parts by Brodie McGhie Willcox of Cheshunt, Hertfordshire and Joseph Addison McLeod of Fenchurch Street. This was the only property identified in his will. McGhie left funds for mourning to his son-in-law, Thomas Bridges, to Richard Collins Smith, son of his late wife and to Mrs. Elizabeth Willcox, mother of Brodie McGhie Willcox. Richard Collins Smith received a further £50 and to McGhie's sister Ann Sherman, then of Doughty Street, Middlesex, an annuity of £20 was provided. Elizabeth Willcox died in 1843, prior to which she had been living at Dorset Square, London.

On 5th June 1839 Augusta Sherman McGhie married Watkin Charles Kenrick, a mariner, at All Hallows, Tottenham. His father was Charles Kenrick, a gentleman; Augusta's father was described as a merchant. Witnesses to the proceedings were Brodie Aug. McGhie, Thomas Bridges, Augusta's brother-in-law and his sister, who signed as Marianne Evans and Mary and Lucy Johnston (likely to have been daughters of Ebenezer Johnston), their neighbour. The death of Brodie Augustus McGhie at the age of 75, was recorded at Edmonton in January 1841 (*GRO*). His will was proved on 20th February 1841 (*PROB 11/1941/220*).

Within two months of his death, the executors of the late B. A. McGhie put the *Ellen* up for sale. Built by McGhie, Hawks and Carr for their own use, the ship, of some 352 tons, was capable of carrying a large cargo and had frequently travelled from Sydney in New South Wales, Australia (*British Mercury* 10th April 1841)

At the time of the 1841 Census, Augusta, then aged 24, Watkin Charles Kenrick, aged 31 and Sarah Beaston, aged 25, were listed with Elizabeth Hancock, a widow, aged 65, head of house, at West Green, Tottenham, near the Black Boy. Mrs. Hancock lived in a cottage, according to an entry dated 1822 in the Vestry Minutes of Tottenham Church. Augusta and Watkin Kenrick had two children, Augusta Lewin McGhie Kenrick and William Charles Kenrick. Elizabeth Hancock died, aged 76, on 12th January 1851 at West Green.

Thomas Bridges, the son, a solicitor, was living at Coleman Street in 1840. In the census of 1841, he and Ellen (Eleanor) Bridges and their six children were living at Woodberry Down, Stoke Newington. By the time of the census of 1851 the family had moved to Marwood in Devon and had another child, Alice Lucy, her birth having been registered in Barnstable, in Devon. Their other children were born at Clapton, Stamford Hill, Tottenham and Stoke Newington. Thomas Bridges was by that time a farmer.

An indenture (*MDR/1842/5/46*) dated 2nd June 1841 and registered on 5th July 1842, dealt with McGhie's estate. The parties were Brodie McGhie Willcox of St. Mary Axe, a merchant, Joseph Addison McLeod of 16½ Biliter Street, both in the City of London, of the first part (McGhie's executors), the said Willcox, McLeod and Daniel Prince, a merchant of Threadneedle Street in the City of London, of the second part and Arend John George Walstab of Austin Friars, a merchant of the City of London, of the third part. The first and second parties sold to the third party the remainder of the term of 96 year lease for several closes of land. The dwelling house, stables, outbuildings and offices were drawn on the plan in the margin, with three parcels of land and Snares Mead, on the north side of Hanger Lane in the Parish of Tottenham High Cross. References were to the lease from 26th December 1807 and indentures registered 8th August 1815 (*MDR/1815/5/480*) and 8th March 1833 (*MDR/1833/2/379*), the latter dealing with the three parcels of land sold for the new road. It also referred to an indenture of underlease subject to *"the payment of the rents and performance of the covenants"*, contained in an indenture dated 26th December 1817.

Ann Sherman, a widow of Stamford Grove East, Upper Clapton, Middlesex, died on 20th March 1847. Brodie McGhie Willcox, her nephew and one of her executors applied for letters of administration LMA (*DL/C/0524/174/001-002*) for her estate, valued at under £450. She was buried on 26th March at St. John at Hackney, aged 78. Her niece, Augusta Kenrick died in April 1847 in Wokingham, in Berkshire. Watkin Charles Kenrick, of Wokingham, a ship owner, lately of Greenwich, Kent, died in 1856, aged 44 (*The London Gazette*).

The younger Thomas Bridges died aged 65, on 28th December 1870. Ellen Bridges, his widow, then of Marwood Hill, North Devon and Palace Gate,

Exeter and daughter of Brodie Augustus McGhie, died on 5th May 1886, aged 80. Emma Augusta Bridges, her spinster daughter, was sole executor. In the census of 1861 a Thomas McGhie Bridges, son of Thomas and Ellen, was recorded on board a Royal Navy ship at Hong Kong, aged 22.

As to Brodie McGhie Willcox of Portman Square, London, an M.P for fifteen years, he had been a founding member of The Peninsular & Oriental Steam Navigation Company later known as the P&O shipping business (in the census of 1861 his occupation was given as *"land, funds and shareholder"*). He died in 1862 leaving effects valued at under £120,000. His obituary confirmed that his father, Watton was a ship-owner from Rotherhithe. The family of B.M. Willcox is buried in Highgate Cemetery, Camden, where there is an obelisk dedicated to him, his wife and children; it is listed by English Heritage.

Arend George John Walstab (1810-1898)

It is unlikely that Walstab moved into the dwelling house at Hanger Lane but if he did it was for a very short time. According to the electoral register of 1837 and 1838, Walstab was living at Tottenham Green. By the time of the census of 1841, aged 30 and a merchant, he was living at Philip Lane, Tottenham with his wife Frances and his five children, Georgina, Arthur, Henry, Emily and Jean.

Walstab was born on 27th August 1810, but was not baptised until 29th March 1817, at St. Mary, Islington. His father, Arend Hendrick Walstab, a merchant and his mother, Elizabeth, Jacomina Gertruyde, lived at Duncan Place, Islington. Arend married Georgiana Frances Steel at St. George, Bloomsbury on 7th March 1833. They were both of that parish and they married by licence.

Frances died in 1848 in Kensington. On 3rd June 1850, Arend was *"made free of the City of London"* as a foreign timber and coal merchant. By the time of the census of 1851, Arend, then 39 and a widower, recorded as a *Fire wood importer* was living at 16 Gloucester Terrace, Paddington, in the Parish of Marylebone with his Dutch-born mother, Elizabeth, then a widow and his children, Georgina (17) born in Hadley, George (16), Henry (15), Emily (13) and Jean (11) all four born in Tottenham and Frank (8), Arthur (6) a second son of that name, born in Paddington and William (5) born in the Parish of St. James Westminster. Arend left England in 1850 and moved to Brighton, Melbourne. He died, aged 88 on 13th January 1898 and is buried in Brighton Cemetery. He had formerly lived at 18 Darling St., North Yarrs and had been described as a *"colonist of 52"*.

John Jerram (1797-1875)

Walstab's ownership of the land at Hanger Lane was short-lived. The next indenture in the Registry *(MDR/1842/5/47)*, registered on 5th July 1842 and dated 30th June 1842 was between Walstab and John Jerram. Walstab, then shown as a merchant of Austin Friars, of the one part and John Jerram, a wholesale tea-dealer of Fenchurch Buildings in the City of London, of the other part, acquired three closes of land with buildings and two closes known as Snares Mead, subject to the payment of yearly rents and the performance of the covenants for the remainder of the 96-year lease.

The census of 1841 was taken on Sunday, 6th June. It showed that John Jerram, aged 44, with his wife and family, occupied a house at Hanger Lane, Tottenham, despite the pencilled amendments in the Rate Books suggesting that he was not there until 1842.

The will of Samuel Jerram of Duncroft near Staines, in Middlesex, proved on 1st June 1828, explained that "*John Jerram nephew and now partner in the firm of Jerram Beard & Jerram*" was the son of John Jerram. Samuel's nephew received a bequest of interest on £1,000 and his brother and sisters, Charles, Ann, Hannah and Harriet Jerram also received bequests. Samuel had other brothers, Charles, Thomas and William. His executors were his widow, Harriet, his brother Charles, of Chobham, in Surrey and Henry Hulbert, a tea broker. The death of Samuel Jerram, aged 48, was announced in *Jackson's Oxford Journal*, dated 17th April 1824. *The Law Advertiser* reported that the partnership among Thomas Beard, John Jerram and Samuel Jerram, of Poultry, wholesale tea dealers, was dissolved on 27th May 1824.

John Jerram was listed in the Electoral Registers of 1847, 1848, 1849 and 1853 at Hanger Lane, as the leaseholder and occupier of the house and land. The Electoral Registers for Tottenham Polling District in the County of Middlesex identify "*voters in respect of property including tenant occupiers at a rent of not less than £50*".

In the census of 1851, Jerram's address was given as 1 Hanger Lane, the first house on that road. Below is a table with information given on the census form:

Table of occupants in 1851 at 1 Hanger Lane.

Address	Name	Age	Occupation	Where born
1 Hanger Lane	John Jerram	54	Wholesale Tea Dealer	Nottinghamshire
	Jane Ridley Jerram	42		Chobham Surrey
	Jane Harriet Jerram	14		All Hallows Tottenham
	Hannah Jerram	12	Scholar	Tottenham
	Charles Jerram	8		"
	Ellen Douglas Jerram	6		"
	Arthur Jerram	3		"
	Sidney Jerram	2		"
Hanger Lane Woodbury Lodge	James Stevens	40	Under Gardener	
	Frances Stevens	30		

The main residence was not yet named but Woodbury Lodge was occupied by an under-gardener, his wife and family. This was probably an entrance lodge.

In *The Standard* of 11th July 1829, the marriage on 3rd July 1829 was reported of John Jerram to Miss Rowell, daughter of the late W. Rowell of Grove House, Chobham, in Surrey. In 1824, John's uncle, the Reverend Charles Jerram lived at Chobham and the church records show that he officiated at the ceremony. John gave his address as Poultry, London and his wife was of the Parish of St. Lawrence, Chobham. The baptism of Jane Harriet Jerram, born on 26th May 1836, was recorded at St. Katherine, Coleman on 21st June 1836. Her father's address was shown as Fenchurch Buildings in the Parish of St. Katherine Coleman and his occupation was that of a tea dealer. Hannah was baptised on 29th May 1838 at St. Katherine, Coleman; Samuel was baptised on 13th May 1841 at the same church. Charles and Edward Jerram were baptised on 13th December 1842 at All Hallows, Tottenham. The births of the youngest children were also recorded at Edmonton.

The name of John Jerram, Esq., is recorded on a plan drawn in the margin of an indenture registered on 8th April 1851 (*MDR/1851/4/669*) between Thomas Temberton and John Jay, Esq., made after the death of Ebenezer Johnston. It also records that the parcel of land (*1a 2r 18 p*), in Tottenham, Middlesex, was once owned by Thomas Coxhead Stevens.

An indenture is archived at the Middlesex Deeds Registry (*MDR/1854/1/150*), registered on 5th January 1854 and dated 31st December 1853. It was between John Jerram of Fenchurch Buildings, a wholesale tea-dealer, of the one part and John Giblett of Woodberry Vale, Stoke Newington, a cattle salesman of the other part. It recited an indenture dated 26th December 1807 (between John Wood and Thomas Coxhead Stevens) leased for 96 years, for parcels of land including *Oatfields* along with the house erected on the site and two closes called *Snaresmead*. It recited an indenture of 1833 for the new road, to be known as Seven Sisters Road, from Stamford Hill Road in the Parish of Tottenham to Camden Town, then in the Parish of Islington. The proportion of the yearly rent payable for the land and house was to be £245 from the following 25th December, less £12 for the rental from the portions of land used for the roads. John Jerram passed the land and house where he had been living to John Giblett and his heirs at a rent of £233. Giblett rented and did not own the land and house at this time and was recorded there in the Rate Books from April 1854 until June 1857. More of him and his family later.

In 1855 Jerram was recorded in the electoral register at Highbury Hill House, Islington. Jane Harriet Jerram's marriage was announced in *The Standard*, dated 7th November 1856. On 6th November 1856, at St. Mary Islington she married William Winterbotham, Esq., of Tewkesbury, in Gloucestershire. In *The Morning Chronicle* of 19th November 1857, it was reported that John Ridley Jerram (18), a midshipman and eldest son of John Jerram, of Highbury Hill and Fenchurch Buildings, had drowned on 20th August 1857 at Sidney Head in the wreck of the *Dunbar*. On 31st May 1860, Hannah Jerram married Thomas Applebee at St. Mary, Islington. By the time of the census of 1861, John Jerram was living at Breadford House, Guildford Road, Chobham in Surrey. His sons, Samuel, aged 19 and Charles, aged 18, were recorded at 14 Fenchurch Buildings (written underneath the entry is the name John Jerram). Samuel was a clerk to a wholesale tea dealer and his brother was a ribbon warehouseman.

In *The London Gazette* it was announced that the partnership of John Jerram, Son & Company, operating from 14 Fenchurch Street, was dissolved on 16th January 1866; the announcement was signed by John and Samuel Jerram. The death of John's wife, Jane Ridley Jerram, aged 60, was registered at Chertsey, in the third quarter of 1868. Her daughter, Hannah Applebee, died in childbirth, on 11th March 1872, at the age of 34, leaving six children. John Jerram died in 1875 and his will was proved by his spinster daughter, Ellen Douglas Jerram.

Samuel Lloyd Stacey (1830-1923)

An indenture of lease (*MDR/1861/14/481*) dated 8th November 1858 and registered on 7th October 1861 was made between John Giblett of Hanger Lane, Tottenham in the County of Middlesex, a salesman, of the one part and Samuel Lloyd Stacey of 300 High Holborn, Middlesex, a chemist and druggist of the other part. Giblett leased to Stacey and his heirs the farm and dwelling house known as Woodbury Lodge on the south side of Hanger Lane, Stamford Hill, together with the pleasure grounds, gardens, walks, the entrance Lodge and the kitchen garden and a parcel of land in front of the back lawn bounded by a wire fence containing three acres more or less. Giblett reserved the right of way for his servants and others but passed it over to Stacey and his heirs from the 28th September 1858 for a term of 21 years at a yearly rent. Thomas Bentley Hudson of Tokenhouse Yard, a solicitor, witnessed the signing by John Giblett. It might be presumed that Stacey moved into Woodbury Lodge on 29th September 1858. It also suggests that Giblett had leased the land and possibly the Lodge from the heirs of John Wood before that date.

Samuel Lloyd Stacey was the son of George Stacey and Deborah Lloyd; Samuel was baptised on 2nd October 1830 at Tottenham and he married Mary Barclay (baptised on 29th March 1827) on 12th May 1854. The marriage was registered at Edmonton. In 1857, a few years after his marriage, Samuel's father, George died, aged 70.

The census of 1861 shows that Samuel L. Stacey, aged 30, born in Tottenham and his wife Mary, aged 34, were living at Woodbury Lodge, Tottenham, Middlesex. He was a wholesale druggist and they had four children, Henry George, aged 6, born at St. John's Wood, Middlesex, John B., aged 4, also born at St. John's Wood, Ernest L., aged 2 and baby Mary, 10 months were born at Tottenham. The family had a nurse, parlour maid, nursery nurse and other servants. By a separate entry under *Woodbury Lodge* (gardener's cottage) was John Winder and his wife, Elizabeth and their five children. They had only recently arrived in the area as their baby of eight months was born in Stoke Newington. In the next entry, Daniel Pelling was listed at Hanger's Lane, Shepherds Cottage with his wife Sarah and sons Daniel and Robert. Then was John Watson, a civil engineer, his wife, Elizabeth and family at Albion Lodge.

In 1863, the birth of Wilson Stacey was registered in Hackney; he was baptised on 24th September 1862 at Upper Clapton. The maiden name of the child's grandmother was Wilson. Adelaide Mary was born in Clapton on 19th

February 1864 and Helen Beatrice in Tottenham on 29th September 1865. Samuel L. Stacey was recorded in the electoral register in 1863 and 1865 at a house in Upper Clapton, so the family stayed for only a few years at Woodberry Lodge. Another brother, Robert Hugh Stacey was born on 21st January 1867 in Tottenham. Samuel Lloyd Stacey, his family and their many servants were living at Tottenham Green at the time of the census of 1871. He was then a wholesale and retail chemist and druggist. In 1881 they were living at "*Elmhurst*", Bruce Grove.

All the children were baptised years later at St. Ann's Tottenham; John Barclay on 1st January 1873, Henry George, Ernest Lloyd and Mary Deborah on 29th April 1874, Wilson on 9th September 1877 and Adelaide Mary, Robert Hugh and Helen Beatrice on 22nd May 1882. Henry George Stacey married Mary Josephine Howard at St. Ann's, Tottenham on 5th October 1887. She was the daughter of Joseph Howard, M.P. for Tottenham and Henry was living at St. Ann's Vicarage at the time of the marriage. Mary, Adelaide and Helen never married.

In 1890, Samuel Lloyd Stacey and his sons Henry George Stacey and Wilson Stacey were co-partners in the firm of Corbyn Stacey and Company. Samuel Lloyd Stacey was living at 45 Fellows Road, South Hampstead when he died on 5th May 1923.

John Black (1802–1866)

In May 1862 William James Black (*John Black*), Samuel Lloyd's successor at *Woodberry Lodge*, was recorded in the Poor Rate Books as the occupier of a house at Hanger Lane. An Indenture registered on 28th March 1862 (*MDR/1862/5/729*) dated 30th September 1861, was made between Samuel Lloyd Stacey of 300 High Holborn in the County of Middlesex, a chemist and druggist, of the one part and John Black, of Bow Lane in the City of London, a gentleman, of the other part. It recited an indenture of lease dated 8th November 1858, made between John Giblett, of the one part and Samuel Lloyd Stacey, of the other part (*MDR/1861/14/481*). The land in question was south of Hanger Lane, near Stamford Hill, Tottenham and included Woodberry Lodge, pleasure grounds, gardens, entrance lodge and kitchen garden. Besides this there was a parcel of land of some three acres bound by a wire fence, with a back lane belonging to the above premises, with the right of way for John Giblett, his servants and others; it was next to premises occupied by Mr. Watson (this was John Watson of Albion Lodge). Samuel Loyd Stacey also had the right of way for himself and his family "*at all reasonable and proper times during the demise to walk over the land of John Giblett held by him under a lease*".

The Glasgow Herald (*British Library's Newspaper Collection*) dated 9th October 1866 has an entry for John Black, late of *Woodberry Lodge*, Stamford Hill who died, aged 64, on 2nd October at the Pier Hotel in Erith in Kent. He was a "*wax vest manufacturer in the lighting business*". The will of John Black confirms that he had previously lived at *The Priory*, Homerton, in

Middlesex and at 15 Bow Lane, Cheapside, in the City of London, as well as *Woodbury Lodge,* Stamford Hill. His widow was Mary Robertson Dalton Black of Erith. Leaving under £12,000, John Rankine Black, his son and John Archibald Fullarton of Edinburgh, a publisher, were executors.

By an indenture dated 31st December 1866, registered on 28th February 1867 (*MDR/1867/5/749*) Mary Robertson Dalton Black of Erith in Kent, widow of the late John Black, John Rankine Black and John Archibald Fullarton of Edinburgh, a publisher, of the first part, Joseph Wood Mason, of Red Cross Street, of the second part and John Giblett of Hanger Lane, Tottenham, Middlesex, of the third part, recited a lease from 29th September 1858 for a term of 21 years, at a rent of £100 p.a., between John Giblett and Samuel Lloyd Stacey. Mary Robertson Dalton Black, John Rankine Black, John Archibald Fullarton and Joseph Wood Mason *"did demise, release and quit claim unto John Giblett and his heirs for the remainder of the lease of 21 years"*. Joseph Wood Mason and John Giblett were attested by William Henry Lee, clerk to Kingsford and Dorman of 23 Essex Street, Strand, Middlesex. Two years later, on 31st May 1868, Mary, then living at 19 The Villas, Erith, died and left her estate to her son and only next of kin, John Rankine Black, of the same address.

In June 1832, Scottish-born John Black was living at Upper Clifton Street as a coal merchant. His son, John Rankine Black was baptised on 12th June 1832 at St. Leonard, Shoreditch, Middlesex. At the time of the census of 1851, John, then 45 years old and a light manufacturer and Mary (40), who was born in England, were living at 75 High Street, Homerton in Hackney with their son John Rankine Black, a student at University College, London. An obituary for John Rankine Black, of Donagh Lodge, Lockgoilhead in Scotland, who died on 20th June 1870, was recorded on 2nd July 1870. It reported that he was also late of *Woodberry Lodge*, Stamford Hill. His will described him as a barrister-at-law *"sometimes residing at Donagh Lodge, Lochgoilhead in the County of Argyle"*, where he died at the age of 37.

36

From the Gibletts at Woodberry Lodge
to Mr. Dorman

The Giblett (sometimes spelt "Giblet") Family History

The Giblett family was involved in every aspect of animal husbandry as farmers, cattle, sheep and pig salesmen, butchers, poulterers, tallow chandlers, curriers, graziers, upholsterers, tanners, boot and shoe makers. Its members were located at various addresses in Hampshire; Hartley Wintney, Elvetham, Sandhurst, Stratfield Turgis, Winchfield, as well as Hartfordbridge, some thirty miles west of London. Wills and administrations serve to identify and explain a web of relationships. Burial records for Hartley Wintney, Hampshire, transcribed by Alice Hamilton, also confirm who were the various members of the Giblett family. The family had businesses in London's West End and homes, land and farms in Hampshire. Some members made great fortunes and others lost them.

James Giblett (died 1765)

A starting point for this branch of the family is with James Giblett, a yeoman of Hartley Wintney, Hampshire who, when he died was buried on 27th October 1765. His wife, Elizabeth Giblett was buried on 10th April 1763. The will of James Giblett was proved on 16th July 1766. He identified his sons, James, William, Thomas, John, Robert, daughter Elizabeth and daughter-in-law, Judith Giblett, widow of his late son, Paul (who was buried on 5th March 1762). Below is a summary of the lives of some of their children.

James Giblett: died 1785 (married Ann Hewett) and his family

James Giblett married Ann Hewett and was the father of James, Thomas, William, Paul, John, Ann, Sarah and Elizabeth Giblett. James *Gilbert* (Giblett), the elder James died intestate and was buried on 25th October 1785 at Hartley Wintney. In November of that year an administration (*PROB 6/161*) was applied for at Southampton, in relation to the estate of James Giblett. Six months later, on 26th May 1786 *"the goods chattels and .... of James Giblett late of the parish of Winchfield in the County of Southampton deceased was granted to James and Thomas Giblett, the natural and lawful sons of said deceased to administer .... Ann Giblett, widow, the relict ... having first renounced the admon of the said deceased"*. This confirms the name of his wife and that she was still alive in May 1786. The burial registered for Ann Giblett, at Hartley Wintney on 4th March 1794, is likely, therefore, to have been for his widow.

In land tax records of 1781, John Giblett was recorded as a poulterer at Tyler Street, London. He was the son of James and Ann Giblett and John, the son, was buried at Hartley Wintney on 23rd March 1800. On 26th July 1781, he had married Sarah Simson (sometimes *Simpson)*, by licence from the Bishop of London at St. James, Piccadilly, in Westminster, in the presence of Alexander Simson, John Richards and Elizabeth Brown (*Marriage in register: No 225*). Sarah, baptised, on 24th September 1758, was the daughter of Alexander and Susannah Simson and her brother, William Simson was baptised in 1760, also at St. James. Their children, Sarah and John Giblett, were baptised in 1790 and 1793.

John Giblett's will was written on 8th March 1800 but not proved until 26th September 1801, almost a year later. He had been living in Davies Street in the Parish of St. George, Hanover Square and he made his mark, rather than sign, perhaps due to frailty. He referred in his will to his brothers, James Giblett of Hartley Row, Southampton, Hampshire and Paul Giblett, a butcher, as executors, along with his brother-in-law William Simson of Bond Street, an upholsterer. He left £1,000 to his daughter and an additional £500, if his wife died. Sarah Giblett, a widow, from London, was buried in 1805 at Hartley Wintney.

Alexander Simson of 4 New Bond Street, with property at Tyler Street, in his will, written in 1787 and proved in 1793, identified his wife Susannah, son William, daughters Anna and Sarah Simson and grandchild Susannah Godby. Anna Simson married John Godby on 29th June 1778 at St. Martin-in-the-Fields, in the presence of John Richards and Sarah Simson. Both the bride and groom were from that parish.

In 1810, a Sun Fire Office Policy (*MS 11936/453/839938*) was taken out by William Simson, an upholsterer of 4 New Bond Street and James and Paul Giblett, of the same place, in trust to the will of John Giblett, deceased, on a house at Davies Street, Berkeley Square, in the tenure of Mr. Baily, a poulterer. The value of the brick house, household goods, china and glass was £1850, a substantial amount of money. John Giblett's son was not then 21 and his uncles were acting on his behalf.

An indenture (*MDR/1812/3/422*), dated 20th March 1812, gives evidence that the minor, John Giblett, as he had been two years earlier, was the son of John Giblett. Parties to the indenture were William Simson, James Giblett and Paul Giblett, executors of the will of John Giblett of Davies Street, who died in 1800, of the one part and John Giblett, an upholsterer, the only son, of the other part. Reference was made therein to another indenture (*MDR/1808/4/14*) of 1808 and to Robert Grosvenor. The witness for James Giblett was his son, James Giblett junior, of Crown Office Row, Inner Temple; for Paul Giblett, William Robert Burgess and for William Simson, John Baily, a poulterer of Davies Street. The witness for John Giblett junior, who had come of age, of the other part, was Anna Godby of New Bond Street, a widow. His uncle and aunt, William Simson and Anna Godby, stood in place of his parents.

Sarah Giblett was the daughter of John Giblett who had died in 1800. Sarah wrote her will on 6th March, died on 8th March and Ansley Bishop of 15

Cork Street, was a witness who appeared personally to add a statement dated 21st March 1838 to confirm that the deceased had formerly lived at New Bond Street, Middlesex. The will was proved on 23rd March 1838. In her will, she was described as a spinster of 15 Cork Street in the Parish of Westminster, Middlesex. She made bequests to seven cousins, namely Elizabeth Giblett, Mary Giblett, Alicia, wife of Mr. Francis, Sarah Hunt, wife of Mr. Hunt, Fanny Giblett, Jane, wife of Mr. Gomm, all of whom were daughters of her uncle Paul Giblett and George Osborn, the latter a butcher of Lower Grosvenor Street, who was the son of Sarah and George Osborn. Sarah Giblett, according to *Pallott's Marriage Index*, married George Osborn around 1788. George was living at Chatham Place, Blackfriars in 1793. Sarah Osborn was still alive in 1818 when her brother James wrote his will. She made bequests to her brother, John Giblett, to Jane, wife of William Giblett of Elvetham in Hampshire and to her friend Marianne, aged 21, who married James Brewster of 22 Madox Street, Hanover Square, at St. George, Hanover Square, on 15th August 1834.

Paul Giblett (father of John Giblett of Woodberry Lodge) died 1848

James (son of the earlier James) and Ann Giblett's son, Paul Giblett, married Elizabeth Blagrove by licence on 24th October 1784 at St. James, Piccadilly, Westminster in the presence of Mary Robinson and John Beresford. The bride and groom were both living in that parish and both were over the age of 21. In church records, Paul and Elizabeth Giblett were shown as parents of William Giblett, baptised on 8th January 1788, Elizabeth, baptised on 7th May 1789, Susannah Ann Giblett, baptised on 14th August 1790 and Mary, baptised on 4th January 1792, all at St. James, Westminster. Other children were baptised at St. George, Hanover Square; Alicia was born in 1792, Sarah in 1795, Frances (Fanny) in 1801 and John Giblett was born on 20th March and baptised on 4th May 1803. Some of the children were included as beneficiaries in the will of their cousin, Sarah Giblett, who died in 1838. There was another daughter named Sophia born around 1802.

An indenture of lease at LMA (*MDR/1796/5/173*) was registered 30th September 1796 between brothers James Giblett of 138 New Bond Street, of the one part and Paul Giblett of Carnaby Street, of the other part, which referred to an earlier lease (*1794 B5 330*) between John Giblett Esq., of Mary Le Bone and Thomas Davies, a hatter, of Bond Street. This indenture was for the unexpired term of lease for premises on the west side of New Bond Street. A month later Paul Giblett, a butcher, took out an insurance policy dated 29th November 1796, recorded in the *Sun Insurance Office Policy Registers Old Series at LMA* (*MS 11936/407/660291*). It included cover for a brick house at his address valued at £300, wearing apparel, £100 and utensils and dead stock in the slaughterhouse behind the other house also built of brick, £100; total £500. On 3rd February 1800, an Indenture of lease tripartite *LMA* (*MDR/1800/1/326*) involved Paul Giblett of New Bond Street, William Virgo of Upper James Street, Golden Square and William Stokes, a trustee of William Virgo. It related to the messuages, tenements and shop that were situated on the west side of New Bond Street. Included was another reference to the earlier memorial lease dating from 9th September 1794 (*MDR/1794/5/330*).

Documents at the *LMA* show that around 1800 Paul Giblett was supplying meat to the Clerkenwell Correction Centre and Newgate Prison. It has been suggested in some sources that the Giblett family was providing meat for the King.

An advertisement in *The Morning Chronicle* in March 1803 put up for sale a valuable freehold estate including a brick dwelling house, coach house, stabling and outbuildings, pleasure gardens, meadow and grazing land of some 104 acres at Kilburn, Middlesex, two miles from Oxford Street, possessed by Mr. Giblett and Mr. Newport, described as its tenants but presently on lease to Mr. Henlock for eight years at £370 per annum. The Mr. Giblett in question is most likely to have been Paul Giblett.

An Indenture (*MDR/1804/1/213*) in 1804 between Paul Giblett of New Bond Street and John Davies of Oxford Street related to land at Kilburn, Brondesbury. It made reference to the previous indenture (*MDR/1794/5/330*) from 9th September 1794 between John Giblett and Thomas Davies relating to the premises on the west side of New Bond Street, including a public house, then called the *Dog and Duck*.

In October 1805, insurance policies *LMA* (*MS 11936/434/779796 and 781455*) show that Paul Giblett owned two properties, a house at Kilburn Priory in his own tenure and built from brick and tiles, valued at £500 and another at 138 New Bond Street, London, complete with attached building and contents, valued at £550.

In 1807, an Indenture *LMA* (*MDR/1807/1/174*), between John Montagu, Esq., of 15 Harcourt Buildings, Inner Temple, of the one part and Paul Giblett, a butcher, of New Bond Street, of the other part, was for purposes of assigning land on the west side of Bond Street, originally a lease and release on 9th April 1796 (*MDR/1796/3/228*). It referred to land held in trust by James Giblett, a butcher of Bond Street, John Giblett, a poulterer and Stephen Randall of Hammersmith, executors named in the will of John Giblett, who died in 1790.

The Indenture (*MDR/1807/1/175*) registered in 1807, was an assignment of mortgage dated 24th May 1806 for 40 years, when Paul Giblett paid John Montagu £6,000. The land was assigned in trust to the three executors, James Giblett, John Giblett and Stephen Randall. Two of the executors had died; John Giblett, in 1800 and Stephen Randall in 1802. The land to which reference was made in this indenture was that detailed in 1800.

In 1807 Paul Giblett was recorded in *The Morning Post* as the treasurer of Smithfield Society of Agriculturalists and Breeders. In 1808 *The Farmer's Magazine: Proceedings of the Smithfield Club*, recorded and confirmed his place of business as 138 New Bond Street and details were given of sheep that he had butchered. In 1809 Paul was listed together with William Giblett as butchers.

In 1810, a lease *LMA* (*MDR/1810/8/525*) among Paul Giblin, James Thornhill and John Morley, cutlers related to a newly built messuage with workshops and cellar on the west side of New Bond Street, once numbered

137 and now 144, the house next to one owned by Paul Giblett. The original lease was for 21 years and the rent was for £200 per annum until 1821. On 6th November 1810, another lease referred back to an indenture of lease from 1807 (*MDR/1807/9/98*) between Paul Giblett and John Montagu. Montagu was related to Giblett as John Giblett, who died in 1790, married Elizabeth Montagu, making them Paul Giblett's uncle and aunt.

Paul Giblett's character is revealed in a story. A book, stored at the British Library includes a section *The Refuter refuted: A reply to Mr. Giblett's Pamphlet entitled A Refutation of the Calumnies of George Harrower with appendix* by Captain George Harrower and published by him in 1816, in order to present his side of the story. He wanted "*to spare the feelings of his wife*" and said that he had no desire "*to wound the feelings of the younger branches of Mr Giblett's family*". In it, he was answering the allegations of his father-in-law, Paul Giblett in the latter's pamphlet, responding to character assassination and abuse. The following account is complied from Harrower's pamphlet, newspaper reports of the day, British Library Collections and Old Bailey Proceedings.

George Harrower left Bombay on board the *Caroline*, arriving back in England some time after May 1812 (*British Library, Asian and African Studies*). Anne Bulley, in her book *The Bombay Country Ships: 1790-1833,* suggests that Harrower had owned ships. He did not meet Mr. and Mrs. Giblett until later in 1812 and he described them as a "*respectable, religious and well educated family*". He was interested in meeting Mr. Giblett because the latter was well-versed in the science of agriculture. They met through Mr. Thompson, a coachmaker, who came with his daughter and Mr. Harrower to visit Mr Giblett, his wife and family. Having expressed an interest in buying property in the country Harrower went with Mrs. Giblett, her daughter and Mr. Thompson to see Micklefield Hall, a large 18th century country house, which was for sale by auction, with a seventeen-year lease unexpired. They all approved of the property and on Mr. Giblett's advice Harrower made an offer to it's owner, Mr. Boyd and secured the house and land by a private contract.

Harrower had already lent Giblett £2,000 and Giblett tried to persuade George to purchase his three houses in Bond Street which Giblett said had cost him £15,000. George did lend Giblett £5,000 and Giblett assured Harrower that the houses were "*freehold, unencumbered and his own property*".

After Harrower moved in, most of the Giblett family went to stay with him for three weeks at Micklefield Hall. Harrower visited the Gibletts and a relationship developed with their daughter, Susan. Paul Giblett alleged that it was when the family came to stay at Micklefield Hall, Harrower declared his intention to marry Susan, settling £10,000 on her marriage portion. Mrs. Giblett was heard to remark when she saw the letter that it was "*as good as £10,000*". Harrower, answered this allegation saying that it was not until he made a journey to Scotland that he wrote to Susan on 3rd August 1812 and made the decision to settle £10,000 as a marriage portion. When he returned, although he liked the estate, he decided that there was too much work in managing it. Before the wedding he wrote to his brother, Robert, asking if he wanted to buy Micklefield Hall and Robert agreed.

A *Faculty Office marriage allegation* was made on 17th October 1812 and the couple married at St. George, Hanover Square, London. The entry in the church records is as follows:

> George Harrower, bachelor, of the parish of Rickmansworth in the County of Herts. and Susannah Ann Giblett, spinster, of this parish, were married, in this church, by licence, the 20th day of October in the year 1812 by J. Grenville, curate. In the presence of Paul Giblett, Elizabeth Giblett, Mary Giblett and Alicia Giblett.

Then, as a favour to his wife's brother, to help him start in business, George changed his mind and agreed to sell Micklefield Hall to William Giblett for £4,000, with interest, at the price he bought it from Mr. Boyd. William had to pay back the bond in five years, in September, 1817. Harrower and his wife agreed to rent back the house, although William retained restricted use of certain parts of it.

The marriage settlement had been drawn up in great secrecy by Paul Giblett's solicitor, Mr. Stokes, as Giblett was reluctant to tell his prospective son-in-law his business. Therefore, Harrower did not see the marriage settlement until a year after his marriage and had signed it without reading. He later discovered that William Giblett and not William's father, Paul, was named as a trustee, along with Harrower's brother, Robert. Giblett was in great need of this money, not for his daughter but to settle his debts. He did confide to Harrower that some of his wealthier clients were very slow to pay their bills.

Paul Giblett again asked his son-in-law to buy his three houses in Bond Street but Harrower was reluctant to oblige, as the loans were not secured. Giblett was most anxious to sell them to Harrower for £10,000 and when this did not happen, Harrower lent him money on a mortgage. Giblett must have been desperate as he declared that he had bought the houses for £15,000, the properties in question being, probably, the messuages and shops referred to in a number of indentures in the *Middlesex Deeds Registry*. Apparently Giblett had also borrowed money from a near relative. Harrower agreed to keep the mortgage secret from Mr. Thompson or anyone else. However, Giblett had not told Harrower the whole truth about the houses and he owed money on them and was unable to pay the mortgage. Harrower asserted in his pamphlet, that he wanted to buy a house in the country and not in Town and that Giblett had also borrowed £1,270 from him to pay part of £2,800 for the tithes on his farm at Kilburn.

William Giblett acted in a somewhat ungracious manner to his sister and George Harrower and Susan were obliged to leave Micklefield Hall. In *The Morning Chronicle,* dated 10th December 1813, it was William Giblett, a grazier, who was reported as residing at Micklefield Hall. Harrower then purchased *The Retreat*, at Stanmore, using borrowed funds that he was required to repay in a very short time. Documents dating from 6th October 1813, held at *Hertfordshire Archives*, show that Captain George Harrower had also bought from Charles V. Hunter a house, cottage, barn, plants, fittings and 30 acres of land at Caldicott Hill, Aldenham, Hertfordshire. So, on 12th August, 1814, Harrower had to sell *The Retreat* and 28 acres of land, and he went with his wife and one of her sisters to Scotland to introduce her to his family, having had to ask Giblett to repay some of the money he owed to fund the visit. Giblett broke his promises and Harrower's agent was told that he could take Giblett to court and he would starve before he retrieved the money that he was owed. An advertisement in *The Times*, dated 19th December 1814 reported that Harrower was quitting his residence (*Retreat Cottage*) and it was for sale by auction. He had lent so much money to Giblett that he was in financial difficulty himself.

The debt of Paul Giblett (£1,020 and £500 secured by bond) was referred to in an indenture, registered on 12th November 1814, *LMA* (*MDR/1814/7/163*). The three parties had been John Montagu, Paul Giblett and John Westcar, a grazier. The premises, with a lease of 40 years, were on the west side of Bond Street. In 1807 Paul Giblett had mortgaged the premises to Montagu for £6,000; the indenture was signed by Paul Giblett, in the presence of Eliza Giblett, a spinster of New Bond Street, his daughter.

Mr. Thompson, the coachmaker, in a letter to Harrower dated 17th January 1815, wrote that Giblett was to be bankrupt and Harrower's money was worth nothing. He had heard that William Giblett was to carry on the family business and Paul Giblett had offered to pay some money to his creditors. In an Indenture *LMA* (*MDR/1815/2/236*) registered on 12th March 1815, Paul and William Giblett made a plea of debt for £1,000 and cash. There was confusion in Bond Street and Thompson called on his lawyer to visit Giblett to retrieve some of his money. In *The London Gazette* in November 1815, Paul Giblett of New Bond Street in the Parish of St. George, Hanover Square and William Giblett of Micklefield Hall, in the County of Hertford, butchers, dealers and chapmen, partners under the name of Giblett and Son, were declared bankrupt. In December 1815, Micklefield Hall was auctioned; William Giblett was in debt to Harrower for £4,000 and Paul Giblett to him for upwards of £17,000. Harrower declared that Giblett, "*his wife and numerous offspring participate in his calamity*". There were at least ten children. John Giblett, later to be associated with Woodberry Lodge, was twelve at the time and the youngest member of the family, Jane, was only nine years of age.

Harrower the Bigamist

It is possible that William was aware at this time that Harrower was a bigamist but did not do anything as Harrower had been effectively financially supporting the Giblett family. However, it was around this time that Paul Giblett heard from someone who had returned from India that his son-in-law was already married and had a wife in India. In 1794 in Bombay, Harrower had married Mary Usher but with a history of lunacy in her family, she had been declared a lunatic. He brought his wife back to Scotland but this did not work out so his sister accompanied Mary back to India, where he provided money for her to be cared for by her family. Harrower argued in the pamphlet that he believed that his wife had died in December 1813 and offered to go to India to find proof.

Giblett made it known that Harrower was a bigamist and tried to drive a wedge between Susan Harrower and her husband by encouraging his daughter to return to her family home at Bond Street but she refused. Giblett wanted Harrower in court in the hope that his son-in-law would be transported and he not have to pay back the money he owed to Harrower. Giblett suggested that Susan destroy the marriage settlement but instead Susan Harrower arranged for a carriage to take the couple to France, fearful that there was a chance that her husband would be incarcerated for breaking the law. Harrower, in his own defence, admitted that he went to France, Scotland and England but had been open about his business. He was eventually apprehended while investigating Giblett's accounts of bankruptcy.

Harrower was put under arrest at Bow Street, held at Newgate Prison and was indicted at the Old Bailey on 17th February 1816. Eliza Giblett, according to *The Times*, attended court to support her sister, Susan Harrower and gave evidence that she and other sisters had attended the wedding. Eliza moved out of the family home when it became clear that her father was exploiting the situation for as much as he was able. The jury, after half an hour's deliberation, convicted Harrower on the charge of bigamy but recommended mercy. He was confined for six months and fined one shilling.

There was no mercy, however, for Paul Giblett. An indenture (*MDR/1816/5/244*) was registered on 22nd August 1816 between Thomas Giblett, a farmer, of Hartford Bridge, along with two cattle salesmen of Newgate and Leadenhall Market, of the one part and the Commission of bankruptcy of the other part. The Commission was acting against Paul Giblett, of New Bond Street and William Giblett of Micklefied Hall, butchers, dealers and chapmen and partners in Giblett & Son; Thomas Giblett, the farmer, was Paul Giblett's brother. Perhaps the cattle salesmen were trying to resolve the Giblett family's dilemmas.

It was reported in *The Times* on 7th December 1816 that Paul Giblett was committed, on 19th November, to the same cell as his son-in-law in Newgate prison for giving unsatisfactory answers to the bankruptcy commissioners. In his pamphlet, Harrower included his accounts of money loaned to Paul and William Giblett over the years (£17,617). He analysed those presented by Giblett who conveniently left out that he had won £2,500 on the Lottery and sold his farm at Kilburn for £9,770 and had been receiving £500 per annum in rent from it on a twenty-one year lease. Giblett's figures were at odds with Harrower's. The newspapers suggested that Captain Harrower and his wife retired happily to live out their days in relative obscurity in Scotland. Paul Giblett's wife died around this time.

George Harrower was buried in St. Margaret's churchyard, Edinburgh on 14th August 1829 and his widow, Susannah Ann, by then wife of John Hutchinson, a wood merchant, was buried in the same place on 18th May 1848 (*Scottish Record Society Edinburgh: Index to the Register of burials in the Churchyard of Restalrig 1728-1854*). The National Records of Scotland, Edinburgh, retain a will for Captain George Harrower (*SC70/4/48/601-638*), dated 11th August 1830, indicating that George Harrower, formerly of Micklefield Hall, Herts. was then living at Claremont Cottage, near Edinburgh. He referred to his marriage settlement which involved George Harrower, of the first part, Susannah Ann Giblett, daughter of Paul Giblett, of the second part, William Giblett of New Bond Street, of the third part and Robert Harrower of Drumming, Clackmannanshire, North Britain of the fourth part. He identified his three children as Eliza Susan Ann Harrower, Mary Ann Harrower and George Kerr Harrower. Executors of the will were Susannah Ann Giblett or Harrower, his wife, Charles Kerr, of Fletcher & Alexander of London, Walter Riddell, George Hewat, Esq., a merchant of Edinburgh and William Hunt, writer to the Signet. As the middle name of his son was Kerr and Charles Kerr was one of his executors, it is likely that the last named was a family member. George Harrower's will was proved by one of his trustees, Charles Kerr on 16th October 1856.

William Giblett (1788-1854), brother of John Giblett of Woodberry Lodge

On 17th April 1816, an advertisement in *The Morning Chronicle* announced that Paul Giblett's premises at New Bond Street, on a 14 year lease equivalent to a freehold, were to be sold by auction as part of a Commission of Bankruptcy, as directed by the mortgagees. It included a dwelling house, large shop, counting house, yard, greenhouse, slaughterhouse and buildings to carry out the trade of butcher, stable and also the adjoining houses, showroom and workshop.

Despite being declared bankrupt, William Giblett moved on with his life. A *Faculty Office marriage allegation* dated 24th February 1817 confirmed that William Giblett, a bachelor, intended to marry Mary Jane Stansfeld, a spinster; both were over the age of 21 and Mary Jane was five years older than William. They married at Rickmansworth on 15th March 1817. An indenture dated 8th March 1817 included in the will of John Stansfeld, a timber merchant who died on 15th June, 1828, confirmed that William Giblett had left Micklefield Hall, near Rickmansworth and was living at New Bond Street. The value and benefit of the marriage settlement may have tipped the balance and put William back in business. William Giblett was one of the executors of John Stansfeld's will along with Stansfeld's wife, Frances.

Not long after the wedding, Elizabeth Giblett, Mary Giblett and Alicia Giblett of 110 New Bond Street, described as butchers, were listed in a Sun Insurance Office Policy Register, with a policy *LMA* (*MS 11936/476/931378*) dated 11th June 1817. They insured their brick dwelling house at the address along with household goods, printed books, wearing apparel and plate valued at £840, musical instruments £10, pictures and prints for £20, China and glass for £80 and utensils and dead stock £50; total £1,000. This was a valuable property. Perhaps there were steps being taken to deal with the effects of the bankruptcy proceedings against William and Paul.

William Giblett had four children baptised at St. George, Hanover Square between 1818 and 1825. Mary Jane, Frances Elizabeth, Sophia and Alicia Stansfeld Giblett. Frances Elizabeth and Sophia were born when their parents were living at 53 Lower Brook Street and then they moved to 2 South Molton Street, where Alicia was born.

The butchery business continued and in 1820 William Giblett was operating at 110 New Bond Street. In *The London Gazette* dated 4th November 1823, under a sub-heading of *Dividends*, on 29th November, was the following statement, *"Paul Giblett of New Bond Street butcher (carrying on trade in New Bond Street with Wm. Giblett of Micklefield Hall, Hertfordshire, under the firm of Giblett and Son)"*. This would suggest that there was still a relationship between Paul Giblett and his son. In the *Butchers' Company, Freedom Register 1800-1844* held at the Guildhall in London, William Giblett of Bond Street in the County of Middlesex, a butcher, was admitted into the freedom of the Company by redemption and sworn, around 5th December, 1830.

In 1827, *The London Gazette* announced that the partnership was dissolved as among William Giblett, E. Giblett, M Giblett and A. Giblett of 110 New Bond Street, followed by – *"E. Giblett, M. Giblett and A. Giblett of 61, Lower Brook Street, dressmakers and milliners"*, William's sisters.

In 1828 William Giblett was still in the livestock business, recorded in an account of the Smithfield Club Cattle show as keeping pigs. On 17th October of the same year in *The Times*, he was cited in an article entitled *"The Butchers of the Metropolis"*. The article outlined a meeting of butchers to oppose legislation to set up public slaughterhouses outside the City. Mr. Giblett, in his capacity as chairman of the Master Butchers of London, spoke about defending their rights to carry out business without interference and said that for the past nine months he had extensive premises for slaughtering his cattle at Bayswater, near Kensington but was now willing to pay any rent to move this operation closer to his shop in Town (Bond Street).

An entry in *The Law Advertiser, Volume 8,* for the year 1830 (*page 222*) identified a link between William Giblett of New Bond Street and his brother John Giblett of Bayswater, both of Middlesex, beast and sheep salesmen, when their partnership was dissolved by mutual consent on 2nd February 1830 (*Gazette*). In the Census Return of 1841, John Giblett declared *"sheep salesman"* as his occupation.

The British Library has a copy of the *Islington Market Bill* published by W. Tyler and described as:

> The address of Mr William Giblett upon summing up the evidence produced by him as an agent for the trade of butchers, to the Committee of the honourable House of Commons 3rd January 1834 (author William Giblett).

William Giblett was by then a man with some power and influence.

In March, 1838 William was again in *The Morning Post* having been elected as Vestryman at St. George, Hanover Square, giving evidence of his religious beliefs. In the census of 1841, he was recorded with his children, Mary, Frances, Sophia and Alicia Giblett (15).

William Giblett, then 68, of St. James, Swain's Lane in the Parish of St. Pancras, was buried in Highgate Cemetery (*burial 10756, plot 709*), on 16th June 1854. He wrote his will in 1847 and it was proved on 24th July 1854. George Stansfeld Furmage was a trustee. He left his estate to his wife and his "*four dear daughters*". Frances Elizabeth Giblett married Reverend William Hamilton in November 1853, before her father died and her sister; Mary Jane Giblett married Henry Mallory, a widower from Cheltenham after the death of her father in October 1854 at St. George, Hanover Square.

The *BMD Index* includes notification of the death of Mary J. Giblett (83) in the *Apr/May/Jun quarter 1866* (*6a 295*). A burial (*31038*) was recorded at the London Cemetery Company, Highgate at St. James Swain's Lane, in the Parish of St. Pancras for a Mary *Ann* Giblett, aged 83, who was buried there on 1st June 1866. Her address was shown as 9 Grosvenor Street, Cheltenham where she may been living with her daughter and son-in-law. Her name may have been transcribed incorrectly. Mary Jane Giblett died intestate and her daughter, Alicia Giblett, a spinster, administered the estate. When Henry Mallory, an ironmonger, died in 1892 he left his estate to his son, Francis Stansfeld Mallory, who died in 1921 and he in turn left his estate to Leslie Stansfeld Mallory and Mary Elizabeth Stansfeld Mallory. Alicia Stansfeld Giblett died on 9th August 1913, aged 90 at 12 The Avenue, Brondesbury, Middlesex (*The Times*). Another daughter, Frances Hamilton was still alive at the time of the 1881 Census.

Elizabeth Giblett, the wife of Paul, had died between 1812 and 1822, evidenced by a *Faculty Office* marriage allegation dated 16th August 1822 that was recorded for Paul Giblett, a widower and Leonora Hewson, a spinster. Paul had moved from New Bond Street, as the couple were then living in the Parish of St. Mary, Southwark. Their son, Richard Henry Le Warner Giblett, was baptised at St. John, Waterloo, London on 14th August 1829. Paul Giblett, late of Bond Street and then Brighton was named in an indenture (*MDR/1838/1/749*) *Gregory to Giblett*, registered on 7th February 1838 and dated 2nd January. It related to a lease for 41 years for premises at South Molton Street which were transferred by Mary Gregory, executor of Samuel Hewitt, with the consent of Paul Giblett and William Simson, the executors of John Giblett, formerly of Davies Street, to John Giblett's son and John Giblett, late of Peppard near Henley-on-Thames, Oxfordshire, then living at Torquay in Devon.

Richard Henry Le Warner Giblett married Mary Brown on 16th April 1845 at St. Mary Magdalene, Bermondsey. Both were over the age of 21, making his year of birth around 1824; he was baptised some years after his birth. On the marriage certificate it was recorded that he was a butcher and his father, Paul Giblett, a gentleman. The father of the bride, Timothy Brown, was a clerk. Sarah Elizabeth Giblett was baptised on 19th April 1846 when her parents were living at Cross Street and her father's occupation shown as a butcher. The death of Richard Henry Le Warner Giblett was registered in Bermondsey, Lambeth in the second quarter of 1848. On 17th December 1848, in Brighton,

Paul Giblett died of natural causes, as he was 86 years of age (*death certificate*). A death was registered for Leonora Giblett in Islington in the second quarter of 1855. A death was registered for Elizabeth Sarah Giblett (22) (*BMD Oct/Nov/Dec 1868*). A burial (*51724*) was recorded at Norwood Cemetery for Elizabeth Sarah Giblett, aged 22, on 19th November 1868. She had been living before her death at "*Fleurier Street*", Walworth.

William and John Giblett's sisters

Evidence can be seen of the lives, activities and fortunes of Paul Giblett's daughters as they matured, with 1827 being a critical year for weddings.

A *Faculty Office* marriage allegation to show their intention to marry was made between Jane Giblett, a spinster over the age of 25 of the Parish of Christchurch and John Gomm, also over the age of 25 of the Parish of St. Marylebone on 13th March 1827. John Gomm, by then 50, born in 1801, of 31 Edward Street, Portman Square, died on 31st January and his will was proved by his widow, Jane on 21st February, 1851. At the time of the census of 1851, Jane (48) was recorded at the same address with her children William Francis Gomm (21) an architect, Jane (20), Henry (18), a clerk, and Elizabeth (15) a scholar. On the night of the census, another two of her children, Octavia Gomm (10) and Mary Gomm (9) were visiting their uncle and aunt, William and Mary Giblett and their four daughters. The Gomms had another son named Alfred, aged (2) at the time of the census of 1841 but he was not at home in 1851. Jane Gomm, widow of John, aged 66, died intestate at 63 Leighton Road, Kentish Town on 14th June 1867. She was buried at Kensal Green, All Souls, on 20th June 1867.

Sarah Giblett married William Hunt around 19th November 1827 at St. Mary, Bryanston, which had just been opened in the Parish of St. Marylebone, Westminster. Anomalously, John Giblett appeared to have a married sister named Eliza Hunt, recorded in the census of 1861 but it was Sarah Giblett who married William Hunt in 1827 and Sarah Hunt who was named in the will of her cousin, Sarah Giblett in 1838.

A *Faculty Office* marriage allegation on 27th September 1827 to show their intention to marry was made between Alicia Giblett, a spinster, over the age of 32, of Christchurch, Marylebone, Westminster and William Webb Francis, a bachelor, over the age of 30, born in the Parish of St. George. They married on 4th October at St. George, Hanover Square in the presence of William Giblett, William Francis, Mary Giblett, Frances Giblett (her sisters) and Maria Francis. In the census of 1851, it was shown that William Webb Francis was an upholsterer, employed three people and was living at 104 New Bond Street with his wife, Alicia, and daughter Alicia, like her mother, born in the Parish of St. James, Piccadilly, aged 20. In 1853 William, of the same address signed over all his personal estate and effects to his creditors. In 1871 William was 74, his wife Alicia 75 and their daughter Alicia was 40. William died on 17th July 1875 at 2 Cambridge Street, Hyde Park Square, aged 78. His son Frederick John Francis was sole executor of his will. His effects were valued at under £450.

A *Faculty Office* marriage allegation was dated 26th December 1835 for James Patison, Esq. and Sophia Giblett, both over 21 and of the Parish of St. Marylebone. James Patison, of Grove Terrace, Notting Hill married Sophia Giblett of Greville Place, Kilburn Priory at St. Marylebone on 5th January 1836 (*The Times*). James Patison (64) died intestate on 4th June 1864 at 27 Carlton Villa, Maida Vale (*The Times*). The death intestate of Sophia Patison (65) was registered in Marylebone in May 1867, suggesting that she was born around 1802

> 10th May – Letters of administration of the personal estate and effects of Sophia Patison, late of 27 Carlton Villas, Edgeware Road, in the County of Middlesex, widow, deceased, who died 23rd April, 1867 at 27 Carlton Villas aforesaid was granted at the Principal Registry to John Giblett of Woodberry Lodge, Hanger Lane, Tottenham, in the County aforesaid, gentleman, the brother and one of the next of kin of the said deceased he having been first sworn. Effects under £450.

In records of the *Sun Fire Office Policy Register LMA* (*MS 11936 516/1072579*) dating from 21st February 1828, Sophie and Frances Giblett of Greville Place, Kilburn Priory, Middlesex, schoolmistresses, took out a policy on their "*now dwelling house being two houses communicating*" valued at £1,500. This may have been the house insured and declared by their father, Paul Giblett in 1805. On the same date another policy *LMA* (*MS 11936/516/1072580*) was initiated for them, showing the same address and occupations, for their house at Buck Field, with household goods, wearing apparel and books worth £500, musical instruments worth £60 and china and glasses; totalling £600. Both sisters were recorded as teachers, operating a school for ladies. By the time of the census of 1841, it was Elizabeth, Mary and Fanny Giblett who were running the school for ladies at Greville Place, Kilburn. Alicia Giblett (15), likely to have been the youngest daughter of William Giblett was a pupil there along with Eliza Giblett (11), eldest daughter of John Giblett. In 1851, Elizabeth (61) was described as the proprietor of a ladies school at 12 Greville Place, Marylebone, Middlesex and Mary (59) and Fanny Giblett (49), sisters of the head of house, were governesses or teachers. In 1861, Mary and Fanny were heads of household but Elizabeth had disappeared from the census records. Miss Elizabeth Giblett's death at Greville Place, Kilburn Priory was announced in *The Morning Chronicle* on 29th July 1858 and was registered in the third quarter of 1858 at Marylebone. In 1871, John Giblett's wife, Mary (66) was a visitor to the house at 8 Clarence Square, Brighton of Mary Giblett (77), who was head of household and Fanny Giblett (70), her sister, both unmarried and living off annuities. The death of Mary Giblett (86) was registered in the last quarter of 1876 at Brighton, confirming that she was still living there prior to her death. At the time of the census of 1881, Frances (Fanny) Giblett, then aged 80, was living with her niece, Frances E. Hamilton (61). Her children were all born in Lanark, Scotland. The death intestate of Fanny Giblett (86) was recorded at Hackney (*1b 265*) in 1887.

James Giblett (1795-1873) son of John and Sarah

Records for St. Andrew Holborn show that a John Giblett was baptised there on 16th March 1794; James Giblett on 7th June 1795; Thomas Giblett on 26th March 1797 and Richard Giblett on 26th May 1799. All were children of John and Sarah Giblett and their address was recorded as Gray's Inn Lane. John Giblett, a bachelor of St. Andrew, Holborn had married Sarah Whitfield, a spinster born around 1766, on 30th April 1793 at St. Mary Le Bone, Middlesex, by banns. Witnesses were Ellen Whitfield and John Jackson. Several other Giblett children were baptised at the Old Church, St Pancras, Camden, Middlesex. There were Ellen in 1801, Sarah in 1803, William in 1806, Jackson Giblett, born on 17th February 1808 and baptised on 17th April 1808 and Henry John Giblett in 1814. They were also children of John and Sarah Giblett.

The will of John Jackson, a gentleman of St. Marylebone, was written in 1800. Jackson was a wealthy man who made bequests to relatives but left his leasehold property at Camden Town to his niece, Sarah Giblett, for her natural life. All his wearing apparel and books were to go to her children and his freehold and leasehold estate was to be divided among her children. He made reference to the debts of John Giblett and provided money to maintain and educate Sarah's children. John Hunter and John Giblett, both husbands of Jackson's nieces, were named as executors. By way of a number of codicils after their births, in 1801 he made a bequest to Ellen Giblett and in 1803, to Sarah Giblett, both daughters of Sarah Giblett. Then in 1807, shortly before he died aged 77, he made a bequest to Sarah's son, Thomas.

Sun Fire Office Policy Registers from around this period, held at the *LMA*, show that on 23rd July 1793, John Giblett of Red Lion Street, in the Parish of St. Andrew, Holborn, a currier (*a person who dresses and colours tanned leather*), entered into a policy (*MS 11936/395/617543*) to insure his brick dwelling house for £100, utensils and stock for £600, totalling £700. He moved to that address a few months after his marriage but by 20th February 1794, in policy (*MS 11936/398/626005*), John, identified as a currier and leather cutter, was living at 15 Gray's Inn Lane, Middlesex, which was on the corner of what was then known as Gray's Inn Lane (there was also a Little Gray's Inn Lane) and Little James Street; Gray's Inn Lane became Gray's Inn Road.

He was still at that address, doing the same job, when he insured his premises on 21st April 1800 (*MSS 11936/418/702068*). His household goods, wearing apparel, prints, books and plate in his stone dwelling house, "*roomed office behind with workshops and store room all adjoining and communicating, in brick timber and yard*" were valued at £180, china and glass £20 and stock and utensils £799; total £999. Business was improving; earlier, on 14th September 1794, he had taken on an apprentice, William Welch.

Land Tax records show that in 1804, 1806 and 1807 John Giblett was at 15 Gray's Inn Lane, in the Parish of St. Andrew and George the Martyr, where the proprietor was John Dick. Between the years 1809 and 1816, the records show that John Giblett was at Drury Lane in the Parish of St. Giles in the Fields and St. George, Bloomsbury, in property owned by the Earl of Guildford. Indeed, records indicate that Giblett may have had his Drury Lane premises in 1798.

On 23rd December 1815 John Giblett, then of the Parish of St. Giles in the Fields, Middlesex and of Pratt Street, Camden, wrote his will (*PROB 11/1578/51*) which was proved on 2nd March 1816. He left all his property to his wife, Sarah. He made his mark and did not record his occupation. A further statement, was written in the margin, beside his short will, noting:

> On 22nd February 1836 admon with the will annexed of the goods of John Giblett, late of Drury Lane in the parish of St Giles in the Fields and of Pratt Street, Camden Town in the parish of St Pancras deceased by Sarah Giblett widow deceased whilst living the relict and universal legatee.........and granted to Jackson Giblett one of the natural and lawful children of the deceased having been first sworn duly to administer, no executor and the residuary legatee being.... on the death of said Sarah Giblett ... (some parts illegible)

The leasehold property at Camden Town, referred to in the will of John Jackson, may have been at Pratt Street.

In 1834 Mrs. Sarah Giblett, aged 68, daughter of Mrs. Ellen Whitfield, was buried alongside her late mother in the tomb of John Jackson at the City Road Chapel in London, next to Wesley's House. On 2nd August 1834, the *Register of Burials* for 1779-1839 at City Road Wesleyan Chapel, in the Nonconformists *BMD* registers (*RG4/4333*), records Sarah's burial, her previous place of abode having been North Brixton. Mrs. Whitfield, who had died aged 80, was buried with her brother John Jackson in 1808, the year after his death.

Sarah's sister, Ellen Whitfield, born in 1762, married John Hunter at St. Marylebone in 1794. Ellen, a "*beloved wife*", died at their home, aged 68 on 1st April 1832, at Brixton Place, Surrey; her death was reported in *The Times*.

A will for Sarah Giblett, a widow of North Brixton in Surrey, proved on 14th August 1834 and pronounced:

> I make this my last will or testament giving or bequeathing unto my daughter Sarah Giblett the whole of my property whatsoever find or ....either by me or but to me at my decease for her own pri-vate use. Signed Sarah Giblett. Witnessed by Richard Giblett and Robert Christie on 21st May 1832. On 14th August 1834 admon with the will annexed of the goods, chattels and credits of Sarah Giblett, late of Claremont Place, North Brixton, in the County of Surrey, widow deceased were granted to Sarah Giblett, spinster,

the daughter, the universal legatee named in the said will having been first sworn duly to administer there not being any executor named in the said will.

An insurance document held at *LMA* dated 1830, referred to John and James Giblett, curriers, of 24 Drury Lane, London. They were the sons of John Giblett, a currier, who died in 1816. They occupied or owned other properties at Broker's Alley, King's Head Yard, Duke Street and Lincoln's Inn Fields. In *The Times*, John and James Giblett, curriers, were two of the signatories, among many named on 30th June 1832, who were opposed to City of London officials' intention to move the Leadenhall Leather Market to Bermondsey because there was not enough capacity to display and sell at Leadenhall. The debate continued because in 1833 there was a response from officials to allow for a new skin market three days a week at Farringdon Market; Leather Lane, Skinner Street and Shoe Lane still exist today. John Giblett was given the Freedom of the City, by redemption, on Tuesday 29th January 1833.

On the back of the *Old Ordnance Survey Maps of Stamford Hill (The Godfrey Edition), 1868*, there is a reference to James Giblett of Woodberry Lodge. The name of Giblett at Tottenham can be found in 1837, when John Giblett was recorded in the *Poor Rate Books* as an overseer at Tottenham High Cross. In the Electoral Register for 1838 John Giblett (*747*) and James Giblett (*757*), probably brothers, were shown to reside at Lordship Lane, Tottenham as owners or occupiers of a house and land. In the census of 1841 James Giblett, aged 47, was recorded as a merchant living at Elm Lodge, Tottenham, in Edmonton, together with another merchant by the name of William *Whitten* (50), his wife, Mary (35), daughter Elizabeth (4) and son William (8 months).

The *Tottenham Tithe Map and Tithe Award Book (1844)* at Bruce Castle Museum, clarifies that James Giblett rented land from William Hobson, the builder to whom reference is made earlier in the book but the land was north of White Hart Lane and not at South Tottenham. The table below shows the numbers and sizes of the fields rented by James Giblett:

Table with information in Rent Charge Book 1843.

Owner	Occupier (renting)	No. on plan	Fields and closes
William Hobson	James Giblett	1819	6 acres meadow
		1820	7 " "
		1865	Kitchen Garden
		1866	House and yard
		1867	Buildings and yard
		1868	8 acres meadow
		1869	7 " "
		1870	3 " "
		1871	5 " "
		1897	5 " "

Ann Tooth, a widow, married James Giblett on 31st October 1844 at All Hallows in the Parish of Tottenham and both bride and groom were resident in the parish. He lived in Lordship Lane and his father was recorded as John Giblett, a merchant; Ann's father, Samuel Rackwitz, was a gentleman. Samuel Rackwitz was a witness to the wedding. Ann Rackwitz had previously married James Tooth on 20th May 1822 at St. Sepulchre, Holborn, Middlesex and her first husband died intestate.

In 1845, John and James Giblett were recorded in the Post Office Directory for London and Birmingham as leather merchants of 31 Vere Street, Clare Market, which is between the Strand and Drury Lane. Another John Giblett was recorded as a cattle salesman.

James Giblett continued to be recorded in the Electoral Registers for Tottenham in 1847, 1848 and 1849, as occupier of a house and land at Lordship Lane. An advertisement in *The Times* dated 1st July 1850 confirms the location and extent of James Giblett's residence at Tottenham:

> Forty dozen of choice old port and other wines, part of the household furniture...pony chaise, harness stocks of hay, farming stocks and effects. By Mr Richards on the premises, Elm Lodge, Lordship Lane, Tottenham on Thursday 4th July at 11 by order of James Giblett, Esq. leaving the residence.
>
> About 50 loads of prime old meadow hay, narrow wheel wagon, hay tumbrel (cart) and market carts ditto on springs clothes and poles, sheep troughs, iron pig ditto and various agricultural implements, three promising two year old well bred colts, 400 choice greenhouse plants, garden engines, iron roller, garden seats, targets, bows and arrows, brewing and dairy utensils, useful materials, large hog house and viewing on morning of sale. Catalogues at the Lodge and of the auctioneers, Tottenham, Middlesex.

James left the Tottenham area after July 1850. As seen from the census of 1851, James Giblett, aged 55, described as a leather merchant and his wife Ann, aged 50, were then living at 19 Royal Avenue, Chelsea, two families living in the same house. The form noted that James was born in the Parish of St. Andrew, Holborn and Ann at St. Sepulchre, Middlesex.

The death on 30th December 1867 of Ann Giblett (66), wife of James Giblett of Pratt Street, Camden Town, London, was recorded in *The Morning Post*. On 1st September 1870, James Giblett, a widower of 57 Pratt Street, married Emma Hyslop, a spinster of 7 Market Street, at St. Mary, Islington, London. His father's name was shown as John Giblett, a currier and Emma's as John Hyslop.

In the 1871 Census, *Thomas* Giblett, then aged 75 and described as a retired merchant, was recorded living at 57 Pratt Street, Camden with his wife Emma, aged 47. He was shown to have been born in the Parish of St. Andrew, Holborn and she at Blackfriars, Surrey. Emma's details were correct but James' Christian name was not. The Electoral Register for the Borough of Mary-Le-Bone, Parish of St. Pancras, Ward 3 at Camden Archives shows that James Giblett and not *Thomas* Giblett was registered as a voter at the address in 1870 (*No.21906 pg 439*) and 1871 (*No. 21515 Pg 431*).

James Giblett (78) died at 57 Pratt Street on 7th December 1873 (*BMD Pancras 1b 103*). His will was proved by his wife, Emma Giblett, the relict and sole executor. His effects were valued at under £14,000. In May 1877, an assignment of lease (*LMA A/CSC/2845/8*) for 57 Pratt Street was transferred from E.T.S. Delevingne to Emma Giblett, a widow.

In the census of 1881, Emma Giblett, a widow aged 57 was recorded at 144 Junction Road, Upper Holloway, Middlesex and her place of birth was shown as Christchurch, Blackfriars, in Surrey. Her death was registered in *BMD, Index, Oct/Nov/Dec 1885 (61)* in Islington. Many articles in the *British Library Newspaper Collection*, reported the circumstances of her death at home on 27th December 1885. A Christmas party for friends and relatives had gone significantly wrong. The hostess, Emma Giblett, dressed up as *Winter* in a white dress with cotton wool representing snow. Her outfit caught fire and in a matter of seconds she was engulfed in flames and later expired from her injuries. Her nephew attended the inquest and explained what happened. Her will was proved by her brother William Alfred Hyslop, a pawnbroker of High Street, Hemel Hempstead and one of her next of kin and was granted on 23rd June 1886. Following her death, the lease (*A/CSC/2845/9*) for Pratt Street was transferred by William Alfred Hyslop to Isaac Thwaites of Hampstead, Middlesex.

John Giblett (Born 1803, married 1826, died 1893)

It was John Giblett who was living at Woodberry Lodge in 1868. John Giblett was the son of Paul and Elizabeth Giblett, as evidenced from census returns and his baptism at St. George, Hanover Square.

A *London Diocese* marriage licence confirms that John Giblett, a bachelor, of the Parish of St. George, Hanover Square, married Mary Ann Joyner, a spinster born in Putney or Chelsea, of the Parish of St. Mary, Aldermary, London. Both were over the age of 21. They married on 7th January 1826 at St. George, Hanover Square, witnessed by George Thomas Platt and John George Leigh.

It can be seen recorded in *The Examiner* that on 25th September 1836, John Giblett of Coles Terrace, Islington, applied for a permit to shoot game. John Giblett appeared in census returns over the years at different addresses in Islington, Stoke Newington, Hackney and Tottenham. The table below includes ages, addresses and places of birth accurately or otherwise declared:

Table showing John Giblett at addresses in census returns.

Census	Age	Address	Parish	Place of birth
1841	35	Barnsbury Road Coles Terrace	Islington	Not given
1851	47	5 Green Lanes, Hackney	St. Mary, Stoke Newington	St. George Hanover Square, Westminster

1861	55	14 Farleigh Villas, Pembury Road	St. John, Hackney	Westminster
1871	66	Woodberry House, St Ann's Road	St. Ann, Tottenham	St. George, Middlesex
1881	72	Paradise Row, 2 Glebe Place	St. Mary, Stoke Newington	Bond St, Middlesex
1891	88	9 Northampton Pk	St. Paul, Islington	Bond St, Middx.

There are a number of discrepancies in John Giblett's age in the various census returns. His birthday was on 20th March, around the time of the census but specific dates of censuses vary. Glebe Place, Paradise Row, is close to St. Mary's Church, next to Clissold Park in Stoke Newington. Glebe Place no longer exists.

Elizabeth, daughter of John and Mary Ann Giblett, was baptised at St. Mary Abbots Church in Kensington and Chelsea on 30th June 1830. At that time John was a cattle salesman living at Notting Hill Place. The 1841 Census shows that John, then a sheep salesman and Mary Giblett were both aged 35 and their children were Elizabeth (11), Mary (8), John (6), William (4), Fanny (2) and Frederick (1 month). At the time of the census of 1851, their daughters, Elizabeth (20), Mary (18), Fanny (12), and sons John (16), Frederick (10) and Arthur (6) were all said to have been born in Islington. John Giblett, as noted earlier, rented the dwelling house later known as *Woodberry Lodge* for £233 a year from 5th January 1854. He was in Hackney at the time of the 1861 Census when, aged 55, he was listed with his wife Mary (54) and sons John (25) a cattle salesman, Fred (19) a cattle salesman and Arthur (15), a scholar. Also recorded in the household was Eliza Hunt, married, aged 60, described as the sister of the head of house and born in London. At the time of the census of 1871, John Giblett, aged 66, was recorded at *"Woodberry House"*, at St. Ann's Road, Stamford Hill, with his son Arthur, aged 24, a wine merchant. William A. Jourdan, 32, a local man born in Stoke Newington and head gardener and his wife Sarah, 35, were living in *"Woodberry Lodge"* and Daniel Pelling and his family were listed at *"Woodberry Farm"*. The grounds of the estate were extensive. The *Old Ordnance Survey map of Stamford Hill, of 1868*, marked the main house as *"Woodberry Lodge"*. In the census records of 1881, the age of John Giblett was given as 72 and for his wife Mary as 73. Also in the house were his son, Arthur, a wine merchant, aged 34 and two servants. There may have been a transcription error as the parents ages should have been 76 and 75. By the time of the 1891 Census John Giblett, aged 88, a cattle merchant and a widower was living with his son Arthur, aged 45, then secretary to his father.

It was announced in the *Bradford Observer* in April 1860, that Guerrier, Giblett and Giblett junior, Metropolitan Cattle Market and graziers at Hangers *Land* (sic.), Tottenham, beast and sheep salesmen, had dissolved their partnership. This was John Giblett and his son, John. "Hangers *Land*" should have read "Hanger Lane".

A number of weddings took place in John Giblett's family during the period 1860 to 1866. In 1860 it was announced in *The Morning Post* that

Mary Giblett, second daughter of John Giblett, Esq., of Farleigh Villas, Lower Clapton married, at St. John at Hackney, John Walpole Holloway, eldest son of Joseph Richard Holloway of Highbury Grange. It was reported in the *Caledonian Mercury* that on 11th January 1865 in Edinburgh, John Giblett of 5 Highbury Park West, Islington, eldest son of John Giblett of Church Street, Stoke Newington, married Isabel Shiel Swan, youngest daughter of John Swan. It was announced in *The Pall Mall Gazette* dated Wednesday 17th October 1866, that Fanny Giblett, the youngest daughter of Mr. J. Giblett of Glebe Villas, Stoke Newington and Woodberry Lodge, Stamford Hill, married Mr. W. Stone of Nightingale Road, Lower Clapton, on 13th October 1866 at St. Mary's Stoke Newington.

John Giblett, was certainly living at 1 Glebe Place, Stoke Newington from July 1864 (*MDR/1864/15/490*) and in December 1867 (*MDR/1867/30/341*) as his name appeared in indentures at those times. A letter was published in *The Times* from John Giblett, dated 11th August 1865, showing that address. He argued in the letter that it was not the foreign imports of livestock which introduced diseases to England. He believed, from his thirty years in the cattle business, that they were more "*sound*", as he put it, than those cattle from England, Scotland and Ireland. He continued "*... the most particular in their investigation, viz the Jews. No class of people pay so much attention to the cleanliness, wholesomeness and sound state of their meat: Priests are appointed to see their oxen killed*". The government was suggesting a quarantine period for foreign imports, which Giblett said would create a problem in meeting the demand for meat.

Giblett's name is recorded on maps in 1864 on the northwest side of Seven Sisters Road, which is now part of the Tewkesbury Estate. John Giblett sold land in 1867 to the Tottenham and Hampstead Junction Railway and the Great Eastern Railway, Cambridge and the Midlands Railway Companies. The junction of the two railway lines, near what is now St. Ann's Road, was close to the site of Woodberry Lodge and the line would have cut through the land that he owned.

In January 1870 (*MDR/1870/4/117*) Giblett recorded his address as *Woodberry Lodge* and in the same year he was listed in the Electoral Registers as the occupier of a house at St. Ann's Road, Stamford Hill. According to the Electoral Register for Tottenham, in 1872 and 1873 John Giblett was occupying a house and land at *Woodberry Lodge*, Hanger Lane, with a rental income in excess of £100 per annum, suggesting that Giblett perhaps no longer owned the land.

In *The Pall Mall Gazette* of Tuesday 23rd April 1872, the death was announced in Sydney, on 9th February 1872 of Charles F. Giblett, son of John, of Woodberry Lodge, Stamford Hill, confirming that John Giblett was still in residence there. Charles F. is likely to have been the son called Frederick, who was aged one month at the time of the census of 1841. In 1874 (*MDR/1874/26/409*) John Giblett was back at Glebe Place, Stoke Newington.

John Giblett and The Tottenham and Hampstead Junction Railway Company

A number of documents held by *The National Archives (C 16/345/G166)* outline a dispute between John Giblett and *The Tottenham and Hampstead Junction Railway Company*. The plaintiff, John Giblett, a cattle salesman, recorded his address as No.1 Glebe Place, Stoke Newington Middlesex. Below is a summary of the Bill of Complaint in Chancery, dated 15th November 1866.

1. The Lands Clauses Consolidation Amendment Act 1860 gave power created by the Tottenham and Hampstead Junction Railway Act 1862, to make a railway from Tottenham to join the Hampstead Junction Railway to be *"of great local and public advantage"* and for that company now to purchase, *"take hold and dispose of lands"*.
2. The plaintiff, John Giblett, was described as the owner in fee simple of certain lands in the Parish of All Hallows Tottenham, Middlesex, required for the purpose of the railway works authorised.
3. The Company gave notice dated 25th June 1863, that *"they require to purchase or take all the lands and hereditaments"* described on a plan and to pay compensation for any damage caused. The Company demanded that Giblett's *"estate and interest in the land and hereditaments"* be outlined. There were three plots of pasture land identified, numbered 7, 9, 13, in the Parish of All Hallows, Tottenham, in the County of Middlesex.
4. No.7 was held by the plaintiff as yearly tenant but given up by him in 1863.
5. Negotiations took place between surveyors for both parties to establish the amount of compensation
6. Surveyors unable to agree by 20th July 1864, so the Company started work without paying any compensation.
7. On 6th September 1864, £575 was paid as security into the Bank of England.
8. The plans for railway work were originally presented in November 1861.
9. The railway company started work on land numbered 9 and 13, which was then in their possession.
10. Reference to a document dated 25th June 1863 with plans of three portions of land for which the railway company now agreed, on 29th March 1865, to give £1,000 for the purchase of land and compensation.
11. On 26th April 1865, a letter was sent to *"John Giblett and to all persons having or claiming any estate or interest"* and £1,000 was to be paid as compensation to Giblett. However, Giblett had no interest in land numbered 7 on the plan and a special jury was set up by Sheriff of the County of Middlesex to determine the sum of money paid in compensation to Giblett for 9 and 13 (not 7, which he no longer owned) or any land which he is *"enabled to sell and convey"*, in compensation for railway and works.
12. On 23rd May 1865, the special jury agreed the sum of compensation as £2,325.

13. An abstract of the Plaintiff's title to the said land was sent to the Railway's solicitor. After a long delay and many applications by the solicitors for the Plaintiff, the draft was returned on 30th May 1866, with the approval on behalf of the plaintiff and the mortgagees.

14. Circumstances changed with the mortgagees on the said lands, causing an alteration in conveyance, which was redrafted and approved on 4th October 1866 by all parties.

15. On 19th October 1866, the plaintiff's solicitor sent a letter outlining the circumstances of the redrafting, explaining that a sub-mortgage on the property made an alteration necessary and reconveyance. They wanted to move the process along, threatening further legal action.

16. The solicitor for the railway company made an appointment to transfer the mortgage and requested costs from the plaintiff.

17. On 30th October 1866, another letter was sent to the defendant requesting settlement for the purchase.

18. On 31st October 1866, a letter was sent to Giblett's solicitors, including the following statement *"On examining the abstract of the reassignment of the mortgage to the Misses King at Cranbrook, I found that you had never supplied me with any abstract of the assignment by them to Wollaston and others. Messrs Neve and Company promised to supply you with this abstract to enable you to let me have it and I have been expecting to receive it daily. Until I have had this I cannot finally approve the draft conveyance"*.

19. A letter was sent from the plaintiff's solicitor on 3rd November 1866, again insisting that it was sent but now sent again and threatening further legal action for a speedy resolution and payment of purchase money.

20. The said £575 was with the Bank of England but not agreed purchase price of £2325.

21. The defendant's company refused to complete the conveyance, despite the plaintiff having provided requested information, documentation and informed interested parties.

The plaintiff requested payment of £2325 and interest of 5% per annum from 20th July 1864 or threatened that an injunction be used to restrain the defendants from continuing possession of the said land until such money has been paid. The plaintiff argued that he had *"a lien as unpaid vendor on the said lands of £2325 and interest"* and *"if necessary a receiver of the rents and profits of the said lands or of the monies and effects, income and revenue of the defendants company may be appointed"*. The Bill was filed by Messrs. Kingsford and Dorman of 23 Essex Street, Strand, Middlesex.

On 18th January 1867, in Chancery, an answer was filed to the above Bill in which the defendants agreed the sequence of events. John Giblett was the owner of No. 9 and 13 but not 7, marked on plan of land at All Hallows, Tottenham and entitled to compensation. The sum of £575 was paid into an account and compensation of £2325 agreed. An abstract of the title to the said lands was eventually furnished by the plaintiff's solicitors. Some alterations took place with the mortgage which involved a reconveyance. The defendant's company denied that it refused to complete the sale and purchase of land but that any delay in drafting the conveyance was to clarify the situation relating to the plaintiff and the mortgagees to execute a conveyance giving him title. All purchase money was now to be paid to the plaintiff, the mortgagor, John Giblett.

Deaths of John and Mary Ann Giblett

Mary Ann Giblett, wife of John Giblett, died on 8th January 1890, aged 85 at 28 Petherton Road, at which time John Giblett was listed in the Electoral Register at that address. Three years later, on 28th October 1893, he died at Northampton Park, Canonbury, in his ninety-first year. Probate was granted almost a year later on 15th October 1894. He was described as a cattle salesman and his effects, amounting to £154 8s. 8d., went to his son John, a cattle salesman. In the *London Gazette* of 25th January 1895 it was reported, under a section on County Court Jurisdiction relating to creditors, that John Giblett, the elder, formerly of 18 West Smithfield and Deptford, in Kent but lately of 9 Northampton Park, Canonbury, Middlesex, had died.

William Jones

After Giblett, the next person to live at *Woodberry Lodge*, Stamford Hill, was William Jones who, late in 1863, married Miriam Emma Lane. In the Census of 1861, Jones, described as a grocer and wine merchant living at Windsor in Berkshire, was married to Maria Elizabeth, the mother of his three children, Percy Edward, Henrietta Ann and Douglas William Jones. Maria died there on 17th January 1863. At the time of the census of 1871, William Jones, aged 36, was listed as head of house at Penge, in Surrey, with Miriam Emma, aged 42. He was born in Islington around 1835 and she at Wycombe in Buckinghamshire. Jones gave his occupation as an auctioneer or valuer. By 1st June 1874 he recorded his address as *Woodberry Lodge*, Stamford Hill, when he was one of the parties named in a transfer (*MDR/1874/16/861*) of *Woodberry Lodge*, coach house and other buildings by John Giblett, then of 1 Glebe Place, Stoke Newington, to Thomas Wheeler and Daniel Clarke, both of Chipping Wycombe, Buckinghamshire. In this indenture he was described as having been formerly a wine merchant. In a supplement to the London Gazette, dated 27th February 1875, William Jones was listed as a banker at 33 Abchurch Street, possibly a business address, along with Percy Edward Jones, a clerk, Douglas William Jones, a minor, Henrietta Anne Jones, a minor and Miriam Emma Jones of Mount Pleasant, Oxford Road, Wycombe, described as a married lady. In October of the same year the *Times* and *Leeds Mercury* record a legal case under the heading of *"Prosecution of the Directors of the City and County Bank"* in which William Jones of *Woodberry Lodge*, Stamford Hill was described as the managing director of that bank. He had been charged and appeared in court because the bank had allegedly communicated to shareholders information which was misleading and fraudulent. The directors of the bank created an impression that they were more successful than they were when in fact they owed more than £50,000.

The Electoral Registers for Tottenham shows that William Jones was qualified to vote as the occupier of a freehold house at *Woodberry Lodge*, St. Ann's Road, Stamford Hill, in the years 1876 to 1879. William Jones left Stamford Hill some time around 1877. *The London Gazette* dated 6th October 1882 included a report of proceedings in the London Bankruptcy Court. It was a *"resolution for liquidation"* of the affairs of William Jones, of *"no occupation"* but late a managing director of a bank, by then of 93 Talbot Road, Bayswater, Middlesex and late of 3 Adelaide Place, London Bridge in the City of London and of Woodbury Lodge, Stamford Hill, Middlesex. Miriam Emma Jones (wife of William) of Chapel Road, Worthing, West Sussex died on 27th August 1898, aged 76; Miriam was a good deal older that her husband. Her estate passed to Daniel Clarke, a solicitor.

Abraham Briggs is also recorded in the Electoral registers for Tottenham in the years 1872 to 1876, qualified to vote as occupying a house and land with a rental value exceeding £150 per annum at Stamford Hill, Tottenham. During the years 1877 to 1882, his address was given as Craven Farm, Stamford Hill, Tottenham but he was qualified to vote as the owner of a freehold house based on the address at Woodberry Lodge. However, in the census of 1881, Abraham Briggs (42), a dairy farmer, his wife Emma (40) and their children were recorded at Bailey's Lane, East View, Stamford Hill, in Hackney. Their son Harold (8) was born at Stamford Hill. The last year in which Briggs was registered to vote as the freeholder of Woodberry Lodge was 1882. In the census of 1871, Abraham Briggs was recorded as a cow-keeper at Pritchards Road, Hackney, suggesting that the two were one and the same.

Document (*DL/T1/AA/44/018*) from 1880, held at the LMA, confirms the ownership of various parcels of land at Tottenham prior to development. A drawing is included that matches the numbered parcels of land, owners, occupiers, description and sizes. The document states:

> Altered Apportionment of the Rent Charge in lieu of Tithes on certain lands in the parish of Tottenham in the County of Middlesex.
>
> Whereas a certain Instrument of Apportionment of Rent Charge made on the Commutation of the tithes of the parish of Tottenham in the County of Middlesex was duly confirmed by the Tithe Commissioners for England and Wales on or about the thirtieth day of September, one thousand eight hundred and forty four.
>
> And whereas an instrument of Altered Apportionment of Rent Charge in respect of certain lands in the said parish was duly confirmed by the said Tithe Commissioners on or about the twentieth day of November, one thousand eight hundred and seventy three
>
> And whereas by the said last mentioned Instrument certain lands therein described as the property of John Giblett and containing in the whole twenty seven acres one rood thirty seven

perches are charged with the following Rent Charges that is to say the sum of five pounds ten shillings and nine pence payable to the Vicar of the said parish and the sum of six pounds five shillings and six pence payable to the appropriators

And whereas Abraham Briggs, Charles Dorman, George Russell and William Anthony Tharp being the present Owners of portions of the said lands as set forth in the Schedule hereunto annexed have applied to the said Tithe Commissioners to alter the Apportionment and Altered Apportionment of the said Rent Charge so far as regards the said lands

Now we the undersigned Tithe Commissioners for England and Wales by and with the direction and consent of the said Abraham Briggs, Charles Dorman, George Russell and William Anthony Tharp and by virtue of the powers of the Statute in that behalf provided do by this instrument in writing under our Hand and Official Seal alter the said Apportionment and Altered Apportionment in such manner and in such proportions as are mentioned in the said Schedule hereunto annexed.

In Tottenham whereof We have hereunto subscribed our respective names and caused our Official Seal to be affixed this seventeen day of June in the year of our Lord one thousand eight hundred and eighty.

Signed G. Ridley(LS) James Caird

(City of London, London Metropolitan Archives)

The table below contains much of the information on the Schedule drawn on one page of the document which included owners and occupiers:

Table of owners and occupiers in 1880.

Owner	Occupier	Plan annexed to confirm App. & Altered apport.	Number on plan in margin	Name and description of land & premises	Quantity in statute measure A R P
Abraham Briggs	Himself		1461a	House buildings pleasure grounds gardens & water	3 2 0
Charles Salisbury Butler	Himself	1468a	1468a	Building land	0 2 7
Charles Dorman	Edmund Wood	1466a	1465a 1466a	Building land Building land	19 2 0 0 3 36
				Total	20 1 36
George Russell	Himself	1469	1469	Building land	0 3 0
William Anthony Tharp	Hicklin	1468b	1468b	Building land	2 0 34
				Total	27 1 37

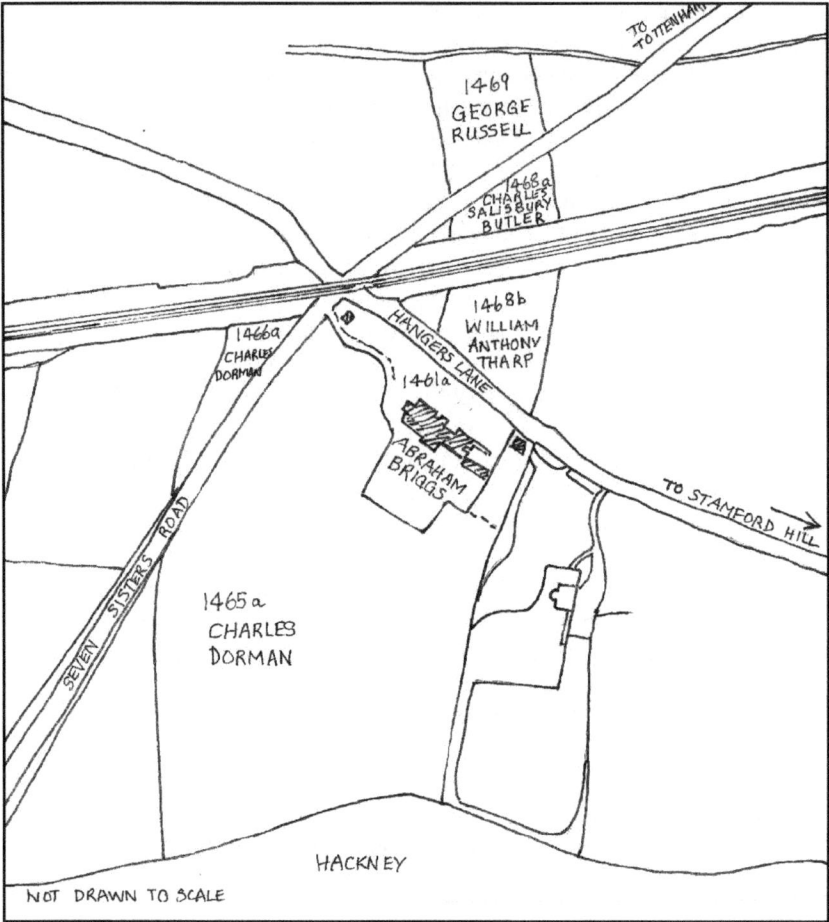

36.1 Author's Map from DL/T1/AA/44/018 showing ownership in 1880.

This document confirms that John Giblett was the owner of the property in 1873 but the above-named parties were owners by 1880. The name of Charles Salisbury Butler is marked on the drawing but not included in the statement above. He was for many years the M.P. for Tower Hamlets and lived at "*Cazenoves*", Upper Clapton, Middlesex. He died on 11th November 1870, aged 58, at 48 Princess Gate, Hyde Park, London. Charles Salisbury Butler had acquired 3 roods and 20 perches in March 1867 (*MDR/1867/7/ 213*).

In 1870, William Anthony Tharp owned freehold land at Hanger Lane, according to the electoral register. He acquired the land at Tottenham before that time. He died in October 1889. In 1886, George Russell, a piano forte manufacturer, was living at 28 Beaconsfield Road, West Green, in the High Cross polling district. The company was established in 1842 and was known for its upright pianos. He continued to make them between 1880 and 1910. The last known address for the company was 2 Stanhope Street. Middlesex.

Summary and Conclusion Regarding Land Ownership

The following summary attempts to highlight the sequence of events and the ownership of the land including *Woodberry Lodge* based on indentures memorials and other documents:

When he died in 1634, Edward Barkham left parts of his land at Tottenham to his sons Edward and Robert. Around 1661, Robert's son, also Robert Barkham, acquired a share of the land at Hanger Lane and Edmonton, which passed to his son, Robert. After the younger Robert's death in 1691 it passed to his eldest son, Robert who sold it in 1694 to Henry Hayter. When Henry died in 1716, it was inherited by his brother, Thomas Hayter. Around 1720/1, William Lethieullier, the barber surgeon and merchant, bought it. This was a year after the death of his father, Sir John Lethieullier, the merchant who, with his brothers, had lent money to Sir William Barkham and his daughters. When William Lethieullier died in 1739, the land passed to his widow, Mary and on her death in 1746/7, to their youngest son, Samuel Lethieullier. Samuel died in 1752, so the land then passed to his widow, Sarah Lethieullier, who in 1756 married Stephen Holland. Stephen died in 1768 and the land reverted again to his widow. It was Sarah's wish that after her death in 1779, the farm and other land at Tottenham should be left to her nieces, Rachel Waller and Margaret Lethieullier, later Pinckard, as tenants in common. It was they who, around 1798, sold what remained of the land in Tottenham to John Wood and George Stacey, respectively a stockbroker and a chemist. John Wood died in 1813 and his heirs owned what still remained of the land, unsold, for the next fifty years. It was leased to Thomas Coxhead Stevens, the stave and timber merchant. What later became known as Woodberry Lodge was constructed at his own expense after 1807 by Thomas Coxhead Stevens. It then passed to Brodie Augustus McGhie, the ship broker, Arend George John Walstab, the firewood importer, John Jerram, the wholesale tea importer, Samuel Lloyd Stacey, the druggist and chemist, John Giblett, the cattle salesman and then to John Black, the "*wax vest*" manufacturer in the lighting business.

In 1859, the heirs of John Wood conveyed the tenancy to John Nesbitt Malleson, the solicitor. The remaining members of the Wood family continued to own the freehold until 1864. Edmund Heysham Wood lived for a time at Muswell Hill as did John Lucas, his brother, William and his son Joseph Lucas. John Giblett would have known them as he had grazed his cattle at Hanger Lane in Tottenham. Giblett was directly involved in leasing the land during the next twenty years.

In 1864, ownership of *Woodberry Lodge* and the land transferred from Edmund Heysham, George and Herbert William Wood to John Giblett, the cattle salesman and Jonathan Seaman Mallett, the clerk at Kingsford and Dorman, solicitors. In the same year, Caroline Mary and Marianne Augusta King became the new tenants in common of the land owned by John Giblett.

In 1865, James Kingsford, the solicitor, mortgaged *Woodberry Lodge* and buildings with the surrounding meadow land from John Giblett.

The Woodberry Lodge Estate, of some forty-one acres, was sold in October 1866, probably by Kingsford or John Giblett, with the intention of developing the land to build detached and semi-detached villas. Early in 1867, Giblett officially acquired part of Bushey Hangers adjoining Oat Fields. The land, of some 4 acres, 3 roods and 31 perches, was purchased from Joseph Lucas, a solicitor and his cousin, Joseph Lucas of Hitchin, both executors of John Lucas' estate. In 1870, Giblett transferred ownership of thirty-eight acres to Charles Dorman and his heirs. In 1874 Caroline Mary King, Thomas Nightwick, James, Thomas and Charles Dorman, John Giblett, William Jones, the banker and his wife Miriam, agreed to lease *Woodberry Lodge* with all the land and outbuildings but not the fish pond, to Thomas Wheeler, a banker and brewer and Daniel Clark, a solicitor and their heirs. This agreement referred to a small part of the estate, approximately seven acres. It was part of William and Miriam Jones' marriage settlement, involving Wheeler and Clarke, in December 1863.

Charles Dorman appears to have taken sole ownership of the remaining twenty three acres as from 1874. Although John Giblett was involved in conveyances after this date, James Kingsford and Charles Dorman are the main names appearing after 1870.

The development of the *Woodberry Lodge Estate*, that is, the area surrounding the *Lodge*, partly owned by James Kingsford and/or Charles Dorman, solicitors, accelerated rapidly. According to *"The Victorian Villas of Hackney"* by Michael Hunter, houses were erected on a speculative basis. It was a way for a builder or speculator to take particular plots of land on building leases from their owners, who then raised capital, often from solicitors, to pay for the cost of erecting houses. The solicitors, in those days, would have the funds of their clients to invest. When a building was nearly finished, the builder put it up for sale or rent to pay off his loan or debts. The explosion of investment in the development of property and land in Victorian London was at full pace, with freehold land and leases rapidly and profitably changing hands, sometimes with deeds being written after the buildings were erected. This might explain the relationship between George Candler, the builder and estate agent and Charles Dorman, the personally wealthy partner at Kingsford, Dorman & Co. who handled many conveyances and owned properties to let. In all likelihood, George was the leaseholder of the properties in the area, including 54 Vartry Road and Charles Dorman along with other rich clients and after his death, his sons, were the freeholders or mortgagors.

Kingsford Terrace was named after James Kingsford and Charles Street, later to become Richmond Road, named after Charles Dorman. Lawrie Road, later renamed Berkeley Road, was probably named after Lawrie Park where Charles Dorman lived in Sydenham. Candler Street, developed around 1878 by Edmund Wood, may have been named after Samuel Horace Candler, George Herbert Candler's brother but more likely the early Candler local landowners. The earliest houses in Candler Street were built before George Candler arrived in the area as the street was referred to in the census of 1881.

Plans were submitted by Weatherall and Green in 1877 and 1878 for new roads on the *Woodberry Lodge Estate* and in 1879 and 1880, by a Mr. Eve for further new roads. In 1878, Edmund Wood submitted plans for shops on

Seven Sisters Road. In April 1880, J.T. Lee submitted plans for 14 houses in Vartry Road. In 1882, the same Edmund Wood, the builder and developer of some of the first houses in the area who was listed as living in the *Woodberry Hotel*, 15 Church Street, Stoke Newington and at *The Angel Inn* in Highgate during 1882, submitted plans for a new road on the *Woodberry Lodge Estate*. The 1881 Census identified Edmund Wood(s) as a land agent; he and his family lived at Truro Road, *Warwick Lodge*, Tottenham, Middlesex and he is cited in documents relating to 13-37 Albert Road. George Candler later gave this address when he began submitting building applications in 1890 when it was still owned by Kingsford, Dorman & Co. In the *Rate Books* of 1900, held at Bruce Castle Museum, there were only a few references to E. Wood, which would suggest that by that time Wood had transferred the leases to other parties. The name *Woodberry Lodge Estate* was used by George Candler on his rent books for the tenements and houses in the local area.

In 1879, the *Woodberry Hotel* was situated next to what is now the *Woodberry Tavern*, a local public house on Seven Sisters Road. Kingsford Terrace was the row of shops on the left hand side of Seven Sisters Road, leading up to the junction of the railway lines. Charles Dorman negotiated with the *North London Tramway Company* on the 18th January 1884 to lease the land for the turning of the trams between the railway line and the back of Kingsford Terrace; there still exists today a gap in the terrace where the trams used to enter in order to turn.

In 1890 Thomas James, who resided at 71 Amhurst Park, submitted plans for nine houses on the south side of Vartry Road probably Nos. 134-150. Other wealthy local residents from Amhurst Park, which backs onto Vartry Road, were involved in the building of houses in Vartry Road and owned some of the freeholds. Over the next few years the number of deeds increased dramatically as Charles Dorman enlarged his investment in and management of property and land sales in the area. A number of significant ones in Vartry Road are outlined later.

A deed (*MDR/1897/8/504*) for the freehold land and messuages at Nos. 26-58 Vartry Road was first registered in 1897 by Charles Dorman and Selina Noys (*see Appendix 1*). Charles Herbert Dorman, as one of the executors and trustees of Charles Dorman's will, took the place of his father in 1903 (*MDR/1903/10/300*) and in 1906 (*MDR/1906/29/30*) with his brother Francis, when his sister, Julia Frances, retired from the trusteeship. After Charles Herbert Dorman died in 1915, Francis Dorman took the place of his eldest brother in the *Memorial of a Land Registry Document* for messuages in Vartry Road in a conveyance (*MDR/1915/6/546*). In 1925, a reconveyance was registered (*MDR/1925/20/404*) by George Thomas Noys and Nora Madeline Noys after the death of Selina Noys, their mother. In 1926, Francis Dorman appointed his son, Laurence Charles Dorman, as trustee of his father's will (*MDR/1926/1/226*). Francis died in 1931 and Lady Emily Shackleton became a trustee. She died in 1936 and Charles John Paget Dorman, her nephew, was appointed trustee in December, 1936 of his grandfather's will (*MDR/1936/61/165*). The latter's father, Arthur Dorman, had died in January

1914 and his obituary explained that his wife had died before him and Charles John Paget was his only son; Charles John Paget Dorman died in 1939. Nora Noys died in 1944 and Barclays Bank and her brother George Noys inherited her estate; he died in 1945 and Edith his wife inherited his estate.

Electoral Registers for Tottenham, St. Ann's Ward, confirm that the shared owners of the freehold of the Woodberry Estate were James Kingsford in 1882, 1891 and 1895, the year that he died and Charles Dorman in 1882, 1889, 1890, 1891. The Registers had voters classified by ownership, occupation or as lodgers. In 1904, they showed that Charles Herbert Dorman, Francis Thomas Dorman, Julia, Emily, Maude and brother, Arthur William Dorman owned the freehold of the *Woodberry Estate.* This included Vartry Road, Richmond Road, Franklin Street, Manchester Road, Heysham Road, Berkeley Road and St. John's Road. The name of James Henry Kingsford was recorded in deeds in 1913 and 1915, the year he died, in connection with properties at Franklin Street, Vartry Road and St. John's Road. George Herbert Candler managed those properties in 1913, in addition, from around 1900, to flats owned by Kingsford, Dorman & Co. and also the Dorman family.

The *Poor Rate* books do suggest George Candler as the owner of many properties during the time he lived in the area but he may only have been the leaseholder. The only houses that there is evidence of him owning, forming part of his estate in his will, were the two houses at 21 and 22 Casselden Road, Harlesden, one of which still had a mortgage.

It is certain that in 1951, when No. 54 Vartry Road was first registered with the Land Registry, Laurence Charles Dorman was a director of the *Woodberry Lodge Estate Company. The London Gazette* of 22nd May, 1951 records that the freehold land in question was about to be registered and any objections had to be notified before 5th June, 1951. It was listed by the *Woodberry Lodge Estate Company* as the *Woodberry Lodge Estate*, Tottenham, Middlesex. Mr. H. W. C. Davies, who had an office in Southgate, was a director of the *Woodberry Development Company* in this year but later both were wound up.

Laurence Charles Dorman's name appeared many times in the *London Gazette* over the years at various addresses. At the end of the War, Kingsford, Dorman & Co. was at Effingham House, 1 Arundle Street, Strand, WC2. In October 1964, Kingsford, Dorman & Co. was at Old Square, Lincoln's Inn, London WC2A 3UA and Laurence Charles Dorman and his son, Charles Swinford Dorman, were both solicitors in the firm; in 1972 they were still practising from 13 Old Square. Laurence Charles Dorman died in February 1993.

Appendices

Appendix 1

Some deeds relating to South Tottenham, 1859–1936

The Middlesex Deeds Registry, held at the London Metropolitan Archives, records freehold land and land held on leases of over 21 years. Below are summaries of deeds and extracts from the registers relating to the land at South Tottenham, some already discussed, starting with John Wood and bringing the account up to the time of Dorman family. They are in chronological order. Where there are transcriptions of original documents, words may be abbreviated. The author has concentrated on the parcels of land known as *Oat Field or Oat Fields,* sometimes *Oatfield or Oatfields,* as the houses on Vartry Road were built on the edge of that parcel of land on the border between Hackney and Tottenham. Other parcels of land including *Snares Mead* are cited in earlier indentures before various parcels of land were sold. The sizes of the parcels of land were not always identified and sometimes varied over the years. In terms of measurement, there are four roods to one acre and forty perches to one rood. The MDR reference includes the year, book/volume and the number of the deed, with the date it was registered. Registration followed the signing and in some cases this was some time after the deed was dated (some of the deeds also have original document references). The deed indexes include the main parties to the exchange although not all participants are named. The summaries below include the parties named, a description of the lands affected, some with plans and some are annotated. Where parts of the indentures are quoted, they are recorded with the date of registration, followed by the book or volume number and the number of the indenture, e.g. B10 No. 574.

MDR/1859/10/574 registered 22nd July 1859

Summary: Wood to Malleson. Dated 13th June 1859. Parties: Edmund Heysham Wood and others to John Nesbitt Malleson. Conveyance. Description of lands affected: <u>Oatfield and Snares Mead (38 acres)</u>. The deed included a drawing of the various parcels of land and their sizes. Below is a transcription of the deed *(Some of the words are abbreviated)*:

> Indenture bearing date 13th June 1859 and made between Edmund Heysham Wood of New House Rickmansworth in the County of Herts., Esq. and Sophia Wood his wife of the 1st part, Edmund Heysham Wood, George Wood of No 85 Westbourne Terrace in the County of Middlesex Esq. and Herbert William Wood of No.

16 Lansdowne Terrace, Cheltenham in the County of Gloucester, Esq., of the 2nd part and John Nesbitt Malleson, of No. 11 Austin Friars in the City of London, Gent of the 3rd part purporting to be a Conveyance to the sd John Nesbitt Malleson To the uses and upon the Trusts therein mentioned of All those three closes of meadow or pasture land commonly called or known by the several names of the Twelve acres the Five acres and the Six acres but heretofore called or known by the name of The Oat Field and being formerly 2 closes containing together by estimation 26 acres more or less lying in the Parish of Tottenham High Cross in the County of Middlesex afsd near unto a certain place called or known by the name of Stamford Hill abutting South upon the Lands heretofore of Sir Robert Smith, Knight & North upon Hangers Lane together with the Messuage or Tenement erected and built thereon And also All those 2 closes of Meadow or Pasture ground containing together by estimation 12 acres be the same more or less commonly known by the name of Snares Meads adjoining South upon Hangers Lane aforesaid All which and last mentioned two closes & premises were also lying & being in the Parish of Tottenham afsd (save and except from the above mentioned closes or pieces or parcels of Land and Ground All that piece or parcel of Land situate lying and being in the Parish of Tottenham aforesaid abutting on Hangers Lane towards the North & containing 1 acre and 7 perches be the same more or less and all that piece or parcel of land situate and lying and being northward of Hangers Lane aforesaid and abutting south westwardly on land now or late belonging to James Collins, Esq., and containing 1 acre & 30 perches be the same more or less And also all that piece or parcel of Land situate lying and being North Eastwardly of the last mentioned piece or parcel of land abutting north eastwardly on Land formerly belonging to John Clarkson, Esq., & containing 1 rood & 5 perches be the same a little more or less which sd 3 several lastly described pieces or parcels of Land have been thrown into & form part of a New Road from the Stamford Hill Road in the Parish of Tottenham to the Camden Town Road in the Parish of Islington and which are the same piece or parcels of Land which in the year 1833 were conveyed by Frances Wood, William Varden, Edmund Heysham Wood, George Wood, Herbert William Wood and Frances Ellen Wood To the use of the sd Commissioners for carrying into Execution certain Acts of Parliament for consolidating the Trusts of certain Metropolitan Turnpike Roads and which sd Closes or pieces or parcels of Land are more particularly described in the Plan drawn on the back of the 3rd skin thereof & in the margin hereof And all and singular other (if any) the Freehold heredits situate in the Parish of Tottenham afsd devised by the Will of John Wood & now remaining unsold with the appurts. Which

Indre as to the Execution thereof by the sd Edmund Heysham Wood, George Wood and Herbert William Wood is witnessed by Andrew Goring Pritchard of No.11 Austin Friars in the City of London, Clerk, to Messrs. Wadeson and Malleson of the same place Solrs And as to the Execution by Sophia Wood is witnessed by John Nesbitt Malleson of Austin Friars afsd Solr And the same Indenture is hereby required to be registered by the sd Edward Heysham Wood As witness his hand & seal this 13th day of June in the year of our Lord 1859- E:H: (LL)Wood – Signed and Sealed in the presence of A. Goring Pritchard, No.11 Austin Friars, clerk to Messrs. Wadeson & Malleson – E. Webber- same place, clerk. (City of London, London Metropolitan Archives)

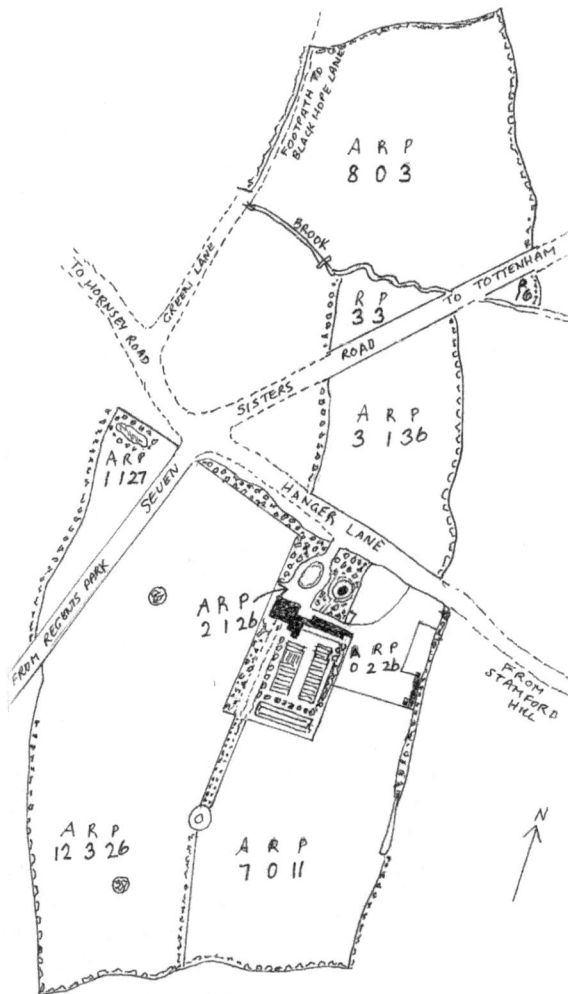

App.1.1 Map of MDR/1859/10/574.

In the indenture of 1798 relating to the land at Tottenham, the firm of solicitors cited was Wadeson and Malleson. Here was another family connection. In 1858, with the death of John's widow, Frances Wood, the above Indenture was written. Parties cited in the will and in earlier indentures, namely William Varden and Frances Ellen Wood, a spinster, the daughter of John Wood, were by this time also dead. In 1859, the heirs of John Wood were Edmund Heysham Wood, his wife Sophia and George and Herbert William Wood, the sons and daughter-in-law of John Wood. The freehold land defined as Oat Fields and Snares Mead remaining unsold in the Parish of Tottenham, left in the will of John Wood, then deceased, was conveyed to John Nesbitt Malleson of 11 Austin Friars. John Nesbitt Malleson's obituary in *The Times* (1907) reported that from 1847-1892 he was a partner in Wadeson and Malleson and had a large family and conveyance practice. He was also a close friend of Charles Dickens. By this time, only Oat Fields and Snares Mead were in the possession of the new owners, minus the parcels of land used for the new road. Plans showed that when the dwelling house and grounds were transferred in 1842 from the executors of Brodie Augustus McGhie to Walstab and then Jerram, the layout remained the same until 1859, when the executors of John Wood conveyed it to John Nesbitt Malleson. By 1867, the grounds had been extended, remodelled and many new trees had been planted, probably by John Giblett.

MDR/1864/15/490 registered 8th August 1864

Summary: Wood to Giblett. Dated 19th July 1864. Parties: Edmund Heysham Wood, formerly of Muswell Hill and now of No.37 Kensington Gardens Square, Bayswater, of the first part, George Wood, formerly of Woodford and now of No. 85 Westbourne Terrace, Middlesex, of the second part, Herbert William Wood of No. 61 Kensington Gardens Square, Lieutenant Colonel in the Indian Army, of the third part, John Giblett, of No. 1 Glebe Place, Stoke Newington, cattle salesman of the fourth part and Jonathan Seaman Mallett of No. 23, Essex Street, Strand, a gent, of the fifth part.

Edmund Heysham Wood, by the power of the indenture of 13th June 1859, had an equal undivided third part share of land and heredits, together with George Wood and Herbert William Wood. Edmund Heysham Wood, George Wood and Herbert William Wood granted their respective shares to John Giblett and his heirs and if forfeit to the use of Jonathan Seaman Mallett during the life of John Giblett. Description of lands affected: <u>indenture included a tracing, shaded in green, of the 26 acres, known as Oat Fields, including a house and 12 acres known as Snares Mead.</u> The land conveyed for the new Seven Sisters Road in 1833 by William Varden, Frances Wood and her heirs to the Commissioners for Roads, as in indenture above (1 acre & 7 perches, 1 acre & 30 perches, 1 rood & 5 perches) was cited. John Nesbitt Malleson of No.11 Austin Friars was a witness for the Wood family and Charles Dorman for John Giblett.

This would appear to be the last time that the heirs of John Wood were involved in ownership of this land. Jonathan Mallett, of the Essex Street address, was a clerk at Kingsford Dorman and was listed in the census of 1881 as a law stationer. He married Lucy Mask at St. Marylebone in 1858. In 1861 he was listed as a solicitor's managing clerk, living in Marylebone. He was living at 17 Shepperton Cottages in the Parish of St. Mary Islington when his mother, then a widow, who was visiting, died suddenly in 1865. Her husband had been a tailor/woollen draper when they were living at Woodbridge in Suffolk.

MDR/1864/15/491 registered 8th August 1864

Summary: Giblett to King. Dated 20th July 1864. Parties: John Giblett, No.1 Glebe Place, Stoke Newington of the one part and Caroline Mary King and Marianne Augusta King, spinsters, from St. Leonard's on Sea, Sussex, of the other part (they became tenants in common with their respective heirs). Description of lands affected: <u>land outlined above, known as Oat Fields and Snares Mead in the Parish of Tottenham High Cross.</u>

It described the land for the new Seven Sisters Road acquired in 1833 by the Commissioners for roads from William Varden, Frances Wood and her sons. Charles Dorman witnessed the proceedings for John Giblett.

In 1861 Caroline King, 67 and head of house, was listed with her daughters and servants at 3 Uplands Terrace, Hastings. She was registered as a fund holder and had been born in Ireland. Caroline, her daughter, was unmarried and was then aged 37. The sisters may only have been visiting at Easter, as the will of Marianne Augusta King, who died in 1868, gave alternative addresses for both sisters.

MDR/1865/9/24 registered 2nd May 1865

Summary: King and others to Wollaston and others. Dated 27th April 1865. Parties: Caroline Mary King and Marianne Augustus King, both of St. Leonards-on Sea, spinsters, of the one part to Alexander Luard Wollaston of Southampton, the Honourable Somerset Richard Maxwell of Arley Cottage, Cavan, Ireland, the Reverend William Henry Cleaver of Brighton, Sussex, clerk and Philip Bryan Davies Cooke of Owsten Park, Doncaster, of the other part. Endorsed in the indenture registered in Middlesex on 8th August 1864 (*MDR/1864/15/491*) between John Giblett of No. 1 Glebe Place, Stoke Newington, Middlesex, cattle salesman, of the one part and Caroline Mary King and Marianne Augustus King, both of St. Leonards on Sea, Sussex, spinsters, of the other part. Description of lands affected: <u>land and premises situated in the Parish of Tottenham, Middlesex.</u>

The parties involved were from various parts of England and Ireland.

MDR/1865/17/770 registered 25th August 1865

Summary: Giblett to Kingsford. Dated 25th April 1865. Parties: John Giblett of No. 1 Glebe Place, Stoke Newington, Middlesex, cattle salesman, of the one part and James Kingsford, of No. 23 Essex Street, Strand, Middlesex, of the other part. The indenture of mortgage was granted and conveyed to James

Kingsford and his heirs. Description of lands affected: <u>all those parcels of land</u> <u>(26 acres including the Oat Fields and 12 acres including Snares Mead)</u>. The indenture referred to the land that had been conveyed for the new Seven Sisters Road in 1833 (1 acre & 7 perches, 1 acre & 30 perches and 1 rood & 5 perches) by Frances Wood, William Varden, Edmund Heysham Wood, George Wood, Herbert William Wood and Frances Ellen Wood.

MDR/1866/24/102 registered 31ˢᵗ October 1866

Summary: Giblett to Dorman. Dated 28ᵗʰ September 1866. Parties: John Giblett of No. 1 Glebe Place, Stoke Newington, Middlesex, cattle salesman of the one part to Charles Dorman of No. 23 Essex Street, Strand, Middlesex, gentleman, of the other part. John Giblett granted it unto Charles Dorman and his heirs. Description of lands affected: <u>three closes of meadow 12, 5 and 6 acres known</u> <u>as Oat Fields (26 acres) at Tottenham High Cross and 12 acres known as Snares</u> <u>Mead adjoining south on Hanger Lane.</u>

It made reference to an indenture dated 19ᵗʰ July 1864 (*MDR/1864/15/490*) and to the new road from Tottenham to Camden Road constructed in 1833 (not including 1 acre & 7 perches, 1 acre & 30 perches, and 1 rood & 5 perches) and the Tottenham and Hampstead Junction Railway Company. Norton, Trist & Co. received instructions to offer for sale the Woodberry Lodge Estate of approximately 41 acres in October 1866 but the sale also included as part of Lot 1, a piece of land *(No. 6) of 4a 3r 31p*, not being part of Oat Fields or Snares Mead.

MDR/1867/7/213 registered 20ᵗʰ March 1867

Summary: Giblett and his mortgagees to Butler. Dated 15ᵗʰ March 1867. Parties: Caroline Mary King and Marianne Augustus King, both of St. Leonards on Sea, Sussex, spinsters, of the 1ˢᵗ part, James Kingsford, of No. 23 Essex Street, Strand of the 2ⁿᵈ part, Charles Dorman, of the same place, of the 3ʳᵈ part, John Giblett of No. 1 Glebe Place, Stoke Newington, Middlesex, of the 4ᵗʰ part, Charles Salisbury Butler of Upper Clapton, of the same county, Esq., of the 5ᵗʰ part and Charles Edward Kingston Butler of Bishopsgate Street in the City of London, Esq., of the 6ᵗʰ part. It recited an indre dated 19ᵗʰ July 1864 (*MDR/1864/15/490*), when Edmund Heysham Wood, of the 1ˢᵗ part, George Wood, of the 2ⁿᵈ part, Herbert William Wood, of the 3ʳᵈ part, John Giblett, of the 4ᵗʰ part and Jonathan Seaman Mallett of the 5ᵗʰ part, transferred all those two meadows or pasture ground, estimated at 12 acres, known as Snares Mead, then in the hands of John Giblett and Jonathan Seaman Mallett. By the deed in 1867, Caroline Mary King, Marianne Augusta King, James Kingsford, Charles Dorman and John Giblett, mortgagees, now grant, release and convey to Charles Salisbury Butler and his heirs. Description of lands affected: <u>a parcel of land, situated between Seven Sisters Road and</u> <u>the Tottenham and Hampstead Junction Railway, containing 3 roods and 20</u> <u>perches (*coloured brown on the plan*) once part of Snares Mead)</u>, discharged of the mortgage securities and land tax. The plan showed the new railway bridge over Hanger Lane erected by the Great Eastern Railway Company. Charles Edward Kingston Butler was the son of Charles Salisbury Butler. The layout of buildings and gardens on the plan is below:

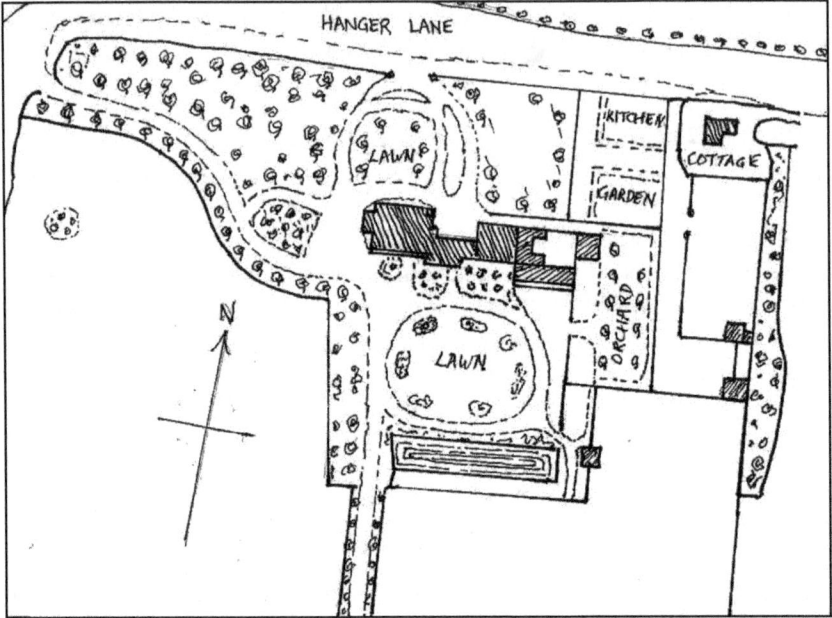

App.1.2 Section of MDR/1867/7/213.

MDR/1867/10/134 registered 26th April, 1867

Summary: Lucas to Giblett. Dated 31st December 1866. Parties: Joseph Lucas and Joseph Lucas to John Giblett and Jonathan Seaman Mallett. Description of lands affected: a parcel of land, part of Bushey Hangers, at Tottenham High Cross measuring 4a. 3r. 31p. between Seven Sisters Road and land owned by John Giblett on the border of Hackney.

> Indenture dated the 31st December 1866 made between Joseph Lucas of Upper Tooting in the County of Surrey Esq. and Joseph Lucas of Hitchin in the County of Hertfordshire, Esq. devisees in trust named in the last Will and Testament of John Lucas Esq. deceased who was a devisee named in the last Will and Testament of Joseph Lucas Esquire deceased and which said Joseph Lucas of Upper Tooting and Joseph Lucas of Hitchin parties hereto are in the now mem. Indenture called the Vendors of the 1st part John Giblett of Stoke Newington in the County of Middlesex of the 2nd Part and Jonathan Seaman Mallett of No. 23 Essex Street, Strand in the said County of Middlesex

gentleman of the 3ʳᵈ part Whereby it was witnessed that for the consons therein mentioned They the said Vendors did and each of them did by the now memorialising Indenture grant and confirm unto the said John Giblett and his heirs All that triangular piece or parcel of land situate in the Parish of Tottenham High Cross in the County of Middx containing in the whole by estimation 4a 3r 31p be the same more or less bounded on the west by the Seven Sisters Road on the north east by other land of the said John Giblett and on the south east by land now or late of Wilson Esquire which said piece of land intd to be by now memg Indenture granted is more partially delineated and described in the Map or plan drawn in the margin of the 1ˢᵗ Skin of now memorialising Indre and therein coloured Green and the same is part of cerain heredits wch were formerly described as All those the 3 formerly 4 closes or pieces or parcels of arable meadow or pasture land commonly called or known by the name of Bushey Hangers containing by admeas. 47 acres situate lying and being in the Parish of Tottenham High Cross in the said Coy of Middlesex heretofore customery freehold holden of the Manors of Tottn. Pembroke Bruces Dawbens and Mockings some or one of them in the said County of Middlesex and some time since duly and legally enfranchised and which said closes pieces or parcels of land were late in the occupation of John Remington or Edward White his undertenant but are now in the possess of Edward Scales Together with the site of such of the buildings as were lately standing and being thereon or on some part thereof as have been totally demolished or permitted to go to ruin or decay Together with all and singular ways mounds hedges ditches waters watercourses liberties privils casements heredits and apurts.....

(City of London, London Metropolitan Archives)

It was passed to John Giblett and his heirs and if he should forfeit it during his lifetime for the use of Jonathan Seaman Mallett and his heirs. Joseph Lucas of Hitchin had as his witness Charles Cecil Lucas, clerk to Messrs. Lucas & Showler, 1 Trinity Place, Charing Cross, solicitors and the witness for Joseph Lucas of Upper Tooting and John Giblett was William Henry Lee, Clerk to Messrs. Kingsford and Dorman, solicitors 23 Essex Street, Strand. It was sealed in the presence of Charles Dorman.

This extra piece of land was numbered 1475 on the Tithe Map of 1844 and No. 922 on the Old Ordnance Survey Maps of Stamford Hill 1868 and became part of the Woodberry Lodge Estate. On it was built part of Vartry Road, the Baptist Church, Stamford Hill School and the houses beside the church on Seven Sisters Road before 1894. Manchester, Heysham and Berkeley Road were built after that date. *Drawing below:*

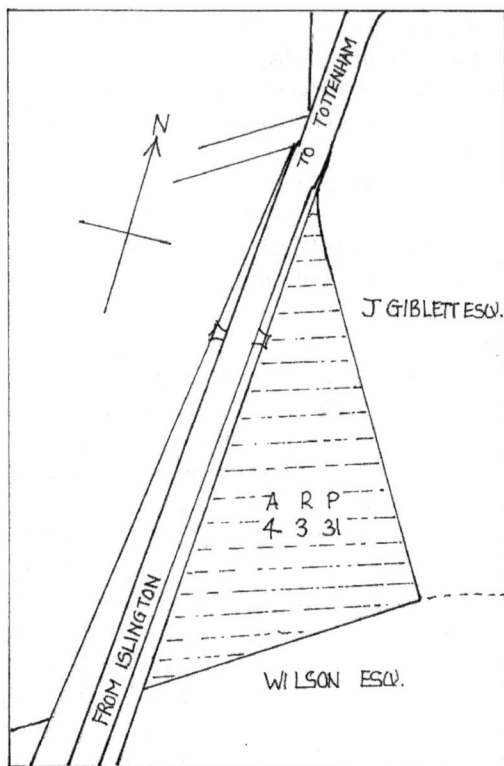

App.1.3 Map of MDR/1867/10/134.

MDR/1867/30/340 registered 19th December 1867

Summary: Dorman to Giblett. Dated 13th December 1867. Endorsed on an indenture dated 28th September 1866, registered 1866 (*MDR/1866/24/102*), made between Charles Dorman of No. 23 Essex Street, Strand, of the one part and John Giblett of No. 1 Glebe Place, Stoke Newington, Middlesex, cattle salesman, of the other part. Description of lands affected: all land and heredits outlined in indenture in the Parish of Tottenham.

MDR/1867/30/341 registered 19th December 1867

Summary: Kingsford to Giblett. Dated 13th December 1867 Endorsed in an indre dated 25th April 1865 (*MDR/1865/17/770*). Parties: James Kingsford of No. 23 Essex Street, Strand, Middlesex, of the one part and John Giblett of No. 1 Glebe Place, Stoke Newington of the other part. Kingsford granted and released unto John Giblett and his heirs. Description of lands affected: all land and heredits outlined in indenture in the Parish of Tottenham.

MDR/1867/30/478 registered 20th December 1867

Summary: Giblett to Dorman. Dated 14th December 1867. Parties: John Giblett of No. 1 Glebe Place, Stoke Newington, of the one part to James and Thomas Dorman, both of Sandwich in Kent, Esqs. of the other part. The indenture identified land at Tottenham High Cross for the use of James and Thomas Dorman and their heirs. Description of lands affected:

1. A triangular piece of land (4a 3r 31p) bounded on the west by Seven Sisters Road on the northeast by the following land and on the southeast by land formerly owned by Wilson Esq. (part of Bushey Hangers)
2. Messuage, stables, outbuildings, cottage, yards, gardens, orchard and two pieces of meadow land estimated as 23 acres and 34 perches (Oat Fields)
3. 3 roods & 4 perches (part of Oat Fields)
4. 1 acre, 3 roods and 5 perches (part of Snares Mead)
5. 8 acres, 3 roods and 6 perches (two parts of Snares Mead- 8a 3p & 3r 3p)
6. a triangular piece of land 16 perches (part of Snares Mead)

Some parcels were bounded by the Tottenham & Hampstead Junction Railway, Seven Sisters Road, Hanger Lane and land on the south then or late owned by Wilson. The parcels of land, except No. 1, were part of Oat Fields, estimated at 26 acres and Snaremead, 12 acres. Some of the land had been acquired by the Tottenham & Hampstead Junction Railway.

MDR/1868/16/255 registered 29th June 1868

Summary: Giblett to Dorman. Dated 14th June 1868. Parties: John Giblett of No. 1 Glebe Place, Stoke Newington, cattle salesman, agreed payment to James and Thomas Dorman from Sandwich in Kent. Description of lands affected: land described at Tottenham High Cross, Middlesex. Transcription of deed below:

> Indenture bearing date the 14th June 1868 (endorsed upon an Indre bearing date the 14th day of December 1867 registered the 20th December 1867: B30 No. 478) & made between John Giblett described in the said Indre of the 14h day of December 1867 as of No 1 Glebe Place Stoke Newington in the Coy of Middlesex, Cattle Salesman of the one part and James Dorman and Thomas Dorman described in the last mentioned Indre as both of Sandwich in the Coy of Kent Esqs of the other part whereby for the consons therein mentioned Indre it was thereby agreed & declared & the said John Giblett did thereby for himself his heirs exors & admors covenant with the said James Dorman & Thomas Dorman their exors admors & assigns All and singular the messuages & other heredits by the within written Indre expressed to be granted with their rights casements & appurts should be & remain a security for & stand charged with the payment to the said James Dorman & Thomas Dorman their exors admors or assigns of as well the sum of £600 & interest for the same according to the covenant in

the now memorial Indre contained as the said within mentioned sum of and £5,700 & all interest due & to grow due for the same and that the same messuages & heredits & premises should not in anywise be redeemed or redeemable but upon payment by the said John Giblett his heirs exors admors or assigns to the said James Dorman & Thomas Dorman their exors admors & assigns as well of the said sum of £600 & interest for the same according to the covenant therein before contained in that behalf as of the said sum of £5,700 & the interest to grow due for the same & which said premises are in the herein within written Indre described to be situate in the Parish of Tottenham, High Cross in the Coy of Middx And which now memorial Indre as so the execution thereof by the said John Giblett is witnessed by William Henry Lee Clerk to Messrs Kingsford & Dorman of No. 23 Essex Street Strand, Solrs And the same is now required to be registered by the said John Giblett. As witness his hand and seal this 16th day of June 1868 John Giblett (LS) signed and sealed by the said John Giblett in the presence of Chas. Dorman Solr, Essex St Strand, Wm. H Lee, Clerk to Messrs Kingsford & Dorman, Solrs Essex St Strand"

(City of London, London Metropolitan Archives.)

(Admors: administrators Exors: executors Consons: possibly consolidated funds.)

MDR/1870/4/117 registered 10th February 1870

Summary: Giblett to Dorman. Dated 1st January 1870. Parties: John Giblett of Woodberry Lodge, of the one part to Charles Dorman of 23 Essex St. Strand, gent of the other part. Giblett granted it to Dorman and his heirs. Description of lands affected: <u>a triangular piece of land of some 4 acres, 3 roods & 31 perches, bordered on the northwest by Seven Sisters Road, on the southeast by land now or late of Wilson Esq., and on the northeast by a messe, stables, outbuildings, cottage, yards, gardens, orchards and other heredits and the surrounding meadows, known as Oat Fields and Snares Mead. The land in question contained by estimation 23 acres 34 perches (once part of 26 acres called Oat Fields, including 3r 4p), (1a 3r 5p and 8a 3r 6p, once part of 12 acres known as Snares Mead).</u>

MDR/1873/11/128 registered 23rd May 1873

Summary: Swinford and others to Great Eastern Railway Company. Dated 9th April 1873. Parties: Reverend Smithett Swinford, Esq. of Ashton Keynes, Wiltshire, clerk, Thomas Francis Swinford, late Captain 98th Regiment of Infantry but then of Minster in the Isle of Thanet in Kent and Charles Dorman of No.23 Essex Street, Strand, of the first part, John Honck of Homebridge House, Tottenham, Middlesex, cattle salesman, of the second part and the Great Eastern Railway Company of the third part. This deed was consequent upon the passing of the Metropolitan Station and Railways Act 1864. Swinford, Swinford, Dorman and Honck granted the land to the Great Eastern Railway Company. Description of lands affected: <u>two parcels of land containing by estimation 2 roods and 30 perches (made up of 10 perches and 2 roods and 20 perches). The drawing marked the two plots beside a proposed road in between the Seven Sisters Road and the Tottenham and Hampstead Railway</u>.

According to the Census of 1851, members of the Swinford family were listed at Abbey House, Minster, Thanet in Kent. Below is a summary of details:

Name	Relation	Age	Occupation or profession
John Swinford	Head	64	Farmer 413 acres- 12 men and 6 boys
Frances H. "	Wife	50	Wife
James S. "	Son	26	Manufacturing chemist
Anne "	Daughter	23	Farmer's daughter
Frances E. "	Daughter	19	Farmer's daughter
Smithett "	Son	16	Scholar
Jane/Janie "	Daughter	15	At home
Mary A. "	Daughter	13	" "
Mary C. "	Daughter	8	" "
Emily "	Daughter	6	" "
Mary Sackett	Visitor	61	No occupation

John Swinford's wife was Frances Hudson Smithett. His son was James Smith Swinford; his daughters were Frances Elizabeth, Mary Ann and Mary Charlotte. Mary Sackett was the sister of Ann, his first wife. Theirs was a large household and they had seven servants. Their sons, Thomas Francis Swinford, aged 11 and Alfred, aged 10, were at boarding school in Dulwich. Thomas was a first-class cricketer and later joined the Army. John had other children by his first wife, namely John Sackett Swinford, Daniel and Henry Herbert. He also had a young son named Alfred, who was seven months-old in 1841, at the time of the census. Charles Herbert Dorman may have been named after his uncle.

John Swinford died on 16th February 1869. His will was proved on 16th March and his executors were his sons, Smithett Swinford, Thomas Francis Swinford and son-in-law, Charles Dorman; his effects were valued at under £30,000. The letters of administration of John Sackett Swinford, a bachelor, who had died in October 1868, was granted on 25th March 1869 to Charles Dorman, one of the executors of John Swinford, the father and next-of-kin of John Sackett Swinford. Francis Thomas Dorman was one of the executors of the wills of sister and brother Mary Ann and Alfred Swinford, when they died. Laurence Charles Dorman was executor for Mary Charlotte Swinford, then a spinster, when she died in 1939.

MDR/1874/16/861 registered 29th July 1874

Summary: King and others to Wheeler. Dated 1st June 1874. Parties: Caroline Mary King, of St. Leonards on Sea, Sussex, spinster, of the first part, Thomas Nightwick of Benenden, Kent, gent, of the second part, James and Thomas Dorman of Sandwich, Kent, of the third part, Charles Dorman, of No. 23 Essex Street, Strand, of the fourth part, John Giblett of No. 1 Glebe place, Stoke Newington, cattle salesman, of the fifth part, William Jones, formerly wine merchant in New Windsor and now bank manager of Woodberry Lodge, Stamford Hill and Miriam Emma Jones, his wife, of the sixth part and Thomas Wheeler, banker and Daniel Clarke, gent, both from Chipping Wycombe in the County of Buckingham, of the seventh part.

Reference was made to a marriage settlement made between William Jones, of the first part, Miriam Emma Jones, then Miriam Emma Lane, spinster, of the second part, and Daniel Clark and Thomas Wheeler, of the third part, dated 22nd December 1863.

The following statement, with many abbreviations, includes a description of the lands affected:

> Caroline Mary King, Thomas Nightwick, James Dorman, Thomas Dorman & Charles Dorman with the privity of the said John Giblett did & each of them did thereby grant & release & the said John Giblett in virtue of his Power of Appointment under an Indre of the 19th day of July 1864 and every other power enabling him in that behalf did thereby appoint & in virtue of his estate & interest did thereby grant and confirm unto the said Thomas Wheeler & Daniel Clarke their heirs All that messe or tenement called Woodberry Lodge with the coach house stables outhouses cottages and buildings yards gardens land orchard & other heredits thereunto belonging situate in the parish of Tottenham High Cross in the Coy of Middx. containing in the whole [some missing due to ink blot] 3 acres and 1 rood (exclusive of the site of the fish pond) as the same heredits premes [*premises*] are delin-eated and described in the Map or Plan endorsed in the second skin of the memlg [*memorialising*] Indre & also endorsed on this Memorial and are thereon coloured green Together with a certain wall & gates to be erected within twelve months from the 4th day of September 1874 between the points marked A and B on the said plan And also together with a right of way & passage ingress egress & regress for the said Thomas Wheeler and Daniel Clarke their heirs tenants & assigns & other persons going to or from the same premes in common with other persons either with or without horses carts & carriages or otherwise by through or over a Road or Way 20 feet wide from the High Road along the ground adjoining the said premes thereby granted on the east by means of the said gates to be erected as afsd [*aforesaid*] & unto & to the use of the said Thomas Wheeler & Daniel Clarke their

heirs & assigns forever Nevless [*nevertheless*] upon & for such of the trusts intents & purposes & with under & subject to such of the powers provisos agreements and dictons in & by the said Indre of Settlement of 22nd day of December 1863 expressed declared & contained of and concerning the heredits & premes therein comprised or referred to as were then subsistg & capable of taking effect Which said Indre as to the exons thereof by the said Caroline Mary King is witnessed by Henry Jeffreys Farrar of Cranbrook in the Cy of Kent, Attorney at law & as to the exon [*execution*] thereof by the sd Thomas Nightwick is witnessed by John Elliot Wilson of Cranbrook afsd Attorney at law as to the exon thereof by the said James Dorman and Thomas Dorman respectively is witnd by James Mann of Sandwich in the said Cy of Kent, Inn keeper and as to the exon thereof by the sd John Giblett & Charles Dorman is witnessed by William Henry Lee of No.23 Essex St Strand, clerk to Messrs Kingsford & Dorman of the same place, Solicitors & as to the exon thereof by the said William Jones & Catherine Emma Jones his wife witnessed by Douglas William Jones of Woodberry Lodge, Stamford Hill afsd Gent & as to the exon thereof of the said Thomas Wheeler & Daniel Clarke resply is witnessed by William Tyrell Pycraft of High Wycombe in the Cy of Buckingham, Clerk to Daniel Clarke of the same place Attorney at Law As witnessed the hand and seal of the sd [*said*] Daniel Clarke Signed and sealed in the presence of T. Jesse, Wm. T. Pycraft, Clerks to Mesr D Clarke, Solr, High Wycombe.

(City of London, London Metropolitan Archives)

Included with the deed was a tracing which marked *Hanger Lane*. It is notable that the wall to be built in 1874 and referred to in the indenture was identified in a map of 1894 as the back wall of a row of houses on Henrietta Road, off St. Ann's Road on the site of the Woodberry Lodge Estate. Towards the end of the document, Catharine Emma Jones was named as the wife of William Jones and not Miriam Emma Jones. William Jones married Miriam Emma Lane, a spinster, in the last quarter of 1863 (*2b 46*), in Hastings. Douglas William Jones was the son of William. John Giblett's son was also a wine merchant so he may have known Jones in connection with his business.

Brothers James and Thomas Dorman were cousins of Charles Dorman. James Dorman died in Sandwich in Kent in 1886 and left £25,000 in his will. Thomas Dorman died in 1894; neither brother had children. According to the census of 1871, Thomas Wheeler (57) was head of house and was described as a banker and brewer, employing three clerks and twenty men. His wife, Gertrude was 44. They were living at 93 Easton Street, Chipping Wycombe, Buckinghamshire. Daniel Clarke (34), head of house, an attorney at law and solicitor, was living with his wife Elizabeth (37) and four children at 90 Easton Street. Wheeler and Clarke were neighbours.

MDR/1874/26/409 registered 2ⁿᵈ December 1874

Summary: King and others to Kingsford. Dated 2ⁿᵈ June 1874. Parties: Caroline Mary King, spinster of No. 1 Church Road, St. Leonard's on Sea, Sussex, of the first part, Thomas Nightwick, Gent of Benenden, Kent, of the second part, John Giblett of Glebe Place, Stoke Newington, Middx., of the third part and James Kingsford, No. 23 Essex Street, Strand, Middx., Gent., of the fourth part. Reciting a mortgage dated 20ᵗʰ July 1864, on land at Tottenham High Cross, including Oat Fields and Snares Mead, which made reference to the land sold in 1833 by the heirs of John Wood for the new road, as 1 acre 7 perches, 1 acre 3 perches and 1 acre 5 perches (*there was a mistake in the transcription as this last one should have read 1 rood 5 perches*).

It also referred to six parcels of land, *shaded in pink*, listed in an indenture dated 20ᵗʰ July 1864, certain portions of which had been sold. They were recorded on a drawing as:

* 3 roods 23 perches (Tottenham and Hampstead Junction Railway);
* 2 roods 1 perch (Tottenham and Hampstead Junction Railway);
* 3 roods 20 perches – Sold March 1867 (*MDR/1867/7/213*);
* 16 perches – Described in December 1867 (*MDR/1867/30/478*);
* 1 acre 3 roods 5 perches- Described in December 1867 (*MDR/1867/30/478*);
* 3 acres 1 rood (exclusive of the site of the fishpond) together with messuage. July 1874 (*MDR/1874/16/861*).

This indre stated that Caroline Mary King, Thomas Nightwick and John Giblett granted and confirmed unto James Kingsford and his heirs any land designated not already sold. This was the last indenture that included Caroline Mary King.

MDR/1874/26/410 registered 2ⁿᵈ December 1874

Summary: Giblett to Dorman. Dated 1ˢᵗ August 1874. Endorsed on an indre dated 1ˢᵗ January 1870, registered on 10ᵗʰ February 1870 (*MDR/1870/4/117*) and made between John Giblett of Woodberry Lodge, Tottenham, Middx, cattle salesman, of the one part and Charles Dorman of No. 23 Essex Street, Strand, Middx., gent, of the other part, "*Whereby after reciting that since the date of the there within written Indre certain portions of the heredits comprised therein viz the piece of land there within described as containing 16 perches, the piece of land there within described as containing 1 acre 3 roods and 5 perches and the messuage stables outbuildings cottage yards garden and a piece of land containing 3 acres and 1 rood including the sites of the buildings but exclusive of the site of the fishpond therein being a portion of the land there within described as containing 23 acres and 34 perches had been sold and conveyed to the respective purchasers*" (Nos. 4, 5 & 6 in the previous indenture).

John Giblett covenanted with Charles Dorman for the land except for the parts unsold and declared himself to "*stand charged with the payment to Charles Dorman*". Description of lands affected: parts of Snares Mead and

<u>Oat Fields.</u> This indenture confirms that Giblett resided at Woodberry Lodge in 1870.

MDR/1876/13/316 registered 20ᵗʰ May 1876

Summary: Kingsford and others to Trevor and others. Dated 28ᵗʰ April 1876. Parties: James Kingsford of No. 23 Essex Street, Strand, Middlesex, of the first part, James and Thomas Dorman of Sandwich in Kent, of the second part, Charles Dorman of No. 23 Essex Street, Strand, Middlesex, of the third part, John Gilbert of No. 2 Glebe Place, Stoke Newington, cattle salesman, of the fourth part, Edwin Howard of No.77 Kew Bridge Street, Blackfriars, gent, of the fifth part, Frederick Anthony Trevor, of No.5 Charles Street, Berkeley Square, Middlesex, Barclay Field of Ashurst, Tunbridge Wells, Kent, Esq., Robert Bryce Hay of Mordington House, Bognor in Sussex and Reverend Augustus William Gurney of Bewdley, Worcestshire, clerk in Holy Orders, all of the sixth part. Kingsford, Dorman, Dorman, Dorman, Gilbert and Howard transferred to Trevor, Field, Hay and Gurney, part of a larger plot known as Oat Fields, with a plan, *shaded in pink*. Description of lands affected: <u>12 messuages Nos. 1-12 on a new road called Charles St, off St. Ann's Rd, formerly known as Hanger Lane.</u>

The plan confirmed that the land and premises on the other side of Charles Street belonged to Messrs. Wheeler and Clark. Charles Street was later renamed Richmond Road. John Gilbert was a neighbour of John Giblett, a former owner of the land. Edmund Wood submitted plans for houses on St. Ann's Road in July 1876. This was the start of the development of the Woodberry Lodge Estate.

MDR/1877/2/289-296 all registered 10ᵗʰ January 1877

Deed	Parties	Date	Nos. of properties
289	Kingsford to Wood	4ᵗʰ Dec 1876	25-29 Charles St (5)
290	Kingsford to Wood	5ᵗʰ Dec 1876	30-34 Charles St (5)
291	Kingsford to Wood	6ᵗʰ Dec 1876	35-39 Charles St (5)
292	Kingsford to Wood	7ᵗʰ Dec 1876	76,77,78,79 Charles St (4)
293	Wood to Dorman	6ᵗʰ Dec 1876	30,31,32,33,34 Charles St (5)
294	Wood to Dorman	5ᵗʰ Dec 1876	25-29 Charles St (5)
295	Wood to Dorman	7ᵗʰ Dec 1876	35-39 Charles St (5)
296	Wood to Dorman	8ᵗʰ Dec 1876	76-79 Charles St (4)

There was much exchanging of properties among the owners and lease-holders, James Kingsford and Charles Dorman and Edmund Wood, the builder.

MDR/1877/13/380 registered 23ʳᵈ January 1877

Summary: Dated 15ᵗʰ January 1877. Wheeler and others to Briggs. Parties: Arthur Vernon of High Wycombe, Buckinghamshire, architect and surveyor, Luke William Pearson of Cheltenham, Gloucestershire, auctioneer and Robert Vernon of High Wycombe, Buckinghamshire, coal merchant, of the first part,

Thomas Wheeler and Daniel Clarke of Chipping Wycombe, Buckinghamshire, gents, of the second part and William Jones, late of New Windsor Berkshire, wine merchant but now of Lancaster Gate, Bayswater, Middlesex. gent and Miriam Emma Jones, his wife of the third part. The above granted it to Abraham Briggs and his heirs. Description of lands affected: <u>Woodberry Lodge with coach house, stables, outhouses, cottage, buildings, gardens, land, orchards and other heredits, excluding site of fish pond at Tottenham High Cross, Middlesex recently measured as 3 acres and 1 rood and shaded green on the plan</u>. This included the right of way on a road, from St. Ann's Road, 20 feet wide adjoining the site on the east side by means of a gate.

MDR/1877/5/516 registered 16th February 1877

Summary: Kingsford to Wood. Dated 9th December 1876. Parties: James Kingsford of No. 23 Essex Street, Strand, lessor, of the one part and Edmund Wood of No. 13 Charles Street, St. Ann's Road, Stamford Hill, builder, lessee, of the other part. Description of lands affected: <u>five messuages in course of erection or completion Nos. 71-75 Charles Street</u>, known later as Richmond Road.

The 99 year leases were first issued from 25th December 1874. Albert Street was also marked on the plan. It was later known in the 1894-96 Ordnance Survey Map as Albert Road.

MDR/1877/5/517 registered 16th February 1877

Summary: Kingsford to Wood. Dated 11th December 1876. Parties: James Kingsford of No. 23 Essex Street, Strand, lessor, of the one part and Edmund Wood of No. 13 Charles Street, St. Ann's Road, Stamford Hill, builder, lessee, of the other part. Description of lands affected: <u>six messuages in course of erection or completion Nos. 65, 66, 67, 68, 69, 70 Charles Street</u>. The 99 year leases were first issued from 25th December 1874. Reference on the plan was also made to Albert Street.

MDR/1877/5/518 registered 16th February 1877

Summary: Wood to Dorman. Dated 11th December 1876. Parties: Edmund Wood of No. 13 Charles Street, St. Ann's Road, Stamford Hill, builder, lessee, of the one part and Charles Dorman, gent of No. 23 Essex Street, Strand of the other part. Description of lands affected: <u>five messuages in course of erection or completion Nos. 71, 72, 73, 74, 75 Charles Street</u>. This was a lease. The plan showed two new roads named Albert Street (became Albert Road 1894) and Charles Street.

MDR/1877/5/519 registered 16th February 1877

Summary: Wood to Dorman. Dated 12th December 1876. Parties: Edmund Wood of No. 13 Charles Street, St. Ann's Road, Stamford Hill, builder, of the one part and Charles Dorman, gent, of 23 Essex Street, Strand, Middlesex of the other part. Description of lands affected: <u>six messuages in course of erection or completion Nos. 65, 66, 67, 68, 69, 70 Charles Street</u>. This was a lease. The plan showed two new roads, Albert Street and Charles Street.

MDR/1877/7/22 registered 6th March 1877

Summary: Dorman to Wood. Dated 14th December 1876. Parties Charles Dorman of the one part and Edmund Wood of Tottenham in Middlesex of the other part. Description of lands affected: <u>Nos. 19-24 Charles Street</u>.

MDR/1877/7/23 registered 6th March 1877

Summary: Wood to Dorman. Dated 16th December 1876. Parties: Edmund Wood of Tottenham in Middlesex of the one part and Charles Dorman of the other part. Description of lands affected: <u>Nos. 19-24 Charles Street</u>.

MDR/1877/13/380 registered 10th May 1877

Summary: Dorman & others to Prudential Insurance Company. Dated 8th May 1877. Parties: James Kingsford of No. 23 Essex Street, Strand, Middlesex, gent, of the first part, James and Thomas Dorman of Sandwich, Kent, of the second part, Charles Dorman, of No. 23 Essex Street, Strand, Middlesex, of the third part and Prudential Insurance Company of the fourth part. Description of lands affected: <u>three parcels of ground at a place near Hanger Lane now called St. Ann's Road, on a new road called Charles Street part of 26 acres more or less known as Oat Fields with 30 messuages Nos. 25-39 Charles Street, inclusive and Nos. 65-79 Charles Street, inclusive</u>.

MDR/1877/19/344 registered 9th July, 1877

Summary: Dated 13th June 1877. Kingsford to Russell. Parties: James Kingsford of 23 Essex Street, Strand, Middlesex, of the first part, James and Thomas Dorman of Sandwich, Kent, of the second part, Charles Dorman of 23 Essex Street, Strand, of the third part, John Giblett of 2 Glebe Place, Stoke Newington, cattle salesman, of the fourth part, Charles William Willoughby, of 9 Parson's Mead, Croydon, Surrey, gent, of the fifth part and George Russell of Stanhope Street, Euston Road, Middlesex, piano forte manufacturer of the sixth part. The first five granted to the sixth, George Russell. Description of lands affected: <u>all that piece of land (3r 3p), in two parts, *shaded green and pink*, part of two closes known as Snares Mead (12 acres), adjoining south on Hanger Lane and North-west of Seven Sisters Road. Under indres 20th July, 1864, 2nd June, 1874, 14th December, 1867 and 14th June, 1868</u>. George Russell was named on the Tithe Map of 1880 as owner of this piece of land.

MDR/1877/19/346 registered 9th July, 1877

Summary: Dated 24th July 1876. Kingsford to Russell. Parties: James Kingsford, of 23 Essex Street, Strand, Middlesex, of the first part, James and Thomas Dorman of Sandwich, Kent, of the second part, Charles Dorman of 23 Essex Street, Strand, of the third part, John Giblett of 2 Glebe Place, Stoke Newington, cattle salesman of the fourth part, Charles William Willoughby, of 9 Parson's Mead, Croydon, Surrey, gent., of the fifth part and George Russell, of Stanhope Street, Euston Road, Middlesex, piano forte manufacturer, of the sixth part. The first five granted to the sixth, George Russell. Description of lands affected: Firstly all that parcel of land at Tottenham High Cross, north-west of Seven Sisters Road, shaded pink on plan, containing by estimation 8a 12 p, part of two closes known as Snares Mead containing 12 acres; Secondly a smaller parcel of land shaded blue (no size given), adjoining the first, under indres 20th July 1867, 14th June 1868, 1st January 1870, and 1st August 1874.

The plan showed the adjacent parcel of land in the previous indenture (*MDR/1877/19/344*) on which was written "*The property of Charles Dorman Esq.*".

MDR/1878/2/913 registered 17th January 1878

Summary: Kingsford to Dorman. Dated 24th December 1877. (Original indenture of mortgage dating from 1874 (*MDR/1874/26/409*) made between King and others and James Kingsford for the land at Tottenham.) Parties: James Kingsford of the one part and Charles Dorman, of No. 23 Essex Street, Strand, gent., of the other part. Since 1874 certain portions of land had been sold including 12 messuages (Nos. 1-12 Charles Street), recently erected, 12 messuages (Nos. 13-24 Charles Street) and a piece of land being part of two closes known as Snares Mead situated on the north west of Seven Sisters Road, containing 8 acres and 12 perches. Since an indre dated January 1877, three further pieces of land had been sold with 30 messuages recently erected (Nos. 25-39 and Nos. 65-79 Charles Street) and another piece of land on the north side of Seven Sisters Road remaining unsold part of two closes formerly known as Snares Mead. Description of lands affected: all other land in Oat Fields or Snares Mead remaining unsold. Charles Herbert Dorman was a witness for James Kingsford. Charles Street was renamed Richmond Road.

MDR/1878/2/914 registered 17th January 1878

Summary: Dorman to Dorman. Dated 24th December 1877. (Endorsed in an indre dated 14th December, 1867 (*MDR/1867/30/478*) and made between John Giblett of Stoke Newington of the one part and James and Thomas Dorman of Sandwich in Kent of the other part.) Parties: James and Thomas Dorman of the one part to Charles Dorman of No. 23 Essex Street, Strand, gent., of the other part. That since the date of the indenture dated June 1868 certain portions of land had been sold: A triangular piece of land containing 16 perches; a piece of land containing 1 acre, 3 roods and 5 perches; a piece of land with a house known as Woodberry Lodge, containing 3 acres 1 rood; a piece of land with 12 messuages (Nos. 1-12 Charles Street); a piece of land with 12 messuages (Nos.

13-24 Charles Street) the last three being part of 23 acres and 34 perches; a piece of land containing 8 acres and 12 perches and another small piece of land, part of *8a 3r 6p*. Since another indenture of January 1877, further portions had been sold; three pieces of land, with 30 messuages had been newly erected, Nos. 25-39 and Nos. 65-79 Charles Street; also part of the 23 acres 34 perches and a remaining piece of land part of 8 acres 3 roods 5 perches before mentioned. Description of lands affected: <u>remaining pieces of land part of Oat Fields</u>.

MDR/1878/2/915 registered 17th January 1878

Summary: Dorman to Dorman. Dated 26th December 1877. Parties: Charles Dorman of No. 23 Essex Street, Strand, of the one part to James and Thomas Dorman of Sandwich in Kent, of the other part. Description of lands affected: <u>nine pieces of land to be known as Nos. 1-9 Woodberry Villas on Seven Sisters Road</u> (identified on plan as nine detached villas starting at the junction of St. Ann's Road and Seven Sisters Road up to junction of Albert Road with a gap between houses 2 and 3 for a road named *The Crescent*).

MDR/1878/22/46 registered 25th July 1878

Summary: Dorman to Wood. Dated 23rd & 25th March, 1878. Parties: Charles Dorman Esq., of the one part to Edmund Wood of No. 3 Woodberry Villas, of the other part. Description of lands affected: <u>Public House to be known as the Woodberry Hotel on Seven Sisters Road</u> in the Parish of Tottenham.

The rent was £100 per annum and the lease for 80 years was made originally on 25th December 1877 and expired on 25th December 1957. The indenture included a floor plan of the ground floor of the building. Around the same time another indenture (*MDR/1878/22/48*) explained that Charles Dorman lent Edmund Woods £3,600.

MDR/1879/9/327 registered 19th March 1879

Summary: Dorman to Wood. Dated 2nd December 1878. Parties: Charles Dorman, of the one part to Edmund Wood, of the other part. Description of lands affected: <u>messuage and shop adjacent to the Woodberry Hotel on Seven Sisters Road, Tottenham (No. 1 Albert Road)</u>. The rent was £8 8s per annum and the lease for 80 years was made originally on 25th December 1877 and expired on 25th December 1957. On the same day there was registered (*MDR/1879/9/328*), a mortgage to secure £3,600 and interest. There were numerous indentures recorded for the owners and Woodberry Hotel over the years and it eventually was owned by Watney's Brewery (*LMA ACC/1399/198, 199, 200*).

MDR/1882/25/873 registered 28th July 1882

Summary: Banks to Dorman. Dated 24th December 1881. Parties: Henry William Banks, Cannon Street, chartered accountant, of the one part and

Charles Dorman of No. 23 Essex Street, Strand, of the other part. Description of lands affected: <u>No. 2 Franklin Street, west side (*first house Albert Road end*)</u>.

This was reciting an indenture dated 23rd December 1879 between Charles Dorman and Edmund Wood (99 year lease), rental £4 10 shs. per annum.

MDR/1882/25/874 registered 28th July 1882

Summary: Dorman to Humphreys and others. Dated 24th June 1882. Parties: Charles Dorman, gentleman, of the one part and Robert Humphreys of No. 7 Windsor Road, Denmark Hill, Camberwell, Surrey, gentleman, James Francis Frith, of No. 9 Mincing Lane, City of London, merchant and James Henry Kingsford of No. 23 Essex Street, Strand, of the other part. Description of lands affected: <u>Nos. 11-18 Woodberry Pavement on the south east side of Seven Sisters Road</u>. (Nos. 11 & 12 were on a site formerly known as 6 Woodberry Villas and No. 13 on what had been No. 7 Woodberry Villas).

The plan showed that the terrace started at the junction of St. Ann's Road with the railway line, up to a shop adjoining Woodberry Hotel on the corner of Albert Road (*what is now the Woodberry Tavern*). This is now part of the Sir Fred Messer Estate. The tower blocks on this Estate are called Oatfield and Twyford House. Henrietta House took its name from Henrietta Road.

MDR/1882/25/875 registered 28th July 1882

Summary: Dorman to Homer. Dated 12th July 1882. Parties: Charles Dorman, vendor, of the one part to Edward Charles Homer, purchaser, of Mansion House Chambers, No. 11 Queen Victoria St., civil engineer, of the other part. Description of lands affected: <u>parcel of land with a frontage of 80 feet on Vartry Road.</u>

The plan showed three plots of land on either side of the site belonged to Charles Dorman. At the back was the Parish of Hackney. Opposite the site were marked Charles Street (Richmond Road), Franklin Street and St. John's Church. A current map indicates that this plot is now made us of four houses, Nos. 80 to 86 Vartry Road, of a different style to those built by Candler. By 1894, Edward Charles Homer was living at 62 Amhurst Park.

MDR/1882/39/1011 registered 2nd December 1882

Summary: Wood to Dorman. Dated 16th October 1882. Parties: Edmund Wood of No. 37 Albert Road, Seven Sisters Road, Stamford Hill, of the one part to Charles Dorman, gent of No. 23 Essex Street, Strand, of the other part. Description of lands affected: <u>No. 9 Woodberry Terrace, dwelling house and shop.</u>

Originally leased in June 1878 for 99 years by Charles Dorman to Edmund Wood. It was on the south-east side of Seven Sisters Road.

MDR/1882/39/1012 registered 2nd December 1882

Summary: Wood to Dorman. Dated 1st November 1882. Parties: Edmund Wood of No. 37 Albert Road, Seven Sisters Road, of the one part to Charles Dorman, gent, of the other part. Description of lands affected: Nos. 5-24 Kingsford Terrace.

Leased for 99 years by Charles Dorman to Edmund Wood in September 1878, May 1879 and January 1880.

MDR/1882/39/1013 registered 2nd December 1882

Summary: Wood to Kingsford. Dated 1st November 1882. Parties: Edmund Wood of No. 37 Albert Road, Stamford Hill, of the first part, Charles Dorman of No. 23 Essex Street, Strand, of the second part and James Kingsford, gent, also of No.23 Essex Street, Strand of the third part. Description of lands affected: 19 messuages recently erected at Nos. 1-19 and 2-18, Candler St.

Leased in June 1878, in May 1879 and April 1880 for 99 years by Charles Dorman to Edmund Wood.

MDR/1882/39/1014 registered 2nd December 1882

Summary: Wood to Dorman. Dated 1st November 1882. Parties: Edmund Wood of No. 37 Albert Road, Stamford Hill, of the one part to Charles Dorman, gent, of the other part. Description of lands affected: Nos. 1&3, 5&7, 9&11, 13&15 and 6&8, 10&12, 14&16 Franklin Street.

Originally leased in June 1878 for 99 years by Charles Dorman to Edmund Wood.

MDR/1882/39/1015 registered 2nd December 1882

Summary: Wood to Kingsford. Dated 1st November 1882. Parties: Edmund Wood of No. 37 Albert Road, of the first part, Charles Dorman of No. 23 Essex Street, Strand gent, of the second part and James Kingsford, gent, of the third part. Description of lands affected: Nos. 11-25 and 2,4,6,8,10,12 Townsend Rd.

Originally leased in 1878 for 99 years by Charles Dorman to Edmund Wood. Planning books from the Council show that as early as 1875, someone by the name of Woodbridge submitted plans for the new Townsend Road on the Woodberry Farm Estate. The road may have been initially named after John Townsend, who was a local magistrate for Middlesex and Westminster. In 1886, Townsend Road became St. John's Road, taking its name from the iron church in Franklin Street known as St. John's Church or the new St. John's Church in Vartry Road. Some of the streets cited in the deeds were renamed and renumbered.

MDR/1884/4/131 registered 26th January 1884

Summary: Dorman to Company. Dated 18th January 1884. Parties: Charles Dorman, of the one part to North London Tramway Company, hereafter called the Company of the other part. Description of lands affected: triangular parcel of land between the Midland Railway Company Line, behind Nos. 10-20 Kingsford Terrace, Seven Sisters Road and a gateway between this and No. 21

Kingsford Terrace with right of way for carriages, wagon, trams and engines to access the workshops behind the terrace and allow the trams to turn.

A small pocket of land next to the railway line was marked on the map as leased by Edmund Wood. Mr. Todd owned land west of the site.

MDR/1886/16/208 registered 17th June 1886

Summary: Giblett to Rowland and others. Dated 15th June 1886. Parties: John Giblett of Petherton Road, Highbury, cattle salesman, of the one part to Frederick Arthur Alexander Rowland, of No. 14 Clements Inn, gent, and Samuel Augustus Barnett of St. Jude's Vicarage, Commercial Street, Whitechapel, in Holy Order of the other part. This was a transfer of original mortgage to the new mortgagees. Description of land affected: triangular parcel of land in Tottenham bordered on the west by the Tottenham and Hampstead Junction Railway (Midland Railway Company) and St. Ann's Rd in the south (five houses and part of No. 1 Market Terrace, St. Ann's Road).

MDR/1889/18/378 registered 25th June 1889

Summary: Dorman to Woolf. Dated 24th June 1889. Parties: Charles Dorman of the one part and Montague Woolf, No. 20 Wormwood Street in the City of London, gentleman, of the other part. Leases originally granted in September 1878 to Edmund Wood, builder. Description of lands affected: seven parcels of land, four of them being east side and three on the west side of a new road or intended to be called Franklin Street (Nos. 17-37 and 18-56) in June 1878.

Premises leased by Charles Dorman to Edmund Wood now assigned to Montague Woolf. New 99 year leases from 24th June 1889. A tracing of the site showed the position of the original iron chapel in Franklin Street, which was opened in 1880.

MDR/1889/32/552 registered 20th November 1889

Summary: Dorman and others to Woolf. Dated 16th November 1889. Parties: Charles Dorman of No. 23 Essex Street, Strand, mortgager, of the first part, James Kingsford formerly of 23 Essex Street and now of "*The Wood*", Sydenham Hill, trustee, of the second part and Montague Woolf of No. 20 Wormwood Street in the City of London, of the third part. The original 99 year leases were between Charles Dorman and Edmund Wood in June 1878 at an annual rent of £10 10s. (9) with one at £5 5s. Leased again in May, 1879 and in April 1880. Description of lands affected: five double messuages Nos. 1&3, 5&7, 9&11, 13&15, 17&19 Candler Street and 2, 4&6, 8&10, 12&14, 16&18 Candler St. one single and four double messuages making 19 messuages in all. The houses had a single square bay on the ground floor and backed onto the rear of houses on Albert Road.

MDR/1889/32/553 registered 20th November 1889

Summary: Woolf to Dorman. Dated 18th November 1889. Parties: Montague Woolf of 20 Wormwood Street in the City of London, of the one part and Charles Dorman, of the other part. Description of lands affected: <u>Nos. 1-19 and 2-18 Candler St (19 messuages)</u>. Original 99 year leases in June 1878, then in May 1879 and April 1880 for ten parcels of land by Charles Dorman to Edmund Wood at an annual rent of £10 10s. with one at £5 5s.

MDR/1889/32/554 registered 20th November 1889

Summary: Dorman and others to Woolf. Dated 16th November 1889. Parties: Charles Dorman, of the first part, James Kingsford of "*The Wood*", Sydenham Hill, gent, of the second part and Montague Woolf of 20 Wormwood Street in the City of London of the third part. Description of lands affected: <u>Nos. 11, 13, 15, 17, 19, 21, 23, 25 Townsend Road and 4, 6, 8, 10, 12 Townsend Road (13 messuages)</u>. Charles Dorman to Edmund Wood, 99 year leases at an annual rent from September 1877 and again in December 1878. Townsend Road was renamed St. John's Road. The houses on Townsend Road were double fronted, each with two bays.

MDR/1889/32/555 registered 20th November 1889

Summary: Woolf to Dorman. Dated 18th November 1889. Parties: Montague Woolf of "*The Wood*", Sydenham Hill, gent, of the one part to Charles Dorman of No. 23 Essex Street, Strand, of the other part. Description of lands affected: <u>Nos. 11, 13, 15, 17, 19, 21, 23, 25 Townsend Road and 4, 6, 8, 10, 12 Townsend Road</u>.

The 99 year leases were originally from Charles Dorman to Edmund Wood in 1877, at an annual rent of £83 13s. and again in 1878. Remainder of the lease from 29th September 1889.

MDR/1889/32/556 registered 20th November 1889

Summary: Dorman to Woolf. Dated 19th November 1889. Parties: Charles Dorman, lessor to Montague Woolf, lessee. Description of lands affected: <u>five double messuages Nos. 1&3, 5&7, 9&11, 13&15, 17&19 Candler Street and 2, 4&6, 8&10, 12&14, 16&18 Candler St., one single and four double messuages, 19 messuages in total</u>.

Annual rent £99 15s. The 99 year leases were from 29th September 1889.

MDR/1889/32/557 registered 20th November 1889

Summary: Dorman to Woolf. Dated 19th September 1889. Parties: Charles Dorman, lessor to Montague Woolf, lessee. Description of lands affected: <u>Nos. 11, 13, 15, 17, 19, 21, 23, 25 Townsend Road and 4, 6, 8, 10, 12 Townsend Road</u>.

Annual rent of £68 5s. The 99 year leases were from 29th September 1889.

MDR/1890/32/864 registered 15ᵗʰ April 1890

Summary: Dorman to Trustees of the Hearts of Oak Building Society. Dated 20ᵗʰ March 1890. Parties: Charles Dorman, the vendor, of the one part to William George Bunn, George Wood, Maxwell Samuel Hardy and John Thomas Sleepwash, Trustees of the Hearts of Oak Benefit Building Society, the purchasers, of the other part. Description of land affected: <u>Nos. 4-12 and 11-25, Townsend Rd, 1-19 and 2-18, Candler Street and Nos. 18-56 and 17-37 Franklin Street on the Woodberry Lodge Estate.</u>

There was a detailed plan of the area included with the indenture showing the street layout along with other streets including Albert Road, Woodberry Mews, Charles Street, Vartry Road and a proposed road, with location of the houses. It also showed a building beside No. 56 Franklin Street called The Mission Room, described on some plans as St. John's iron church.

MDR/1890/31/654 registered 19ᵗʰ November 1890

Summary: Dorman to Jewell. Dated 17ᵗʰ November 1890. Parties: Charles Dorman, the lessor to Mrs. Rachel Jewell of 86 Amhurst park, Stamford Hill, widow, the lessee. Description of land affected: <u>plan showed that the proposed house "intending to be known as 10 Stanley Terrace" was on the south side of Vartry Rd with a frontage of 38 feet and 97 feet deep.</u>

The rear of the site backed on to the back gardens of the houses on Amhurst Park Road. On one side of the site the premises had been demised to Mrs. Rachel Jewell and on the other side were premises belonging to Thomas Jones, Esq. There was a peppercorn rent for the first year and thereafter rent of £28 10s. for the 99 year lease. This house is now numbered 132 Vartry Road. Mrs. Jewell's son was called Stanley, hence the name of the terrace. In the census of 1891, he was listed as a contractor and his mother was living on her own expenses. By 1897 Mrs. Jewell was living at 92 Kensington Gardens.

MDR/1890/31/653 registered 19ᵗʰ November 1890

Summary: Dorman to Jewell. Dated 18ᵗʰ November 1890. Parties: Charles Dorman, the lessor, of the one part to Mrs. Rachel Jewell of 86 Amhurst Park, Stamford Hill, widow, the lessee, of the other part. Description of lands affected: <u>plan showed that the three lots of land were for three houses to be known as Nos. 11, 12 and 13 Stanley Terrace on the south side of Vartry Rd.</u> Land belonging to Charles Dorman was on one side of the site and the other was 10 Stanley Terrace, just demised to Mrs. Jewell. There was a peppercorn rent for the first year and thereafter rent of £28 10s. for the 99 year lease. These houses are now numbered 126, 128 and 130 Vartry Road.

MDR/1890/31/656 registered 19ᵗʰ November 1890

Summary: Dorman to Jewell. Dated 17ᵗʰ November, 1890. Parties: Charles Dorman, the lessor, of the one part to Mrs. Rachel Jewell of 86 Amhurst Park,

Stamford Hill, widow, the lessee, of the other part. Description of lands affected: No. 1 to 6 Florence Villas, on the north side of Vartry Road.

On the one side were the premises belonging to the Tottenham School Board and on the other side was land belonging to Charles Dorman. There was a peppercorn rent for the first year and thereafter rent of £28 10s. for the 99 year lease.

MDR/1890/32/936 registered 29th November, 1890

Summary: Dorman to Woolf. Dated 25th November 1890. Parties: Charles Dorman, gent, of the one part to Montague Woolf, surveyor of Wormwood St, in the City of London, of the other part. Description of lands affected: Nos. 39&40, 41&42, 43&44 and 45&46 Albert Road, four pieces of land and eight messuages (semi-detached houses).

There were references to an earlier indenture dated 4th December, 1878 and to Edmund Wood.

MDR/1890/32/937 registered 29th November 1890

Summary: Dorman to Woolf. Dated 25th November 1890. Parties: Charles Dorman, of the one part to Montague Woolf, surveyor, of the other part. Description of lands affected: strip of land, ten feet wide, at rear of houses in Albert Road (No. 39 to 46) and at the rear of houses in Candler Street (No. 1,3,5,7,9 and 11) presently belonging to Mr. Woolf.

MDR/1891/26/720 registered 30th September 1891

Summary: Dated 29th September 1891. Parties: John Jeken Cockburn of Sussex and James Kingsford of "The Wood" Sydenham, of the first part (mortgagees), Charles Dorman (vendor), of the second part and James Davison of 531 Holloway Road, Middlesex (purchaser) of the third part. Description of lands affected: Nos. 1-6 Florence Villas, Vartry Road at the junction of Lawrie Road (known now as Berkeley Road) and the north side of Vartry Road, next to Stamford Hill School.

A plan showed the location and marked the land beside the Villas as belonging to Charles Dorman. There was a reference to another Indenture of 17th November 1890 between Rachel Jewell and the vendor, Charles Dorman. In other documents she was referred to as Mrs. Jewell.

MDR/1891/12/406 registered 4th May 1891

Summary: Dorman to Conor. Dated 20th March 1891. Parties: Charles Dorman, of the one part to Albert William Conor and Eliza Jane Conor, his wife of No. 8 Woodberry Pavement, of the other part. Description of lands affected: two messuages and shops at No. 8 & 9 Woodberry Pavement on Seven Sisters Road, bound by Townsend Rd.

In the same book two further memorials were registered: (*MDR/1891/12/407*) when Conor transferred to Thomas Nothard and John Lowe and (*MDR/1891/12/408*), dated 27th March, when Conor transferred it back to Charles Dorman.

MDR/1894/10/346 registered 3rd April 1894

Summary: Dorman to Swinford. Dated 10th February 1894. Charles Dorman, of the one part to James Smith Swinford, of the other part. Description of lands affected: Nos. 33-73a, 54, 56, 58 Townsend Road, which was renamed St. John's Road; Nos. 61-67a, 71-89, 91a-103a, 91-105 Vartry Road (these tenements are now numbered 61-75, 87, 89-99(3), 101-111(6), 113-139(7) Vartry Road), Manchester Road and Heysham Road (houses had not been constructed).

Reference was made in the Indenture to the Woodberry Lodge Estate. James Smith Swinford, born in 1825, was the son of John Swinford and his first wife Ann Sackett. Charles Dorman's wife, Janie, was the daughter of John Swinford and his second wife, Frances Hudson Smithett. James Smith Swinford died on 11th March 1909; his nephew, Charles Herbert Dorman was one of his executors.

MDR/1896/1/824 registered 7th January 1896

Summary: Dorman to Blackwell. Dated 6th January 1896. Parties: Charles Dorman of No. 23 Essex St. Strand, gent, of the one part to Arthur William Blackwell of No.11 St. John's Road, Stamford Hill, Middlesex, civil servant, of the other part. Description of lands affected: No. 78 Vartry Road.

The Indenture showed that the land to the left of 78 was owned by Charles Dorman Esq. and the land to the right was sold to Mr. Homer, who lived at 62 Amhurst Park. At the rear were the houses in Amhurst Park Road backing onto the site.

MDR/1897/8/504 registered 5th March 1897

Summary: Dorman to Noys & Dorman. Dated 22nd January 1897. Parties: Charles Dorman of No. 23 Essex Street, Strand, Middlesex (mortgagor), of the one part and Selina Noys of No. 221 London Rd, Thornton Heath, Surrey, widow and said Charles Dorman (mortgagees), of the other part. Description of lands affected:

> All that piece or parcel of land situate partly in the parish of Tottenham and partly in the parish of Hackney, both in the County of Middlesex on the south side or south west side of a road called Vartry Road and having a frontage thereto of 194 feet 10 inches or thereabouts bounded on the east by St. John's Hall, on the west by a double messuage known as No 60 and 62 Vartry Road and on

the south by the gardens of the messuages, situate in Amherst Park Road, Hackney together with the nine messuages or tenements and buildings therein erected (8 of such messuages being double and one a single messuage) and known as Nos 26, 28, 30, 32, 34, 36, 38, 40, 42, 44, 46, 48, 50, 52, 54, 56, 58 Vartry Road aforesaid all which said piece or parcel of land with the messuages or tenements therein were made particularly delineated and described with the dimensions, boundaries and abuttals thereof in the plan drawn in the margins.

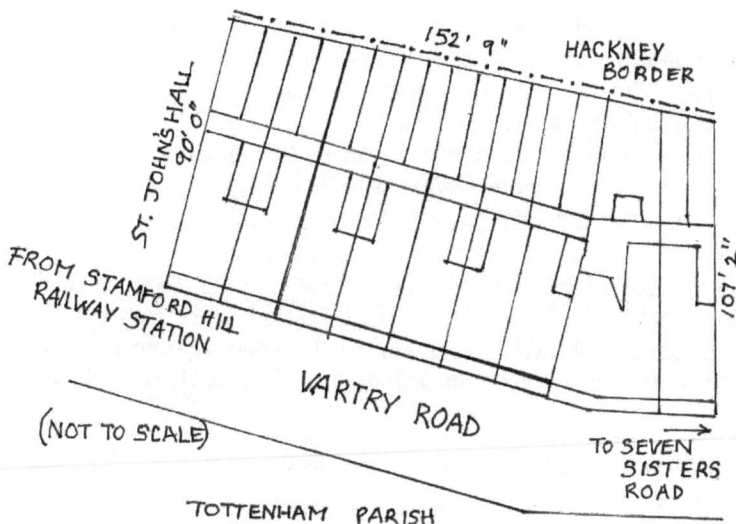

App.1.4 Map of MDR/1897/8/504.

A plan showed the layout of the house and double messuages. This is the house referred to on deeds for the first time being owned by Charles Dorman as mortgagor and then as mortgagee with Selina Noys. Number 54 is half-way along Vartry Road and its back garden is on the border between Tottenham and Hackney.

In the census of 1871 George Walter and Selina Noys and their daughter, Nora Madeline, then seven months old, were recorded in Croydon. Jemima Smith, aged 63, mother-in-law to the head of house, was visiting. By the time of the census of 1881, the family had grown; the children were listed as Nora Madeline (10), George Thomas (9), Margaret A. (7) and Ethel W. (4) and they were still in Croydon. Jemima Smith, formerly of No. 181 St. James Road, Croydon was living with her daughter at 221 London Road, Thornton Heath, when she died on 12th September 1891. Her daughter, Selina Noys and Jemima Mordaunt (wife of Charles Cooke Mordaunt) were her executrices when the will was proved on 16th October 1891. Effects were £1,733 4s. 4d.

George Walter Noys of No. 221 London Road, Thornton Heath, Surrey, a salesman, died on 29th August 1893, aged 59. Administration took place 30th

November 1893 by his widow, Selina Noys. Effects were valued at £7 7s. 4d. Selina Noys was 55 years of age when in 1897 she became the joint mortgagee with Charles Dorman. Dorman may have given Candler the right to live in No. 54 Vartry Road, as whole or part payment for developing the tenements and houses in the Woodberry Lodge Estate and in his capacity as house agent, as in the Rate Books Candler is recorded as owning them in 1900 and 1913.

MDR/1898/11/486 registered 24th March 1898

Summary: Swinford to Dorman. Dated 22nd March 1898. It was endorsed on a deed dated 10th February 1894 made between Charles Dorman of 23 Essex Street, Strand, in the County of Middlesex, gentleman, of the one part and James Smith Swinford of *"The Shrubbery"*, Basingstoke, in the County of Hants., Esq., of the other part (*Reg:MDR/1894/10/346*). Parties: James Smith Swinford, of the one part to Charles Dorman of the other part. Description of lands affected as in indenture (*MDR/1894/10/346*):

Nos. 33-73a, 54, 56, 58 Townsend Road, which was renamed St. John's Road;

Nos. 61-67a, 71-89, 91a-103a, 91-105 Vartry Road (these tenements are now numbered 61-75, 87, 89-99(3), 101-111(6), 113-139(7) Vartry Road);

Manchester Road and Heysham Road (houses had not been constructed).

James Smith Swinford was the half brother of Janie, Dorman's late wife.

MDR/1898/11/487 registered 24th March 1898

Summary: Dorman to Pedder. Dated 23rd March 1898. Charles Dorman, of the one part and Stephanie Henrietta Pedder of 38 Victoria Street, Kensington (widow) of the other part. Description of lands affected:

Nos. 61-75 Vartry Road (4 double messuages);

Nos. 56-62 Richmond Road (2 double messuages);

Nos. 39-53 Franklin Street (4 double messuages);

Nos. 1-39, 41(10 double messuages and one single) and Nos. 2-48 Manchester Road (12 double messuages) bound by land owned by Charles Dorman in Heysham Rd.

When Pedder bought them in 1899 she would have been 75 years of age.

MDR/1898/13/681 registered 5th April 1898

Summary: Dorman to Kingsford and others. Dated 1st April 1898. Parties: Charles Dorman, of the one part to James Henry Kingsford, Reverend William Harrison and Lionel Hope Cockburn, of the other part. Description of lands affected: Nos. 71, 73&73a, 77&77a, 79,81,83,85,87,89 now known as Nos. 87-111 Vartry Road, including 3 double messuages, 91&91a to 103&103a, now known as Nos. 113 to 139 Vartry Road (7 double messuages) and Nos. 54,56,58 St. John's Road.

MDR/1899/31/428 registered 12th August 1899

Summary: Dorman to Noys. Dated 1st August 1899. Parties: Charles Dorman of 23 Essex Street, Strand, Middlesex, gentleman (mortgagor), of the one part and Selina Noys of No. 221 London Road, Thornton Heath, Surrey, widow and said Charles Dorman (mortgagees) of the other part. Description of lands affected: parcel of land with a frontage of 239 feet and 7 inches by 76 feet depth, north of Berkeley Road which ran between Vartry Road and Seven Sisters Road formerly Lawrie Road with 15 messuages to be known as Nos. 1-29 Berkeley Road, inclusive.

Selina Noys already shared a mortgage with Charles Dorman on Nos. 26 –58 Vartry Road from 1897. The plan showed that there was an area of land next to the first house (No. 1 Berkeley Road) without any building on it. The paper used for the deed was provided by Cox & Sons of No. 102 Chancery Lane, stationers, who were related by marriage to George and Samuel Candler. The empty plot is now the Telephone Exchange at 554 Seven Sisters Road, opened on 22nd March 1934 *(British Telecom Archives)*.

MDR/1900/9/762 registered 5th April 1900

Summary: Dorman to Kingsford. Dated 8th March 1900. Parties: Charles Dorman, of the one part to James Henry Kingsford of No. 44 Royal Parade, Eastbourne, Sussex, gentleman and Frank Kingsford of 23 Essex Street, Strand, gentleman, of the other part. Description of lands affected: 12 messuages on the west side of Richmond Road (formerly called Charles Street) Nos. 32-54 Richmond Road (formerly known as Nos. 53 to 64 Charles Street).

The original indenture of mortgage was dated 25th March 1891 *(MDR/1891/12/406)*. James Henry and Frank Kingsford were brothers.

MDR/1900/32/94 registered 22nd November 1900

Summary: Dorman to Dorman. Dated 15th November 1900. Parties: Charles Dorman, of the one part and Charles Herbert Dorman, of the other part, both of 23 Essex Street, Strand and gentlemen. Description of lands affected: all that piece or parcel of land situate in the Parish of Tottenham on the north east side of a road called Heysham Road together with 7 double messuages known as Nos. 1&3, 5&7, 9&11, 13&15, 17&19, 21&23 and 25&27 Heysham Road.

Charles Dorman was transferring the land to his eldest son.

MDR/1901/9/680 registered 16th January 1901

Summary: Dorman to Browne. Mortgage, dated 15th January 1901. Parties: Charles Dorman, of the one part and Charles Edmund and Charles Alexander Browne of Southend House, Bury St. Edmunds, Suffolk, of the other part. Description of lands affected: land and freehold, including 15 double messuages, Nos. 2&4 to 58&60 Heysham Road.

MDR/1901/9/681 registered 16th January 1901

Summary: Dorman to French and Candler. Dated 15th January 1901. Parties: Charles Dorman of 23 Essex Street, Strand, of the one part and Jane Sophia French of 6 Torrington Park Villas, North Finchley, aforesaid spinster and Samuel Horace Candler of 23 Essex Street, Strand of the other part. Description of lands affected: <u>all that several pieces or parcels of land forming part of an estate called Woodberry Lodge Estate Nos. 33&33a to 73&73a St. John's Road, odd numbers inclusive</u>.

MDR/1902/12/565 registered 6th May 1902

Summary: Memorial of probate of a will. Dated 2nd May 1902. Charles Dorman of No.19 Wetherby Gardens, South Kensington, solicitor. It included *"All my real estate and all my personal estate and effects whatsoever and wheresoever not otherwise disposed of by this my will or any codicil hereto"*.

MDR/1902/12/566 registered 6th May 1902

Summary: Dorman to Goodall. Dated 2nd May 1902. Endorsed on a deed dated 28th March 1887 made between Charles Dorman, gent, of the one part and John Goodall of No.17 Kingsford Terrace, Seven Sisters Road, Stamford Hill, Corn Chandler of the other part. Parties: Julia Frances Dorman of No.19 Wetherby Gardens, South Kensington, spinster and Charles Herbert Dorman of No.23 Essex St, Strand of the one part and John Goodall of No.17 Kingsford Terrace of the other part. Description of lands affected: <u>No.17 Kingsford Terrace, Seven Sisters Road</u> with *"All and singular leasehold hereditaments and premises comprised in or demised by within written indenture"*.

This was a transfer from Charles Dorman, following his death, to the executors named in his will.

MDR/1903/10/299 registered 7th April 1903

Summary: Noys to Noys and Dorman. Dated 30th March 1903. Parties: Selina Noys of 221 London Road, Thornton Heath, Surrey but then of St. Martin's, London Road, Deal, Kent, widow, of the one part and Selina Noys and Charles Herbert Dorman, gent, of the other part. Supplemental to a deed made between Charles Dorman and Selina Noys registered 5th March 1899 (*MDR/1899/31/428*). This was a mortgage. Description of lands affected: <u>parcel of land in Berkeley Road with 15 messuages Nos. 1 to 29 Berkeley Road</u>. Due to death and probate of Charles Dorman.

MDR/1903/10/300 registered 7th April 1903

Summary: Noys to Noys and Dorman. Dated 30th March 1903. Parties: Selina Noys of 221 London Road, Thornton Heath, Surrey but then of St. Martin's, London Road, Deal, Kent, widow, of the one part and Selina Noys and Charles Herbert Dorman, gent, of the other part. Supplemental to a deed made between Charles Dorman and Selina Noys registered 5th March 1897 (*MDR/1897/8/504*). Description of lands affected: parcel of land in Vartry Road with 9 messuages known as Nos. 26&28, 30&32, 34&36, 38&40, 42&44, 46&48, 50&52, 54 and 56&58, eight double messuages and one single. Due to death and probate of Charles Dorman.

MDR/1906/7/163 registered 12th March 1906

Summary: Dorman to Hodgson and Dorman. Dated 21st December 1905. Parties: Julia Frances Dorman and Charles Herbert Dorman, of the one part and Margaret Anne Hodgson and Charles Herbert Dorman of the other part. Description of lands affected: freehold ground messuage and shop No.12 Woodberry Pavement but now known as No.634 Seven Sisters Rd. Registered 1896 (*MDR/1896/25/542*).

MDR/1906/7/594 registered 16th March 1906

Summary: Dorman to Dorman. Dated 22nd December 1905. Parties: Julia Frances Dorman, of Queen Anne's Mansions, St. James Park and Charles Herbert Dorman, of the first part, Frank Thomas Dorman, of the second part, Reverend Arthur William Dorman of Bath, of the third part, Emily Mary Shackleton of Edinburgh, of the fourth part and Maude Isabel Dorman of Queen Anne's Mansions, St. James Park, of the fifth part. Description of lands affected: all Charles Dorman's real estate and personal estate and effects.

Grantor was Charles Herbert Dorman although Julia Frances Dorman's name was also listed as a grantor. Julia Dorman, then aged 46 married Charles Sarolea on 28th December 1905 at Christ Church, Westminster and went to live in Scotland.

MDR/1906/7/742 registered 19th March 1906

Summary: Dorman to Hodgson and Dorman. Dated 15th March 1906. Parties: Charles Herbert Dorman and Francis Thomas Dorman, both of 23 Essex Street, Strand, solicitors, vendors, of the first part, Margaret Ann Hodgson, formerly of Bath but now of No. 4 Princes Mansion, Victoria Street, Westminster, spinster and Charles Herbert Dorman, mortgagees, of the second part and Tottenham Urban District Council, purchaser, of the third part. Description of lands affected: parcel of land (eight feet of footpath) in front of Nos. 612, 614, 616 Seven Sisters Road near the corner of Albert Road.

This deed would appear to confirm that Julia Frances Sarolea was no longer a trustee as Francis Thomas Dorman was listed jointly with Charles Herbert Dorman.

MDR/1906/9/212 registered 31st March 1906

Summary: Hodgson and Dorman to Dorman and Cobb. Dated 20th March 1906. Parties: Margaret Anne Hodgson of No.2 Lansdown Place, Bath but now of No. 4 Princes Mansions, Victoria Street, Westminster, spinster and Charles Herbert Dorman, of the one part and Charles Herbert Dorman and

Francis Cecil Cobb of Margate, Kent, of the other part. Supplemental to following deeds (called the Principal Indentures):

1. Deed dated 26th May 1887 registered 28th May 1887 (*MDR/1887/14/453*) between Caroline Irons of the one part and John Bownas Crawhall and George Nelson Emmet of the other part.

2. Deed dated and registered 28th September 1895 (MDR/1895/B30/666) between John Bownas Crawhall and Robert William Emmet.

3. Deed dated 18th October 1900 registered 8th November 1900 (*MDR/1900/30/667*) between Robert William Emmet, of the one part and Charles Herbert Dorman of the other part.

4. Deed dated 5th February 1901, registered 1st June 1901 (*MDR/1901/14/792*) between Charles Herbert Dorman, of the one part and Margaret Anne Hodgson and Charles Herbert Dorman of the other part.

5. Deed dated 9th September 1901 registered 1st September 1902 (*MDR/1902/23/605*) between Margaret Anne Hodgson, of the one part and Margaret Anne Hodgson and Charles Dorman of the other part.

Description of lands affected: <u>three leasehold messuages shops and premises except small portion of forecourt recently sold to Tottenham Urban District Council for the purpose of widening the highway Nos.1,2&3 Woodberry Terrace but now known as Nos. 612,614,616, Seven Sisters Road, Tottenham.</u>

MDR/1906/9/213 registered 31st March 1906

Summary: Hodgson & Dorman to Howard. Dated 20th March 1906. Parties: Margaret Anne Hodgson of No.4 Princes Mansions, Victoria Street, Westminster, spinster and Charles Herbert Dorman, mortgagees, of the one part and Arthur Howard of No. 634, Seven Sisters Road, Tottenham, hardware merchant, mortgagor, of the other part.

> Supplemental to a deed dated 31st May,1895 between Arthur Howard and Lavinia Charlotte Howard, his wife of the one part and Charles Dorman of the other part being a mortgage on a piece of ground in Tottenham together with messuage and shop known as No. 12 Woodberry Pavement but then as No. 634 Seven Sisters Road, registered 1896 (B25 No. 542) also indenture dated 21st December 1905 made between Julia Frances Dorman and Charles Herbert Dorman of the one part and said Margaret Anne Hodgson and Charles Herbert Dorman of the other part registered 1906 (B7 No. 163) relating to the sale of a piece of land nine feet eight inches wide part of forecourt.

Description of lands affected: <u>a piece of ground, messuage and shop at No. 634 Seven Sisters Road</u> except the piece of land that was sold.

MDR/1906/9/807 registered 5ᵗʰ April 1906

Summary: Dorman & Dorman to Dorman & Candler. Dated 30ᵗʰ March 1906. Parties: Charles Herbert Dorman and Francis Thomas Dorman, of the one part and Francis Thomas Dorman and Annie Candler, widow of the other part. Description of lands affected: Nos. 22&22a to 36&36a (8 double messuages) St. John's Road.

MDR/1906/17/500 registered 26ᵗʰ June 1906

Summary: Dorman to Dorman. Dated 15ᵗʰ January 1901. Parties: Charles Dorman, of the one part and Charles Herbert Dorman of the other part. Description of lands affected: Nos. 29-57 Heysham Rd (7 double messuages and one single dwelling (No. 49) and No. 62&64, 66&68 (2 double messuages).

MDR/1906/17/501 registered 26ᵗʰ June 1906

Summary: Dorman to Hodgson & Dorman. Dated 30ᵗʰ April 1906. Parties: Charles Herbert Dorman, transferor, of the one part to Ferdinand Robert Hodgson, No.2 Halsey House, Red Lion Square and Charles Herbert Dorman, transferees, of the other part. Supplemental to a deed, 5ᵗʰ January, 1901 made between Charles Dorman, transferor, to Charles Herbert Dorman. Description of lands affected: Nos. 29,31-55,57 (7 doubles) Heysham Rd also 62&64 and 66&68 (2 doubles) Heysham Rd, registered 1906 (*MDR/1906/17/500*).

MDR/1906/29/30 registered 5ᵗʰ November 1906

Summary: Dorman to Noys & Dorman. Dated 12ᵗʰ September 1906. Parties: Charles Herbert Dorman and Francis Thomas Dorman, mortgagers, of the one part and Selina Noys and Charles Herbert Dorman, mortgagees, of the other part. Supplemental to a deed registered 1897 (*MDR/1897/8/504*) and supplemental to a deed dated 30ᵗʰ March, 1903 (*MDR/1903/10/300*) between Selina Noys and mortgagers of the other part. Description of lands affected: Nos. 26&28-50&52, 54, 56&58 Vartry Road.

MDR/1906/29/31 registered 5ᵗʰ November 1906

Summary: Noys & Dorman to Collins & Dorman. Dated 12ᵗʰ September 1906. Parties: Selina Noys formerly of No. 221 London Road, Thornton Heath and now of St. Martin's, London Road, Deal, Kent, widow and Charles Herbert Dorman transferors, of the one part and Lionel Collins of Airlie Ripley Road, Worthing Sussex, and Charles Herbert Dorman, transferees, of the other part. Description of lands affected: piece of land with 15 messuages Nos. 1-29 Berkeley Road. Supplemental to a deed registered 1899 (*MDR/1899/31/428*) between Charles Dorman, of the one part and Selina Noys and Charles Dorman, of the other part and another dated 30ᵗʰ March, 1903 (*MDR/1903/10/299*).

MDR/1909/3/460 registered 3rd February 1909

Summary: Dorman to Dorman. Dated 22nd December 1909. Parties: Julia Frances Dorman and Charles Herbert Dorman, transferors, of the one part to Charles Herbert Dorman and Francis Thomas Dorman, transferees of the other part. Supplemental to a deed dated 2nd June 1880 (*B13 No. 657*) between Edmund Wood and Charles Dorman. Description of lands affected: <u>a dwelling house, shop and bake house with gateway" at No. 21 Kingsford Terrace</u>. Supplemental to a deed from November 1882 between Edmund Wood and Charles Dorman (*MDR/1882/39/1012*).

MDR/1909/3/461 registered 3rd February 1909

Summary: Dorman to Wieffenbach. Dated 1st February 1909. Parties: Charles Herbert Dorman and Francis Thomas Dorman of 23 Essex Street, Strand, solicitors, of the one part and Ferdinand Jacob Wieffenbach of 70 Grove Road, Holloway, baker and confectioner, of the other part. Recital of deed dated 1st January, 1880 between Charles Dorman and Edmund Wood. Description of lands affected: <u>dwelling house, shop and bake house with gateway then known as No. 21 Kingsford Terrace and now known as No. 523 Seven Sisters Road</u>.

MDR/1913/11/869 registered 11th June 1913

Summary: Dorman to Candler. Dated 7th April 1913. Parties: Charles Herbert Dorman and Frances Thomas Dorman, of the one part to Annie Candler of Abbotsford, Torrington Park, North Finchley, widow of the other part. Description of lands affected: *"All that parcel of land situated in the Parish of Tottenham in Middlesex on the north west side by a road known as St. John's Road (formerly known as Townsend Road) and having a frontage of 154 feet 6 inches or thereabouts and a depth therefore of 80 feet bounded on the north and northeast by a road known as Manchester Road and on the south side by Heysham Road together with the eight double messuages or tenements and buildings erected therein and known as <u>Nos. 38&38a to 52&52a St. John's Road even numbers inclusive</u>"*.

MDR/1913/11/870 Probate registered 2nd June 1913

Summary: Kingsford & Dorman to Dorman & Dorman. Dated 31st May 1913. Parties: James Henry Kingsford, gent of No.18 Wolverton Gardens, Ealing Common and Charles Herbert Dorman, gent, of the one part and Charles Herbert Dorman and Francis Thomas Dorman of the other part. Recital of an Indenture dated 23rd March 1898 (*MDR/1898/11/487*) and made between Charles Dorman, of the one part and Stephanie Henrietta Pedder of No. 38 Victoria Street, Kensington, widow, of the other part. Description of lands affected:
<u>Nos. 61-75 Vartry Road (4 double messuages) between 59 Vartry Road and Richmond Road and Richmond Terrace, then known as 61&61a, 63&63a, 65&65a and 67&67a</u>;

Nos. 56-62 Richmond Road (4 double messuages) between 54 Richmond Road and the rear of St. John's Almshouses;

Nos. 39-53 Franklin Street (4 double messuages) from 37 Franklin Street

Nos. 1-39, 41(10 double messuages and one single) and Nos. 26-48 Manchester Road (6 double messuages).

Stephanie Henrietta Pedder died on 6th July 1912. She left her estate to James Henry Kingsford Esq. and Charles Herbert Dorman, solicitor.

MDR/1913/11/871 registered 11th June 1913

Summary: Kingsford & Dorman to Dorman & Benn. Dated 2nd June 1913. Parties: James Henry Kingsford and Charles Herbert Dorman of the one part, transferors, to Charles Herbert Dorman and Arthur Benn of No.108 Coleherne Court, Kensington, transferees, of the other part. Description of lands affected: Nos. 2&4 to 22&24 on the south side of Manchester Road inclusive (6 double messuages).

The land was described in an indenture of mortgage on 23rd March 1898 (MDR/1898/*11/487*).

MDR/1914/13/559 Deed/Probate registered 23rd June 1914

Summary: Dorman to Dorman & Dorman. Dated 12th June 1914. Parties: Charles Herbert Dorman, of the one part and Charles Herbert Dorman and Francis Thomas Dorman of the other part. Description of lands affected: 4 double messuages on the north side of Heysham Road Nos. 13&15, 17&19, 21&23 and 25&27.

In November 1900, Charles Dorman transferred to his eldest son, Charles Herbert Dorman, the parcel of land and buildings at Nos. 1-27 Heysham Road. In April 1900, Kingsford, Dorman & Co was listed as owning Nos. 1-23 Heysham Road. Charles Herbert Dorman became joint owner of the land and tenements with his brother Francis Thomas Dorman.

MDR/1914/13/600 Deed/Probate registered 23rd June 1914

Summary: Dorman & Dorman to Candler. Dated 12th June 1914. Parties: Charles Herbert Dorman and Francis Thomas Dorman, both of 23 Essex Street, Strand, gentlemen, of the one part and Annie Candler of Abbotsford, Torrington Park, North Finchley, Middlesex, widow, of the other part. Description of lands affected: 4 double messuages on the north side of Heysham Road Nos. 13&15, 17&19, 21&23 and 25&27 at Tottenham.

It was stamped on 23rd June 1928 when a receipt was received at the Registry to prove that the mortgage was discharged on 20th June 1928.

MDR/1915/6/546 registered 7th May 1915

Summary: Dorman to Dorman. Parties: Charles Herbert Dorman to Francis Thomas Dorman. Deed dated 21st January 1897. Charles Dorman of 23 Essex Street, Strand, of the one part and Frances Anne Paterson of "*Heatherdown*", Ascot in Berkshire, spinster, of the other part. It was for "*all that piece of land situated partly in the parish of Tottenham and partly in the parish of*

Hackney, both in the County of Middlesex, south side of a road called Vartry Road and having a frontage of 107 feet 2 inches bounded on the south side by the gardens of the messuages situated in Amhurst Park Road, Hackney" and secondly with another frontage of 187 feet 8 inches. Description of lands affected: three double messuages on Vartry Road Nos. 60&62, 64&66, 68&70 and three single messuages 72, 74 and 76 bordered by Nos. 56&58 on one end and at the other end by 78 Vartry Road. Another ten messuages: two single messuages Nos. 90 and 92 and eight double messuages Nos. 94&96, 98&100, 102&104, 106&108, 110&112, 114&116, 118&120 and 122&124 bordered at one end by No. 88 and at the other by No. 126 Vartry Road.

This memorial arose from the death of Charles Herbert Dorman on 6th February 1915. The deed was dated 21st January 1897 and carried Charles Dorman's signature but it was not registered until 7th May 1915. The mortgage passed to the surviving trustee of Charles Dorman, Francis Thomas Dorman. The tracings showed that Nos. 60-76 were once owned/leased by Mrs. Blackwell and Nos. 90-124 was owned/leased by Mrs. Worrall, who lived at No. 64 Amhurst Park, backing on to Vartry Road. However the latter died on 29th April, 1895 (*The London Gazette, July 8 1896*). The will of Amelia Emily Worrall, widow, was proved by her son, Thomas Edward Worrall, feather merchant, in June 1895. The drawings were not updated. George Candler was listed as the owner of Nos. 56-76 Vartry Road in the 1913 Rate Books but he was probably the leaseholder.

MDR/1915/8/158 registered 8th June 1915

Summary: Dated 7th June 1915. Parties: Reverend William Harrison, Lionel Hope Cockburn of the first part, the mortgagers, Francis Thomas Dorman, trustee, of the second part and William Eve of No. 10 Union Court, Old Broad Street of the third part. Transfer of mortgage. Supplemental to an indenture (*MDR/1898/13/ 681*) herein called the "*mortgage*" dated 1st April 1898 and made between Charles Dorman, the testator, of the one part and James Henry Kingsford and the mortgagees of the other part. Description of lands affected: Nos. 87-139 (odd numbers) Vartry Road and Nos. 54, 56, 58 St. John's Road, Stamford Hill.

All the hereditaments granted by the mortgage on which are now vested in the "*mortgagees*". Francis Thomas Dorman was listed as a trustee, presumably that of the will of his father, Charles Dorman. James Henry Kingsford, son of James Kingsford, died on 14th May 1915 and was this event was probably the reason for this memorial a few weeks after his death.

MDR/1915/10/281 registered 19th July 1915

Summary: Hibburd to Public trustees. Dated 14th July 1915. Transfer of mortgage. Parties: Ernest Wilby Hibburd of Elm Grove, Crouch End, of the one part and the Public Trustees of Nos. 3&4 Clements Inn, Strand, Middlesex of the other part. Supplemental to a deed (*MDR/1915/6/46*) between Charles

Dorman and Frances Anne Paterson "*being a mortgage of freehold land messuages and tenements*". Description of lands affected: <u>Three double messuages on Vartry Road Nos. 60&62, 64&66, 68&70 and three single messuages 72, 74 and 76 bordered by Nos. 56&58 on one end and at the other end by 78 Vartry Road. Another ten messuages: two single messuages Nos. 90 and 92 and eight double messuages Nos. 94&96, 98&100, 102&104, 106&108, 110&112, 114&116, 118&120 and 122&124 bordered at one end by No. 88 and at the other by No. 126 Vartry Road.</u>

A notification for claims to the estate of Frances Anne Paterson of "*Heatherdown*", Ascot, Berkshire, spinster, deceased, who died on 21st January 1905 (*The London Gazette, 24th March 1905*) were being dealt with by Kingsford, Dorman & Company of 23 Essex Street, Strand, Middlesex. Her will was proved on 18th February 1905 by her executors, Ernest Wilby Hibburd of No. 23 Hewitt Road, Hornsey, Middlesex, gentleman, Kenneth Durnford Iliff of No. 28 Granvile Road Hove, Sussex, Clerk in Holy Orders and Charles Herbert Dorman of 23 Essex Street, Strand, Middlesex, gentleman. The executors were intending to disperse her assets (Effects £72,649 18s.3d.).

MDR/1921/31/786 registered 2nd December 1921

Summary: Dorman to Dorman. Dated 15th November 1921. Parties: Constance Margaret Dorman of No. 23 Lawrie Park Road, Sydenham, widow and Francis Thomas Dorman, solicitor, of the one part and Francis Thomas Dorman of the other part. Reconveyance supplemental to a deed (registered 22nd November 1900 (*MDR/1900/32/94*). Description of lands affected: <u>parcel of land on north side of Heysham Road with 7 double messuages Nos. 1&3, 5&7, 9&11, 13&15, 17&19, 21&23 and 25&27</u> for "*securing the principal sum of two thousand one hundred pounds and interest*". These houses were transferred from Charles Dorman to his son Charles Herbert Dorman in 1900 and after the latter died in 1915 they went to his wife Constance and were then held jointly with her brother-in-law. Constance Margaret's daughter, Pamela Dorman, only six when her father died, achieved notoriety when, on or around 19th December, 1933 she married Ian Dundas, chief-of-staff of the British Union of Fascists. Their marriage, at St. Michael's Church, Chester Square, Westminster, London, had Sir Oswald Mosley as the best man. Pamela was given away by her brother, Geoffrey Charles Herbert Dorman. Pamela married three times.

MDR/1923/15/547 registered 24th March 1923

Summary: Dated 20th March 1923. Parties: Charles Edmund Brown and Francis Thomas Dorman, of the first part, Francis Thomas Dorman, of the second part and William Henry Lee of the third part. Memorial of a reconveyance of freehold. Description of lands affected: <u>15 double messuages Nos. 2&4 to 58&60 Heysham Road, Tottenham, even numbers inclusive.</u>

Described by recital of a mortgage (*MDR/1901/9/680*) dated 15th January, 1901, made between Charles Dorman and Charles Edmund Browne of Brunton, near Chathill, Northumberland, formerly a captain in the Cavalry and Charles Alexander Browne, of Southend House, Bury St. Edmunds, Suffolk.

MDR/1923/15/548 registered 31ˢᵗ March 1923

Summary: Dorman to Noys & Robinson. Dated 20ᵗʰ March 1923. Parties: Francis Thomas Dorman of No. 23 Essex Street, Strand, of the one part and George Thomas Noys of No. 4 Sydenham Road, Sydenham, Kent and Percy Robinson of No. 9 Albert Road, South Norwood, Surrey, of the other part, both gentlemen and mortgagees. Description of lands affected: <u>12 messuages Nos. 32-54 Richmond Road formerly Nos. 53 to 64 Charles Street</u>.

The deed was stamped after a receipt was produced to state that this mortgage (or charge) had been discharged 29ᵗʰ October 1929. In 1900, the messuages at Nos. 32-54 Richmond Road were acquired by James Henry Kingsford.

Selina Noys, of 47 Beckenham Road, Beckenham Kent died on 8ᵗʰ March 1923, leaving her estate, valued at £1,530. 5s. 2d. to George Thomas Noys, auctioneer and to Nora Madeline Noys, spinster. Probate was not granted until August that year. The beneficiaries were her son and daughter. George Thomas Noys owned his home at No. 4 Sydenham Road, Sydenham, according to the H.M. Office of Land Registry (*The London Gazette, 6ᵗʰ December, 1921*).

MDR/1924/34/397 registered 30ᵗʰ September 1924

Summary: Reconveyance dated 24ᵗʰ May 1923. Parties: Francis Thomas Dorman and Annie Candler, widow, of the first part, Francis Thomas Dorman, of the second part and William Henry Lee, gentlemen, of the third part. Description of lands affected as below:

> Supplement to a Deed dated 16ᵗʰ January 1901 (B9 No. 681) when a principal Indenture was made between Charles Dorman of 23 Essex Street, Strand and Jane Sophia French of 6 Torrington Park Villas, North Finchley aforesaid spinster and Samuel Horace Candler of 23 Essex Street, Strand, aforesaid of the other part hereinafter referred to as the principal indenture. All that several pieces or parcels of land forming part of an Estate called Woodberry Lodge Estate. Description of property affected <u>33, 33a-73, 73a St. John's Road</u>, odd numbers inclusive.

The last deed was a memorial of an instrument operating to transfer or create a legal estate (No. 6 Torrington Park Villas was later renumbered No. 14).

William Henry Lee had been the clerk for Kingsford, Dorman & Co. in respect of all the Deeds and Memorials relating to the area. This was the only Indenture in which Jane Sophia French, who was Annie Candler's sister and Samuel Candler, a partner in Kingsford, Dorman & Co, in a recital of a will dated 21ˢᵗ May 1903, appear to have been directly involved with Charles Dorman. Annie was later to move to *"Abbotsford"*, No. 94 Torrington Park, after her husband died on 11th March 1903. Her sister, Jane French died in 1905 and a later Indenture records her death and grant of probate, registered on 20th October 1905. In 1913, Annie took ownership of Nos. 38-52a, St. John's Road, probably renumbered, from Charles Herbert and Francis Thomas Dorman. Charles Herbert Dorman, also cited in the sale documents, was the eldest son of Charles Dorman.

MDR/1924/35/818 registered 9th October 1924

Summary: Dated 6th October 1924. Parties: Francis Thomas Dorman, solicitor and Thomas Alexander Mason Esq. Description of lands affected: <u>piece of ground situated in Seven Sisters Road between Manchester Road and Heysham Road in Tottenham</u> (this is now Manchester Gardens). Below is a transcription of extracts from the Deed held at the City of London, London Metropolitan Archives.

> Memorial of a Conveyance dated 6th October 1924
>
> Parties: FRANCIS THOMAS DORMAN of No. 23 Essex Street, Strand in the County of London Solicitor (herein after called the "Vendor" of the one part and THOMAS ALEXANDER MASON of Temple Court Reigate in the County of Surrey, Esq.,(hereinafter called the "Purchaser") of the other part
>
> By recital of a Deed dated 19th May 1893 and made between the said Charles Dorman of the one part and John Jeken Cockburn and James Kingsford of the other part …
>
> Registered 25th May 1893 Book 16 No. 783

The following deeds were listed on the back (*MDR/1924/35/818*):

> By RECITAL of another Indenture dated the 16th day of January 1901 and made between the said Charles Dorman of the one part and Jane Sophia French and Samuel Horace Candler of the other part
>
> REGISTERED 24th March 1923 Book 9 No 681
>
> And by a RECITAL of the Will dated 2nd day of May 1901 of the said Charles Dorman, his death and grant of probate,
>
> Probate REGISTERED 6th May 1902 Book 12 No. 565
>
> And by a RECITAL of the Will dated 21st May 1903 of the said Jane Sophia French her death and grant of probate.
>
> Probate registered 20th October 1905 Book 26 No.650
>
> And by RECITAL of another Indenture dated 22nd day of December 1905 and made between the said Julia Frances Dorman and Charles Herbert Dorman of the 1st part, the Vendor (Francis Thomas Dorman) of the 2nd part, the said Arthur William Dorman of the 3rd part, Emily Mary Shackleton (formerly the said Emily Mary Dorman) of the 4th part and the said Maud Isabel Dorman of the 5th part.

REGISTERED 16th March 1906 Book 7 No. 594

And by a RECITAL of the Will dated 14th December 1903 of the said John Jeken Cockburn, his death and Grant of Probate.

Probate REGISTERED 18th February 1914 Book 4 No. 17

And by a RECITAL of another Indenture dated 17th day of March 1923 and made between the said Edith Cockburn and Lionel Hope Cockburn of the one part and the Vendor of the other part (supplemental to the herein before recited Indenture of 19th May 1893) REGISTERED 14th June 1923 Book 18 No. 854

And by RECITAL of another Indenture dated 24th day of September 1924 and made between the Vendor and the said Annie Candler of the 1st part, the Vendor of the 2nd part and William Henry Lee of the 3rd part (supplemental to the herein before recited Indenture of the 16th of January 1901)

REGISTERED 30th September 1924 Book 34 No. 397

These recitals of indentures explain why some of the people appeared in the Memorials at various times. Jane Sophia French died 13th June 1905. Samuel Horace Candler died 12th March 1903.

MDR/1924/38/197 registered 27th October 1924

Summary: Dorman to Middlesex County Council. Dated 8th October 1924. Conveyance of freehold to "*transfer or create a legal estate*". Parties: Francis Thomas Dorman, vendor, of the one part and the Middlesex County Council of the other part. Description of lands affected: <u>piece of land, 44ft. wide, fronting on Seven Sisters Road by 120ft. deep on Manchester Road Seven Sisters Road, Tottenham</u>.

Beside Francis Thomas Dorman's name was written "*free of Charles Dorman*". The Weights and Measures Office – No. 590 Seven Sisters Road.

MDR/1925/20/404 registered 29th May 1925

Summary: Memorial of a Reconveyance dated 19th May 1925. Parties: George Thomas Noys of No. 4 Sydenham Road, Sydenham in the County of Kent, estate agent and Nora Madeline Noys of St. Martins, No. 47 Beckenham Rd, Beckenham, in the County of Kent, spinster, of the one part and Francis Thomas Dorman of 23 Essex Street, Strand in the County of London, gentleman, of the other part. Supplement to a deed dated 22nd January 1897 made between Charles Dorman of the one part and Selina Noys and the said Charles Dorman of the other part. Registered 5th March 1897 (*MDR/1897/8/504*) Description of lands affected: <u>Nos. 26/28 to 56/58 Vartry Road, Tottenham, including No. 54 Vartry Road</u>. The grantors were George Thomas and Nora Madeline Noys.

Also supplemental to a Deed dated 30th March 1903 made between Selina Noys, of the one part and Selina Noys and Charles Herbert Dorman of the other part. Registered 7th April 1903 (*MDR/1903/10/300*). Arising from will and probate and Charles Dorman's death.

Also supplemental to a Deed dated 12th September 1906 made between Charles Herbert Dorman and Francis Thomas Dorman, who were then the trustees of the will of the said Charles Dorman, of the one part and Selina Noys and Charles Herbert Dorman of the other part. Registered 5th November 1906 (*MDR/1906/29/30*).

In 1925, George Thomas Noys was recorded in the *MDR Indexes of the Memorials* (*LMA*) for the years 1919-1938 for Vartry Road, as were Nora Madeline and Selina Noys. The only other entry was for George Thomas Noys, for property at Whittington Road, Edmonton. When she died, Selina had a mortgage on Nos. 26 to 58 Vartry Road, recorded in 1925 in the *MDR* indexes.

This reconveyance continued to link No. 54 Vartry Road with the Noys family and Francis Thomas Dorman, as a trustee of the will of Charles Dorman. Francis Thomas Dorman died on 8th February 1931. His estate passed to his wife Ada Mary Dorman and son Laurence. Nora Madeline Noys of No. 47 Beckenham Road, Beckenham, Kent, spinster, died in February 1944 and left £4,747 13s., *inter alia,* to George Thomas Noys, described as a surveyor and estate agent. Hers was the same address as that of her mother when the latter died twenty years earlier. In the census of 1911, Selina (69) and her two spinster daughters, Nora (40) and Margaret Anne (37) were shown to be living with their mother. George Thomas Noys of No. 40 Valley Road Shortlands, in Kent, died at Grafton Villa, Blisworth, Northamptonshire on 4th March 1945 and left £33,407 16s.11d, *inter alia*, to his wife Edith Bertha Noys. Margaret Anne Noys died in 1955.

MDR/1925/20/405 registered 29th May 1925

Summary: Public Trustee to Dorman. Dated 7th May 1925. Parties: The Public Trustee, of the one part and Francis Thomas Dorman of 23 Essex St, Strand, in the County of Middlesex, gentleman of the other part. Witness to sealing of the Deed, J. H. Higgins, public trustees and L.M. Sewell, civil servant, Public Trustees Department, Kingsway, WC2. It was a reconveyance.

Supplemental to a Deed dated 21st January 1897 made between Charles Dorman, of the one part and Frances Anne Paterson of the other part. (*MDR/1897/6/546*). Description of lands affected: Nos. 60&62, 64&66, 68&70 to 124 Vartry Road, Tottenham.

Also supplemental to a Deed dated 14th July 1915 made between Ernest Wilby Hibburd, of the one part and the Public Trustees of the other part. Registered 19th July 1915 (*MDR/1915/10/281*). (Ernest Wilby Hubbard released himself from the mortgage.)

And by a recital of a Deed dated 22nd December 1905 and made between Julia, Charles Herbert, Francis, Arthur, Emily and Maude Dorman. Registered 16th March 1906 (*MDR/1906/7/594*). (Julia Frances Dorman relinquishing herself as a trustee of her father's will.)

MDR/1926/1/226 registered 1st January 1926
Summary: Dated 30th December 1925. Parties: Francis Thomas Dorman, solicitor and Laurence Charles Dorman, gentleman. Below is a transcription of extracts from the deed held at the City of London, London Metropolitan Archives:

Memorial by copy
This indenture made thirtieth day of December one thousand nine hundred and twenty five between FRANCIS THOMAS DORMAN of No 23 Essex Street, Strand, Solicitor of the one part and LAURENCE CHARLES DORMAN No 23 Essex Street Strand Gentleman, of the other part WHEREAS these present are supplemental to an Indenture dated 22nd December, one thousand nine hundred and five and made between Julia Frances Dorman and Charles Herbert Dorman of the first part, the said Francis Thomas Dorman of second part Reverend Arthur William Dorman of third part, Emily Mary Shackleton of the fourth part and Maude Isabel Dorman of fifth part being a Deed of Appointment of the said Francis Thomas Dorman as a Trustee of the Will of Charles Dorman deceased in the place of the said Julia Frances Dorman who thereby retired from the Trusteeship and jointly with the said Charles Herbert Dorman, the continuing trustee of the said Will, such deed also conferred certain additional powers upon the Trustees and Whereas since the date of the before mentioned Deed further parts of the residuary estate of the said Charles Dorman consisting of stocks, shares and freeholds and lease-hold houses have been sold and the proceeds thereof have been applied by the trustees in reducing the Mortgages on the parts of the said residuary estate and whereas the sum of three thousand pounds referred to in the before mentioned Deed and which the said Charles Dorman had covenanted to pay to the trustees of the Marriage Settlement of the said Arthur William Dorman has to the sum of two hundred pounds been paid to such Settlement Trustees and the Trustees of the will of the said Charles Dorman, have given to such Settlement Trustees, a Mortgage upon freehold property forming part of the said residuary estate, to secure the balance of two thousand eight hundred pounds and Whereas the said Charles Herbert Dorman died on sixth February one thousand nine hundred and fifteen and Whereas the said Francis Thomas Dorman is desirous of appointing the said Laurence Charles Dorman to be a trustee of the will in the place of the said Charles Herbert Dorman deceased.

He the said Francis Thomas Dorman doth hereby appoint the said Laurence Charles Dorman to be a trustee of the said Will of the said Charles Dorman And the said Francis Thomas Dorman doth hereby declare that all real and personal estate (including things in action and the right to recover and receive the same) which is now subject to the trusts of the said will of the said Charles Dorman and is capable of being vested by this declaration, shall vest in Francis Thomas Dorman and Laurence Charles Dorman for all the estate and interest now subject to the trusts of the said will of the said Charles Dorman upon the trusts and subject to the powers and provisions applicable to the same respectively by virtue of the said will.

It was signed and sealed by Francis Thomas Dorman and Laurence Charles Dorman (the place, "*The Woodberry Lodge Estate*", in the Parish of Tottenham was written in the margin of the Memorial, then crossed out beside Francis Thomas Dorman's name and replaced with "*appointment of new trustee*"). Francis Thomas Dorman, trustee, appointed Laurence Charles Dorman, his son, as a trustee of the will of Charles Dorman. The only sons and daughters of Charles Dorman still alive were Francis Thomas Dorman, Lady Emily Shackleton, *née* Dorman and Julia Frances Sarolea, *née* Dorman, who, according to this document, had given up being a trustee.

MDR/1928/22/508 registered 11th June 1928

Summary: Stamped in red, on memorial was written "*On 11th June 1928 a receipt was produced in the Registry to the effect that this mortgage (or charge) had been discharged on 31st May 1928*" on a mortgage dated 21st December 1905. Parties: Julia Frances Dorman of Queen Anne's Mansions, Westminster, spinster, Charles Herbert Dorman, gentleman, of the first part, Charles Herbert Dorman, Julia Frances Dorman, Rev. Arthur William Dorman, Vicarage, Hinton, Charterhouse near Bath, Emily Mary Shackleton No. 14 Learmonth Gardens in the City of Edinburgh, Frances Thomas Dorman and Maude Isabel Dorman of Queen Anne's Mansions, Westminster, of the second part and Charles Herbert Dorman and Francis Thomas Dorman of the third part. Description of lands affected: <u>Nos. 79&81, 83&85, 87&89 and 91&93 Richmond Road (formerly 1&1a, 2&2a, 3&3a and 4&4a, Charles Street)</u>.

Charles Herbert Dorman died in 1915 and Maude Isabel Dorman on Easter Sunday, 23rd April, 1916.

MDR/1930/1/857 registered 28th March 1930

Summary: Dorman and Dorman to Andrews. Dated 25th March 1930. Parties: Francis Thomas Dorman, gent and Laurence Charles Dorman, gent, to Henry Augustus Andrews, builder and contractor, of No. 81 Avenue Road, Tottenham, Middlesex. Description of lands affected: <u>parcel of land at the junction of Candler Street and St John's Road.</u> The houses later constructed on this triangular piece of land are of a different style to others.

MDR/1931/14/794 registered 3rd May 1931

Summary: Dorman & Shackleton. Dated 9th April 1931. Parties: Laurence Charles Dorman (already a trustee), solicitor of No. 23 Essex Street, Strand and Dame Emily Shackleton appointed as testators and personal representatives of land under the will of Charles Dorman, following the death of Francis Thomas Dorman, in February.

MDR/1936/61/165 registered 10th December 1936

Summary: Dorman to Dorman. Dated 3rd December 1936. Appointment of new trustee of the will of Charles Dorman following the death of Lady Emily Shackleton. Parties: Laurence Charles Dorman and Charles John Paget Dorman of Brockley Court, Somerset, Captain in His Majesty's Reserve Forces.

Supplemental to deed dated 22nd December 1905 and registered 16 or 17th March 1906 (*MDR/1906/7/594*) among Julia Frances Dorman and Charles Herbert Dorman, of the first part, Francis Thomas Dorman, of the second part, Rev. Arthur William Dorman, of the third part, Emily Mary Shackleton, of the fourth part and Maude Dorman, of the fifth part.

Deed dated 30th December 1925 between Francis Thomas Dorman, of the one part and Laurence Charles John Dorman of the other part registered 11th January, 1926 (*MDR/1926/1/226*).

A deed dated 25th March 1931 between Laurence Charles Dorman, of the one part and Dame Emily Mary Shackleton of the other part registered 9th April 1931 (*MDR/1931/14/794*).

Description of lands affected: <u>Nos. 612 and 614 Seven Sisters Road and land at other places in London.</u>

Some of the deeds overlapped in content because the earlier ones would be added as new people became involved with the ownership, as trustees or arising from death and probate. Charles Paget Dorman died in 1939.

After 1938, Deeds were no longer recorded in this way and land was registered at H.M. Land Registry. In the first part, the freehold land is now shown and numbered on an H.M. Land Registry General Map, with a parcel number and the date of first registration. It also states in which borough is the property. The second part is the proprietorship register which states the nature of the title, name, address and description of the proprietor of the land and any entries affecting the right of disposal thereof. This is the *title absolute*. The third part is the charges register containing charges, encumbrances, etc. adversely affecting the land and registered dealings therewith. This is usually where building societies' interests are recorded.

Appendix 2

Miscellaneous deeds and documents for Hanger Lane, Tottenham

Some of these indentures relate to the land owned in 1619 by Edward Barkham, north and south of Hanger Lane but sold by various people over the years. Some names for the parcels of land vary from maps of 1619 and 1798.

BARNFIELD

A lease and counterpart 1798 (*ACC/1028/111*) from George Stacey of Holborn, chemist, to Thomas Withington, of Abchurch Lane, broker, of Middlesex. The 21 year lease for eight acres of land, known as "*Barnfield*", north of Hanger's Lane on what is now St. Ann's Road, including barn, sheds, stables, office gardens and meadow. Barnfield belonged to the heirs of Stephen Holland before 1798.

Document *LMA* (*ACC 1028/112*) dated 1799 was a receipt for payment of tax on land and premises situated in Hanger Lane, near Stamford Hill, occupied by Thomas Withington. The will of Thomas Withington of Old Pay office, Old Broad Street and Chapman's Green, Lordship Lane, Tottenham, Middlesex but then living at Buxton in the County of Derby, bachelor, was proved in 1805. He left his estate to his widowed mother, brother Richard and sisters, Elizabeth and Susan.

Some time after this, on 30th December 1819, a new lease *LMA* (*ACC 1028/114*) was granted by George Stacey, son of George Stacey, chemist, to Mr. John Saint Barbe of Austin Friars. John St. Barbe (1778-1862) married Elizabeth Thomas at Edmonton in 1808. The last name had been crossed out, in pencil and replaced with the name of Thomas Gibson of Milk Street, Cheapside, City of London, silk merchant. The annual rent was £84 for premises at Hanger Lane, Stamford Hill (Barnfield). Written on the back were the years "*1819, 14 years lease and 1833*".

A new lease *LMA* (*ACC 1028/115*), was made on 25th April 1822 between John Saint Barbe and Thomas Gibson then of Trump Street, silk merchant, for the remainder of the lease of 14 years, for "*Barnfield*". A counterpart of lease (*ACC 1028/116*) dated 21st January 1829 was made again between George Stacey, the son, to Thomas Gibson, of Milk Street, Cheapside, silk merchant, for the same eight acres known as Barnfield. The names of Deborah (Smith) Dermer, who lived west of the land and Bannister Flight, to the east of the land were recorded in this indenture. George Stacey's name appeared in the

Poor Rate Book for High Cross, Tottenham, 1837 as the owner of land at Hanger Lane, then still occupied by Thomas Gibson.

ALBION LODGE (KNOWN LATER AS VARTRY LODGE) AND CLAYHANGERS

MDR/1806/5/331 registered 2nd August 1806

Summary: Hunt to James. Dated 14th December 1805. Parties: Philip Thomas Hunt, farmer, to Richard James, Esq. It was a lease (and counterpart) for 99 years from 24th June, 1804. A plan of the premises showed that it was situated on the north by Hanger Lane near Stamford Hill, on the south and east was land owned by Joseph Stonard and on the west by land owned by Thomas Coxhead Stevens. Description of lands affected: <u>8 acres known as Gallowfield or Gallows Hill with mansion house and other buildings erected by Richard James</u>. Rent £60 yearly.

The plan in the margin showed that Mr. Burnand had the house. Another document (*ACC/0489/003*) at LMA dated 22nd August 1804, recorded that Philip Thomas Hunt had demised the land, which had been formerly occupied by Nicholas Carter, to Richard James for £3,000, leased for 99 years.

MDR/1812/1/525 registered 24th January 1812

Summary: Nicholson and James to Burnand. Dated 2nd August 1811. Parties: Ralph Nicholson, of the first part, Richard James, of the second part and Lewis Burnand of the third part. It was an Assignment of lease from Nicholson and James to Burnand. Description of lands affected: <u>8 acres known as Little Gallow Field or Gallows Hill, Stamford Hill, with dwelling house and other buildings</u>.

This indenture also referred to an earlier indenture of lease for 99 years, dating from 14th December 1805, registered on 2nd August 1806 *(MDR/1806/5/331)*, when Philip Thomas Hunt demised to Richard James. Another document *(ACC/0489/005)* at LMA showed that £5,000 was paid by Lewis Burnand to Nicholson and £2,500 to Richard James.

MDR/1812/1/526 registered 24th January 1812

Summary: Dated 4th and 5th August 1811. Parties: Abraham Watson Rutherford, Thomas Wagstaffe and Richard James to Lewis Burnand. The lease and release was among Rutherford, Wagstaffe, James, Burnand and Blunt of Broad Street. Description of lands affected: <u>1 acre, 2 roods and 30 perches part of a parcel of land known as Clay Hangers, next to Little Gallows Field</u>.

The plan showed the parcel of land was south of Hanger Lane and shown in writing on it was Mr. Burnand's allotment and next to it was Mr. Rutherford's allotment

MDR/1812/1/527 registered 24th January 1812

Summary: James to Burnand. Dated 5th August 1811. Parties: Richard James of Tottenham, Esq., of the one part to Lewis Burnand of South Street, Finsbury Square, merchant, of the other part. The indenture of Assignment made reference to an earlier lease of 95 years unexpired, dating from 2nd January 1809, made between Thomas Coxhead Stevens, of the one part and Richard James of the other part. In this instance Richard James sold, assigned and transferred the land to Lewis Burnand. Description of lands affected: <u>two closes lying on the north side of Hanger Lane in the Parish of Tottenham High Cross at or near a place called Stamford Hill commonly called Snares Mead</u>.

These parcels of land were known as Little Snare's Field and Great Snares Mead in 1619 and 1798.

MDR/1826/10/415 registered 8th November 1826

Summary: Dated 12th & 13th October, 1826. Conveyance and assignment of freehold and leasehold premises at Hanger Lane, Stamford Hill in Middlesex by lease and release from Lewis Burnand, Esq. to Ebeneezer Johnston of Bishopsgate St., London, ironmonger and John Coles of Frogmorton St. *"trustee of bar dower"*. Description of lands affected: <u>1 acre, 2 roods and 30 perches, part of parcel of land (3½ acres) known as Clay Hangers at Hanger Lane</u> once owned by Abraham Watson Rutherford and Richard James 1812 (*MDR/1812/1/ 526*), mansion house and other buildings registered 2nd August, 1806 (*MDR/1806/5/331*) and parcel of land, dated 7th April 1817 but not registered until August 1825 (*MDR/1825/9/539*).

Johnston paid £4,200 to Burnand. Documents (*ACC/0489/007-008*) cover the same transaction.

MDR/1876/30/861 registered 29th November, 1876

Summary: Conveyance: Dated, 27th October 1876. Parties: The Great Eastern Railway Company, of the one part to George Holmes, Esq. of Norfolk Road, Hackney, Middlesex, gent, of the other part. Description of lands affected: <u>parcels of land outlined in pink including 1,4,5 & 6 (4 acres 2 roods 20 perches) marked on Company Parliamentary plans and with the letters A,B & C in the parish of Tottenham between Amhurst Road and Hanger Lane</u>.

The plan showed the parcel of land with a footpath on the west of the site. The area next to the railway line was marked as a new road 40 feet wide, which was to be made by purchaser.

Another document in the Holmes Family Collection (*ACC/0489/025*) adds further information. The road marked between A&B, already owned by the Great Eastern Railway Company; the purchaser, George Holmes, had to obtain permission to continue the road from B to C so that private dwelling houses, with an annual value not less than £45 per annum, could be built. There was to be absolutely no building of warehouses on the site; it was sold for

£3,815.12s.6d. Earlier indentures were shown in the schedule of acquisitions *as MDR/1870/14/496 and MDR/1868/1/392.* The land was on the parcel of land formerly known as *Clayhanger.*

BUSHEY HANGERS

MDR/1808/9/613 registered 6th December 1808

Summary: Lucas to Hindle & Hindle. Dated 30th November 1808. Parties: John Lucas of South Ville House, Lambeth and now of Upper Tooting, Surrey, of the first part, John Hindle of Chancery Lane, of the second part and James Hindle, also of Chancery Lane, of the third part. Description of lands affected: cottage or tenement *"lately erected by John Birkenhead"*, in the north west corner of one of the fields and two acres behind it (113 × 822 × 99).

Hanger Lane was on the north, east and south was land owned by John Lucas and on the west was land owned by Edward Scales. This was included in an indre dated 30th June 1802 between Joseph Lucas and John Birkenhead. The lease was for 31 years at an annual rent of £31 10s. John Lucas had inherited this land from his uncle, Joseph Lucas when the latter died in 1807. In the Poor Rates book for Tottenham Wood, Green Ward, 1810 was an entry *"John Hindle land of Lucas"* and written alongside was *"Elsom paid the preceding rate acknowledging himself to be the occupier"*. This entry was followed by an entry for De Zoete for house, garden and two acres of land.

MDR/1810/7/603 registered 12th September 1810

Summary: Lucas to De Zoete. Dated 28th August 1810. Parties: John Lucas of South Ville House, Lambeth and now of Upper Tooting, Surrey, of the one part, a devisee of the last will and testament of Joseph Lucas, deceased and Samuel De Zoete of Mincing Lane, City of London, merchant, of the other part. Description of lands affected: plan showed land on the east was owned by Lucas, occupied by James and or John Hindle or their undertenants, south by Lucas land, west on land owned by Edward Scales and north was waste land fronting onto Hanger Lane.

The waste land was to be fenced in by De Zoete at his expense and included part of a pond on the south east corner of the plot. The lease was from 29th September 1816 for 23 years at an annual rent of £12 15s to Samuel De Zoete, his executors and administrators. It was John Lucas, Joseph's nephew of whom, on 4th April 1809 William Robinson wrote *"same day Mr John Lucas had leave to enclose a piece of the waste in front of Mr. Derzotte's in Hanger's Lane for which he paid £25"*. Samuel was the father of Samuel Herman De Zoete, born there in 1810 who in 1838 married Ellen Simon.

MDR/1821/9/637 registered 20th December 1821

Summary: Stutfield to Howard. Dated 19th December 1821. Parties: Charles Stutfield of Ratcliffe Highway, Middlesex, of the one part and William Howard of Tottenham of the other part, in consideration of £500 paid by Howard to Stutfield for the lease. Description of lands affected: *"All that other and these pieces or parcels of land situate at Hanger Lane"*.

This may have included other pieces of land besides the house, garden and paddock. Stutfield, a wine and brandy merchant whose business was in the Parish of St. George in the East, Middlesex, died in 1826.

MDR/1822/3/418 registered 3rd April, 1822

Summary: Lucas to Howard. Dated 23rd March 1822. Lease. Parties: John Lucas of South Ville House, Lambeth and now of Upper Tooting, Surrey, of the one part and William Howard of Hanger Lane in the Parish of Tottenham, Middlesex, of the other part. It referred to previous leases between Lucas and Hindle, registered 16th December 1808 (*MDR/1808/9/613*), Lucas to De Zoete, registered 12th September 1810 (*MDR/1810/7/603*) and Stutfield to Howard registered 20th December 1821 (*MDR/1821/9/637*). This indenture vested it to William Howard for the *"residue of said several terms"* of 31 years, 29 years and 23 years. John Lucas had agreed with Howard to add three quarters of a year to the lease upon a further payment of £10 15s per annum added to the existing rent of £31 10s and £12 15s. Description of lands affected: one messe or tenement with outhouses, stables, yards, gardens, and adjoining paddock on the north, abutting on Hanger Lane, east on land and premises belonging to John Lucas, occupied by William Howard, south also on land belonging to Lucas and occupied by Howard and on the west on land belonging to or occupied by Mr. Scales.

The lease commenced from 25th December 1822 for the term of 31¾ years at an annual rent of £55; declared in lieu of rent £31 10s., £12 15s. and the extension of lease. A plan was drawn in the margin and named the messe as Suffolk House. It was later rebuilt or remodelled and shown on the Old Ordnance Survey Maps of Stamford Hill 1868 as Suffolk Lodge. This indenture was the result of the extension of the lease. The house had been extended by De Zoete or Stutfield around 1810 with a carriage drive laid out on the forecourt where the waste land had been enclosed. The garden and paddock were larger in size than when De Zoete had ownership.

Appendix 3

Tables of owners in 1900 and 1913

The "*owners*" of flats and houses on Woodberry Lodge Estate, compiled from Tottenham Parish Rate Book, St. Ann's Ward, 19th April 1900.

George Candler	Charles Dorman	Kingsford Dorman	Notes on freehold, leases and house construction
Vartry Rd 26-52,**54**, 56-70 **72,74,76 90,92,** 94-124 61-75,**87,** 89-99, **101-111,** 113-139			**1894** Building approval for 25 houses on south side of Vartry Rd to be built between existing houses. **1895** Candler "*owned*" 61-67, 71-103 **1896** Building approval for conservatory at 54 Vartry Rd in December **1897** 60-76, 90-124 mortgaged by Frances Anne Paterson and Charles Dorman. 26-58 mortgaged by Selina Noys and Charles Dorman **1898** 87-139 C. Dorman to J. H. Kingsford, W. Harrison and L Cockburn, mortgagees. 61-75 Charles Dorman to Stephanie Henrietta Pedder. **1899** Candler listed as occupier and "owner" of 54 & 115 Vartry Rd. Selina Noys and Charles Dorman mortgagees. Joseph Owen lived at 59 Vartry Rd 1892 (electoral register) and held leases for 51-59. **1900** W Blackwell held lease of 78 Vartry Rd, occupied by Samuel Blackwell. Mrs Worrall owned coach house & stables at 88 Vartry Road, occupied by Richard Cook. She lived at "*Ledbury*" 64 Amhurst Park until her death in 1895.
	Richmond Rd **26-62,** 79-125		**1874** E Wood owned 30-34,70-76,77 **1877** E Wood owned 25-29 (numbered differently, prior to houses built by George Candler) **1898** 56-62 C. Dorman to Stephanie Pedder
		Berkeley Rd **1-29**	**1899** plans approved for 15 houses. (originally called Lawrie Rd)
		Heysham Rd	**1898-99** plans approved for 31 houses **1900** Charles Dorman transferred 1-27 to son Charles Herbert Dorman
		Manchester Rd 2-48, 1-41	**1898** Nos.1-39, 2-48 Freehold land from C. Dorman to Stephanie Pedder. Plans approved for 22 houses 1898-1899
St John's Rd 33,33a-37, 37a,49a-55	St John's Rd **2,**22,22a52,52a, **54,65,58,**7,11, 39,39a-47 55a-73,73a	Land & sheds at corner of St Johns Rd, Candler St	**1878** E Wood leased Nos. 11-23&25 also 4 -12 **1898** Nos. 54,56,58 C. Dorman to J. H. Kingsford, W. Harrison and L Cockburn, mortgagees. **1900** Candler rented land and shed at corner of St John's & Candler St from Kingsford, Dorman & Co. Daniel Amhurst Tyssen owned the freehold of 1,3,5,7 St John's Rd
		Franklin St 1,38	**1878** E. Wood 2-56 (N28),1-53 (S23) **1898** 39-53 Freehold from C. Dorman to S. Pedder

George Candler	Charles Dorman	Kingsford Dorman	Notes on freehold, leases and house construction
		Candler St **5,17**	**1878** E Wood owned leases 1-19 (N10), 2-18 (S9)
		Albert Rd **29-38,12-28**	**1900** 12-24, 13-27 owned by E Wood
	S.S.R **610-616**, **618**,644, 652, 656	Seven Sisters Rd **483,485**	No. 618 was a Tavern The shops had living accommodation above

The table below shows the houses "*owned*" by George Candler, compiled from the Tottenham Parish Rate Book, St. Ann's Ward, half-year to September 1913.

Table of owners in September 1913.

House nos.	Notes
Vartry Rd 30-52,**54,** 56-70, **72,74,76,78** 90,92, 94-124 61-75, 87,89-99,**101-111,** 113-139	**1901** Charles Dorman died. Freehold of land transferred to his sons and daughters. Probate (B12 No. 565). **1907** Samuel and Arthur William Blackwell occupied 78 Vartry Rd. James William Brock and Charles Edward Homer lived at 62 Amhurst Park, Stamford Hill but owned freehold stables at back of 80 & 82 Vartry Rd. **1905 & 1910** Rate Books show 54 Vartry Rd owned by executors of Dorman. The leasehold of 115 Vartry Rd was held by George Candler. Selina Noys and Charles Herbert Dorman were still mortgagees. **1913** 61-75 Recited indenture of mortgage made between Charles Dorman & Stephanie H. Pedder in 1898 now J. H. Kingsford and C.H. Dorman to C. H. Dorman & F. T. Dorman. Pedder died in 1912 and left estate to them. 22-28 Vartry Rd. owned by Baroness Amhurst of Hackney. George Candler listed as "owner" of 54 and 115 Vartry Rd. Gross rental value £50 a year. Rental per week 19s. for house, when other flats 9s. 6p. Nov. 1903 Candler was residing at 115 Vartry Rd (marriage certificate)
Richmond Rd (Charles St) **32-62,** 79-125	**1913** Nos. 54-62 Recited indenture of mortgage made between Charles Dorman & Stephanie H Pedder in 1898 now from J. H. Kingsford & C. H. Dorman to C.H. Dorman & F.T. Dorman.
Berkeley Rd 1-29	**1899** mortgaged by Selina Noys and Charles Dorman (died 1901). **1903** transferred to Noys and Charles Herbert Dorman **1906** Noys transferred to Lionel Collins and Charles Herbert Dorman.
Heysham Rd 147,49, 51-57, 2-68	**1900** 1-27 Charles Dorman to Charles Herbert Dorman, his son. **1914** 13-27 Freeholds bought by Annie Candler from C.H. & F.T. Dorman. The mortgage was discharged on 23rd June 1928.
Manchester Rd 2-48, 1-41	**1913** 1-39, 2-48+41 Recited indenture of mortgage made between C. Dorman & Stephanie H. Pedder in 1898 to James Henry Kingsford, C H & F T Dorman. She died in 1912 and left her estate to them.
St John's Rd 22,22a-52,52a **54,56,58,** 33,33a-73, 73a,	**1901** 33-73a bought by S. H. Candler, Jane S. French and W. H. Lee from Charles Dorman on 16th January. **1913** 38-52a bought by Annie Candler from C.H. & F.T. Dorman. **1915** 54,56,58 transfer of mortgage W. Harrison & L. H. Cockburn, mortgagers F.T. Dorman, trustee and William Eve.
Franklin St 39-53	**1913** Nos. 39-53 Recited indenture of mortgage made between C Dorman & Stephanie H Pedder in 1898 to J H Kingsford, C H & F T Dorman & CH Dorman as she left her estate to them in her will.
Seven Sisters Rd **612, 614**	612 tenement and ground floor 614 house and shop

Appendix 4

Table of numbers of houses and flats in 2014

Street	Houses (highlighted) Number of flats in brackets	Notes, about owners, planning applications, changes to street names and numbers
Vartry Rd	26-52(14), **54**, 56-70(8) **72, 74, 76, 78, 90, 92,** 94-124(16) 61-75(8), **87**, 89-99(6) **101-111**(6), 113-139(14) 81(10) Almshouses 152-182 (30) Devonshire Terrace built 1901&1903 14a/14b coach house	Candler made planning applications for 7, 14, 2 units in 1892, 25 units in 1893/4. Planning for 51-59, 141-151 (then 1-6 Florence Villas) 80-86, 88, 120-130, 132-150 in different style and built earlier, possibly by Wood. 152-166, 168-182 Devonshire Terrace built in 1901&1903, possibly by Candler but no records to prove it' 81 (10 units) only number between 75 tenement and 87 house.
Richmond Rd (Charles St)	26-44(10), **56-62**(4) + 18 24(8), 43-113(45)+5 fill in	Some demolished to build new estate. 1890 12, 11+1 units proposed by Candler
Berkeley Rd (Lawrie Rd)	**1-29** (15)	Candler proposed 15 (1-29) in 1898
Heysham Rd	1-47(24), **49**, 51-57(4) 2-68(34)	Candler proposed 31 (1899) + **25** (1)
Manchester Rd	1-39(20), 2-48(24), **41**	Candler proposed 23 (1896)
St. John's Rd (Townsend Rd)	33-73(40), 22-52(16) **54, 56, 58** (49-55, 61-69, 108-124, 87-137)	Candler proposed 20 (1980) 16 (1891) 3 (1892) Rest demolished to build new Estate. Original hall wallpaper still existed in 2003 at 39 and photographs taken.
Franklin St	1-37(S19),39-53(S8) 2-56(N28)	Old street demolished. New housing for disabled people in 1960s. Old rate book for tenant from upstairs flat (57)
Candler St	2-18 (S9) 20,22(1) 1-19 (N10)	Built around 1890. 20/22 are in a different style.
Albert Rd	24 (N semis) 8+1, 8+1,+ 4 (S) houses	Leased from 1877 by Wood, builder. Original houses no longer exist. There are now blocks of flats and some houses built at the same time as the estate.

Appendix 5

Table of Ownership of land at South Tottenham
1152–1952

1152	Henry of Scotland gave Ughtred, Augustinian Canoness of Clerkenwell, 140 acres in the "hanger".
1160–3	Henry's son, Malcolm IV of Scotland, granted the property to Robert, son of Swein of Northampton.
1165–1176	Robert, son of Swein of Northampton, gave it to St. Mary's Priory between these years and the nuns held it until the Dissolution of the Monasteries.
1345	Sir Thomas Heath held the "fealty" which included the house and land including Oatfield, Snaresmead and Great Hanger, although he often defaulted to the prioress.
1455	Sir William Kingston bought the reversion of the lease and the house and land including Oatfield, Snaresmead and Great Hanger.
1540	Sir William Kingston granted it to Edmund Jerringham, his stepson, who died in 1546.
1546	Sir Anthony Kingston inherited from his stepbrother, Edmund Jerringham.
1546	Sir Anthony Kingston surrendered 140 acres called Great Hanger to Henry Jerringham and Oatfields to Edward Pate. Later in the year Henry Jerringham surrendered Great Hanger also to Edward Pate.
1553	Pate conveyed Oatfield to William Parker, draper and his 140 acres to Auguste Hinde, alderman.
1554	August Hinde succeeded by his infant son Rowland Hinde.
1560	Michael Lock, a London Mercer, was granted the land.
1561	Oatfield was conveyed by William Parker to Thomas More.
1619	Sir Edward Barkham (Oatfields, Snaresmead and Thistlefield were part of the estate of Edward Barkham).
1631	Dame Jane Barkham (wife of Sir Edward Barkham) and Sir Edward Barkham (son of above).
1654	Sir Robert Barkham.
1661	James Huxley, executor of will, then Robert Barkham (son of above).
1691	Frances Barkham (widow of Robert) and son, Robert Barkham.
1694	Henry Hayter.
1716	Thomas Hayter (brother of Henry).
1720	Thomas Hayter, Whitfield Hayter (brothers).
1721	Thomas Hayter, Mary Morland, sister of Thomas Hayter, John Otway and Rebecca, his wife, cousin of Thomas Hayter to William Lethieullier.
1724	William Lethieullier (son of Sir John Lethieullier).
1739	Mary Lethieullier (widow of above).
1746/7	Samuel Lethieullier (son of above).
1752	Sarah Lethieullier (widow of above).
1757	Stephen Holland (husband of above).
1768	Heirs of Stephen Holland – Sarah Holland (widow of above).
1779	Heirs of Stephen Holland – Rachel Waller and Margaret Lethieullier (sisters and nieces by marriage of Sarah Holland).
1791	Heirs of Stephen Holland – Rachel Waller, Margaret and Richard Pinckard (husband).
1798	Samuel Weyman Wadeson, George Wilson, John Wood.
1815	Heirs of John Wood leased for 96 years from 1807 to Thomas Coxhead Stevens (38 acres).
1815	Leased by Thomas Coxhead Stevens to Thomas Coxhead Marsh (38 acres) £4,000.
1821	Leased by Thomas Coxhead Stevens and Thomas Coxhead Marsh to Joseph Henley (38 acres) £2,500.

1821	Leased by Solly and Bainbridge, administrators of T. C. Stevens, Joseph Henley and T.C. Marsh to Brodie Augustus McGhie for remainder of 96 year lease (38 acres).
1842	Leased by Willcox, McLeod, executors of Brodie Augustus McGhie to Arend George John Walstab for remainder of 96 year lease (38 acres).
1842	Leased by Arend John George Walstab to John Jerram for remainder of 96 year lease at a yearly rent (38 acres).
1854	Leased by John Jerram to John Giblett for remainder of 96 years lease at an annual rent of £245 (38 acres).
1859	Heirs of John Wood-Edmund and Sophie Wood, George and Herbert William Wood to John Nesbitt Malleson (38 acres).
1861	Leased by John Giblett to Samuel Lloyd Stacey, house, lodge, pleasure ground and gardens for 21 years from 1858 (3 acres) rent £100.
1864	Sold by Edmund and Sophie Wood, George and Herbert William Wood to John Giblett and if forfeit to Jonathan Seaman Mallett (38 acres).
1864	Leased by John Giblett to Caroline Mary King and others (38 acres).
1865	Leased by Caroline Mary King and others to Alexander Luard Wollaston and others (38acres).
1865	John Giblett to James Kingsford (38 acres).
1866	John Giblett to Charles Dorman (38 acres).
1867	John Giblett and others to Charles Salisbury Butler part of Snaresmead (3r 20p).
1867	Joseph Lucas and other to John Giblett (4a 3r 31p) part of Bushey Hangers.
1867	Charles Dorman to John Giblett (41 acres).
1867	James Kingsford to John Giblett.
1867	John Giblett to James and Thomas Dorman (4a 3r 31p) house and 23 acres and 34 perches, part of Oat Fields (1a 3r 5p; 3r 4p; and (8a 3r 6p), part of Snares Mead.
1868	John Giblett to James and Thomas Dorman for £5,700 and £600 of interest for remaining land at Tottenham as parts of Snares Mead had been sold.
1870	John Giblett to Charles Dorman (4a 3r 31p) and remaining part of Oat Fields and Snares Mead unsold.
1874	Caroline Mary King and others to Thomas Wheeler and Daniel Clarke – 3 acres & 1 rood including Woodberry Lodge, part of Oat Fields.
1874	Caroline Mary King and others to James Kingsford – remainder of Oat Fields and Snares Mead.
1874	John Giblett to Charles Dorman remainder of Oat Fields and Snares Mead.
1877	James Kingsford and Charles Dorman – Development of Woodberry Lodge estate with Edmund Wood and others.
1877	James Kingsford and others to George Russell – two parts of Snaremead once twelve acres (8a 12p) and another part.
1877	Thomas Wheeler and others to Abraham Briggs – Woodberry Lodge (3a 1r).
1882, 1891, 1895	James Kingsford shared owners of Woodberry Lodge Estate.
1882, 1889, 1891	Charles Dorman shared owners of Woodberry Lodge Estate.
1896	Charles Dorman.
1901	Charles Dorman.
1902	Charles Herbert Dorman and Julia Dorman, trustees of Charles Dorman's will for Arthur, Francis, Emily and Maude Dorman.
1915	Charles Herbert Dorman ⅛ share (last year ownership of Woodbury Estate included in electoral registers). He died that year. Francis Thomas Dorman then became trustee of his father's will. In 1926 his son, Laurence Charles Dorman, became a trustee.
1931	Lady Emily Shackleton became a trustee when Francis Thomas Dorman died. After Lady Emily died in 1936, Charles John Paget Dorman took her place. He died in 1939.
1952	Laurence Charles Dorman director of Woodberry Lodge Estate Company and H.W.C. Davies director of Woodberry Development Company.

Literature, documentation and associated reading

General

A-Z, Geographers' London Atlas
AA Road Atlas of Britain, 1990
Boyd's Marriage Index, 1538-1840
Bebbington, Gillian, *London Street Names*, 1972
Census Returns for England, Wales and the Isle of Man, 1840-1911
Concise Oxford Dictionary
Electoral Registers for England
Foster, Joseph, ed., *Alumni Oxonienses*, 1500-1714, Vol. 1-4: 1715-1886 Vol.1-8
Foster, Joseph, ed., *London Marriage Licences 1521-1869*, 1887 (from excerpts by Colonel Chester)
Foster, Joseph, ed., *The Register of Admissions to Gray's Inn 1521-1889, together with the register of marriages in Gray's Inn Chapel 1695-1754*, 1889
Harleian Society Publications – London Parish Registers: baptisms, marriages and burials
Index of Vicar General Marriage Allegations, 1660-1850, Lambeth Palace Library
Index of Faculty Office Marriage Allegations, 1632-1850, Lambeth Palace Library
Indexes and allegations for Vicar General and Faculty Office on microfilm at Society of Genealogists
Map for Earl of Dorset ("Mannors of Pembrooke Bruses Dawbneys and Mockings in the Parishes of Tottenham and Edmonton in the County of Middlesex", 1619) reduced from the original by T.T. Barrow and engraved by W.C. Walker, 1823, for the supplement to Robinson's History and Antiquities of Tottenham, Middlesex.
O'Farrell, John, *An Utterly Impartial History of Britain*, 2008
Old Ordnance Survey Maps (The Godfrey Edition), Stamford Hill, London, Sheet 21, 1868, 1894, 1913
Oxford Dictionary of National Biography, Volumes 1-60
Pallott's Marriage Index, 1780-1837
Phillimore Parish Registers
Venn, J. and J.A., *Alumni Cantabrigienses*: Part I from the earliest times to 1751, Vol.1-4
Venn, J.A., *Alumni Cantabrigienses* Part II 1752-1900 Vol.1-6

Part 1

Alcock, Joan P., *Sydenham and Forest Hill History and Guide*, 2005
Ford, W.J., *A History of the Cambridge University Cricket Club, 1820-1901*, 1902
Forrest, Katherine, A., *Manx Recollections, Memorials of Eleanor Elliott*, 1894
Golden, Jennifer, *Hackney at War*, 1995
Huntford, Roland, *Shackleton*, 1985

...tory, 1908/9

...s, *Fashions and Fashion Plates 1800-1900*, 1943

...pographical Society, *The London County Council, Bomb Damage Maps, 1939-1945*, 2005

..., William, R., *A Naval Biographical Dictionary*, 1849

...ice Directories, London, 1856, 1878, 1904, 1908/9, 1921, 1937

r... /ffice Directory, Isle of Man, 1863

Russell, Helena, *Cleveland Bridge 125 years of History*, 2002

Tottenham Street Directory, 1908/9, 1923

Part 2

Andrews, Jonathan *et al*, *The History of Bethlem*, 2013

Atwater, Edward E., *History of the Colony of New Haven to its absorption into Connecticut*, 1881 *(Section Emigration of Planters of New Haven)*

Aubrey, John, and Rawlinson, Richard, *The Natural History and Antiquities of the County of Surrey, Volume 3*, 1718 (pp. 273 and 277)

Baker,T.F.T., ed., *The Victoria History of the Counties of England: A History of Middlesex, Volume 5*, 1976

Brooke, Iris, *English Costume of the Eighteenth Century*, 1929, Drawn by Iris Brooke and described by James Laver

Brooke, Iris, *English Costume of the Nineteenth Century*, 1931, Drawn by Iris Brooke and described by James Laver

Bulloch, William, *Bullock's Roll*, Royal Society, 1663-1940

Calendar of State papers, Domestic Series, for the relevant years. BL

Calendar of State Papers, Treasury Books, for the relevant years. BL

Calendar of State Papers Colonial, America and West Indies, Volume 10, 1677-1680, Miscellaneous, 1679 (No. 1248)

Campbell, James W. P, *Building St. Paul's*, 2007

Carswell, John, *The South Sea Bubble*, 1993

Clark, Lynn, *A History of Stoke next Guildford*, 1999

Collinge, J.M, *Navy Board Officials 1660-1832*, 1978

Cox, John Edmund, *Annals of St. Helen Bishopsgate*, 1876

Crossley, Alan, *et al.* eds., Victoria County History: *A History of the County of Oxford, Vol. 11, Wootten Hundred (northern part)*, 1983

Davies, J. D., *Gentlemen and Tarpaulins*, 1991

Dexter, Franklin B., ed., *Ancient Town Records, Volume 1, New Haven Town Records, 1649-1662* (New Haven Colony Historical Society), 1919

Dexter, Franklin B., ed., *Ancient Town Records, Volume 2, New Haven Town Records, 1662-1684* (New Haven Colony Historical Society), 1919

Diaries and Consultation Books of the East India Company for relevant years (BL)

Diary of Samuel Sewall, Volumes 1&2, 1674-1708

Dictionary of American Biography

Duncombe, Rev. John, *The History and Antiquities of the two Parishes of Reculver and Herne, in the County of Kent*, 1784

Fell-Smith, Charlotte, *John Dee (1527-1608)*, 1909

Fisk, Fred, *The History of Tottenham*, 1913

Gater, G.H., and Godfrey, Walter. H., general eds., *Survey of London: Volume 15, All Hallows, Barking-by-the-Tower*, 1936

Graham, Thomas William, M.A. (rector), *Some Account of the Parish of Stoke near Guildford*, 1933

Hammond, Paul, and Hopkins, David, eds., *John Dryden: Tercentenary Essays*, in a chapter by John Barnard, "Dryden, Tonson and the Patrons of *The works of Virgil* (1697)", 2000

Heal, Sir Ambrose, *The London Goldsmiths 1200-1800*, 1972

Hoadley, Charles J., *Records of the Colony and Plantation of New Haven, 1638-1649*, 1857

Journals of the House of Commons, Volume 10, 1688-1693(BL)

Journals of the House of Commons, Volume 11, 1693-1697(BL)

Journals of the House of Lords, Volume 18, 1705-1709 (BL)

Journals of the House of Lords, Volume 19, 1709-1714 (BL)

Lambert, Edward R., *History of the Colony of New Haven*, 1838

Latham, Robert, and Matthews, W., eds., *The Diary of Samuel Pepys, Volumes 1-10, Index Volume 11*, 1995

Lincolnshire Archives Committee, Report 22

London inhabitants inside the City Walls 1695, introduced by D.V. Glass, published by London Record Society, 1966

Lysons, Daniel, *The Environs of London: being an historical account of the towns, villages, and hamlets, within twelve miles of that capital: interspersed with biographical anecdotes: Volume 3 (Tottenham, pages 517-557)*, 1795

Lysons, Daniel, and Lysons, Samuel, *Magna Britannia: Vol. 2, Part 1, Cambridgeshire*, 1808

Manning, Owen, and Bray, William, *The History and Antiquities of the County of Surrey Volumes 1 &2*, 1804-14

Massachusetts Historical Society Collection (Transcript and foot notes for Winthrop Papers), Volume VI, 1650-54, edited by Malcolm Freiberg, M.H. S., 1992

Memoranda, Collection of the Massachusetts Historical Society Sixth series, Vol. 1, The Letter-book of Samuel Sewall, 1886

Milevsky, Moshe, *King William's Tontine: Why the retirement annuity of the future should resemble its past*, 2015

Milton, John, *Milton's Letters to Cromwell*, 1743, Pg. 54 (Society of Antiquaries)

Noble, Mark, *Memoirs of the Protectoral House of Cromwell, Vol. 2*, 1784, 1787

O'Donaghue, Rev. Edward G., *The Barkham Family*, Bethlem Royal Hospital Archives and Museum, Beckenham, Kent

Peacock, John, *Costume 1066-1966*, 1986

Pickford, Ian, ed., *Jackson's Silver & Gold Marks of England, Scotland & Ireland*, 1989

Protz, Christine, *Tottenham: A History*, 2009

Robinson, William, *The History and Antiquities of the Parish of Tottenham High Cross in the County of Middlesex*, 1818

Robinson, William, *The History and Antiquities of the Parish of Tottenham in the County of Middlesex*, two Volumes, 1840

Sainty, John C., *Admiralty Officials 1660-1870*, 1975

Savage, James, *Genealogical Dictionary of the First Settlers of New England, Vol. 2*

Tomalin, Clare, *Samuel Pepys: The Unequalled Self*, 2002

Torrey, Clarence Almon, *New England Marriages Prior to 1700*, 1987

Waters, Henry Fitz-Gilbert, *The New England Historical and Genealogical Register, Vol. 45*, 1891

Westfall, Richard S., *Never at Rest: A Biography of Isaac Newton"*, 1980

Part 3

British Library (BL): Asian and African Studies Collections:

Despatches to England, Volumes covering years 1694-1751

Despatches from England, Volumes covering years 1680-1758

EIC Court Minutes (IOR/B/43) 1699-1702, EIC Court Minutes (IOR/B/51)1710-1712

Factory Records, Surat, G/36/118

Farrington, Anthony, *A Biographical Index of East India Company Maritime Service Officers, 1600-1834,* London (British Library) 1999

Index of East India Company Court Minutes, Volumes covering years 1678-1853

IOR Indexes, Z-N (and Microfilms):

Bombay Baptisms, 1709-1948, Bombay Marriages, 1709-1948, Bombay Burials, 1709-1948

Bengal Baptisms, 1713-1948, Bengal Marriages, 1713-1948, Bengal Burials, 1713-1948

Madras Baptisms, 1698-1948, Madras Marriages, 1698-1948, Madras Burials, 1698-1948

Letter Book (10), Old Company (IOR/E/3/93), 1698-1709

Letters to Fort St. George, Volumes covering years 1681-1765

Letters from Fort St. George, Volumes covering years 1679-1763

McNally, S.J., *The Chaplains of the East India Company*, 1976,(OIR 253.0954)

Selections from the letters, despatches and other state Papers, preserved in Bombay Secretariat: Home Series, Volume 2, 1660-1781

Borrowman, R., *Beckenham Past and Present,* 1910

Colwell, Stella, *Family Roots: Discovering the Past in the Public Record Office,* 1992

Glinert, Ed, *East End Chronicles,* 2005

Grainger, James, *A Biographical History of England: From Egbert the Great to the Revolution,*1824

Harleian Society Register, Volume 31, St. Helen Bishopsgate

Hasted, Edward, *The History and Topographical Survey of the County of Kent, Vol.2,* 1800

Hibbert, Christopher, Weinreb, Ben, *et al.*, eds., *The London Encyclopaedia,* 1995

Hoare's Bank, A Record, 1672-1955, The Story of a Private Bank, 1955

Journals of the Board of Trade and Plantations, Vol. 3, March 1715-Oct., 1718

Maziere Brady, D.D., William, *Volume 2, Clerical and Parochial Records of Cork, Cloyne and Ross compiled from Parish Registers and Family Papers,*1863

McAuliffe, Roma, *The Story of the Bloomsbury Dispensary* (Pamphlet), 1973

Musgrave, William, *Musgrave's Obituary, Prior to 1800,* 1900

Nichols, John, *Illustrations of the Literary History of the Eighteenth Century*: *Consisting of authentic memoirs and original letters of eminent persons,*1831

Pinckard, George, *Notes on the West Indies: Written During the Expedition Under the Command of the Late General Sir Ralph Abercrombie in 1806*

Price, Frederick George Hilton, *A Handbook of London Bankers,* 1890 (reprinted in 2013)

Roseveare, Henry, *Markets and Merchants of the Late Seventeenth Century, The Maresco-David Letters, 1668-1680,* 1991

The Faculty Office Marriage Licence Index, 1701-1725

The History of Parliament: the House of Commons, 1690-1715

The London and Surrey, England, Marriage Bonds and Allegations, 1597-1921, LMA

The National Trust, *Stourhead, Wiltshire,* 1985

The Records of the Honourable Society of Lincoln's Inn: Volume I, Admissions, from A.D. 1420 to A.D. 1799, 1896

Part 4

Bulley, Anne, *The Bombay Country Ships: 1790-1833,* 2000

Glover, Stephen, *History of the County of Derby, Part 2,* 1829

Harcourt, Freda, *Flagships of Imperialism: The P & O Company and the Politics of Empire from its origins to 1867,* 2006

Hunter, Michael, *The Victorian Villas of Hackney,* 1981

Post Office Directory, London, 1845

Richardson, Moses Aaron, *A Collection of Armorial Bearing Inscriptions in the Church of St. Nicholas, Newcastle on Tyne (Ebook)*

Scottish Record Society Edinburgh: *Index to the Register of burials in the Churchyard of Restalrig, 1728-1854*

Newspapers, magazines and articles

17th and 18th Century Burney Collection newspapers (online database) BL

19th Century British Library Newspapers, 1800-1900 (online database) BL

Chown, Claude Henry Iyan, *The Essex Review,* 1927

Milevsky, Moshe, *Portfolio choice and longevity risk in the late seventeenth century: A re-examination of the first English Tontine, Netspar discussion papers, 2014*

North West Kent, Family History Society, Volume 1, Autumn, 1978-1980,

Parker, Roy and Parker, Dorothy, *The Rise of the English Drugs Industry: The role of Thomas Corbyn in Medical History, 1989,* page 286

Proceedings of the Huguenot Society, XXV II (2), Article, 1999.

Taylor, John, ed., *Weekly Parish Registers Northamptonshire Notes and Queries, Volume VI, 1896*

The Candelers of London, Vol. 2, Home Counties Magazine, article

The London Gazette

The Times online 1785-1985

The Weekly Herald, May 28th 1937, Bruce Castle Archives

Thwaite, Nicola, Assistant Libraries Curator (north), The National Trust, *Arts/Buildings/ Collections Bulletin, Spring Issue, May 2013, Article "There and Back again" (pages 14-16)* concerning bible at Blickling Hall

Manuscripts, maps and rare books
British Library (BL)

A List of the Surviving Nominees on the Fund of Survivorship, at Midsummer 1730, printed by Henry King (8285.ee.48)

Egerton MS 2519, Papers of General Desborough, 1651-1659 (1654)

Hill Family Papers, Add MS 5488, Folio 68-72 (pages 28-32), 1756

Lethieullier, IOR L/L/2/3/371/1&2, 1704(deed), IOR L/L/2/372/1&2, 1735 (lease and release to East India Company)

The Million Act (514.k.2.23), printed by Samuel Heyrick, 1694

The Refuter refuted: A reply to Mr. Giblett's Pamphlet entitled A Refutation of the Calumnies of George Harrower with appendix by Captain George Harrower, 1816

Islington Market Bill: The address of Mr. William Giblett upon summing up the evidence produced by him as an agent for the trade of butchers, to the Committee of the honourable House of Commons 3rd January 1834 (author William Giblett), published by W. Tyler, 1834

Bruce Castle Museum

Brochure and plan of the Woodberry Lodge Estate (PS/089), 1866

Electoral Registers Tottenham 1905-1939, 1832, 1836, 1847-1861

Poor Rate Books, High Cross Ward, 1838-1870

Rent Charge Books for Tottenham, 1779, 1780, 1798

Tottenham High Cross Ward Poor Rate Book 1820 (D/PT/SE/7), 1837 (D/PT/SC/18)

Tottenham Manorial Court Rolls 1626-1792, microfilms

Tottenham Parish Rate Book of St. Ann's Ward, 19th April, 1900

Tottenham Parish Rate Book of St. Ann's Ward, September, 1905

Tottenham Parish Rate Book of St. Ann's Ward, September, 1913

Tottenham Tithe Map, and award Book, 1844

Tottenham Urban District Council Registers of deposited plans in the Surveyors Report Books for New Streets and Buildings, indexed by depositor and places, 1890-1901 (1/TLA/B/4/Volumes 3-5),

St. Ann's and its Environs in the Sixties by a One Time Pupil in His Seventies (872)

1864 OS map, Middlesex sheet XII, 7&11 (detail)

1894-6 OS map, Middlesex sheet XII, 7&11 (detail)

Wyburd Map accompanying survey, 1798

London Metropolitan Archives, City of London (LMA)

Some documents have now been digitised and are available on www.ancestry.com

Freedom of the City Admission papers 1681-1925 (database online) COL/CHD/FR/02/0027-0033, COL/CHD/FR/02/0129-0134

Registers of Marriages of St. Dunstan Stepney, 1609/10-1631/2 (P93/DUN/265)

M/093/271 (1691) Counterpart assignment of residue of term

ACC/0401/033&034, Bargain and sale and lease for a year

A Survey of the Parish of Tottenham in the County of Middlesex, 1798, for Henry Piper Sperling, Esq., compiled by James Wyburd (CLC/270/MS12700A)

Holmes Family Collection, ACC/0489/024 – 026, AC/0489/003-008

Weatherall Family Collection, ACC/1028/107, 1798, ACC/1028/109 &110, ACC/1028/113

The Middlesex Deeds Registry. Registers of Memorials. 1708-1938:

Indexes 1709-1919, 1920-1938:

MDR/1720/2/301, ACC/0026/064, MDR/1821/5/538, MDR/1821/5/539

MDR/1859/10/574, MDR/1868/16/255, MDR/1874/16/861, DL/T1/AA/44/018, MDR/1924/35/818, MDR/1926/1/226, M/093/271, ACC/0401/033.

Records of Sun Fire Office, MS 11936/453/839938, MS 11936/434/779796 and 781455, MS 11936/476/931378, MS 11936/516/1072579 and 1072580, MS 11936/395/617543, MS 11936/398/626005, MS 11936/407/660291

DL/C/0514/010/001-003, DL/C/0524/174/001-002, DL/C/426/197 (wills and administrations)

A/CSC/2845/8, A/CSC/2845/9.

The National Archives, Kew (TNA)

Original documents, catalogue and documents online:

Wills: PROB 11, PROB 6/61, PROB 12, PROB 5/2476, IR 26/425/476, abstract of administration, indexes of wills and administrations 1600-1858

C16/933/F43, E134/4 Jas 1/Trin 4, E134/8 Jas 1/Hil 25, C2/Eliz/B2/32, C2/Eliz/C16/60, E 115/267/96, C 47/34/6, C 11/263/36, C 11/245/16, C 10/14/3, E 134/28chas2/east11, CUST 116/28/63, ADM 20/54 Nos. 299, 350, 1025, 1598, ADM 106/488/125, C 111/184, C 111/187, C 111/191, C 111/192,

C 111/207, C 10/246/26, C 9/253/38, C 11/43/36, C 11/151/3, AO 1/1721/138, C 6/295/65, C 16/345/G166, WO 97/1106/38

Manuscripts and rare books at other archives

Cambridgeshire Archives: Holworthy family of Elsworth 279 and catalogue entries for Holworth

C. Hoare & Co., Fleet Street: HE/3/C/1-3, HE/1/A/27, HE/1/A/30, Ledger Volume 69, Folio 231, 1ˢᵗ June, 1768,

East Riding of Yorkshire Archives and Local Studies Service: DDCL/2264-2267

Essex Record Office: D/DGd E38, D/DC 23/774-778, 781-785, 819-821 & 847, D/ABW 98/2/33 (will of Thomas Siggurs)

Hertfordshire Archives and local studies: DE/HL/12302

Lancashire Archives: DDK/471/231&232, DDK/471/254a & 254b, DDK/471/233

Lewisham Local History and Archives Centre: Indenture regarding title of Kent House Farm, A62/6/61

Lincolnshire Archives: 1 PG/3/4/2/1 (mortgage), 1-ANC/9/D/6)

National Records of Scotland, Edinburgh: Record of Testamentary Deeds (SC70/4/48/601-638), 1856

New York State Library, Albany: Edward Eggleston Estate Purchase, Tower of London letters (No. 1308), dated 12ᵗʰ November 1692

Scrap book dedicated to Charlotte Unwin, 1847 (courtesy of Lindsay Clubb)

Society of Genealogists: Charlton Parish Register 1653-1753, Volume 2, transcribed by Francis Ward, Lincolnshire Monumental Inscriptions: (LI/MI), Volume I, 1674-1979, Volume 37 of Lincolnshire Monumental Inscriptions (LI/M37)

The Royal Society: The Journal Book of the Royal Society, Volume XI, 1702-1714

Wellcome Library: Morland, Joseph, Disquisitions concerning the force of the heart, the dimensions of the coats of the arteries and the circulation of the blood, 1713

Westminster City Archives: Probate papers, 2206/5/15, 1722, 2206/8/18, 1733, Act Book 10, Fol.45, Act Book 11, Fol.62, ACC 120, piece no.1902 (will), Poor Rate Records 1783-1793

Yorkshire Archaeological Society: MD355/1/1/33/1 (Marriage settlement), MD/259/K/4 (assignment of mortgage)

Web sites

www.ancestry.com

www.bednallarchive.info/bedcoll/BC2/bc2_851-875.htm

www.british-history.ac.uk

www.britishnewspaperarchive.co.uk

www.familysearch.org (IGI was the forerunner of this web site)

www.findmypast.co.uk

www.gov.uk/search-will-probate

www.historyofparliamentonline.org

www.innertemplearchives.org.uk/biog_sources.html

www.nationalarchives.gov.uk/a2a

http://shissem.com/Hissem_Thornton-Heyshams.html

www.nottingham.ac.uk/manuscriptsandspecialcollections/researchguidance/deedsindepth/introduction.aspx

www.victorianlondon.org

Archives

British Telecom Archives, 268-270 High Holborn, London WC1 7EE

Bromley Public Libraries, Local Studies and Archives

Bruce Castle Museum (Haringey Culture Libraries & Learning)

Camden Local History Centre
City of London, London Metropolitan Archives
City of Westminster Archives Centre
Edinburgh, The National Records of Scotland
Essex Record Office: S.E.A.X – Essex Archives Online
Hackney Archives
Islington Local History Centre
Goldsmiths' Company, Library
Guildhall Library: The Library of London History
Lewisham Local History and Archives Centre
New York State Library, Albany
New Haven Public Library, Connecticut
New York Public Library, Bryant Park
Norfolk Records Office
Royal Society
Society of Genealogists, London
Surrey History Centre Archives
The National Archives, Kew
Wellcome Library

Index